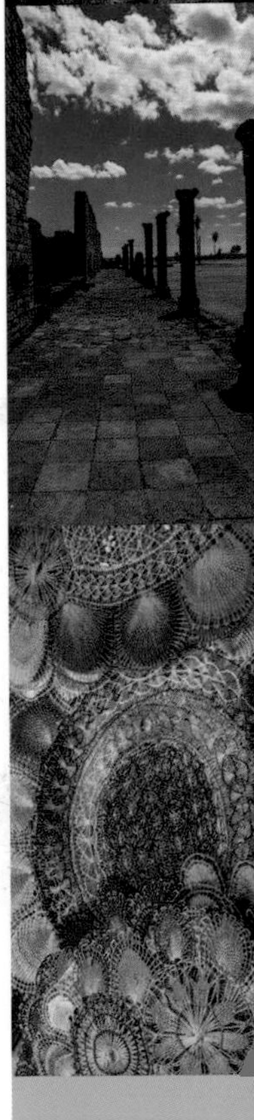

Paraguay

the Bradt Travel Guide

Margaret Hebblethwaite

edition 2

www.bradtguides.com

Bradt Travel Guides Ltd, UK
The Globe Pequot Press Inc, USA

Bradt
N
BOLIVIA
BRAZIL
0 100km
0 100 miles
KEY
Capital City
Departamento capitals
Other towns
Trunk road
Other road
Departamento boundary
Airport
Ferry
Cabrera-Timane NP
Cerro Chovoreca NP
Río Negro NP
Río Negro NP
Cerro León
Defensores del Chaco NP
Médanos del Chaco NP
Alto Paraguay
General Eugenio A Garay
Campo Iris NR
Teniente Enciso NP
Puerto Bahía Negra
Puerto Leda
Fuerte Olimpo
Río Negro
Paraguay
Miranda
Apa
Verde
Pilcomayo
Ruta 9
Ruta 9
Ruta 9
Boquerón
Mariscal Estigarribia
Filadelfia
Boquerón
Puerto Casado
Vallemí
Serranía San Luis NP
Paso Bravo NP
Bella Vista NP
Cerro Corá NP
Pedro Juan Caballero
Concepción
Amambay
Ruta 5
Ruta 5
Ruta 3
The Pantanal: Fuerte Olimpo is the gateway into Paraguay's tropical wetlands
pages 377–83
Cerro Corá National Park: a remote national park tinged with historical sadness, the site of Mariscal López's death
pages 351–4

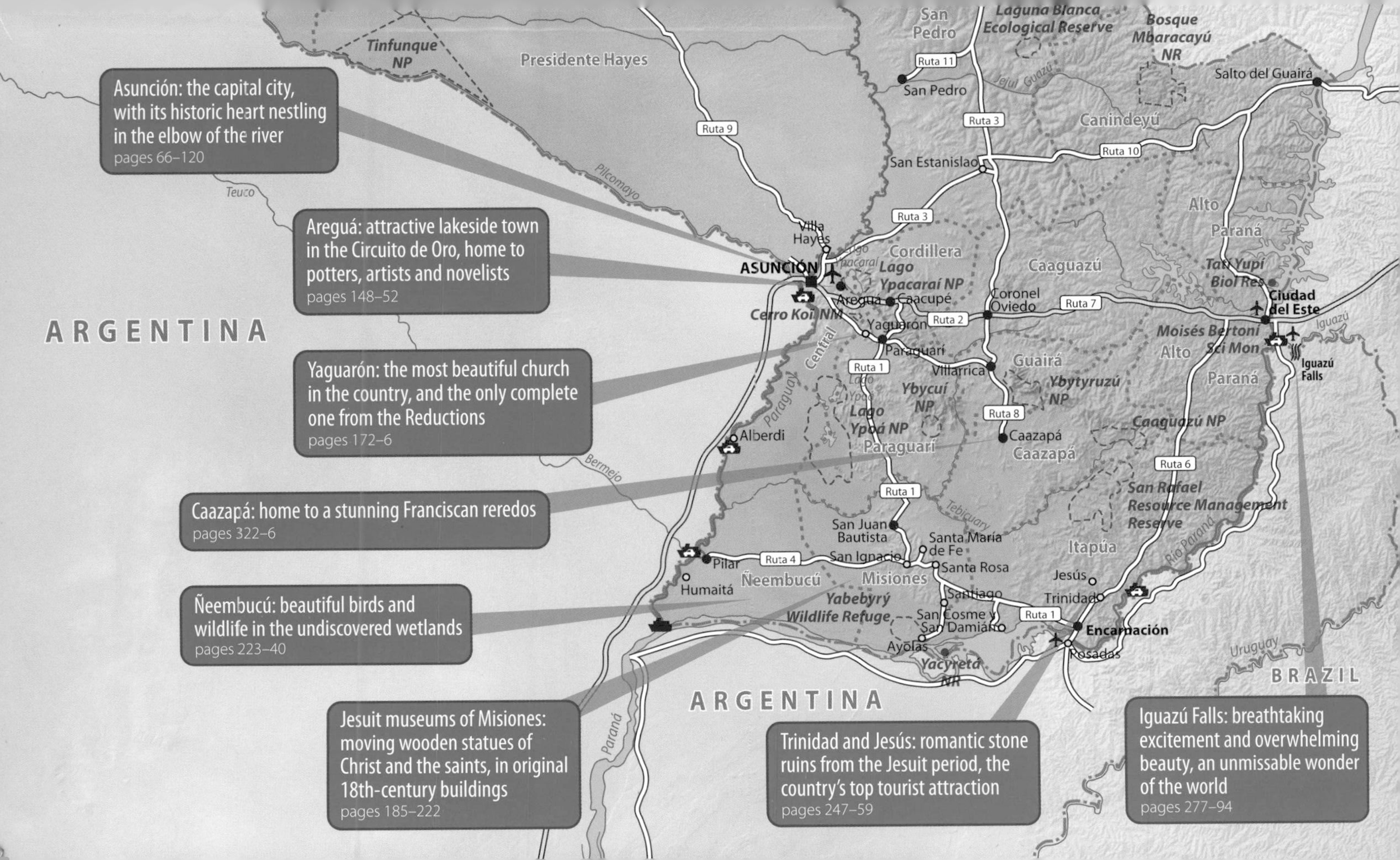
Asunción: the capital city, with its historic heart nestling in the elbow of the river
pages 66–120
Areguá: attractive lakeside town in the Circuito de Oro, home to potters, artists and novelists
pages 148–52
Yaguarón: the most beautiful church in the country, and the only complete one from the Reductions
pages 172–6
Caazapá: home to a stunning Franciscan reredos
pages 322–6
Ñeembucú: beautiful birds and wildlife in the undiscovered wetlands
pages 223–40
Jesuit museums of Misiones: moving wooden statues of Christ and the saints, in original 18th-century buildings
pages 185–222
Trinidad and Jesús: romantic stone ruins from the Jesuit period, the country's top tourist attraction
pages 247–59
Iguazú Falls: breathtaking excitement and overwhelming beauty, an unmissable wonder of the world
pages 277–94
ARGENTINA
ARGENTINA
BRAZIL
Tinfunque NP
Presidente Hayes
San Pedro
Laguna Blanca Ecological Reserve
Bosque Mbaracayú NR
Salto del Guairá
Canindeyú
Ruta 9
Ruta 11
Ruta 3
Ruta 10
San Estanislao
Pilcomayo
Teuco
Villa Hayes
ASUNCIÓN
Cordillera
Lago Ypacaraí NP
Caaguazú
Alto Paraná
Tati Yupi
Ciudad del Este
Areguá
Caacupé
Coronel Oviedo
Ruta 7
Ruta 2
Cerro Koi NM
Yaguarón
Paraguarí
Central
Moisés Bertoni
Iguazú
Iguazú Falls
Villarrica
Guairá
Ybytyruzú NP
Ruta 1
Ybycuí NP
Lago Ypoá NP
Paraguay
Alberdi
Ruta 8
Caazapá
Caaguazú NP
Bermejo
Ruta 6
San Rafael Resource Management Reserve
Tebicuary
San Juan Bautista
Santa María de Fe
Itapúa
Pilar
Ruta 4
San Ignacio
Santa Rosa
Jesús
Humaitá
Ñeembucú
Misiones
Santiago
Trinidad
Yabebyrý Wildlife Refuge
San Cosme y San Damián
Encarnación
Ayolas
Posadas
Uruguay
Yacyretá NR
Paraná
Río Paraná

Paraguay Don't miss...

Paraguayan harp
The country's answer to the classical harp has a frame made entirely of wood
(MM) pages ix–x

The *campo*
It is in the countryside that Paraguayan traditions live on most strongly (EH) page 49

Iguazú Falls
This wonder of the natural world just over the border into Argentina or Brazil is a must-see for most visitors to Paraguay (MM)
pages 277–94

Jesuit-Guaraní Reductions
Trinidad is one of the famous 'Paraguayan Reductions' that were started as missions for the Guaraní indigenous (MM)
page ix

The craft towns
Areguá is one of the key towns on the Circuito de Oro, and specialises in ceramics (YG)
pages 148–52

Paraguay in colour

left & above The pleasantly bookish Café Literário and the perennially popular Lido Bar are among the best-known eateries in the centre of Asunción (MM) pages 84 and 85

below left The Casa de la Música Agustín Barros is the finest of the bicentenary houses restored to their original splendour in the centre of the capital (MM) page 114

below right The remarkable Museo de la Silla is five floors of innovative and often eccentrically designed chairs (MM) pages 102–3

above left The Cabildo, the former seat of the Senate, is a symbol of Asunción and is stunningly illuminated at night (MM) pages 99–100

above right Trains no longer run from the Estación de Ferrocarril, but the old station building now houses a museum dedicated to the railway (MM) pages 104–5

right The ornate Palacio de Gobierno, otherwise known as the Palacio de López, is the grandest building in Asunción (MM) page 112

below A stained glass window in the Panteón, which houses the remains of some of Paraguay's most important historical figures (MM) page 111

We're 40... how did that happen?

How did it all happen? George (my then husband) and I wrote the first Bradt guide – about hiking in Peru and Bolivia – on an Amazon river barge, and typed it up on a borrowed typewriter. We had no money for the next two books so George went to work for a printer and was paid in books rather than money.

Forty years on, Bradt publishes over 200 titles that sell all over the world. I still suffer from Imposter Syndrome – how did it all happen? I hadn't even worked in an office before! Well, I've been extraordinarily lucky with the people around me. George provided the belief to get us started (and the mother to run our US office). Then, in 1977, I recruited a helper, Janet Mears, who is still working for us. She and the many dedicated staff who followed have been the foundations on which the company is built. But the bricks and mortar have been our authors and readers. Without them there would be no Bradt Travel Guides. Thank you all for making it happen.

Hilary Bradt

Celebrate our anniversary and get a 40% discount on all titles with the code BRADT40.

Available from www.bradtguides.com

AUTHOR

Margaret Hebblethwaite began her writing career as a theologian, and is the author of ten religious books in the areas of feminist theology, spirituality and Latin American liberation theology. She worked as assistant editor on *The Tablet* from 1991 to 2000, when she gave up her job to pursue her interest in Latin American liberation theology, by moving to a poor *campesino* community in South America.

She has lived in Santa María de Fe, Misiones, Paraguay since 2000, where her time has been consumed by working for a number of community projects. She founded and runs the charity Santa María Education Fund (*www.santamariadefe.org*); works with the sewing co-operative Taller de Hermandad to help them with their marketing (*www.santamariadefe.com*); and founded the Santa María Hotel, which is run as a community project with all profits going to the local people (*www.santamariahotel.org*). This is the first book she has written since her move to Paraguay.

AUTHOR'S STORY

When I decided to emigrate to Paraguay in the year 2000, I never imagined that one day I would be writing a guidebook. On my first visit to the country in 1996 I had fallen in love with Santa María de Fe, a small town in Misiones which had originally been a Jesuit mission (or Reduction) for the Guaraní indigenous, and I waited four years for my youngest child to grow up before I could realise my dream of moving here.

Paraguay was (and is) mercifully free of *gringos* and I wanted to keep it to myself. But there was a contradiction. I had come here to immerse myself in a poor community, inspired by the thinking of liberation theology. As well as learning from the poor, I had to respond to the needs of the poor. They needed education, and soon the Santa María Education Fund was born (see page 63). However, education was not enough. People also needed work, and they needed money.

It was clear what the untapped resource was, what Santa María – and Paraguay as a whole – had to sell to the rest of the world: tourism. The contribution I could make was not only to help bring donations into the country, but to help bring in trade and people. I had to stop being selfish about the wonderful place I had discovered. The Santa María Hotel was started; and the *Bradt Guide to Paraguay* began to be written.

PUBLISHER'S FOREWORD

Adrian Phillips, Managing Director

They say actions speak louder than words. The actions of Margaret Hebblethwaite are certainly compelling: four years after her first visit, Margaret moved to Paraguay permanently, and in the decade since has devoted herself tirelessly to projects in support of the local community of Santa María de Fe. It's this passion and local knowledge that make her the perfect Bradt author – and her words speak pretty loudly of the merits of this wonderful country too!

Second edition published November 2014 First published 2010

Bradt Travel Guides Ltd, IDC House, The Vale, Chalfont St Peter, Bucks SL9 9RZ, England
www.bradtguides.com
Print edition published in the USA by The Globe Pequot Press Inc, PO Box 480, Guilford, Connecticut 06437-0480

Project Manager: Maisie Fitzpatrick
Cover image research: Pepi Bluck, Perfect Picture

ISBN: 978 1 84162 561 4
e-ISBN: 978 1 84162 797 7 (e-pub)
e-ISBN: 978 1 84162 698 7 (mobi)

British Library Cataloguing in Publication Data
A catalogue record for this book is available from the British Library

Photographs Alamy: Florian Kopp/imagebroker (FK/I/A); Dreamstime: Aguina (A/DT); Ysanne Gayet (YG); Margaret Hebblethwaite (MH); Emily Horton (EH); James Lowen (JL); Carlos Masi (CM); Marco Muscarà (MM); Dorota Sakwerda (DS)
Front cover Campesinos, Caaguazú (FK/I/A)
Title page Detail of the Yaguarón tabernacle (MM); Jesuit ruins of Jesús (MM); *Ñanduti* lace (MM)
Back cover Jesuit ruins of Trinidad (MM); decorations made from woven rushes (MM)

Maps David McCutcheon FBCart.S

Typeset from the author's disc by Ian Spick, Bradt Travel Guides and Wakewing, High Wycombe
Production managed by Jellyfish Print Solutions; printed in India
Digital conversion by the Firsty Group

Acknowledgements

I am indebted to the excellent work by Peter T Clark on national parks and wildlife; to the Paraguayan guidebook *La Magia de Nuestra Tierra* published by the En Alianza foundation (see section on guidebooks in *Appendix 4*, page 399); and to the Servicio Geográfico Militar for producing the first reliable maps of Paraguayan terrain. I acknowledge the continuing help and support of Senatur, the government tourist office, and of the group that works closely with them, Touring, who are responsible for promoting the Ruta Jesuítica. They also produce the best road maps, and the guidebook *Paraguay: Guia Túristica TACPy*.

In terms of individuals, I wish to thank the historian Ignacio Telesca, and the Jesuit linguist Bartomeu Meliá, for being constantly available on email to answer questions; the historian Margarita Durán for helping on the Franciscan Reductions, both in her published work and on the telephone; James Lowen for checking the section on fauna and supplying full, accurate names of species; and the Argentinian historian Ernesto Maeder, for reading and commenting on the section on San Ignacio Miní. I also thank Miguel Del Puerto for welcoming me to his modest abode in Filadelfia and acting as a superb guide to the central Chaco; Crystian Arevalos, guide at Trinidad, for taking me to the statues of Trinidad and to the Colonias Unidas and for his prompt and informed reply to any query; Adrian Soto for updating the material on Concepción; Isabelino Martínez for being a walking encyclopaedia, particularly on Guaraní questions; María Gloria García and Ruben Dario Maidana for checking and correcting the Spanish language section; Ben Hebblethwaite for driving me around while I took notes, and for showing me some of the cheapest eating places in Asunción; and Rosa María Ortiz and Sister Margot Bremer for giving me research bases in Asunción.

I wish also to thank the English volunteers who kept the English-teaching programme in Santa María running constantly without my help throughout the period of writing and editing: Lisa Kiernan, Mollie Iggulden, Chloe Pilpel, Nicola Hands, Katy Hardman, Richard Coombs, Dorota Sakwerda and Alice Gimblett.

For the second edition I acknowledge with gratitude the contribution of Noelia Mendoza in checking the section on Concepción, of Miguel Del Puerto in checking the section on Filadelfia, of India Dowley in contributing some additional bars and restaurants to the chapter on Asunción, and my volunteers Eleanor Redpath and Julia Smyers for keeping the English programme running virtually unaided during the re-writing period.

Contents

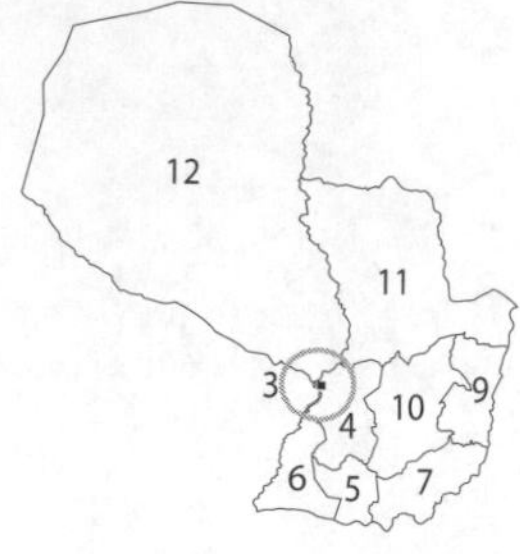

Introduction viii

PART ONE GENERAL INFORMATION 1

Chapter 1 **Background Information** 3

Geography 3, Climate 4, Natural history and conservation 4, History 10, Government and politics 18, Economy 18, People 19, Language 20, Religion 21, Education 22, Culture 23

Chapter 2 **Practical Information** 28

When to visit 28, Suggested itineraries 29, International tour operators 29, Red tape 31, Embassies and consulates 32, Getting there and away 33, Health 38, Safety 44, What to take 46, Money 46, Budgeting 48, Getting around 49, Accommodation 52, Eating and drinking 55, Public holidays and festivals 56, Shopping 57, Arts and entertainment 58, Visiting museums and churches 58, Media and communications 58, Cultural etiquette 61, Travelling positively 62

PART TWO THE GUIDE 65

Chapter 3 **Asunción** 66

History 66, Getting there and away 67, Orientation 67, Getting around 68, Tourist information, tour operators and agencies 73, Where to stay 77, Where to eat and drink 84, Entertainment and nightlife 89, Shopping 91, Other practicalities 95, What to see and do 97, Excursions 119

Chapter 4 **Circuito de Oro** 121

Getting out of Asunción 123, Suggested circuits 128, Fernando de la Mora 131, Travelling along Ruta 2 131, San Lorenzo 132, Capiatá 135, Itauguá 138, Ypacaraí 140, Caacupé 141, Itacurubí de la Cordillera 144, Towns north of Ruta 2 144, Luque 144, Areguá 148, San Bernardino 153, Altos 156, Emboscada 157, Atyrá 158, Tobatí 159, Vapor Cué 162, Towns south of Ruta 2 162, Pirayú 163, Piribebúy 163, Valenzuela 167, Sapucai 168, Travelling along Ruta 1 169, Itá 170, Yaguarón 172, Paraguarí 176,

Carapeguá 177, Ybycuí 178, La Colmena 179, Salto Cristal 179, San Roque González 180, Quiindý 181, Parque Nacional Lago Ypoá 181, Caapucú 183

Chapter 5 **Misiones and the Jesuit Reductions** **185**
Villa Florida 187, San Miguel 190, San Juan Bautista 191, San Ignacio Guasú 196, Santa María de Fe 205, Santa Rosa 210, Santiago 212, Ayolas 214

Chapter 6 **Southwest to Ñeembucú and the Old Battlegrounds** **223**
Pilar 225, Humaitá 232, Fishing pueblos along the Río Paraná 235, Northern Neembucú 240

Chapter 7 **Southeast to Itapúa and the Ruins** **241**
San Cosme y Damián 241, Carmen del Paraná 247, Trinidad 247, Jesús 256, Colonias Unidas 259, Excursion to San Ignacio Miní 260, Excursion to San Rafael Nature Reserve 267, Encarnación 268

Chapter 8 **Excursion to the Iguazú Falls** **277**
Puerto Iguazú 279, Foz do Iguaçu 286

Chapter 9 **Ciudad del Este and the East** **295**
Ciudad del Este 295, Itaipú 304

Chapter 10 **Villarrica and Central Eastern Paraguay** **309**
Coronel Oviedo 311, Yataitý 312, Independencia 313, Villarrica 315, Excursions from Villarrica 320, Caazapá 322

Chapter 11 **Concepción and the Northeast** **329**
Getting there and away 329, Travelling along Ruta 3 330, San Pedro de Ycuamandyyú 334, Concepción 337, The far north 342, Pedro Juan Caballero 346, Parque Cerro Corá and the surrounding area 351, The far north of Cerro Corá 354, The east-northeast 354

Chapter 12 **The Chaco** **361**
Within reach of Asunción 363, Travelling along the Ruta Transchaco 364, The humid Chaco, up to Pozo Colorado 366, Filadelfia 367, Boquerón 371, Loma Plata 372, Salt Lakes 373, Mariscal Estigarribia 374, The Pantanal 377

Appendix 1 **Language** **384**
Appendix 2 **Glossary** **392**
Appendix 3 **Selective list of fauna** **397**
Appendix 4 **Further information** **399**

Index **405**
Index of Advertisers **412**

HOW TO USE THE MAPS IN THIS GUIDE

Keys and symbols Maps include alphabetical keys covering the locations of those places to stay, eat or drink that are featured in the book. Note that regional maps may not show all hotels and restaurants in the area: other establishments may be located in towns shown on the map.

Grids and grid references Several maps use gridlines to allow easy location of sites. Map grid references are listed in square brackets after the name of the place or sight of interest in the text, with page number followed by grid number, eg: [72 C2].

LIST OF MAPS

Areguá 150
Asunción overview 72–3
Asunción access roads 126
Asunción city centre 74–5
Asunción, Villa Morra Carmelitas 79
Caazapá 323
Central Eastern Paraguay 310
Chaco, The 362
Circuito de Oro 122
Ciudad del Este 298
Concepción 338
Eastern Paraguay 296
Encarnación 270
Foz do Iguaçu 289
Franciscan towns 124
Iguazú Falls 278
Itapúa 242
Lago Ypoá region 182
Misiones 186
Nature reserves 8
Ñeembucú 224
Northeast, The 328
Paraguay 1st colour section
Pedro Juan Caballero 348
Pilar 227
Puerto Iguazú 281
Salto Cristal 180
San Bernardino 154
San Ignacio Guasú 198
San Ignacio Miní 264
San Juan Bautista 193
San Lorenzo 133
San Pedro de Ycuamandyyú 335
Santa María de Fe 205
Trinidad 249
Villarrica 317
Villarrica city centre 319

FEEDBACK REQUEST AND UPDATES WEBSITE

At Bradt Travel Guides we're aware that guidebooks start to go out of date on the day they're published – and that you, our readers, are out there in the field doing research of your own. You'll find out before us when a fine new family-run hotel opens or a favourite restaurant changes hands and goes downhill. So why not write and tell us about your experiences? Contact us on ☎ 01753 893444 or e info@bradtguides.com. We will forward emails to the author who may post updates on the Bradt website at www.bradtupdates.com/paraguay. Alternatively, you can add a review of the book to www.bradtguides.com or Amazon.

LIST OF BOXES

Accommodation price codes 53
Address forms in Paraguay xii
Aimé Bonpland 208
Aloft Asunción 77
Augusto Roa Bastos and his contemporaries 92
Bus timetable: Asunción – Misiones 188–9
Bus timetable: Asunción – Pilar 226
Bus timetable: Pilar – Humaitá – Paso de Patria 233
Buses: Asunción tel numbers 50
Buses to and from neighbouring countries 36
Chartering planes 381
Emergency 390
Estancias in the Apatur network 54
Fish dishes 217
Flights to northern Paraguay 380
Folk dance costume 23
Franciscan and Jesuit Reductions compared 174–5
Franciscan Reductions and towns with a strong Franciscan influence 146–7
Franciscan Reductions: history 125
Houses in the *campo* 185
Iguazú: the name 279
Indigenous groups and regions 19
Legend of Iguazú, The 285
Liberation theology and the Christian Agrarian Leagues 209
Long-haul flights, clots and DVT 43
Luis Bolaños 326
Mangoré 196
Marzo Paraguayo 108
Mennonite towns 368
Moíses Bertoni 308
National anthem 17
Nazis and Paraguay 14
Paraguay at a glance 2
Paseo Carmelitas 87
Pedro Juan Cavallero 346
Reduction: a typical town layout 200
Restaurant price codes 55
Roque González 114–15
Saints and their iconographical symbols 138
San Juan fiesta 194
Sunday in Asunción 106
Tereré etiquette 26
Train journey 119
Travellers with disabilities 45
Triple Alliance War: interpretations, The 352
Tropic of Capricorn 383
Virgin of Caacupé: the legend 142
Where different crafts are made 25

FOLLOW BRADT

For the latest news, special offers and competitions, subscribe to the Bradt newsletter via the website www.bradtguides.com and follow Bradt on:

- www.facebook.com/BradtTravelGuides
- @BradtGuides
- @bradtguides
- www.pinterest.com/bradtguides

SEND US YOUR SNAPS!

We'd love to follow your adventures using our guide, so send us your photos and stories via Twitter (@BradtGuides) and Instagram (@bradtguides) using the hashtag #Paraguay. Or you can email your photos to e info@bradtguides.com with the subject line 'Paraguay pics' and we'll tweet and instagram our favourites.

Introduction

'Paraguay is fabulous. I was deeply taken with the place, the scenery, birds, people, frogs, toads and wood sprites.' Simon Barnes's comment in *The Times* of 14 June 2008 may surprise a lot of people, for whom Paraguay is a blank on the map. And there are literally a lot of blanks if you search Google maps, although they are being filled in bit by bit. You find, for example, contours marked on western Brazil up to the border, and then as you cross into Paraguay they turn into flat grey. You go to a beach resort like Cerrito and not a single street name is given. You go into the heart of Asunción, the capital city, on Google Earth, using the 'street level' function, and you are skating across flat ground with just three or four drawings of buildings (not even photographs) standing up here and there. You come across backpackers who say, 'Don't go to Paraguay – there's nothing to see', but it is just that they do not know where to look.

Paraguay is one of last holiday paradises waiting to be discovered, with 300 days of sun a year. Only two special interest groups have so far discovered Paraguay in a big way: Brazilian fishing folk, who come over in their busloads to the remotest places in the south, on the banks of the Río Paraná; and US pigeon shooters, who come over in their privately chartered planeloads to the remotest places in the north, buried in the midst of the Paraguayan Chaco. Apart from these people, there is no tourist rush to Paraguay. It is, to a large extent, pure, virgin, undiscovered territory. You do not want to tell other people about it, for fear of spoiling it for yourself. And yet, at the same time, you do want to spread the word because you love it so much.

True, Paraguay is poor country. It is one of the poorest in the continent of South America, generally classified as a close second to Bolivia. Paraguay has only a third of the per capita income of Brazil and Argentina (UN figures for 2012). No-one would want to visit Paraguay who was uncomfortable with this fact. If you only wanted to see gleaming buildings and travel on motorways, you would not go to Paraguay. Yet for some travellers, the poverty is a reason to come, rather than to stay away. They may come out of a desire for solidarity, in the spirit of liberation theology, whereby the poor can teach the rich the message of the gospel. Or they may come out of a curiosity to see the kind of culture you can no longer find in Europe or North America. (For more figures on poverty, see page 20.)

When Simon Barnes came, he was taken by the wildness of the nature reserves and the richness of the birdlife, one of Paraguay's main attractions (see pages 6–7). But there are other key characteristics that mark the country. If you ask people who know something about Paraguay, even if only a little, what words they associate with the country, they may well mention poverty, the Guaraní language, the indigenous people, the Jesuit Reductions, the harp, craft, football, *tereré* and *mate*. Each of these aspects is outlined below, while more information can be found within the body of the guide.

GUARANÍ LANGUAGE It is well known that Paraguay is a bilingual country: 77% of the population can speak Guaraní, although this has gone down markedly from

87% in 2002. In the *campo* (countryside) almost everyone speaks Guaraní as their mother tongue, but unless you go deep into the *campo*, almost everyone is fluent in Spanish as well. This gives Paraguay a unique richness among Latin American countries. There are other countries that have a strong use of indigenous languages in certain regions, but none where the country as a whole is bilingual.

You will find that if you speak Spanish you will have no difficulty travelling all over the country, because no-one will think of speaking to you, as a foreigner, in Guaraní. You will hear a lot of Guaraní spoken, but unless your Spanish is good you may not realise it because the frequency of Spanish words in Guaraní discourse may lead you to think they are talking Spanish. For more on Guaraní, see pages 20–1 and 389–91.

THE INDIGENOUS The indigenous population (as measured in the census of 2012) is 112,848, which accounts for only 1.7% of the total population. Although this is scandalously low, it is more than 25,000 up on the figure in the 2002 census, and is higher than in some other South American countries. You are very aware that there is an indigenous presence as soon as you set foot in Paraguay: you see them selling their crafts in the airport, the bus terminal and on the streets of central Asunción – often wearing bright feather headdresses to attract the tourists.

The country is divided by the Río Paraguay into the west (the Chaco) and the east (where most people live). Approximately half of the indigenous live in the east and half in the west, but because the west is so sparsely populated by other groups, the indigenous are more evident there. There is a movement towards more urban living, but the majority still live in the countryside. A division of the ethnic groups into different language groups is given in a table on page 19.

THE REDUCTIONS The famous 'Paraguayan Reductions' were missions for the Guaraní indigenous, distinguished by their high development of architecture, sculpture, music and other arts. The term 'Reductions' is somewhat confusing (*Reducciones* in Spanish), but it dates back to their origin and refers to a semi-nomadic people moving into fixed settlements. There were Jesuit Reductions and Franciscan Reductions, but the Jesuit Reductions are much better known: they were more pioneering in their artistic and cultural development, and bolder in the kind of independent political utopia that they established.

The Jesuit-Guaraní Reductions were far flung in the initial period, starting from 1609, and subject to destruction by slave-traders from São Paulo, but they gradually consolidated themselves and in their heyday numbered 30 towns (the Treinta Pueblos). These Treinta Pueblos then formed a region stretching across three present-day countries: eight in Paraguay, seven in Brazil, and 15 in Argentina. They are sometimes all loosely referred to as the Paraguayan Reductions, because they were all in the original Jesuit province of Paraquaria (Latin). At the time, this Jesuit region was practically a nation in itself – part of the Spanish empire but independent of the jurisdiction of the other Spanish colonies in South America.

Most of the Argentinian and Brazilian Reductions unfortunately fall outside the scope of this book, although San Ignacio Miní (Argentina) has been included as a popular, nearby excursion from Paraguay (see pages 260–7). For more information on the Reductions, see chapters 5 and 7.

HARP The Jesuit Anton Sepp, who taught the Guaraní to make musical instruments, is called the father of the Paraguayan harp. This beautiful instrument – not the classical, European harp, but the Paraguayan harp, which is different in a number of ways – is now an icon of Paraguay. It is made entirely of wood, with no metal to its frame, so it is considerably lighter, and the wood of the sound box is usually carved with plant motifs. It has no pedals, so you cannot change key without retuning the whole instrument; to make a semitone, the player will press a string with their metal tuning key, or even with a finger, but some new harps are now being made with a row of levers at the top of the strings, called Salvi levers. For more on the harp see page 23.

CRAFT Paraguay is renowned for its craftwork, and especially for some traditional forms of lace, meticulously fashioned by hand and taking a vast amount of time. One of these is *ñanduti* (Guaraní 'spiderweb'), because it is circular; this is particular to Paraguay and made in Itauguá (see pages 138–40). Another textile is the distinctive and beautiful *ao po'i* (Guaraní 'cloth fine'), which can refer to the cloth itself or to the embroidery on it. On occasions this can be turned a kind of lacework. The best quality *ao po'i* is made is Yataitý (see pages 312–13). Paraguayan men who can afford it will wear a shirt embroidered with *ao po'i* for special occasions: President Lugo wore such a shirt for his investiture. A third kind of lace is *encaje ju* (Spanish 'lace'; Guaraní 'needle'), which is made in a number of places.

The intricate craft of ***filigrana*** (filigree) silver jewellery is associated with Luque (see pages 144–8): since the amount of silver used in this painstaking work is not great, and labour is cheap in Paraguay, the brooches, earrings and pendants are very reasonably priced.

Also enormously time-consuming is the decorative ***poncho de sesenta listas*** which is still made by hand, entirely out of cotton thread: this comes from Piribebúy (see pages 163–7).

There are many crafts that make use of natural materials native to the country: leather, for bags; palm leaves, for hats; rushes, for table mats; vegetable fibres, for shoulder bags; bamboo, for furniture; *palo santo* wood, for statues of saints; clay, for pottery; wool, for ponchos; cotton, for hammocks; and more besides. Each of these crafts is connected with a particular town, and often with a particular family. This makes a craft tour of Paraguay a particularly rich experience. See also pages 25–6.

FOOTBALL Another key characteristic of Paraguay is football, far and away the country's leading sport. It has even been claimed that the game originated in the Jesuit Reductions, because José Manuel Peramás, a contemporary Jesuit historian, reported in 1793 that the Guaraní 'would play with a ball which, although it was all of rubber, was so light and quick that it would go on bouncing without stopping … They did not hit the ball with the hand as we do, but with the upper part of a bare foot, passing it and receiving it with great agility and precision.'

Paraguay qualified for four consecutive World Cups between 1998 and 2010, which is an amazing feat for a country with such a small population, lack of infrastructure and general level of poverty.

The team is renowned for its steely spirit and never-say-die approach. BBC football commentator Tim Vickery says: 'Paraguayan football has always been able to count on fighting spirit. The game brings out the warrior in the people, who knit together naturally to build teams feared all over the continent for their durability.'

Unfortunately, Paraguay did not qualify for the 2014 World Cup in Brazil, but in 2010 they made history by making the quarter-final stage of the World Cup for the first time, and the team that defeated them in a penalty shootout – Spain – went on to win the tournament. For many people around the world this was the first time they sat up and took account of the little-known country of Paraguay. See also page 27.

TERERE You cannot think Paraguay without thinking *tereré*. If you have not been to Paraguay yet, you may not know what the word means, but you may well have heard of *mate*, because it is drunk in Argentina and Brazil as well. *Mate* is a tea made with boiling water, and *tereré* uses the same leaf, but infused in iced water.

Everywhere you go in Paraguay you will find people sitting in little groups and passing round the *tereré*. It is served in a common cup (*guampa*) and drunk through a metal straw (*bombilla*). Paraguayans really adore their *tereré*, and do not understand how other nations can live without it. See also pages 26–7 for instructions on how to participate in this ritual.

THE FUTURE? At the turn of the century, tourism was at a very low ebb, following the murder of a vice-president in 1999. The country teetered on the brink of a coup both in 1999 and in 2000. After that the Argentinian economic crisis hit Paraguay hard – many families here have relatives sending money back from Buenos Aires – and there was no money for investment in anything. Paraguay was a country in deep recession, where the poor were getting poorer and the rich were getting poorer too. Craft shops in Asunción struggled not to go bankrupt. Even professional people were saying, 'I have never known it as bad as this'. The *campesinos*, as always, suffered the most.

But from 2004 onwards, the economic crisis levelled out, and there began to be increasing movement on the tourist front, with the appointment of a series of good ministers of tourism (women who were professionals in tourism rather than politicians). There was investment in two major tourist programmes, the Ruta Jesuítica and the Camino Franciscano; the publication of local tourist materials such as guides, maps, leaflets and reviews, none of which existed five years earlier; and the sprouting up of new hotels, especially in Asunción. The number of foreign tourists has risen every year since 2003, by between 2% and 15%, and reached 610,000 in 2013. Of these, 88% are from other countries in Latin America, and of the rest the highest numbers come from Spain, Germany, Japan, Italy and France. More than half of tourists come for business or for professional events, and one third for holidays and sightseeing. Accommodation for tourists in hotels rose 34% between 2007 and 2012, and was predicted to double between 2012 and 2016.

Paraguay's interest in promoting tourism has been reflected in recent years by the nomination of some famous personalities as '*embajador turístico del Paraguay*': Arnaldo André (a film and television actor), Roque Santa Cruz (a footballer), and – most recently and most dramatically – an orchestra from one of the poorest *barrios* of Asunción, which plays on musical instruments knocked together out of old tins and boxes. Known as *La Orquesta de Instrumentos Reciclados de Cateura*, this group has rightly become quite famous internationally. You can listen to their beautiful music on YouTube. In the Cateura barrio, where they live, people scratch together a living by going through rubbish bins and sorting materials for recycling; but never before has there been such an imaginative use of recycled materials as this.

The Guaraní indigenous had a dream of 'a land without evil' – *la tierra sin mal* in Spanish, or *yvý maraneý* in Guaraní – 'a land without stain, without pollution'. In their semi-nomadic existence they were always looking for this paradise. Something of the romance of the Guaraní dream under Jesuit tutelage was captured in Roland Joffé's powerful film about the Paraguayan Reductions, *The Mission*. But it was not fiction; the film recounted historical events. The historians have called the creation, and destruction, of those Jesuit-Guaraní Reductions, 'the Forgotten Arcadia'. With the help of this guidebook, it will be much easier for people of other cultures and other continents to come and search, nomad-like, for the land without stain, here, where it was first dreamt of, in the lost paradise of Paraguay.

ADDRESS FORMS IN PARAGUAY

This guide has not attempted to change the Paraguayan way of writing addresses, but it will not be comprehensible without some explanation. The name of the street may or may not be followed by the number, but it will almost certainly be followed by c/ or by esq or by e/ … y …

c/ means *casi* ('nearly'), which means that the name is given of the nearest cross street.
esq means *esquina* ('corner'), which means that the house is on the corner of the two streets mentioned.
e/ …y … means *entre* … y … ('between … and …') which means that the house is between the named side streets.

For example:

Agyr 25 de mayo 1767 c/ Mayor Fleitas – means that the office of Agyr is on the street called 25 de mayo, at number 1767, which is close to the junction with the street called Mayor Fleitas.

National Yegros 501 esq Cerro Corá – means that the office of National is on the street called Yegros, at number 501, which is on the corner, at the junction with the street called Cerro Corá.

Turismo Ami Pampliega e/ Adrián Jara y Pa'í Pérez – means that the office of Turismo Ami is on the street called Pampliega, on the stretch between the side street called Adrián Jara and the side street called Pa'í Pérez.

A curiosity is that many people in the interior do not know the name of the streets in their town, sometimes not even of the street they live on. They use different points of reference.

In the interior, addresses on the main roads are often pinpointed by giving the number of kilometres from Asunción. For example:

San Ignacio Country Club Ruta 1 km230 – means that it is on Ruta 1, 230km from Asunción.

Occasionally, the number of kilometres is measured from another city. For example, in the context of Ciudad del Este.

Churrasquería Interlagos Ruta 7, km5 – means that it is 5km from Ciudad del Este.

Part One

GENERAL INFORMATION

PARAGUAY AT A GLANCE

Location Paraguay is in the centre of South America, without a coastline. Its neighbours are Brazil, Argentina and Bolivia.
Area 406,752km^2
Climate Subtropical, generally hot and humid, particularly in January, with a few cold weeks from June to August. Heavy thunderstorms are common, as are months of drought. The Chaco has a rainy season and a dry season.
Status Republic with a president
Population 6,600,284
Origin of the population Indigenous from many peoples but especially Guaraní; Spanish and their *mestizo* (mixed race) descendants; more recent immigrants, especially Brazilians, Argentinians, Germans and Koreans
Life expectancy 67 years
Capital Asunción, population 515,588
Other main towns Ciudad del Este, Concepción, Encarnación, Pedro Juan Caballero, Villarrica
Administrative structure 17 *departamentos* plus the capital
Principal exports Hydro-electric power, beef, soya, leather, wood, cotton, sugar, tobacco, *yerba maté*, marijuana
GDP US$3,878 per capita in 2012
Official languages Spanish and Guaraní
Currency Guaraní (Gs)
Exchange rate US$1 = Gs4,305; £1 = Gs7,226; €1 = Gs5,595 (August 2014)
Airport Silvio Pettirossi, Asunción
International telephone code +595
Internet domain .py
Time GMT –4 (but because the summertimes of the two hemispheres are different, Paraguay is 3 hours behind London from October to March, and 5 hours behind from March to October)
Voltage 220V
Weights and measures Metric; kilograms and kilometres
Flag Red, white and blue horizontal bands, with the shield of the republic in the middle on one side of the flag, and a lion in the middle on the other side
National anthem *Paraguayos, ¡República o muerte!* (first line of chorus)
National flower Passion flower (Guaraní *mburucuyá*)
National holidays See page 57
National tree Lapacho (Guaraní *tajý*)
National bird Bellbird (*pájaro campana*)
Most successful sport Football
Most famous writer Augusto Roa Bastos
Most famous composer Agustín Pío Barrios (Mangoré)

NB: figures are from the 2012 Dirección General de Estadística, Encuestas y Censos (DGEEC) and the Enciclopedia Concisa de Py.

1

Background Information

An outline of some of the key features of Paraguay appears in the *Introduction* (see pages viii–xii). This chapter concentrates on more detailed facts and figures.

GEOGRAPHY

Paraguay covers 406,752km^2 and is shaped like a lopsided butterfly. The eastern half is where 97% of the people live; it is a little over 150,000km^2 of largely fertile lowland, interrupted occasionally by wooded hills. Further to the east it rises around 400–500m into the Paraná tableland. The western part is called the Chaco, which is larger (almost 250,000km^2), but has less than 3% of the population, because it is so inhospitable.

RIVERS AND LAKES The two principal rivers are the Río Paraguay, which divides the country in two (like the body of the butterfly), and the Río Paraná, which forms the frontier with Corrientes and Misiones in Argentina.

The Río Paraguay rises in the Brazilian Pantanal and has an average width of 500m, with numerous tributaries on both sides. They include (from north to south on the eastern side) the Río Apa (frontier with Brazil), the Aquidabán (great beaches north of Concepción), the Jejuí Guazú, the Manduvirá, the Río Salado (which runs into the great Lago Ypacaraí) and further south, on the border of Misiones, the Río Tebicuarý. The next river that flows into it from the east is the great Río Paraná.

The tributaries flowing in from the west (north to south) begin with the Río Negro of the Pantanal (which forms the boundary with Bolivia for a short distance, where the Río Paraguay comes in from the northeast and the Río Negro follows the line directly north–south). Then there are many small rivers called *riachos* along the stretch that has Brazil to the east, ending with the Riacho Mosquito just north of Puerto Casado. Then come the Río Verde, the Río Montelindo, a second Río Negro, the Río Aguaray Guazú, the Río Confuso and finally the Río Pilcomayo, which forms the boundary between the Paraguayan Chaco and the Argentinian Chaco.

The Río Paraná rises in the Brazilian state of Paraná, and is a swift-flowing river, 150m deep and narrow near Ciudad del Este, ranging to 15m deep and 1,500m wide near Encarnación. This is the river that has been exploited for the Itaipú and Yacyretá hydro-electric dams, and that will soon be harnessed again, for the Corpus dam (near Trinidad).

The country has two principal lakes: Lago Ypacaraí and Lago Ypoá (see pages 153 and 181–3).

HILLS Paraguay is generally a flat country. This is particularly so in the Chaco, where the only hill is the Cerro León (604m, though it is really a grouping of about 46 hills). In western Paraguay, there are two *cordilleras* (hill ranges). The smaller one, close to Asunción, runs through the *departamento* (province) called Cordillera, and includes the hills to the north of Paraguarí (good for views and adventure tourism), the hills to the south of Areguá (of notable geological characteristics, page 152) and the hills around Tobatí and Atyrá (eg: that of Casa del Monte, page 158).

The larger *cordillera* runs from the northeast corner of Paraguay, at Cerro Corá (see pages 351–4), south along the Brazilian border to the Bosque Mbaracayú (pages 356–8), where the range divides. One finger takes a turn east (and the frontier follows it) to reach Salto del Guairá on the Río Paraná. After this, the frontier follows the river southwards.

The other part of the *cordillera* goes in a southwesterly direction from Mbaracayú, through the San Joaquín area, and eventually reaches the reserve of Ybyturuzú, where Paraguay's highest hill is found: Cerro Tres Kandú, at 842m (see pages 321–2). From this point the *cordillera* sweeps southeast, and then southwest again, where it is named the Cordillera de San Rafael, at 455m (see pages 267–8).

CLIMATE

The climate of most of Paraguay is subtropical. According to the official dates, spring is 21 September to 20 December, summer is 21 December to 20 March, autumn is 21 March to 20 June and winter is 21 June to 20 September. Although there can be long periods of drought, fatal for the crops, there is generally a good level of rainfall, producing a very green landscape. The rain most typically falls in violent thunderstorms, which are not infrequent.

The average maximum temperature is 36°C in January (the hottest month) in the Chaco (Mariscal Estigarribia), and 32°C in Encarnación (the most southerly city). The average minimum in those two places in January is 23°C and 20°C respectively.

In July (the coldest month) the average maximum temperature is 26°C in Mariscal Estigarribia, and 21°C in Encarnación. The average minimum in those two places in July is 12°C and 9°C respectively. See also pages 28–9.

NATURAL HISTORY AND CONSERVATION

Paraguay has a very rich biodiversity, due to its being located in the subtropics, and having five distinct ecoregions – the Chaco (subdivided into dry north and wet south), the Pantanal (on the west bank of the Río Paraguay in the far north), the Pampas (or savannah or grasslands, eg: in the Misiones area), the Cerrado (mixed dry woodlands and grassland, in the north of the eastern region) and the Atlantic Forest (now largely deforested, but in the east of eastern Paraguay). There is a great extent of wetlands, encouraging a wealth of species, not only in the northern Pantanal, but also to the east of the Río Pilcomayo where there is the Tinfunque reserve, and to the east of the Río Paraguay in the *departamentos* of Ñeembucú, Paraguarí and Central.

The Chaco (which is mostly in Paraguay, with a part in Argentina and a part in Bolivia) is considered to be the world's largest natural area after the Amazon. The country is beginning to receive more attention as a tourist destination by those who want to see nature in its pristine state, in all its splendour.

FAUNA More than 398 species of fish, 173 species of mammals, 177 species of reptiles, 87 species of amphibians and 713 species of birds have been recorded (see

Birdwatching, page 9) in Paraguay. It is also extraordinarily rich in butterflies: there are at least 381 species. Here is a brief summary of some of Paraguay's best-known animals and birds, but for comprehensive information look at the Fauna Paraguay website (*www.faunaparaguay.com*). For a selective list of fauna names in English, Latin, Spanish and Guaraní, see *Appendix 3*.

Mammals

Jaguar Without doubt Paraguay's most dramatic and handsome animal, the jaguar is the biggest feline in all America. Paraguayans commonly translate *jaguareté* (Guaraní) as *tigre*, but it is a spotted jaguar, not a striped tiger. The body length is up to 1.85m, plus the tail which can be 0.75m. Solitary and territorial, it is a dangerous hunter, feeding on capybaras, peccaries, tapirs, caimans, fish and birds. If you come across one, you should not turn around, but make a lot of noise, talking loudly, and waving your arms about holding anything you have to hand, so as to appear bigger than you are. Then withdraw slowly, but without turning your back. There are few jaguars in eastern Paraguay but in the Alto Paraguay region of the Chaco they are quite common.

Puma Another name for the puma is the mountain lion (there are many more, such as cougar). It is tawny yellow but the young have dark speckles. The end of the tail is almost black. It can grow even bigger than the jaguar, but it is a lighter cat, and feeds on smaller prey, including porcupines and vipers. It is found in both halves of the country.

Black howler monkey This is one of two kinds of monkey common in Paraguay, and there are plenty of them in both halves of the country. The males are big and black, so that they look a different species from the females, which are brown. When they howl, they make a loud repeated ululating noise somewhere between a croak and a snore. There is a family of howler monkeys that lives in the plaza of Santa María de Fe, and they are a great attraction, as they come quite close to the visitors to accept pieces of banana.

Black-striped capuchin monkey Slightly smaller than the howler monkey, and the male does not have a different colouring from the female. It is found only in eastern Paraguay.

South American coati This is not quite a racoon, but almost. It has a triangular head with a long snout, and the tail has horizontal stripes all the way down. It lives in low thorn and humid forests, is a rapid climber, and eats almost anything. There are a great number at the Iguazú Falls, and their behaviour has become problematic because the visitors feed them, which changes their natural habits and makes them greedy and aggressive.

Maned wolf Known as *aguará guasú* in Guaraní, this has long reddish hair, with long ears, long black legs and a kind of mane in a black line along its back. It is nocturnal and omnivorous, and lives in wetlands all over the country.

South American tapir A big animal that has a long snout with an extended upper lip, which almost becomes a short trunk. It has hooves and a stumpy tail, and is up to 2m in length. It is herbivorous, nocturnal and solitary, and is found in both regions of the country.

Peccary There are different types, but the Chacoan peccary – which was believed to be extinct but has been rediscovered – is like a boar with long hair that sticks up in spikes. It is herbivorous and feeds on cacti. There is also a collared peccary and a white-lipped peccary, which are found in both regions, while the Chacoan peccary lives only in the west.

Giant anteater This huge anteater is grey with a diagonal band of black, edged with white, running from its back to under the neck. The front limbs have three powerful claws, and the long, thin snout has an even longer and thinner tongue that shoots out. It has long, bristly fur and is found in both halves of the country.

Capybara Called *carpincho* in Spanish – a well-known word for what, in Paraguay, is a common animal in both regions, while few people are familiar with the term 'capybara' in English. It is herbivorous and lives where there is water, in wetlands and on riverbanks. It is more than 1m long and is a good swimmer and diver, with interdigital membranes. It is hunted by Paraguayans for its meat, and is now a protected species – not that that means anything in Paraguay. It is the world's largest rodent, with a rectangular profile to its face, and tight, reddish brown hair.

Armadillo There are different types and sizes, ranging from 25cm for the southern three-banded armadillo to 1m for the giant armadillo. It has a shell divided into little segments arranged in rows, giving the impression of armour. It feeds on ants, termites, larvae, etc, and the giant armadillo also eats honey.

Reptiles

Caiman Known by its Guaraní name *yacaré*, which in correct contemporary Guaraní should be spelt *jakaré*, though the old spelling persists. When translated into Spanish, people call it a *cocodrilo*, but strictly speaking it is a caiman, which belongs to the alligator family, rather than the crocodile. Like the capybara, the *yacaré* is a protected species which is nonetheless commonly hunted for its flesh, which tastes like a cross between meat and fish. The caiman lives on both sides of Paraguay, and there are plenty at the Iguazú Falls.

Birds

Greater rhea This bird is what many people call an ostrich but is actually subtly different, because it has three toes instead of the two that the African ostrich has. They are large, flightless, silent birds. Many rheas have been semi-domesticated because of their use in eating up pests and keeping the grass and weeds down. Unusually among birds, it is the male who sits on the eggs to incubate them and raises his brood: even more unusually, the eggs come from several different females.

Toucans One of the most famous and most colourful birds of Paraguay, the toco toucan has an enormous yellow and orange beak tipped with black. It is a big black bird (53cm) with a yellow circle round its eyes, a white bib, and a white stripe near the end of its tail. It lives in jungles and forests, in both east and west Paraguay.

Macaws Macaws are a type of parrot. The red-and-green macaw is the most vividly colourful of the Paraguayan parrots. The hyacinth macaw is blue, and is the largest of the family. These magnificent birds are scarce on both sides of the country, but can be seen in several zoos, eg: Casa del Monte in Atyrá, or the Atinguý refuge outside Ayolas.

Chilean flamingo The Chilean flamingo can be observed in the Chaco without too much difficulty. This beautiful long-legged bird, which likes standing on one leg, has pink feathers, a black beak, and red knees and feet. It measures 70cm and inhabits lagoons and marshes in the western region.

Tinamous Called a *perdiz* in Spanish, which is usually translated as 'partridge' in a dictionary, but the distinctive kind of *perdiz* carved in wood and stone in the Jesuit-Guaraní Reductions has a crest on its head, and is a very regal-looking bird. This is the brushland tinamou or the quebracho crested-tinamou, found in the Chaco. There are other species of tinamou elsewhere in Paraguay; all are cryptically coloured brown and buff.

Herons and egrets These birds have long legs, usually white bodies, and they eat mostly fish. There are several kinds, and the snowy egret is common in both regions of Paraguay. They are beautiful in flight, and very distinctive, owing to the retracted neck.

Southern lapwing This shorebird has a distinctive name in Spanish, *tero tero*, though is mostly known by its Guaraní name of *teteú*. It is an elegant bird with a few purple and green highlights on its grey and white body, and a red beak. It occurs in both halves of the country.

Bare-throated bellbird The bare-throated bellbird or *pájaro campana* is particularly loved by Paraguayans because there is a famous piece of harp music named after it which evokes its song. It has been declared the 'national bird' by the Congress. The song can be heard from hundreds of metres away, and resembles the echo of a little hammer on metal. It is a vulnerable species, but good numbers have been recorded recently in the Mbaracayú reserve and in some reserves of Itaipú.

Hummingbirds Often seen in Paraguay, extracting the nectar wherever there are flowers, with its wings whirring. There are various species, but one of the most common is the glittering-bellied emerald, which is (as its name suggests) a dark emerald colour. The males have a red beak, and the females a grey beak. It is a small bird, only 9cm long, with a 2cm beak, and its name in Spanish, *picaflor*, refers to its pecking of the nectar. The *mainumbý* (to give it its Guaraní name) was regarded in old mythology as having existed before the creation of the world and having a special relationship to God, for which reason it has been used in the murals of San Ignacio to represent the Holy Spirit (instead of a dove).

FLORA The national flower of Paraguay is the *mburucuyá* which was portrayed by the artists of the Jesuit-Guaraní Reductions as their principal flower motif, in stone and wood carving: it has been captured in the logo of the Ruta Jesuítica tourist programme. The *mburucuyá* fruit – the passion fruit – has a delicious, tangy flavour: it gives a kick to any fruit salad, makes an excellent mousse and can also be turned into a fruit juice drink.

The *lapacho* (Guaraní *tajy*) is regarded as the national tree, and with its abundant pink blossom it gives a very distinctive appearance to Paraguay in springtime. The tree is tall and produces a wood which is hard and strong, and is used for pillars, door and window frames.

The *cocotero* is the distinctive and most typical tree of the *campo* in the western region – a skinny palm tree with long, sharp spines and a fragrant yellow flower that appears at Christmastime, and is customarily placed before the crib. It is very abundant. Other kinds of palm tree found in the country are the *pindó,* the *coco phoenix* and (in the Chaco) the tall *karanda'ý* with its fan-like leaves, which produces an excellent hardwood used in building. For more details of the flora, see the sections on national parks and reserves in the regional chapters.

NATURE RESERVES There are a large number of nature reserves in Paraguay, some belonging to the state – the national parks – and others in private hands – the protected wild areas (*áreas silvestres protegidas*). The map below shows their distribution around the country, and information on these will be found within each regional chapter.

In order to visit the national parks, you need to contact the Secretaria del Ambiente (SEAM) (*021 615806; www.seam.gov.py*). They can give you advice on the access roads into the reserve, on where you can stay, and can put you in touch with the park ranger (*guardaparque*), who can give you a guided tour. But visiting without prior notice is not forbidden.

There is a bilingual guide to the national parks, and it is still in print although it may not be easy to get hold of: *Guide to Paraguay's National Parks and other Protected Wild Areas* by Peter T Clark (see *Appendix 4*). Try the Servilibro bookshop, Quijote, Servilibro or El Libro en Su Casa; see *Bookshops*, pages 93–4, or buy one direct from the author (*021 391371;* e *petertomclark@hotmail.com*).

BIRDWATCHING Paraguay is an exceptional country for birdwatchers, so do not forget your binoculars if you have a pair. It is said that expert birdwatchers can add from 400 to 450 new species to their list in just a couple of weeks in the country. Paraguay has 57 IBAs (Important Bird Areas), including Laguna Blanca (see pages 333–4), the Tagatijá stream (see pages 342–3) and the Bosque Mbaracayú (see pages 356–8) in the northeast; Arroyos y Esteros (see page 330) in the centre; and Lago Ypoá (see pages 181–3), the Yabebyrý Wildlife Refuge (see page 220), Yacyretá island (see pages 219–20) and the San Rafael Nature Reserve (see pages 267–8) in the south. The most accessible of the IBAs is the Bay of Asunción, which is rich in migratory birds, even though the construction of the Costanera (coast road) has not been good for bird habitats. The organisation Guyrá Paraguay (see details on page 76) organises regular birdwatching days in the Bay, and can also be approached to arrange a guided trip for visitors. The tour operator Wildlife Tours (m *0981 920296; www.wildlife.com.py*) also specialises in birdwatching (see page 77).

In the Chaco, which is an arid zone with vast *estancias* (country estates), there are seven species of tinamou. This is a regular stopping place for many migratory species, including flamingoes; the time of migration is September and October. North of the tropic of Capricorn, in the uninhabited dry region of the Chaco, lucky birders find the black-legged seriema walking beside the road, or the crowned eagle flying overhead.

The Pantanal, the biggest wetland in the world, begins in the northeast of the Chaco. As you travel up the Río Paraguay towards the Río Negro, you see a great contrast to the arid western zone of the Chaco, with palm trees, gallery forests and extensive wetlands. Crossing the area on horseback, by rowing boat or on foot, you can observe aquatic species like herons, cormorants, storks, ducks, southern screamers and terns hunting the river for their next catch. The swallow-tailed hummingbird and the toco toucan are among the 280 species registered so far that inhabit the area.

In the north and centre of the eastern region you find the cerrado, which is characterised by a mixture of low forests and grassland, on nutrient-poor well-drained soils, like sand. (There is also cerrado in Brazil and Bolivia.) The national parks of Paso Bravo, Bella Vista and Cerro Corá are examples of this landscape. A little further south, the private reserves of Mbaracayú (the eastern part, see pages 356–8) and Laguna Blanca (dedicated to agriculture and tourism, see pages 333–4) offer a good example of this kind of territory, and Mbaracayú additionally has a very extensive tract of Atlantic Forest. The red-legged seriema is common and, if you go exploring at night with a lamp, you may see nightbirds such as the white-winged nightjar, a globally threatened bird that was discovered in Paraguay as recently as 1995.

The principal remnant of the Atlantic Forest is found in the southeast of the country, in the San Rafael reserve. From the hilltop you can see natural grasslands with paths disappearing into the forest in the direction of the reforestation projects. Again, the bird life is stunning: in the grasslands you find a great variety of tinamous, and also endangered species like the marsh seedeater and the chestnut seedeater. In the Atlantic Forest you can see the ochre-collared piculet and the chestnut-bellied euphonia, and other colourful birds. A highlight of a night walk may be a common potoo, an extraordinary creature. By day it sits motionless on top of a dry stick, with the appearance of bark but with a long, barred tail, and at dusk it emits a long cry like a human wail. At night it metamorphoses into an agile aerial hunter.

REFORESTATION Paraguay has been massively deforested, and the illegal logging is continuing at a terrifying pace because it is always difficult to enforce laws in

Paraguay, where the level of corruption is so high. In 1845, 55% of the eastern half of Paraguay was forested; in 1991, 15%; and in 2002, only 4%. The Atlantic Forest originally covered nine million hectares, at the time of writing only 700,000ha remain, and these are not continuous but scattered, which impedes the ecological function of the forest.

In the first 11 months of 2012 alone, 268,084ha were deforested in the Paraguayan Chaco, attracting attention in *The Guardian* and *The New York Times*: it has been calculated to be continuing at the rate of a hectare a minute. These are terrifying figures. Paraguay has been classed as the worst country in the Americas for deforestation, and the second worst in the world. According to University of Maryland data, Paraguay has lost almost 4 million hectares of tree cover since 2000. Between 130 and 140 thousand hectares of woodland are cut down each year. Amazingly, however, nearly every species that has ever been recorded here still remains.

There is now a campaign, '*A todo pulmón*', to reforest the countryside, particularly in the Atlantic Forest region, with 50 million trees: *lapacho*, cedar, *yvyrapytã*, *timbó*, *kurupa'ý* and others. (See *Travelling positively*, page 62).

The best-preserved parts of the Atlantic Forest are the Bosque Mbaracayú (see pages 356–8) and the Reserva San Rafael (see pages 267–8). Both have good facilities for receiving visitors.

AQUIFER The Guaraní Aquifer, which Paraguay shares with Brazil, Uruguay and Argentina, is the third-biggest subterranean water reserve in the world, with a volume of 37,000km^3. Out of its total extent of 1,190,000km^2 (an area greater than Spain, Portugal and France put together), 5.9% is in Paraguay, that is, 70,000km^2. The aquifer is found underneath the Atlantic Forest ecoregion, in the *departamentos* of Caaguazú and Alto Paraná, and about 200 wells in Paraguay go down deeply enough to reach it. The aquifer is replenished by rainwater.

HISTORY

The original inhabitants of what was to become Paraguay were the **indigenous**, principally the Guaraní, though there were also other peoples, including war-like tribes such as the Guaicurú. The Guaraní lived a semi-nomadic agricultural life, cultivating maize and mandioc, and hunting deer, monkey, coati, tapirs and anteaters. They made pots and baskets, and from time to time travelled in long wooden canoes. They lived in long huts or *chozas* made of branches and adobe, with up to 60 related families in each. When they moved on, every couple of years, they dreamt that they were pursuing the *yvý marane'ỹ* (Spanish *la tierra sin mal*, 'the land without evil'). Later, when they were evangelised, this legendary paradise became identified with the promised land.

THE CONQUEST The New World was carved up in advance by the 1494 **Treaty of Tordesillas** that gave Portugal everything to the east and Spain everything to the west of a north–south line running 370 leagues west of the Cape Verde islands (approximately through where São Paulo is today). But the treaty could not cope with the changing situation on the ground and incursions were frequent. The first European to discover Paraguayan territory was the Portuguese explorer **Alejo García**, who crossed the land from Brazil to reach the Peru of the Incas with their famous gold. He filled up his boat with precious metals, but was murdered by hostile indigenous on his way down the Río Paraguay, approximately at San Pedro de Ycuamandyyú in 1525 (see pages 334–7).

The conquest of Paraguay began with the Spanish expedition led by Pedro de Mendoza, who established the first (short-lived) port of Buenos Aires in 1536, and sent his lieutenant **Juan de Ayolas** upriver. Ayolas stopped briefly in Lambaré (on the outskirts of the future Asunción), where he left his deputy **Domingo Martínez de Irala**, before going further north. Ayolas never returned, and Irala, who was more a politician and a diplomat than a soldier, made this area the headquarters of the invasion. Irala made a pact with the Guaraní, who were more pacific than the tribes around Buenos Aires. The invaders were allowed to have relations with the Guaraní women, so laying the foundations for a *mestizo* bilingual society in which children learned Spanish from their fathers and Guaraní from their mothers.

Juan de Salazar y Espinoza is regarded as the founder of Asunción in this period, because of the fort he established on a bend of the Río Paraguay on 15 August 1537, the feast of the Assumption. The first Buenos Aires was abandoned, to be re-founded from Asunción towards the end of the century, and the new town growing up around the fort (with its first *cabildo* or town council inaugurated in 1541) was seen as important for its strategic position on the river which led towards Peru and its gold. The hope was that this river would become as important for silver as Peru had been for gold: hence, the Río de la Plata (river of silver).

In 1556 the ***encomienda*** system began, in which the initially peaceful co-existence of Spanish and Guaraní was seen in its true colours, as cruel exploitation. The men were sent to work in the fields of the Spanish, who treated them harshly as though they were slaves, and the women cared for the homes and the sexual appetites of the Spanish in Asunción.

MISSIONS 1541 saw the arrival of the first Franciscan missionaries, who worked within the colonial system and tried to make the best of it. From 1580 onwards they formed Reductions for the Guaraní (see box on *Luis Bolaños* on page 326).

At this stage the whole huge area south of Peru and east of the Andes was called the Provincia Gigante de Indias, and was subject to Peru, which in turn was subject to Spain. An important governor based in Asunción from 1598 to 1617 was Hernando Arias de Saavedra (known as **Hernandarias**) who was a *criollo* (son of Spaniards, born in South America) and attended to the interests of the indigenous. With his support, a group of **Jesuits** arrived from Peru in 1607 to found a new Jesuit province of Paraquaria (the origin of the name Paraguay), with the brilliant young Antonio Ruiz de Montoya (henceforth **Montoya**) among them. With them, a new era began in which the Jesuit Reductions did not work within the Spanish colonial system, but outside of it, in a territory that the Europeans were forbidden to occupy. The Spanish and Portuguese were thus deprived of slaves, and had the embarrassment of seeing those who they regarded as semi-human natives develop a civilisation of art, architecture and music superior to their own. (For more on the Jesuit Missions see page ix and chapters 5 and 7.)

The resentment, jealousy and hostility this aroused was eventually to result in the order by Carlos III of Spain in 1767 for the **expulsion** of the Jesuits from South America, which was carried out the following year, in 1768. Although the Treinta Pueblos of the Jesuit-Guaraní Reductions were over-run, exploited and depopulated within only a few decades of the expulsion, those 150 years of protected life laid bases which have never been completely annihilated, most particularly in the survival of the Guaraní language in a country that is still truly bilingual.

UPRISING SUPPRESSED Before the expulsion, however, there was upheaval in Asunción, with a rebellion led by **José de Antequera**, who taught that 'the power of the commoner in any republic, city, town or village, is more powerful than the power of the king himself'. Yet again, the hunger for slaves lay at the root of the troubles, for the landowners in Asunción were seeking slaves for their estates through the capture of indigenous from the Chaco, their source of indigenous labour in the east having been denied them by the protected territory of the Treinta Pueblos. When the Jesuits obtained the ruling that the Chaco indigenous too should be handed over to them to save them from slavery, the people of Asunción wanted to rid themselves of Jesuits and of Spanish power all at the same time. Known as the **Revolución de los Comuneros** (Revolution of the Commoners) the uprising began in 1717; the first armed confrontation was at the Battle of Tebicuarý in 1724, but the uprising was suppressed at the Battle of Tabapý in 1735, with the help of Guaraní soldiers from Misiones fighting in both battles on behalf of the Spanish crown.

BUENOS AIRES The old rivalry with Buenos Aires (which had been an offspring of Asunción) continued as Asunción grew constantly stronger: in 1776 it was made capital of a new viceroyalty of Río de la Plata, with Paraguay under its jurisdiction. When Buenos Aires declared independence in 1810, Asunción refused to go into the new republic: according to an often-repeated anecdote, the future president of Paraguay, José Gasper Rodríguez de Francia (henceforth **Dr Francia**), placed two pistols on the table in Congress, declaring, 'My arguments in favour of my ideas are these: one is destined against Fernando VII [of Spain] and the other against Buenos Aires.' The Argentinian General Manuel Belgrano invaded to try to force Paraguay into their independent republic, but was repelled in the battles of Paraguarí and Tacuarí (19 January and 9 March 1811).

INDEPENDENCE A year later, Paraguay decided to go for its independence as a separate state, and the so-called Próceres de la Independencia (agents of independence) achieved their goal in a cunning plan – with the threat of violence but without a shot being fired. The Próceres slipped out of the Casa de la Independencia on the night of 14 May 1811 to take over the army barracks in the Plaza of Asunción. The Paraguayan soldiers submitted to the leadership of the Próceres, who then released political prisoners, prepared weapons and sounded the cathedral bells. They took eight cannons to set in position in front of the house of the Spanish governor Bernardo de Velasco, who capitulated without a fight early on the morning of 15 May. (See also *Casa de la Independencia*, pages 98–9, and the box on page 346.)

The initial years of freedom were unsettled, as the Próceres, Fernando de la Mora, Francisco Xavier Bogarín, Fulgencio Yegros, Pedro Juan Cavallero and Dr Francia, tried to work out a regime of governance.

DR FRANCIA In 1814 Dr Francia was elected dictator, and three years later secured the position for life. He adopted a rigidly isolationist policy, closing the frontiers to all imports, in order to force the Paraguayan people to become self-sufficient – and hence stronger – and to forge a strong sense of national identity, on a more egalitarian basis than in other South American countries. He led a life of extreme and almost monkish personal austerity. (When President Fernando Lugo took power in 2008 he declared he would take Dr Francia as his model, for his witness against greed and corruption.)

THE TWO LÓPEZ PRESIDENCIES After the death of Dr Francia in 1840, a brief power vacuum was resolved when **Carlos Antonio López** became second president of the country in 1844. He ended the policy of isolationism and brought in English engineers to build a railway system, which at that date was at the cutting edge of new technology. Most of the fine buildings of Asunción were constructed under his presidency.

On the death of Carlos Antonio in 1862, power was seized by Francisco Solano López (henceforth **Mariscal López**). He introduced a telegraph network and began a couple of new buildings in Asunción (the Panteón and the Palacio de López), but his main passion was building up the army, which he turned into the most powerful force in Latin America. Accompanied by his Irish mistress and consort, Eliza Lynch (henceforth Madame Lynch), he embarked in 1864 on an ill-conceived aggression against his neighbours.

WAR OF THE TRIPLE ALLIANCE Mariscal López began the war in 1864 with an attack on Brazil, after it had intervened in Uruguayan politics. When he was refused permission to cross Argentinian territory to take his army down to Uruguay, he responded by taking the town of Corrientes in 1865. The result was that all three countries – Brazil, Uruguay and Argentina – formed a Triple Alliance against López. (See also *Piribebúy*, pages 163–6.)

At an early stage of the war, Mariscal López turned down the peace offer that depended on his going into exile, and his refusal to negotiate or surrender led his country into six years of utter destruction, from which Paraguay has never properly recovered. Paraguay won the next battle – that of **Curupaytý** – near the point where the rivers Paraguay and Paraná meet, in the far south (see page 235). But, inevitably, the combined forces of the allies won through with time, and once Humaitá fell, after continuous bombardment over six months (see pages 232–5), the advance of the allies was unstoppable.

Mariscal López was chased north to Asunción, then east to Piribebúy (to where he had moved his capital), and by this time his adult army had been virtually eliminated. Undeterred, he sent out an army of 3,500 children under 15 years of age, with moustaches painted on their faces to make them look like grown men, and they were wiped out in the shameful massacre of the **Battle of Acosta Ñú** in 1869.

From there on, the pace of retreat quickened, and Mariscal López resorted to executing thousands of his own people for supposed treachery. Finally, Mariscal López was cornered at **Cerro Corá** in the far northeast corner of the country, and with his death on 1 March 1870 the war was over (see pages 352–3). The destruction on Paraguay's side was horrific beyond words: the calculation of the numbers of Paraguayan dead varies from 58% to 75% of the population. Of males, the death toll is calculated as over 95%, and of adult males (over 20 years old) as over 99%. We owe the survival of the Paraguayan people to the children of that day, but it is not surprising that, despite a high birth rate, Paraguay is still, 140 years on, an underpopulated country. (See also the box on page 352.)

COUPS In the aftermath of the war, Brazil and Argentina annexed large parts of Paraguay in compensation for war expenses, and they occupied the country until 1876. In the next stage of Paraguayan history, a constitution and an electoral system emerged, with two main parties (which persist up to the present day): the Colorados and the Liberales. But, in fact, power changed hands through coups, rather than through the ballot box. There were coups or assassinations of presidents in 1874, 1877, 1880, 1902, 1904 and 1911.

CHACO WAR In the 1930s another war broke out, the War of the Chaco (1932–35), against Paraguay's neighbour in the other direction, Bolivia. For a long time the boundary had been uncertain, with Paraguayans believing that all the Chaco

NAZIS AND PARAGUAY

It is often said, with justification, that Paraguay harboured Nazis fleeing after World War II, but it can easily be blown out of proportion. There is an enormous German population in Paraguay today, with whole German areas, such as Filadelfia, Loma Plata and Neuland in the central Chaco, Nueva Germania in San Pedro, the Colonias Unidas in Itapúa, and Independencia in Guairá. Not only that, but very many of the best hotels have some element of German management. Good hotel almost equals German hotel. But it would be a great mistake to suspect all Germans in Paraguay of having a Nazi background.

Nonetheless, the first Nazi party outside of Germany was formed in Paraguay, around 1930. During World War II, the Paraguayan government distanced itself from Nazism. The country declared war on Germany in 1945, but only three months before the defeat of Hitler. But when the dictator Stroessner (himself of German ancestry) came to power in 1954, he felt a bond with the authoritarian methods of the Nazis, and received around a dozen Nazi leaders into the country.

There is even a theory (expounded by the Paraguayan writer Mariano Llano) that Hitler did not die in his Berlin bunker but fled to Argentina in a submarine, and about ten years later passed into Paraguay incognito, but with the knowledge and consent of Stroessner, where in due course he died in anonymity. This theory has recently been developed at length in a book by Abel Basti, *Hitler en Argentina* (2014). At first, said Basti, he did not believe the stories that Hitler had escaped to Argentina and Paraguay, because he had the official version of the suicide in the bunker so stuck in his head, but as he met more and more witnesses who said they had been with Hitler in South America, he became convinced. After the fall from power in Argentina of President Juan Domingo Perón, says Basti, Hitler came to live in Paraguay under the pseudonym Kurt Bruno Kirchner, where he died on 5 February 1971. Basti maintains he is buried in an old Nazi underground bunker, now covered by an exclusive modern hotel.

Whatever the truth, it is not disputed that there was an organisation called Odessa which helped Nazis escape to South America, and among those who did so was Josef Mengele, the doctor who performed medical experiments on Jews in Auschwitz. Mengele subsequently obtained naturalisation in Paraguay, and lived for some years in the 1960s in a house that used to belong to the Krug family in Hohenau, a house with multiple underground secret tunnels. It has been suggested that the time is coming to develop a Nazi tourist circuit, but it does not seem likely, principally because the fugitives became liked and respected within the communities where they hid. Other Nazis believed to have found refuge in Stroessner's Paraguay were Edward Roschmann (commandant of the Riga concentration camp), Martin Bormann, Erwin Fleiss, Marko Colak and Ante Pavelić. All these Nazis spent part of their exile in Argentina and part in Paraguay.

belonged to them, and Bolivians believing that it was theirs. Until oil was mooted to be present in the Chaco, it did not much matter who it belonged to, because no one wanted to live in such inhospitable territory (see *Chapter 12*), but now a host of military outposts (*fortines*) were established by both sides. Paraguayans believe that imperialist interests from the USA and Europe, through rival petrol companies, contributed to the outbreak of the conflict.

Paraguay won the **siege of Boquerón** in 1932, against the Bolivian forces that had taken the fort three months earlier, but it took another three years to push the war to its final truce, with tragic loss of life on both sides (about 100,000 in all), either from bullets or from thirst and disease. A famous film by Paz Encina, *Hamaca Paraguaya*, which won a prize at the Cannes film festival in 2006, is set at the end of this Chaco War. Paraguay felt that by winning the War of the Chaco it had regained dignity after its defeat in the previous War of the Triple Alliance, but even after peace was declared the borders remained disputed, until an international commission finalised them in 1938, with both sides feeling hard done by.

MORE COUPS Presidential power continued to change hands by coups, in 1936 and 1937. A new left-wing group called the Febreristas took power in the aftermath of the war. It nationalised major enterprises, gave land to war veterans, and took steps to begin a social welfare programme. In 1939, the war hero General José Félix Estigarribia won the presidential election and introduced the 1940 constitution, only to be killed in a plane crash the same year. He turned out to be the last non-Colorado president for 60 years, for another coup put the Colorados into power, cancelled the socialist reforms and imposed military rule. In 1947 there was a mini **civil war** as an armed uprising of Febreristas and Liberales was suppressed, and a large number of the educated classes were forced into exile, including the renowned writer Augusto Roa Bastos (see box on page 92). There was another coup in 1949 and again in 1954.

STROESSNER DICTATORSHIP This time, in 1954, it was **Alfredo Stroessner**, the son of a German immigrant, and head of the armed forces, who pushed himself to the head of government. Paraguay had known dictatorships in the past – that of Dr Francia had lasted 26 years – but now this new and rather different form of dictatorship was to last as long as 34 years, during which time Stroessner was seven times 're-elected'. He established a vast network of paid spies (Guaraní *pyragué*) in every inch of the interior, and the alleged hunt for communists was the front for a savagely repressive system in which three people or more, gathered together, could constitute an illegal meeting.

A secret organisation was formed of (principally middle-class) opponents, called the **OPM** – variously deciphered as the Organización Primero de Marzo (the date of Mariscal López's death) and the Organización Politico-Militar. When the details of this organisation were discovered – principally through torturing one of its members and his pregnant wife in his presence – a full-scale repression was unleashed which swept into its path the Christian *campesino* (peasant) organisation, the **Ligas Agrarias Cristianas** (one of whose members happened to have been also a member of the OPM). Thousands of innocent *campesinos* endured long periods of imprisonment and regular, savage torture (see *Museo de las Memorias*, pages 105–6). A dozen foreign Jesuits (the Society of Jesus having returned to Paraguay in 1927) were sent into exile on the grounds that they were subversives: virtually all returned after the end of the dictatorship.

COLORADO PRESIDENTS Stroessner's control was so absolute that only a relative of his could break it. **Andrés Rodríguez**, whose daughter was married to one of Stroessner's sons, was a senior commander in the army, and he took power in a coup of February 1989. Nine months earlier, **Pope John Paul II** had visited Paraguay, which effectively broke the ban on meetings and gave an opportunity for people to mobilise in great numbers. Rodríguez introduced contested elections, and won the first one himself, in May 1989, standing for the same party, the Colorado party, which was in power throughout Stroessner's regime. He freed political prisoners, allowed press freedom and introduced a new constitution in 1992, under which no president could serve a second consecutive term. The second president in the newly free Paraguay was **Juan Carlos Wasmosy** (1993–98), again from the Colorado party. In his period of office a lot of banks went bankrupt, in a domino effect. In 1996 a fellow Colorado party member (or *coreligionario* as the term is), **Lino Oviedo**, mounted a coup against him, which was unsuccessful, and landed Oviedo with a ten-year prison sentence. He spent the next years being put in prison, managing to get himself released, and then being returned to prison to continue his sentence.

Lino Oviedo was a populist ranter with a suspiciously huge fortune, and he won himself a large following among the *campesino* population, wooed with gifts. He was later to die in a mysterious helicopter crash on 2 February 2013, shortly before the April election when his rival Horacio Cartes was voted President. But in 1998, when he was barred from standing in the election, he put up a colleague as his puppet, Raúl Cubas, who won the election and released Oviedo from prison. When the Supreme Court ordered Cubas to return Oviedo to jail and the president refused, a constitutional crisis was unleashed, which was exacerbated by the murder of the vice-president, Luis María Argaña. A massive uprising in the plaza outside the Congress resulted in the events of the **Marzo Paraguayo** (see box on page 108), and the fleeing of both Cubas and Oviedo into exile.

In the national euphoria surrounding the flight of Cubas and Oviedo, and in a situation where the vice-president had been murdered, the president of the Senate, **Luis González Macchi**, was made president by popular acclamation, and the country united for a brief time into a government of national unity. The pact was short-lived and disillusionment with González Macchi soon set in. The 2003 election was won by **Nicanor Duarte Frutos**, who made some half-hearted efforts at the beginning of his presidency to attack corruption, but was widely considered by the end of his presidency to have become as corrupt as any of his predecessors.

LUGO In 2008 a resigned bishop committed to liberation theology, from the poor diocese of San Pedro de Ycuamandyýu (see pages 334–7), **Fernando Lugo**, came forward to stand as a presidential candidate without a party, but supported by an alliance of most of the small parties together with the Liberales, called the Alianza Patriótica para el Cambio (Patriotic Alliance for Change). He won, and the 60-year rule by the Colorado party, which had customarily filched national funds to bribe voters, briefly came to an end. Lugo renegotiated the Itaipú treaty with Brazil in Paraguay's favour, introduced free healthcare and extended free education to the end of secondary, but he suffered a blow to his reputation when it emerged that he had fathered at least one child when he was still a bishop. His policy of *cambio* (change) was constantly plagued by opposition from Parliament, in which the Colorados still held a majority, and in which the second party, the Liberales, proved to be no longer the allies that had helped him win power.

One year before the end of his term, on 22 June 2012, the Colorados and the Liberales joined forces to remove Lugo in what is commonly referred to as *el golpe* (the coup), even though it was achieved by the constitutional means of impeachment. Lugo's Liberal running mate, Federico Franco, achieved his long-held and undisguised ambition to take over as President. The Liberal party so came

NATIONAL ANTHEM

The national anthem (*himno nacional*) was written in 1846, in the presidency of Carlos Antonio López, ie: after independence and before the Triple Alliance War. Although it was actually written by a Uruguayan, Francisco Acuña de Figueroa, it expresses something very deep in the Paraguayan soul – pride in their independence, grief and courage in their defeats, and a sense of patriotism as the chief virtue. Paraguay is still a very formal society and the anthem is carefully taught to all schoolchildren and sung with great reverence at most public events. The first verse about the victory of independence is sung in a very slow and stately fashion, and then the chorus – which includes the catchphrase 'República o Muerte!' ('Republic or Death!') – changes to a rapid and galloping pace.

A los pueblos de América, infausto
Tres centurias un cetro oprimió,
Mas un día soberbia surgiendo,
¡Basta! dijo … y el cetro rompió;
Nuestros padres, lidiando grandiosos,
Ilustraron su gloria marcial;
Y trozada la augusta diadema,
Enalzaron el gorro triunfal.

Paraguayos, República o Muerte!
Nuestro brío nos dio libertad;
Ni opresores, ni siervos alientan
Donde reina unión, e igualdad.

The peoples of America were sadly oppressed for three centuries by a sceptred power,
But one day pride rose up and cried, 'Enough!'… and the power was broken.
Our predecessors, great leaders, showed their martial glory:
The august diadem was shattered, and they lifted aloft the cap of triumph.

Paraguayans, Republic or Death!
Our spirit brought us freedom.
Neither oppressors, nor servants are encouraged
Where there reigns union and equality.

Paraguay celebrated the bicentenary of its independence in style on 15 May 2011.

to power for the first time in over 60 years, and held power until they were heftily defeated the following April, in what was seen as a punishment vote for their part in the coup. The neighbouring South American countries were so outraged by the twisting of democratic processes in the coup that they suspended Paraguay's membership of Mercosur until the next election.

CARTES When the next election came in April 2013, the left was in disarray. Not only did Lugo lack a party to follow on in his footsteps, but the small remaining alliance of pro-Lugo groups became split over their candidate. The old tradition of payment for votes was stronger than ever, and power returned to the Colorado party with Horacio Cartes as president. Cartes is a rich businessman, trading in tobacco and fizzy drinks, whose name has been linked with drug trafficking and money laundering, especially in Wikileaks. He had entered politics so recently that he had to negotiate a change in Colorado party regulations to enable such a new member to run for president. His first year of office showed once again the tensions that result when a President is at odds with the political party that brought him to power, as his efforts to replace the 'jobs for the boys' tradition with a meritocracy proved completely fruitless. The Colorados – stung by their short period out of power – re-established their hold with massive layings-off of public employees who had been contracted during the Lugo and Franco years, replacing them with Colorado party members.

GOVERNMENT AND POLITICS

The President of the Republic is directly elected by the people for a period of five years. Under the constitution, he or she cannot stand for re-election. The term of office always begins on 15 August, the date of the foundation of Asunción.

The lower house is called the Cámera de Diputados and has a minimum of 80 members. The upper house is called the Cámera de Senadores and has a minimum of 45 members. The judges of the Supreme Court are chosen by the National Congress, and there has been much complaint over the way that party interests, principally of the Colorado party, have produced corrupt judges.

The country is divided into 17 *departamentos*, each of which has a regional government known as the *gobernación*. Within each *departamento* are many *municipios*, corresponding to each small town; the local government (and its building) are called the *municipalidad*.

ECONOMY

One third of the population are classified as self-employed, and another third as private labourers. Unpaid family workers, ie: principally mothers, account for 8%, while domestic workers in other people's houses number 6%. The level of state employees is very high, at more than 9%.

The country imports far more than it exports, particularly in the way of electrical goods. The main exports are beef, soya, sugar, wood, cotton, tobacco, *yerba mate*, leather and hydro-electric energy from the two dams. The principal crop is soya – largely from estates owned by Brazilians, who buy up Paraguayan land to plant genetically modified crops, using toxic pesticides, and for that reason have attracted a degree of resentment from the local people. Five times as much land is used for soya plantation as is used for the next largest crop, which is maize. Paraguay is the fourth largest exporter of soya beans in the world.

Another enormous area of production is cattle-raising. There are ten million head of cattle, while the human population is only just over six million. Paraguay is the eighth largest beef exporter in the world.

An economic structure that is very strong in Paraguay is the co-operative movement. It is easier to open an account in a *cooperativa* than in a bank, and many people prefer to feel they are sharing the profits rather than lining the pockets of bankers. People pay in a minimal amount monthly, and this enables them to take out a loan; almost everyone you meet is paying off a loan. *Cooperativas* also sell good quality electrical goods and even cars to their members at discount prices, usually purchased on a hire purchase basis.

PEOPLE

The population of Paraguay is six million – a tiny population for a developing country, due principally to the loss of life and practical elimination of the male population in the Triple Alliance War, which ended in 1870 and from which the country is still recovering today. Just over half a million of that number live in greater Asunción. Paraguay, therefore, has one tenth of the population of Britain, in a territory almost twice the size. Some 39% of Paraguayans are under 18, and 51% are between 18 and 59. In other words, just under 10% are 60 or over. This is a young country, with an expanding population, and with room for that expansion.

The **indigenous population** – 112,848 in the 2012 census – has also been slowly increasing, both in eastern and western Paraguay, though the increase in the east is notably more than that in the Chaco. In 1991 less than a third of indigenous lived in eastern Paraguay, but by 2012 that had risen to 52%. In the eastern half of Paraguay, the indigenous are Guaraní, though from different subgroups, such as the Mbyá, the Áva, the Aché and the Paĩ Tavyterã. This was the area where the Franciscans and Jesuits founded their Reductions for the Guaraní. They are in most *departamentos*, except for the southwest part of the eastern half (Central, Paraguarí, Ñeembucú and – ironically – Misiones, where they were once so strong). The Guaraní make wooden animals: different groups make them in different sizes and styles.

In the western half of the country, the indigenous fall principally into three areas. Along the west bank of the Río Paraguay, you find the Zamuko family (of whom the Ayoreo make the fibre shoulder bags, a popular craft item). Along the east bank of the Río Pilcomayo and pushing a good way inland, you find the Mataco/Mataguayo family, of whom the better known groups are the Nivaclé (who are Christian

INDIGENOUS GROUPS AND REGIONS

Linguistic family	Region	Ethnic group
Tupí Guaraní	East	Mbyá Guaraní
		Aché
		Paĩ Tavyterã
	East, West	Guarayo-Chiriguano
	East, West	Guaraní Ñandeva o Tapiete
Zamuko	West	Chamakoko
		Ayoreo
Mataco/Mataguayo	West	Nivaclé
		Maká
		Nanjui
Guaicurú	West	Toba-Qom
Lengua/Maskoy	West	Toba Maskoy
		Lengua-Enxet
		Sanapana
		Angaite
		Guana

The warlike Guaicurú, with whom the famous San Roque González de Santa Cruz first worked (see box, pages 114–15), are now very few, but those that survive from this language group live closer to Asunción.

and produce crucifixes) and the Maká (which is the group you can visit close to Asunción). And scattered right across the centre of the vast Chaco wilderness you find the Lengua-Maskoy group. (See also page ix and the box on page 19.)

Although there are laws to protect the indigenous, they are often flouted: for example, they were badly hit culturally and economically when groups were relocated for the construction of the two hydro-electric dams. The battle for land still goes on.

While **poverty** is one of the characteristics of the country, the Paraguayan people have become quite skilled at hiding it, and a sense of dignity leads the majority to dress as well as they can. But scratch the surface and you find this same majority have no money in their purses to take a bus or make a phone call, they have a pile of debts at local shops to clear or reduce every time they earn a little money, and they live hand to mouth with no food in their fridge for the morrow. In Asunción there are more people with proper jobs, but in the *campo* few people other than teachers and civil servants earn the minimum wage.

The 2012 census threw up a lot of new figures for the economic condition of the people. The proportion of unemployed or under-employed people is 14%. Of those who are working, only 45% are in employment, whether public or private, as opposed to being self-employed or doing domestic work in the home. The average monthly income of those working is US$395. The illiteracy rate is 5%. Those without any medical insurance, not even the state-run system of IPS, number 73%, and more than one third of the population (38%) are sick or injured. Electrical supplies reach the great majority (98%) and thanks to the hydro-electric dams energy is not expensive. But 29% still cook on firewood, and 41% have no system of rubbish collection, whether public or private. Homes without a fridge (in the sweltering climate) number 17%; those without a television, 11%; and those without a mobile phone, 8%. If this last figure seems surprising, bear in mind that those without communication will not be given work, so a mobile phone is an essential investment, and is not expensive. Most people use it only to receive calls or to send text messages.

Motorbikes, too, have been transforming the economy in the last decade. Homes with motorbikes number 50%, while those with cars number 27%. A surprising 25% of homes now have a computer connected to the internet, and half of the population aged between 20 and 24 use the internet. The internet growth area now is in smartphones. (Source: *Resultados Principales, Encuesta Permanente de Hogares 2012*.)

LANGUAGE

In Asunción 79% of people speak Spanish as their first language, and 20% Guaraní as their first language (with only 1% having a different mother tongue). The mother tongue is Guaraní in 82.5% of rural homes, and 42.6% of urban homes, making an average of 60% of homes where Guaraní is the first language.

While effortless bilingualism is the rule, the languages are not interchangeable. People will use Guaraní for common household matters like cooking, playing and building; and also for countryside matters like the names of animals, birds and trees. But they are unlikely to know the Guaraní words for a host of other things, particularly things that relate to education and the conceptual world.

This extends even to numbers. A Guaraní speaker is unlikely to use a Guaraní word for any number above one, and in traditional Guaraní the numbers only went up to five anyway, the word for 'five' being the same as 'hand': *po*. If you ask a *campesino* the word for 'brother' in Guaraní, he is unlikely to know, because he always says *hermano* (Spanish). In traditional Guaraní there are three words for brother, depending on whether it is an older or a younger brother and whether the speaker is male or female, and another three words for sister; but in the *mestizo* (mixed race) society, these subtleties from indigenous life have been lost.

What this means is that a mixture of Guaraní and Spanish runs right through daily life, and there is a word for this mixture: *jopará*. It will be evident throughout this guidebook, in such common terms as *sombrero pirí* (Spanish 'hat'; Guaraní 'of palm leaf') or *corredor jeré* (Spanish 'colonnade'; Guaraní 'going all around'). (See also *Appendix 1*.)

The survival of Guaraní owes a great deal to the Jesuits. They were responsible for turning the purely oral language into a written language, with the systematic formation of grammars and dictionaries (after some initial grammatical and vocabulary notes made by the Franciscan Luis Bolaños; see box on page 326). This work has enabled Guaraní to take its place in the world as a survivable language. Even today, the Jesuits lead the field in this respect. For example, the leading Guaraní grammar still being used is that written by the Spaniard Antonio Guasch SJ in 1961, and the first translation of the Bible into Guaraní was done by Diego Ortiz SJ, published in 1996.

Another reason why the Jesuits have been responsible for the survival of Guaraní is that through the Reductions (see page ix), in which the Jesuits did not permit Spaniards to enter for more than two or three days at a time, they created enclaves where both the Guaraní race and the Guaraní language could continue in a pure form for 150 years, until the Expulsion of the Jesuits of 1768. Meanwhile, in the rest of the continent, the process of integration of the indigenous into Spanish life began much earlier. Once the Jesuits were expelled, the Guaraní were soon assimilated through intermarriage, but the language survived.

The Guaraní indigenous are quite distinct from the *mestizo* majority (referred to by the indigenous as *los blancos* 'the whites', although European whites may sometimes have difficulty distinguishing the colour of the *mestizos* from the indigenous), and their indigenous language is purer. But increasingly the Guaraní language of the indigenous is being overtaken by the common Paraguayan Guaraní language, with all its *jopará*.

There is also the interesting phenomenon that people's first language for writing may be different from their first language for speaking. For example, a *campesina* taking notes at a base community meeting will write down notes in Spanish about a discussion held in Guaraní, and when the time comes for reading them back, will give her report in Guaraní. It is always harder for people to read and write in Guaraní than in Spanish, and the older generation cannot do it all. With the educational reforms, reading and writing in Guaraní is now taught from the first grades of primary school, all over the country, but there is no threat to the dominance of Spanish as a language of education. Although promoters of Guaraní have invented a whole new bank of Guaraní words, for days of the week, months of the year, household appliances and so forth, some people think there is something artificial about the attempt: Guaraní was not made for that. (See also the *Introduction*, pages viii–ix.)

RELIGION

Paraguay is still one of the most Catholic countries of Latin America, with an 87% Catholic population (not so far overtaken by the wave of charismatic new Protestant churches that has swept over Brazil and other nations). It is so Catholic that its three principal cities are named after three Catholic doctrines: the Assumption, the Incarnation and the (Immaculate) Conception. It has ten dioceses and one archdiocese (Asunción), and two apostolic vicariates, not yet ready to form dioceses (both in the Chaco). It is one of the few South American countries without a cardinal.

While Protestant churches are small in number, their members tend to be more active than the Catholic majority. The largest Protestant churches are Pentecostal, though Seventh-day Adventists and Mormons also have a notable presence.

The Catholic present of Paraguay is very much linked to the Catholic past, which in the case of Paraguay began with the famous Reductions (see also *Introduction*, page ix). This guide uses the term 'Jesuit-Guaraní Reductions', bearing in mind that there were Jesuit Reductions that were not for the Guaraní (in Bolivia, for example) and Guaraní Reductions that were not founded by the Jesuits (but by the Franciscans). More attention will be given to both kinds of Reduction later in this guide. Jesuit Reductions will be dealt with in *Chapter 5* (the museums) and *Chapter 7* (the Ruins); Franciscan Reductions will figure in chapters 4, 10 and 11.

EDUCATION

Education is still very formal in Paraguay, despite there having been a certain level of educational reform since the dictatorship. Young schoolchildren sit at desks. A lot of emphasis is placed on the children memorising, rather than thinking for themselves. Standards of spelling and punctuation are low, even among educated people. Essay writing is not taught either at school or at university.

Paraguay has the lowest rate of enrolment in secondary education within South America (UNESCO Institute for Statistics 2010). Although compulsory and free education supposedly runs right up to the end of secondary school, only a minority actually finish school. No follow-up measures are taken against parents of children who do not attend school. Of working adults, only 12% have had 12 or more years of schooling, and 15% have been to school for only three years or fewer.

State schools now have *prescolar* (nursery) classes, and some have a *jardín* (kindergarten – a year younger); these classes are known as *Educación Inicial*. Then *Escolar Básica* runs from *Primer Grado* (at six years) to *Noveno Grado* (at 14 and over). Pupils who do not pass their exams have to repeat the year. It is normal in state schools to have two shifts, so that one set of children have class in the morning (07.00–11.00) and another group in the afternoon (13.00–17.00). After *Noveno Grado*, there are three more years of secondary schooling, called *Educación Media – primer año, segundo año y tercer año.* A secondary school is called a *colegio*, and a superior kind of secondary school, that teaches a skill as well as the basic subjects, is called a *colegio técnico*. All school exams are written and marked by the teachers, so that the more reputable universities and institutes of higher education set their own entrance exams, preceded by a *cursillo* (short course, though it may last as long as a year in some subjects).

University education is usually in the evenings (on the assumption that people can afford to study only if they are working at the same time), and as a result a degree usually takes from four to six years to complete. The two universities that are traditionally considered to have the best reputation are the state-run Universidad Nacional and the private Universidad Católica, both of which have branches all around the country. In recent years a plethora of private universities have opened, most of them competing with each other to offer the lowest fees and to require the lowest number of class hours per week, in an attempt to make higher education more affordable. Some universities have classes only on Saturdays. The two hydro-electric dams (Itaipú and Yacyretá) fund a number of university scholarships, but you are eligible for one only if you have already begun to pay for your university yourself and can produce the receipts.

CULTURE

MUSIC AND FOLK DANCE Music came to Paraguay in a big way with the Jesuits in the early 17th century, and their Baroque compositions, principally by the Jesuit Domenico Zipoli (a contemporary of Vivaldi), were adored by the Guaraní, whose nascent musical sense had until then been expressed in rhythmic, repetitive music to the beat of a *maraca* (gourd filled with seeds). Soon the Guaraní orchestras were the best in the continent, and their polyphonic choirs were considered by visitors to rival music in the finest cathedrals of Europe.

The Jesuits introduced the harp to Paraguay (see pages ix–x) but today the Paraguayan harp has 36 strings, thanks to the musician who did more than anyone since Anton Sepp to develop it, Félix Pérez Cardozo (1908–52). He added four more strings at the bass end, so as to play *Pájaro Campana* ('Bellbird') – one of the most famous pieces in the Paraguayan folk repertoire, for which he wrote the complex setting we hear today. He also wrote *Llegada* ('Arrival'), *Despedida* ('Departure') and *Tren lechero* ('The Milk Train') – one of the most exciting pieces of music for a single instrument (or a duo) that you will ever hear, full of steam shunts and whistles and clickety-clicks, produced by harp notes.

In terms of Paraguayan popular music today, there are basically two types: the *polka* – which, though lively dance music, is not the same as the European polka – and the *guarania*, which is the nostalgic, slower version of the same rhythm, in

FOLK DANCE COSTUME

WOMEN

- long, full skirt (Spanish *pollera*) with a well-starched petticoat (Spanish *miriñaque* or Guaraní *saiguý*)
- blouse (Guaraní *typói*) with short sleeves made out of *encaje ju* or *ñanduti* or crochet
- shawl (Spanish *chal*) of *encaje ju* or *ñanduti* or crochet
- necklace (usually a rosary with artificial pearls)
- earrings (large costume jewellery type, to match necklace)
- a false plait of hair hanging right down the back
- artificial flowers in hair, which hide where the plait is attached
- make-up on face (originally with natural dyes from fruit)
- dance slippers (originally of leather) or bare feet
- a bottle or a water jug (Guaraní *kambuchí* or Spanish *cantero*) to carry on the head

MEN

- black trousers or breeches (Guaraní *bombacha*)
- leather boots (Spanish *botas*)
- shirt embroidered with *ao po'í*
- colourful striped woven sash as a belt (Spanish *faja*)
- neckerchief (Spanish *pañueleta*)
- hat with brim (Spanish *sombrero*) made of leather (Spanish *cuero*) or palm leaf (Guaraní *karanda'ý* or *pirí*)
- leather horse whip (Spanish *guacha*)

For *encaje ju* and *ñanduti* see page 24.

a minor key. The *guarania* was invented in 1925 by another of the great figures in Paraguayan musical history, José Asunción Flores (1904–72), with the famous piece 'Jejuí'; he later wrote the famous romantic *guarania* 'India'. Both the polka and the *guarania* are syncopated: the right hand plays in 6/8 time while the left hand plays in 3/4. One of the great joys of travelling in Paraguay is hearing this fantastically lively music on harp and guitar, sometimes accompanied by accordion, played by musicians dressed in colourful *ao po'i* shirts (see below under *Craft*, and for the harp see box, pages ix–x). Without its distinctive music, Paraguay would lose its heart.

In October 2013 a huge group of 420 harpists gathered in Asunción to beat the Guinness World Record for the maximum number of harps playing together at the same time. The quality of the playing was high and the atmosphere enormously exciting. Many of the young harpists who travelled there from all over the country had received lessons provided on behalf of the charity Sonidos de la Tierra, founded by conductor Luis Szarán to take music classes to the far corners of the interior.

Another enormously enjoyable musical experience is seeing folk dance, which, particularly in the *campo*, is very much a live tradition, in which young people of both sexes eagerly take part. The dances have romantic themes, and the colourful folk costumes are very decorative. One dance has a humorous element, with people falling off chairs. Another has the girls dancing with water jugs on their heads. Some of them have the men snapping their horse whips through the air, and stamping their boots on the ground, while the girls flirt with them. There is a dance in which a girl has an ever-increasing number of bottles placed on her head, one on top of another.

Becoming a dance teacher requires a great deal of training, as everything must be done according to time-honoured tradition. The best place to see folk dance is at a festival or a big event like the Santiago fiestas (see pages 212–13), when there is sometimes a competition for the best dance group.

CRAFT Paraguay is notable for its craftwork. Most famous are its traditional forms of lace, painstakingly done by hand. One of these kinds of lace is called ***ñanduti*** (Guaraní 'spiderweb'), because it is circular; this is made in Itauguá (see pages 138–40). Another exquisite craft is ***ao po'i*** (Guaraní 'cloth fine'), which can refer to the cloth itself or to the embroidery on it, and which can at times turn into a kind of lacework. It is made all over Paraguay, but the town that boasts the best quality products is Yataitý (see pages 312–13). A third kind of lace is ***encaje ju*** (Spanish 'lace'; Guaraní 'needle'), which is made in a number of places.

Another intricate craft of great beauty that is particular to Paraguay is the ***filigrana*** (filigree) silver jewellery associated with Luque (see pages 144–8), and prices are low due to the small amount of silver used.

Also enormously time-consuming is the decorative ***poncho de sesenta listas*** which is still made by hand, entirely out of cotton thread: this comes from Piribebúy (see pages 163–7).

As you travel around you may encounter many other crafts that use natural materials native to the country, such as leather for bags; palm leaves for hats; rushes for table mats; vegetable fibres for shoulder bags; bamboo for furniture; *palo santo* wood for statues of saints; clay for pottery; wool for ponchos; and cotton for hammocks. Crafts tend to be associate with a particular town or even with a particular family. This makes a craft tour of Paraguay a particularly interesting, personalised experience (see also chart opposite).

WHERE DIFFERENT CRAFTS ARE MADE

Places not in the Circuito de Oro are followed by their *departamento*.

Kind of craft	Place where it is made
ao po'í (embroidery)	Yataitý, Guairá; and elsewhere
Appliqué embroidery	Santa María de Fe, Misiones
Bamboo souvenirs and furniture	Tañarandý (*compañía* of San Ignacio)
Banana-leaf models	Itá
Encaje ju (lace)	Yataitý, Guairá; Carapeguá (with a thicker thread); San Miguel, Misiones; and elsewhere
Fibre weaving, hats of palm leaf (*karanda'ý or pirí*), rush tablemats	Limpio, Tobatí, Maká indigenous
Leathercraft	Areguá; Asunción; Luque; Ypacaraí; Concepción; and elsewhere
Musical instruments (harps and guitars)	Luque
Ñanduti (spiderweb lace)	Itauguá
Poncho de 60 listas	Piribebúy (workshop of Rosa Segovia and family)
Pottery	Itá; Areguá; Tobatí
Silver filigree jewellery (*filigrana*)	Luque
Stone carving	Santa María de Fe, Misiones (workshop of the Rotela family in the *compañía* of San Gerónimo); Trinidad, Itapúa (workshop of Vicenta Morel)
Wood carving of saints	Tobatí (workshop of Zenón Páez); Capiatá (workshop of the Rodríguez family)
Wood carving	Indigenous peoples: the Nivaclé; the Mbyá Guaraní; Tobatí; Santa María de Fe, Misiones; San Ignacio, Misiones
Wooden furniture	Escuela Pa'í Pukú in the Chaco
Woollen ponchos and blankets, hammocks, tablecloths	San Miguel, Misiones; Carapeguá; and elsewhere

Craftspeople in Paraguay are beginning to be organised at both local and national level, for better publicity. Most of the craft towns are covered in *Chapter 4*. There is normally an association or co-operative for those working at the same craft in the same town. An Expoferia de la Artesanía Paraguaya takes place in the central railway station of Asunción, usually in the first two weeks of June. See also the section on craft shops on pages 91–3. In addition, there are a couple of national networks:

Instituto Paraguayo de Artesanía (IPA) 021 614896/899; e ipa@artesania.gov.py; www.artesania.gov.py. A network organised by the government, to help small craft enterprises.

Cámara de Empresas Artesanas del Paraguay (CEAP) Mariscal López 957, PB Oficina N° 6; 021 490951; e info@ceap.org.py; www.ceap.org.py. An organisation of craftspeople making more expensive, high-quality goods.

***TERERE* AND MATE** *Tereré* is explained in the *Introduction* (see page xi), along with how important this traditional drink is to Paraguayans. When people from other countries have a tea break or a coffee break, Paraguayans have a *tereré* break. When Paraguayans drink *mate*, it tends to be a more solitary custom in the early morning, as a wake-up drink – unless the weather is very cold, in which case they may drink *mate* during the day as well. Unlike the Argentinians, Paraguayans never put sugar in *mate*.

Both *mate* and *tereré* are made with *yerba mate*, which means '*mate* leaf', but people usually just say *yerba* for short. The cup for the leaves is called a *guampa*, and there are different types for *tereré* and for *mate*. For *tereré*, a cow's horn is generally used, with the point cut and filled in with a wooden stopper, so that it will stand up. For *mate*, people usually use a wooden *guampa*, because it has to be something with insulation against the heat of the water. In both cases a metal straw is used, called a *bombilla*, which has a flattened end with a strainer on it, so that the *yerba* leaves do not pass up the straw. Only one *guampa* and one *bombilla* is used, and it is passed around the group for each to drink in turn. This can be found distasteful by many foreigners, who are afraid of getting infections, but in fact that is very unlikely, although not totally unknown.

Just as there are two kinds of *guampa*, there are two kinds of vacuum flask. The one that holds hot water for *mate* is similar to the kind of Thermos you can buy in other countries. But the kind for holding iced water has to have a much broader mouth, because the ice is made in thick bars of about 4cm diameter. This fat kind of vacuum flask uses polystyrene as the insulation material, and is very light to carry. Beautiful souvenir vacuum flasks are made with a decorated leather casing, and *guampas* can have details of silverwork on them. You will see a lot of these in Luque.

Along with the *yerba* it is customary to add other plants, which are known as *remedios*, because they have medicinal qualities as well as enhancing the flavour. These are usually mashed in a pestle and mortar, and can be added to the *yerba* in the *guampa*, but are more often added to the iced water in the flask. Some *yerba* mixtures come ready prepared with *remedios*, usually mint and *boldo*. Other *remedios* used (some for *mate*, others for *tereré*) are *burrito*, *cedrón*, eucalyptus, aniseed, camomile, avocado leaves, sage, and other plants with untranslatable Guaraní names. When you go to somewhere like Mercado Cuatro in Asunción and see a variety of strange green leaves or roots laid out near a large pestle and mortar, these are *remedios* to put in *tereré* or *mate*.

Growing *yerba* is very difficult, and depends on the right kind of soil, which is found only in this region of South America. Under the Jesuits, the Guaraní became expert at it, to the point where the major part of their export sales was for *yerba maté* – which became known as 'green gold'. Aimé Bonpland (see box on page 208) also became proficient in its production, 50 years after the Jesuits were expelled.

TERERE ETIQUETTE

The ritual of serving *tereré* is very strict, with one person acting as host, and serving the others in strict rotation. There is a lot to learn about how to serve *tereré* correctly, but all the visitor needs to know is how to respond when it is offered. If you are offered *tereré*, it is not rude to refuse, but it would be rude to wipe the *bombilla* before drinking. If you accept, you should drink all the water in the *guampa* and then return it to the host. If you do not want another turn you say '*gracias*', which in Paraguay means 'No thank you' or 'Thank you, that's enough now', rather than 'Yes thank you'.

A plantation of *yerba* trees is called a *yerbal*. After the leaf is plucked, it has to be dried and lightly toasted, mashed into little pieces, and then stored for several years in a dry place for its flavour to develop, before finally being packeted. The Selecta *yerba mate* factory in Bella Vista welcomes visitors, to show them their production process (see page 260). *Yerba mate* is a stimulant, a digestive and a laxative. Because of its very bitter flavour, you cannot eat while drinking *tereré*, and so it also acts as a dietary aid.

FOOTBALL As well as qualifying for the World Cup in 1998, 2002, 2006 and 2010 (see pages x–xi), the talented and determined Paraguayan team also reached the final of the Olympics held in Greece in 2004, winning Paraguay's first and only Olympic medal. They lost the final 0–1 to their great rivals Argentina.

A rock-solid defence has always been a strong point of the Paraguayan side. In 1998 and 2002 they reached the second round of the World Cup, suffering dramatic late 1–0 losses to France and Germany respectively. Eccentric goalkeeper José Luis Chilavert captained the side in both of those tournaments. He was generally considered to be the best goalkeeper in the world at the time, and led his team from the back – even scoring some stunning free-kicks for his country.

But the 2009 team moved to a more open and attacking style of play, with three strikers where previously they would only have had one – the most famous of whom has been Roque Santa Cruz, who transferred to Manchester City in 2009 for £20 million. In 2009 they even qualified ahead of Argentina, who are among the top favourites in any World Cup.

In 2010, when they made the quarter-final stage of the World Cup, they suffered an agonising 1–0 defeat in a thrilling contest against eventual winners Spain. Both teams missed a penalty, and Paraguay had a goal badly adjudged to be offside. Unluckier still was the fate of their star player Salvador Cabañas, who was shot in the head in a Mexican nightclub a few months before the tournament. Miraculously, he survived the shooting and made an eventual recovery, but his football career was over.

Paraguayan resilience was again on display in the 2011 Copa America (South America's equivalent of the European Championships) when they managed to reach the final without winning a single game. However, manager Gerardo 'Tata' Martino had apparently lost faith in his side as an attacking force and decided to step down after the tournament. His absence was sorely felt by the Paraguay team, however, who got through three managers during the qualifiers for the 2014 Brazil World Cup, before finishing bottom – due to having conceded one more goal than Bolivia. Meanwhile, Tata's own managerial career went from strength to strength, winning the Argentinian league title in 2013 with Newell's Old Boys before going to Barcelona, where he holds what is arguably the most prestigious managerial job in club football.

Paraguay's most famous **club sides** are Olimpia (with a black and white strip) and Cerro Porteño (red and blue): in battles between the two sides, known as *el Clásico*, Cerro Porteño have won more often, but Olimpia have done better in the Copa Libertadores (South America's equivalent of the Champions' League), winning it three times. In recent years a third team, Libertad, has been added to the mix, largely thanks to the financial investment of Horacio Cartes, the current President of the Republic, who still owns the club. All three sides are based in Asunción, yet almost every Paraguayan in the country is either an Olimpia supporter or a Cerro Porteño supporter.

Paraguay's **women's team** have yet to qualify for the SWorld Cup at senior level, but they recently qualified for the under 20's version of the tournament for the first time, due to be held in August 2014 in Canada.

2

Practical Information

WHEN TO VISIT

Visiting Paraguay at any time of year you are likely to have good, sunny weather. However, some months are a bit unpredictable, so if nothing else is determining the time of your trip, here are some factors to bear in mind.

December to February are the hottest months and June to August are the coldest ones. By the middle of September the cold weather is over. If you are looking for temperate weather, therefore, the ideal time to come is between September and early December (before the fares go up for the pre-Christmas rush) or between late February and May. Over Easter would be ideal if it were not the time when all the Paraguayans are enjoying their holiday of Semana Santa, which is Maundy Thursday to Easter Sunday. Easter Monday is back to work. Book your hotel ahead for those crucial three days if you want to be in Paraguay over Easter, and be prepared for everywhere to be closed.

If you cannot come in spring or autumn it is up to you to decide if you prefer to be hot or cold. Paraguayans have a long summer holiday from December to February, and in January those who can afford it tend to go to the Brazilian beaches, or to the Paraguayan beaches of San Bernardino, Villa Florida or Ayolas. Educational institutions also have a short winter break in the first fortnight of July (*la quincena de julio*). The weather in July is very variable: it can be as agreeable as an English summer, but there is also the risk that it may be unpleasantly cold, and with every year's increasing climate change, the cold snaps of winter are becoming more frequent and more bitter. The old wisdom used to be that July was a good month to come, because it would not be too hot (average temperatures in Asunción in July are 10–22°C), and that if there was cold weather it would last only three or four days. With climate change, that needs to be re-assessed. June and August are generally all right, but cannot be guaranteed.

This would not matter if there was adequate heating in the buildings, but Paraguayans are not accustomed to cold weather, and take few precautions against it – it is quite normal for people to sit indoors with the door and windows wide open and their overcoats on. Even if you are in a hotel with good-quality air conditioning, which produces either hot or cold air, you may sometimes find staff who do not know how to make the hot air come out, because they are not used to having heated buildings. (The trick is to adjust not just the temperature, but the mode.) In fact, you may find that they automatically turn on the air conditioning when you go into your hotel room, even in the midst of winter, so making a cold room even colder, because in Paraguay, quality equals air conditioning.

In January it is always hot (average temperatures in Asunción in January are 23–33°C, but it can exceed 40°C). You will need either a fan or air conditioning to get a good night's sleep, but virtually all hotels have air conditioning nowadays. The cheaper hotels, however, have the noisy kind in square boxes, rather than the long rectangular device set high in the wall which is separated from the motor that makes the noise, and is called a split. Even the poor will have a fan going all night. People sometimes walk around under a black umbrella, which in Paraguay is not usually called *paraguas* (the word used in Spain, 'for waters') but *sombrilla* (shade).

Heavy and dramatic thunderstorms are fairly frequent – in Asunción there were 99 days with storms in 2012 – but there is no way of planning to avoid them. There can also be long spells of drought.

SUGGESTED ITINERARIES

A 'classic tour' of Paraguay might go something like this: fly into Asunción; a day or two in Asunción; a day or two doing part of the Circuito de Oro; a day or two going south to visit the museums of Jesuit-Guaraní art in Misiones, perhaps stopping at a few places on the way; a day or two to get to and visit the ruins of Itapúa; a day to get to the Iguazú Falls (ideally travelling through Argentina); a full day at the Iguazú Falls; then fly out from Foz. Alternatively, return to Asunción for the flight out, crossing over the middle of Paraguay, and perhaps taking a day or two to visit Villarrica and Caazapá, or more towns on the Circuito de Oro.

Within the central area of the country you can stay at *estancias* (country estates): these are little paradises, and it is a lovely idea to try to build in one full day at one of these (see pages 53–4). People with an adventurous streak may want to go to Concepción, the Río Paraguay, and perhaps even the Pantanal (see pages 377–83), but that all takes time: you should allow at least a week for going to the Pantanal, and plan the dates carefully to see if it can, in fact, be accomplished in that time. Even getting to the well-presented Bosque Mbaracayú nature reserve (see pages 356–8) is complicated and time-consuming. It is a more feasible idea for nature lovers, and just as beautiful, to make an excursion of a day or two to the wetlands of Ñeembucú (see pages 223–40) after visiting the Jesuit museums of Misiones and before visiting the ruins of Itapúa.

The more hardy travellers who want to go on to another country after Paraguay may want to travel overland to Bolivia by bus (which is not very expensive), crossing the vast expanse of the Chaco desert; others with more financial resources and more time will want to see more of the wildlife of the Chaco by paying for a driver-guide. Those interested in the Reductions can make the excursion to the Argentinian missions (a day or two, see pages 260–7) and to the Brazilian missions (four days or more). A longer trip to a less frequented area would take you to the park of Cerro Corá (see pages 351–4), in the extreme northeast, taking upwards of three days, at least.

Almost everyone wants to see a little of Asunción, a little of the Circuito de Oro, a little of Misiones, the Reductions, and the Iguazú Falls. But it should be remembered that you can also do a tour of Paraguay using Foz do Iguaçu as your base, and never setting foot in Asunción. Since there are no direct flights to Paraguay from other continents, you will be making just one change at São Paulo in either case.

INTERNATIONAL TOUR OPERATORS

The best international tour operators for Paraguay are the little ones, as the bigger companies do not yet have much (if any) experience of the country. Paraguay-based tour operators can be found on pages 76–7.

IN THE UK

Audley Travel New Mill, New Mill Lane, Witney OX29 9SX; ☎ +44 1993 838650; **e** mail@audleytravel.com; www.audleytravel.com; ⌚ 09.00–18.00 Mon–Thu, 09.00–17.30 Fri, 10.00–16.00 Sat & Sun. A high-class operator specialising in quality, tailor-made journeys, & one of the few major operators ready to do trips to Paraguay. They offer visits to Asunción, Encarnación & the Chaco. The Latin America Regional Manager, Susan Middleton, has lived in Paraguay.

Journey Latin America 12 & 13 Heathfield Terrace, Chiswick, London W4 4JE; ☎ +44 20 8747 8315; e tours@journeylatinamerica.co.uk; www.journeylatinamerica.co.uk; ⏰ 09.00–18.00 Mon–Fri, 09.00–17.00 Sat. The great specialists in Latin American travel offer attractive tours all over the continent. Paraguay currently only figures in their tour programmes on the drive from the Iguazú Falls to catch a plane in Asunción, as part of a trip that takes you from Brazil to Bolivia & Peru in less than 3 weeks. This is no way to visit Paraguay,but they do offer tailor-made ('bespoke') holidays as well as the ready-made tours.

Last Frontiers The Mill, Quainton Rd, Waddesdon, Bucks HP18 0LP; ☎ +44 1296 653000; e info@lastfrontiers.com; www.lastfrontiers.com. Specialists in tailor-made holidays all over Latin America, including Paraguay, where they offer a 14-day Wildlife & Ruins itinerary.

Santa María Hotel (See ad, page 184) Lee Cottage, Blockley, Moreton-in-Marsh GL56 9HH; e info@santamariahotel.org; www.santamariahotel.org. This hotel in the Paraguayan *campo* has a base & a bank account in Britain & it is set up to receive & look after visitors from airport to airport, especially those who do not speak Spanish. The tours are tailor-made, but they typically involve visits to Reductions & the Iguazú Falls.

IN THE USA

Frontiers PO Box 959, Wexford PA 15090 0959; ☎ +1 800 245 1950; e info@frontierstravel; www.frontierstravel.com. Pigeon shooting in the Chaco. They say: 'A true Mecca of sorts for shooting at featured destinations in Argentina, Uruguay & Paraguay [...] These game-rich countries are teeming with high volume duck, dove, perdiz & pigeon. The absolute hunt of a lifetime awaits you.' Shooting pigeons is not everyone's cup of tea but this aspect of tourism is part of the total picture, whatever you think of it. The Paraguayan tourist body Senatur supports it pointing out that it falls within the requirements of sustainability, that the large number of pigeons is a pest to crops & other species are not put at risk, that the hunting season is limited by law (in 2014 it was 1 Apr–31 Jul), that the companies who offer this are registered with the government & that the sport brings in important income.

Trek Safari 1503 The Greens Way, Jacksonville Beach, Florida 32250; ☎ +1 904 273 7800; e trek@treksafaris.com; www.treksafaris.com. They say that Paraguay is 'one of the fastest growing wingshooting venues today for pigeon hunting [...] Outfitter Erik Von Sneidern has developed an excellent program near the small co-operative from area called Neuland [...] This is a unique hunt in that pigeons, both the gray/blue & the beautiful Picazuro, are the primary focus of the trip [...] The new Picazuro Lodge is by far the best place to stay for a pigeon shoot in Paraguay.' See above for more on the practice of pigeon shooting.

Trico Tours www.tricotours.com. This small, family-operated agency specialises in customised tours to Paraguay, Uruguay & Argentina. Paraguayan harpist Nicolás Carter & family members living in Paraguay & Uruguay assist in guiding private tours for individuals, families & small groups. They can be trusted to know the country well, take you off the beaten track to experience the heart & soul of Paraguay, & to provide attentive, personal service.

IN ARGENTINA

Viditerra 1915 Av Roque Saenz Peña 615 7° of 710, Buenos Aires, Argentina; ☎ +54 11 4393 4160, 0810-666-3977; e info@viditerra1915.com; www.viditerra1915.com. Formerly called Exprinter Viajes, this good-quality tour operator specialises in pilgrimages & has experience of offering a 2-week trip through the Jesuit-Guaraní Reductions in Paraguay, Argentina & Brazil.

IN BRAZIL

Missões Turismo Av dos Jesuítas, 305, sala 01, São Miguel das Missões, RS; ☎ +55 55 3381 1319; e missoesturismo@terra.com.br; www.missoesturismo.com.br; ⏰ 08.00–12.00 & 13.30–18.00 Mon–Sat. Excellent Portuguese-speaking company with much experience of doing the route of the 30 pueblos, bringing visitors to the Paraguayan Reductions as well as the Brazilian & Argentinian ones.

RED TAPE

Visitors from most EU countries (including the UK) do not require **visas**, but they are required for visitors from most African and Middle Eastern countries, and some Asian countries including India and China. Nationals of Canada, USA, Australia, New Zealand, Russia and Taiwan need to buy what is called a *visa de arribo* when they arrive at passport control: the price is currently US$135–160, depending on the country of origin. Check with your local Paraguayan embassy or download the *Guía para el Turista que visita Paraguay* from www.senatur.gov.py.

Do not forget that you will probably be going to the Iguazú Falls, which are just outside the Paraguayan boundary, so you need to think about Argentina and Brazil as well. **Argentina** does not require a visa for visitors from most EU countries (including the UK), Russia, Australia, Canada, the USA or most of South America. However, US citizens have to pay a 'reciprocity fee' online before they arrive at the Argentinian border (currently US$160); this allows multiple visits for ten years or until your passport expires. **Brazil** does not require a visa for visitors from most EU countries (including the UK) and Canada. (However, see page 288 for relaxed rules on visiting the Iguazú Falls. See also page 279 for a way of crossing from Paraguay to Puerto Iguazú, Argentina, by ferry, without passing through Brazil.) Be sure to check with the Paraguayan Embassy in your country before departure.

A normal **tourist stamp** when you enter the country will last for 90 days. If you want to spend longer than this in Paraguay, you can renew the stamp once for a further 90 days quite easily by going to Migraciones in Asunción (*Caballero N° 201 e/ Eligio Ayala; ☎ 021 446673/446066/492908; ⌚ 07.00–13.00 Mon–Fri*) and paying a fee (currently Gs403,010, or approximately US$70). There is no problem about doing this: Paraguay likes to have foreigners in the country who bring in money, and likes to collect fees from them, but they may ask you to come back the next day to collect your passport, which could be a nuisance if you are not staying in Asunción. Alternatively, you can over-run your time and pay a small fine when you leave the country (currently Gs210,468, or approximately US$50, so this is the cheaper alternative, illogically). A third option is to make a short trip over the frontier and get a new stamp (but if you go to the Iguazú Falls make sure they actually do stamp your passport, as they will prefer to wave you through without doing so, and then you will be fined on departure from Paraguay). What is not advised is to get a visa for a longer stay: it will take you time, money and frustration to assemble all the necessary documents, and when you arrive in the country the passport officer may give you a 90-day tourist entry stamp anyway. When you leave the country after your 90 days you will then be fined, even though you paid for a visa. At least, that has been the experience of some travellers. If you want to stay longer than two periods of 90 days, you can apply for a **resident's permit**. You must start with a temporary permit and can progress to a permanent permit after a year. Getting these permits is a long, expensive and frustrating business, but if you do want to apply for one there are certain documents you will need to bring from your country of origin, which will need to be legalised both by the Foreign Office of your country and by the Paraguayan Embassy there: birth certificate; marriage certificate, divorce or separation certificate, or death certificate of spouse (to prove if you are single, divorced, separated or widowed); and proof of employment or income and professional qualifications relevant to your work. The police certificate and health certificate can be obtained in Paraguay, and the translation of the documents must be done in Paraguay by an authorised translator: Migraciones will give you a list of these.

If you have questions about any of these matters, it may be difficult to get through to Migraciones in Asunción because the phone is usually engaged, but you can get advice by ringing the office of Migraciones in one of the other cities: Ciudad del Este ☎ 061 503545; Concepción ☎ 0331 241937; Encarnación ☎ 071 206286; Pedro Juan Caballero ☎ 0336 272195; Salto del Guairá ☎ 046 243536.

EMBASSIES AND CONSULATES

These are embassies unless marked as consulates. Most receive only the public in the mornings, and the safest times are between 08.00 and 11.00, Monday to Friday.

Argentina España y Perú; ☎ 021 212320; ⏲ 07.30–14.00. Consulate: Palma 319, 1° Piso; ☎ 021 442151
Australia (Consulate) Procer Arguello 208 e/ Mariscal López y Bollani; ☎ 021608740
Austria (Consulate) Aviadores del Chaco 1690; ☎ 021 613316
Belgium (Consulate) Ruta 2 km17.5, Capiatá; ☎ 028 33326
Bolivia Campos Cervera 6421 c/ R.I.2 Ytororó; ☎ 021 621426/614984
Brazil Coronel Irrazábal esq Eligio Ayala; ☎ 021 2484000. Consulate: ☎ 021 232000
Canada Prof Ramírez c/ J de Salazar; ☎ 021 227207
Chile Capitan Neudelmann 351 esq Campos Cervera; ☎ 021 662756/613855
China Mariscal López 1133 c/ Vicepresidente Sánchez; ☎ 021 213361/2
Colombia Coronel Brizuela 3089 esq Ciudad del Vaticano; ☎ 021 229888
Costa Rica Torreani Viera 831 c/ Pacheco; ☎ 021 624909
Cuba Luís Morales 766 c/ Luís de León; ☎ 021 222763
Denmark (Consulate) Nuestra Señora de la Asunción 766 c/ Humaitá; ☎ 021 490617
Dominican Republic Santa Cruz de la Sierra 1118 esq San Alfonso ; ☎ 021 210324
Ecuador Dr Bestard 861 esq Juan XXIII; ☎ 021 614814/665060
European Union América 404 e/ Mariscal López y España; ☎ 021 206069
France España 893 esq Padre Pucheu; ☎ 021 213840/211680
Germany Av Venezuela 241; ☎ 021 214009
Greece (Consulate) Nicolás Bo esq Guaraníes; ☎ 021 312318
Honduras Andrade 2203 c/ Raúl Carmona; ☎ 021 606889
Italy Quesada 5871 c/ Bélgica; ☎ 021 615620
Japan Mariscal López 2364; ☎ 021 604616
Lebanon San Francisco 629 c/ República Siria; ☎ 021 229375
Malta Mariscal López 2307; ☎ 021 602130
Mexico España 1428 c/ San Rafael; ☎ 021 6182000
Netherlands (Consulate) Artigas 4145 c/ Teniente Delgado; ☎ 021 283665
Norway (Consulate) Tte Jara Troche 655 e/ Juan de Salazar y Sociedad; ☎ 021 221492
Panama Carmen Soler 3912 esq Radio Operadores del Chaco; ☎ 021 211091
Peru Acá Carayá 215 esq Corrales; ☎ 021 607431
Philippines (Consulate) Perú 1044; ☎ 021 214688
Poland (Consulate) Palma 685; ☎ 021 447266
Portugal (Consulate) Herrera 195 c/ Yegros; ☎ 021 451950
Russia Molas López 689 c/ San Martín; ☎ 021 623733
South Korea República Argentina Norte 678 esq Pacheco; ☎ 021 605606/605401
Spain Yegros 437, Edificio San Rafael 5° y 6° Piso; ☎ 021 490686/7
Switzerland O'Leary 409, esq Estrella, 4° Piso; ☎ 021 448022
UK Edificio Citicenter, 5° Piso, Av Mariscal López y Cruz del Chaco; ☎ 021 3285507
Uruguay Boggiani 5832 c/ Alas Paraguayas; ☎ 021 664244
USA Mcal Lopez 1776 esq Kubitschek; ☎ 021 213715
Vatican City State Ciudad del Vaticano 350 c/ 25 de mayo; ☎ 021 211037
Venezuela Soldado Desconocido 348 c/ España; ☎ 021 664682

GETTING THERE AND AWAY

BY AIR Paraguay is a cheap country to holiday in, but is not a cheap destination to fly to, because there are no direct intercontinental flights. People usually change in São Paulo. Buenos Aires is also an option for changing, particularly if you are coming from Australia. The name of the international airport in Asunción is Silvio Pettirossi.

The international flights to Asunción at the time of going to press are the following:

From Sao Paulo: TAM (*www.tamairlines.com*), GOL (*www.voegol.com.br*)
From Buenos Aires: TAM, Aerolineas Argentinas (*www.aerolineas.com.ar*)
From Montevideo and Salto: BQB (*www.flybqb.com*)
From Santiago de Chile: TAM/LAN (*www.lan.com*)
From Santa Cruz: TAM, Amaszonas (*www.amaszonas.com*)
From Lima: TACA (*www.taca.com*)
From Panama: COPA (*www.copaair.com*)
From Miami: American Airlines (*www.aa.com*)

The flight situation is rapidly changing. Four airlines have started flying to Asunción in the last few years, while three have stopped doing so in the same time span. Two more – Air Europa and Aerolap (Paraguay's own new airline) – have announced plans but have not begun yet. So you need to check on the situation when your time comes to travel.

The airfare varies according to season: high season is July, August and December. At present the companies flying **from São Paulo** are TAM Airlines and GOL; and **from Buenos Aires**, Aerolineas Argentinas and TAM. GOL is a cheap-flight company, principally for online booking, with all the disadvantages of that.

If you are travelling **from London**, the route preferred by most people at present is TAM to São Paulo followed by TAM to Asunción. The best-known specialist travel agency in the UK for Latin American flights is Journey Latin America (*+44 20 8747 3108; www.journeylatinamerica.co.uk;* *see page 30 for full listing*). But the cheapest way may be to book online with TAM, since most people choose to fly TAM to São Paulo followed by TAM to Asunción. Unfortunately, the website is not an easy one to use, but TAM is a very good airline. It has consistently come top (with LAN, its partner in the LATAM airline group) of the SkyTrax World Airline Survey for South American airlines, taking into account the check-in process, catering, comfort of seats, on-board entertainment, etc. LATAM is now part of the Oneworld alliance (with British Airways and other major airlines).

Bear in mind that the **morning flights from São Paulo to Asunción** tend to get booked out about three weeks in advance, so you need to book ahead if you want to avoid waiting all day in São Paulo until the less busy evening connection. If you do not get your second boarding pass at your point of departure, then you can obtain it in São Paulo by gate 2 in Terminal 1, marked 'Passageiros em Conexão'. If there is no-one there, just wait until a member of staff appears, which will be in sufficient time before your flight.

The other route from London that some people are beginning to choose is American Airlines via Miami, which sometimes works out cheaper. However, there are a number of disadvantages in flying this route. One is that the total flight path is longer, the wait in Miami around five or six hours, you may need a second stop in another US city, and the whole journey takes considerably longer – around 24 hours or more, compared to around 16 with TAM via São Paulo. Another disadvantage is that at the time of writing you are only allowed one bag of 23kg, whereas TAM are very generous with their luggage allowance, permitting two bags of 32kg, totalling 64kg. A third disadvantage is that to pass through the USA you need either a visa, or (in the case of nationals from visa waiver countries – see *travel.state.gov* for the full list) something called an ESTA, even if you are just in transit and not going to do anything more than change planes. An ESTA currently costs US$14, and lasts two years, and you should apply for it when you have your full details of your flights and passport to hand, but at least 72 hours before travel. You have to apply online, (*www.esta.cbp.dhs.gov/esta*).

If you are travelling to Paraguay **from the USA**, then American Airlines, changing in Miami, is the obvious route. But alternative and possibly cheaper routes are Delta to São Paulo, followed by GOL to Asunción; LAN to Santiago, followed by TAM to Asunción; or TAM all the way, changing in São Paulo. Other options are COPA via Panama, and TACA via Lima, which can both work out very competitively priced.

In order to get your **full luggage allowance** you need to book your flights 'on the same ticket', which means you book them at the same time through the same agent. Then the intercontinental luggage allowance carries on to your destination of Asunción, and you do not need to retrieve your bags and check them in again in São Paulo (or wherever you change planes). On an international flight which is not intercontinental (eg: São Paulo to Asunción) you usually get just 20kg in all, and would have to pay high excess luggage surcharges on anything over that.

If you are going to more than one place in South America, you should find about **air passes**, which can offer you more economical prices if you are taking several flights. A Mercosur air pass, for example, has to be purchased in advance overseas in conjunction with your intercontinental flight, so you need to think about this from the start. The LATAM group have recently introduced a new South American air pass. Some basic pointers are given on *www.airtimetable.com*, and then choose 'Air Pass programmes', but this may be an area where you need the advice of a good travel agent.

By plane to Foz Another excellent route is to fly to Foz do Iguaçu, just over the Brazilian border. You will probably fly in with TAM from São Paulo, and the airport code is IGU. It makes sense to fly there because you will undoubtedly want to visit the Iguazú Falls during your visit. You can also do an 'open-jaws' flight, arriving in Foz and leaving from Asunción, or vice versa. Fuller details are given on page 287.

By plane to Posadas Less commonly done, but quite feasible, is to fly to Posadas, just over the Argentinian border. This makes sense if you want to visit Buenos Aires on the same trip, and if your interest is more focused on the Jesuit Reductions than on Asunción. You will arrive on an Aerolineas Argentinas flight from Buenos Aires, and the airport code is PSS.

BY BUS

From Buenos Aires Only one-third of the people entering Paraguay arrive at the airport. The majority are Paraguayans, coming from Buenos Aires by bus. If you wish to do the same, don't assume that you will save money by flying to Buenos Aires and taking the 18-hour bus to Asunción instead of getting a second flight. You might save a little on the flights, but by the time you have taken into account your costs of getting in from the airport, taxis, tips, extra luggage charges and your lunch in Argentina while you wait for the evening buses, as well as the fare in a *coche cama* or *semi cama* (see opposite), you will might well be spending more overall.

And although you can do the journey out to Paraguay by spending one night on the plane and the next on the bus, to return from Paraguay you will almost certainly need a night in Buenos Aires to be sure that delays at the frontier do not cause you to miss your flight, so this cost needs to be factored in as well.

However, if you are spending time in Buenos Aires anyway, then it makes perfect sense to take the bus to Asunción as an alternative to flying. The bus goes from the Retiro bus terminal, and will cost US$66–100 (Gs300,000–450,000), depending on what class you choose. *Común* is also called *convencional* and has ordinary bus seats, which recline a bit; *semi cama* ('half bed') is also called *diferencial* and the seats recline more; in *coche cama* they recline more still and you get a blanket and a pillow; *cama total* is also called *ejecutivo* and the seats recline practically to the horizontal and you get a blanket and pillow.

You can pay by credit card in Buenos Aires, and at some bus companies in Asunción for the return journey; Retiro bus terminal is well provided with telephones, internet (middle floor near Puente 2), shops and cash machines (top floor near Puente 2 and middle floor near Puentes 1 and 3). Asunción bus terminal has a cash machine, in the middle of the ground floor. It has telephones near the cash machine.

Nuestra Señora de la Asunción is the same company as Chevalier, so their buses may have either name. Nuestra Señora de la Asunción and Godoy have *depositos* where they can receive luggage earlier in the day, but Crucero del Norte does not. You will be expected to pay a small tip for each bag as it is loaded in the bus.

From São Paulo From São Paulo to Asunción is a longer bus journey – about 22 to 26 hours. Buses typically leave the bus terminal, Rodoviária Tietê (☎ *6221 2900/9977*), in the evening, around 18.00. The bus terminal is on the metro line so it is easy to get around.

When you get to Tietê with your luggage you will find the only lifts from the platforms to the first floor are at the far ends (before platform 1 or after platform 50). The left luggage (Guarda-Volumes) is back on the ground floor; you have to go up to the first floor and then down again to the ground floor, but this time the lift is in the middle. There is no direct access to Guarda-Volumes from the platforms, but a porter will bring your luggage to your platform 15 minutes before your bus leaves. If you are arriving by taxi, you can ask it to stop right by the Guarda-Volumes. There are luggage lockers upstairs, if your bag is not very big. There are also cash machines and internet.

The cheapest bus for the journey to Paraguay is currently the Brazilian Pluma (*Tietê:* ☎ *0800 6460300; Asunción:* ☎ *021 551758*). Once a week there is a *coche cama* (leaving São Paulo on Friday at 18.00) but you pay almost double for it. However, there is a daily *semi cama* service, which is almost as comfortable; it leaves at 18.30. The fare is around US$66–77 or Gs300,000–350,000. The other companies making the journey are the Paraguayan companies Nuestra Señora de la Asunción, Rysa and Expreso Guaraní. With Pluma you stop to buy your meals on the journey, which is quite nice because the eating places are good and you get half-hour stops to stretch your legs, but you need to calculate for this when working out the fare. The other companies provide food on the bus (*servicio a bordo*). If you are on Pluma and your bus leaves at 18.30, you are likely to stop for supper around 22.00, for breakfast around 06.30, and reach Foz do Iguaçu around 10.00, where you may have to change to another Pluma bus. It will be around midday by the time you have passed the frontier; then you stop for a late lunch in Coronel Oviedo and arrive at Asunción about 18.00. (Paraguayan time is usually one hour behind.)

BUSES TO AND FROM NEIGHBOURING COUNTRIES

For telephone numbers see the box, page 50.

Country	**Cities**	**Principal bus companies**
Argentina	Buenos Aires, La Plata, Córdoba, Corrientes, Posadas, etc	Crucero del Norte, Encarnacena, Expreso Sur, Nuevo Godoy, Nuestra Señora de Asunción, Pycasú, Río Paraná, Rysa, Santaniana, Sol, Yacyreta
Bolivia	Villa Montes, Santa Cruz	Pycasú, Río Paraguay, Stel Turismo, Yacyretá
Brazil	Rio de Janeiro, São Paulo, Brasília, Camboriú, Porto Alegre, Florianopolis, Foz	Caterinense, Nuestra Señora de Asunción, Pluma, Rysa, Transcontinental
Chile	Santiago, Iquique; connectons to Peru, Ecuador, Colombia, etc	Pullman del Sur (dep. Santiago 13.00 Tue & Fri; dep. Asunción 09.00 Tue & Fri; 30 hours)
Uruguay	Montevideo	EGA (dep. Montevideo 13.00 Mon, Wed & Sat; dep. Asunción 08.00 Mon, Wed & Sat; 22 hours)

These are the bus companies with websites. Those that say they offer online purchase are marked with * but this sometimes turns out to be only for nationals of the country of the bus company.

Catarinense	www.catarinense.net/en
Crucero del Norte	www.crucerodelnorte.com.ar *
Rio Paraná	www.rioparanasa.com.ar *
EGA	www.ega.com.uy
Encarnacena	www.laencarnacena.com.py *
Expreso Sur	www.expresosur.com.ar
Nuevo Godoy	www.empresagodoy.com.ar *
Nuestra Señora de la Asunción	www.nsa.com.py *
Pluma	www.pluma.com.br *
Pullman del Sur	www.pdelsur.cl
Rysa	www.rysa.com.py
Sol	www.soldeparaguay.com.py *

Going back in the other direction, Pluma leaves the Asunción Terminal at 10.00. On Sunday there is an additional *coche cama* service that leaves at 11.00.

From Bolivia Buses from Bolivia to Asunción leave from Santa Cruz, going through Villa Montes *en route*, near the Paraguayan border. This journey is only for the hardy or the impoverished, and you may find the bus stuffed with cargo that can take up not only the luggage room but the aisles leading to the toilets as well. Villa Montes is reputed to be the hottest and most mosquito-infested town in Bolivia: the hotels there are cheap and grim, and the places to eat (in the main plaza) are basic. Santa Cruz is a much bigger and much more civilised place, but it is a long drive from there to Villa Montes, before you even begin on the vast Chaco desert.

Stel Turismo, Rio Paraguay and Yacyretá are all the same company for this route. The bus leaves Santa Cruz daily at 20.00, and Asunción daily at 20.00 going in the other direction. Pycasú is the other company that does the Bolivia route, but it only goes once a week, leaving Santa Cruz on Sundays at 17.00, and Asunción on Thursdays at 19.00. Theoretically, the time from Villa Montes to Asunción is 17–18 hours and from Santa Cruz to Asunción 20–23 hours, but this is extremely variable, depending on bus breakdowns, rain, road closures and smuggling negotiations at the borders. For telephone numbers of the bus companies see the box on page 50. The fare is Gs250,000, (about US$55) whether to Villa Montes or to Santa Cruz. The last stop within Paraguay is Mariscal Estigarribia, at Migraciones in that town (see page 374).

BY BOAT

Ferries from Argentina There are a number of ways that you can cross from Argentina to Paraguay across the Río Paraguay or the Río Paraná – in addition to the principal bus routes from Clorinda to Falcón (see pages 364–5), and Encarnación to Posadas (see page 261).

A ferry (*Facebook: Copanatra SRL – Servicio de Balsas*) travels down the Río Paraguay from Clorinda, Argentina, to **Puerto Itá Enramada** on the edge of Lambaré, just to the south of the Cerro Lambaré. The ferries leave on weekdays every half-hour between 06.30 and 17.00 from Paraguay. (Remember that Argentina is one hour ahead, except in the Paraguayan summertime; in 2009 Argentina decided not to change its clocks for summertime.) On Saturdays and Sundays the last half-hourly crossing leaves at 13.00. The distance from Asunción to Clorinda via the ferry is only 11km, whereas it is 60km via the Puente Remanso.

On the Río Paraguay there is a well-established ferry route from Formosa, Argentina to **Alberdi**, Paraguay; this is a place where smuggling is difficult to detect, and it is also reputed to have been the route used by former politicians fleeing Argentina after the end of the military dictatorship.

Then there is Pilar to Puerto Cano (see page 226), where you can cross either as a foot passenger or with a car, and Paso de Patria, Paraguay, to Paso de la Patria, Argentina (see page 235) which is for foot passengers only.

On the Río Paraná there are ferries linking **Bella Vista** with Corpus (see page 262), and linking **Presidente Franco** with Puerto Iguazú (see page 280). You can take cars on both of these ferrics.

OVERLAND There are surprisingly few crossing points overland into Paraguay. Between Argentina and Paraguay there is always a river to cross, and between Bolivia and Paraguay there is the almost impassible Chaco desert (but see page 280 on taking a bus across the Chaco).

Between Brazil and Paraguay, from Salto del Guairá southwards there is the River Paraná to cross (with bridge crossings at Foz do Iguaçu into Ciudad del Este, and at Guairá into Salto del Guairá). Continuing north from there, there is the barrier of the *cordillera*, which again makes crossing difficult. It continues until you reach Pedro Juan Caballero, where it is so easy to cross to and from Ponta Porã, Brazil, that it happens to you in the middle of the street before you have realised.

After that the frontier follows the Río Apa, but you can cross over the river from Bela Vista, Brazil, to Bella Vista, Amamby (not to be confused with Bella Vista, Itapúa). On the Río Paraguay, Paraguayan boats will stop at Porto Mortinho, Brazil, which is another easy way to get from one country to the other.

HEALTH *with Dr Felicity Nicholson*

Needless to say, **travel insurance** is important in the developing world, to cover for health problems, as well as for accidents, theft, loss of luggage and mishaps generally. It is also recommended to carry a written note of your blood group with you – it is standard for Paraguayans to have this information shown on their driving licences – and also written information about any health condition you may have (eg: diabetes) and any medicines you need to take regularly. The only **vaccine** required under the International Health Regulations to enter Paraguay is yellow fever if you are coming from an endemic area. Paraguay has not had a case of yellow fever reported since 2008 and does not wish to have another one. The vaccine takes ten days to be fully effective and the certificate lasts for ten years though vaccine coverage is much longer. A yellow fever certificate, or if the vaccine is not suitable then an exemption certificate, will be provided, and you should carry it with you when you travel, although it is unlikely that you will be asked to show it at the border. For safe travelling in Paraguay you should consider visiting your GP or a travel clinic several weeks before departure. It is wise to be up to date on tetanus, polio and diphtheria (now given as an all-in-one vaccine, Revaxis, that lasts for ten years), and hepatitis A. Hepatitis A vaccine (Havrix Monodose or Avaxim) comprises two injections given about a year apart. The course costs about £100, but may be available on the NHS; it protects for 25 years and can be administered even close to the time of departure. Hepatitis B vaccination should be considered for longer trips but especially for those working with children, in hospitals or in situations where contact with blood is likely eg: contact sport. Three injections are needed for the best protection and can be given over a three-week period, if time is short, for those aged 16 or over. Longer schedules give more sustained protection and are therefore preferred if time allows. Hepatitis A vaccine can also be given as a combination with hepatitis B as Twinrix, though two doses are needed at least seven days apart to be effective for the hepatitis A component, and three doses are needed for the hepatitis B. Again this schedule is only suitable for those aged 16 or over.

The newer injectable typhoid vaccines (eg: Typhim Vi) last for three years and are about 75% effective. Oral capsules (Vivotif) may also be available for those aged six and over. Three capsules over five days gives protection lasting for approximately three years but may be less effective than the injectable forms if they are not taken properly. They should be encouraged unless the traveller is leaving within a few days for a trip of a week or less, when the vaccine would not be effective in time. For vaccination against dengue fever, see below.

DENGUE FEVER As well as updating your innoculations, you need to know something about dengue fever, which is not uncommon in Paraguay. This mosquito-borne disease may mimic malaria but there is no prophylactic medication against it. Only the aedes aegypti mosquitoes carry the dengue fever virus; they are characterised by black-and-white striped legs. The *aedes aegypti* mosquitoes bite during daylight hours, though predominantly first thing in the morning and later in the afternoon. However, it is worth applying repellent if you see any mosquitoes around. The repellent should always be used after applying sunscreen and in accordance with the manufacturer's recommendations: 50–55% DEET should be used twice a day; less concentrated DEET needs to be used more often. There have been a lot of cases of dengue in Paraguay in recent years, especially in 2007 and 2013, but 85% of the last outbreak was in Asunción and its surrounding areas (as far as Capiatá, Itá and Itauguá). The few patients in other areas were mostly considered to have been infected when passing through Asunción. Dengue is like a severe flu, and should be suspected when a high fever is accompanied by two of the following symptoms: strong headaches, pain behind the eyes, nausea, rashes, joint and muscle pains. Viral fevers usually last about a week or so and most patients are completely recovered within a couple of weeks. Complete rest and paracetamol are the usual treatment; plenty of fluids also help. Some patients are given an intravenous drip to keep them from dehydrating. The test for dengue is not cheap (about £20) and is only done by laboratories in Asunción, but all those suspected of having dengue are asked to report to a doctor. People with dengue need to be monitored, and they should be protected by a mosquito net to prevent mosquitoes carrying the infection on to someone else. There are four serotypes of the virus that causes dengue and three of them are present in Paraguay (types 1, 2 and 4).It is especially important to protect yourself if you have had dengue fever before, since a second infection with a different strain can increase the risk of developing the potentially fatal dengue haemorrhagic fever (also known as severe dengue), which has abdominal pain, persistent vomiting, bleeding and breathing difficulty.

Paraguay is far from the only country where there is dengue: 40% of the world's population are at risk of contracting the disease. Paraguay, however, has been commended by the World Health Organisation for its success in controlling the spread of dengue (from 10,000 cases per week in April 2013, down to only 326 in April 2014), principally through house-to-house searches of exposed, still water such as in old tyres or bottles, which are breeding grounds for mosquitoes. The good news is that after 70 years of searching for a dengue vaccine, a French laboratory now seems to have been successful, and has done clinical trials in Thailand. It is hoped that the vaccine will be available to the public in mid-2015. The bad news is that a new illness similar to dengue but a little milder, Chikungunya, has now developed in Africa and at the time of going to press had reached Brazil (with eight cases). It is likely to reach Paraguay in the future and the forthcoming dengue vaccine will not offer protection against it.

MALARIA There is no or negligible risk of malaria, unless you are going to the eastern *departamentos* of Alto Parana and Caaguazú, and there it is found only in certain municipalities, mainly in the benign form (*P vivax*) throughout the year. If you are expecting to travel to those areas, the prophylactic drug of choice is chloroquine, as the drug is still effective. It is both cheap and easy to take and has been used for many years quite safely. It is not suitable for those with epilepsy, bad psoriasis, some heart conditions, myasthenia gravis and for those with severe liver disease. When chloroquine is contraindicated then paludrine may be suitable. Preventing mosquito bites by wearing long-sleeved clothing and trousers, applying insect repellents containing 50–55% DEET to exposed skin and sleeping under impregnated bed nets will all help to prevent infection.

RABIES There has not been a case of human rabies in Paraguay since 2005, although it was a problem in the past. Rabies is carried by mammals including bats, and is passed on to humans through a bite, scratch or a lick of an open wound. Because rabies is such a serious illness, if you are bitten you should assume the animal is rabid, and seek medical help as soon as possible, to be on the safe side. The local hospitals in Paraguay generally have the post-exposure treatment, but if they do not the doctors can direct you to the specialist rabies centre within the Universidad Nacional in San Lorenzo, on the outskirts of Asunción. Meanwhile, scrub the wound with soap under a running tap or while pouring water from a jug.

Find a reasonably clear-looking source of water (but at this stage the quality of the water is not important), then pour on a strong iodine or alcohol solution of gin, whisky or rum. This helps stop the rabies virus entering the body and will guard against wound infections, including tetanus.

Pre-exposure vaccination for rabies is ideally advised for everyone, wherever they are travelling to, but it is recommended for those who are likely to be in contact with dogs, bats and other mammals, eg: biological researchers or people exploring caves, especially if they are likely to be more than 24 hours away from medical help. The pre-exposure course consists of three doses of vaccine taken over 28 days, but if time is short they can be given over 21 days. Contrary to popular belief, these vaccinations are relatively painless (though this was not so in the past), but they are expensive in the UK.

If you are bitten, scratched or licked over an open wound by a sick animal, then post-exposure prophylaxis should be given as soon as possible, though it is never too late to seek help, as the incubation period for rabies can be very long. Those who have not been immunised will need a full course of injections (five doses of rabies vaccine over about a month). Even if you have had all three doses of the pre-exposure vaccination you will still need post-exposure treatment, but in a slightly reduced form. This treatment is free in Paraguay. At the beginning of treatment you will ideally also be given rabies immunoglobulin (RIG) – human, if available, but horse (equine) will do, to prevent the rabies virus from binding to the nervous system.

The benefit of having had all three doses of the pre-exposure vaccine is that you will no longer need the RIG, and post-exposure treatment will then just involve two doses of vaccine given three days apart. If all this advice appears excessive for visiting a country where there has not been human rabies for some years, remember that, if you do contract rabies, mortality is almost 100% and death from rabies is probably one of the worst ways to go.

LEISHMANIASIS Leishmaniasis is a disease producing ulcers on the skin, mouth and nose, and around 100 cases were reported in Paraguay in 2013, mostly in the central and eastern areas of the country. (Many other countries, particularly in India and Africa, have much higher rates.) The disease is caused by parasites that are spread by bites of infected sandflies, known in Paraguay as *karachãs*. Dogs can be infected and pass the disease on to humans, but transmission from human to human is rare. The sores erupt weeks or months after you have been bitten; they are open initially, and when they heal they leave an unsightly scar. Diagnosis is by a blood test, and treatment is highly successful. One strain, visceral leishmaniasis can be fatal if untreated: the symptoms are recurrent fever and abdominal swelling, as red blood cells become reduced and the spleen and liver become enlarged.

CHAGAS DISEASE Chagas disease is an illness found principally in Latin America, and a team from Médecins Sans Frontières discovered 200 cases in the Boquerón *departamento* of the Chaco within six months when they arrived in 2011 to screen the local population for it. Often the disease escapes diagnosis because the symptoms are mild for a long time, although a simple blood test can give a result in 15 minutes. The Ministry of Health in Paraguay declared in June 2013 that the disease had been much reduced and it was hoped that the country would obtain certification for being free of Chagas disease within two years.

The name comes from Brazilian doctor Carlos Chagas who identified the disease in 1909. It is transmitted through the faeces of a kind of beetle (triatomine bug) that carries a parasite *trypanosome cruzi*. The bug, which is known in Paraguay by the name *vinchuca* or *chicã guasu*, lives in the cracks of the walls or roofs of poorly constructed houses and emerges at night to suck blood. Treatment with benznidazole or nifurtimox is practically 100% successful in the initial acute stage of the disease, which lasts about two months after infection and has flu-like symptoms (fever, headache, muscle pains) combined sometimes with difficulty in breathing and purple swelling on one eyelid. In the subsequent, chronic phase, parasites can lodge in the heart and cause cardiac problems and progressive deterioration of the heart muscle, or can affect the nervous system or the digestive system, and treatment becomes progressively more difficult.

PIQUE If you get little black flecks in your feet that look like dirt or a small splinter, but are irritating, then you have *pique* – a little mite that burrows under the skin and lays eggs. It is easily treated: dig out the *pique* with a sterilised needle, but make sure you get it all out, or in a few days you will have a blister filled with a white liquid which has the eggs in it, and it will spread. You can dribble iodine (*yodo*) or clear alcohol (*alcohol rectificado*) over the wound (both easily obtainable in *farmacias*) and keep the wound covered so it does not get infected.

SNAKEBITE Snakes rarely attack unless provoked, and bites in travellers are unusual. You are less likely to get bitten if you wear stout shoes and long trousers when in the bush. Most snakes are harmless and even venomous species will dispense venom in only about half of their bites. If bitten, then, you are unlikely to have received venom; remembering this may help you to stay calm. Many so-called first-aid techniques do more harm than good: cutting into the wound is harmful; tourniquets are dangerous; suction and electrical inactivation devices do not work. The only treatment is antivenom. In case of a bite that you fear may have been from a venomous snake:

- Try to keep calm – it is likely that no venom has been dispensed.
- Prevent movement of the bitten limb by applying a splint.
- Keep the bitten limb BELOW heart height to slow the spread of any venom.
- If you have a crêpe bandage, wrap it around the whole limb (eg: all the way from the toes to the thigh), as tight as you would for a sprained ankle or a muscle pull.
- Evacuate to a hospital that has antivenom.

And remember:

- NEVER give aspirin; you may take paracetamol, which is safe.
- NEVER cut or suck the wound.
- DO NOT apply ice packs.
- DO NOT apply potassium permanganate.

If the offending snake can be captured without risk of someone else being bitten, take this to show the doctor – but beware since even a decapitated head is able to bite.

MOSQUITO CONTROL Mosquitoes may be a nuisance by day and especially if you go somewhere like the Pantanal. At night they can be a menace and stop you sleeping. The most common way Paraguayans deal with them is to use a **fan** or **air conditioning** – mosquitoes cannot fly while the air is circulating. Some people have metallic netting on the windows of their houses to stop the mosquitoes getting in.

You should use a DEET-based **insect repellent** to put on all exposed skin both day and night, although this never offers complete protection. You may wish to supplement it with a **plug-in** insect repellent indoors – readily available in Paraguay (*un enchufe contra mosquitos*) – and a **spiral** outside – which again can be easily bought locally (*un espiral contra mosquitos*). You should not use the spiral indoors, and you should not sleep with a plug-in closer than 2m to your face.

Some Paraguayans use **mosquito nets**, but most do not. Paraguayans tend to say they feel restricted inside a net, and they prefer to keep mosquitoes at bay with a fan or air conditioning. Very few Paraguayans use nets nowadays and very few hotels provide them. But there is no better protection than the barrier method, and if other methods have failed it is a great relief to be able to drop a net over yourself when you get bitten in the night, and so complete the night undisturbed. It is best to buy your own from your home country to ensure that is does not have holes in it and is freshly impregnated with permethrin to kill the mosquitoes on contact. Nets not only keep mosquitoes from biting you, but also keep bats (which may carry rabies) at bay. There is a technique to using a net: it should be tucked in all around so the mosquitoes do not get in underneath; and if your toe or arm touches the net then it is likely to be bitten through it. But a net without a means of stringing it up is useless: one of those stretchy travel clothes lines with hooks on the end might be useful here.

You can use an **insecticide spray** against mosquitoes, but it needs a bit of organisation to use it correctly. The Paraguayan sprays – usually known by the brand name Mapex – are very strong, so it is more than usually important to air the room thoroughly before sleeping in it. You may wish to close the windows of your bedroom before dusk, as that is when most mosquitoes enter, so you need to be around at the right times: spray about an hour before dusk with the window shut. Wait outside the room for at least 15 minutes. Then go in and open the window and put the fan on, to drive out the toxin and at the same time discourage mosquitoes from entering. Then close the window, before it begins to get dark, and do not open it again until it is light the next morning.

EATING, DRINKING AND HEALTH There is no need to avoid local water when it comes from a central system where it has been treated. But if you are in a remote area where there is no mains water, it is not a good idea to drink water from wells directly without filtering it as sometimes this can make you very unpleasantly ill, for up to a week. If you are visiting *campesinos* in a land occupation (*asentimiento*), for example, it is not a good idea to share *tereré* with them, even if you feel it might look discourteous to decline.

There are delicious fruit juices to drink but if you are in an area without mains water and are not sure about where the water in a fruit juice has come from, it is better to be safe than sorry. (In Paraguay, a *jugo de fruta* always has water added to the squeezed juice.) You can buy bottled mineral water all over the country, though it is not available as readily as fizzy drinks. If you are going to remote areas then you might want to take a filtration bottle with you such as Aquapure. One bottle will filter 350 litres of water and can be used to filter any water from tap to river. It removes impurities and all protozoa, viruses and bacteria without any chemicals.

There are plenty of cheap foods on sale in the street and on buses, which it is quite unnecessary to avoid, *empanadas* and *chipas* among them. It is up to you whether you want to accept the invitation to share *tereré* with the local people. The risk of infection from the shared *bombilla* is very small, because metal does not readily harbour germs, but the risk is not non-existent. Fresh milk – what Paraguayans call *leche de vaca* ('cow's milk') as opposed to long-life milk – must be boiled (or pasteurised) before drinking, but this is not anything you need to worry about as no-one is going to serve you milk that has not been boiled.

That said, be sensible and ensure that the food is properly cooked. Do not eat food that is lukewarm when it is meant to be piping hot. If you do get a bout of diarrhoea then it will usually settle down over 24 to 48 hours. Make sure you rehydrate yourself with plenty of fluids and rebalance salts, with rehydration sachets such as Electrolade. Alternatively, you can make your own with a bottle of Coca-Cola and a three-finger pinch of salt added to it. If the diarrhoea doesn't settle or you have a fever, blood and/or slime in the stool then you are likely to need antibiotics. Seek medical help as soon as you can. If this is not possible then ciprofloxacin or norfloxacin usually work well in this situation, so if you are going to be somewhere remote then you might consider carrying them. They are only available on prescription in the UK.

PERSONAL FIRST-AID KIT A minimal kit contains:

- A good drying antiseptic, eg: iodine or potassium permanganate (don't take antiseptic cream)

LONG-HAUL FLIGHTS, CLOTS AND DVT

Dr Felicity Nicholson

Any prolonged immobility, including travel by land or air, can result in deep-vein thrombosis (DVT) with the risk of embolus to the lungs. Certain factors can increase the risk and these include:

- Having a previous clot or a close relative with a history of clots
- Being over 40, with increased risk in over 80s
- Recent major operation or varicose-veins surgery
- Cancer
- Stroke
- Heart disease
- Obesity
- Pregnancy
- Hormone therapy
- Heavy smoking
- Severe varicose veins
- Being tall (over 6ft/1.8m) or short (under 5ft/1.5m)

A deep-vein thrombosis causes painful swelling and redness of the calf or sometimes the thigh. It is only dangerous if a clot travels to the lungs (pulmonary embolus, PE). Symptoms of a PE – which commonly starts three to ten days after a long flight – include chest pain, shortness of breath and sometimes coughing up small amounts of blood. Anyone who thinks that they might have a DVT needs to see a doctor immediately.

PREVENTION OF DVT

Keep mobile before and during the flight; move around every couple of hours
Drink plenty of fluids during the flight
Avoid taking sleeping pills and excessive tea, coffee and alcohol
Consider wearing flight socks or support stockings (see *www.legshealth.com*)

If you think you are at increased risk of a clot, ask your doctor if it is safe to travel.

- A few small dressings (plasters or Band-Aids)
- Suncream
- Insect repellent; anti-malarial tablets; impregnated bed-net or permethrin spray
- Aspirin or paracetamol
- Antifungal cream (eg: Canesten)
- Ciprofloxacin or norfloxacin, for severe diarrhoea
- Tinidazole for giardia or amoebic dysentery
- Antibiotic eye drops for sore, 'gritty', stuck-together eyes (conjunctivitis)
- A pair of fine-pointed tweezers (to remove splinters, the thorn of the *cocotero* tree, etc)
- Alcohol-based hand rub or bar of soap in plastic box
- Condoms or femidoms
- Digital thermometer (for those going to remote areas)

TRAVEL CLINICS AND HEALTH INFORMATION A full list of current travel clinic websites worldwide is available on www.istm.org. For other journey preparation information, consult www.nathnac.org/ds/map_world.aspx (UK) or http://wwwnc.cdc.gov/travel/ (US). Information about various medications may be found on www.netdoctor.co.uk/travel. All advice found online should be used in conjunction with expert advice received prior to or during travel.

SAFETY

As is well known, where there is poverty, the crime rate is higher. In Asunción and the other cities, particularly Ciudad del Este and Pedro Juan Caballero, you need to be careful and take a few simple precautions.

When you arrive at any airport, go to the taxi rank, where all the drivers are known and registered, or to a window which says 'Taxis'. In the case of Asunción Airport, the official taxis are no longer the yellow ones that you find in the rest of the city, but smarter cars that have been selected for their greater comfort. They are not recognisable as taxis, and there are officials at the door who are responsible for seeing that travellers get directed to an approved taxi. Do not accept an offer of 'Taxi?' from someone who approaches you in the airport or bus terminal, and leads you to a private car. Most likely, the only harm you will come to is to find yourself with someone who does not know the city well, and will waste time looking for the address you are going to, although it could lead to a more serious assault. Some of the porters at Asunción Airport have been known to try to get work for their relatives this way, by fixing 'taxis' for the people whose bags they are carrying.

Do not go into the poorest areas of cities, even by day and even with a companion, unless that companion is someone known to the local people. This applies to the *bañados* in Asunción – the areas along the riverbank which get periodically flooded, and where there are only hovels. It also applies to a lesser extent to some of the adjacent barrios to the *bañados* such as Barrio Republicano.

Some people make a point of always travelling by taxi after dark, in the cities. This is a matter of individual decision, and others consider it excessively cautious and expensive. Avoid crossing open spaces, especially at night: it is better to walk around a deserted square at night than to walk through it, where passing cars and pedestrians would not witness any problem or assault. It is probably better not to go for a walk in the Parque Caballero in Asunción even by day. Avoid unpopulated streets, or at least be alert to who might be following you, crossing the road to avoid isolated male walkers. Thieves work alone sometimes, but often they operate in groups.

TRAVELLERS WITH DISABILITIES

Mark Davidson

Unlike many countries in South America, Paraguay has been slow to begin to take into account the needs of people with disabilities, but awareness is in its early stages and will grow. As with other countries in the region, there are a large number of people lacking basic healthcare.

PLANNING AND BOOKING At present there are no tour operators who specifically deal with wheelchair-bound travellers wishing to visit Paraguay. It is possible that some companies may be able to offer trips suited to your individual needs.

GETTING THERE Silvio Pettirossi International Airport at Asunción has very limited facilities for those in wheelchairs. The airport at Ciudad del Este may have a lower standard of facilities than the international airport.

ACCOMMODATION Some of the larger hotels in Asunción have facilities for those with disabilities and those in wheelchairs such as the Hotel Chaco (*Caballero; ☎ 021 492066; see page 78*). In Ciudad del Este, Centro Hotel and Asunción Gran Hotel advertise themselves as catering for those with disabilities.

SIGHTSEEING Many of the streets in Asunción are in need of repair so any wheelchair users will have to proceed with care when travelling around the city. Some of the walkways that allow you to view the Iguazú Falls are wheelchair accessible but it is advisable to check beforehand.

As a result of Paraguay's infrastructure, it would not be that easy for anyone with a disability to get around the country unaided. Seeking information in advance will be a necessity if you want to see some of the nation's rarer species of animal and plant life.

TRAVEL INSURANCE There are a few specialised companies that deal with travel to Paraguay. A number of operators deal with pre-existing medical conditions such as Travelbility (*☎ 0845 338 1638; www.travelbility.co.uk*) and Medici Travel Insurance (*☎ 0845 880 0168; www.medicitravel.com*).

The main hospitals in the country are located in the capital, such as Centro Médico Bautista, and have limited facilities for those with disabilities.

FURTHER INFORMATION The tourist information office for Paraguay may be able to provide more information for those with disabilities and can be contacted via Senatur (*e infosenatur@senatur.gov.py*).

A good website for further information on planning and booking any accessible holiday is www.able-travel.com, which provides many tips and links to travel resources worldwide.

Bradt Travel Guides' title *Access Africa – Safaris for People with Limited Mobility* is aimed at safari-goers, but is packed with advice and resources that will be useful for all adventure travellers with disabilities.

Be careful in public buses: a lot of theft occurs in them. There is no need to avoid taking buses, but be cautious if the bus is either very full or empty. Although it is unlikely you will have any trouble, be aware that from time to time problems can occur. Pockets can be picked, handbags can be sliced into with sharp knives, and jewellery can be snatched from your neck, so for extra safety put pendants inside your clothes. Do not expect the other passengers or driver necessarily to assist you in the case of an attempted theft: they may be at risk of reprisals.

Do not wear a money belt around your waist, unless it is well hidden and does not protrude. Otherwise all it does is announce to the thief where the valuables are, and make an assault more likely. Paraguayans will hide their money in their socks or bra rather than in a money belt. Split up your money, so if you are robbed you have at least a little emergency money in another place. It is a good idea to also carry a smaller amount of money in a secondary wallet, that you can hand over with less serious loss if assaulted. Paraguayan thieves are not usually interested in credit cards and do not know how to use them: all they want is cash, jewellery, mobile phones and other electrical devices.

If you are held up at knifepoint or with a gun or by a group, do not resist. Your life and health are of more value than your money and holiday.

All of the above applies to the cities. When you go to the *campo* you need have no fear of going to isolated areas or poor communities.

WOMEN TRAVELLERS There are no special rules for women travellers. Although Paraguayan men can be pushier than European men, there is no particular safety risk for women, and it is not necessary for women to be escorted or to dress differently from how they would at home.

WHAT TO TAKE

The only foreign **mobile phones** that can be relied upon to work in Paraguay are quadband phones which have all the frequencies, and the various smartphones like BlackBerry, iPhone etc. But it is easy to buy a phone when you arrive, or just a SIM card (*un chip*) for use in Paraguay (see pages 58–9).

If you like to travel with a **laptop**, most hotels, apart from the most modest ones, now have Wi-Fi. In terms of electric plugs, Paraguay uses two-pin plugs such as are used in Europe, and has 220 voltage (the same as Europe, different from the USA and Brazil). A universal plug adaptor is a good idea as well as a simple adaptor to two-pin. In a thunderstorm you should unplug any electrical devices: computers in particular are vulnerable to being burned out, and most Paraguayans even unplug their fridges.

Some people will wish to bring **insect repellent**, long-sleeved shirts for the evening, and possibly a mosquito net, but see the section above on *Mosquito control*, page 41. If you use suncream, it is probably best to bring it with you: you cannot rely on being able to buy it in every part of Paraguay. A soft, squashable **sun hat** is a good idea. Good walking sandals are necessary for most of the year.

If you are going to be here between June and August you should bring, at least as a precautionary measure, an overcoat, scarf, gloves and sweaters. Some people may also want to bring a hot water bottle, which are hard to find outside of Asunción.

MONEY

EXCHANGE RATE The guaraní is the oldest currency of South America, dating back to 1943. Despite this, it is not much known outside of Paraguay, and most internet currency conversion websites do not include it. Sites that do include www.oanda.com and www.xe.com. At the time of writing there were just over Gs7,000 to the pound (though this has fluctuated in recent years up to more than Gs8,000 in August 2009 and down to under Gs6,000 in March 2013), nearly Gs6,000 to the euro, and a little over Gs4,000 to the US dollar.

ARGENTINIAN MONEY It can be confusing when you are in a tourist spot in Argentina (eg: to see San Ignacio Miní or Puerto Iguazú), and see prices written as $, to know whether they are in Argentinian pesos or US dollars. The safest way is to ask: 'dólares, or pesos?' Another tip is that dollars are sometimes written with a double vertical line through, while the single vertical line $ usually refers to the Argentinian currency.

CASH MACHINES If you are coming from Argentina or Brazil you may be able to change cash for guaraníes before you arrive, but otherwise you will have to wait until you get to Paraguay to get guaraníes from a cash machine (*cajero*). You can do so straightaway at Asunción airport, where the cash machines are nearly always in working order. Or you can change dollar notes at the bank (if you arrive in banking hours).

After your passport, probably the most important single thing to bring is your credit cards, and if possible a **Visa card**. All cash machines accept Visa cards, whether credit or debit cards, with the exception of the machines of the Banco Nacional de Fomento, which are designed to enable Paraguayan state employees to withdraw their salaries. Some cash machines do not accept MasterCards, Maestro, Cirrus and other cards, even when they have a notice up saying that they do, but this is much less of a problem than it used to be. In general, a Visa card is the most reliable card in Paraguay. While you will always be able to find a cash machine for the other cards in Asunción, when you are travelling in the interior it could be a problem.

Sometimes travellers have found that their bank blocks their card as soon as they attempt to use it in South America, so try to check with your bank that this will not happen before you travel. In fact, you should take a phone number for your bank with you that works from abroad (ie: not an 0845 number) because you may find that, despite your prior notification, your card still gets blocked and the only way to unblock it is to ring up. There are now plenty of cash machines all over Paraguay. They are limited in the amount of money you can take out at a time: currently the maximum is Gs1,500,000, but that is plenty to keep you going for a while.

CASH It is always advisable to bring more than one way of accessing money, in case of theft: the best backup to your credit card (apart from another credit card) is cash. This is not quite as easy-peasy as you may think, because some banks (eg: Banco Continental) will not change cash except from Paraguayans, as they have to enter their identity card number into their system. Others, however, (eg: Banco Visión) will change cash without any fuss. In any case, as long as you can find a Paraguayan to help you, it should not be a problem.

The best currency to bring in cash is **US dollars**. These can be changed all over the country, and for that reason people will usually accept payment in dollars if you do not have enough guaraníes, if you round the figure up to allow for loss on the exchange. If you bring euros or pounds these can be exchanged too, in banks or *financieras* in Asunción or other major cities, but you may have great trouble changing them in the interior. However, there is no problem in changing euros or pounds in Asunción at a place like MaxiCambios (Shopping del Sol/Shopping Multiplaza/Shopping Mariscal López/Super Centro/bus terminal) or Cambios Chaco (Palma 364/Shopping Villa Morra/Shopping Multiplaza/Super Centro among other branches in Asunción, and in nine other cities including Encarnación, Ciudad del Este and Pedro Juan Caballero).

It is a good idea to bring a **five-dollar note** for tipping the porter at the airport, who is likely to grab your bags, leaving you with little choice but to tip him. (You probably will not have guaranies until you have entered the country, certainly not in small denominations.) Remember that he has to struggle to make a living, and is not allowed to work every day as a porter because of the competition for places.

Banking hours are at least 08.30–13.30, Monday to Friday, but some banks are open later.

TRAVELLERS' CHEQUES Travellers' cheques (*cheques viajeros*) are now completely useless, since not even banks will accept them, not even if they are paid into a bank account rather than changed into cash.

NOTES The guaraní is one of the top six currencies of the world in terms of having a lot of zeros. With all those noughts it is easier to recognise notes by their colour rather than by the numbers on them. The highest note is Gs100,000. Here is a colour code:

Pale mauve	Gs2,000 (Adela and Celsa Speratti, educational reformers)
Red	Gs5,000 (head of Carlos Antonio López, president)
Dark brown	Gs10,000 (head of Dr Francia, president)
Slate blue	Gs20,000 (head of *la mujer paraguaya*, in folk dance costume)
Blue	Gs50,000 (head of Agustín Pio Barrios, the guitarist known as Mangoré)
Green	Gs100,000 (head of San Roque González, Jesuit saint and martyr)

The purple Gs1,000 note (head of Mariscal López) is now almost obsolete, replaced by a new coin.

In 2009 it was announced that three noughts would be removed from the currency in 2011, so instead of Gs5,000 you would just have Gs5. But it has not happened, and no more word has been heard of the plan. You just get used to saying '*cinco mil*' instead of '*cinco guaraníes*'.

TIPPING The general rule in Paraguay on tipping is to do it as often as you can. A suggested tip is Gs10,000–30,000 or US$2–6 for a guide in a church or museum (depending on their knowledge); Gs5,000–10,000 or US$1–2 for a porter; Gs1,000 for a supermarket assistant carrying your bags to your car or to a street kid washing your windscreen. You can pay less if you are a backpacker, tight for money yourself, but you should pay more if you turn up leading a party of foreigners. Remember that people are very poor, and deserve to get something when they have helped others who are so much better off than themselves.

Keep in mind that the guide at a church or a museum, or the porter at the airport, may not be getting any wage for their work, and if they are it will be a very low wage. In fact, the better a guide is, the less likely it is that he or she has a wage: those who have jobs often have them through family or political connections, so those who can survive by doing a job without a wage are doing it because they are good at it.

BUDGETING

Compared to other countries – even compared to nearby Brazil or Chile – Paraguay is cheap. Travel may be in buses of poor or indifferent quality, but you can cross the country from Asunción to Encarnación (on the southern border) or to Ciudad del Este (on the eastern border) for around US$15. You can sometimes get a cheap bed for US$7, and for US$35 you can get somewhere quite nice to stay. Backpacker survival food might cost you US$7 a day, and for US$18 you can get a good meal. If you want luxury, of course you can spend a lot, and you may be tempted to splash out on beautiful, labour-intensive craftwork. But even so, you will be spending almost nothing on museums, which are mostly free.

Here are the costs of some basic items:

2-litre bottle of mineral water	under US$1 in a shop
Half-litre bottle of mineral water in a restaurant	US$1.50
Litre of beer	US$2.50
Bottle of decent wine	US$6
Loaf of bread	US$1.20
Street snack	US$0.50–1
Sweet snack	US$0.50
Postcard	US$1.20
T-shirt	US$8
Litre of petrol	US$1.80

GETTING AROUND

The *campo* (countryside) is where the national traditions live on most strongly, whether of food, dance, architecture, Guaraní language or cultural expectations. When you get into what they call the interior you get inside the country, in more than one sense. The capital, by contrast, has a lot of foreign influence.

The word *pueblo* literally means 'people' but is used for a town or a village. Most towns in the interior are small, of the size that would be called a village in Europe, so *pueblo* captures well the sense of community, in which everyone knows everyone.

The country map on pages ii–iii of the first colour section shows the different *departamentos* of the interior, with their capitals.

BY BUS As Paraguay is a poor country, where only a minority have cars, it is fair to assume that you can get to anywhere by **bus**, if you have enough time and patience. Travel by bus can be tiring and uncomfortable, but it gives you more of a feel of the country to be travelling with the local people. The website of the bus terminal in Asunción (*www.mca.gov.py/webtermi.html*) is some help with finding how to get to places, but it would be wise not to depend solely on this, as it may not be up to date. For greater convenience, there is a list of the Asunción telephone numbers of bus companies that operate all over the country on page 50. A call (in Spanish) to the general information number of the Terminal (*021 551740*) will identify which bus companies go to the area you want to reach, if you have not already got that information from the relevant section of this guide.

Paraguay has the worst road infrastructure in South America, according to a 2014 report by the World Economic Forum, and in addition many buses are old and uncomfortable, so bus travel is always likely to be a bit penitential. But a few of the companies travelling to the interior now have more comfortable buses with reclining seats, and the number of asphalted roads has increased very substantially since 2000.

BY TAXI If you want to travel a bit more comfortably and conserve your energy for where you are heading, there are a lot of **private transport companies** that can hire you a car or minivan with a driver (see list in *Chapter 3*, page 71). Vehicles hired from Asunción for the benefit of tourists can generally be relied upon to have air

BUSES: ASUNCIÓN TELEPHONE NUMBERS

Terminal information 021 551740/1; 551732; 552154
Alborada 021 551612
Beato Roque González 021 551680
Boquerón 021 551738/550880
Canindeyú 021 555991
Caterinense 021 551738
Chaqueña 021 422975
Citta 021 553050
Ciudad de Pilar 021 558393
Cometa Amambay 021 551657
Crucero del Este 021 555082
Crucero del Norte 021 559087/224555
EGA (Empresa General Artigas) 021 559795
Encarnacena 021 290385/293289
Expreso Guaraní 021 551664
Expreso Sur 021 557766
Flecha de Oro 021 551641
Godoy 021 558795/557369
Guaireña 021 551727
JC 021 553050
Mariscal López 021 551612
Misionera 021 551590
Nasa 021 551731/558451/555534
Nuestra Señora de la Asunción 021 551660; 289124/7
Ñeembucú 021 551680
Ortega 021 558198
Ovetense 021 551737
Paraguaya 021 559720
Pilarense 021 551736
Pullman del Sur 021 551553
Pluma 021 551758
Pulqui 021 555235
Pycasú 021 557700, 551735
Río Paraguay 021 558051
Río Paraná 021 551733
Rysa 021 557201/10
San Jorge 021 554877, 551705
San Juan 021 555728
San Luis 021 551705
Santaniana 021 551607/551722
Sirena del Paraná 021 553820
Sol del Paraguay 021 551763
Stel Turismo 021 551680/558051
Tigre 021 558196
TTL 021 553050
Uneleste 021 557360
Yacyreta 021 551725
Ybytyruzú 021 551727
Yuteña 021 558774

conditioning and insurance, though it is worth checking. Taxis in the interior of the country are not generally insured, and very few private cars are insured. This is illegal but it is not regarded as either shocking or abnormal – it is just one of those laws that is more honoured in the breach than the observance. The Paraguayan approach is that you do not worry about what you are never going to be able to afford to do anyway, and that if you are stopped by the police then the *coima* (bribe) will be less than the cost of the insurance.

CAR HIRE If you want to go for self-drive **car hire**, there are good international companies in Asunción, and also in Ciudad del Este, and one now in Encarnación, but nowhere else in the country (see pages 70, 300 and 273). Unfortunately, if you want to hire a car over the border in Posadas or in Foz do Iguaçu and bring it in to Paraguay, you will probably find that the small print does not allow it.

The driving rules for Paraguay that you need to know are:

- Have your headlights on even by day if you are driving on the *rutas* (main roads); it is not necessary on small country roads or in cities. If you do not do this you are likely to be fined.
- Everyone should wear a seatbelt. (This may be surprising since people rarely put on seatbelts, but that is what the law says.)
- Carry a first-aid box, two warning triangles and a fire extinguisher.

- Do not wear flip flops that leave the heel loose when driving.
- The simplest rule on speeds is 40km/h in towns and 80km/h on the *rutas*. In fact, some urban areas allow 50 or 60km/h, and if there is no speed limit marked on the *ruta* then you can go up to 110km/h.

Be prepared for a lack of road signs. Particularly tricky is negotiating your way out of Asunción and for this you need detailed instructions (see pages 123–7).

BY AIR If you want to fly, there are hardly any **domestic flights**, as most of those that were started had to be discontinued due to lack of passengers. You can fly to Ciudad del Este by TAM (*021 645500; www.tam.com.br*), which will get you a little more quickly to the Iguazú Falls, if you are not planning to visit anywhere along the way. There is only one flight a day, leaving Asunción at 17.20 and leaving Ciudad del Este at 09.40. The flight takes 45 minutes and costs around US$50 each way (see page 299).

There is now a new service to towns on the Río Paraguay, which operates three times a week, run by SETAM, the Servicio de Transporte Aéreo Militar (see page 378). You can charter a plane, though you are unlikely to want to do that, even if you are rich, unless you are going to the Chaco (details are on page 381).

MAPS The use of maps is growing, although Paraguayans have not been much accustomed to using them in the past. If you get out a map in the *campo* and ask to be shown where you are and where the place is you want to get to, most people will be at a loss to say. In cities in the interior, it is quite difficult to get hold of a map, and it is not very easy even in Asunción. However, there are a few options.

Senatur (the government tourist office) produces a map of the country that can be picked up free at Turista Roga (Guaraní 'Tourists' House'), and maybe at the tourist desk at the airport too. They can also give you a free *Asunción Quick Guide*, which includes a number of maps, including the principal roads of the city, the centre, and the fashionable Villa Mora area. These guides are excellent (though stuffed with advertising).

Touring (see pages 75–6) do some of the best maps. They have a road map of the east of the country, a road map of the west (ie: the Chaco), and there are good maps in their guidebook (see *Appendix 4*). For their map of Asunción, see pages 71–2. They also do street maps of the Gran Asunción towns: Fernando de la Morá, Lambaré, Luque, Mariano Roque Alonso, San Lorenzo and Villa Elisa.

Ictus also do good maps, and they come in narrow packets which are easy to fit into pockets. For their map of Asunción see page 71. They also do an excellent map of Ciudad del Este. Their map of the country is similar to, but not quite as good as, the free map distributed by Senatur. A bookshop that generally has Ictus maps is Librería La Plaza (see page 93).

Servicio Geográfico Militar have done a large number of detailed maps covering the whole country, and these are on sale, distributed by Meier (*021 301804*). They are hard to find, but there is a newsagent on the ground floor of the Shopping del Sol (see page 94) which stocks them. However, these maps, though of a high quality from the cartographical point of view, are so out of date that they are useful only for physical features and underlying street layout. They have also done a single, whole-country map which is good, and has detailed tables of distances from town to town.

JB Ediciones is a publicity company that has from time to time produced useful city maps – mostly free, paid for by advertising. But their only readily available publication is their *Asunción Quick Guide*, which has maps of different areas of

Asunción and customarily features another area of the country at the back. You can pick these up in hotels or at Turista Róga (*Palma 468 c/ Alberdi*).

www.jma.gov.py has an interactive webmap of Asunción, which usefully marks all the one-way streets.

ACCOMMODATION

Paraguay was slower than most other Latin American countries at getting modern backpacker hostels. But there are now a number in Asunción, although very few yet in the rest of the country. However, there are plenty of cheap hotels; these may be called *hotel* or *hospedaje* or *pensión* or *alojamiento*, or (more in Argentina) *residencial*, or (rarely) *hostal* (which is also and more often used as a Spanish translation for 'hostel'). You never hear any reports of bedbugs or such things, so you can feel safe in using cheap accommodation in Paraguay.

In the last few years a few towns have begun to advertise ***posadas***. A posada is a family bed and breakfast, and the term *posada túristica*, together with a simple logo of a house with a roof, is used by establishments that have been vetted by Senatur and can be relied upon to offer a good standard of accommodation, tastefully decorated, clean, with comfortable beds, no dodgy electrical fittings, maybe some craft decorations or photos of tourist sites on the walls, perhaps a hammock strung up outside, often a private bathroom, and so on. They are not necessarily the cheapest places to stay – a price of at least Gs50,000 per person per night is normal, whereas most small hotels would charge per room, which often works out cheaper – but they do offer a welcome degree of reliability. The term *posada* is now beginning to be used by a few small bed and breakfasts that are not part of the approved Senatur network, but to distinguish the approved ones look for the logo and the two words *posada turística*. In this guide I have omitted the word *turística* for brevity, but have not included any of the 'non-approved' *posadas*.

It is important to know what the word ***motel*** means in Paraguay, as there are a very large number of these and they are not motels in the English sense. A *motel* is a hotel where you can hire a room by the hour to have sex with your companion. They usually have names like *amor* (love) or *bosque* (wood) or *luna* (moon) and have a discreet car park that cannot be seen from the road. Occasionally, a hotel serves both purposes, but if it is called 'hotel' rather than 'motel', you can expect to be quoted a price for the night rather than a price per hour.

Many of the best hotels in Paraguay are run by Germans or have some level of German management, at least in the past. This is true not just in the German towns like Loma Plata, Independencia and Bella Vista, but all over the country.

At the other end of the scale from the country *hospedajes* are a rapidly increasing number of **luxury hotels** in Asunción. Because Paraguay is a cheap country, it is a good place to hold international **conferences**, for which many hotels now have ample facilities. The Paraguay Convention and Visitors Bureau (*Serrati 386 c/ General Santos;* ☎ *021 221986/7; www.paraguayconvention.com*) was set up to help those considering Paraguay as a site for an international conference, of any size from 50 to 2,000 participants.

A continental **breakfast** means coffee or tea or *cocido* with bread and jam and probably fruit juice. An American breakfast means there is also cereal, fruit, ham, cheese, eggs, yoghurt, cakes, etc. In this guide, these terms have not been used, but 'good breakfast' indicates that more than a continental breakfast can be expected.

A **sommier** bed means a good-quality, comfortable bed with a sprung mattress of considerable depth. Until a few years ago, the only mattresses on sale in Paraguay were made of foam, in varying densities. Now most hotel owners want to be able to advertise that there are sommier beds in at least some of the rooms. Some *posadas* have sommier beds too.

Although many hotels have a central water heating system, in all private houses and smaller hotels the water is heated by an electrical device in the shower-head. There is a technique to getting the maximum heat out: turn down the water flow as low as possible without cutting out the electrical device altogether. From the taps, only expect cold water, unless in a luxury hotel. There are not many plugs for basins, but you could bring a universal-fit plug.

Air conditioning is now so common, even in the cheapest hotels and hostels, that it has not been mentioned within the listings in the guide, but if there is the option of getting a cheaper room with a fan then this has generally been stated. If you prefer a fan to air conditioning, some hotels have both in the same room, but most do not. The better kind of air conditioning is called a split, because it is split into two parts, making the air conditioning a lot quieter and smoother in operation. It can also be used for heating in winter. Only a few years ago, splits were found only in expensive hotels, but now they are common even in cheap guesthouses. Cable **television**, again, is so common it has not normally been mentioned. It is common to find one double and one single bed in your room, enabling it to be used by a couple or by two sharers; quite often rooms have four beds or more. **Credit cards** are accepted in an increasing number of hotels, so this is not generally mentioned unless in the case of a mid-range hotel where it might be in doubt. No **stars** have been given for hotels because there is no official rating in Paraguay, so the classification is useless. Some hotels will call themselves four-star when someone else would call them two-star. **Wi-Fi** is now so common in hotels that this has not generally been commented on: as a rule you would expect it in a hostel or in a mid-range hotel.

Where hotels have websites, an email address has not generally been included as well, as the website is the surer way of making contact. Mobile phone numbers have usually been included as well as landlines, because it is often easier for a foreigner to send a text message in Spanish than to talk on the phone, and it is easy and cheap to buy a mobile phone with a Paraguayan SIM card (see pages 58–9). In fact, text messaging is now so common in Paraguay that some smaller hotels have discontinued their landlines so as to receive all messages and calls on their mobile.

In the case of hostels, where most people sleep in dormitories, the number of rooms has not been given but rather the number of people that can sleep there. Even in hostels, air-conditioning and cable TV are so common they have normally not been mentioned, though split air conditioning may be mentioned.

ESTANCIAS Strictly speaking, an *estancia* is a large country estate where there is a farm and a farmhouse, but out of these, some have developed their houses to

ACCOMMODATION PRICE CODES

Based on a standard double room in high season.

$$$$$	Gs1,000,000+	US$230+
$$$$	Gs400,000–1,000,000	US$92–230
$$$	Gs250,000–400,000	US$57–92
$$	Gs125,000–250,000	US$28–57
$	<Gs125,000	<US$28

ESTANCIAS IN THE APATUR NETWORK

Book through the Central de Reservas (*021 210550;* e *turismo@tacpy.com.py; www.turismorural.org.py*). Distances are number of km from Asunción.

***CHAPTER 1* – ASUNCIÓN**

Ykuá Satí; **$$$**; page 83

***CHAPTER 4* – CIRCUITO DE ORO**

Oñondivemí 27.5km; **$$$**; page 170
Los Manantiales 59km; **$$$**; pages 160–1
La Quinta 82.5km; **$$$**; page 166
Santa Clara 141km; **$$$**; page 183

***CHAPTER 10* – VILLARRICA AND ITS SURROUNDINGS**

Don Emilio 138km; **$$$**; page 132
Loma Linda 206km; **$$$**; page 326
Golondrina 252km; **$$$**; page 311

***CHAPTER 11* – CONCEPCIÓN AND THE NORTHEAST**

Mbuni 50km; **$$$**; page 330
Laguna Blanca 287km; **$$**; page 333

receive paying guests, operating like hotels. A stay in an *estancia* involves driving into the countryside and spending at least a day enjoying the facilities. Typically they are lovely houses, well furnished, and with excellent food, so it is an enjoyable way to spend part of a holiday, in a very Paraguayan environment. You will probably be charged a daily rate for full board, and you will have access to a variety of activities, which typically include observation of farming processes such as planting, harvesting or seeing cows milked; swimming in a pool or a stream; other sports such as football, volleyball or ping pong; riding or going for a ride in a sulky or horse cart; boating or fishing; lounging in a hammock; walking, bicycling, etc. There are also hotels and country clubs which offer similar activities and are not technically *estancias*. Note that there is a *veda* period when fishing is forbidden, in November and December to let the fish stock recover.

If you do not have a car to get to an *estancia*, the owners may be able to pick you up from the nearest bus route, so do not be deterred from asking. You will probably need to give at least one day's notice of your arrival; you cannot just turn up.

The network of *estancias* that receives visitors is called Apatur (*Asociación Paraguaya de Turismo Rural*), and they have an office in Asunción at the Touring y Automóvil Club Paraguayo (*Brasil c/ 25 de mayo, 8th Floor;* *021 210550 int 126;* e *turismo@tacpy.com.py; www.turismorural.org.py*). No-one there speaks English, but if you email they should be able to cope with an English request in writing. The furthest *estancias*, such as those north of Concepción, do not belong to Apatur, and for these see pages 342–3. The *estancias* in Misiones belong to a different network, Emitur, instead of Apatur, and most of these are around Santiago (see page 212). Refer to the box above for a list of the principal Apatur *estancias*, divided according to the chapters in this book where they are featured, and in order of distance in kilometres from Asunción.

EATING AND DRINKING

You can eat very well in Asunción, and even vegetarians will find plenty of good salads to fill their plates, even (indeed, especially) in the *churrasquerías* (restaurants serving roast meals). But most restaurants and bars in the interior of the country are very basic. Every town will have a bar which serves *empanadas* (like cornish pasties) and *milanesas* (escalopes), beer and fizzy drinks, and not much else. Most ordinary restaurants serve a small variety of meat dishes, accompanied by chips, rice salad, potato salad or a mixed salad (lettuce, tomato, onion), and it is usual to skip dessert entirely.

Petrol stations are good places to find cheap and readily available food, as many are open 24 hours and serve hot dogs (*panchos*), croissants (*media lunas*), capuccinos and other fast foods. A *super pancho* is a long hot dog with fillings of onion, sweet corn, cabbage, etc. Youths who go out at night in Asunción to bars or night clubs often finish with breakfast in a petrol station.

Many of the European staples are missing in Paraguay. It is not a tea country, or a coffee country, or a wine country; it is not a bread country or a cheese country. You can get good wine readily (imported from Chile and Argentina), and Hornimans do a Classic London Blend of tea. However, it is difficult to get good coffee, bread or cheese outside of good restaurants and specialised shops in Asunción. Instead of tea and coffee, the people drink *tereré* or *cocido*. Instead of wine they drink beer or *gaseosa* (fizzy drinks). They may drink a *jugo* (fruit juice) with their meals: these delicious mixtures blend fresh fruit with extra water and sugar, to make a longer drink in this thirsty climate. Instead of bread, *mandioc* or *sopa paraguaya* or *chipa* is eaten.

If you are in Asunción and want to buy good bread, you can try La Palmera (*Montevideo 149 esq Benjamín Constant;* ☎ *021 492833*). For cheese you can try La Quesería (*O'Higgins 989 c/ España;* ☎ *021 662580; www.laquesria.com.py;* ⏲ *09.00–21.00 Mon–Sat, 09.00–13.00 Sun; delivery).*

An increasing number of restaurants both in Asunción and in the interior are offering what they call in English 'delivery', which means you can order on the phone and they will deliver to your address.

The concept of **opening hours** for restaurants often does not apply. With smaller restaurants or those in the interior you can usually assume, unless it says to the contrary, that the restaurant will be open from whenever the first member of staff turns up, probably around 07.00 in the morning, until the last person leaves, probably not before 23.00. On the whole, if people go out to dinner (particularly in Asunción) they eat late: 20.00 is the earliest you should arrive at a restaurant. Lunchtime, however, happens at midday like clockwork, all over the country, but a bit more flexibly in Asunción. It is worth knowing that a number of expensive restaurants have a cheap weekday lunch menu called the *menú ejecutivo*, which can

RESTAURANT PRICE CODES

Based on the average price of a main course.

$$$$$	Gs75,000+	US$15+
$$$$	Gs50,000–75,000	US$10–15
$$$	Gs30,000–50,000	US$6–10
$$	Gs15,000–30,000	US$3–6
$	<Gs15,000	<US$3

enable you to enjoy a good restaurant at a much lower price than normal; this is normally not available in the evenings or at weekends.

PUBLIC HOLIDAYS AND FESTIVALS

MAJOR FESTIVALS AND SPECIAL EVENTS Dates should be checked annually with the local *municipalidad* or another source, as they are liable to vary. For more details of these events, see under their respective towns.

Saints' days and hence patronal feast days do not vary. They are preceded by a *novena* (nine days), usually with a daily mass and some kind of evening event.

Date	Place	Event
2 January	Pilar	Fiesta Hawaiana
6 January	Capiatá, Fernando de la Mora	San Baltasar
First weekend January	Santiago	Festival de la Doma y el Folklore
January	Valenzuela	Festival de la piña
Third Sunday January	Piribebúy	Ñandejára Guasú
Weekend mid January	Santiago	Fiesta de la Tradición Misionera
Last weekend of January	Laureles	Fiesta de la Tradición y el Folklore
25 January and preceding Thursday–Sunday	Caazapá Bolaños	Fiesta de Ykuá
Up to 2 February	Areguá	Festival de Alfarería
Early February	Filadelfia	Arete Guasú
3 February	Piribebúy, Itá	San Blas
Four weekends in February/March before Lent	principally Encarnación, but also Asunción barrio San Jerónimo, Atyrá, Caacupé, Hernandarias, San Ignacio, Paraguarí, Salto del Guairá, Villa Hayes, Villarrica	Carnival
Thursday, Friday and Saturday of Holy Week	all over the country	Semana Santa
Good Friday	Tañarandý; Yaguarón	Procesión de Viernes Santo
Easter Saturday/Sunday	Santa María de Fe	Tupãsy Ñuvaitĩ
Second weekend June	San Miguel	Ovechá Ragué
15 June and 16 July	Sapucai	train trip
29 June	Altos (*compañía* Itaguazú)	Feast of St Peter and St Paul, Kamba Ra'anga
Two weeks mid-July	Asunción (Mariano Roque Alonso)	Expo (*www.expo.org.py*)
31 July	San Ignacio	San Ignacio
End July to end September	Areguá (*compañía* Estanzuela)	Expo Frutilla
End August/early September	Concepción	Expo Norte (*www.exponorte.org*)
8 September	Santa María de Fe	Natividad de la Virgen
Last weekend September	Chaco	Transchaco Rally (motor racing)

Ten days in November or December	Yataitý	Expoferia de ao po'í
Second weekend November	Asunción (Conmebol)	Fitpar (tourism exhibition)
October or November	Asunción (Teatro Municipal)	Festival Mundial del Arpa
8 December	Caacupé	Inmaculada Concepción
18 December	Itapé	Virgen de Itapé

NATIONAL HOLIDAYS (*FERIADOS*) Since 2013 the national holidays (*feriados*) have moved to the nearest Monday, to give people a long weekend.

1 January	Año nuevo (New Year)
1 March	Día de los héroes (Heroes' Day – anniversary of death of Mariscal López)
Variable	Maundy Thursday and Good Friday
1 May	Día del trabjador (Workers' Day)
14 & 15 May	Día de la Independencia (Independence Day)
12 June	Día de la paz del Chaco (Peace after the Chaco War)
15 August	Fundación de Asunción (The Assumption)
29 September	Aniversario de la Victoria de Boquerón (Victory of Boquerón in the Chaco War)
8 December	Fiesta de la Virgen de Caacupé (The Immaculate Conception – feast day of Caacupé)
25 December	Navidad (Christmas)

The following are also generally celebrated nationwide:

30 July	Día de la Amistad (friendship day, when people give little presents to their friends)
21 September	Día de la Juventud (day for young people, when there is often a parade of floats by educational establishments; it is also the first day of spring)

SHOPPING

Business hours are from 08.00 (or 07.00 for manual workers or schools) until midday. Shops re-open in the afternoon, generally at 13.00, and small family shops never close. Some businesses open only in the mornings, Monday to Friday. Others work through to 13.00 or 14.00 or 15.00, in lieu of having a long lunchtime and a return to work in the afternoon, as used to be the pattern. Few people work on Sundays, apart from in family shops.

It is common to see **armed guards** outside shops and banks in the cities, with rifles or revolvers. This is supposed to make you feel safer, not more nervous.

Outside the capital it may prove difficult to find a range of goods. Chemists (*farmacias*) are well stocked all over the country, and have long opening hours. But you may have to go to Asunción or one of the other big cities if you want to buy, for example, a good corkscrew, cheese that is not *queso paraguayo,* a decent pack of coffee, an unsweetened yoghurt, a pack of biological detergent or a novel, even in Spanish. Traditional craft can be bought in its town of origin, but craft from all over the country can be readily bought in Asunción (see pages 91–3); there are not many generalised craft shops outside of the capital.

ARTS AND ENTERTAINMENT

Festivals of music and folk dance are quite common in the *campo* but you will not find cinemas outside of the cities. Asunción has a few small theatres and a number of exhibition halls (see pages 89–91). Pirated DVD films are readily available all over the country, to play on a laptop. For paintings and sculpture, see under *Museums* in *Chapter 3* and under San Ignacio, Santa María de Fe, Santa Rosa and Santiago in *Chapter 5* and San Cosme y Damián and Trinidad in *Chapter 7*.

VISITING MUSEUMS AND CHURCHES

Most local town **museums** in the interior of Paraguay (with the exception of the museums in the Reductions) have very predictable contents: relics from the wars such as bullets, cutlery and metal plates, rusty sabres, as well as old typewriters, old telephones, old radios and the like. When you have seen one, you may feel you have seen them all. The museums of Jesuit-Guaraní art, however, are in a totally different league.

Most museums in Paraguay are free, and most of those that are not free (like the Jesuit museums of Misiones) charge only Gs5,000 entrance. If you want to visit a church or a museum and it is closed, do not just go away. Find out who has the key and go and ask them if you can visit. Usually they are more than happy to come and open up, and expect to be informed when a visitor comes, as they would waste a lot of time sitting in an empty building waiting for visitors, who may turn up only once a week or less. However, do not omit to tip them a dollar or two if they have come out specially for you, or more if they have specialised knowledge.

In Europe you are asked not to walk around during a service in **church**, but to wait until it is over. In Paraguay, however, you may sometimes need to take the opportunity to look at the church during the liturgy because when it is over the church will be locked up. In this case you should obviously be very discreet, and it is much better to do it before the mass (or funeral, or baptism) than during it.

MEDIA AND COMMUNICATIONS

TELEPHONES Outside of Asunción, it is more common to have a **mobile phone** (*celular*) than a landline (*linea baja*). A lot of telephone numbers in this guide are mobile numbers, and can be easily recognised because they begin with 09. In 2013, as many as 93% of households had a mobile phone, the second highest proportion in Latin America after Colombia. Most people, however, will not be able to afford to make calls, but only to receive calls or to send texts.

Some people have more than one mobile number, for the different networks: 097x for Personal, 098x for Tigo and 099x for Claro. (There is also 096x for Vox, but that only works in Asunción.) Some of these people swap their SIM cards round once a day to pick up any messages; others have a phone that takes two SIM cards, both working at the same time. Since 2013 it has been possible to change your network without changing your phone number, so you can no longer be sure that an 098x number is Tigo, or an 097x number Personal. In the past people would change their number frequently, as their mobile got lost, or more likely stolen, but nowadays people can recover their number onto a new SIM card so phone numbers are far more stable than before.

Remember that your mobile phone from home may not work in Paraguay, unless it is a smartphone or quadband. But it is easy to get up and running with a mobile phone when you arrive, even for a short period, as you will not be expected to take out a contract (*un plan*). Nearly everyone has pay-as-you-go (*prepago*). You can buy a phone for around Gs150,000, and a *chip* (SIM card) to give you a number currently costs as little as Gs15,000, which includes Gs10,000 worth of credit. Topping up is easy: everywhere you go you will find *librerías* and other shops that do a *mini carga* (Tigo) or a *maxi carga* (Personal): you just say what your number is and how much money you want to put on it (Gs 20,000 should be more than enough at a time). You are recommended to get a mobile phone running on a Paraguayan network for your visit, so that you can send and receive messages at minimal cost and make bookings, check opening hours and contact keyholders, with very basic written Spanish and without needing to talk on the phone.

A very convenient and inexpensive (4%) way of sending money is by Giro Tigo, which you might perhaps need for making reservations in some places. If you do not have Tigo, ask your hotel to help you. You go to one of the many shops that sell credit for a Tigo phone, and give the name and phone number of the recipient and the phone number and *cédula* number of the sender. Then they can withdraw the money from any Tigo shop in their locality.

If you want to leave a message for someone who is not answering their phone, do not leave a voice message, as it will cost them money to retrieve it, and they may not even know the number to ring to retrieve voice messages. Send them a text message, which is cheap for you and free for them.

A new kind of mobile has recently been introduced by Copaco with a service called **Linea Alta** that uses an Asunción prefix even though the line is situated somewhere in the interior of the country. *Linea alta* means 'high line' (as opposed to *linea baja* – 'low line' or landline) and the service picks up the signal in a similar way to a mobile phone, though it has the lower tariffs of a landline. The numbers begin 021, like an Asunción number, but are followed by 7 digits instead of 6. They are beginning to be installed in rural areas where there is no cable for a landline, or where the landline numbers are oversubscribed.

There were a lot of changes in **landline codes** in Paraguay a few years ago, as towns were switched over to digital networks and had extra numbers added. Normally a code now has two or three numbers and after the code there is a number with six or seven digits. Asunción numbers all begin 021, so if you find a number with that prefix in the interior of the country, it may mean that the people have an Asunción office, or that they live in Asunción during the week. However, if it has 7 digits after the 021 it is more likely to mean that it is one of the new *linea alta* phone numbers.

You may need **Argentinian mobile phone numbers** if you make the excursion to Puerto Iguazú or San Ignacio Miní; these can be confusing. Within the country they have two digits more than landlines, with the number 15 inserted between the area code and the phone number. If you are dialling from outside the country you drop the 15 and put in 9 earlier on, between the country code and the area code. For example:

from Argentina 0376 15 4540395
from abroad +54 9 376 4540395

This guide includes a lot of telephone numbers, whether landline or mobiles, so that Spanish-speakers can easily contact organisations for the latest information. As much detailed information as possible has been included. Even though things are liable to go out of date, this gives you something to check, rather than leaving you in the dark as to what kind of services might be on offer. It is recommended to ask a Spanish-speaker to telephone and check on such rapidly changing details as opening times, bus fares, etc. Do not trust website information on that kind of detail as it is often outdated.

The national company for landline phones is called **Copaco**, but it used to be called Antelco, and you still occasionally come across the old name. Every small town has a Copaco office, where people can go to make calls, and where the operator knows the numbers of all the people in the town. These Copaco numbers, therefore, are invaluable for updating local information – whether it is for knowing if a hotel is still functioning, or to find out who is the new person responsible for opening the museum, or to ask if the road to the town has yet been asphalted. For this reason, a large number of Copaco telephone numbers have been included in this guide, under the name of the town.

Also included are a large number of phone numbers for the ***Municipalidad*** (town hall) because there will sometimes be someone there responsible for tourist matters, but it will be open only Monday to Friday, in the mornings. The Copaco number is a very useful one because it works all day long.

At the start of each chapter is the number for the ***Gobernación*** of the *departamento*, because there is always someone there responsible for tourism, though once again they will only work mornings (usually 07.00–13.00). In addition, every *departamento* now has a tourist website beginning *www.siente*, eg: www.sientemisiones.com.

There used to be a large number of shops wherever you went offering public telephone facilities, called ***cabinas*** because the phones are in enclosed booths. But since mobile phones have swept all over the country and are now possessed by every family, many of these *cabinas* have closed down. Occasionally, the booths are divided into those for landline calls, and those for different mobile networks.

The **international code** is not 00 as in other countries, but 002. The number for local **directory enquiries** is ☎ 112, or (for the office in Asunción) ☎ 021 112, ☎ 021 2192018 or ☎ 021 2192176. Asunción can give you other numbers for directory enquiries around the country. The word for '**extension**' is *interno*. Paraguayans write phone numbers in the form 021 645600 int 364.

INTERNET It is often the case that **email addresses** and **websites** are inactive or discontinued. This is a characteristic of the poor communications of Paraguay generally. For this edition every effort has been made to eliminate web addresses which are no longer active, even when they are advertised, and also those which are 'under construction' but have nothing on them, unless there seems a serious possibility that they may soon spring into life. Many people have email addresses but do not check their mail boxes regularly, or at all, so you may find you only get replies from the larger hotels and companies. However, regular and efficient use of email and websites is rapidly growing.

Internet cafés are called *cybers*, but with the growth of smartphones and personally owned computers they are less common than they used to be. But you will be able to find one at least in the big shopping malls (Spanish *shoppings*) and it generally costs around Gs5,000 to use a computer for an hour (under US$1). To compensate for the loss of *cybers* there are now Wi-Fi connections in a number of plazas, especially in Asunción, and in a number of cafés and restaurants.

POST Post offices are rare, even in Asunción; it has never been in the culture to send letters, and the postal service has got progressively slower and more expensive at the same time. People are more likely to send a document by bus, as an ***encomienda***, than to send it by post. Rural towns (*pueblos*) usually have a post office of sorts, but it may not be advertised as such, almost certainly will not sell stamps, and will maybe only receive correspondence for the local government office or for foreign missionaries living there. Even the word for post – *correo* – now means 'email', rather than overland post.

MEDIA The principal **newspapers** are *ABC-Color* and *Ultima Hora*, with *La Nación* coming in third place, and a couple of popular papers with scandals and pin-up girls, *Crónica* and *Popular*. However, newspapers are expensive for Paraguayans, and most people cannot afford them. They are not sold in *librerías* but in on-street *kioskos* (in Asunción and larger towns) or through individual newspaper-sellers on foot. If you have not bought one in the morning you are unlikely to get one, though the Asunción Terminal generally has them later in the day.

The Paraguayan **television** channels are Red Guaraní (2), Telefuturo (4), Paravisión (5), SNT (9), Latele (11) and Canal Trece (13). There are news programmes at 12.00 (Red Guaraní and Canal Trece), 12.30 (Telefuturo and SNT) 18.50 (Canal Trece), 20.00 (Telefuturo), 21.00 (Paravisión), 23.00 (Telefuturo) and 23.15 (Canal Trece). In Asunción you can get the state network begun by President Lugo, TV Pública (14/15.1 or cable 2/3), which began as a culturally and historically brilliant channel, but lost its heart through censorship at the time of the 2012 coup.

The principal **radio** stations are all on AM: Radio Uno (650), Radio Caritas (680), Radio Cardinal (730), Radio 1° de Marzo (780), Radio *Ñanduti* (1020) and Radio Fe y Alegría (1300). Of these, only Radio Cardinal goes out on FM: 92.3FM. The FM system is generally only used for local radio, which is what people listen to more than the national programmes, unless they are in Asunción.

CULTURAL ETIQUETTE

When it **rains**, people assume that everything is suspended (school, social events, etc) without requiring notice of cancellation. This applies not only when the rain is heavy, but when it is a light drizzle, when it looks as though it might rain, and for quite a long time after it has stopped. This is particularly so in the *campo* where there are more dirt roads, and in state schools, where the teachers like to have a holiday as well as the pupils. In Asunción, only 9% of the capital's roads have drainage, so in times of heavy rain, you should travel only if it is essential, as some of the roads, such as Aviadores del Chaco, will turn into virtual rivers.

Paraguayans generally take a **shower** every afternoon around 16.00 or 17.00, and you may be expected to do likewise. It is very important to know that you should not put your **toilet paper** into the toilet, but in a bin at the side; otherwise you will block the pipes.

In Asunción many people have doorbells to their houses, which are usually located outside, on the street. In the *campo*, people do not normally have either bells or door-knockers, but the method of attracting attention is by clapping your hands in the street outside. When you go into someone's house you should say '*Permiso*' ('[With your] permission') as you enter, to which the reply is '*Adelante*' ('Go ahead'). You should not visit people, telephone or play a radio, etc between midday and 13.00 or 14.00, which is when people are having their lunch and resting a little, though few people actually have a nap. If you are invited to eat a meal in someone's home, it is polite to say that it is '*muy rico*' ('very nice').

There is plenty of sexual behaviour between unmarried couples in Paraguay, but it takes place entirely in private (at a motel or in the fields) and it is not the done thing to flaunt it. You do not see couples holding hands or kissing in public places. There is a high level of homophobia but if gay couples ask for a room for two, they will often find themselves with a double and single bed anyway.

There are very few facilities for people with disabilities, and unfortunately it is still very rare to see someone in a wheelchair in a public place (see also box on page 45).

You may be unfortunate enough to find yourself in a situation where the easiest way to extract yourself is to pay a **bribe**. Resist it all you can, as giving in to expectations of bribes perpetuates the system, but it is understandable if people sometimes feel that they have little choice, for example if their passport has been taken away and they have a plane to catch and cannot communicate well in Spanish. Police or customs officers may make up a rule you have supposedly broken to get a bribe out of you, or you may indeed have broken one of the detailed rules that seem to exist for little purpose other than to enable bribes to be taken. The person seeking the bribe will present it as a way in which he can do you a favour, to help you get over the higher cost of a fine. The word for 'bribe' is *coima*, but it has strong negative connotations, and anyone seeking a bribe would not use that word, but a euphemism like *propina* (tip), *colaboración* (collaboration), *arreglo* (settling up) or *aceite* (oil). More likely there will be no discussion, but you will just be delayed until you hand over some money (Gs50,000 might be enough, or more likely Gs100,0000). You will know if you have paid a bribe, rather than a fine, because a fine will have some paperwork. In the case of visitors to the country, the police are supposed to give you a ticket, which you take to Senatur (*Secretaria Nacional de Turismo; Turista Roga, Palma 468 c/ Alberdi;* ☎ *021 494110;* ⏲ *07.00–19.00 inc Sun*). Senatur want to know about cases of police asking for bribes, because they want to put a stop to the practice.

There are three kinds of policeman: *policia caminera* in grey uniforms; *policia nacional* who have recently changed their beige uniforms for dark blue; and *policia municipal* in white shirt and black trousers, or light blue shirt and dark blue trousers.

TRAVELLING POSITIVELY

The best way to help is usually financial, but where volunteer opportunities exist this has been mentioned.

If you would like to help with the care of orphaned or abandoned children, **SOS Children's Villages** (*Asunción office: Cerro Corá 1155, Asunción;* ☎ *021 227345;* **e** *ana.medina@aldeasinfantiles.org.py; www.aldeasinfantiles.org.py*) have five homes for children known as the Aldeas ('Villages'), in San Ignacio, Hohenau, Asunción, Luque and Belén. You can make a donation online, or become a godparent or a friend of the Aldeas.

If you would like to help on environmental projects, the **World Wide Fund for Nature** is working on reforestation in Paraguay (*Coordinación de voluntariado, WWF Paraguay Atlantic Forest Ecoregional Office, Las Palmas 185 c/ Av Argaña, Ciudad de Lambaré, Asunción:* ☎ *+595 21 331766/21 303100;* **e** *voluntariado@wwf.org.py; www.wwf.org.py*). It is trying to conserve the Atlantic Forest in Alto Paraná, and aims to plant 50 million trees in a project called *A todo pulmón – Paraguay respira* ('With all its lungs, Paraguay breathes').

A charity called **Para La Tierra** (*contact Karina;* **m** *0985 260074;* **e** *karina@paralatierra.org; www.paralatierra.org*) takes volunteers to an interesting site in the Cerrado, Laguna Blanca (see pages 333–4). You pay to volunteer, but can go for as short a time as one week. The work involves conservation and recording wildlife.

The **Fundación Paraguaya** does good work in offering microfinance and entrepreuneruial education, and they have a website in English (*www.fundacionparaguaya.org.py*). They have helped two excellent agricultural schools to get up and running on a self-sufficient basis (Hotel Cerrito in the Chaco, page 364, and Mbaracayú Lodge in the North East, page 357). They take volunteers if they have excellent Spanish and are over 20, but this has a cost (click 'Internships' on the website).

Dequení (*www.dequeni.org.py*) is a well-established foundation that works primarily with children from poor communities. It offers protection to children at risk, runs community centres and gives training to help young people from poor communities find work.

If you would like to help with the nutrition of poor children living in the *bañado* of Asunción, there are daily lunch canteens run by the organisation **Ko'eju** (*15 de agosto 10, opposite the Congress;* ☎ *021 445446/497333; www.koeju.org*), which means 'dawn' in Guaraní. The canteens began in 2002 in the Chacarita, where 350 children are still fed daily, and they have spread now to 20 other areas. Ko'eju is run by Luis and Olga Manfredi, pastors of the Centro Familiar de Adoración church.

The Jesuit programme for the education of the poor in Latin America is called **Fe y Alegría**, and naturally there is a Paraguayan branch (*O'Leary 1847, c/ Séptima Proyectada;* ☎ *021 371659/390576;* **e** *comunicaciones@feyalegria.org.py; www.feyalegria.org.py*). It does excellent work, running schools for the poor, training programmes for community leaders, and radio schools to teach literacy, particularly in Guaraní. Sometimes they take volunteers, particularly from Spain, but not for short periods.

A charity that works principally in giving scholarships for tertiary level education to bright students from poor homes is the **Santa Maria Education Fund** (*UK registered charity no.1105031;* **e** *info@santamariadefe.org; www.santamariadefe.org*). It was founded by the author of this guide, and its projects can be visited in Santa María de Fe, Misiones. It takes a limited number of volunteers as English teachers, but they must be fluent in Spanish and fill specific job slots – usually five months to a year. Short-term visitors can sometimes help by transporting books from England.

If you live in England, one way of helping is via the Anglo Paraguayan Association (**e** *anglopysociety@yahoo.com*; *www.paraguaysocietyuk.org*). It has a very small fund which it administers, in order to help a number of different projects. Because the organisation is largely composed of Paraguayans who have come to live in England, they have excellent feelers for small projects that deserve aid.

Part Two

THE GUIDE

3

Asunción

Asunción is not one of Latin America's loveliest cities, though it grows on you. A certain amount has been done in the last few years to clean buildings, remove over-large hoardings, widen pavements and install pergolas, benches and period streetlamps in the key areas of the city centre. There is much more to be done, as many fine 19th-century buildings are in a state of near collapse, but could be magnificent if restored. However, a start has been made, in the renovated Casas del Bicentenario. If you know where to go, you can find a lot of great interest and a little of great beauty.

As the capital, Asunción brings together the best artistic and intellectual life of the country, and a cultural and political awakening is undoubtedly taking hold, particularly among young people. It can be seen in the recent political protests, summoned through social networks, and in the rise of a new wave of design that is simultaneously more modern and more heritage-based. There was an artistic creativity and an inspiring eloquence in the peaceful street demonstrations that followed the 2012 coup, and there is still a tangible buzz in the air – influenced inevitably by the northern hemisphere, but nonetheless with a pride in distinctive Paraguayan culture. At the same time, economic growth over the last five years has resulted in a plethora of innovative new bars and restaurants.

Seen at its worst, Asunción has roads and pavements in terrible condition, rubbish littering the streets, and children in ragged clothes begging on buses. BBC journalist Tim Vickery once wrote: 'The place and the people have a certain serene charm, but one of the abiding impressions is of mangy dogs snoozing on shattered paving stones.' But seen at its best, Asunción is immensely rich in green spaces, with plazas, parks, the Jardín Botánico and the Costanera. Particularly good places for walking are the new coast road and the Parque de la Salud (see pages 116 and 117). It is always a joy when some of the trees are blossoming, with the pink of the national tree, the famous *lapacho* (*tajý* in Guaraní), the yellow of another variety of *lapacho*, the red of the *chivato*, and the blue of the *jacaranda*. The blossom is seen not only in spring but whenever a burst of warm weather misleads the trees into thinking spring has arrived.

HISTORY

Asunción is so named because it was founded on 15 August 1537, the feast of the Assumption of Mary, by Captain Juan de Salazar de Espinosa, whose bronze statue, with its conquistador armour and outstretched sword, stands in the centre of the plaza in front of the Cabildo today. He had arrived in the ship of Don Pedro de Mendoza, in the first Spanish voyage to discover the Río de la Plata area by sailing upriver from the big estuary at what is now Buenos Aires.

Asunción was sited on a sharp bend of the river, rendering it a good lookout post. Today the stretches of river immediately to north and south of the bulge where Juan de Salazar placed his fort are known as Bañado Norte and Bañado Sur.

They are where the poorest live – those who have come up to the capital from the poor interior in search of work, and find themselves relegated to makeshift hovels on land which is central enough but floods from time to time.

In 1541 the first Cabildo was created, converting Asunción from a military fort to a civilian town with a local government. In due course, settlers from Asunción went to found other cities, such as Buenos Aires, Corrientes, Santa Fe and Santa Cruz de la Sierra, giving rise to the saying that Asunción is 'the Mother of Cities'.

Paraguayans are proud of the fact that they gained their independence without a drop of blood being spilt. The actions of the Próceres de la Independencia are commemorated in the Casa de la Independencia. The first president, Dr José Gaspar Rodríguez de Francia (dictator 1814–40), began to put some town planning into what had previously been haphazard growth. Under his successor, Carlos Antonio López, the railway was inaugurated, and some of the handsome 19th-century buildings went up. The following president, Mariscal Francisco Solano López, in the short period before he embarked on his catastrophic War of the Triple Alliance, was responsible for building the grandest of the city's buildings – the Palacio de López.

During the Chaco War of 1932–35 many buildings in the city became hospitals and barracks. Since then, the city has continued to expand in population and area, until now one continuous urban spread unites it with what are supposedly distinct towns – Lambaré, Villa Elisa, Fernando de la Mora, San Lorenzo, Luque and Mariano Roque Alonso – to form Gran Asunción. This populated area is all on the east bank of the Río Paraguay, as no bridge has yet been built to enable the city to expand to the northwest. (To the west and southwest is Argentina.) Today there are half a million inhabitants in Asunción itself, but two and a half million in the greater Asunción area. This may not sound too cumbersome, until you consider that there is no metro, and that the overcrowded buses often have to jolt their slow way over cobbled roads, making travel in the capital rather trying.

GETTING THERE AND AWAY

Full information on how to get to Asunción can be found on pages 33–7. Most people who are not South Americans arrive by a flight from São Paulo, after their intercontinental flight. It is also possible to arrive by overnight bus from São Paulo or from Buenos Aires. Travellers who have entered the country at another border point – eg: Encarnación, Ciudad del Este, Salto del Guairá, Pedro Juan Caballero or through the Chaco – will find travel information under the relevant section.

ORIENTATION

The city is like a fan, with its nub in the bend of the river where Juan de Salazar placed his fort. Alternatively, you could think of the city's access roads as being like the five fingers on a hand that has its palm placed over the city centre. From north to south these five fingers are:

- The Ruta Transchaco (the road from Argentina, from Bolivia, from the Chaco), turning into Artigas, which is a broad, fast road, with the Bañado Norte to one side, and the burnt-out shell of the Ycuá Bolaños supermarket to the other.
- The Autopista (the road from the airport), turning into Aviadores del Chaco, which goes past the Sheraton Hotel, then the Shopping del Sol. It then changes its name to España and comes into the centre through quite a middle-class area.

- Mariscal López (one of the roads from San Lorenzo), which comes in past the Shopping Villa Mora and the Shopping Mariscal López (one behind the other); later the Mburuvichá Róga (house of the president), the US Embassy, the football club Olimpia, and so to the centre.
- Eusebio Ayala (the other road from San Lorenzo), a broad street lined with buildings and household shops: plumbing supplies, furniture, lighting, domestic appliances, beds, etc. Then it buries itself in Mercado Cuatro and disappears.
- Acceso Sur, turning into Fernando de la Mora, which goes past the Terminal and is lined with shops until it changes into Próceres de Mayo and runs through the thick of Mercado Cuatro. From that point on it is called Pettirossi.

The **Terminal** (☎ *021 551740*) sits diagonally on the corner of República Argentina and Fernando de la Mora. There is a VIP lounge with computers and Wi-Fi for passengers of the buses run by Nuestra Señora de la Asunción, which is one of the better bus companies travelling to the interior and to international destinations. The terminal has a cash machine, money-changing facilities and a left-luggage office. In the **centre** the roads are one-way and run in parallel lines. When they reach the level of the east side of the Plaza de la Democracia they change their names. For example, Mariscal Estigarribia becomes Palma, 25 de mayo becomes Estrella, Cerro Corá becomes Oliva, Azara becomes General Díaz and Herrera becomes Haedo.

Continuing down the grid of these parallel streets you come to the major road Dr Francia. This becomes Ygatimí, which has the church of Cristo Rey on its far west corner, where it meets with Colón. From this point downwards, the parallel streets are popularly referred to as (**Proyectada** or **Avenida**) Primera, Segunda, Tercera, etc, even though they have other names marked on the map.

The end of many bus lines, beyond the centre, where the city hits the river, is barrio **Sajonia**, so any bus to Sajonia will be going to the centre first. South of Sajonia is Tacumbú, which is where the prison is, then the Bañado Sur, and then the Cerro Lambaré.

The **Villa Morra** area is becoming Asunción's second city centre, as can be clearly seen on the map on page 79, with a concentration of hotels and restaurants, the shopping centres of Mariscal López Shopping and Villa Morra Shopping and the restaurants of Paseo Carmelitas. Another shopping centre and more smart hotels and restaurants adjoin this barrio to the east, in the Shopping del Sol area. This area is now considered fashionable, although it is not rich in historic buildings.

Lambaré itself is a wedge shape on the map to the southwest of the Terminal. Most maps do not show its streets because it is technically a separate town, but it juts up into Asunción and is indistinguishable from it.

GETTING AROUND

Flights to Asunción Airport have been covered in the previous chapter (see pages 33–4). You will want to get some guaraníes before you leave the airport. There are two Itaú cash machines at the airport and they can generally be relied upon to be in working order; they accept all credit and debit cards. If you are changing money, there is a Cambios Chaco on both floors of the airport, open 24 hours. There is a tourist information office at the airport run by Senatur (☎ *021 645600 int 2349;* ⏲ *10.00–18.00*).

GETTING IN FROM THE AIRPORT Silvio Pettirossi Airport [73 H2] (☎ *021 645600/5*) is half an hour (20km) from the centre of town, in a northeasterly direction towards Limpio, down the road known as the Autopista (although it is not a motorway). To get from the airport into town, you have three choices: taxi, bus or hired car.

The people who organise the **taxis** stand by the exit door, and will make sure you get an official taxi, even though it will not have 'taxi' written on it. These airport taxis (☎ *021 645851; www.taxiparaguay.com*) are better quality than the usual yellow taxis of Asunción. There are flat rates from the airport, currently Gs120,000 to the centre, and Gs110,000 to the bus terminal. Ask before you get in.

To take a taxi in the other direction, from the Terminal to the airport, there is generally a set fee, currently Gs90,000, which is more than driving to anywhere else in town but is by no means excessive.

To take a **bus** from the airport is amazingly cheap (Gs2,000) and it now runs all night, at approximately half-hourly intervals. You can now get on right outside the airport, where the taxi rank is. The bus number is 30-2 and it has a big 'A' displayed in the front window. Make sure you are going into the centre (*el centro*) and not in the other direction, to Luque.

In the other direction, the airport bus runs from the micro-centre along España, past the Shopping del Sol on Aviadores del Chaco, and then along the Autopista.

If you **hire a car**, there are seven companies to choose from, including Avis and Hertz (see *Car hire*, page 70). You can also return a car here if you have hired it from a central car-hire office that is closed on Sunday.

BY TAXI There is a vast network of yellow taxis, with a lot of underemployed drivers waiting for work, and innumerable taxi ranks (*paradas de taxi*). Some of the taxis rattle as they drive along or have broken door handles, but nothing seriously wrong. If you get a taxi that you like, you can also ask what they would charge for taking you on trips to the interior: a recent rate for this has been Gs3,000 per kilometre.

At night you pay a supplement over what you read on the meter; the drivers carry a written table to show what night rate corresponds to the meter reading. The *paradas* all have telephone numbers, and wherever you are in the city you can ask people to ring a taxi for you. Radio taxis include Radio Taxi Asunción (☎ *021 311080*) and Radio Taxi Coop (☎ *021 550116*).

BY BUS There are approximately 50 local buses, or *lineas*, run by different companies, so that each line has a slightly differently coloured bus. Bus maps are almost impossible to find. You pay when you get on, and it is a flat fare on all buses for all distances, which rose in July 2014 to Gs2,400. Try to have the change, or at least nothing bigger than a Gs10,000 note. There are plans to introduce electronic tickets within the next year or two. Buses used to stop running at 22.00 but the condition set for the price rise was that they should continue running until 04.00. At the time of going to press it was too soon to know how this will work out in practice.

Here are a few of the useful lines to know:

8	from the Terminal to the centre via Fernando de la Mora
18	from the Terminal to the junction with España, via San Martín
23	from the Ruta Transchaco, IPS Hospital, España, Colón, Cuarta
30-2	from the airport to the centre
31	from the Terminal to the centre via Mariscal López
38	from the Terminal to the centre via Fernando de la Mora

48	from the Terminal to the centre via Eusebio Ayala, then Artigas
13, 23, 30, 18, 35, 37	go along España
2, 3, 6, 12, 15, 16, 18, 28, 30, 31, 55, 56	go along Mariscal López
2, 3, 18, 28	go along San Martín
12, 26, 56	from San Lorenzo 'desvío Luque' run along Mariscal López into the centre of Asunción and turn left along Colón

On the way out of the city centre most buses run along Oliva, which turns into Cerro Corá.

METROBUS PROJECT There is not yet a Metrobus, and the plan, which was launched in 2011, has met with continued resistance, partly from traders who think that a fast public transport route into the city centre would have a negative effect on their sales. The planned Metrobus would run from San Lorenzo 18km to the centre of Asunción, with dedicated bus lanes; there would be 16 feeder bus routes and 26 stops where you could get on the bus. The latest proposal to break through the deadlock is to have a monorail running above street level instead of the Metrobus.

CAR HIRE Most of these have branches at the airport in addition to their central reservation offices below, and the airport branches are usually open on Sundays. Localiza has additional branches in Encarnación, Ciudad del Este and Pedro Juan Caballero (see pages 273, 300 and 349).

Avis Eligio Ayala 700 esq Antequera, Plaza Uruguaya; 021 496181; e reservas@avis.com.py; www.avis.com.py. Also branches in the Sheraton & Ibis hotels & on Aviadores del Chaco 3075 (*021 446233*).

Fast Rent a Car Prof. Chávez 1276 c/ Santa Rosa; 021 605462/610811; e info@fast.com.py; www.fastrentacar.com.py. Cars with or without driver.

Hertz Av Eusebio Ayala km4.5; 021 5197310/13; m 0971 328086; e hertz@diesa.com.py

Localiza Av Santa Teresa 3190 esq Austria; 0800 115432 / 021 683892/3; www.localiza.com.py

National España 1009 esq Washington; 021 232990/4; m 0981 622622; e info@national.com.py; www.national.com.py

Touring Cars Yegros 1045 c/ Tte Fariña; 021 375091/447945; e reservas@touringcars.com.py; www.touringcars.com.py. They hire out cars, buses, motorboats & also 4x4 vehicles, which is what you will need if you want to go on dirt roads. But they come at a cost. For 1 day, with a km limit of only 100km, you would pay around US$100, & for a week with a km limit of 2,000km you can expect to pay nearly US$1,000.

Trans-Guaraní Rent-a-car Denis Roa 1455; 021 662071; e autos@transguarani.com; www.transguarani.com. Anne Marie speaks English.

Travel Rent-a-car Airport; 021 645600/9 int 2364/021 645666; m 0983 237187; e travelrc@conexioncom.py; www.travelrentacar.com.py

AVENIDA ÑU GUASÚ Controversially, a stretch of the railway line has been taken up to replace it with a fast road that is now being completed. Although trains were not running anyway, they had been until a bridge required maintenance, and they could have been started again if the road had not usurped their track. The road will run from the centre of Luque via the swish Conmebol Hotel near the airport and across the Ñu Guasú park, to the Jardín Botánico, reducing the journey time to just eight minutes and from there providing a rapid entry to the centre along the broad and fast Avenida Artigas.

CYCLING The use of bicycles in growing in Asunción and there is pressure for cycle lanes, though as yet there has not been a lot of progress on these. Do not make the mistake of the English couple who thought they would bicycle around Asunción and out into the nearby towns in December, having done this successfully in Argentina in the same month. It is much too hot and humid in Paraguay, and the roads are far too bad. After falling off seriously a few times, the couple parked their bikes with a friend and took the bus.

WALKING Asunción is generally safe to walk around in the day. Indeed, exploring the centre on foot is the best way to delight in the mismatch between the crumbling glory of colonial buildings interspersed with sleek, modern hotels and indigenous street traders selling their wares. Be careful not to stumble into one of the *bañados*, however, (such as the Chacorita, behind the Cabildo) where the poorest live, unless you are with someone who is known in that locality. It is not advisable to walk around the quiet streets in the city centre after dark, particularly for women.

TRANSPORT COMPANIES The following have minibuses for small or medium-sized groups (six–19 people). See also page 69 on taxis.

JQ Busses Moleón Mariscal López 638 c/ República Francesa; 021 222352/229778; m 0981 412632; e jqbusses@hotmail.com; Facebook: JQ Busses. Run by Jorge Quintana. Has chauffeur-driven cars as well as different sizes of minibus & bus.
Travel Service Mariotti esq Pres. Santiago Leon; 021 282529; m 0981 450207, 0976 450207; e travelservice@internetpersonal.com.py; www.travelserviceparaguay.com Very professional, reliable outfit run by Martin Molinas. Range of cars, minibuses & buses.
Hummer Presidente Franco 973 c/ Coón; m 0982 444463. Has motor boats & luxury cars with chauffeurs.

HELICOPTER RIDES For an hour's helicopter ride over the Bay of Asunción, Lago Ypacaraí and nearby nature reserves, try Helitáctica (m *0971 911000;* e *commercial@helitactica.com.py*). Currently, a trip costs US$935 for three people, or US$1320 for five people.

MAPS The three maps of Asunción in this guide are inevitably limited in what they can show, and are not a substitute for getting hold of a map of the city with all the road names. The free map of Asunción showing hotels called *Asunción Map Guide* is good: it has amplifications of the city centre and the Villa Morra area, but lacks an index of roads. You can pick this up at Senatur (*Palma 468 e/ Alberdi y 14 de mayo*) or at the airport if the tourist desk is open there. The best maps you can buy are the ones by Ictus, which fold into a thin slip case, have a road index, and are colour-coded for ease of finding your way around. Also, their amplification of the city centre is not nearly as good as that of the free map. You can buy the Ictus maps in a lot of bookshops, including the Librería la Plaza and most of the other bookshops of the Plaza Uruguaya, and El Lector on San Martín. Another good and slightly larger map is by Touring; it is comprehensive, has a road index, and is easy to write on as it is printed in pale pink and yellow; but it has few landmarks shown to help you locate yourself, does not include Lambaré and lacks any amplification of the city centre. You can buy this in some service

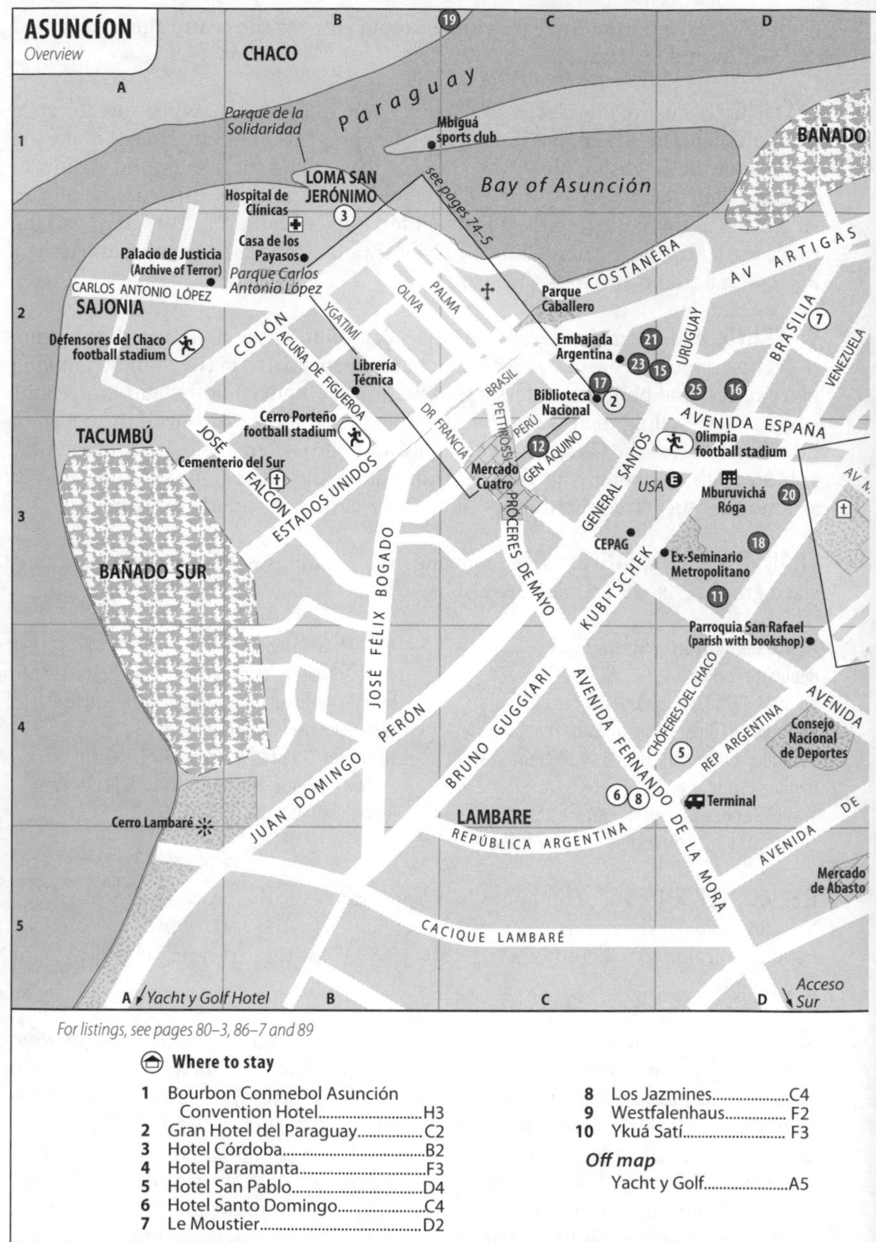

stations and from the shop at the offices of Touring (*Brasil c/ 25 de mayo;* ☎ *021 210550;* ⏲ *08.00–17.00 Mon–Fri*). Apart from these, there is a booklet like a small A–Z called *TAP Guia Asunción*, which is probably the best for finding obscure small streets; it is published by the Hotel Westfalenhaus. You can buy it from the hotel (*Sgto 1° M Benitez 1577 c/ Santísima Trinidad;* ☎ *021 292374/292966*), which unfortunately is rather a long way from the centre.

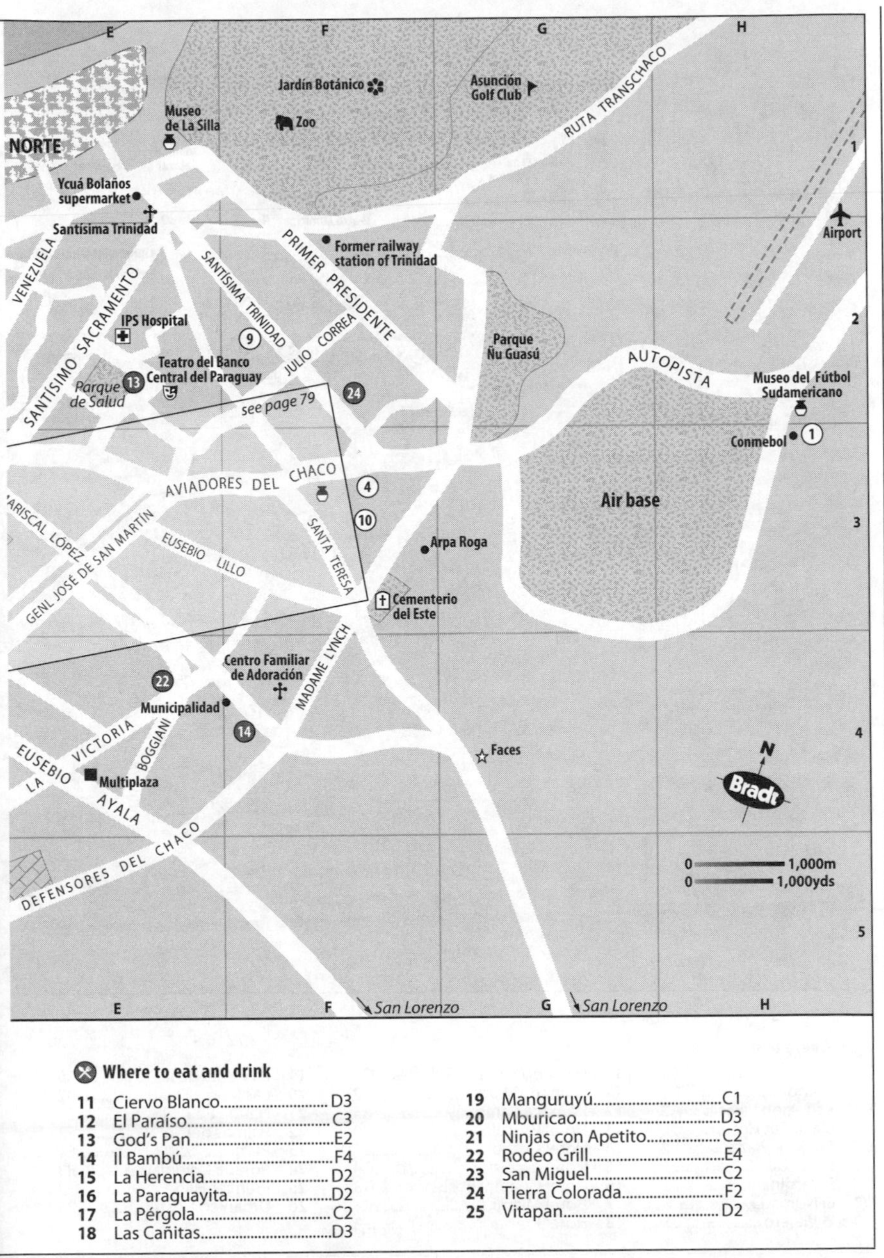

TOURIST INFORMATION, TOUR OPERATORS AND AGENCIES

The website for the city of Asunción is www.mca.gov.py and it has a link to an interactive map. **Senatur** (Secretaría Nacional de Turismo) has its building, Turista Róga (House of the Tourists), on the shopping street Palma in the heart of the city [74 C2] (*Palma 468 e/ Alberdi y 14 de mayo; tourist information* ☎ *0800 113030/021*

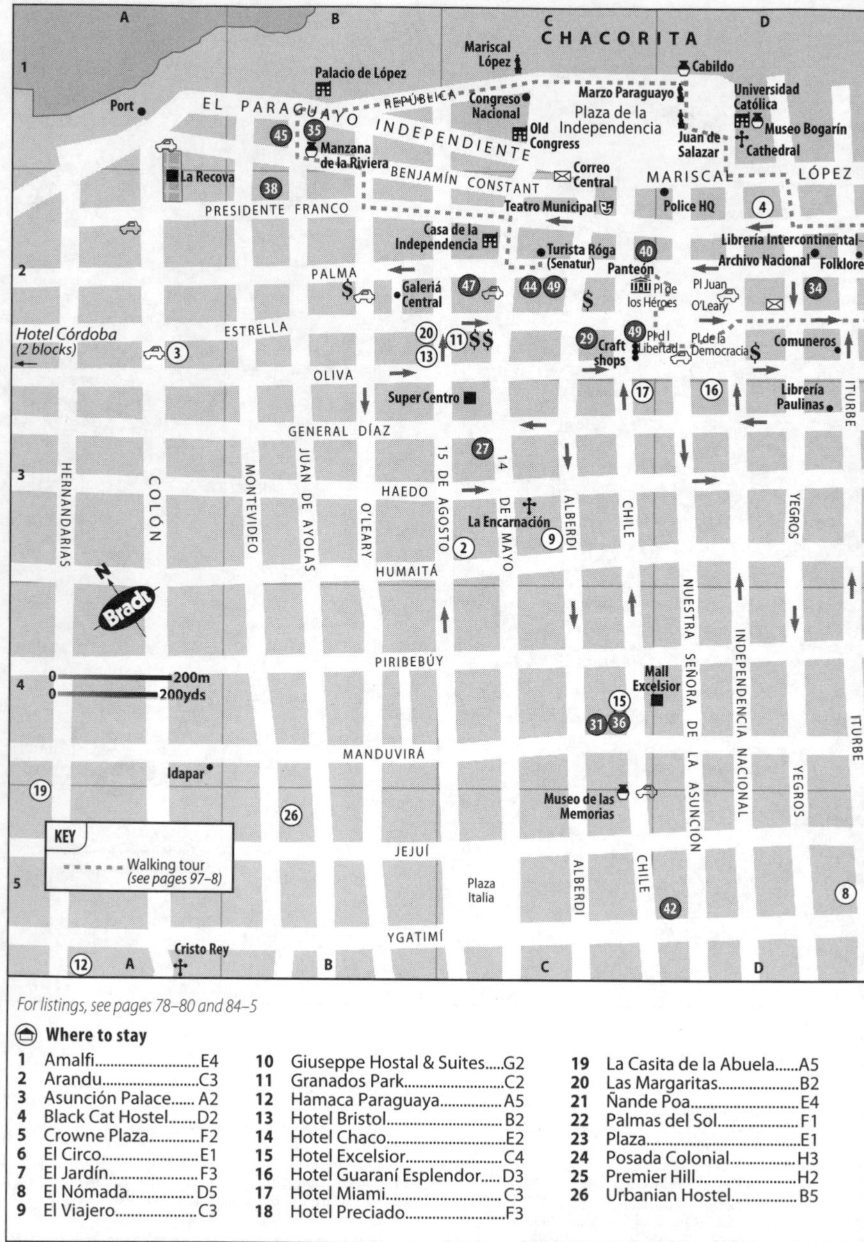

494110; **e** *senator@pla.net.py; www.senatur.gov.py or www.paraguay.travel;* ⌚ *07.00–19.00 daily inc Sun & holidays*). As well as being an excellent place to buy souvenirs (see *Craft shops*, pages 91–3) this is the central tourist information office, and is usually able to provide free maps of the country if you ask, probably as good as or better than the maps you can buy, as well as leaflets and verbal information. Do pick up the latest monthly editions of the excellent *Asunción Map Guide*

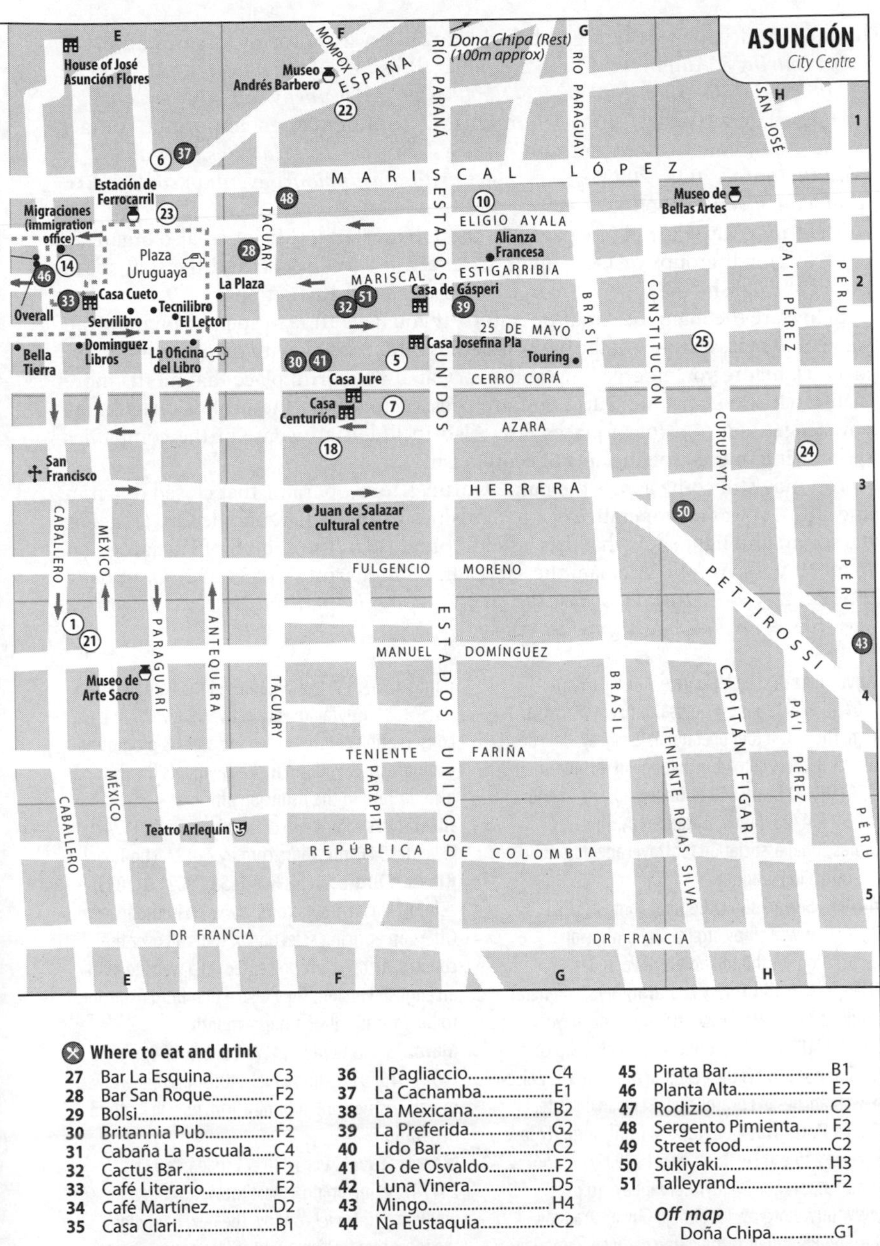

and *Asunción Quick Guide*. These can also be picked up at the airport and at the following hotels: Chaco, Crowne Plaza, Excelsior, Granados, Guaraní Esplendor, Gran Hotel del Paraguay, Las Margaritas, La Misión, Armele, Sheraton, Villa Morra Suites and Yacht y Golf Club.

Another body much involved in tourist information and publications is TACPy, usually referred to as **Touring**, which publishes a lot of materials for tourists, and is generally a good deal more than a motoring organisation [75 G2] (*Touring y Automovil Club Paraguayo, Brasil c/ 25 de mayo; ☎ 021 210550; ⏰ 08.00–17.00 Mon–Fri, 08.00–12.00 Sat; info@tacpy.com.py; www.tacpy.com.py*). For anyone wishing to organise a conference, an important contact is the Asunción Convention and Visitors' Bureau (*De las Residentas 987 c/ Washington; ☎ 021 200952; e raquel.britos@asuncionconvention.com; www.asuncionconvention.com*).

The Santa María Hotel (see page 30), though located in Misiones, also organises tours for small groups or individuals 'from airport to airport', and the staff speak excellent English. They specialise in tours of the Jesuit Reductions.

Below are the main local tour operators. If you have time to spend, you may find some of the classic tours of the big companies rather rapid, with many hours sitting in a bus, before you emerge limp and weary at a wonderful place that merits more than a whistle-stop tour. But if you are pressed for time, the professionals know how to get you to a lot of places fast. Also included are some of the companies specialising in the growing area of ecotourism.

You may still come across the name **Cotur**, a tour operator that closed down in mid-2014. It was a cooperative of small businesses in the Circuito de Oro area. For the sound and light show that they used to organise in the church of Yaguarón, get in touch with Antolín Alemán, the sacristan of Yaguarón (☎ *0533 232198; m 0982 995122), or with Osvaldo Codas, the creative spirit behind the Hotel del Lago (see page 153; e osvaldocodas@gmail.com*).

Agyr Ruiz Díaz de Melgarejo 700, Villa Morra; ☎ 021 614393; e info@agyrsa.com; www.agyrsa.com. The oldest tour operator in Paraguay. Now deals mostly in tours abroad, including Puerto Iguazú.

ASATUR O'Leary 650 e/ General Díaz y Haedo; ☎ 021 494728; www.asatur.org.py. The professional association for travel agents & tour operators in Paraguay.

AIHPY Serrati 386 c/ General Santos; ☎ 021 202650; www.aihpy.org.py. The professional association for the top hotels of Paraguay.

DTP (Desarrollo Turístico Paraguayo) General Bruguez 353 e/ Mcal Estigarribia y 25 de mayo; ☎ 021 221816; e dtp@dtp.com.py; www.dtp.com.py. Some say this is the best tour operator. They also have branches in Encarnación & Ciudad del Este.

Guyrá Paraguay Gaetano Martino, fomerly José Berges, 215 esq Tte Ross; ☎ 021 229097/223567; e guyra.paraguay@guyra.paraguay.org.py; www.guyra.org.py; Facebook: Guyra Paraguay. 'Birding Paraguay' is the name of Guyrá Paraguay's sustainable tourist arm. Rodrigo Zarate is currently in charge of their tourist programme (*m 0981 126594; e rzarate@guyra.org.py*). He & his assistant, Andrea Ferreira, speak very good English. Their various biological stations that can be visited: Estación Kangueŕy in Parque San Rafael (see pages 267–8), Campo Iris in the northern Chaco (see pages 376–7) & Tres Gigantes in the Pantanal (see page 383). Guyrá are very active in developing conservation centres in remote areas & promoting ecotourism, & you can make payments for visits on a credit card in the Asunción office.

InterTours Perú 436 c/ España; ☎ 021 211747; e ventas04@intertours.com.py. See Martin Travel.

Klassen Tours Denis Roa 1455; ☎ 021 612035; e info@klassentours.com; www.klassentours.com. Offers an enticing selection of tours all over the country, attractively presented on a website with an English version. They take a tour from Asunción to the Iguazú Falls 3 times a month.

Maral Sacramento esq Walt Disney 920; ☎ 021 615507; e info@maralturismo.com; www.maralturismo.com. A family firm, now in its third generation.

Martin Travel Peru 436 c/ España; ☎ 021 211747; e incoming@martintravel.com.py; www.martintravel.com.py. The new name for the receptive tourism wing of Intertours, a major company with a lot of experience. It has the advantages & disadvantages of a big company, ie: loads of confidence but sometimes seems in a rush.

OPPY Ruiz Díaz de Melgarejo 609 esq Alberto Souza; ☎ 021 622919-20; e contacto@oppy.com.py; www.oppy.com.py. This lively company was founded in 2009.

Paraguay Safari Soldado Ovelar 527, Fernando de la Mora; m 0971 545659; e paraguaysafari@gmail.com; www.paraguaysafari.com A new organisation offering attractive nature tours at very reasonable prices, in Spanish or in English, minimum 2 people, to the Atlantic Forest, Dry Chaco, the Cerrado Forest, Río Manduvirá, Yvycuí & elsewhere. The guides are 3 wildlife biologists: Rodrigo Ayala, who has done research on lizards & snakes; Johanna López, whose interest is in amphibians, monkeys & jaguars; & Alejandro Bonzi, who has studied bats & small mammals.

San Rafael Peregrinaciones 021 623467/662758. Travel agency specialising in religious tourism & based in the San Rafael parish (see also page 94). Began 12 years ago.

Travel Service Mariotti, esq Pres. Santiago Leon; 021 282529; m 0981 450207, 0976 450207; e travelservice@internetpersonal.com.py; www.travelserviceparaguay.com Primarily a transport company, but Martin Molinas can organise guided tours too.

VIPs Tours Mexico 782 c/ F R Moreno; 021 441199; e vipstour@vipstour.com.py; www.vipstour.com.py. One of the major companies; can do everything from organising tours to airport pickups.

Wildlife Tours Benito Juárez 1150 c/ Saturnino Mereles, Luque; m 0981 920296; www.wildlife.com.py. Two specialist ornithologists run this new company, based in Luque.

WHERE TO STAY

Asunción has a surprisingly large and growing number of **luxury hotels**, not all of which can be represented here. Some are in the centre, and others scattered. In terms of prestige (and price) the big three would be the Bourbon Conmebol (see page 81), the Hotel La Misión (see page 80) and the Sheraton (see page 81). **Hostels** are a new thing in Paraguay: when the first edition of this guide came out there was only one (Black Cat), but now there are nine in Asunción, and around the time of going to press they seemed to be opening at the rate of almost one a month. They are just beginning to spread to other cities. Not everywhere that calls itself a hostel is one in the generally accepted sense, but those listed in the *Hostels* section (see pages 82–3) can be relied upon to offer the usual facilities: dormitory accommodation usually in bunks at low prices as well as private room options, lockers for security, kitchen and laundry area for use of the guests, common sitting room and terrace. They tend to have Wi-Fi and friendly hosts who can be regarded as a source of tourist information. There will normally be English speakers and usually a family atmosphere. In Paraguay, often they have no sign, or a rather invisible one, but you find them from the street number and perhaps from colourful murals along the outside walls; many do not have websites but have Facebook pages.

All places to stay are marked on the maps; a page number refers you to the correct map in each case.

ALOFT ASUNCIÓN

As if the Sheraton, Bourbon Conmebol and La Misión were not sufficiently opulent in this land of poverty, construction is currently underway on a 'green hotel' that will be covered in foliage from top to bottom of its 15 storeys and will use wind turbines. The Aloft Asunción (see map, page 79), next to the Shopping del Sol and opposite the new World Trade Centre being being built on Aviadores del Chaco, is costing US$8 million and will be one of 80 Aloft hotels in the world (of which half are still in construction). Completion is projected for December 2014.

HOTELS

City centre

Map, pages 74–5.

Crowne Plaza (74 rooms) Cerro Corá 939 e/ Tacuari y Estados Unidos; 021 452682; www.crowneasuncion.com.py. Very smart, opened 2005, looks a bit institutional on the outside but is nicely furnished inside. Standard, executive or presidential rooms, & honeymoon suite. Has quiet zones for better sleeping. Pretty central, but not as much as Granados Park, Las Margaritas & Guaraní Esplendor. Hosts conferences. **$$$$$**

Granados Park Hotel (71 rooms) Estrella esq 15 de agosto; 021 497921; www.granadospark.com.py. Directly opposite Las Margaritas & opened in the same year, but with more swish & less imagination than Las Margaritas. In terms of centrality, you cannot do better than this location. Business centre, gym, sauna, massage room, jacuzzi, pool & Wi-Fi. Live music in piano bar. Swimming pool & hydromassage on roof terrace with views over the river. Parking for 100 cars. Free transfer from the airport. **$$$$**

Hotel Excelsior (116 rooms) Chile 980 y Manduvirá; 021 495632; www.excelsior.com.py. Equipped for conferences & can host up to 800 people. Business centre, swimming pool, sauna, massage, tennis. Rooms with striped wallpaper, deep pile carpets, quilted bedcovers. Opposite the Mall Excelsior shopping centre, which is a 5min walk from city centre. 2 restaurants, both with separate entrances onto street: Il Pagliaccio has recently opened with a new presentation & décor, & Cabaña La Pascuala is a favourite with tour agencies, for its live folk music & dance (see *Where to eat*, page 84). **$$$$**

Hotel Guaraní Esplendor (110 rooms) Oliva esq Independencia Nacional; 021 452099; www.guaraniesplendor.com. Recently re-opened with 'Esplendor' tagged onto the name, this tall, triangular building was originally one of Stroessner's prestige works, & it is a famous landmark in the very centre of the city. The land was acquired in 1956, the hotel completed & opened in 1961, remodelled in 1986, & closed in 1995. It fell into increasing disrepair, but was eventually restored & re-opened in 2008. The design is smartly minimalist if a bit boring, & the AC in the rooms is noisy – no doubt the result of being based on 50-year-old ducting. **$$$$**

Las Margaritas (60 rooms) Estrella esq 15 de agosto; 021 448765; www.lasmargaritas.com.py. Fantastic central location. Possibly the most tasteful of the luxury hotels, with pleasing colour matching (especially the green of the daisies after which the hotel is named) & objects of Paraguayan art & craft in the corridors & rooms. Fine view from open top floor, swimming pool, sauna, gym, games room, business centre, Wi-Fi & secure internal car park. Recommended. **$$$$**

Hotel Chaco (70 rooms) Caballero 285 esq Mariscal Estigarribia; 021 492066; www.hotelchaco.com.py. It may be ugly on the outside, but this is a friendly & surprisingly cheap place that has been constantly recommended. Gym, roof terrace, Wi-Fi, parking. Conveniently situated one block from the Plaza Uruguaya & right by the best craft shops & the Librería Intercontinental. Helpful staff; the manager speaks English fluently. Good reductions for groups. One free transfer to or from the airport. **$$$**

Premier Hill Hotel (30 rooms) 25 de mayo y Curupayty; 021 215005; www.premierhill.com.py. Proud of its English style. Each of the floors has a different name & a different design scheme,

ASUNCIÓN *Villa Morra/Carmelitas*
For listings, see pages 80–1 and 87–9

Where to stay

1	Aloft Asunción	E2
2	La Misión	B3
3	Los Alpes, S Teresa	G3
4	Los Alpes, Villa Morra	C3
5	Portal del Sol	G3
6	Sheraton	F2
7	Villa Morra Suites	B2

Where to eat and drink

8	Acuarela	C3
9	Be Okay	B3
10	Café de Acá	D2
11	El Dorado	C2
12	El Mercadito	B4
13	Hacienda Las Palomas	C3
14	Hippie Chic	B1
15	Il Capo	D2
16	Kamambú	A4
17	La Roca	D3
18	Le Sucre Bistro Bar	D3
19	O Gaucho	A3
20	Para Cuando la Vida	E1
21	Paseo Carmelitas	D1
22	Paulista Grill	C3
23	Piegari	F2
24	Rolandi	B2
25	Smuchi	C3
26	Un Toro y Siete Vacas	C2

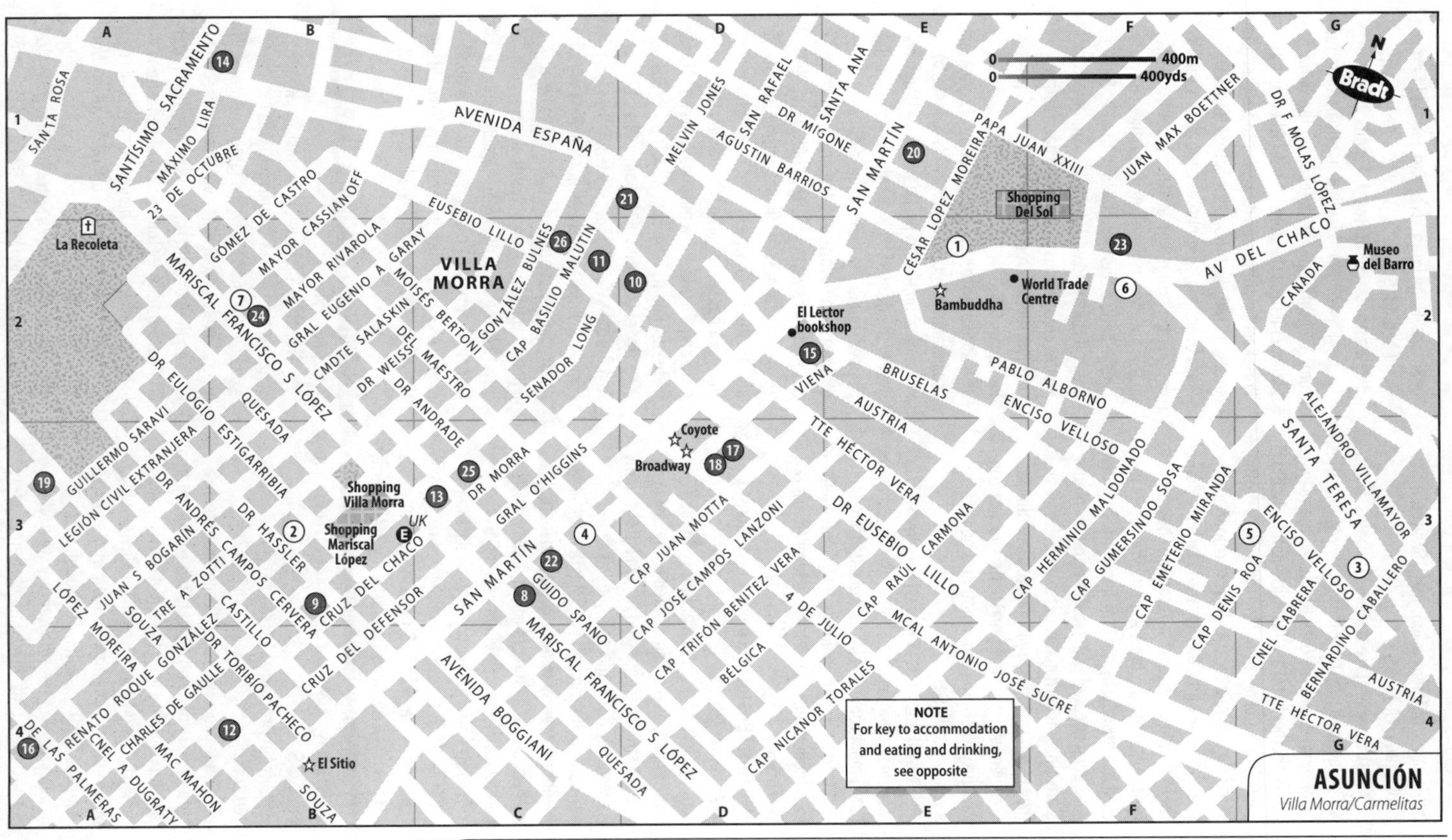
ASUNCIÓN
Villa Morra/Carmelitas
NOTE
For key to accommodation and eating and drinking, see opposite
VILLA MORRA
Shopping Del Sol
World Trade Centre
Bambuddha
El Lector bookshop
Museo del Barro
Coyote
Broadway
Shopping Villa Morra
Shopping Mariscal López
UK
El Sitio
La Recoleta
0 400m
0 400yds
AV DEL CHACO
AVENIDA ESPAÑA
AVENIDA BOGGIANI
MARISCAL FRANCISCO S LÓPEZ
SAN MARTÍN
SANTA TERESA
ALEJANDRO VILLAMAYOR
ENCISO VELLOSO
PABLO ALBORNO
BRUSELAS
AUSTRIA
VIENA
TTE HÉCTOR VERA
DR EUSEBIO LILLO
MCAL ANTONIO JOSÉ SUCRE
CÉSAR LÓPEZ MOREIRA
PAPA JUAN XXIII
JUAN MAX BOETTNER
DR F MOLAS LÓPEZ
CAÑADA
SANTA ANA
SAN RAFAEL
DR MIGONE
AGUSTÍN BARRIOS
MELVIN JONES
EUSEBIO LILLO
CAP BASILIO MALUTIN
SENADOR LONG
GONZÁLEZ BULNES
MOISÉS BERTONI
DEL MAESTRO
DR ANDRADE
DR WEISS
CMDTE SALASKIN
GRAL EUGENIO A GARAY
MAYOR RIVAROLA
MAYOR CASSIANOFF
GÓMEZ DE CASTRO
DR MORRA
GRAL O'HIGGINS
GUIDO SPANO
QUESADA
DR HASSLER
CRUZ DEL CHACO
CRUZ DEL DEFENSOR
SOUZA
SANTÍSIMO SACRAMENTO
SANTA ROSA
MAXIMO LIRA
23 DE OCTUBRE
DR EULOGIO ESTIGARRIBIA
GUILLERMO SARAVI
LEGIÓN CIVIL EXTRANJERA
DR ANDRÉS CAMPOS CERVERA
JUAN S BOGARÍN
TRE A ZOTTI
CASTILLO
DR TORIBIO PACHECO
LÓPEZ MOREIRA
RENATO ROQUE GONZÁLEZ
CHARLES DE GAULLE
MAC MAHON
CNEL A DUGRATY
DE LAS PALMERAS
CAP JUAN MOTTA
CAP JOSÉ CAMPOS LANZONI
CAP TRIFÓN BENITEZ VERA
BÉLGICA
4 DE JULIO
CAP RAÚL CARMONA
CAP NICANOR TORALES
CAP HERMINIO MALDONADO
CAP GUMERSINDO SOSA
CAP EMETERIO MIRANDA
CAP DENIS ROA
CNEL CABRERA
BERNARDINO CABALLERO

according to different woods used. Swimming pool, sauna, Wi-Fi. **$$$**

Asunción Palace Hotel (25 rooms) Colón 415, esq Estrella; 021 492151/3; www.geocities.com/aphotel. Like the Gran Hotel del Paraguay, this is another hotel in a historic building. Built in 1858, it was the house of Mariscal López's brother Venancio, & is marked by 3 rows of colonnades, one above the other, on the façade facing Colón. There are old photos in the reception showing also the time during the Triple Alliance War when it was used as a hospital by the Brazilian army. The rooms have been updated with pleasing simple colours & are quite modern in feel. Sizeable balconies: they look over a noisy road, but you can glimpse the river. One room has a real bath – very rare in Paraguay. Wi-Fi. You can negotiate a good discount if you pay cash. **$$**

Hotel Amalfi (19 rooms) Caballero 877 c/ Manuel Domínguez; 021 494154/441162; www.hotelamalfi.com.py. A lot nicer inside than the slightly garish sign would suggest. Good standard for a modest hotel, with friendly receptionist & Wi-Fi. **$$**

Hotel Bristol (19 rooms) 15 de agosto 472 c/ Oliva; 021 494254; www.hotelbristol.com.py. Next door to Las Margaritas & under same management. Remodelled in the last few years. A striking painting on the wall of the lobby is practically the icon of this hotel: it shows 2 red-earth paths through the fields, a *tatakuá* traditional oven, & some boys playing football. Every room has a different colour & style, all in perfect taste. Wi-Fi. Excellent value. **$$**

Hotel Miami México 449 c/ 25 de mayo; 021 444950; e hostelmiami@gmail.com. If you want somewhere cheap & dead in the centre & are not too fussy, the Miami is practically at the corner of Plaza Uruguaya, up a staircase. It calls itself a hostel but is really just a cheap hotel. Takes credit cards. **$$**

Hotel Preciado (18 rooms) Félix de Azara 840 c/ Tacuary; 021 447661/453937; e hotelpreciado@yahoo.es. Economic hotel in a 19th-century building, close to the centre. Internal parking (entrance from the street Herrera). Wi-Fi, cable TV. A good way of combining lower mid-range quality & a central position with a building of architectural character – although there is nothing to see of the 19th-century style when you get past the façade. Much improved from a few years ago. Huge internal car park reached from the street behind. **$$**

Palmas del Sol Hotel España 202, c/ Tacuary; 021 449485; www.hotelpalmasdelsol.com. A recently opened hotel under the same management as the popular but rather far-out Portal del Sol. Although it faces onto a rather grimy street, it's only just round the corner from the Plaza Uruguaya, so counts as central. Beautifully designed, it brings a great sense of refreshment in this hot, sweaty & polluted city: there is white everywhere, a courtyard filled with trees & plants, & a 2nd courtyard with a small swimming pool. Rooms are spacious & so are the bathrooms. German-run, like most of the best hotels in Paraguay. **$$**

Plaza Hotel (about 40 rooms) Eligio Ayala esq Paraguarí; 021 444196/444772/448834: www.plazahotel.com.py. On the Plaza Uruguaya, next to the disused railway station. A bit dated & chipped, but in a good location. **$$**

Posada Colonial (20 rooms) P'ai Pérez 637 e/ Herrera y Azara; 021 200821; m 0991 763046; www.posadacolonial.net. No sign up outside this hotel, which is not really a hostel though it has some of the same characteristics, including a laundry & a microwave oven for the use of guests. Rooms have Split AC & fridges. **$$**

Hotel Córdoba (18 rooms) Oliva 1275 c/ Don Bosco; 021 495388; www.hotelcordoba.com.py. If you want a cheap hotel in easy walking distance of the centre & do not want to be in a hostel, you cannot do better than here, with private bathrooms, AC, Wi-Fi, garden, cable TV, bar, laundry & airport transfers. Sgl, dbl, trp & quad rooms, at a price much lower than you would pay elsewhere. Some sommier beds. **$**

Villa Morra/Shopping del Sol area

Map, page 79.

Hotel La Misión (36 rooms) San Roque González esq Eulogio Estigarribia, Villa Morra; 021 621800/610519; www.lamision.com.py. This luxury hotel has real style, with the architecture echoing themes from the Ruins of Trinidad & Jesús, & large paintings by Nino Sotelo of Reductions' life in the reception. Tucked behind the Mariscal López Shopping., & a close neighbour of the future World Trade Centre & Blue Tower. **$$$$$**

Hotel Villa Morra Suites (30 rooms) Mcal López 3001 c/ Yaraví Yaraví; 021 612715; www.

villamorrasuites.com.py. Designed by a Uruguayan & opened in 2002, large-scale family-run business, suites all with kitchen & nearly all with lounge, some have actual baths. Has Wi-Fi. Plenty of trees despite being on main road. **$$$$$**

Sheraton (100 rooms) Av Aviadores del Chaco 2066 y Santa Teresa; 021 6177000; www.sheraton.com/asuncion or www.sheraton-asuncion.com.py. One of the smartest & best-known hotels, opened 2004. Not central but on busy road to airport, handy for Museo del Barro & Shopping del Sol. Hosts conferences. **$$$$$**

Los Alpes Santa Teresa (172 rooms) Santa Teresa 2855 e/ Coronel Cabrera y Bernardino Caballero; 021 607348; m 0981 552066; www.hotellosalpes.com.py. A successful hotel in San Bernardino has now opened 2 lovely hotels in Asunción. This was the first to open & is the larger, though it is further from the centre than the other. **$$$**

Los Alpes Villa Morra (18 rooms) Del Maestro 1686 c/ San Martín; 021 606286; www.hotellosalpes.com.py. The second Los Alpes of Asunción. Has a garden & pool. The attic floor of this hotel is used as a superior-quality dormitory by Peace Corps volunteers coming in from all over the country. **$$$**

Portal del Sol (50 rooms) Av Denis Roa 1455 c/ Sta Teresa; 021 609395/607880; www.portaldelsol.com. Good, middle-range hotel with lovely 2,000m^2 garden with lots of birds, shady terraces & a swimming pool. Good food & friendly people. Calls itself a 'traditional German hotel'. Free transfers & Wi-Fi. The downside is that the hotel is a long way from the centre, & not close to anywhere you would want to go to except the Museo del Barro, the Shopping del Sol & the musical instrument shops along the road towards Luque. There are rooms & apts. **$$$**

Hotels near the bus terminal

Map, pages 72–3.

Los Jazmines (6 rooms) Alcides González 160 c/ Fernando de la Mora; 021 553096; www.losjazmines.com.py. Closer to the main road than Santo Domingo. Elegant family B&B with rooms named after varieties of jasmine, all with fridges & en suite bathrooms. The best have a tiny terrace, but the others are a bit dark. Garden with pool. **$$$**

Hotel Santo Domingo (31 rooms) Alcides González esq O Kallsen; 021 550130/555001; www.santodomingo.com.py. 5mins' walk from Terminal, 1 block from main road, garden with a swimming pool, this is quite a smart hotel. Free transfers from airport. **$$$**

Hotel San Pablo Tte Alcides González 1578 c/ Tabapý; 021 552149; m 0981 980130; www.hotelsanpablo.com.py. Inexpensive hotel offering good value accommodation very close to the Terminal. It remains cheaper than most other places despite having improved its accommodation notably in the last few years, with a modern building out the back, a new b/fast room, a large enclosed car park & a *quincho* area where you can eat food you have bought at one of the nearby supermarkets. All rooms have split AC, Wi-Fi & cable TV. B/fast includes a hot toasted sandwich. To get to the hotel, head towards the right as you leave the Terminal, cross the main road (República Argentina) & go up the road facing you which has a taxi rank on the corner. After a short distance there is a corner where you turn right & the hotel is almost at the corner, on your left. The presence of the taxi rank offers security at night, & the hotel is open 24 hours. **$**

Other areas

Map, pages 72–3.

Bourbon Conmebol Asunción Convention Hotel (168 rooms) Avenida Sudamericana 3104; 021 6591000; www.bourbon.com.br. Adjacent to the Conmebol Conference Centre & Confederación Suamericana de Fútbol, with its giant black & white football, this is the closest hotel to the airport & one of the most luxurious of the new hotels in the capital. Part of the Brazilian Bourbon chain. The perfect place for highly paid visiting football stars. It is also a beguilingly pleasant place to hang out, with a simple mammoth lounge occupying the ground floor & stretching up to the top of the building, soothed with sounds of multiple waterfalls & pianos playing without human hands. The rooms open off galleries on various levels above it, with grand internal views from the walkways. Rooftop pool, jacuzzi, spa with eastern aromas, etc. The weekend lunches have a surprisingly reasonable set price of GS99,000: Saturdays *feijoada*, Sundays pasta. **$$$$$**

Gran Hotel del Paraguay (54 rooms) De la Residenta 904 y Padre Pucheau; 021 200051/2; www.granhoteldelparaguay.com.py. A famous hotel in a historic building. Originally the house of Madame Lynch, it has been a hotel since it was bought by an Italian immediately after the War of the Triple Alliance, & has been known as the Gran Hotel del Paraguay since a German took it over in 1921. The dining room dates from the López era & has a painted ceiling. Wi-Fi, pool, tennis, huge & magnificent grounds full of toucans & other birds, only a short distance from city centre. Sat eve may have live folk music. An excellent venue for a buffet lunch because you can eat in the garden. **$$$$**

Hotel Paramanta (28 rooms) Av Aviadores del Chaco 3198 e/ Chacore y Capitan Meza; 021 607053; www.paraguay-hotel.de. The internet suffix .de always indicates a German-run hotel. This one is more convenient for the airport than for the city. Next door is the Candlewood Apart Hotel, under the same management, which has small flats with a little kitchen, at the same price for one night, but with a monthly rate that works out a lot cheaper pro rata. **$$$$**

Le Moustier (28 rooms or suites) Teniente Insaurralde 347 c/ Brasilia; 021 283740; www.lemoustier.org. Lovely 2-storey building with arches around a courtyard with a fountain, beautifully lit at night, this was previously a retirement home for Francophones, but was converted in 2010 into a hotel where nearly every room is a suite with kitchenette. Pool, gym, business centre, Japanese garden, mini cinema, free transfers from airport & Restaurant Chantecler with French Provençale cuisine. **$$$$**

Westfalenhaus Sgto 1° M Benitez 1577 c/ Santísima Trinidad; 021 292374/292966; www.paraguay-hotel.com. Immaculate hotel with an excellent reputation. It looks like a whole street of houses, & has a pool, honeymoon suites, rooms for people with disabilities, good conference facilities & all mod cons. Massage, reflexology & chiropractice. Russian cuisine, big buffet b/fast. English spoken. The hotel produces the *TAP Guia Paraguay* (see page 399) & the *TAP Guia Asunción* (see page 72). The drawback is that it is inconveniently located, in a quiet neighbourhood. **$$$$**

Yacht y Golf (128 rooms) Av del Yacht 11; 021 906121; www.hotelyacht.com.py. The rooms are spacious & have a view of the river or the garden, while the luxury suites have direct access to a private beach. Golf course, 14 tennis courts, 2 squash courts, aquatic sports, gym, basketball, ping-pong, hockey, bicycling, Play Room Club for children, car hire. It's a long way from the centre, & is more for business people wanting the facilities of a resort, or for conferences, rather than for people wanting to explore the city. Free transfer to & from the airport. **$$$$**

HOSTELS

Map, pages 74–5.

Urbanian Hostel (sleeps 40) Montevideo 1029 e/ Jejuí y Manduvira; 021 441209; www.urbanianhostel.com. The newest & most expensive hostel (but with good reason). This calls itself the city's first boutique hostel & has been featured in design magazines for its industrial-chic interior in a beautifully renovated townhouse, using recycled doors & windows & solar-heated hot water. Exposed brickwork, scrubbed wood & custom-built bunk beds (so you can sit up on the bottom bunk). Excellent bar & grill open to the public (*11.00–midnight*) with produce from the organic garden. Spotless, Wi-Fi, computers, pool, TV room, AC & garden. Helpful staff. Bicycle hire, transfers from airport. One drawback: there is no kitchen. **$$**

Black Cat Hostel (sleeps 50) Eligio Ayala 129 e/ Yegros e Independencia Nacional; 021 449827; m 0981 986594; www.blackcathostel.com. Paraguay's first backpacker hostel & still unsurpassed in what it can offer, given its central location, helpful service & the good English spoken there. Not only that, but is one of the most economical. Violeta had the idea after discovering hostels when backpacking to Machu Picchu; her mother is joint owner of the hostel with her. Good English spoken. Pool. Some rooms have fans. Cheap laundry service. Bikes for rent by the hour. **$$**

Giuseppe Hostel (sleeps more than 50) Eligio Ayala 1037 e/ Brasil y Estados Unidos; 021 211479/200397; www.giuseppehostalandsuites.com. On the east side of the centre, this early 19th-century house combines an elegant, minimalist hotel downstairs with dormitories on the upper floor (hence the term 'hostal'). It opened in Jun 2014. The owner speaks English. **$$**

Ñande Poa (sleeps 20) Manuel Dominguez 489 esq. México; 021 449480, m 0985 958430; e hostelnandepoa@gmail.com. Name means 'our fortune'. Slightly more expensive than the other hostels. Traditional house with central courtyard, 1 block from Museo de Arte Sacro. English not spoken. Slightly puzzling notice by the door bell is meant to deter those looking for a daytime bed for sex. As well as dorms, nice private double room with own bathroom & garage. Photos on Facebook page: search for Hostel Nande Poa. **$$**

Arandu (sleeps 28) 15 de agosto 783 c/ Humaitá; 021 449712; m 0981 711852; www.aranduhostal.com. Means 'wisdom' in Guaraní. Fairly close to centre, good-quality rooms & design, mirrors, spacious modern bathrooms & well-equipped kitchen, almost more like the feel of a hotel than a hostel. English not spoken. Very slightly more expensive than some other hostels, & a towel is extra. Terrace with vine & barbecue. Cable TV. Book exchange shelf. Reduced prices for long-stay guests. Credit cards. **$**

El Circo (sleeps 22) Manuel Golondra esq. Mariscal López; 021 441000; www.circo.com.py. Centrally located behind railway station in what used to be a radio broadcast studio, recognisable from the red & yellow chequer pattern outside. The wildest & wackiest of the hostels, with 1 of the most original bars in Asunción, La Cachamba, functioning in a train graveyard next door (see page 86). English is spoken. Large kitchen. **$**

El Jardín (sleeps 20) Azara 941 e/ Estados Unidos y Tacuary; m 0982 369487/0984 860340; e eljardinhostal@hotmail.com. Centrally located; buses from airport & from bus terminal go by the door. Family feel, run by Swedish Thomas & his Paraguayan bilingual wife Carolina, daughter of a political exile in the dictatorship. Big lockers & pool. Provides a good free map. B/fast includes homemade bread, eggs, fruit, cereal & yoghurt. Supermarket around the corner. Photos on Facebook page: search for El Jardin Hostel; website imminent. **$**

El Nómada (sleeps 28) Iturbe 1156 c/ Rodriguez de Francia; m 0992 272946; e elnomadahostal@hotmail.com. Excellent quality & family feel, with both Paraguayan Patricia & French Guillerme speaking good English. Widely recommended. Some rooms have fans. Good b/fast with croissants, chocolate, cereal, fruit & French crêpes. Some other hostels are more central (& others are further out). Cheap laundry service. Transfer to airport cheaper than taxi. **$**

El Viajero (sleeps 60) Alberdi 734 e/ Haido y Humaitá; 021 444563; m 0972 120037; www.elviajerohostels.com. Closest to the centre after Black Cat & el Circo. Tucked along the side of Encarnación church, which you see from the terrace. Has a big sign but so high up you can miss it. Part of a chain of 7 hostels run by Uruguayans. It is professional & provides lots of info, but inevitably lacks the family feel. Big dorms with split AC & a spacious feel. Live-in manager & 1 receptionist speak English. Claims to be the only hostel with a pool & AC in all rooms. Outsiders can use pool if they buy a drink: often turns into a lively mix of Paraguayans & travellers at night. Big lounge with fireplace for winter. **$**

Hamaca Paraguaya (sleeps 36) Hernandarias 1247 c/ Ygatimí; 021 482690; m 0994 151054; www.facebook.com/hamacaparaguaya.hostel. One of the nicest hostels, though not very close to the centre. Family feel, little pictures on handpainted notices make you feel at home. Good English spoken by Carolina, who has lived in USA & Switzerland. Reading lights, cable TV & barbecue. Open 24 hrs. Ham & cheese for b/fast. Games room with pool & bar football. Cash only & in advance. **$**

La Casita de la Abuela, Hostal Verde (sleeps 24) Hernandarias 1074 e/ Jejuí y Manduvirá; m 0981 468090; e lacasitadelaabuelahostalverde@gmail.com; Facebook: La Casita De La Abuela Hostal Verde. One of the friendliest & most relaxed hostels, owner Javier lived in USA for a year, & all staff speak English. Small rooms & tiny bathroom. All guests welcome to paint on the walls, as has been very well done for the Little Prince mural in the garden. Not very central but not too far either. 24 hours, cable TV. **$**

ESTANCIA

There is an *estancia* where you can stay without ever leaving the city, though it is only really suitable for big groups, companies or conferences. Map, page 73.

Ykuá Satí (beds for 250) Mayor Evacio Perenciollo Merlo 2150, esq. Dr Bestard; 021 601230 / 600058; www.quintaykuasati.com.py. Very comfortable & professionally run, with riding, swimming pool, Wi-Fi & restaurant. Not far from Shopping del Sol & the Museo del Barro. Take the Santa Teresa turn off Aviadores del Chaco (where the Hotel Sheraton is), then 5th right to the end of the road & it is a short distance away to the right, at the corner. **$$$**

WHERE TO EAT AND DRINK

You can eat very well in Asunción. Most restaurants are open every day; assume this, unless otherwise specified. Key times for eating are midday for lunch, and from 20.00 for dinner (no earlier). There used to be a shortage of places where you could eat outside, in the hot Paraguayan weather, because Paraguayans prefer to eat indoors with air conditioning, but an increasing number of the fashionable new places now have outside space. If you are looking for a restaurant with a garden, not on a main road, try the Gran Hotel del Paraguay; you can ask them to serve you outside, and it is very reasonably priced. Or try La Paraguayita, Casa Clari, El Dorado, Il Capo (on Austria), El Mercadito, Para Cuando la Vida, Las Palomas, La Roca, the Café de Acá or one of the places at Paseo Carmelitas on the Senador Long side. Luna Vinera and Ciervo Blanco also have outside space, but note that they are open only in the evening.

You are advised to take a long-sleeved garment to a restaurant when eating inside as the air conditioning is often turned up high and you can be cold, even (and especially) when it is sweltering outside.

CITY CENTRE

Map, pages 74–5.

Talleyrand Mcal Estigarribia 932, e/ Estados Unidos y Tacuary; 021 441163/661618. A 30-year-old establishment discreetly placed in the centre; gourmet food but on the dear side as Paraguayan restaurants go; décor with low beams & tapestry chairs, a bit like an English pub, nice atmosphere but not a lot of customers. *Pato a la naranja* (duck with orange) is their signature dish, & *Tournedos Talleyrand* (beef fillet) is also a popular choice. They also have a restaurant in the Shopping del Sol, 1st floor (*021 611697*) & in the Costanera Centro de Eventos (*021 232778*). $$$$$

Cabaña La Pascuala Manduvirá c/ Chile; 021 495632 int 1420; Tue–Sun. The other restaurant run by the Hotel Excelsior. Serves Paraguayan cuisine & a grill, with folk music & dance at 21.30 every night on a tiny stage, looking out onto a garden with a swimming pool. (A better stage for dancing is found at Ciervo Blanco, see page 86.) $$$$

Il Pagliaccio Manduvirá esq Chile; 021 495632 int 1861; Mon–Sat. Italian & international cuisine, run by Hotel Excelsior next door. $$$$

La Preferida 25 de mayo 1005 c/ EEUU; 021 210641/202222. One of the many delights in this beautiful & intimate 1st-floor restaurant is the ghostly piano that greets you with its playerless music as you walk up the stairs. Everything here is quality. Under same management as Hotel Cecilia next door. $$$$

Bar San Roque Eligio Ayala 792 esq Tacuary; 021 446015; 09.00–15.30 & 19.00–midnight Mon–Sat, 10.00–16.00 Sun. This is the oldest restaurant in the country, & is recommended for its food, authentic Paraguayan ambience & reasonable prices. On the corner is a bar, & the restaurant opens off there. Try the *puchero* & don't miss the *mousse mburucuyá*. $$$

Bolsi Estrella 399 esq Alberdi; 021 491841/2. Conveniently placed in the heart of the centre, Bolsi has a café & pastry shop section, & a smallish restaurant with excellent food. It is quite elegant but surprisingly reasonable. It has been open since 1960, which in Paraguayan terms means it is an old establishment. Recommended. $$$

Café Literario Mariscal Estigarribia 456; 021 491640; 16.00–midnight Sun–Thu, 16.00–02.00 Fri & Sat. Though the service is slow, this is a place of such restful enjoyment that you may find yourself returning again & again – annoyed only by the limited opening hours. There is nothing very substantial in the way of food – sandwiches & snacks rather than full meals – but the fruit juices are splendid & the atmosphere exquisite. Not only are there papers to read, but a large & very interesting variety of books to buy, or simply to browse through while you sip your banana & strawberry juice. A wall display of writers' photos provides an education in Paraguayan literature. Upstairs in a discreet gallery are comfortable armchairs. It's a great place to recover your energy after footing it round town. $$$

✕ **Lo de Osvaldo** Cerro Corá 883 e/ Tacuary y Estados Unidos; m 0982 128140; Facebook: Lo de Osvaldo. Steakhouse located in a beautifully restored building next to the Crowne Plaza Hotel, walls covered with historic football photos. The 'Osvaldo' refers to Colorado politician Osvaldo Domínguez Dibb, for many years President of the Olimpia football team, but even if he is not your favourite politician you cannot deny that his restaurant is a good one. Grilled steaks with traditional sides such as *chipa guasu*. High ceilings & exposed brick walls are dotted with signed shirts, newspaper clippings & other vintage football memorabilia. Spacious courtyard at the back. They often have live music. $$$

✕ **Luna Vinera** Ygatimi 250 c/ Chile; ☎ 021 491604; ⏱ Tue–Sun, eves only from 19.00. Delightful restaurant full of character with internal courtyard open to the balmy night air & full of plants. Imaginative food, very reasonable. Attractive rooms for private dinners or events. Large chess set of Indians versus Conquistadors in the bar area. Live music sometimes. $$$

✕ **Café Martínez** Mariscal Estigarribia y Yegros; www.cafemartinez.com/paraguay; ⏱ all day every day. This well-known Argentinian café chain specialising in gourmet coffee has now opened a branch in a fine 19th-century building on a corner in the city centre. There are also branches in Pinedo Shopping, Shopping del Sol & Shopping Mariscal López. $$

✕ **Casa Clari** Ayolas 129 e/ Benjamin Constant y Paraguayo Independente; ☎ 021 4964 76. This building within the Manzana de la Rivera has a café with a pretty 1st-floor terrace overlooking the Palacio de López (spectacular at night when illuminated). Bars in this lovely but little known location have closed down before so it is to be hoped that this one will be a success. Simple good food such as pizza & *picada* alongside an extensive cocktail list. $$

✕ **Ña Eustaquia** Palma e/ Alberdi y 14 de mayo; ☎ 021 297480. Chic little café/restaurant right opposite Turista Roga, where it is bound to attract custom from visitors. They boast of doing 'slow & fast food'. Branches in most of the shopping centres & home delivery (☎ *021 449449;* ⏱ *07.00–21.00*). $$

✕ **Rodizio** Palma 591 e/ 14 de mayo y 15 de agosto; ☎ 021 451281; www.rodizio.com.py; ⏱ Mon–Sat & Sun lunch. Pay-by-weight *churrasquería*, excellent value, packed every lunchtime. $$

✕ **Sukiyaki** Constitucion 763 c/ Herrera; ☎ 021 222038/203037; Facebook: Sukiyaki. Sushi & a range of other authentic Japanese dishes, with many cooked on a hot plate in front of you. Separate smoking area at the back. $$

✕ **Bar La Esquina** 14 de mayo 614 y General Díaz. The best value buffet in town. Packed at lunch but people move on quickly so you will find a seat. $

✕ **Doña Chipa** España y Brasil; ☎ 021 228440. This is the central house of a new chain of cafés, serving a delicious range of *chipas*, with tantalising smells, to eat on the spot or take away. The *chipa a 4 quesos* ('with 4 cheeses') is particularly good, but so is the rest of the range, which includes *mbejú* (see page 396). $

✕ **Lido Bar** Palma y Chile; ☎ 021 446171. On the corner opposite the Panteón, this is a well-known & long-established café, always jam-packed at lunchtime, with all the customers eating around a big circular bar. Prices are cheap & the atmosphere pure Paraguayan. The fish soup is a speciality & there is a good variety of fruit juices. Tables on the pavement give a stunning view of the colourfully illuminated Panteón by night. $

✕ **Mingo** Mayor Fleitas e/ Teodoro Mongeles y Herminio Giménez; ☎ 021 203580. Upstairs buffet with salad, downstairs other dishes. Near Mercado 4, this is an example of how cheaply you can eat in Asunción & still get good quality & variety. $

✕ **Street food** There are tables in the street where you can eat well enough for very little. In Palma there is one such place, though you need to be prompt at midday before the food runs out, & you might feel it inappropriate to be taking cheap food out of the mouths of the Paraguayans. In the Plaza de la Libertad, next to the craft stalls, is another open-air improvised restaurant. $

🍷 **Britannia Pub** Cerro Corá 851 c/ Tacuary; ☎ 021 43990; www.britannia-pub.com; ⏱ Tue–Sun. Bar with theme of British pub, a popular hangout, always full, sells food. Free entry except on certain nights when there is something special on. Recently expanded kitchen & food good value, in fact half-price until 20.30. Among its choice of beers is its own Britannia Beer – which is a German style beer made in Paraguay.

Cactus Bar 25 de Mayo 887 e/ Tacuarý y Estados Unidos; m 0982 320062. A new bar located in a restored townhouse near the city centre; high ceilings, pillars & stone seating dotted with foliage. Serving a standard selection of cocktails alongside *picada*, the outside space gets busy at weekends when local Paraguayan DJs pull in a young crowd.

La Cachamba Manual Gondra c/ Mcal López, 2300; m 0982 127363. Next to El Circo Hostel, this new bar is set in a train graveyard (an old steam train & scattered carriages remain, with the bar itself inside). Industrial décor & fairy lights combined with Art Deco touches & imaginative cocktails (such as vodka with basil & watermelon), served in mismatched enamel cups with a *bombilla*. Perfect for a relaxed midweek drink; great pizza *picada* & hamburgers too. At the weekend, contemporary Western music draws Paraguayans & tourists alike to the sunken open air dance floor.

La Mexicana Presidente Franco c/ Ayolas. A bar until midnight, then they move the chairs & tables & it becomes a disco playing a mix of Latin & dance music.

Pirata Bar Ayolas y Benjamín Constant; 021 452953–4; www.piratabar.com.py; from 18.00 Nightclub with a pirate theme, capacity for 2,000 people. Central, near the Manzana de la Rivera with a view over the Bay of Asunción from La Terraza bar. Salsa night on Wed, live shows on Thu, including sometimes a magician dressed as a pirate.

Planta Alta Caballero 294 y Mariscal Estigarribia. Next door to the Overall craft shop is a discreet doorway that is opened in the evening to give access to a bar upstairs on the upper floor (*planta alta*). The only indication of this by day are the letters PA carved in stone high above the doorway. Artworks & balconies with a view. Open from around 17.30 to 03.00.

Sargento Pimienta Tacuary esq/ Mariscal López; 021 449960; 18.30–05.00 Tue–Sat. Bar with discotheque, salsa.

BETWEEN THE CITY CENTRE AND VILLA MORRA/SHOPPING DEL SOL

Map, pages 72–3.

Mburicao Prof Antonio González Rioboó 737; 021 660048; 12.00–14.30 & 20.00–00.30 Mon–Fri, 12.00–14.30 Sat, closed Sun. Definitely expensive but high quality. Tricky to find: from Mariscal López turn down Chóferes del Chaco, then first right down Chaco Boreal, & first left down González Riobóo. Minimalist design with Scandinavian feel, wood, beige & white, bright lights, good waiters. Outside space viewed through glass walls. Gourmet international menu, very big helpings, very expensive. $$$$$

Ciervo Blanco Jose Asunción Flores 3870 c/Radio Operadores del Chaco; 021 214504/212918; from 21.00 Tue–Sat, show starts at 22.00, on Fri & Sat the show goes on until the early hours, closed Sun. A great place for a night out, with a show of music & folk dance in the semi-open while you eat grilled meat; it works out a little on the pricey side, but is worth it for the ambience & entertainment. $$$$

La Pérgola Peru 240 e/ Rio de Janeiro y Jose Berges; 021 214014. Smart restaurant with upmarket cafeteria next door. On the dear side for Paraguay, but offers quality food, imaginatively presented, though the décor is angular & rather plain, & the restaurant lacks atmosphere. There is a floodlit fountain outside, but it is on the main road & you cannot sit out there. Every table gets a big basket of warm cheese-breads with a dip & liver paste. Close to the Gran Hotel de Paraguay. $$$$

Las Cañitas Carmen Soler 4105; 021 605936; Mon–Sat. Fantastic atmosphere in the wine cellar of this excellent little wine bar & bistro. Quality food & huge wine list. They serve good wine by the glass, with clear descriptions to help you choose. $$$$

La Paraguayita Brasilia y República Siria; 021 204497; daily. Has a roofed outside area far enough from the main road España to make a quiet place to eat in the open air. The restaurant is frequented by Paraguayan media stars. Extensive menu, including traditional dishes, & the food comes beautifully presented. $$$

San Miguel España 1165 c/ Padre Cardozo; 021 200555/206047; Mon–Sun lunch. One block before St Andrew's Anglican Church, this restaurant is famous for its *milanesas*, some of which come stuffed with vegetables. It has a garden, but it is right on the main road. Paraguayans prefer to eat inside anyway, with AC. Live music Fri 21.00. $$$

El Paraíso Herminio Giménez 1743 c/ M Fleitas y República Francesa, with another entrance on Adela Speratti 1740; 021 206810. Chinese restaurant, inexpensive & popular. $$

La Herencia Juan de Salazar 698 esq Tte Morales; 021 222824; www.laherencia.com.py; 07.00–23.00 Mon–Sat, 16.00–23.00 Sun. Brilliant café full of olde worlde character, close to the Anglo language school, with an elegant period design similar to the Café de Acá (see page 88). This café is the latest development of a long-established family firm, *Hijas de Feliciana de Fariña* (which has a restaurant opposite the Café de Acá) that began with a woman cooking *chipa* in Caacupé & bringing it to Asunción by bus to sell. Wi-Fi. Sandwiches, pizzas, salads. The bathroom is almost a museum piece. $$

Ninjas con Apetito Padre Cardozo 578 c/ Juan de Salazar ; m 0992 280977. The owner once had a van permanently parked in the same place, with tables & stools that he put on the pavement in the evening. He cooked & served from the van. Now he has graduated to a fixed site & the place is booming. Great selection of unusual beers. $

Vitapan España e/ General Santos y Teniente Delgado; 021 207844; 06.00–midnight. Not just a bakery – they have a choice of 3 good local lunch dishes every day at a low price. They also do deliveries. $

VILLA MORRA/SHOPPING DEL SOL AREA

This is now the most fashionable area for going out in the evening, with the Paseo Carmelitas on España y Senador Long playing a leading role. The buses that go down España are 13, 18, 23, 30, 35 & 37. Map, page 79.

El Dorado Senador Long 642, c/ Dr. Eusebio Lillo; 021 665164; closed Mon. This recently relocated restaurant is heralded by some as the best in Asunción. Elegant & contemporary in both food & décor, modern art & splashes of colour adorn the grey walls while the international fusion menu (from pheasant to ceviche) is imaginative & fresh, with each plate artistically presented. Extensive wine cellar. Pretty garden at the back. $$$$

Hacienda Las Palomas Guido Spano 1481, esq Senador Long; 021 605111; every eve Mon–Sat, & Sun lunch. Live music Fri & Sat. Mexican cuisine, very good, lovely décor. Recommended. Close to Shopping Villa Mora. $$$$

Rolandi Mcal López esq Mayor Infante Rivarola; 021 610447/609663; www.restauranterolandi.com; Mon–Fri & Sat eve &

PASEO CARMELITAS

Map, page 79

Paseo Carmelitas, where España and Senador Long meet, is home to a whole colony of smart restaurants, cafés & other trendy shops for a cosmopolitan new generation. Not all of them are expensive, and they are open until late. Among the selection on offer are the following, starting with those on España and going round the block in an anti-clockwise direction:

Bellini 021 623968. Choose 8 ingredients for your own pasta sauce – fun & inexpensive.

El Bar 021 600095. Style of Rio de Janeiro, does pizzas & *picadas*.

El Ojo del Amo 021 615349. Upmarket *churrasquería*.

Kamastro www.kamastro.com. Restaurant with art gallery.

Sushi Club 021 623724. Japanese food & music. Expensive, but good sushi.

Tiam Caffé 021 614427. Bistro with Polynesian influence.

Cover Singing Bar 021 623170. Drinks, karaoke & live music. Wed is a big night, Fri is for singles.

Kilkenny Pub 021 609688. Irish, good bands, expensive.

Long Bar 021 600644. Nice garden with coloured bunting & a pretty fountain. Good cocktails.

Moby Dick www.mobydick.com.py. Chain of bars from Uruguay. Another at Aviadores del Chaco c/ Santa Teresa.

Sheridan's Pub 021609688. Victorian décor, lunches, whiskies.

Sky Lounge 021 600940. Drinks, food, electronic music.

Sun lunch. Italian cooking by highly regarded chef Fabio Rolandi, with an emphasis on food cooked in the *tatakua* with its delicious wood flavour. Pasta & bread are specialities. $$$$

✕ **Un Toro y Siete Vacas** Malutín 703 esq Eusebio Lillo; 021 604763/600425; lunchtime & eve daily. Excellent cooking, good service, recommended. $$$$

✕ **Acuarela** Mariscal López c/ San Martín; 021 605183/601750; daily. Brazilian *churrasquería* with extensive buffet & excellent salad selection. Not a lot of ambience but good food & very reasonable. $$$

✕ **Hippie Chic** España esq Dr Antonio Bestard; Facebook: Hippie Chic, soul food; 20.30–03.00 Thu–Sun. Decorated with old boxes as tables, beach chairs & strips of old cloth, Hippie Chic is fashionable to the point of being over-crowded, with consequent slow service. The prices are high, so you are paying a premium to eat your meal off an old box instead of an elegant table. But a fun place if you have time & money to spare. $$$

✕ **Il Capo** Austria 1689 esq Viena; 021 608704; daily for lunch & dinner. Italian cuisine, out of the centre but close to the Sheraton Hotel. Has a nice garden for eating out. They do a *Petto di pollo Mburucuya* (chicken breast cooked with passion fruit). Another branch of the same restaurant is opposite La Pérgola at Perú 291 c/ José Berges; 021 213022. $$$

✕ **Kamambú** Las Palmeras 4890 esq Teniente Zotti; 021 610594. Restaurant dedicated to traditional Paraguayan cooking, just a little to the south of the Villa Morra área. $$$

✕ **La Roca** Capitan Brizuela 750 e/ Lillo y Sucre; 021 600311; www.laroca.com.py; daily except Sat lunch & Sun eve. Elegant restaurant in the amazing house of the late artist Carlos Colombino, where you cross a little bridge & enter a huge round hole in a white wall. Extensive menu of international gourmet cuisine. Sunday buffet. Executive lunch on weekdays at only Gs35,000 for 2 courses & coffee. Sober beige & purple décor, outside terrace roofed with flounced cloth. $$$

✕ **O Gaucho** Dr Toribio Pacheco 4444 esq Mac Arthur; 021 608596. In the small streets behind the La Recoleta cemetery, this Brazilian *churrasquería* has live music & a great atmosphere, & is packed with ordinary Paraguayans enjoying a night out. Fixed-price buffet all inclusive & eat as much as you like. Recommended for vegetarians because of the wide choice of salads as well as meats. $$$

✕ **Para Cuando la Vida** San Martín 1314 e/ Dr Migone y Nuestra Señora del Carmen; 021 615579; www.paracuandolavida; 11.00–midnight Tue–Thu, 11.00–14.00 Fri–Sat, 09.00–midnight Sun, closed Mon. Set back from the main road, tucked behind the Shopping del Sol, this restaurant opened in 2012 has unbelievably romantic décor & imagination, like a Victorian conservatory wrapped up like a present with huge curtains of muslin. The food is good too. One of the most memorable restaurants you could go to. $$$

✕ **Paulista Grill** Av San Martín c/ Mariscal López; 021 608624/611501. Big *churrasqueria* with nothing to offer in the way of décor or ambience, but the grill is excellent with an extensive selection of meats, & the parking is safe because you can sit & look at your car right outside the window. Live music Fri & Sun. $$$

✕ **Piegari** Av del Chaco 2059; 021 622925; www.piegari.com.py. Branch of a top international chain of restaurants; specialises in pasta. $$$

✕ **Be Okay** Hassler esq Cruz del Chaco; +595 21 3275667; m 0981 444433. This new vegetarian/ vegan restaurant has received a lot of hype as the first of its kind in Asuncion, where the health food craze is in its genesis. Choose from a large selection of salads, raw foods & other dishes designed to 'make your body happy', washed down with the house speciality 'green juice'. $$

✕ **Café de Acá** Teniente Vera 1390 esq Dr Morra; 021 623583; 08.30–23.00 Tue–Sun. A short block from Carmelitas, on Teniente Vera, this is now one of the busiest & most delightful cafés in the city, exquisitely decorated in a style from the past. You can also have a proper meal here. Tables out the front & out the back as well as in several rooms inside. $$

✕ **El Mercadito** Alberto Souza Esq Cruz Del Defensor; 021 621355; m 0981 975900. A new gourmet restaurant serving traditional yet refined Paraguayan food with a modern twist. Inside, it channels shabby-chic; scrubbed wooden tables, storm lanterns & chequered parquet flooring, with a wagon surrounded by hay bales in 1 corner. Pretty outdoor seating area with a fountain. Good service & reasonably priced, reservations are a must: it is always packed. $$

♀ **Bambuddha** Aviadores del Chaco 1780 y Vasconsellos; 021 664826; www.bambuddha.

com.py. Bamboo walls & images of Buddha set the theme for this bar, which is very much dedicated to drink after drink. Loud music but with vaguely eastern resonances.

Broadway Mariscal Antonio José de Sucre e/ San Martín y Capitán Brizuela New nightclub with lots of big neon words outside, live show, good music & ambience.

Coyote Mariscal Antonio Jose de Sucre c/ Avenida San Martín; 021 662114. Asunción's premier nightclub; palm trees at the entrance, sparklers shooting out of drinks, a massive dance floor & food from the nearby Sushi Club. If you want to be out until the early hours among Paraguay's elite crowd, this is the place to go.

El Sitio República Argentina 1035 c/ Souza; 021 612822; 22.00–04.00. One of the top discotheques for young people, karaoke Tue & Thu.

Smuchi Dr Francisco Morra 245 e/ Spano y Andrade; 021 604685; 09.00–22.00 Mon–Fri; 14.00–22.00 Sat & Sun. A fun & colourful café decorated with bunting, lanterns & parasols, popular with the young Paraguayan crowd. Sandwiches, wraps, smoothies, etc. Outdoor seating area, lit up by fairylights & dotted with deckchairs. $

Other areas

Map, pages 72–3.

Tierra Colorada Santísima Trinidad 784 y Teniente Fernández; 021 663335; www.tierracoloradagastro.com; 12.00–14.30 Wed, Thu & Fri, from 20.00 Mon–Sat, closed Sun. Run by prize-winning Uruguayan chef Rodolfo Angenscheidt, who also appears regularly on television. He does imaginative things with mandioca, & the VIP room is full of light & green plants. Various steaks. The food is laid out on the plate like a work of art $$$$

Rodeo Grill Boggiani c/ Dr Hassler; 021 606805; www.rodeogrill.com.py; from 11.30 daily. *Churrasquería* a little further out but with live show of harp & folk dance at 21.30 on Thu nights – but ring to double check. All the beef is from tender Brangus cattle. A cheaper option is the adjoining pizzeria (*from 19.00 Fri & Sat*). $$$

Il Bambú Mariscal López esq. Dr Riart; 021 508266. Near the Municipalidad of Asunción, this pizzería is situated in an attractive building made of bamboo. They have gluten-free pizzas. $$

God's Pan Argento Marecos y Cabo 1o Pujol; 021 292938; www.godspan.com.py; 07.00–21.00 daily. Situated by the entrance to the Parque de Salud, this good café completes the visit. Wide menu, lots of pastas. There are also branches at República Argentina 809 esq Souza (*021 600823*) & at Santísima Trinidad 3164 esq Bogotá (*021 280212*). They also do deliveries. $

Salemma Supercenter (off map) This huge supermarket with a monster sign saying 'S' inside 2 red circles that you pass on your way into (or out of) Asunción on Eusebio Ayala provides a handy place to eat with convenient parking on the long crawl through the suburbs of the capital, if you have missed (or cannot wait for) the Frutería in Paraguarí. It has a *churrasquería* as well as a café. $

Faces Mariscal López 2585 c/ Insaurralde, Fernando de la Mora; 021 672768. The largest & most popular nightclub in Asunción, accommodating over 3,000 people across 8 bars, 2 VIP areas, a lounge & terrace. Regularly hosts events ranging from live music to bikini contests.

ENTERTAINMENT AND NIGHTLIFE

There are **cinemas** at the Shopping del Sol [79 E1] (*021 611763*), Shopping Mall Excelsior [74 D4] (*021 443015*), Shopping Villa Mora [79 B3] (*021 605795*), Cinecenter Hiperseis (*Mariscal López y Teniente Casco; 021 613390*) and Patio Real Cines (*Acceso Sur c/ Usher Rios; 021 525309*). See below for details of the shopping centres.

Some young people from Asunción like to stay out all night and round it off with breakfast. If the selection of bars and nightclubs in the box on page 87 is not enough for you, you will find many more at www.asunfarra.com.py/directorio.php.

CULTURAL SPACES There are a number of places around Asunción – some indoors and some outdoors – where cultural or sporting events are often held, and which are difficult to find because they are not usually marked on maps and the addresses are rarely given. You are just expected to know. The events may range from lectures to exhibitions, from films to football matches.

Football games can be on Saturdays or Sundays, at times ranging from 15.00 to 21.00. The hotter the weather, the later the games tend to be played. The three most important football stadiums are Defensores del Chaco, Cerro Porteño and Olimpia. Generally you can pick up tickets easily at the stadium before the match, but if it is an important game (Olimpio versus Cerro Porteño, or an international) you will need to buy them beforehand from Sanri (*Mariscal Estigarribia 1097, esq Brasil; 021 600385/220940; www.sanri.com.py*). In ascending order of price you can buy graderia, platea or preferencia. Sanri sell tickets to concerts, carnivals, congresses and exhibitions (such as the Expos) as well as to sporting events.

Here is a list of useful addresses:

Alianza Francesa [75 G2] Mariscal Estigarribia 1039 c/ EEUU; 021 210382; www.alianzafrancesa.edu.py or/ www.alfran.com. The French cultural centre. It has exhibitions & films.

Arpa Roga [73 F3] Dr Patricio Maciel 559 c/ Sinforiano Buzó; 021 672557; e info@arparoga.com; www.arparoga.com. 'The house of the harp' (Guaraní) is a venture of the Pedersen family of musicians. (Cristóbal is a guitarist & his son Kike & brother Rito are harpists.) The centre has some harps of famous musicians on display, & occasionally hosts concerts & tourist events. It is just outside the ring road & is hard to find on maps, but Buzó is the first turning off Madame Lynch to the north of the junction with Santa Teresa, & Dr Maciel is the first road parallel to Madame Lynch.

Casa de los Payasos [72 B2] Hernandarias 961 e/ Manduvira y Piribebuy; m 0985 894514; www.lacasadelospayasos.blogspot.com. The House of Clowns; a cultural space created by artists due to the lack of circus performance in the city. Paraguayan & foreign artists live & rehearse in the house, where they have constructed their own theatre. This urban circus features jugglers, stunts & acrobats. Afternoon shows for children, night time performances for the older crowd.

Centro Paraguayo-Japonés Julio Correa y Domingo Portillo; 021 607276; www.centroparaguayojapones.blogspot.com/; Facebook: Centro Paraguayo Japonés. The Japanese cultural centre. It has a theatre.

Cerro Porteño [72 B3] Acuña de Figueroa y Cerro León, barrio Obrero; www.clubcerro.com/historia.html. One of Asunción's 2 most high-profile football clubs. Red-&-blue strip (*azulgrana*).

Club de Olimpia [72 D3] Mariscal López 1499 y Pitiantuta; 021 200680/200780; e info@olimpia.com.py; www.clubolimpia.com.py. The other high-profile football club in Asunción. Black-&-white strip. It has won the Copa Libertadores 3 times.

Conmebol [73 H3] Autopista esq Petrona Almirón de Leoz; 021 650993. The conference centre of the Confederación Suamericana de Fútbol, with the Football Museum, on the way to the airport.

Consejo Nacional de Deportes [72 D4] Eusebio Ayala e/ República Argentina y Av de la Victoria. Huge sporting area with a jockey club.

Embajada Argentina [72 C2] España esq Perú; 021 212320/4; www.embajada-argentina.org.py. It has a theatre, Leopoldo Marechal, with capacity for 300.

Estadio Defensores del Chaco [72 A2] Juan Díaz de Solis y Orihuela, barrio Carlos Antonio López, near barrio Sajonia. The principal football stadium, used for international matches & high-profile league games such as Cerro Porteño v Olimpia. Capacity for 36,000.

Ex-Seminario Metropolitano [72 D3] Kubitschek e/ 25 de mayo y Speratti. No longer used as a seminary, this is a large site that is sometimes used for other events.

Instituto Cultural Paraguayo-Alemán Juan de Salazar 310 c/ Artigas; 021 226242; www.icpa-gz.org.py. The German cultural centre.

Juan de Salazar [75 F3] Tacuary 745 c/ Herrera; 021 449921; www.juandesalazar.org.py. The Spanish cultural centre. It hosts a lot of exhibitions & films.

Municipalidad de Asunción [73 F3] Mariscal López 5556 y Capitán Bueno; 021 663311/20. The town hall of the city.

Teatro Arlequín [75 F5] Antequera 1061 y República de Colombia; 021 442152; e info@arlequin.com.py; www.arlequin.com.py. Small theatre, interesting shows.

Teatro del Banco Central del Paraguay [73 E2] Federación Rusa y Sgto Marecos (next to IPS Hospital); 021 6192243; www.bcp.gov.py. From the home page go to Aspectos Institucionales & then Complejo Edilicio. The theatre has capacity for 1,100.

Teatro Municipal [74 C2] Presidente Franco e/ Chile y Alberdi; 021 445169; www.teatromunicipal.com.py. Has a good new website with lovely harp music.

SPECIAL EVENTS

Expo For the first two weeks of July every year, a large exhibition called the Expoferia Internacional de Ganadería, Industria, Agricultura, Comercio y Servicios, or the Expo for short, takes place in the town of Mariano Roque Alonso on the outskirts of Asunción. It attracts an average of 70,000 visitors. Take a bus marked 'Expo' from the Terminal, going south down Fernando de la Mora, and then north around the ring road Madame Lynch, until it passes the Expo on the right-hand side, almost an hour later.

The Expo has many special events each day, ranging from lectures to dance performances, fashion shows to motorbike displays. There are funfairs and restaurants, and almost every conceivable kind of company has a stand there. One novelty for foreign visitors is the emphasis on animals. You can observe how the typically Paraguayan Brahma (grey with a hump and floppy ears) is crossed with an Angus to produce the Brangus, which is very hardy, particularly in a hot and humid climate like Paraguay's. There are also a lot of fine horses, including Arabs, the skewbald spotted paint horse and the handsomely spotted Appaloosa.

Festival Mundial del Arpa The annual World Harp Festival has taken place in Asunción every October or November since 2007, involving Paraguayan harpists living inside and outside of the country, as well as other international harpists who play different kinds of harps. During the day they have workshops, and on three consecutive evenings the Teatro Municipal hosts concerts.

San Baltasar Strictly speaking, Fernando de la Mora is not Asunción but a separate town, but it adjoins it in a continuous urban sprawl. In its Loma Campamento barrio, the African-American community holds a renowned music festival to celebrate the feast of the Epiphany and San Baltasar (traditionally the black king). A dance group called Kamba Kua performs in red and yellow costumes, with torches and drums, on the outside stage of the María Auxiliadora chapel (*Capitan Rivas y 6 de enero, near the Club de Leones*). This will probably happen on the Saturday night closest to 6 January, but for further information contact the *municipalidad* (*021 500007*) or Lázaro Medina (**m** *0982 374736*).

SHOPPING

Craft shops See *Craft*, page x, for information about various Paraguayan crafts.

The tourist office of **Senatur** (Secretaría Nacional de Turismo) is housed in the building called Turista Róga or 'the house of the tourists' [74 C2] (*Palma 468 e/ Alberdi y 14 de mayo; 021 441530;* **e** *infosenatur@senatur.gov.py; www.senatur.gov.py*). It has an excellent indoor marketplace of typical crafts, not huge but of the best quality, including silver *filigrana* jewellery, *ao po'i* embroidered clothes, carved saints, *ñanduti* lace circles and wonderful wooden and feather creations by the indigenous. This is also the central tourist information office, and is usually able to provide free maps of the country if you ask. Do pick up the latest editions of the excellent *Asunción Map Guide* and *Asunción Quick Guide*.

AUGUSTO ROA BASTOS AND HIS CONTEMPORARIES

Undoubtedly Paraguay's most renowned literary figure, Augusto Roa Bastos (1917–2005) was born in Asunción but spent his childhood in Iturbe, a small village in the *campo*, and writes brilliantly about the life of *campesinos* in one of his most famous novels, *Hijo de Hombre* (1960). He was one of a generation of literary figures that shone in the *Grupo de 1940* (also known as the *Vy'á Raty*, 'Nest of Joy') and regarded as the fathers of Paraguayan literature, but were then mostly forced into exile for their left-wing views in the 1947 repression, leading up to the dictatorship of Stroessner (1954–89).

Roa Bastos had to go into exile for political reasons in 1947 (after hiding in the water tank on the roof when his house was ransacked by a right-wing group), and could not permanently return until after the end of the dictatorship. In exile he wrote his most acclaimed work, *Yo El Supremo* (1974), allegedly about the dictatorship of Dr Francia (who called himself 'El Supremo') but with an implicit attack on the regime of Stroessner. This novel won the Brazilian Premio de Letras del Memorial de América Latina (1988), the highly esteemed Spanish prize Premio Cervantes (1989), and the Condecoración de la Orden Nacional del Mérito (1990) in his own country as soon as the dictatorship was ended. He was later decorated with Cuba's highest honour, the Orden José Martí (2003). He wrote five novels and several collections of short stories and of poetry. His works have been translated into 25 languages.

A charming man who called himself 'something of an atheist' and remained deeply socialist to the end of his days, Roa Bastos returned to live in Asunción in 1996, where he died ten years later. 'Literature is capable of winning battles against adversity,' he wrote, 'with no more arms than letter and spirit, with no more power than imagination and language.'

The other literary figures of his generation include the poet Hérib Campos Cervera (1905–53), the poet Elvio Romero (1926–2004), the playwright Julio Correa (1890–1953), the novelist Gabriel Casaccia (1907–80) and the multi-skilled Josefina Plá (1909–99), who was born in the Canary Islands but adopted Paraguay as her home in 1927, where she was prolific as an essayist, poet, journalist and academic historian, not to mention as an potter of beautiful ceramic works.

There is an outdoor market of little **craft stalls** [74 C2] in the Plaza de la Libertad, behind the Panteón, which is enjoyable to walk through and to browse here and there.

On the other side from the centre, near the port, is a run of older craft shops under an arcade, known as **La Recova** [74 A2]. The arcade was designed in 1850 by the Italian Alessandro Ravizza, one of the principal architects to renew the face of Asunción in the time of President Carlos Antonio López, and who also designed the Cathedral, Panteón and Trinidad church. At that time the port was where travellers arrived, whereas now they arrive at the airport or the bus terminal. It has been used as an arcade for craftwork since 1945, and although the decline of the port has led to a corresponding decline of visitors, it is still an attractive and traditional place to shop. On the way to La Recova, walking down Palma, you will pass the best shops of leatherware, selling a huge variety of bags, sandals, belts and other accessories. The three main shops selling attractive Paraguayan crafts are all in the same barrio near the Plaza Uruguaya: Overall, Folklore and Bella Tierra.

Overall [75 E2] Caballero c/ Mcal Estigarribia; 021 448657; 08.00–18.00 Mon–Fri, 08.00–12.30 Sat. Beautiful craft shop next to the Librería Intercontinental, particularly strong on Christmas cribs & tablecloths, traycloths & napkins. There is also a branch in the Shopping del Sol (*021 611739*), which does not close on Sat afternoon.

Bella Tierra [75 E2] 25 de mayo 370 c/ Iturbe; 021 447891; also Shopping Villa Morra, Local 19, PB, 021 604395; 08.00–18.00 Mon–Fri, 08.00–noon Sat. Sells a tempting selection of leather, wood, silvercraft, clothes & sometimes even furniture.

Folklore [74 D2] Mariscal Estigarribia esq Iturbe; 021 450148. The most visible of the craft shops because it has big wooden carvings of Guaraní mythical figures on the pavement outside.

BOOKSHOPS Most shops in Paraguay called *librería* only sell stationery, but Asunción has a good number of genuine bookshops. Every June there is a Libroferia in the car park underneath the Shopping Mariscal López.

The Plaza Uruguaya [75 E2] is the centre for **bookshops**, with several shops in the vicinity and three situated in the middle of the plaza itself: **El Lector** (*021 491966/493908*), and in two identical pavilions, **El Libre en Su Casa** (*021 442855*) and **Servilibro** (*021 444770*).

Books [79 C3] Mariscal López 3791 esq. Dr Morra; 021 603722; www.libreriabooks.com. Mostly English books, but an excellent Spanish selection too. Opposite Shopping Villa Morra, with a second branch in Shopping del Sol, *local* 154.

Café Literario [map, pages 74–5] Mariscal Estigarribia 456; 021 491640; 15.30–midnight Mon–Thu, 15.30–02.00 Fri & Sat. A bookshop as well as a café. Have a drink while you browse, maybe flopping into an armchair in the privacy of the discreet balcony area upstairs (see page 84). The walls are covered with pictures of Paraguay's leading literary figures, & not just Augusto Roa Bastos (see box opposite). Right next door is a splendid shop for horse tack, fleeces & riding boots, called CasaVera, that is fun to look around (*021 445868; see YouTube: Casa Vera – Asunción Paraguay*).

Comuneros [74 D2] Cerro Corá 289 c/ Iturbe; 021 446176/444667; e rolon@conexion.com.py; 07.30–noon & 15.30–18.00 Mon–Fri, 07.30–noon Mon–Sat. One of the best secondhand bookshops, also close to the Plaza Uruguaya.

Dominguez Libros [75 E2] 25 de mayo 458 c/ Caballero; 021 445459. A smaller bookshop – also close to the Plaza Uruguaya. Now building up a good stock in secondhand books.

El Lector [75 E2] Av San Martin c/ Austria; 021 610639/614258/614259; Facebook: El Lector. The main store is in a large, modern building 5mins' walk from Shopping del Sol; another branch is in the Plaza Uruguaya, see above.

La Oficina del Libro [75 E2] 25 de mayo 640, entrepiso, Edificio Garantia; e laoficinadellibro@hotmail.com. Run by the dedicated & talkative Julio Rafael Aquino & hidden away up a staircase (technically between the ground & 1st floors), with nothing visible from the street. Tiny rooms bulging with antiquarian & secondhand books lead one into another, until you wonder where it will end.

Librería de Ediciones Montoya/CEPAG [72 C3] Vicepresidente Sánchez 612 c/ Azara; 021 233541; www.cepag.org.py. The Jesuit publishing house has a bookshop here, selling important books on history, the Reductions & the Guaraní language, as well as the Jesuit monthly *Acción*.

Librería Intercontinental Caballero 270 c/ Mariscal Estigarribia; 021 496991/449738; e agatti@libreriaintercontinental.com.py; www.libreriaintercontinental.com.py; 08.00–noon & 15.00–19.00 Mon–Fri, 08.00–noon Sat. One of the best bookshops especially for academic books, dictionaries & books about Paraguayan history. They take credit cards, but have to ring through first. Closed for 3hrs at lunchtime.

Librería La Plaza [75 E2] Antequera y Mcal Estigarribia; 021 440073/492853. Good secondhand stock hidden inside a discreet exterior, halfway down the side of the Plaza Uruguaya facing the taxis. One of the best bookshops in town although little known.

Librería Paulinas [74 D3] Azara 279 c/ Iturbe; 021 440651; e paulinas@pla.net.py; 08.00–18.30 Mon–Fri, 08.00–noon Sat. Catholic bookshop. Another branch in Shopping Villa Morra (*021 3287142*).

Librería Técnica [72 B2] Blas Garay 106 (Cuarta) c/ Independencia Nacional; ☎ 021 496778/390396; e ventas@etp.com.py or etprentas@cmm.com.py. This is hidden away, not only in its location but also in its storefront, but once you step inside & work your way from room to room, you will find it a treasure trove – principally of academic books. There is another branch in Carmelitas (*Quesada e/ Charles de Gaulle y Cruz del Chaco, local 81;* ☎ *021 611717*).

Parroquia San Rafael [72 D4] Cruz del Chaco 1690 c/ Alfredo Seiferheld; ☎ 021 661607/ 613513; ⌚ 08.00–noon, 15.30–20.00 Mon–Sat. This Catholic parish bookshop specialises in books on the Jesuit Reductions written or edited by the prolific P Aldo Trento. They also sell the best postcards currently available of Jesuit-Guaraní Baroque art (which is not saying much). The parish also does a great deal of good work through the Fundación San Rafael (*www.sanrafael.org.py*) in running an orphanage, hospice, hospital for the poor, hostel for pregnant girls, etc.

Quijote [74 D4] Shopping Mall Excelsior, local 118; ☎ 021 443015 int 1118; www.quijote.com.py; ⌚ 08.00–18.00 Mon–Fri, 09.00–noon Sat. A bookshop that reaches out more to popular tastes & to tourists, with attractive shopfronts in the most frequented shopping areas. It sells CDs as well as books & also has branches in Shopping Mariscal López (*local 224;* ☎ *021 608455*), Shopping del Sol (*local 160;* ☎ *021 611813*) & Shopping Mariano (☎ *021 761960*).

SHOPPING CENTRES If you need quality and reliable goods, it is best to go to one of the shopping malls. Most of them have supermarkets attached, decent eating places of an international self-service style, and clean public toilets. All have cash machines and there is often a Wi-Fi spot. The new shopping centres in the wider area of Gran Asunción are useful if you are travelling in or out of town.

A **World Trade Centre** is currently being built on Aviadores del Chaco opposite the Shopping del Sol, with four towers and 20 floors. As well as retail, it will have restaurants, offices, flats and parking for 1,000 cars. And if that were not enough, an even higher **Blue Tower** is now projected, following investment by a Guatemalan millionaire, to stand next to the World Trade Centre. It will have two towers of 23 floors each, curving this way and that, a three-level shopping mall, and parking for 3,300 cars.

In the city

Mall Excelsior [74 D4] Chile e/ Manduvirá y Piribebuy; ☎ 021 443017/8. Good range of shops, slightly south of the centre, but comfortable walking distance.

Multiplaza [73 E4] Eusebio Ayala 4501, c/ Av RI 18 Pitiantuta. A very large shopping centre 5km from the centre, but inside the Madame Lynch ring road. It has generally cheaper goods & is much frequented by Paraguayans, who get off their buses there on the way in from the countryside.

Shopping del Sol [79 E1] Aviadores del Chaco c/ César López Moreira; ☎ 021 611780/1. Perhaps the most famous of all the shopping centres. On the road to the airport.

Shopping Mariscal López [79 B3] Quesada y General Charles de Gaulle; ☎ 021 611272. Confusingly, the shopping mall on the road Mariscal López is called the Shopping Villa Mora, while the Shopping Mariscal López is directly behind it, in the next block. On Tue there is an all-day market of vegetables, cheeses, etc in the car park underneath the shopping centre, called the Agroshopping.

Shopping Villa Morra [79 B3] Mariscal López y General Charles de Gaulle; ☎ 021 601137/8. Some 3 blocks towards the centre from the junction with República Argentina.

Super Centro [74 C3] Oliva y 14 de mayo. Less grand than the newly built malls, but dead central & has a lot of useful shops, plus a good salad bar in the middle. Some useful computer shops.

Gran Asunción

San Lorenzo Shopping Ruta 2 km 15. On the left as you leave San Lorenzo by Ruta 2.

Shopping Mariano Carlos Antonio López (ex Transchaco) c/ Manuel Irala Fernández. On the left (north) on the way to Mariano Roque Alonso, before you reach the bridge Puente Remanso.

Shopping Pinedo Mariscal López y 26 de febrero. On the left (north) as you approach San Lorenzo from Asunción on Mariscal López.

DEPARTMENT STORES Palma is traditionally known as the quality shopping street in Asunción, and these department stores are all on or adjacent to it.

La Riojana Estigarribia 171 esq Yegros; ☎ 021 492211. Slightly old-fashioned, more typically Paraguayan.

Nueva Americana Mariscal Estigarribia 111 esq Independencia Nacional; ☎ 021 492021; ⏰ 09.00–20.00 Mon–Fri, 08.30–13.00 Sat

Unicentro Palma esq 15 de agosto; ☎ 021 445309/10; ⏰ 09.00–21.00 Mon–Sat, noon–21.00 Sun & holidays. Good shop spread over 8 floors. They also have a branch at the Shopping del Sol, 1st floor.

MERCADO CUATRO [72 C3] The Mercado Cuatro is the equivalent of a department store for ordinary Paraguayans – a vast market of little shops all jammed on top of each other, some inside and some outside, where all the shops selling the same kind of product are grouped together, eg: towels, cutlery, clothes, folk-dance accessories, CDs. Prices are very low, and it has a great buzz – a must for anyone who wants to feel the heart-throb of the city. It is located in the triangle between the streets Pettirossi, Dr Francia and Perú.

The market had its historical origins in the *Mercado Guasú* ('Big Market') of old Asunción, and it moved to its present site in the 1940s. Although it is called the fourth market, no one ever speaks of markets one, two or three. The brilliant, prize-winning film *Siete Cajas* was shot in Mercado Cuatro, and captures authentic Paraguayan life down to a T.

GALERÍA CENTRAL The Galería Central (sometimes called the Galería Palma) is an arcade of shops offering computer equipment, mobile phones and cameras, mostly run by Koreans and at prices well below what you will pay in the shopping centres. It is a covered arcade running from Palma to Estrella, between the streets 15 de agosto and O'Leary.

OTHER PRACTICALITIES

MEDICAL AND EMERGENCIES For Paraguayans, there are two general **hospitals** in Asunción. IPS [73 E2] (*Instituto de Previsión Social; c/ Dr Manuel Peña, Santísimo Sacramento*) is for state employees and their families, who have a level of medical insurance. It is one of the well-known landmarks in Asunción. The other is the Hospital de Clínicas [72 B2] (*Guillermo Arias y Mazzei*) for the poor, with no insurance, and is on the other side of the centre. A recommended hospital for foreigners is the Centro Médico Bautista (*República Argentina y Andrés Campos Cervera; ☎ 021 6889000; appointments ☎ 021 609996 ⏰ Mon–Fri 06.30-20.00, ☎ 021 612444, ⏰ Sat 07.00–11.00; emergencies ☎ 021 607944, ⏰ 24hrs, e info@cmb.org.py; www.cmb.org.py*). Not only is it a good hospital but it has doctors who speak English and is conveniently located in the Villa Mora area. You can book an appointment online as well as by phone.

There are a large number of chemists (*farmacias*) and they keep much longer hours than other shops, including many that are open 24 hours.

The telephone number for police in emergencies is 911 (free); for medical emergencies, dial ☎ 140 or ☎ 021 204800. In case of fire, ring ☎ 131 (police fire-fighters) or ☎ 132 (volunteer fire-fighters; most fire-fighters in Paraguay are volunteers). You can also supposedly ring ☎ 911 to report any malpractice or law-breaking, with the place, date and time of the offence, and your message will be recorded, though whether anyone actually ever uses this service is unclear.

BANKS The central branches of most banks are to be found on or around the street Estrella in Asunción. The **main banks** include Itaú (*Oliva 349 c/ Chile*), BBVA (*Yegros 435, esq 25 de mayo*), Amambay (*Estrella 580 c/ 15 de agosto*), Continental (*Estrella c/ 15 de mayo*), GNB (*Palma y O'Leary*), Sudameris (*Cerro Corá y Independencia Nacional*), Banco Visión (*Palma esq Nuestra Señora de la Asunción*) and Banco Familiar (*Chile 1080 esq Jejuí*). There is also Citibank (although it has closed almost all its branches), Itaú, Banco do Brasil, Banco Itapúa and Banco Regional.

The Banco Nacional de Fomento is a state bank, and generally people only use it for state-run businesses, There is still a certain distrust of banks, deriving from a bad patch in the mid-1990s when a number went bankrupt, with a domino effect. In 2002 one of the biggest banks, the Banco Alemán, also went bust, but this time without bringing down any others with it. Since then, however, no bank has gone bust, and confidence in banks is slowly building up.

As well as the banking system there are ***financieras*** (finance companies) which change money and make loans. Over the last few years a number of these have converted into banks, eg: Visión and Familiar, reflecting a general move in the population towards using a banking system. There are also ***cooperativas*** (credit unions), which are by far the most popular places for Paraguayans to keep their money, but are of less use to the tourist. Finally, there are ***casas de cambio***, specifically for changing money.

Most of the places specifically offering **money-changing** are on Palma (near the junctions with Alberdi or 14 de mayo) or on 25 de mayo (near the junction with Yegros). There are plenty of street money-changers too, near the corner of Estrella and the Plaza de los Héroes, but with casas de cambio so close, which can give a proper receipt, there is little advantage in using them. One of the biggest places for changing money is Norte Cambios (*Palma 403 esq Alberdi; ☎ 021 453277; ⊕ 08.30–17.00 Mon–Fri, 08.30–noon Sat*). Cambios Chaco and MaxiCambios have already been mentioned (see page 47). MaxiCambios (*Super Centro; ☎ 021 494637; also in Shopping del Sol & Shopping Multiplaza*) has facilities for receiving MoneyGram transfers Cambios Chaco has branches in town as well as at the airport (*Palma 364; ☎ 021 445315; also in Super Centro, Shopping Villa Morra & Shopping Multiplaza*).

POST OFFICES The central post office is at Alberdi y Paraguayo Independiente, adjoining the Plaza in front of the Congress [74 C1] (*☎ 021 498112/6; ⊕ 07.00–18.00 Mon–Fri, 07.00–noon Sat;* for the museum, see page 104). There is also now a new and modern post office centrally located one block along from the Plaza de la Democracia (*25 de mayo y Yegros*). There are also branches at the airport, the Terminal, Shopping del Sol (rather hidden away – you may need to ask for it), Shopping Villa Mora (upstairs), on Mariscal López opposite the Shopping Villa Mora, in the shopping Mall Excelsior and on Defensa Nacional e/ Padre Cardozo y Washington (*Airport & shopping centre branches ⊕ 07.00–18.00 Mon–Fri, 09.00–21.00 Sat & Sun*).

COURIERS There are two major international courier companies operating in Paraguay, though neither offer a very fast service, given the transportation difficulties. They will deliver in Asunción and other big cities like Ciudad del Este and Encarnación, but to reach other areas they work with the growing number of national courier companies, such as Tiemsa, Sky Postal and Asunción Express.

DHL General Santos 1170 c/ Concordia (head office) or Independencia Nacional 375 e/ Palma y Estrella (central office); 021 2162000; e asucs@dhl.com; www.dhl.com.py; 08.00–17.30 Mon–Fri; 09.00–noon Sat. 9 branches in Paraguay.

UPS Independencia Nacional 821; 021 451960; www.ups.com. Works with local courier Sky, which has an office in San Ignacio.

Tiemsa Amador de Montoya 1460 c/ Dr Benza; 021 562755/559937; www.tiemsa.com.py

Sky Postal Estrella 685; 021 443785; www.skypostal.com.py

Asunción Express España 436 c/ Dr Bestard; 021 6166100; e info@aex.com.py

INTERNET There is now a Wi-Fi spot in the Plaza de los Héroes (where the Panteón is) and its two neighbouring plazas (O'Leary and Libertad), in the Plaza Uruguaya, in the plaza in front of the cathedral, and in front of the Cabildo. There is also Wi-Fi in most of the shopping malls, and most of them have an internet café, although on the streets these are hard to find these days, as the spread of Smartphones has put them out of business.

LANGUAGE COURSES The **Stael Ruffinelli Language Institute** (*Av General Santos 606, en frente de Juan de Salazar; 021 202630; e info@staelenglish.com.py; www.stael.edu.py*) offers Spanish courses, including Business Spanish and Spanish for teaching purposes (as well as courses in English as a foreign language, for which it is better known).

Idipar (*Manduvirá 979–963 c/ Colon; 021 447896; e idipar@cmm.com.py; www.idipar.edu.py*) offers courses in Spanish and in Guaraní, and organises various activities such as trips, cultural workshops and outings. Courses are individual or in a group of up to six students. Prices range from Gs35,000 to Gs60,000 per class, depending on the number of students.

Reasonably priced Guaraní and Spanish classes are also offered at **CELPE** (*Centro de Enseñanza de Lenguas para Extranjeros; Tacuary 721 c/ Herrera; 021 493147; e celpepy@hotmail.com; www.celpe.com.py*), individually or in classes of up to four students, at home or in the school.

SWIMMING POOLS If you want to swim and are not staying in a hotel with a pool, you could try the pool at the Escuela de Educación Física of the armed forces (General Santos c/ Mariscal López, opposite the Las Residentas turn) or the Colegio San José (*España 642 esq San José; 021 226640/1; www.sanjose.edu.py*) where there are swimming classes open to the public (*Mon–Fri 14.00–21.00*). There is also a 50m open-air pool at the Piscina Club Olimpia attached to the Football club of the same name (see page 90). See also Mbiguá (see page 112).

WHAT TO SEE AND DO

A WALK AROUND THE CENTRE Many tour companies do a two- or three-hour 'Cititour' in a bus, with the emphasis on driving around in air-conditioned vehicles. If you find it more fun to explore on foot, here is a two- or three-hour walking tour you can make of the central area, beginning and ending at the Panteón. This is just a summary, so you should read the details of the sites given in the preceding and subsequent sections, and the route is marked on the map on pages 74–5.

Start at the Plaza de los Heróes and visit the Panteón (see page 111), where national heroes are buried. You may want to walk through the outdoor market of craft shops in Plaza de la Libertad (see page 92), behind the Panteón. If you are short of time or energy you can omit the optional extension in this paragraph and jump to the next paragraph. Walk down 25 de mayo towards Plaza Uruguaya, stopping at Bella Tierra (*25 de mayo 370, see page 93*), near the junction with Iturbe. A little further on is the large Plaza Uruguaya (see pages 111–12), with a number of bookshops around it. At the northern end of the square is the Estación de Ferrocarril (see pages 104–5), which contains old steam trains. Ring the bell around the corner in Río Acaraý to get in (*⌚ 07.00–18.00 Mon–Fri*). A pleasant place to stop for refreshments is the Café Literario (*Mariscal Estigarribia 456; ⌚ 15.30–midnight Mon–Thu, 15.30–02.00 Fri–Sat; see page 84*).

Back in the Plaza de los Heróes, head towards the river to reach the Plaza de la Independencia, home to the city's Cathedral (see pages 106–7). There is not a great deal to see inside, but it is impressive in the context of its surroundings. A little way along the square is a statue of Juan de Salazar, the founder of Asunción, carrying a sword, with the Monument to Marzo Paraguayo behind it, commemorating the students who were killed when demonstrating for democracy in 1999 (see pages 107–8). Behind this monument is the Cabildo, once the Senate building but now a pleasant museum (*⌚ 09.00–19.00 Mon–Fri Mar–Dec, 10.00–17.00 Mon–Fri in Jan & Feb, & Sat & Sun all year round; see pages 99–100*). Leaving the Cabildo you turn to your right to cross the plaza to the Congreso Nacional (*⌚ 07.00–12.30 Mon–Fri; free admission; see pages 109–10*), with its new building paid for by government of Taiwan. In front of it is a 12m high sculpture representing a tree trunk, by the artist Hermann Guggiari, in memory of Juan de Salazar's foundation of the first fort here, when it was the custom to plant a tree trunk with the name of the fort: the sculpture is labelled '*Asunción, Madre de Ciudades, cuna de la libertad Americana*' (Mother of Cities, cradle of American freedom'). On the river side of the parliament you can see the statue of Mariscal López, the general who led Paraguay into the Triple Alliance War and is now regarded as a hero.

Continue walking in the same direction, parallel to the river, to reach the Palacio de López, also known as Palacio de Gobierno (see page 112), built to a grand design for Mariscal López. It is now government offices, and visits are only allowed inside by special arrangement. Turning first left after the Palacio de López, you come to the Manzana de la Rivera (also known as Casa Viola), a small museum of history and art (*⌚ 07.00–21.00 Mon–Fri, 08.00–18.00 Sat, 09.00–18.00 Sun, see opposite*).

If you are feeling energetic, or if you want to do the walking tour in two halves, you could now go on to the popular Costanera coast road and beach (see page 116), reached at the end of Colón. If it is a Saturday afternoon you should visit the Puerto Abierto fair (see page 112) at the port, which is also at the end of Colón.

On your way back, browse in the craft shops of La Recova on Colón (see page 92). Then turn left along Palma, Asunción's most famous shopping street, to make your way back towards your starting point. Coming up half a block to your left now is the Casa de la Independencia – the colonial house where independence was planned (*14 de mayo esq Presidente Franco; ⌚ 07.00–18.30 Mon–Fri, 08.00–12.00 Sat; see below*). Returning to Palma, you reach Turista Róga, a centre containing a tourist information office and craft stalls (*Palma 468*).

HISTORY MUSEUMS

Casa de la Independencia [74 C2] (*14 de mayo esq Presidente Franco; ☎ 021 493918; e info@casadelaindependencia.org.py; www.casadelaindependencia.org.py; ⌚ 07.00–18.00 Mon–Fri, 08.00–noon Sat; free admission*) Right in the centre of the city, this is the house where the independence of Paraguay was secretly plotted, and it has been turned into a museum furnished in period fashion, with many items of interest both historically and artistically. The house was the home of Juan

María de Lara, and there used to be meetings here of the so-called Próceres de la Independencia – Fernando de la Mora, Francisco Xavier Bogarín, Fulgencio Yegros, Pedro Juan Cavallero and Gaspar Rodríguez de Francia. At first light on 15 May 1811 Captain Pedro Juan Cavallero led the coup, and they achieved Paraguayan independence without a shot being fired.

The house was built in 1772 of adobe in classic colonial style by a Spaniard, Antonio Martínez Sáenz, married to a Paraguayan, Petrona Caballero. After his death it became the natural place for the plotters of independence to meet, as they were all friends of Martínez Sáenz's children and heirs. It was acquired by the government in 1943 and declared a historic monument in 1961. There are five rooms, including an oratory, all well laid out with furniture of the period (some belonging to the Próceres), portraits of the Próceres, and artworks, including statues carved in Jesuit or Franciscan workshops. Alongside the house is a restored alleyway showing what the street looked like when the Próceres slipped out of the side door there on the decisive night of 14 May 1811, and when Juana María de Lara passed through it a few hours later to ask the clergy of the cathedral to ring the bells continually to call the people to celebrate Paraguay's birth as independent nation.

Manzana de la Rivera [74 B1] (*Ayolas 128 esq El Paraguayo Independiente; 021 442448/447683; e manzana_rivera@yahoo.com; http://museo.mca.gov.py/inicio.php; 07.30–19.00 Mon–Fri, 07.30–18.00 Sat & Sun; free admission*) The Manzana de la Rivera is a block of mostly historic interlinked houses directly opposite the Palacio de López that operates conjointly as an art and study centre. It is principally known for its well-designed museum of the history of Asunción, and is within easy walking distance of the centre.

The **Casa Viola** – as you go in – is the oldest building (1750), and houses a delightfully arranged museum of the city's history, with old maps, postcards, print and newspaper cuttings making it a most interesting place to browse. This museum is sometimes called the Museo Memoria de la Ciudad, but should not be confused with the Museo de las Memorias (see pages 105–6).

While the Casa Viola's exhibition is permanent, the other halls in the complex are for temporary exhibitions. Casa Castelvi, built in 1804, just before independence, has two exhibition rooms. Casa Vertúa (1898) houses a reference library. Casa Ballario is a two-storey block with a balcony, dating from 1901, which houses the UNESCO offices. Casa Clari is an Art Nouveau building with a café (*021 496476; 11.00–midnight Mon–Thu, 11.00–03.00 Fri & Sat, closed Sun*) with a fabulous view over the Palacio de López. Casa Emasa is a modern building with offices and an art gallery called La Galería.

Cabildo [74 D1] (*Av de la República e/ Chile y Alberdi; 021 443094/441826; e cabildoculturalccr@yahoo.com; www.cabildoccr.gov.py; 09.00–19.00 Mon–Fri except during Jan & Feb, 10.00–17.00 Sat, Sun & daily throughout Jan & Feb; free admission*) Formerly the Palacio Legislativo, where the Senate used to meet, this pink building is a distinctive symbol of the city. Its double row of arches on two floors look stunning lit up at night. Don't miss the museum inside (also called the Centro Cultural de la República): it is small but excellently presented and covers different aspects of Paraguay, including history and art.

The first Cabildo was established in 1607, but the present building was begun by Carlos Antonio López in 1842, and was the fifth Cabildo to be built. Historic events that took place here include the election of Mariscal López as president in 1862 (under extreme pressure), the declaration of war against Argentina in 1865 and the approval of the Constitution in various steps (1870, 1940 and 1992). In 1894 the seat of government moved from here to the Palacio de López, but in 1904 the Congress moved into the building. The term *cabildo* dates from the colonial administration, when representatives of the town, including those designated as *alcaldes* (mayors) and *regidores* (governors), would meet to discuss all civil matters, including taxes, police, holidays, justice, health and the cleaning of the city.

In the most recent coup attempt (or according to some, fake coup attempt) in 2000, a tank fired a hole in the top plasterwork. The hole was there for years before it was mended. In 2004, when the new Congress building was opened, the Cabildo was successfully converted into a pleasant museum and cultural centre.

On the ground floor to the right are three rooms beautifully laid out by the staff of the Museo del Barro (see below). The first has examples of intricate traditional Paraguayan craft, such as woven woollen rugs from Carapegua. The second has indigenous artefacts in feather, fibre and wood (but only a taster for the much bigger display at the Museo del Barro itself) and a big wooden canoe stood up against the wall. The third room has Jesuit-Guaraní art with eight beautiful religious statues stunningly displayed against red walls.

To the left of the entrance are rooms devoted to temporary exhibitions of modern art. Around the corner you can see the presidential chair of the López family. There is also an interesting model of the original layout of the Plaza. Upstairs are rooms devoted to Paraguayan films and music, including harps and guitars that once belonged to some of the country's leading musicians. A new section is devoted to the great composer for the classical guitar, Agustín Pío Barrios, known as 'Mangoré' (see box on page 196). Directly above the entrance is the former Senate chamber, now used for conferences.

Stretching out behind the main building is a room used for meetings and seminars, and if you can gain access, you will find windows giving extensive views in all directions. To see the real Asunción, look down directly over the hovels of the Bañado, a poor residential area crammed into the low-lying space between the plaza and the river. It was horrifically flooded by the river in 2014, as it had been from time to time in earlier years as well. The contrast between these thousands of tumbledown shacks and the shimmering new parliament building, also visible from the window, is very stark.

ART MUSEUMS

Museo del Barro [79 G2] (*Grabadores del Cabichuí, entre Emeterio Miranda y Cañada;* ☎ *021 607996; www.museodelbarro.org;* 🕘 *15.30–20.00 Tue, 09.30–noon & 15.30–20.00 Wed–Sat; free admission)* This is the best museum in town, with collections of indigenous work, Jesuit and Franciscan religious art, and modern art, and also an excellent craft shop. The only problem, apart from its obscure position in town, is its peculiar opening hours.

To get to the museum take a taxi or a bus down España (28, 30-2 Aeropuerto, 44 Autopista, Luque-Aregua) to a little way past the Shopping del Sol (on the left near the junction of España and San Martín). Just after you have passed the big turning off to the right called Santa Teresa you will come to the Farmacia Aviadores, on the right-hand side of the main road (which is now no longer called Espana, but Aviadores del Chaco). This marks the corner of Cañada, an unlikely looking rough road, but the one you must take to reach the Museo del Barro. Turn left at the first corner, and the museum is a short distance along on your right. This is five minutes' walk from the Shopping del Sol.

Literally the 'Mud Museum', it is tucked away out of the centre and in a place so discreet that many taxi drivers have never heard of it. If you are in Asunción between Tuesday and Saturday, this museum, with its excellent craft shop attached, is a must. It was founded in 1972 as a travelling exhibition by a group of artists, and reached its current home after the end of the dictatorship. It is imaginatively modern with good displays, and a good dose of imagination. The museum comprises three different collections: indigenous art, *campesino* art (mostly religious figures), and modern urban art. There are also temporary exhibitions.

Most of the permanent collection is on the first floor, and the first rooms you come to are devoted to **religious art** in the form of painted wooden figures, from the Jesuit Reductions or the Franciscan Reductions, or from the workshops of Guaraní artesans who moved from the Reductions after the Expulsion (see page 11). While the museums in Misiones have large figures – life-size or nearly life-size – and there are few of these in the Museo del Barro, by far the largest number are small figures, 15cm or so high. The collection is strong in crucifixes – including the crucified woman Santa Librada – and the Niño Salvador del Mundo (the Child Saviour of the World) – a naked child Jesus holding an orb in his hand. Particularly interesting are the crucifixes that show the Holy Trinity: God the Father stretches out his arms over his crucified Son, while between the two a huge dove of the Holy Spirit breaks forth with wings outstretched. On the walls are large figures of the crucified Good and Bad Thieves similar to those in Santa Rosa, Misiones.

The **ethnic section** opens out of this room and is impressive. There are fibre costumes and feather headdresses made by the Ishir, wooden masks of men and animals made by the Guaraní, huge clay pots and sculpted wooden animals, again by the Guaraní. Among a group of big-bellied wooden fish, one has tigers and birds outlined on its belly in burnt wood. There are bead necklaces and red ceremonial sashes, and a room of smaller craftworks by the Ayoreo, Chamakoko, Lengua and Mbyá Guaraní.

If you go up a gentle ramp from the indigenous section you enter the rooms of **modern art** (and there are more rooms on the ground floor, opening off the courtyard). Some of the founders of the museum have major pieces here: Carlos Colombino has a huge wooden panel, 9.5m x 3.4m, called *La Próxima Cena* (The Next Supper), which is based on the *Last Supper* by Leonardo da Vinci. Ricardo Migliorisi has a sort of circus tent, painted on the inside in brilliant colours with dancers, circus artists, weird sea creatures and a popular procession of the Virgin: it is titled *La Carpilla Sixtina* (*carpa* is 'tent' in Spanish). A couple of rooms downstairs are devoted to the collection of Ricardo Migliorisi.

In the shop you can buy arts and crafts similar to those displayed in the museum: fibre bags by the Aché indigenous, lace (*encajo ju*) tablecloths, clay figures, wooden painted statues of the saints and some prints. A couple of rooms downstairs are devoted to the collection of Ricardo Migliorisi, one of the people who was involved in founding the Museo del Barro.

Museo de Bellas Artes [75 H2] (*Eligio Ayala 1345 c/ Curupayty;* ☎ *021 211578;* ⌚ *07.00–18.00 Tue–Fri, 08.00-14.00 Sat, closed Sun & Mon; free admission*) As national art galleries go, the Museo de Bellas Artes is a small collection, but it includes some interesting paintings and is well worth visiting, although its move in 2012 to a less central address means a ten-minute walk from the Plaza Uruguaya, or a short bus or taxi ride. It is now in a building packed in between some of the private hospitals and medical institutions, in a road thick with parked cars. There are six small exhibition rooms.

The core of the gallery is the collection of Juan Silvano Godoy, a wealthy politician (1850–1926) who acquired foreign art works (mostly late 19th-century paintings) in his 18 years of exile, during the political upheavals of his day. Although there are two brightly painted statues of the Virgin from the Jesuit Reductions, most of the works are oil paintings. The first three rooms show European works collected by Godoy; the fourth room shows works by European artists who had come to Paraguay at the end of the 19th century; and the last two rooms show works by Paraguayans who had gone to Europe to study art.

The room that you enter first contains an amusing late 19th-century portrait of an embarrassed and bored chaperone, titled *Il Terzo Incomodo* ('The awkward third person'), by the Italian Giacomo Favretto. In the room to the right is a striking painting of Gil Blas (the hero of the French novel of that name) being intercepted by a robber as he travels on horseback, by José Moreno Carbonero and dating from 1890. In the room to the left is a portrait of Godoy by Peruvian artist Teófilo Castillo.

The fourth room displays the draft by Guillermo da Ré (a Venetian living in Buenos Aires) for the famous larger painting in the Palacio de López (which is not open to the public) of the moment when Paraguayans seized their independence from Spain, on 14 May 1811. Pedro Juan Cavallero imperiously demands the resignation of the Spanish governor Velasco, by night, and a chair tumbles over symbolically.

Juan Samudio is one of the early 20th-century Paraguayan artists who studied in Europe and whose works hang in the fifth and sixth room – from a Venetian scene with a gondola to a Paraguayan scene of the Panteón. But the most striking painting of the last room is the 2m high *Parejhara* ('Messenger') by Roberto Holden Jara, son of a British father and Paraguayan mother who studied painting in Europe and on his return dedicated himself to painting the indigenous, as in this painting of eight indigenous scrutinising some craft laid out on the ground.

Museo de la Silla de Asunción (MUSA) [73 E1] (*Artigas 4289 c/ Juana Pabla Carrillo;* ☎ *021 297500;* e *museodelasilla@silday.com.py;* 🕘 *08.00–11.30 & 13.30–17.00)* Go to this new and little-known Museum of Chairs if you possibly can: it is a circular tower with five floors of some 400 innovative and amusingly designed chairs. The collection has been put together by Argentinian architect Jorge Nicolás Jury, who has lived in Paraguay for 37 years, and it is housed in a striking modern building of his own design. There is everything from the *apyka* of the Guaraní indigenous to the barber's chair sat in by astronaut Neil Armstrong; from a child-size Chippendale-inspired gem to a 4m-high copy of a ladder-back chair by Charles Rennie Mackintosh (19th-century Scottish pioneer of industrial design); from a 120-year-old German school desk with the pupil's name carved into the top to the Zig Zag chair of Gerrit Rietveld; from a polished wooden hand large enough to sit in to an antique chair with a wonderful carved back, on sale for US$1,300. The Paraguayan artists Carlos Colombino, Ricardo Migliorisi and the two sons of Hermann Guggiari – Sebastián and Javier – are represented here, with useful biographical details. An international library of books on design is planned for the future.

The morning guide Valeriano Amarilla (m *0982 131465*) is finishing a degree in journalism and is well informed about the exhibits and how they illustrate the work of the fathers of modern design. He will happily take photos of you reclining in the chair of your choice, whether it be a recycled tyre with a red cushion on top, an undulating rocking chair made of corrugated cardboard or the 1928 Le Corbusier chaise longue covered in black and white cow's hide. At the top you emerge into the open air and a spectacular view over Asunción in all directions, from the botanical gardens to the river, the 'Icono' skyscraper and the huge façade of the Trinidad church.

The museum is one block from the gate into the Jardín Botánico, in a modern building on the left labelled 'Espacio de Diseño'. You may find the door originally intended as the way in to the museum closed, as you usually now gain access through the Silday industrial design company that shares the building. Ring the doorbell by the sign 'Artigas 4289'.

Museo de Arte Sacro [75 E4] (*Villa Lina, Manuel Dominguez y Paraguarí; 021 497781/445132 (office); 021 449439 (museum); www.museodeartesacro.com; 09.00–18.00 Fri & Sat; Gs25,000; groups of 15 or more people can visit by arrangement at other times and at a small discount*) Part of the renowned private collection of religious art belonging to Nicolás Darío Latourrete Bo is now housed in a museum of beautifully displayed sacred art in a fine, stately building. Most of the art comes from the Reductions, and the six rooms are divided into the following themes: the Angelic Hierarchies, Christ – God made Man, the Saints – men of God, Jesuit Saints – holy Brides of Christ, the Reredos and Mary the Mother of God. At the time of going to press it was closed for building works.

Museo Bogarín [74 D1] Tucked away down an alleyway beside the cathedral, this is one of Asunción's best (but least-known) museums, packed full of items of great artistic and historical interest, but at the time of going to press (and for many months before that) it was closed for renovation. The absence of news about a date for re-opening could be a bad sign, but it is such an interesting museum that it is to be hoped it will soon re-open with an improved display, and that is certainly the hope of architect Ramón Duarte (*021 203819*), who is in charge of the renovation.

The building itself is of some interest, and the alley on which it stands, the Paseo Comuneros, is a pleasant lane with benches, named after the revolutionary movement that precedes Paraguay's independence in 1811. The historic building was originally the house of Fulgencio Yegros (one of the Próceres of independence, see page 12). During the presidency of Dr Francia it served as a prison where another of Francia's former colleagues among the Próceres, Pedro Juan Cavallero, was held for his part in a suspected plot to pass Paraguay under Argentinian control. He committed suicide here in 1821 on the eve of his planned execution, writing in his blood on the wall of his cell that he knew suicide was a sin.

The building subsequently became a seminary, and later a school. At one stage it housed a laundry and even a public swimming pool, and was known as the *ykuá piscina* (Guaraní 'water hole'; Spanish 'swimming pool'). In 1960 it was taken over by the Universidad Católica and in due course was relaunched as a museum to house the magnificent personal collection of Monseñor Juan Sinforio Bogarín (1863–1949), the sixth bishop and the first archbishop of Paraguay.

If in due course the museum re-opens, among its treasures are items of Jesuit-Guaraní art both large and small, including the carved wooden doors of the Ypané church and the reredos from the Guarambaré church (see page 173), silverwork, and the missal used by Pope John Paul II on his visit to Paraguay, with his signature dated 18 May 1988. Among the items relating to the Triple Alliance War is an outspoken account of Mariscal López's killings, whippings and torturings of his own compatriots, written by his sometime chief military apothecary, George Frederick Masterman.

SPECIAL INTEREST MUSEUMS

Museo Andrés Barbero [75 F1] (*España 217 esq Mompox; 021 441696; museobarbero@museobarbero.org.py; www.museobarbero.org.py; 08.00–17.00 Mon–Fri, closed Jan; free admission; buses 8, 12, 23, 24, 30 & 56 pass*) The museum of ethnic and archaeological items is on the last bit of España before it curves round towards the station, opposite the Hotel Palmas del Sol. It is named after an early 20th-century philanthropist who founded the Paraguayan Red Cross and worked in the fields of health, archaeology and indigenous culture. A statue to him stands at the beginning of Artigas. Dr Barbero founded the ethnological museum back in 1929, but it passed into the hands of a succession of other anthropologists to organise and complete: the German explorer Dr Max Schmidt, and after his death the Slovene Dr Branislava Susnik. It is now in the hands of Dr Adelina Pusineri de Madariaga.

The museum includes more than 3,000 items belonging to different tribes, but most are from different branches of the Guaraní family. There are funeral pots called *japepó* – the Guaraní were buried in foetal position in a pot – cooking pots, stone axes, fibre hammocks, fishing nets, feather headdresses, woven cloths, lances, a hollowed-out boat and paddle, and a gallery of photographs. There is also an important library of over 20,000 specialist books.

Correo Central [74 C1] (*Alberdi y Paraguayo Independiente;* ☎ *021 498114/493997;* e *filatelia@correoparaguayo.gov.py; www.correoparaguayo.gov.py;* ⏲ *07.00–19.00 Mon–Fri, 07.00–noon Sat; free admission*) The *correo central* or central post office, a grand but battered building in beige and cream plaster, occupies most of the block facing the plaza in between 14 de mayo and Alberdi. It was built at the beginning of the 20th century as the private house for a rich Italian businessman, Luiggi Patri, who also bought up and improved the rail service in Paraguay (after the Triple Alliance War). After the death of Patri it was acquired by the Paraguayan government, with the intention of using it as the presidential residence. Instead, however, it became the office for Post and Telegraph in 1913.

There is a central courtyard with trees, and a bust of Mariscal López, who established the first national telegraph service in Latin America in 1864. A philatelic office in the far right corner sells past issues of stamps, and there is a little stamp museum. The first postage stamp in Paraguay was printed in August 1870, a few months after Mariscal López's death on 1 March 1870, and showed a lion with its paws in the air. As well as stamps, the museum has an 1896 clock, old scales for weighing letters, an old postman's uniform, and models of the little planes that used to transport the post.

Museo del Fútbol Sudamericano [73 H2] (*Av Sudamericana esq Petrona Almirón de Leoz, Luque;* ☎ *021 645781;* e *museo@conmebol.com.py; www.conmebol.com*) This prestigious building, on the Autopista on the way to the airport, houses a convention centre as well as a football museum.

A huge black-and-white football forms a focus outside the building, while inside you are met by the flags of the ten footballing countries that comprise the Confederación Sudamericana: Argentina, Bolivia, Brazil, Chile, Colombia, Ecuador, Paraguay, Peru, Uruguay and Venezuela. This leads into a hall of cups. The museum is organised with avant-garde design over two levels, and with interactive installations. On the lower level is the Hermanos Americanos room, which commemorates the symbols, history and talents of each of the ten nations. Inside the football itself is a round chamber screening a show about South American footballing history.

Estación de Ferrocarril [75 E2] (*México 145 esq Eligio Ayala;* ☎ *021 447848;* e *cultura@ferrocarriles.com.py; www.ferrocarriles.com.py;* ⏲ *08.00–16.00 Mon–Fri, 09.00-13.00 Sat & Sun; Gs10,000, Paraguayans Gs5,000*) The old railway station on Plaza Uruguaya is a large and splendid building, unmistakably a station, but since there are no longer any trains running it now functions as a delightful museum about the old railway.

The railway was one of the first built in South America, and was constructed by English engineers, particularly Alonso Taylor, who was responsible for the Asunción central station. President Carlos Antonio López began it in 1854, as part of his modernisation in the days when Paraguay was great. By the time the station was finished in 1864, and the line opened as far as Paraguarí, Mariscal López was president and the Triple Alliance War was beginning. The days of glory were short-lived.

It was 1886 before the work began again to continue the line to Villarrica and beyond. In 1907 the ownership of the railway passed to an English company, and in 1913 the railway was extended to Encarnación. In 1961 the Paraguayan government bought back the railway, but it was beginning to become outdated and uneconomic to run, and it stopped functioning in 1999. The short track from the Botanical Gardens to Areguá was opened again for tourist trips in 2004, only to close again in 2009 when engineering work was needed on a bridge. Since part of the track has now been lifted to make way for a fast road, it seems that trains will never run again on this particular stretch of line.

To enter the station as such you must go round the corner to México 145, and find the door with a brass plate marked Ferro Carril Central de Paraguay Administración. If it is not open, ring the bell. There is enough left of old grandeur to get the sense that in its time this was something very technologically advanced and quite a classy way to travel. On the rails by the platforms are two old steam trains: it is fascinating to go inside the dining car, and the luxury sleeping car, with highly polished furniture and moulded plaster ceilings. The first train to run from here to Areguá in 1861 was the *Sapucai*, which is on display. (Sapucai is also the name of the town where the workshops are for building the trains.) You can also see the old ticket offices and a museum of old railway items – clocks, lamps, whistles, big ledgers with bills for firewood in copperplate writing, and huge drawings of the details of steam cars labelled in English. You feel you are in a time warp: nothing has changed.

For more evocation of how it used to be, see the YouTube trailer of Mauricio Rial Banti's prize-winning film *Tren Paraguay*, which won the prize for best documentary in the 2011 Festival Iberamericano in Mexico.

Museo de las Memorias [74 C5] (*Chile 1066 y 1072 entre Jejuí y Manduvirá; ☎ 021 493873; e msedu@rieder.net.py; 🕘 09.00–16.00 Mon–Fri; Facebook: Museo Memorias; free admission*) The Museo de las Memorias is an initiative to record the human rights abuses of the dictatorship, in a building that was previously the torture centre of the Stroessner regime, known then by the discreet name of Asuntos Técnicos (Technical Affairs) or La Técnica for short.

Under the umbrella of Operation Condor (which created intelligence links between a number of dictatorial regimes in the Southern Cone), and supported by the foreign policy of the USA which was intent on wiping out communism, Stroessner was able to kill, maim or exile all his opponents (very few of whom were communists) through the systematic use of savage torture methods. La Técnica was only officially closed on 23 December 1992, a day after the discovery of the Archive of Terror (police records of the imprisonment and torture of dissidents). The museum is an initiative of the Fundación Celestina Pérez de Almada, to which enquiries should be addressed (*Av Carlos Antonio López 2273; ☎ 021 425345/425873; e fundacion@rieder.net.py*).

SUNDAY IN ASUNCIÓN

Asunción is something of a dead city on a Sunday, and you may be at a loss to know what to do. Here are a few options on a Sunday:

- The Cabildo (🕘 *10.00–17.00; see pages 99–100*)
- The Manzana de la Rivera (🕘 *07.30–18.00; see page 99*)
- Loma San Jerónimo (see pages 116–17)
- The Jardín Botánico y Zoológico (🕘 *06.00–17.00; see page 118*)
- Mercado Cuatro; the food section at Perú y Teniente Fariña makes an interesting visit (🕘 *until noon; see page 95*)
- Flea market on Mariscal Estigarribia y Yegros, outside the La Riojana department store.
- The Cathedral (🕘 *10.00–noon; see below*)
- La Encarnación church (🕘 *09.30–noon; see page 112*)
- La Santísima Trinidad church (🕘 *07.00–11.30; see page 117*)
- Watch a football match (see page 90)
- Take a boat from the port to Mbiguá or to Chaco'i (see pages 112 and 120)
- Most popular of all: the Costanera never closes (see page 116)

The museum explains how systematic torture in the dictatorship began when, one year after taking power, Stroessner sent Antonio Campos Alúm to the USA in 1955 to study how to do it. La Técnica includes implements for pulling off fingernails, donated anonymously by a former torturer. There is a telephone used for psychologically torturing the relatives of the victims, as they heard the screams down the line. You can visit the interrogation room and the cells. There is a bath (*pileta*) to illustrate the water torture, where prisoners were nearly drowned and then revived, wrapped up in chains or barbed wire, with a radio playing loudly to drown their screams. A big display board shows the photographs and names of the 600 'disappeared', whose deaths have not been accounted for. It is believed that 10,000 people passed through La Técnica, of which there are written records for 3,500.

At another address, but part of the same area of interest, is the Archivo del Terror or **Archive of Terror**. This is open to the public and is now located on the ground floor of the **Palacio de Justicia** (*Testanova y Alonso;* ☎ *021 424311/15 int 2269;* e *cdya@pj.gov.py; www.unesco.org/webworld/paraguay;* 🕘 *07.00–18.00 daily*). It is a research centre, with all the relevant police records of those detained, imprisoned and tortured under Stroessner, and has a good computer system for searching the archive.

OTHER CITY CENTRE SITES

Cathedral [74 D1] (☎ *021 449512;* 🕘 *10.00–noon, 13.00–17.00 Mon–Sat; mass 11.00 daily inc Sun, also 19.00 Fri*) The Metropolitan Cathedral dominates the eastern end of the long rectangular space known as the Plaza Mayor in the days of colonialisation, around which is the Parliament and the former parliamentary buildings. There is no official name for the entire space, although the space in front of the cathedral bears a sign saying 'Plaza de la Independencia', and the space in front of the parliament building is sometimes referred to as the Plaza de Armas. But the whole open area is usually referred to simply as 'La Plaza' especially in the context of political demonstrations, as for example, most famously, in the Marzo Paraguayo (see box on page 108).

The cathedral is a large but not particularly distinguished building as cathedrals go, more chunky than ornate. It is usually closed when there is not a mass or other event, but if you are able to get inside you will be struck by the theme colours of the flat wooden roof, the pulpit and the high altar, which are two shades of green with touches of gold. The finest artwork inside the cathedral is the altar, with its heavily worked silver panels. There is also a pleasant modern altar facing the people, with wheat and grape motifs carved into the stonework. There is nothing in the way of guides, booklets or postcards.

The foundation stone of the cathedral was laid in 1842, in the ruins of the previous (fifth) cathedral. It was designed by an Italian architect Alessandro Ravizza (who also designed the Panteón and the church of Trinidad) and it was completed in 1846 – one of the first architectural works in the presidency of Carlos Antonio López.

Outside the cathedral stands a stone bas-relief of Domingo Martínez de Irala, who led the first Spanish settlement here, embracing a group of indigenous, while a paper bearing the plan of a cathedral flutters at their feet. It was a gift from a former Spanish ambassador, Giménez Caballero, and was donated in 1965. But the message it conveys, of two races embracing, has been criticised, for the Spanish forcibly exploited the indigenous, reducing them to near slavery, and although they married indigenous women, they had no choice in the matter.

A plaque in the porch reminds us of the important Synod of Asunción in 1603, which set the policy for evangelising the indigenous in their own language, and so laid the basis for the work of the Jesuit and Franciscan missions, with effects lasting to the present day.

The cathedral reached its finest hour in the events of the Marzo Paraguayo, when it became a makeshift hospital for the wounded and dying demonstrators, and a banner proclaiming the names of the martyrs was soon strung up on one of towers.

Universidad Católica [74 D1] Next door to the cathedral is the Universidad Católica, a very pleasant red-brick building of some age and distinction, with a large columned portico facing onto the plaza. In the 19th century it was the Seminario Conciliar, together with the Museo Bogarín, which nestles into the back of the building. The newly formed Universidad Católica took over the former seminary in 1960 and added the second floor in 1965. (This is one of two campuses for the Católica, – the other being in the poor and somewhat dangerous area of Barrio Republicana.) The cathedral and the university are the two buildings on the eastern end of the plaza.

Monument to the Marzo Paraguayo [74 D1] Moving down the plaza, note the black-and-white tiles underfoot. Many of these tiles were torn up and hurled by the pro-democracy student demonstrators against their Oviedista attackers in the famous events of the Marzo Paraguayo in 1999 (see box on page 108). The Oviedistas aimed fireworks (the fierce rockets known as *petardos*) directly among them, and later gunfire, while the students had no other means of self-defence than to lever up the ground beneath their feet.

The demonstrators who were shot dead (six students and a *campesino* leader, with an eighth student dying from his wounds some time later) are commemorated in a composite monument of a rather do-it-yourself nature that incorporates minor changes year by year. It is situated directly in front of the Cabildo. There is a black stone slab reading 'They gave their lives to make us free', and a wooden dove crying 'Justice! Liberty! Democracy!' There is also a cross to the memory of Luis María

MARZO PARAGUAYO

The Marzo Paraguayo refers to the historic events just before Easter 1999, when huge numbers of pro-democracy demonstrators occupied the plaza in front of the Congress, and were shot at by snipers. The attack left eight dead, of whom seven were students and one a *campesino*, and more than 700 wounded, of whom 90 were wounded by bullets. The youth movement Jóvenes por la Democracia flourished after the events, in a brief period of determination to build a better society.

A politician called Lino Oviedo, previously found guilty of a coup attempt in 1996, had been condemned to ten years in prison but nonetheless retained a lot of popular support. He was barred from standing as a presidential candidate in 1999 because of his sentence, but he put a friend, Raúl Cubas Grau, to stand in his place, and won the election. As soon as he was elected, Cubas released Oviedo from prison, but was ordered by the Supreme Court to return Oviedo to serve out his sentence. When Cubas refused, the Congress began procedures to have him removed from power for disregarding the rule of law.

While this procedure was underway, the vice-president, Luis María Argaña, was shot dead in his car, on 23 March 1999, and the finger of suspicion pointed at Lino Oviedo, who was suspected of trying to destabilise the country and create a power vacuum, so that the parliament would be deterred from leaving the country without either a president or vice-president. If this was the tactic, it misfired, and there was a huge popular feeling that the democratic processes should not be threatened by the gun. Students occupied the plaza to protect the communication between the Cámera de Diputados and the Senate, both on the plaza but in different buildings, in order that they could see through to its end the political judgment against Cubas.

Within a few days the occupation of the enormous plaza had become the symbolic battleground for the protection of democratic processes. More and more demonstrators poured in to occupy the plaza, while the police and army, who were being manipulated by Lino Oviedo, a former general, attempted to dislodge them with water cannons, tear gas and rubber bullets. Eventually, on 27 March, a group of unofficial snipers on the high-rise Marlboro building began firing into the crowd. People remembered that Lino Oviedo had promised to make 'rivers of blood' flow in the country.

Public opinion turned decisively against Cubas and Oviedo, who both fled into exile. The president of the Senate, Luis González Macchi, was made the new president of the republic by unanimous popular acclaim, and for a brief period there was a government of national unity. After a number of years Cubas returned, and later Lino Oviedo, and both were put in prison. President Nicanor Duarte Frutos released Oviedo shortly before the 2008 election, to let him stand against Fernando Lugo and so split the opposition vote, but he did not attract enough votes to prevent Lugo winning. Oviedo was going to stand again in the next election in 2013, but he died shortly before it in a mysterious helicopter crash.

Argaña, the vice-president whose murder sparked off the political crisis. From this spot you can see the high-rise building with 'Whirlpool' written on the top, which is where the snipers shot from, into the crowd – though at that date the firm advertised on top was Marlboro.

Statue of Juan de Salazar [74 D1] Directly behind the Monument to the Marzo Paraguayo, but looking away from the Cabildo instead of towards it, is a **statue of Juan de Salazar y Espinoza**, with his sword outstretched. He founded Asunción on 15 August 1537.

Behind the statue of Juan de Salazar is the striking pink Cabildo (see pages 99–100). The former Congress was in the building at the western end of the plaza, next to the modern Parliament. It can still be visited, via the new Congress (see below).

Facing the Cabildo, on the other side of the plaza, is another historic old building, the police headquarters, with a colonnade of yellow arches. It was built by Carlos Antonio López in 1854. On the next block from the police headquarters is the Correo Central (see page 104). Further along the plaza, in front of the new Congress, is a 12m high metal **sculpture of a tree trunk**, by artist Hermann Guggiari, in memory of Juan de Salazar's foundation of the first fort here, when it was the custom to plant a tree trunk with the name of the fort: the sculpture is labelled '*Asunción, Madre de Ciudades, cuna de la libertad Americana*' ('Mother of Cities, cradle of American freedom'). At the far end of the plaza is a striking **statue of Mariscal López**, another of Paraguay's most famous figures on a horse that is rearing up in dramatic fashion.

Congreso Nacional [74 C1] (*14 de mayo y Av República*) It is not widely known that one can visit the new Congress, which was paid for by the government of Taiwan and opened in 2003. It is on the site of the original fort established by the founder of Asunción, Juan de Salazar. You should give notice for larger group visits, though individuals or small groups may be able to be shown around without prior arrangement.

The **Senate** (*Oficina de Relaciones Publicas;* ☎ *021 4144191;* ⏲ *Jan–Feb 07.00–13.00, Mar–Dec 07.00–15.00; free admission*) is reached through a side entrance facing the Plaza. You should give notice for larger group visits, though individuals or small groups may be able to be shown around without prior arrangement.

To visit the **Cámera de Diputados** (☎ *021 4144191;* ⏲ *07.30–13.00 Mon–Wed, Fri, year round*), the lower house, you use the main entrance around the corner. There is a wide stretch of steps up, and inside it is like a huge glass wigwam, set against a white background. Look for the desk marked 'Atención e Información Ciudadana'. Visits to this part of the building are organised separately from the Senate, and a good time to arrive is 09.30. They may be able to arrange an English-speaking guide if you ask in advance. Visits are not normally allowed on Thursdays, unless permission is sought in advance. The public can also attend parliamentary sessions, in the Sala de los Públicos, which generally has room.

If you cross the courtyard, you come in at the back end of the **old Congress building**, which is next door to the new one. This building, which is also known as the Casa de la Cultura, has had an extraordinarily varied history. It was originally a *colegio* opened by the Jesuits ten years after they arrived in 1588. After the 1768 Expulsion of the Jesuits it was briefly used as a tobacco factory, and then in 1780 became the Seminario de San Carlos, the principal institution of higher education in the late colonial period. With independence it became a barracks, eventually turning into a military school. During the Chaco War it served as a hospital, before becoming a military museum, a Casa de la Cultura, and then in 1996 the Cámera de Diputados.

The old **Jesuit chapel** has had its original floor uncovered, which dates back four centuries. This is where San Roque González was ordained priest, and where his body was brought after his martyrdom, except for his heart. It is likely that he is actually buried here, though that is unconfirmed. On the wall is a map of 1731, drawn by a Capuchin, showing the enormous size of Paraguay at that date, occupying territory now belonging to Brazil, Argentina and Bolivia.

Teatro Municipal [74 C2] (*Presidente Franco e/ Chile y Alberdi; ☎ 021 445169*) The Teatro Municipal Ignacio A Pane, to give it its full title, was re-opened in 2006 after extensive renovation. The enchanting 19th-century theatre was closed in 1994 because it was dangerous, and while something of its old magic has been lost, a lot of careful planning has gone into the restoration, to preserve the old while updating it to modern safety standards. One of the advantages of Paraguay having such a small population is that the principal national theatre can be contained in such an intimate space.

The Teatro Municipal is shut most of the time, with performances most weeks on Thursday, Friday, Saturday and Sunday nights at 20.30, and few people know that it can be visited outside of these times. Go to a discreet little door marked '*acceso actores y funcionarios*' around the corner in Chile during the mornings (*⌚ 09.00–noon Mon–Sat*), and a security guide will show you around the theatre. From Wednesday until Saturday you may find the box office open too, on Presidente Franco.

The first theatre in Asunción was called the Teatro Nacional, and was in the same block but not on the same site: that was the theatre that featured famously in the life of Mariscal López when he took his controversial mistress Eliza Lynch to show her off at a performance. In 1889 it was replaced with the present structure, designed by the Catalan architect Baudilio Alió: the theatre is almost entirely circular, with three circles and 12 rows of stalls providing superb views of the stage.

In the foyer, the original walls have been broken in places to allow for new white marble staircases. But where a wall has been removed a vertical line of original bare bricks has been left to show the outline of the original building, and the new walls are constructed in glass.

Plaza de los Héroes [74 D2] If you go southwest from the cathedral (away from the river), you will reach a green space after just two blocks. Apparently one large square divided into four quarters by a road, this is technically four adjoining squares: the Plaza de los Héroes (north), the Plaza Juan E O'Leary (east), the Plaza de la Democracia (south) and the Plaza de la Libertad (west). You are now as much in the centre of the city as you can get. Sometimes the group of four are referred to collectively as the Plaza de la Democracia, and sometimes as the Plaza de los Héroes, but the other two titles are used less frequently.

The **Plaza Juan E O'Leary** used to be the site of the church of La Merced until the mid-19th century, when it became the Mercado Guazú ('big market') until 1909. The square is now attractively developed as a place to sit and pass time.

The **Plaza de la Democracia** has an underground car park. On one side it faces the newly revamped and re-opened Guaraní Esplendor Hotel, icon of the Stroessner era; on another, it faces the elegant 19th-century building of the Banco Nacional de Fomento – which deserves a visit inside to see a perfect period piece.

The **Plaza de la Libertad** is one of the best places to buy craft: they have *ao po'í* clothes, *filigrana* silver jewellery, fibre bags made by the Ayoreo indigenous, hammocks, carved wood figures and *ñanduti* items. The market operates all day, every day, and some people call this square the Plaza de los Artesanos. In the middle is a bronze statue called *La Razón y la Fuerza* ('Reason and Force'), which shows two struggling figures: the burly Force is unable to dominate the winged Reason.

The Plaza de los Héroes (the official name of one of the four squares) houses the Panteón.

Panteón [74 C2] (*Always open, until late*) A small circular oratory with a high dome, the Panteón houses the mortal remains of some of Paraguay's most famous people. The building was begun by Mariscal López in 1863, as an oratory dedicated to the Virgen de la Asunción, designed by the architect Alessandro Ravizza (the architect of the cathedral and the Trinidad church), but it was left incomplete with the outbreak of the Triple Alliance War. It was not completed until 1936 when, at the end of the Chaco War, it was inaugurated as a public place of honour for remains of national heroes, with the remains of Mariscal Francisco Solano López and his son Panchito López brought here from Cerro Corá, together with the body of an unknown soldier from the recently concluded Chaco War. The other early presidents of Paraguay also have their urns here: Dr Francia and Carlos Antonio López.

On the feast of the Assumption, 15 August, it is the statue of the Virgin from this oratory that is honoured in the public mass outside the cathedral. There are always a couple of colourfully attired sentinels keeping guard at the door, in blue breeches, red-and-white jackets, helmets, and lances flying the Paraguayan red, white and blue flag. But do not be deterred: the building is open to the public, and you are encouraged to go inside. The building was whitewashed from head to foot a few years ago, covering up the attractive red tiles on the dome, but has now been beautifully restored as far as possible to its original colours, and adorned with magnificent illumination at night, as red, blue, mauve and white lights alternate in a creative and scarcely predictable sequence.

Archivo Nacional [74 D2] (*Mariscal Estigarribia y Iturbe;* ↘ *021 447311;* **e** *archivonacionaldeasuncion@gmail.com;* ⏲ *07.00–18.00 Mon–Fri*) The National Archive is open to the public wishing to do research among national documents dating back to colonial times. Until recently the upper floor housed the Museo de Bellas Artes (now moved, see page 101), and the whole building of the Archivo Nacional has been restored both inside and out. As many as five coats of paint were stripped off the hallway to reveal the original hand-painted walls. There are inviting reading desks inside for those who would like to step in and browse. Most of the documents are now digitised, and they go back to 1596 and Hernandarias (see page 11).

House of José Asunción Flores [75 E1] (*Salvador Guanes;* **m** *0971 799790*) Equidistant from the Plaza Uruguaya and the cathedral is the adobe house of the famous musician who created the musical form of *guarania*. To reach it, take the extension of Caballero on the other side of Avenida Mariscal López and then follow the road round as it bears right and then straightens out again and opens out into a tiny square. The location is known as Punto Karapá, Chacarita Alta. The building has been restored and opened to the public, and now houses a small library. It is at Punto, and is managed by Enrique and Stela Pereira but unfortunately a cut in government funding means that there are no longer fixed opening times, and there is no money to maintain the building. But you can turn up and take pot luck, and as always, if you want to visit a museum at an hour when it is not attended, do not omit to tip.

Plaza Uruguaya [75 E2] The Plaza next to the railway station was improved in May 2012, after years in which it was used as by thieves and prostitutes, and then as a campsite by indigenous who were making protests, until it reached the point of such squalor that something had to be done. It is now protected by high but elegant railings – as it used to be before 1942 - and is open to the public from 06.00 to 22.00, with replanted gardens, a Wi-Fi service and good lighting. The square was originally known as the Plaza San Francisco, but the name was changed in gratitude for the return by Uruguay of trophies after the Triple Alliance War. The central statue is of the great Uruguayan politician José Artigas (see also page 356), and there are also some Italian statues in a Romantic style dating from 1885.

Palacio de López [74 B1] If you follow the line of the river going west from the parliament, along the street Paraguayo Independiente, you will come to the grandest building in the city, the huge, white and ornate Palacio de Gobierno, otherwise known as the Palacio de López, because it was begun in 1860 by Mariscal López to be his private residence. He dreamed of a home somewhat like the Palace of Versailles, and put the construction in the hands of the Hungarian builder Francisco Wisner, under the direction of the English architect Alonso Taylor. But when the building was on the verge of completion the Triple Alliance War broke out, in 1864, and the Mariscal never enjoyed his new home. It was left in appalling condition when the Brazilian troops eventually withdrew from Asunción, having used it as a barracks and stables for the cavalry, and having removed the fine European furniture and chandeliers to Brazil, but in 1890 it was restored and turned into government offices, which is still its function today. On one side, towards the city, the building has an enormous flagpole and faces the back end of the Manzana de la Rivera (see page 99). On the other side, it faces towards the river, and this view was seen to full advantage during the bi-centenary celebrations when people gathered to see a magnificent film projected onto the walls. If you would like to visit the inside of the Palacio, you can apply in writing to the Dirección General del Ceremonial del Estado (*4140220;* **f** *4140315*).

The Port [74 A1] Asunción's port lies a couple of blocks along the river from the Palacio de López, just where the traffic turns left to go up Colón, and where the arcade of craft shops known as Le Recova begins (see page 92). Like much in Paraguay, this has a quaint charm in an old-fashioned, run-down way. On Saturday afternoons from 15.00 there is a fair on the riverside called **Puerto Abierto** (*'Open Port';* **e** *puertoabiertoasuncion@gmail.com; Facebook: Puerto Abierto*), where there are creative events, shows, activities for children and craft stalls. It began in 2011 and has a very lively atmosphere. Down to the right, at the end of Montevideo Street, you can hop onto a motorboat (*Facebook: Lanchas de la Bahía;* *every half hour 06.30–19.00 daily; Gs3,500 each way*) to cross over to the little village of Chaco'í (little Chaco) where there is a simple beach and an imaginative new open-air restaurant, Manguruyú (see page 120).

There are other boats which do not cross the whole river but only a tributary and take you to the promontory curving round to enclose the bay of Asunción, where there is a beach and a sports club called Mbiguá. The club runs classes in fishing, rowing, and swimming in a 25m salt-water pool (*Facebook: Club Mbigua – Oficial*), and the sound of their occasional night-time parties can sometimes reach across the strait to mainland Asunción. Mbiguá can also be reached by land, but it is a longer way round than taking the boat, taking you through the Bañado Norte area (see page 67 and *Chapter 2*, page 44).

La Encarnación church [74 C3] (*14 de mayo e/ Haedo y Humaitá;* *16.30–20.00 Mon–Sat, 08.00–20.00 Fri; mass: 10.00 Sun, 15.00 Fri, 19.00 Mon–Sat*) Impressive red-brick building of soaring dimensions, built in 1893 on a small hillock in the city centre. It is not in good repair, but if restored would be finer than the cathedral.

San Francisco church [75 E3] (*Herrera y Caballero; ⌚ 08.00–11.30 & 15.00–18.00 Mon–Fri; 08.00–10.00 Sat; Sunday mass 09.00, 10.30, 19.00*) This small Franciscan church in the city centre has been recently restored and is kept open for visits; enter by the door to the right. It was built in 1901 and is Neoclassical in style. The urn of famous Franciscan Luis Bolaños (1550–1629) is here (see box on page 326).

Cristo Rey church [74 A5] (*Colón y Ygatimí; ☎ 021 492870; ⌚ 16.00–20.00 Mon–Fri*) For those who are coming to Paraguay with an interest in the Jesuit Reductions, a visit to the church of Cristo Rey is a must. This Jesuit church on the southwest corner of the city centre is where the (supposedly) incorrupt heart of San Roque González is held. To enquire about seeing the chapel if it is locked, or to ask for a guide, enquire at the Jesuit residence.

A small chapel to the right of the main church is dedicated to Roque González and his companions. In addition to the heart, framed in a glass case on the wall, there is another glass case containing the murder weapon: a stone axe. There is an excellent modern carved statue of the three martyrs, each with their distinctive feature: Roque González, as ever, carries the painting of *La Virgen Conquistadora*; Alonso Rodríguez is said to have nearly gone blind from weeping over the Passion, so is shown carrying a book; and Juan del Castillo carries the cord with which he was dragged by horses along the ground on the day of his martyrdom. A plaque on the wall records the names of the 26 Jesuit martyrs who lost their lives in the Reductions. Outside the chapel is a series of large wall pictures made from painted tiles that tell the life story of the saint (see box on pages 114–15).

Casas del Bicentenario [map. pages 74–5] In commemoration of the bicentenary of the Independence (2011), six historic houses in Asunción were purchased as part of the national heritage, and four of these have now been restored and opened to the public as sites devoted to the arts. There are many other fine 19th-century buildings waiting to be restored, but these six are exceptionally beautiful.

The **Casa Bicentenario de la Literatura** [75 E2] (*México c/ 25 de mayo; ⌚ 09.00–17.00 Mon–Fri*) is right on the Plaza Uruguaya, and is floodlit every night (along with other historic buildings such as the Palacio de López, the Cabildo, the Panteón, the cathedral and the Casa de la Independencia). Six elegant rounded arches face onto the plaza, and behind them is a portico adorned with portraits of the Próceres de la Independencia (see page 12). Inside the building, some of the delicately painted walls have been restored. The house was originally built in the early 1800s, designed by the French architect George Lavand, and is one of the few examples of the French Neoclassical style in the city. Grand though it was, it formed part of the Convento de San Francisco until Dr Francia abolished the religious orders in Paraguay in 1824, and then became a barracks under the command of Mariano Roque Alonso. In time it passed into the ownership of Julia Miranda Cueto, the wife of Mariscal José Félix Estigarribia, hero of the Chaco War, and remained in her family for four generations: it is sometimes known as the **Casa Cueto**, after her. Today the house is used as a centre for literature, with exhibition rooms for books and items belonging to Paraguay's most famous novelist, Augusto Roa Bastos (see box on page 92). There is a library of 5,000 Paraguayan novels, an audiovisual auditorium and a research centre. Book launches are held here.

The **Casa Bicentenario de las Artes Visuales** [75 F3] (*Azara 845 e/ Estados Unidos y Tacuary; ☎ 021 443736; m 0981 713390; ⌚ 09.00–17.00 Mon–Fri, closed Sat & Sun*) – occasionally referred to as the **Casa Centurión** – has a neat square façade,

ROQUE GONZÁLEZ

Roque González de Santa Cruz (1576–1628) is Paraguay's first canonised saint, along with two other Jesuit priests martyred at the same time as him, Alonso Rodríguez and Juan del Castillo. The group is usually known as 'San Roque González and his companions', and they were canonised by Pope John Paul II during his visit to Paraguay in 1988.

San Roque González should not be confused with plain San Roque, the medieval French saint who worked with plague victims, contracted the plague himself, and is shown with a wound in his thigh and a dog bringing him food; there are innumerable statues of him in Paraguay. San Roque González, by contrast, is shown with an arrow through his exposed heart, and a picture of the Virgin in his hands, for reasons that will become apparent.

Roque González was born in 1576 of a half-indigenous Paraguayan mother, though his father was Spanish. He was ordained initially into the diocesan clergy of Asunción, and was made parish priest of the cathedral, but when he realised he was going to be made vicar general of the diocese at the young age of 33, he joined the Jesuits to escape the promotion and dedicate his life to working with the indigenous.

His first mission was to the warlike Guaicurú indigenous of the Chaco, where he succeeded in winning their trust, but for his next mission he was sent among the Guaraní. He was not the founder of San Ignacio Guasú – the first Jesuit Reduction in Paraguay, founded at the end of 1609 – but he was its chief architect, arriving there as superior in 1611. His talent and energy were summed up by his contemporary P Francisco del Valle when he wrote that he was 'carpenter, architect and builder; he does it all himself … he wields the axe and works the wood and transports it to the construction site, yoking up the team of oxen himself'.

Roque González helped to pioneer the shape that all subsequent Reductions would take, with music, dance and theatre; carving, painting and metalwork; an economy built on shared labour rather than money; care for the sick in a mutually

with symmetrical flights of steps leading up to main door. This house is devoted to documenting the visual arts, principally Paraguayan films, and is named after Ignacio Núñez Soler (1891–1983), who used to paint houses, squares, festivals and plays. The house has a fascinating collection of short historical documentaries ranging from two minutes upwards, showing snatches of historical events or indigenous customs: the staff will gladly put on a film of your choice in the little cinema.

The **Casa de la Música Agustín Barrios** [75 F3] (*Cerro Corá e/ Tacuary y Estados Unidos; 021 443736; 07.00–13.30 Mon–Fri, closed Sat & Sun*) is the most stunning of the bicentenary houses, with its broad frontage, narrow columns, rounded corners, high windows and internal rooms opening one onto another. At the heart of the house is a glass-topped cupola where light pours in through blue, yellow and mauve glass. If the gate is locked on Cerro Corá you may be able to gain access through the Casa de las Artes Visuales, as the two houses back onto each other. The house is named after the great classical guitarist (see box on page 196), and it is also sometimes called the **Casa Jure**. The house was formally opened as a museum of music in June 2014. It includes a library, a small auditorium, the harp of Félix Pérez Cardozo (see page 23), and manuscripts of Manuel Ortiz Guerrero (see page 320).

The **Casa Josefina Pla** [75 F2] is just one block away (*25 de mayo 972 c/ Estados Unidos; 08.00–14.30 Mon–Fri*). Although less dramatic on the outside, it has a responsible community; and the use of the native language of Guaraní, rather than Spanish, except for church services (which had to be in Latin).

Not content with staying in San Ignacio, he set out to build more Reductions, travelling always with a picture of Mary as La Conquistadora (the Conqueror), which represented his belief that the true rulers of the Guaraní people were Christ and his mother, who were victorious over the Europeans with their force of arms. He founded 12 Reductions in all, at the rate of about one a year, moving in a southeasterly direction into the region known as Tapé, south of both the Río Paraná and the Río Uruguay, until the year of his martyrdom in 1628.

Sadly, nearly all the Tapé Reductions were overrun and destroyed by the *bandeirantes* (slave-traders) coming from São Paulo, who captured and sold half a million Guaraní in the slave markets of São Paulo, not to mention many more who were killed as being too weak to be of economic use. It was not, however, the *bandeirantes* who were responsible for his death, but a small group of hostile *caciques* (tribal chieftains) who saw their power being eroded, notably Ñesú. He sent assassins who clubbed Roque González to death as he was attaching a clapper to the bell in the new Reduction of Ca'aro, in present-day Missões, Brazil. Alonso Rodriguez heard the clamour and ran out to see what was going on, and he too was murdered, as was an elderly indigenous man who reproached the assassins, and paid for his courage with his life. The Jesuits of today are trying to secure the canonisation of this nameless Guaraní hero, to whom they have given the name Arasunú (Guaraní 'Thunder').

The heart of the dead Roque González is alleged to have reproached the assassins, and they tried unsuccessfully to silence it by piercing it with an arrow, and then throwing it into the fire. The allegedly incorrupt heart of the saint is displayed today in the Cristo Rey church in Asunción (see page 113).

Juan del Castillo was killed two days later, in a nearby Reduction, on the orders of the same Ñesú. The date of his death, 17 November, has been taken as the joint feast day of the three martyrs.

striking long internal courtyard lined with pillars and topped with a pitched glass roof. The rooms along the two sides of this courtyard are offices, mostly of Fondec (the national fund for culture and the arts).

The **Casa del Teatro Edda de los Ríos** [75 F2] (*25 de mayo 993 c/ Estados Unidos*) is devoted to the theatre. It has been renovated and was opened to the public in June 2014, with a photographic collection and a costume once worn by the Paraguayan actress Edda de los Ríos. The house was previously lived in by the De Gásperi family, so is sometimes known as the **Casa de Gásperi**.

The opening of one remaining Casa del Bicentenario is still awaited, the **Casa Zanotti**, which will be the new seat of the IMA (*Instituto Municipal de Arte; Presidente Franco y Montevideo*), where there are schools of dance, singing, drama and elocution, arts for children and a conservatory of music.

Biblioteca Nacional [72 C2] (*De la Residenta 820 c/ Perú; ☎ 021 204670; e binacpy@hotmail.com; ⌚ 07.00–18.00 Mon–Fri*) The large reference library lies close to the Gran Hotel de Paraguay and is open to the public.

Cementerio de la Recoleta [79 A2] (*Mariscal López y Chóferes del Chaco; ⌚ 07.30–17.00 daily*) The church of La Recoleta, begun in 1853, stands at the entrance to this 13ha cemetery, a well-known site in the city. It has some notable monuments, such as the Art Nouveau *La Llorona* (*Av C, calle 57*), the tomb of Madame Lynch's baby daughter, Corinna Adelaide Lynch (*Av A, calle 9*), and the urn of Madame Lynch herself; when you exit the church to the left, turn first right and it is the third tomb.

Costanera The long-awaited 3.8km coast road is open at last, and has transformed the riverside into a place where people go to walk, cycle, hold events and simply pass the time, especially at weekends. The west end begins next to the Port (see page 112), that is, from the end of Montevideo (Colón being one-way in the other direction), and the eastern access is a continuation of General Santos. There is a long beach, but bathing is not recommended due to pollution. The magnificent Palacio de López can be appreciated from its other side. You can hire bicycles from the port end. A second stretch of the Costanera is about to be built, which will extend it from the General Santos access point up to the Avenida Primer Presidente and the Jardín Botánico.

OUTSIDE THE CITY CENTRE

Loma San Jerónimo [72 B1] Asunción's oldest barrio, the hitherto little-known Loma San Jerónimo (*Facebook: Loma San Jerónimo*), was once the centre of Asunción, before it was a city, and today is only marginally off-centre. It has recently been developed in a highly imaginative way, in accordance with the style of the local people, to become what Senatur calls the city's 'first tourist barrio'. The houses on these five or six winding streets and alleyways are painted in vivid yellow, green, purple, orange and pink, and have brightly painted notices and murals. On Saturdays and Sundays from 09.00 to 17.00 they serve as simple bars and restaurants. One home offers its high roof terrace as a viewpoint over the river, and the information centre (*Piravevé 2448;* ☎ *021 452493;* ⏲ *09.00–17.00 Sat & Sun*) has local guides who can show you around for a modest fee. Just on the days when the rest of Asunción shuts up and goes to sleep, you can go to San Jerónimo to find a bit of movement. Because it is close to the port, you can combine it with the Saturday afternoon Puerto Abierto (see page 112).

It is a tricky place to find, although it is tucked right up to the side of the centre, to the west of Colón. One of the streets of San Jerónimo is called Estrella, and this is, in fact, the same street as the Estrella in the city centre, although it looks as though it stops, and you have to climb some steps to find your way through. Alternatively, take the extension of Palma, now called Avenida República, until you come to some steep steps on your left, painted in all the colours of the rainbow. (If you continue straight, you will come to the new Parque de la Solidaridad being constructed on the water's edge.) Or take General Díaz beyond Colón, until you come to a small square, Plaza de Dr Gaspar Rodríguez de Francia. The exit from the plaza immediately to your right will lead you to a sign '*Bienvenidos a Loma San Jerónimo*'. That takes you on to the street Piravevé (Guaraní, 'Flying Fish'), which leads to the Pasaje Bicentenario, then to Estrella, Pasaje Día y Medio, and so to the *mirador* (viewpoint) and eventually to the Oratorio.

On the days when they cook, the gastronomy is both typical and tempting. Casa del Pescador cooks fish dishes; Cocido Literario sells the famous *cocido quemado*; a third cooks beef in a *tatakua* (outside wood-fired oven); you see notices for *pasta frola, torta mermelada, alfajores, chipa guasú, sopa, mbejú* and *empanada*. It is an excellent introduction to the food of the people cooked by the people.

When the conquistadors established the fort that was to become Asunción, this area on the shoulder of the bay was the obvious first place for the new indigenous residents to settle, and the residents are descendants of that original stock. When Dr Francia laid out the capital on the grid pattern, San Jerónimo escaped being squared up, because it was already occupied and was too higgledy piggedly to change. The houses are built directly on rock, without foundations, and the stream Arroyo Jaén, which once went through it, is now buried underneath asphalt. Originally the barrio went right down to the river, but in the time of Carlos Antonio López a naval base was built on the bank, so San Jerónimo perches just above and behind that, with some houses higher than others and irregular steps linking them all together.

The barrio celebrates Carnival and Semana Santa, but most typically the **Day of the Cross** on 3 May, Kurusú Ára, when the bell of the Oratorio rings at 06.00 and people adorn a cross with strings of *chipa* or sweets. At 09.00 there is Mass, and in the evening at 17.00 people drink *cocido* and eat the *chipa* which has been taken down from the cross. It is a feast that has its origins back in the days of the Roman emperor Constantine, when fragments of the true cross of Christ were believed to have been discovered, but it took on a Paraguayan flavour when the Jesuits established it in place of an earlier celebration around the mythological creature Kurupí.

Santísima Trinidad church [73 E1] (*Santísimo Sacramento y Santísima Trinidad;* ⌚ *08.00–11.00 & 15.00–19.00 Tue–Sat & 08.00–11.00 Sat; masses 07.00 Mon–Fri, 19.00 Sat, 07.30 & 10.00 sung & 19.00 Sun*) This imposing church was designed by Alessandro Ravizza (the architect of the cathedral, the Panteón and the Recova). The imposing façade is built up in horizontal layers, topped by an iron cross, and there is an integrated bell tower on the left side, although this was added later. The church was built in 1856 by President Carlos Antonio López, who intended it as his family chapel and future mausoleum, and stole for it the side altars from the beautiful old church in Yaguarón (see pages 173–6). He added the figure of St Charles Borromeo (his patron saint) to the altar on the right, while the saint of his second name, St Anthony, is painted onto the reredos behind the high altar. Meanwhile the saints corresponding to his wife Juana Pabla Carrillo are placed in corresponding symmetry – St John the Baptist behind the left-hand altar, and St Paul behind the high altar. There is a beautiful painted wood ceiling. The grand façade and bell tower are showed off to best advantage when floodlit at night.

Ycuá Bolaños supermarket shrine [73 E1] On 1 August 2004 there was a horrific fire at the huge Ycuá Bolaños supermarket in which 400 people died. The principal reason for the deaths was that when the alarm was given the supermarket owner ordered his staff to lock all the fire escapes so that people could not get out. His idea was to prevent looting in the confusion, but instead hundreds of people were burned alive. Ironically, the supermarket was named after a life-giving spring of water discovered by a Franciscan in the 17th century.

The huge burnt-out shell of the complex is on the corner of Artigas and Santísima Trinidad, in the northeast of the city. It is a massive reddish-brown tiled building, now scrawled with graffiti with messages such as 'Silencio nunca más' ('*Silence, never again*'). Inside the shell, the relatives and friends have made a museum and a shrine and there is a 3m x 6m painting of the tragedy, *Agosto en llamas* ('August in flames').

Parque de la Salud [73 E2] (⌚ *05.00–22.00 daily*) This park is run by IPS hospital (see page 95). It is great for walking and full of shady trees, interesting vegetation, flowers and birds. You need to show your passport or ID card both when you enter and when you leave, and guards patrol, keeping the park safe. Circular paths provide 1,500m of running or cycling track. The names on the trees are in Guaraní and Latin, and there are frequent drinking water fountains. There is good lighting at night. To reach it take Sacramento, then Manuel Peña along the south side of the IPS hospital, where the traffic lights are. Carry straight on until the asphalted bit of the road turns right, and you will see the entrance just after God's Pan café (see page 89).

Jardín Botánico y Zoológico [73 F1] (*Artigas y Primer Presidente; ☎ 021 281389 /90; park ⏲ 06.00–17.00, free admission; zoo ⏲ 09.00–17.00 Tue–Sun; Gs7,000, cars Gs6,000, minibuses GS20,000*) A little further to the northeast from Ycuá Bolaños is the 250ha Jardín Botánico, out of which 12ha form the zoo. The entrance is opposite the beginning of Artigas. Bus 44 will get you there from the centre (Cerro Corá).

The **zoo** has hippopotamuses, chimpanzees, spider monkeys and peacocks, as well as the more familiar Paraguayan animals such as capybaras, peccaries, foxes, tortoises and parrots, not forgetting the magnificent Paraguayan jaguars (with three cubs born in November 2013), and lions and Bengali tigers. There is a lake for caimans and another for fish. There has been some criticism about cages being too small. Some improvements have been made, but more needs to be done.

The zoo contains two interesting houses, which belonged to Carlos Antonio López and his wife Juana Pabla Carrillo. The Casa Baja (Lower House) was converted into a Museum of Natural History in 1912, and houses a ghoulish collection of deformed animal foetuses in preserving jars. A little further on is the Casa Alta (Upper House) which is an elegant two-storey house with colonnade and balcony all around, and now is a museum of antiquities. Features of the extensive gardens include the fountain known as Fuente Kamba'i, the springs of Ykuá Madame Lynch and Ykuá López, the Jardín Romano and the Jardín Japonés.

On the east side of the Jardín Botánico is the **Asunción Golf Club**, nestling up against the curves of the fence. There is a secondary entrance to the garden where the two meet, and opposite is the former railway station of Trinidad, which Carlos Antonio López had built as close as possible to his house. Today this is where the tourist train trip used to start (see the box opposite). On the other side, between the Jardín Botánico and the river, there are plans to develop a Viñas Cué Ecological Park, to include the offices of Guyrá Paraguay (see page 76) and a wildlife rescue centre.

Close to the entrance to the Jardín Botánico is the Museo de la Silla (see pages 102–3), so it is worth combining the visits.

Parque Ñu Guazú [73 G2] (*Autopista*) This park on the way to the airport, just outside the Madame Lynch ring road, is a popular place for people to go walking or bicycling, especially at weekends. It has children's playgrounds, gardens and bars. The name means Big Field, and Guazú (big) is the same word as in San Ignacio Guasú, but here it is usually spelled with a z (the older spelling), although the new Avenida Ñu Guasú is usually spelled with an s.

Centro Familiar de Adoración [72 F4] (*Del Maestro 3471; www.cfa.org.py; ⏲ services 18.00 Sat, 10.00 & 19.00 Sun*) This is not in the run of normal sightseeing, but it is a phenomenon – a simply enormous Protestant church, with seating capacity for 10,000 people, and they are talking about an expansion to take 20,000. It is located just to the north of the junction between Mariscal López and Madame Lynch. Head towards town from the junction and take the first right: the church is one block away. It began as a small Bible study group under pastors Emilio and Betania Abreu, and grew at amazing speed. It has four storeys plus a basement and sub-basement, and from the top gallery of seats the preacher appears so tiny that an enormous blow-up has to be projected onto the walls.

Cerro Lambaré Mirador [72 A4] A tall monument with a cross on top, placed on a hill to the south of the Bañado Sur, occupies a position previously taken by a statue of Stroessner. For a while it was a haunt of drug addicts but has now been cleaned up and has gardens and a view. It is worth a stop if you are in a car, and the 23 bus will take you there if you are not; the 23 also goes to the Jardín Botánico, way on the other side of town (see opposite).

EXCURSIONS

RAKIURÁ RESORT DAY (*América c/ Capitan Brizuela, Luque;* ☎ *021 645021; www.rakiuraparaguay.com*) A popular day out from Asunción is to the sports park near the airport, called Rakiurá Resort Day, where there are three hectares of parkland with

TRAIN JOURNEY

When the railway was built in the mid-19th century by English engineers under Carlos Antonio López, it was at the cutting edge of technology and one of the first railways in the continent. After the Triple Alliance War the line was continued until it reached Encarnación and crossed the river into Argentina. However, eventually motor vehicles were found to go faster than the steam train. The railway then became a means of transport for the poor, who were prepared to spend all day travelling for the sake of saving a little money. Then even that faded. However, some form of a regular service was operating up until the late 1990s, when the train fell off the rails when carrying a Sunday school outing, and a little girl was killed. All services were suspended for many years.

In the first decade of this century the stretch from the Botanical Gardens of Asunción to Areguá was re-opened as a Sunday excursion, with a lot of publicity. It used to be a delight to do this trip, known as the Tren del Lago. The tickets were the original ones: old-fashioned rectangles of thick cardboard with slightly wonky printing. The engine was a proper Thomas-the-Tank-Engine-style chuff-chuff, and it claimed to be the last working steam train in the world to be fired by wood rather than coal. The engine was called appropriately *President C A López*, and it pulled a huge wagon of logs as well as a couple of passenger carriages. It had a shrill whistle and a shiny bell that went dong-dong before the train set off. It travelled at a stately 15km/h, and if that seems slow, consider that it is three times as fast as walking and a lot more restful. You could observe from the windows families coming out to wave at the train going past – evidently proud of this feature of national life.

Suddenly in August 2009 the train journey was discontinued, without a whisper of publicity, and eventually, the word came that a bridge was waiting for engineering repairs. The line would re-open around June 2010, it was said. June came and went, but the line never did re-open. After a few years the rails were taken up to make way for the new Avenida Ñu Guasú (see pages 70–1), so now the train will never run again, at least not on that particular stretch, though it is hoped that it may someday function on other stretches.

However, the railway museum in Asunción is excellent (see pages 104–5), and the old workshops for building the trains, in Sapucai (see page 169), also very interesting. This note is added here for those who are wondering what happened to the famous Tren del Lago trip. RIP.

sports pitches, an aquatic park, a gym and a spa. There are snack bars, and facilities for football, beach volleyball, tennis, putting, golf, swimming and horseriding. To get to Rakiurá, take the airport road but continue on past the airport for less than a kilometre, then double back for half a kilometre on the road América, that joins it from the right. This is technically Luque rather than Asunción, although it is well out of the centre of Luque (see pages 144–8).

CHACO'Í Literally 'little Chaco', this is a very different kind of excursion – a humble little village of some charm on the opposite side of the Río Paraguay (so in the Chaco), with an imaginative new restaurant, Manguruyú, that has become something of a cult (*Río Paraguay c/ Vice Presidente Sánchez; Facebook: Manguruyú; ⌚ dinner, Thu–Sat 20.00–midnight, lunch Fri–Sun 12.30–16.00;* **$$**). The name is the Guaraní for a catfish. There is a building of character right on the water's edge dating back to 1902 but the guests sit outside – originally just on a riverside terrace but now all along the beach. There are striking views at night over the water to the lights of the city, including the floodlit Palacio de López. Begun by Spaniards in February 2014, the restaurant became an instant success and despite capacity for 130 people reservation is now essential, exclusively via the inbox of their Facebook page (name, number of people, contact number), with people booking up to two weeks ahead. There is a wide menu but they specialise in fish dishes and casseroles, all at very reasonable prices. The house sangria includes strawberries, oranges, peaches and a splash of blackcurrant liqueur. The boats from Asunción leave every half hour daily from a point just to the right of the port (*⌚ 06.30–19.00 daily; Gs7,000 return; Facebook: Lanchas de la Bahía*), and after that, when the restaurant is open, they go directly to Manguruyú without charging as the price of the ferry is included in the restaurant bill. The crossing takes 20 to 25 minutes. You can also get there by land – crossing the Puente Remanso, left in the direction of Puerto Falcón as far as the intersection with Ruta 12, then 7km left again – but it is a long way round. Manguruyú was inundated in 2014 when the river flooded, and the staff then devoted their energies to helping distribute flood-relief donations to local families, declaring 'The flood has made us close our doors but has called us to open our hearts'.

INDIAN RESERVE Visiting a village of the **Maká** indigenous, on the edges of Asunción, is easy to arrange. Basically, you can just show up and ask for Rubén Riquelme (**m** *0985 871116*), who is one of the Maká; then you give a voluntary donation. They will have craft to sell. It is always best to let them know in advance of a visit, but it is not strictly necessary. The village is just before the Puente Remanso (where the Ruta 9 crosses into the Chaco), on the right-hand side. To get there, ask for Mariano Roque Alonso (see map on page 126); linea 44 (from Cerro Corá in the centre), or Brújula from the Terminal, are among the buses that go there. Most of the indigenous that you will see in Asunción – at the airport or in the streets, selling their wares – are Maká from this village.

CIRCUITO DE ORO The most popular excursion from Asunción is the Circuito de Oro, which is a tour of the towns close to Asunción noted for their craft or for their Franciscan churches, or for both. See the next chapter for details.

4

Circuito de Oro

Departamentos:
Central; gobernación ☎ *0291 432591/2*
Cordillera; gobernación ☎ *0511 243103/242351*
Paraguarí; gobernación ☎ *0531 432211/432979*

The famous Circuito de Oro, or Golden Circuit, is a collection of small towns to the east and southeast of Asunción, each reachable within about an hour. The great majority of traditional Paraguayan crafts are based in one or other of these towns, so you can do a circuit that takes you from workshop to workshop, seeing (for example) three or four of the following: the production of harps in Luque, silver *filigrana* jewellery, also in Luque, pottery in Areguá, sculpture of wooden saints in Capiatá, *ñanduti* lacework in Itauguá, leatherwork in Atyrá, more sculpture of wooden saints in Tobatí, *ponchos de sesenta listas* in Piribebúy, more pottery in Itá, and so back to Asunción.

In its simplest form, you do it in a day, going out on Ruta 1, crossing over to Ruta 2 on the road that goes through Piribebúy, and coming back on Ruta 2 – or vice versa. However, there are a lot of interesting places just to the north and south of Ruta 2, so with these deviations the route can become more complicated. The road through Luque and Areguá is one such loop. Another loop is San Bernardino, Altos, Atyrá. And a third is Pirayú, which provides a way of foreshortening the circuit, because it provides an earlier link between Ruta 1 and Ruta 2 – with the loss, however, of some of the most interesting places. An even more abbreviated tour can be done by making the crossover from Itá (on Ruta 1) to Itauguá (on Ruta 2). Here is an outline of the considerable number of towns covered in this chapter:

- **Towns on Ruta 2** San Lorenzo, Capiatá, Itauguá, Ypacaraí, Caacupé, Itacurubí
- **Towns to the north of Ruta 2** Luque, Areguá, San Bernardino, Altos, Emboscada, Atyrá, Tobatí, Vapor Cué
- **Towns to the south of Ruta 2** Pirayú, Piribebúy, Valenzuela, Sapucai
- **Towns on Ruta 1** Itá, Yaguarón, Paraguarí, Carapeguá, Ybycuí, San Roque González, Quiindý, Caapucú

This same area is now being promoted simultaneously under two other names, Pyporé (Guaraní 'footsteps') and the **Camino Franciscano**. The latter name draws attention to the fact that many of the old Franciscan Reductions were sited in the same area that is now rich in craft workshops. (The Jesuit Reductions, by contrast, were a little further from Asunción, in the *departamentos* of Misiones and Itapúa). A tour of the Circuito de Oro can therefore take in both historical art and current craft. Capiatá, for example, has an important Franciscan church and a famous workshop of carved wooden saints. Itauguá has a splendid museum of Jesuit and Franciscan statues, and is also the one place in Paraguay where the famous *ñanduti* lace is made. Atyrá has a Franciscan reredos in its church, and makes leather sandals. Tobatí is known for

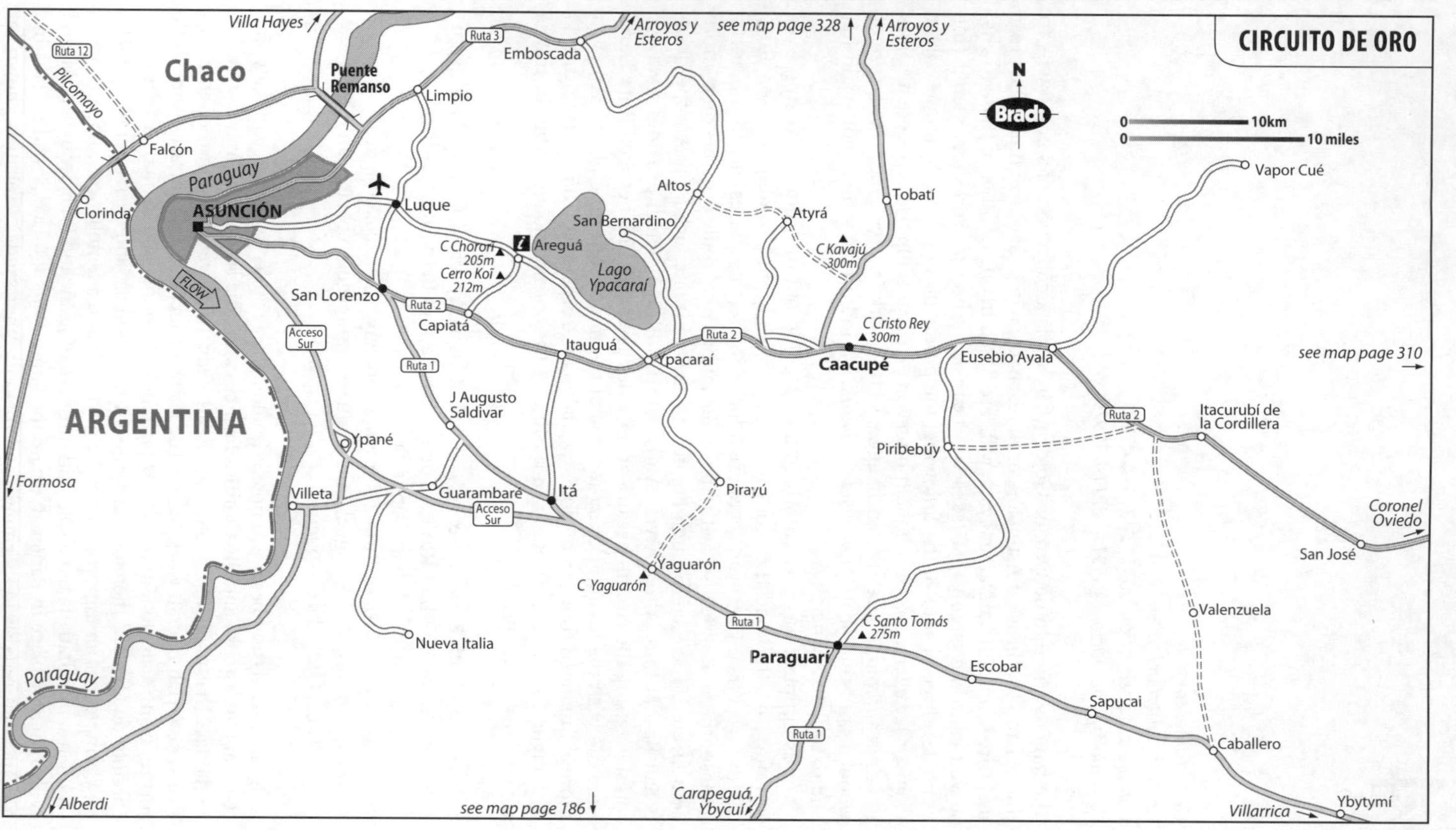
CIRCUITO DE ORO
N
Bradt
0 10km
0 10 miles
Villa Hayes
see map page 328
Arroyos y Esteros
Arroyos y Esteros
Ruta 12
Pilcomayo
Chaco
Puente Remanso
Ruta 3
Emboscada
Limpio
Falcón
Paraguay
Clorinda
ASUNCIÓN
Luque
Altos
Tobatí
Atyrá
San Bernardino
C Kavajú 300m
C Chororí 205m
Areguá
Cerro Koi 212m
Lago Ypacaraí
FLOW
San Lorenzo
Ruta 2
Capiatá
Acceso Sur
Itauguá
Ypacaraí
C Cristo Rey 300m
Caacupé
Eusebio Ayala
Vapor Cué
see map page 310
Ruta 1
J Augusto Saldivar
ARGENTINA
Ypané
Itacurubí de la Cordillera
Piribebúy
Formosa
Villeta
Guarambaré
Itá
Pirayú
Coronel Oviedo
San José
Yaguarón
C Yaguarón
Valenzuela
C Santo Tomás 275m
Nueva Italia
Paraguarí
Escobar
Sapucai
Caballero
Alberdi
see map page 186
Carapeguá, Ybycuí
Villarrica
Ybytymí

craftwork in wood and in pottery, and has the ancient twin statue to the Virgin of Caacupé. Piribebúy has an important Franciscan church with a fine reredos, and is also where the *poncho de sesanta listas* is made. Itá is famed for its pottery, and has an old reredos in a Franciscan chuch with many original features. Its neighbouring town of Yaguarón is famed for having the most beautiful and complete church of that period to be found anywhere in Paraguay.

However, two of the principal tourist attractions on this route are famed neither for their craft nor for their Franciscan heritage. San Bernardino is the most popular holiday town for Paraguayans, because of its beach on Lake Ypacaraí: in January all the hotels are full for the summer holiday, but through the rest of the year there is plenty of availability. And Caacupé, on Ruta 2, is the national Marian pilgrimage centre, and hundreds of thousands of Paraguayans walk to the basilica for the feast of the Immaculate Conception on 8 December. Through the rest of the year it is also well visited, and whether you are a Marian devotee or not, Caacupé represents an important feature of Paraguayan culture.

The Circuito de Oro can be done in an abbreviated form as a long day trip from Asunción, through an agency or with one of the tour companies on pages 76–7. Or you can hire a car (with or without a driver) and create your own route, with the freedom to spend nights along the way. You can also do a form of the circuit on public transport, if time is no object, and if you can stand the rattle and lurching of the buses.

GETTING OUT OF ASUNCIÓN

BY CAR If you hire a car, then getting out of Asunción is one of the biggest challenges you will face, due to the lack of road signs and a decent road map. (The maps you can buy either show the streets of Asunción or the main roads of the whole country, with very few maps providing anything to bridge the way between them.) Most Paraguayans learn to find their way by travelling first with other people. Here, then, is a beginners' guide for foreigners.

The first thing you need to know for negotiating your way out of Asunción is that there is a semi-ring road from northeast to southeast of the city, called **Madame Lynch** on its more northerly stretch, and on its more southerly stretch Defensores del Chaco – but more popularly known as **Calle Ultima** (the last road). **Cuatro Mojones** is the name of the big intersection where Calle Ultima crosses the road called Fernando de la Mora, which leads to the bus terminal.

At this point it would be useful to refresh your memory on the 'five-finger' layout of Asunción access roads (see map, page 126). **To leave the city**, working from north to south around the access roads follow the instructions given in the sections below.

To go north

From the centre, take Artigas, follow the edge of the Jardín Botánico, and you will then be on the **Ruta Transchaco**. Turn left to cross the Río Paraguay at Puente Remanso, after Mariano R Alonso, if you are going to the Chaco or crossing into Argentina at Clorinda: it is now called **Ruta 9**, which is another name for the Ruta Transchaco. Or carry straight on – this is now **Ruta 3** – through Limpio and onwards through Arroyos y Esteros, towards the northeast of Paraguay. Being a new highway, this is one of the few roads to have adequate road signs.

To go to the airport

From the centre, take España, which will change its name to Aviadores del Chaco, and then to the **Autopista** (not a real motorway – these do not yet exist in Paraguay). After you pass the football museum on the right (evident

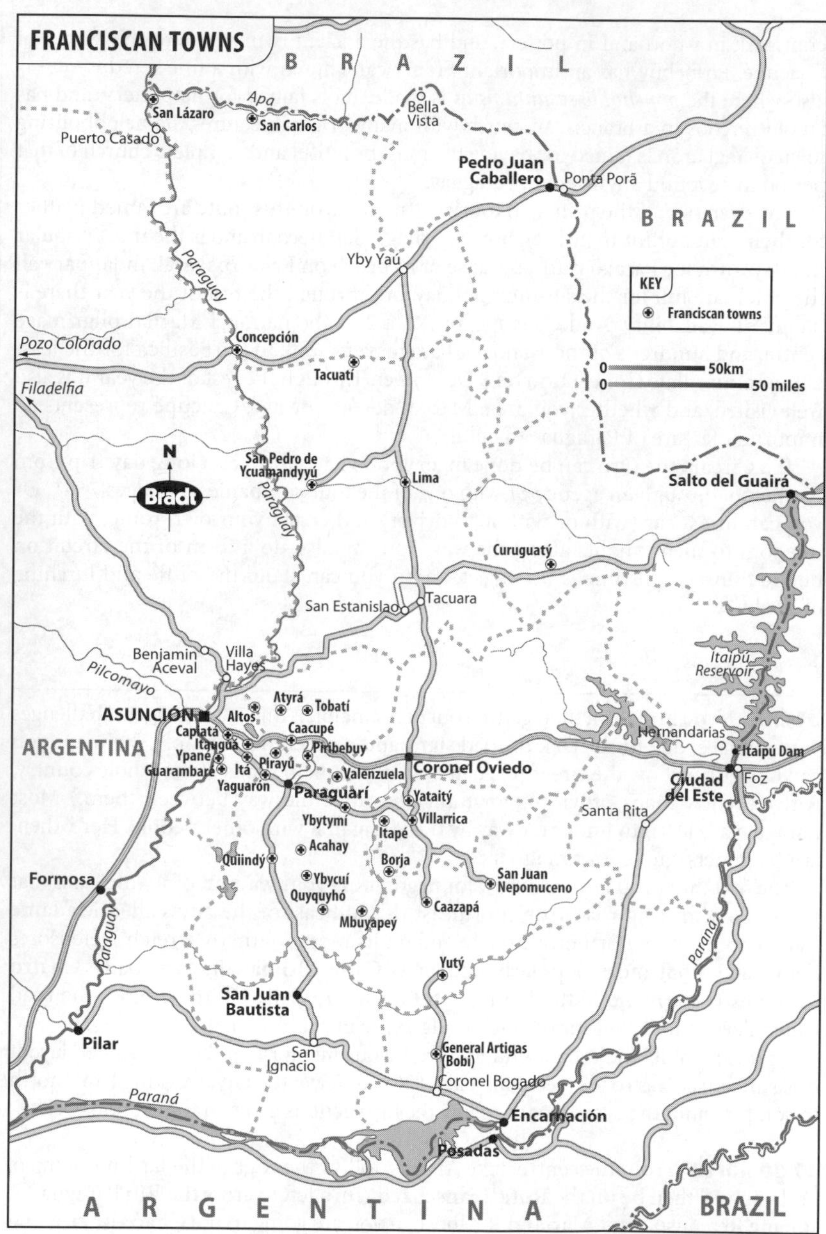

from its huge football outside) you will come to the airport on the left, where there is a roundabout. If you continue on the same road you will reach an urban area and a maze of streets, and eventually come out on Ruta 3, before Limpio.

To go east From the centre do one of the following: (1) take Mariscal López from the start, which will lead you on a straight fast road into San Lorenzo, from where you turn left onto Mariscal Estigarribia to get onto either Ruta 1 or Ruta 2. You want Ruta 2 to go east. Or (2) take España, but after the Shopping del Sol (on the left), take the fork right which is called Santa Teresa. This will join up with Mariscal López after crossing Madame Lynch. Then continue as above. Or (3) take Eusebio Ayala, which later changes its name to Mariscal Estigarribia, and leads you into San Lorenzo some five blocks to the west. Again, you must turn left, and then you will find the road dividing into Ruta 1 and Ruta 2. Because all these routes are complicated, slow and congested, there are plans to construct a new access road bypassing San Lorenzo, which will be called Acceso Este, or Laguna Grande.

Some people favour avoiding San Lorenzo, Capiatá and Itauguá completely by (4) taking a route through Luque and Areguá, and eventually coming out on Ruta 2 at Ypacaraí. There are no road signs for this route, but if you want to try it, follow the directions for driving to Luque on pages 144–5. Once in Luque, go past the

FRANCISCAN REDUCTIONS: HISTORY

The very first Franciscan Reduction was Altos in 1580 (30 years before the first Jesuit Reduction), followed in 1585 by Itá (one of the pottery towns). Soon afterwards came Yaguarón (which today has the only complete church left from the period of the Reductions) and Tobatí (which has a larger version of the Virgin of Caacupé). Next came Guarambaré, Ypané and Atyrá (reputedly 'the cleanest town' in Paraguay, and with leathercraft and an attractive rustic hotel, Casa del Monte).

All of these are early Franciscan foundations, though some, such as Atyrá and Tobatí, started in a different site: they moved from what is now the *departmento* of San Pedro to the present location in 1672 and 1699 respectively, due to attacks from other indigenous tribes. (Indeed, the origin of the twin Virgins carved by the Indio José of Tobatí was in this persecution; see box on page 142.)

Luis Bolaños went south of the Río Paraná in 1615 and left Paraguay to the Jesuits. But after a long gap, the Franciscans returned to founding Reductions in the late 18th century, with Itapé (north of Caazapá) in 1678, and San Lázaro and San Carlos by the Río Apa, along the northern frontier of present-day Paraguay. In the same period the European settlers founded the historic cities of Concepción and San Pedro de Ycuamandyyú in the north, which inevitably were affected by Franciscan influence. The old cathedral of San Pedro, still standing and in good condition, is an example of a church in a Franciscan town (for Fray Pedro de Bartolomé was co-founder and first chaplain to the settlement) that was not founded as a mission for the indigenous. There is still a strong presence of Third Order Franciscans (ie: lay members) in San Pedro.

Further south, in central eastern Paraguay, chapels began to be built in the 18th century to serve the needs of the local people who lived scattered around the region, and while these were not true Reductions (because they were not founded to gather together a group of indigenous in one place) they are rightly regarded as Franciscan towns: Capiatá, Itauguá, Pirayú, Caacupé, Piribebúy, Valenzuela and Bobí.

In 1848 the Franciscan Reductions stopped being Reductions: by order of President Carlos Antonio López, the community lands were appropriated by the state, and the indigenous were granted Paraguayan citizenship. The towns became *mestizo* (mixed race), and were absorbed into the wider Paraguayan population.

two plazas (to your left) and continue straight on until you reach a junction with a broad double avenue. This road is called Humaitá, and you turn right for three blocks, and then left. (There is a small model of the ruins of Humaitá, see page 234.) This turn is called las Residentas and may not look very promising, but it will lead you eventually into Areguá. Find your way through Areguá to the road for Ypacaraí (Ruta Areguá Patiño) with the help of the map on page 150. (You need to move over a couple of blocks to the left.) When you get to Ypacaraí you turn left onto Ruta 2 to continue east. This may sound complicated (and it is) but bear in mind that none of the routes east out of Asunción are easy.

To go southeast From the centre, do one of the following: (1) take Mariscal López, which will lead you into San Lorenzo, as above. Then take Ruta 1. Or (2) take Eusebio Ayala, which later changes its name to Mariscal Estigarribia, and leads you into San Lorenzo, as above. Or, best of all, (3) take the road Fernando de la Mora, which goes past the bus terminal, through Cuatro Mojones, and then straight on. Eventually, it will join up with Ruta 1 on the far side of Itá, some 35km out of Asunción, where there is a big roundabout in the middle of the countryside. This route is called the **Acceso Sur**, and many car drivers prefer it, because it cuts out some of the long crawl out of the city, bypassing San Lorenzo. The buses take the route along Eusebio Ayala and through San Lorenzo, because it gives them more opportunities to pick up passengers on the way.

ASUNCIÓN ACCESS ROADS

To confuse things even more, the *town* of Fernando de la Mora is between Asunción and San Lorenzo, on the roads Mariscal Estigarribia and Mariscal López, and the *road* Fernando de la Mora does not go through it, but only borders it for a short distance.

Finally, some clarification is needed of how to find your way through **San Lorenzo**. nowhere is Paraguay's lack of road signs more frustrating than here, when you are trying to get out of Asunción onto Ruta 1 (towards Encarnación and the south) or onto Ruta 2 (towards Ciudad del Este and the east). If you have come into San Lorenzo on Mariscal López, the secret is to turn left two blocks after the church – which is on your right as you drive through. At this left turn – where many other cars will also be turning left – you can then see ahead of you, above the road, the signs for **Ruta 2** to the left, and **Ruta 1** to the right. From there on, it is all straight driving. If you come in on Eusebio Ayala, you also have to take a right-angle turn to the left, as shown on the map on page 133.

One reader of the first edition wrote in to give the following handy rule for getting out of Gran Asunción when you do not know how to recognise where San Lorenzo begins. You will go past an area where there are no houses: this is the campus of the Universidad Nacional, immediately before San Lorenzo, and it will be on your left if you took Mariscal López and on your right if you took Eusebio Ayala. Call the first street you cross after that 'one' (14 de mayo). Then count the streets and turn right on number 'seven'. You will then be on Mariscal Estigarribia, which soon divides into Ruta 1 and Ruta 2 (see map opposite).

BY BUS If you are leaving Asunción by bus, then you avoid the problem of getting lost. If you are going to a town close to Asunción, you will probably find that the long-distance buses will not take you, even though they pass through those places. You will need to take a medium-distance bus, which you find by going down the underpass from within the Terminal building, to reach the lower level. These buses go to places like Caacupé, passing through other towns *en route*, and the fares are extremely cheap.

There are also local buses (*linea*) which you can pick up on the street, for example from the bus stop on República Argentina immediately outside the Terminal. The bus marked 'ITA' goes to a lot of towns on the Circuito de Oro – San Lorenzo, Capiatá, Itauguá and then Itá. However you take your bus, you will find the travelling bumpy and tiring, so you will probably not want to do more than a couple of towns in a day, and maybe only one.

If you are coming into the city on a bus on Ruta 1 and want to go out on Ruta 2 (or vice versa), then you will save an enormous amount of time if you swap roads in San Lorenzo, rather than going to the Asunción Terminal. You will need to walk one block to pick up one of the buses that go along the other road, and since it is very difficult to describe any landmark in the prolonged urban sprawl, it is best to ask the driver to show you where to get off and which direction to walk.

If you are arriving by bus to visit the capital, then the easiest way is to carry on to the bus terminal in Asunción, and take your bearings from there. But with more experience you can save time by getting off the bus in San Lorenzo at the point where the bus driver calls out '*Desvío Luque*' (shortly after you go past the cemetery, where there is a red-brick wall at the corner), walking around the corner to the right, and then taking a number 12, 26 or a 56 local bus direct to the centre of Asunción, bypassing the slow drag into the southeastern quarter of Asunción where the bus terminal is. Some people get off at the Shopping Multiplaza, which is already in Asunción on the road Eusebio Ayala, and has local buses that go more directly to the centre. And vice versa, if you are confident, you can leave Asunción by the same route.

SUGGESTED CIRCUITS

CIRCUITO DE ORO TOURS OFFERED BY AGENCIES If you would like to follow a suggested route, then the easiest way to do it is on a set tour with an agency. They will know exactly where they are going, so will cover a lot more places, and will build in a presentation that includes scenery, art, traditional culture and legend.

The disadvantage of some of these tours is that they go at such a pace that you spend most of your time driving around in a comfortable air-conditioned vehicle, rather than exploring. The emphasis is on doing a lot of places, rather than on doing each place thoroughly. The advantage is that you get through a lot, without having to do any planning.

A company that is currently advertising a 7-hour tour is **DTP** (*General Bruguez 353 e/ Mcal Estigarribia y 25 de mayo;* ☎ *021 221816;* e *dtp@dtp.com.py; www.dtp.com.py; see also page 76*). The price per person varies according to the number in the group, but they can do it for just one person or for eight or more. Their route takes you to Itá, Yaguarón, Piribebúy, Caacupé, San Bernardino and Itauguá.

A version of the Circuito de Oro called 'Siete Pueblos', which does not go down as far as Ruta 1, is offered by **Martín Molinas** (*Mariotti, esq Pres. Santiago Leon;* ☎ *021 282529;* m *0981 450207/0976 450207;* e *travelservice@internetpersonal.com.py; www.travelserviceparaguay.com*). It takes in San Lorenzo, Capiatá, Itauguá, Yparacaí, San Bernardino (with lunch there), Luque and Areguá. He can add on Caacupé as an optional eighth town.

However, most tour operators will gladly offer you a Circuito de Oro day tour if you ask them, irrespective of whether it is advertised on their website.

DESIGN YOUR OWN TOUR If you prefer to be independent, the information in this chapter is sufficiently detailed for you to plan a circuit that suits you. Here are some suggested routes that you should be able to manage if you hire a car. If you look at the regional map at the beginning of this chapter, you will see the shape of each circuit. If you try to do the tour by public bus, you will only get half of it done because you will be more tired. Be sure to check underneath the individual town information below for fuller details of facilities and opening times, as the times below are only intended as a rough guide and do not reflect variations for weekends and Mondays, nor for winter/summer. For Paraguayans the two highlights are the beach resort San Bernardino and the pilgrimage centre Caacupé, but these may not be priorities for foreigners, so they do not figure prominently in the tours below.

Where to stay Most but not all places have a cheap *hospedaje*, but if you are looking for a better-quality hotel, then here are some of the chief options. Some of them are really special places to stay. But remember you could also use Asunción as your base, and return there each night. Remember also that if you go to an *estancia*, the idea is to spend some time there enjoying nature and the activities, and not just to get a bed for the night.

Areguá – Los Jardines de Areguá or one of the *posadas* (see page 149)
Atyrá – Casa del Monte (see page 158)
Caacupé – Alta Gracia (see pages 141–2)
Capiatá – Hotel Los Lagos or Jardín Alemán (see page 135)
Itauguá – Olimpo Hotel (see page 139)
Paraguarí – Hotel Gabriela (see page 177)

Piribebúy – La Quinta *estancia* or Hotel Parador Chololó (see page 166)
San Bernardino – Hotel del Lago or Linda India (see page 153)
Valenzuela – La Cascada (see page 167)

Where to eat and drink Wherever you go there will be a cheap bar where you can pick up lunch, but if you want something more in the way of a restaurant you should plan in one of the following towns for lunchtime:

Areguá – La Cocina de Gulliver or Los Jardines de Areguá (see page 149)
Atyrá – Casa del Monte (see page 158)
Capiatá – Hotel Los Lagos or Jardín Alemán (see page 135)
Itauguá – Olimpo Hotel (see page 139)
Luque – Restaurant Real (see page 145)
Paraguarí – La Frutería or Hotel Gabriela (see page 177)
San Bernardino – Hotel del Lago, Selva Negra or Café Francés (see pages 153, 154 or 155)
Ypacaraí – El Galpón de Don Ernesto (see page 140)

One-day mini-tour For a mini-tour that is still a circuit beginning and ending in Asunción, while incorporating three craft towns, one old church and two museums, visit **Luque** for its *filigrana* silver jewellery, followed by **Areguá** for its art galleries, good architecture and pottery. You can stop for lunch here, at La Cocina de Gulliver, before continuing on to **Capiatá** with its fine old church (🕘 *14.30–18.00*) and Museo Mitológico (🕘 *08.00–noon and 14.00–17.00*). The last stop on the route is **San Lorenzo**, which has the Museo Boggiani and a shop of indigenous craft (🕘 *09.00–17.30 or later in summer*).

One-day short tour via Itá and Itauguá Here is a slightly longer tour that gets you down to Ruta 1 as well as Ruta 2, and gives you five craft towns, two old churches, and three very different museums. You can do it in either direction, but the suggested version combines better with opening hours. If you possibly can, go just a little further along Ruta 1 to be able to include Yaguarón as well, before doubling back to Itá.

San Lorenzo Museo Boggiani and its shop of indigenous craft (🕘 *09.00–17.30*)
Itá Centro Artesanal, church with reredos (🕘 *07.00–11.30*)
Itauguá *Ñanduti* lace, old streets, museum (🕘 *07.00–10.45 & 14.00–17.00*), lunch at Hotel Olimpo
Capiatá fine old church (🕘 *14.30–18.00*), Museo Mitológico (🕘 *08.00–noon & 14.00–17.00*)
Areguá art galleries, good architecture, pottery
Luque *filigrana* silver jewellery, finish with dinner at Restaurant Real

One-day standard tour via Pirayú Here is a fuller tour that gives still more of the flavour of the route, with five craft towns, four fine Franciscan churches, four very different museums and two towns with interesting or old architecture, although it still leaves out many of the best places. You would need to start early and it does not give you very long in each place. You can do it in either direction, but the suggested version combines better with opening hours.

San Lorenzo Museo Boggiani and its shop of indigenous craft (🕘 *09.00–17.30*)
Itá Centro Artesanal, church with reredos (🕘 *07.00–11.30*)

Yaguarón stunning church (🕘 *06.00–11.00 & 13.30–17.00*), museum (🕘 *09.00–14.00*)
Pirayú church with reredoses
Ypacaraí lunch at El Galpón de Don Ernesto
Itauguá *ñanduti* lace, old streets, museum (🕘 *07.00–10.45 & 14.00–17.00*)
Capiatá fine old church (🕘 *14.30–18.00*), Museo Mitológico (🕘 *08.00–noon & 14.00–17.00*)
Areguá art galleries, good architecture, pottery
Luque *filigrana* silver jewellery, you could finish with dinner at Restaurant Real

Longer tour via Piribebúy and Caacupé Alternatively, with an earlier start and more driving (and probably a hired driver who knows where he is going) you can do the longer circuit through Piribebúy in a day, and reach the famous Caacupé. In principal the tour includes five craft towns, five churches and five museums, but you would need to select from the list below the places that are of most interest to you, as you cannot realistically stop at more than three places in the afternoon without being totally exhausted, even if you are in a car and know where you are going. If you are able to take two or even three days over this route, then good accommodation options midway would be the Hotel Gabriela near Paraguarí, La Quinta near Piribebúy, the Hotel Alta Gracia at Caacupé, the Hotel Olimpo at Itauguá or the Hotel Los Lagos near Capiatá. These hotels have been chosen for quality rather than economy, because it is assumed that if you have a car for making the tour, you are not a hard-up backpacker.

San Lorenzo Museo Boggiani and its shop of indigenous craft (🕘 *09.00–17.30*)
Itá Centro Artesanal, church with reredos (🕘 *07.00–11.30*)
Yaguarón stunning church (🕘 *06.00–11.00 & 13.30–17.00*), museum (🕘 *09.00–14.00*)
Paraguarí a cheap, quick lunch of reasonable quality can be picked up at the Frutería, or a gourmet lunch at La Quinta if you order in advance
Piribebúy museum (🕘 *07.00–noon & 14.00–17.00*); church
Caacupé basilica
Itauguá *ñanduti* lace, old streets, museum (🕘 *07.00–10.45 & 14.00–17.00*)
Capiatá fine old church (🕘 *14.30–18.00*), Museo Mitológico (*08.00–noon & 14.00–17.00*)
Areguá art galleries, good architecture, pottery
Luque *filigrana* silver jewelry, finish with dinner at Restaurant Real

Two-day tour via Valenzuela and Sapucai There is yet another variant of the Circuito de Oro that goes even further than the Piribebúy turn along Ruta 2 before crossing over to Ruta 1. You make the change between the two Rutas by passing through Valenzuela, which has an attractive old church. This route also enables you to include Sapucai in the circuit, which has the old workshop where the trains used to be made, and is an interesting place quite different from anywhere else you will have visited. This circuit, like the last one, can be combined with the northern diversion to San Bernardino, Altos, Atyrá and Tobatí (see above), though if you did that it would become a three-day tour.

Day one
Luque *filigrana* silver jewellery
Areguá art galleries, good architecture, pottery, lunch at La Cocina de Gulliver
Caacupé basilica
Valenzuela old church, night at La Cascada

Day two

Sapucai railway museum (⌚ *07.00–17.00*)
Yaguarón stunning church (⌚ *06.00–11.00 & 13.30–17.00*), museum (⌚ *09.00–14.00*)
Itá Centro Artesanal, church with reredos (⌚ *07.00–11.30*)
Itauguá lunch at Hotel Olimpo, *ñanduti* lace, old streets, museum (⌚ *07.00–10.45 & 14.00–17.00*)
Capiatá fine old church (⌚ *14.30–18.00*), Museo Mitológico (⌚ *08.00–noon & 14.00–17.00*)
San Lorenzo Museo Boggiani and its shop of indigenous craft (⌚ *09.00–17.30*)

FERNANDO DE LA MORA

Before you even get to the beginning of Ruta 1 and Ruta 2 (which both start in San Lorenzo) you must go through Fernando de la Mora, which is a built-up area between Asunción and San Lorenzo such that the boundaries between them are indistinguishable.

The feast of the Epiphany is celebrated in style in Fernando de la Mora with the festival Kambá Kua, when torches and drums herald dancers in red and yellow costumes. The event has African origins and is held in honour of the black king Balthasar, who was traditionally one of the wise men to visit the Christ child. It takes place on the nearest Saturday night to 6 January, beginning at 21.00, on the esplanade of the María Auxiliadora chapel (*by the Club 6 de Enero, Capitan Rivas y 6 de enero, Loma Campamento; entrance Gs25,000*). The festival has been celebrated for more than 20 years and includes other musical artists besides the black dance troupe. It bears some resemblance to the celebration of Kambá Ra'angá in Altos (see page 157).

The origin of the Kambá Kua black community of Fernando de la Mora was a group of 250 people of Kenyan descent who accompanied the Uruguayan politician José Artigas to Paraguay when he came to the country in exile.

TRAVELLING ALONG RUTA 2

Ruta 2 is the highway that runs directly east until it reaches Coronel Oviedo, halfway across eastern Paraguay, on the way to Ciudad del Este. The first 100km of Ruta 2 are dotted with interesting towns, to the right and left of the main road, on the Circuito de Oro.

After San Lorenzo (see pages 132–5) you come to Capiatá, and from then on there are stations of the cross along the road, each bearing the picture of the Virgin of the Schoenstadt movement. When they end, you come to the little drive on the north side of the road, into the Tupãrendá retreat centre (see page 140).

In Ypacaraí the road divides and goes around a large central island. Then you pass an ugly concrete church on the left with a strange octagonal tower. As you leave Ypacaraí you go through a *peaje* (toll station) where you will be charged Gs10,000. The next turning to come up is to San Bernardino, to the north. Between Ypacaraí and Eusebio Ayala you pass a totem pole topped with the figure of Tupã – God the Father in the traditional Guaraní religion.

A bit further on you come to a large white cross with a hollow centre, in the middle of the road, called the Kurusú Peregrino (Guaraní 'Cross'; Spanish 'Pilgrim'). This marks the final stage of the walk to Caacupé, for the annual pilgrimage of 8 December. It is also the point where you turn left if you are going to Atyrá. Carrying on towards Caacupé you pass a number of *viveros* or nursery gardens, which sell flowering plants.

At Caacupé the road divides. Eastbound traffic hugs around the town to the south, and to enter Caacupé you drive all the way round it before finding the left turn marked for the centre and the Basilica: this is the westbound carriageway of Ruta 2.

Between the Piribebúy turn and the Eusebio Ayala turn there is a clutch of excellent ***chiperías***. The Chipería Camellito (km66) is followed by the Chipería María Ana (km69), the Chipería Leticia (km74) and the Chipería Barrero (km79). If you are driving, pull in and buy one of these delicious fresh aniseedy rolls, all soft and spongy inside from the melted cheese. The *chipas* cost only a modest Gs2,000 each. Particularly recommended is the Chipería María Ana.

Beyond Eusebio Ayala you come to a good eating place on the road, **Viva el Sabor** (*km83;* **m** *0982 543605;* **$**). It is opposite a dirt road to Piribebúy (not the asphalted road that you have already passed) and before the dirt road to Valenzuela (see pages 167–8). It does fast food, but is more Paraguayan than North American. It is clean, modern and tastefully designed, and has a high terrace from which you can keep an eye on your car. They serve good homemade *empanadas* and hamburgers, ice cream in lots of different flavours, fresh fruit juice and crisp salad.

In Itacurubí de la Cordillera you pass a pleasant green plaza at the side of the road and a horseracing track. Towards the east of the town is an excellent, popular restaurant on the south side of the road, called **La Curva** (*km88;* *0518 20064;* **$**). The staff are friendly and there are ample portions of *asado*. They even serve breakfast.

Past Itacurubí you come to a lot of little stalls on the road selling fruit and vegetables. The next turn to the left leads to Nueva Londres (see regional map for *Chapter 10*, page 310), which was founded by British emigrants in 1893. After that you come to another toll station and shortly after it the major intersection of Coronel Oviedo (see pages 311–12). You have now passed out of the area of the Circuito de Oro.

SAN LORENZO

Copaco 021 583300; municipalidad 021 582817

San Lorenzo joins Fernando de la Mora and then Asunción in one big urban sprawl, and travelling through by bus one is tempted to curse the place for adding to the long stretch of bumpy crawl that makes arriving or leaving the capital city so unpleasant. (A bus will take at least an hour just to get onto the open road.) But the roads in San Lorenzo that the long-distance bus goes along, with their market squalor, are very different from the town centre, with its church in the middle of the plaza and its dignified houses. And the Museo Boggiani, with its accompanying shop selling indigenous crafts, is so interesting that you should try to fit in a visit there if you possibly can.

GETTING THERE AND AWAY Take a number 12, 56 or 26 local bus (*linea*) to get there. The long-distance buses that pass through the town do not generally like to take passengers who get off so close to Asunción. See also *Getting out of Asunción*, pages 123–7 and *Travelling along Ruta 2*, pages 131–2.

WHERE TO STAY *Map opposite.*

Hotel Liz (72 rooms) Gral Genes 531 e/ Defensores del Chaco; 021 580300/1; **m** 0974 580300; www.hotelliz.py. A 5-storey pink & white building, car park, terrace with panoramic view, sommier beds, minibars, cable TV, pool, restaurant. **$$**

Hotel San Blas (20 rooms) Coronel Romero 498 c/ Defensores del Chaco; 021 570200/576181. A simple place, but well sited opposite the church. Wi-Fi in reception only. **$**

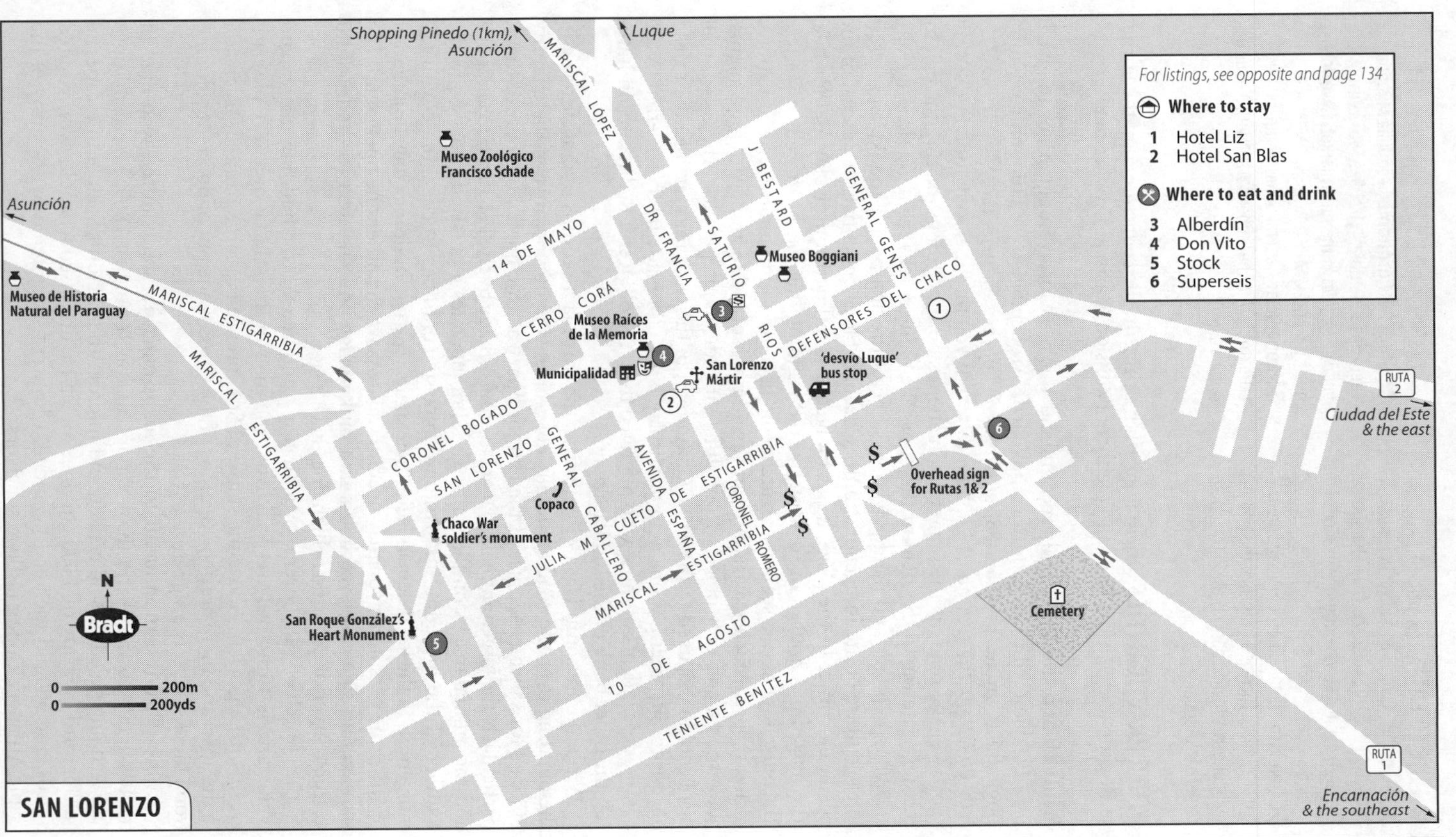
SAN LORENZO
For listings, see opposite and page 134
Where to stay
1 Hotel Liz
2 Hotel San Blas
Where to eat and drink
3 Alberdín
4 Don Vito
5 Stock
6 Superseis
Shopping Pinedo (1km), Asunción
Luque
Asunción
Ciudad del Este & the east
Encarnación & the southeast
RUTA 2
RUTA 1
Museo Zoológico Francisco Schade
Museo de Historia Natural del Paraguay
Museo Boggiani
Museo Raíces de la Memoria
Municipalidad
San Lorenzo Mártir
'desvío Luque' bus stop
Overhead sign for Rutas 1& 2
Copaco
Chaco War soldier's monument
San Roque González's Heart Monument
Cemetery
MARISCAL LÓPEZ
MARISCAL ESTIGARRIBIA
J BESTARD
GENERAL GENES
SATURIO RIOS
DR FRANCIA
DEFENSORES DEL CHACO
14 DE MAYO
CERRO CORÁ
CORONEL BOGADO
SAN LORENZO
GENERAL CABALLERO
AVENIDA DE ESTIGARRIBIA
JULIA M CUETO
ESPAÑA
CORONEL ROMERO
MARISCAL ESTIGARRIBIA
10 DE AGOSTO
TENIENTE BENÍTEZ
N
Bradt
0 200m
0 200yds

WHERE TO EAT *Map, page 133.*

Alberdín Coronel Bogado c/ Dr Francia; 0800 11 2662/021 662972. Only a hamburger & pasta bar, but it serves good-quality food at that level. $

Don Vito Coronel Romero y San Lorenzo; 021 224495. There is a branch of this popular chain of *empanada* bars on the Plaza, on the corner of the square. $

Stock Del Agrónomo esq Julia Miranda Cueto de Estigarribia; 021 575166. As usual, the *patio de comidas* in the supermarkets have good quality & prices. $

Superseis General Genes y Mariscal Estigarribia. Another supermarket with a *patio de comidas*. $

OTHER PRACTICALITIES There is a cash machine in the *cooperativa* on the corner of Bogado and Saturio Rios, and plenty of banks on Mariscal Estigarribia.

WHAT TO SEE AND DO Highly recommended is the **Museo Boggiani**, or to give it its full name, the Museo Antropológico, Arqueológico y Etnográfico Guido Boggiani (*Coronel Bogado 888, e/ Mariscal López y Saturio Ríos; 021 584717; 09.00–19.00 Tue–Sat, until 17.30 in winter*). If you find it closed, look in the craft shop over the road, as the same person attends both buildings, or ring the bell by the next gateway to the right of the door. The name comes from Guido Boggiani, an Italian explorer and painter who was one of the first people to take an interest in the culture of the indigenous in the Chaco. A block and a half to the east of the northeast corner of the plaza, it has indigenous craft both on display and for sale. The museum is housed in an attractive old building that has been well converted. The museum has two sections: an archaeological part, with items from excavations, including prehistoric excavations, and an ethnographical section, with implements, adornments and cult objects from different indigenous peoples. There is a wall display of masks used in the Areté Guasú feast of the Guaraní to invoke their dead ancestors. Surprisingly, one item on display is a violin made by the Guaraní in the Chaco, descendants of those who migrated from the old Jesuit Reductions in Itatín (on the other bank of the Río Paraguay).

While the museum is very interesting, the three large rooms of craft for sale in the building over the road are totally absorbing, not only because of the quantity of items for sale but because of the extraordinary artistic quality of many of them, particularly the larger animals that act as stools (made by the Paĩ Tavyterã Guaraní) and the animal masks on the walls. The shop operates a fair-trade policy and the founder of the museum, José Antonio Perasso, continues to collaborate with the indigenous in the legal demands for their rights. The two buildings may be attended by the same person, so you may need to wait to have the other one opened up. The shop has no sign displayed but is in a pinky-beige building next to the Instituto Técnico Superior en Salud, which does have a sign.

The church of **San Lorenzo Mártir** is a grand neo-Gothic building in grey and white, and is attractively set back from the road in the middle of a very pleasant green with a garden. Above the statue of St Laurence is a large painted Ascension in the apse; and there are good Stations of the Cross made out of different coloured wood blocks, with the signature 'NUMA'.

In the plaza is a **monument to the *niños mártires***, the children who died in the battle of Acosta Ñú (north of Vapor Cué) on 16 August 1869. Mariscal López had virtually no adult soldiers left, and in order to give himself time to escape, he put forward an army of 3,000 children under 15, disguised as adults with painted beards, and 500 old men and wounded, who were slaughtered by the army of the Triple Alliance, leaving just two survivors.

Around the plaza and the neighbouring streets are a good number of old **colonial houses**, with colonnades of round masonry pillars.

On the outskirts of town and opposite the entrance to the Universidad Nacional is the small **Museo de Historia Natural del Paraguay** (*07.30–13.00 Mon–Fri; free admission*), which has collections of flora and fauna native to the country and is run by the government Secretaría del Ambiente, SEAM. (Guided tours to groups can be arranged by ringing 021 585206/8.) Within the Universidad Nacional itself – which spans the distance between Mariscal Estigarribia and Mariscal López – is a similar but larger museum of taxidermy, the **Museo Zoológico Francisco Schade** (*021 585606; 07.00–13.00 Mon–Fri; closed January*). It is part of the Facultad de Ciencias Agrarias, and was founded some 50 years ago. It is full of stuffed birds and animals, and some of it is a bit stomach-churning, such as the two-headed calf.

At San Lorenzo you can take your choice between Ruta 2, heading towards Ciudad del Este and the east, and Ruta 1, towards Encarnación and the southeast. This section pursues Ruta 2, while the route along the other highway, Ruta 1, begins on page 169.

CAPIATÁ

Copaco 0228 634974; municipalidad 0228 634727

Capiatá is interesting on a number of counts. Most importantly, it has a fine, historic church, almost all of it original to the Franciscan Reduction. It has an interesting museum, both for Guaraní mythology and for religious art. The Rodríguez family of saint-makers (*santeros*) have their workshop here. And the folk cult of the black saint Balthasar adds a fascinating touch of popular religiosity.

GETTING THERE AND AWAY The journey by bus takes an hour from the Asunción Terminal, and the best place to get off is after you pass the España supermarket sign on the right-hand side of the road. The turn to the left there (Candelaria) has a taxi rank. If you want to go to the church first, this is the road that leads directly to it, just one block in from the main road.

The museum of mythology is 1km before Capiatá, on the Asunción side. If you are coming by bus and the driver does not want to drop you outside, or if you do not want to have to walk a kilometre into town afterwards, you can go on to Capiatá and take a taxi back, asking it to wait for you. You can also ask the taxi to take you to the workshop of the Rodríguez brothers, which will be the easiest way to locate it, although instructions for walkers and drivers are given below.

See also *Getting out of Asunción*, pages 123–7 and *Travelling along Ruta 2*, pages 131–2.

WHERE TO STAY AND EAT

Hotel y Restaurant Jardín Alemán Ruta 2 Km24; 0228 634025; www.jardinaleman.com.py. Outside town, almost halfway to Itauguá on Ruta 2. Pool. The restaurant (*11.00–14.30 & 19.00–midnight, closed Mon; $$$*) has a buffet service every day, & offers something better than you will find in the town itself. **$$$**

Hotel Los Lagos Avenida Pedro López Bedoy y Paseo Los Lagos; 0228 629019; m 0983 523469/0983 523469; e silva@loslagos.com.py; www.loslagos-aparthotel.com; Facebook: Los Lagos Apart Hotel – Capiata. Two blocks after the turn to the church (which is to the left, you turn right, & some 3.5km along the road the hotel is to your left, opposite the Cooperativa de Capiatá. It has an artificial lake. Recommended for lunch, but you should order it in advance. **$$$**

WHAT TO SEE AND DO The **church** of Capiatá, dedicated to Nuestra Señora de la Candelaria, is Paraguay's second most complete church of the Reduction period, after Yaguarón. It was built in the mid 18th century and completed in 1769. What we have today is nearly all original, but not quite, for the façade has been redone, the bell tower removed, the wooden pillars of the side colonnades replaced with round masonry ones, and a choir balcony removed from the inside. However, the interior is magnificent, and it is surprisingly different from its contemporary Yaguarón. A restoration lasting six years was carried out at the end of the 20th century by Estela Rodríguez Cubero, who also worked on restoration in Atyrá, Yaguarón, Caazapá (both churches) and the cathedral and the Santísima Trinidad in Asunción.

The church is open only in the afternoons, from 14.30 to 18.00 each day. You can confirm these hours by ringing the priest or his secretary (*0228 634237*). There is not a lot of point in going to the church if you cannot get inside, as most of the original outside features have been lost. But if you do succeed in getting in, you will find a glorious extravaganza of dark red, blue and creamy beige. There are large figures of the crucified thieves (the good one and the bad one) on either side of the musicians' gallery over the entrance door. The interior pillars have carved details. The ceiling is fairly plain, but the barrel vault over the chancel is painted. There is a splendid pulpit, an excellent crucifix, two side altars, and an elaborate reredos with the figure of the Candelaría in a central position. It was made by the same artist who did the reredos of Yaguarón, the Portuguese José de Souza Cavadas.

The statue was removed from the church by Mariscal López during the Triple Alliance War, allegedly to prevent sacrilege, and was only identified as belonging to Capiatá many years later, when it was in the cathedral of Asunción. It was returned to its rightful place with great ceremony in 1940. The Christ Child in the Virgin's arms was subsequently stolen from the church, but it was happily recovered and replaced in 1979.

The patronal feast day is 2 February – the feast of Candlemas, or the Presentation of the Christ Child by Mary in the temple.

The **Museo Mitológico Ramón Elías** (*Ruta 2 km19; 02286 34262; 08.00–noon & 14.00–17.00 Mon–Sat, 08.00–noon Sun; Gs5,000*) is the only museum of its kind in the country, but is far more than a museum of mythology. The building itself is magnificent, having been constructed in 1976 by the artist Ramón Elías out of materials recovered from colonial buildings over the period of ten years: huge beams, heavy doors on wooden hinges, carved windows, massive roof tiles, and of course a colonnade with wooden columns and carved capitals.

Inside the museum – which is now looked after by his widow Elsa de Elías – is a gallery of monsters from Paraguayan mythology, which Ramón Elías carved. According to legend, the spirit of evil, Taú, seduced a beautiful girl, Keraná, and she gave birth to seven monsters:

> Tejú Jaguá was a lizard with a dog's head.
> Mbói Tu'ĩ was a big snake with a parrot's head.
> Moñái was a serpent with two spikes on his head and sharp teeth.
> Jasý Jateré was a very blonde, naked goblin who would whistle to attract children to lure them away during the heat of the siesta.
> Kurupí had a penis so long that he had to wrap it round his waist.
> Aó Aó was a fertility god looking like a sheep with sharp teeth, walking upright.
> Luisõ was the most terrible of the monsters, looking like a large black dog but attacking like a tiger.

As well as these seven, Elías carved other traditional figures, including the well-known Pombero, the lord of the night, looking like a short, black, hairy man. He also included the figure of God himself, Tupã, the supreme father and source of goodness, whom the Franciscans and Jesuits identified with the God of Christians. He is portrayed by Elías (and in many subsequent sculptures) as a figure sitting on a bench with arms outstretched, one holding the sun and the other the moon, and with an enormous beard that covers his entire body in place of clothing.

Beyond this big hall of sculptures are three further rooms. One has some old items from the Triple Alliance and the Chaco wars, but the rest of the space is devoted to art from the Reductions. There was a burglary in May 2009 when 25 statues of saints were stolen, worth over US$500,000. Though Elsa de Elías is heartbroken and says that they took all the best pieces, leaving the rooms virtually empty, she has reorganised well and the works of Jesuit art that are left are also very fine. Particularly good are three smallish crucifixes: one, in a cupboard-niche, is quite poignant; another has a twisted body with bright red blood, and mauve and yellow details; and another has God the Father flying out from the top of the cross, and the dove flying out from a mitre on the head of the Father.

On the opposite side of the road from the museum, and 50m in the direction of Asunción, is a well-presented kiosk that sells honey and related products, called **Pan de Miel**. It is just by the service station.

To reach the workshop of the **Rodríguez *santeros*** (saint-makers), take the road Santo Domingo in between the petrol station and the Tuvalu Karaoke, between the museum and the town. The shop is a pale green corner house, one block in. Cándido Rodríguez was well known when he was alive, following in his own father's footsteps as a *santero*; and now his children (Esperanza, Carlos, Justo, Maximiliano, Irenion and Juan) and his widow (Juana) carry on the practice, each with their own slightly distinct style. They employ three methods: painted, part-painted (the face, hands and feet) and unpainted. The figures are typically quite small, and each saint is easily identified by his or her symbol (see box on page 138). These little statues can also be found in the craft shops of Asunción, Overall and Bella Tierra.

The **Oratorio del Santo Rey Baltasar** (Ruta 2, km22.5) is nearly 3km after the town centre, and is thoroughly hidden from the road, so here again you may do better to take a taxi, with a driver who knows where he is going. But if you want to find it on your own, you need to look out on the right-hand side for a red and yellow sign saying 'Taller de moto' immediately after a sign saying 'Pollos Don Juan'. This is immediately opposite 'Sulmetal' on the left-hand side, before you get to the 'Toyota' sign.

Tucked in behind the car mechanic's garage is the oratory with its five arched doorways. An oratory was built here in 1931, but it was replaced by a larger one in 1986. Red and yellow is very much the theme colour, and it sets off beautifully the black skin of King Balthasar, who traditionally was one of the three magi who visited the Christ Child in Bethlehem. Inside the oratory is a yellow altar with a red top, yellow vases with red and yellow flowers in, and the little figure of King Balthasar in a glass case, dressed in red and yellow clothes and carrying a sceptre.

The key to the oratory is held by the mechanic, but if he is not there you can see fairly well through the wrought iron gates. This is in every sense an example of popular religiosity – a shrine tucked behind a mechanic's garage, in memory of a black saint – and it is worth remembering that there were black slaves in Paraguay at least up to 1824. The saint's feast day is 6 January (the Epiphany) when there is mass at 08.30 and a procession to the chapel of San Francisco de Asís, down the road at km23, with local children dressed as kings in red and yellow, and some on horseback. As is customary with patronal feast days, there is a novena for the nine days beforehand, with special prayers every evening at 20.30 at the oratory.

SAINTS AND THEIR ICONOGRAPHICAL SYMBOLS

English name	Spanish name	Typical symbol	Other information
St Peter	San Pedro	keys	apostle and first pope
St Paul	San Pablo	sword	shown next to St Peter
St Antony of Padua	San Antonio	Christ Child in arms	Franciscan
St Anna (or Anne)	Santa Ana	book	mother of Virgin Mary
St Joseph	San José	Christ Child or lily	adoptive father of Jesus
St Roque	San Roque	wound in thigh and dog	medieval French
St Roque González	San Roque González	exposed heart and holding picture of Virgin	Jesuit martyr, first Paraguayan saint
St Barbara	Santa Bárbara	holding tower	early martyr
St Andrew	San Andrés	diagonal cross	apostle
St Isidore	San Isidro	hoe	patron of agriculture
St Francis of Assisi	San Francisco	stigmata	founder of Franciscans
St Blaise	San Blas	mitre	heals sore throats
St Laurence	San Lorenzo	grill	deacon, roasted alive
St Librada	Santa Librada	crucified woman	little known in the northern hemisphere
St Raphael	San Rafael	fish	guardian angel

ITAUGUÁ

Copaco ☎ 0294 221420; municipalidad ☎ 0294 220358/220252

Itauguá is often overlooked by visitors, but it is actually one of the best places to visit on the Circuito de Oro. It is an excellent town for its craft, its museum and its old streets of colonial houses.

Its distinctive craft is the famous *ñanduti* lace, which is the Guaraní word for a spider's web: this is usually circular in shape, and then the circles are sewn together to make a large cloth. Its museum has two sections: one devoted to *ñanduti*, and the other devoted to the art of the Reductions. The streets near the church (one block to the south of Ruta 2) are semi-pedestrianised and date from the time of Dr Francia. With their colonnades, they make the centre of Itauguá one of the most attractive towns in this part of the country.

Among Paraguayans, Itauguá is well known not only for its *ñanduti* but also for having a large state hospital. This is to the east of the road that goes south to connect Itauguá with Itá, and patients come in from all over the country for specialist treatment there.

GETTING THERE AND AWAY See *Getting out of Asunción*, pages 123–7 and *Travelling along Ruta 2*, pages 131–2. Any bus going to Ypacaraí or Caacupé will pass through Itauguá, but you may also pick up a bus going along Ruta 2 and then south past the hospital and on to Itá.

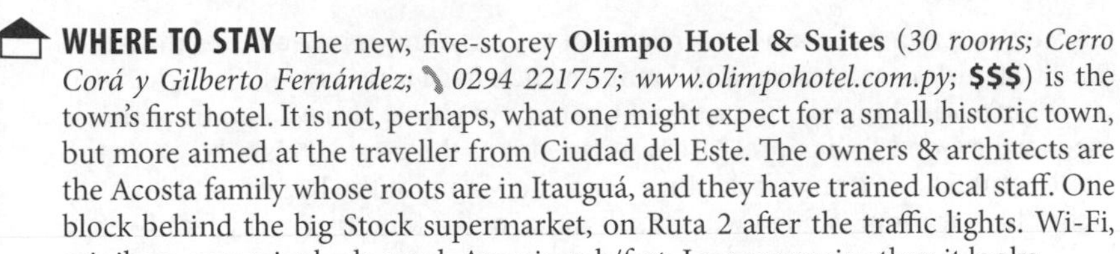

WHERE TO STAY The new, five-storey **Olimpo Hotel & Suites** (*30 rooms; Cerro Corá y Gilberto Fernández;* ☏ *0294 221757; www.olimpohotel.com.py;* **$$$**) is the town's first hotel. It is not, perhaps, what one might expect for a small, historic town, but more aimed at the traveller from Ciudad del Este. The owners & architects are the Acosta family whose roots are in Itauguá, and they have trained local staff. One block behind the big Stock supermarket, on Ruta 2 after the traffic lights. Wi-Fi, minibars, sommier beds, pool, American b/fast. Less expensive than it looks.

WHERE TO EAT AND DRINK For eating, there are a couple of simple local restaurant/bars on Ruta 2, but apart from the Olimpo Hotel, nowhere of higher quality. The best is probably the Guarida de Franki, near the Municipalidad (or town hall). Stock does not have a *patio de comidas* but it does have toilets, telephones and a cash machine. There is also a Banco Visión, two blocks after Stock.

WHAT TO SEE The *ñanduti* **shops** are on Ruta 2, before the traffic lights that mark the junction with General Marcial Samaniego – the road that leads south to Itá. You begin to pass *ñanduti* shops as soon as you reach the town, and they soon come thick and fast. They are an excellent place to browse. One such is Casilda (☏ *0294 220137;* m *0982 250940*).

The traditional *ñanduti* is white, and the most delicate examples of this are exquisite. But while foreign visitors tend to like the whites and natural colours, Paraguayans like bright hues, so *ñanduti* has been developed into multi-coloured tablemats and decorations. Particularly beautiful are the long, elaborate dresses made from *ñanduti*, although they are expensive because they take so long to make. Because the *ñanduti* is starched, it hangs with a good weight, and makes a superb skirt for folk dancing, with richly subtle colour variations as well as a good swing.

There is an annual Festival de *Ñanduti*, usually in June. Check the date with the Municipalidad, or with the association of artisans, Asociación Tejedoras de Ñanduti de Itauguá (*Ruta 2, no 881;* ☏ *0294 22095/21255/20137;* m *0981 673617;* e *tejedorasitaugua@ceap.irg.py; www.ceap.org.py*).

Turn right after the traffic lights to reach the magnificent street of old houses and colonnades that runs parallel to Ruta 2: Teniente Esteban Martínez. On Coronel Francisco Caballero Álvarez (which joins Ruta 2 at the Banco Visión) is a little fountain set into the wall, in memory of the townspeople who have had to migrate to seek work, and one block further along is the plaza with the church.

The **Museo San Rafael** (☏ *0294 220415;* ⏱ *07.00–10.45 & 14.00–17.00 Tue–Fri, 07.00–10.45 Mon & Sat; free admission*) was founded in the 1960s to conserve the statues from the old church and elsewhere. (The current church was finished and inaugurated in 1908, but it incorporates the back wall of the original.) The building itself, adjoining the parish office, is old, dating back to the period of Dr Francia, and incorporates rings in the walls for hanging hammocks, just as in the Jesuit *casas de indios*.

In the *ñanduti* part of the museum, there is a display of dozens of different designs for the circular web of lace, each one only about 9cm wide and woven in fine, white cotton. Most of the designs are based on plants, insects, birds or religious symbols. There is, for example, a *ñanduti* design based on a broom, bread, clouds, bells, a star, an axe, bricks, a daisy, the beak of a toucan, a crab, fish tails, ears of wheat, and even a pregnant tummy. The museum also has on display some vestments made with *ñanduti*.

In terms of religious art, the oldest piece they have and one of the loveliest, which faces you as you go in, is a St Raphael, and it gives the name to the museum. He may have been the patron saint of the original church, but this is not known for certain. Among the most interesting of the large statues are a more-than-life-size St Stanislaus of Kostka, a St Francis which has glass eyes and is articulated (ie: the arms are hinged), and a very fine statue of Christ at the Column, which is used in the Good Friday procession. A reredos of the original church is here too – at least the basic framework of it – with the Virgin of the Rosary in its central niche. The far room is filled with small saints, of the kind that every family once had in their home.

The **church** on the green facing the museum has a large and grand façade, and the view of its frontage is complemented by a golden fountain when you go down the Paseo José Asunción Flores that leads to it. The sacristan is often attending to the well-kept garden, and can let you inside. The Virgen del Rosario, to whom the church is dedicated, is portrayed in pink (as is the other one in the museum, and in Luque too) and with *ñanduti* adornment on her dress. The patronal feast day is 7 October, and on the nearest Sunday the statue is taken through the streets in a painted coach. The coach is kept behind the museum.

YPACARAÍ

Copaco ☎ 0513 432270; municipalidad ☎ 0513 432267

Contrary to expectations, the town of Yapacaraí is not actually on the Lake of Yapacaraí, but it is not far off. The two towns with beaches on the lake are San Bernardino, on the east side, and Areguá, on the west side. Yapacaraí is on the south side, and a few kilometres of marshland separate it from the shore. It is one of the towns that were on the railway, when the line was still running, and the station can still be visited. Ruta 2 divides at the start of the town into separate carriageways, and joins up again after the town.

The name Ypacaraí literally means 'Water, sir?' The town is one of the points of departure used by the pilgrims who walk to Caacupé every 8 December.

GETTING THERE AND AWAY See *Getting out of Asunción*, pages 123–7, and *Travelling along Ruta 2*, pages 131–2. Any bus going to Caacupé will pass through Ypacaraí.

WHERE TO EAT AND DRINK Just three blocks after the rather ugly church you see the notice pointing down a turn to the right. This leads to **El Galpón de Don Ernesto** (*☎ 0513 432223; ⌚ lunch only;* **$$**), a restaurant with blue-and-white check tablecloths serving every kind of homemade pasta. Ring in advance to be sure they make enough pasta that morning for your group.

WHAT TO SEE AND DO The retreat house of the Schoenstatt movement, **Tupãrenda** (*☎ 021 601428/608215*), is on the north side of Ruta 2 before you reach the town of Ypacaraí. It has a beautiful chapel, adorned in excellent taste, and is used for religious conferences. The name means 'God's Place' in Guaraní. The current Bishop of Caacupé, Mons Claudio Giménez, was one of the founders of the Paraguayan branch of this German-based Marian movement, and their key date was the founding of Tupãrenda in 1981.

The city centre is to the south of the main road. The Casa de la Cultura (*⌚ 07.30–12.30 Mon–Sat & 14.00–16.00 Mon–Fri*) has photographs, portraits and objects from the Triple Alliance War. Buried in Ypacaraí are Demetrio Ortiz, who wrote one of the most famous Paraguayan songs of all time, 'Recuerdos de Ypacaraí', and Teodoro Mongelós, a renowned poet who wrote in Guaraní, and was sent to fight in the Chaco War at the age of 17.

As you come into the town from Asunción you pass some places where leather goods are made. Within the town itself there is a turn that runs parallel to the lake, to Areguá, which is not clearly marked, and on this road are some manufacturers of guitars. In the opposite direction is a turn going south to Pirayú, where, for the time being, the asphalt peters out. And just to the east of the town is the turn to San Bernardino, which is clearly marked.

CAACUPÉ *Copaco ☎ 0511 243843; municipalidad ☎ 0511 242382*

The Guaraní name of Paraguay's major Marian centre is a shortened form of *ka'aguy kupe* (Guaraní 'behind the wood'). Caacupé is the spiritual capital of the country, and the feast day of the Immaculate Conception on 8 December with its preceding novena brings in around a million pilgrims, known as the *promeseros*. People make a prayer-bargain with the Virgin along the lines of: if this happens to my favour, I promise to make the pilgrimage to Caacupé on 8 December. Some walk all the way from Asunción, but many take a bus part of the way (buses run all night in a constant stream), to somewhere like Ypacaraí, from where they still have to walk for several hours. Some come on bicycles from faraway towns; some make their way on their knees 18km from Ypacaraí; some walk the 29km from Limpio carrying enormous heavy crosses. The walk is usually made during the night – no-one wants to walk by day in the heat of December – and the arrival is timed for the early morning mass outside the basilica. All along the road on 8 December are makeshift toilets, where the hordes of pilgrims can pay a pittance to enter a screened-off patch of field.

You pass a chapel called Pablito Róga (Guaraní 'Little Paul's house') *en route*. This was erected in memory of a young child who died of thirst on the pilgrimage, while his mother left him to go and look for water: this is between Ypacaraí and the turn for San Bernardino.

During the novena leading up to 8 December, different bishops celebrate early morning mass and deliver sermons, which traditionally is an opportunity for them to aim a shot across the bows of the government. Caacupé is busy with pilgrims all through the year, and not only for the December feast day. It is a cultural phenomenon, and all over the country people have little copies in their homes of the Virgin of Caacupé – a small crowned figure with brown ringlets, in a full white dress decorated with gold and covered with a blue velvety cloak.

GETTING THERE AND AWAY See also pages 123–7 and 131–2. Ruta 2 divides into one-way carriageways at Caacupé, with the eastward traffic making a small circle around the basilica, and the westward traffic passing through the middle of town, just one block away from the basilica.

WHERE TO STAY For a town with so many visitors, one might expect more hotels. But Caacupé is very much a place for Paraguayans who have no money to stay, but go home again on the bus once their mission of reaching the pilgrimage centre is complete. There are a few more simple pensions in addition to the places mentioned below.

Alta Gracia (32 rooms) Mariscal Estigarribia y El Educador; ☎ 0511 242322; www.altagraciahotel.com.py. On the left of Ruta 2 as you approach Caacupé from the Asunción side, at km52.5, before the Puma petrol station & before the 1-way system leads you to turn right. Buses to Caacupé pass the gate. A grand & beautifully designed hotel in traditional style with wooden porticos & pergolas, decorated with muted colours inspired by the elements of earth, water, air & fire.

VIRGIN OF CAACUPÉ: THE LEGEND

The Indio José, who was from the Franciscan Reduction of Tobatí, was being hunted by other indigenous from the Mbayá people (a fierce tribe that no longer exists). As he hid in the forest, terrified for his life, he made a promise that if his life was saved, he would carve a statue of the Virgin from the wood of the tree behind which he was hiding. He fulfilled his promise when the danger was past, but in fact carved two identical Virgins: a larger one, 1.15m high, for the church of Tobatí, and a smaller one, 40cm high, for his personal devotion.

A second strand of legend about its origins is usually combined with the first to provide a sequel. A huge flood in 1603 from Lago Tapaicuá retreated following the prayers of Fray Luis Bolaños (the great Franciscan father of the Reductions). The Indio José (who in this version came from Atyrá – a Reduction close to Tobatí and founded around the same time) swam out to recover a small case, seen floating on the waters. Inside it was the statue of the Virgin, which the Franciscans entrusted to him to carry to the safety of his home.

In 1770 this smaller Virgin was placed in a small chapel in a little place known as Caacupé, where it received such veneration that the church was replaced by a larger one in 1783, and people built houses around it where they could stay at weekends, coming from their work in other towns to attend mass at the chapel: Caacupé began to take on the appearance of a Reduction, though it was not built to be such. A larger church was built, and consecrated in 1846, though the roof was destroyed by a lightning bolt just six years later, and one of the Virgin's fingers was damaged. This church was enlarged three times, the last time in 1856. In 1885 it was replaced by a larger building, which older people still remember fondly as 'the real Basilica' although it no longer exists. Finally, the present basilica was built in the 1980s. The feast of the Immaculate Conception on 8 December attracts around a million pilgrims.

The statue is similar in shape to many other statues of the Virgin in South America, that is, practically pyramidical in shape, as she is clothed in a an expansive cloak, in this case of dark blue velvet embroidered with gold. The Virgin has fairly pale skin, and brown hair falling around her shoulders in waves, and is crowned. Though carved by a Guaraní, she is far less indigenous in style and of lesser artistic quality than the great statue in the church of Santa María de Fe, also carved by a Guaraní, though anonymously. But neither the statue of Santa María de Fe, nor the larger statue by the Indio José in the church of Tobatí have much of a cult for those outside of the area, while huge crowds of pilgrims flock to the little statue of Caacupé.

Business centre, spa, gym, games room, lots of pools. Restaurant De Las Sierras. Very expensive, but it is very lovely. It has promotional prices Mon–Thu, which helps a little. **$$$$**

Hotel Asunción (8 rooms) 8 de diciembre y Juan E O'leary; 0511 243731; e info@asuncionhotel.com.py; www.asuncionhotel.com.py. On a corner right behind the basilica. Wi-Fi, minibars, cable TV, sommier beds. Restaurant. **$$$**

Hotel Katy María (15 rooms) Eligio Ayala esq Dr Pino; 0511 242860/242441. Facing the side of the Basilica. Minibars, Wi-Fi & cable TV. No credit cards. **$$$**

Hotel Mirador (40+ rooms) Padre Solis; 0511 242652. Exactly facing the basilica. **$**

Hotel Uruguayo (10 rooms) Asunción e/ Eligio Ayala y Mariscal Estigarribia; 0511 242977/242222. The oldest established of the hotels. A block & a half from the basilica. Wi-Fi. Restaurant. **$**

WHERE TO EAT AND DRINK

Churrasquería Brasil Ruta 2, km52.5; 0511 243434; daily. About 500m from the basilica in the direction of Asunción, before the 2 parts of Ruta 2 unite, opposite the supermarket Nuevo Super. $$

Chiky Restaurant & Pizzería Ruta 2 e/ Iturbe y Independencia Nacional: 0511 244607; closed Mon & Tue. New place run by Germans, opposite the 8 de diciembre sports club, about 3 blocks from basilica. Caters for vegetarians. $

Restaurant Thais Padre Solis; 0511 242652. Exactly facing the basilica, simple bar. $

WHAT TO SEE AND DO The **basilica** is obviously the chief attraction. It is a distinctive building, with the central dome surrounded by a series of little domes, and a comparatively short nave jutting out, to end in three very high arched doorways. Above these is a space used for putting a written phrase, which changes every year, such as 'A Jesus Cristo por María Inmaculada', and above this is a large semicircular stained-glass window (where a traditional cathedral would have had a circular rose window) representing the rescue of the statue of the Virgin from the flood (see box opposite). Then a long flight of steps leads down to the plaza in front.

Inside, the little statue of the Virgin is at the far end, lifted high on a little hill, with blue light forming an atmospheric background. A stained-glass window records the blessing of the newly completed basilica by Pope John Paul II on his visit of 18 May 1988. Big though it is, for important occasions the basilica is too small, and the mass is then celebrated outside, in the very sizeable forecourt.

Entering by a side door, you can climb a high staircase to the *mirador* at the top of the basilica, and around this stairwell is a striking series of **murals by Nino Sotelo**, presenting the history of the Virgin of Caacupé. He is a marvellous artist, who specialises in large representational paintings of the Reductions. In this case he has painted a Franciscan Reduction, but he has also painted the history of the Jesuit Reductions: of San Ignacio (in the Jesuit house of studies ISEHF in Asunción), of Santa María de Fe (in the town of that name), and of Trinidad in the Hotel La Misión (in Asunción).

A short distance from the basilica, towards the north, is a well of water (Calle Asunción y Pozo de la Virgen) that is considered to have healing properties, called the **Tupãsý Ykuá** (Guaraní 'Water hole of the Mother of God'; where pilgrims fill their water bottles. It is two blocks to the east and then three blocks to the north, from the basilica's forecourt. There is a model of the old basilica here, and the original altar.

There is **leather craft** and **pottery** to be bought at many little stalls, particularly around the basilica and the road that leads south from the southern side of the basilica (Dr Pino).

Outside the town to the north is the hill known as **Cerro Kavajú** (Spanish 'Hill', Guaraní 'Horse'), which is between Atyrá, Caacupé and Tobatí. It has five natural terraces of stone that are said to have been used by the Franciscans to watch over the region. For a guided visit, possibly with abseiling, contact the Secretaria de Ambiente y Turismo of the *departamento* (*0511 43103 or Alba Miranda,* **m** *0971 314306 or Denis Ortega,* **m** *0971 596585*). At the foot of the hill is an ecological complex called **Eco Granja HL** (*Ruta Caacupé-Tobatí km61.5;* **m** *0971 361053*), 6km from Caacupé, where you can find a guide to take you up the hill, and spend a day in farm activities like milking cows and riding in an ox cart. You can also camp.

A smaller hill which has very steep sides is **Cerro Cristo Rey**, a couple of kilometres from the town. There is a procession with a statue to the top of this hill every feast of Cristo Rey (end of November), in which hundreds of people participate.

Just outside Caacupé to the east is a recreational centre, **Itacuá Pesque y Pague** (*Ruta 2 km57;* ☎ *0511 244479;* **m** *0986 375011; Facebook: Itacua, Caacupe*), where you can fish and cook your catch, similar to the Isla Valle Pesca y Pague place near Areguá (see page 152). A couple of kilometres after leaving the town you take a turn left for 500m, then turn 150m right, then 50m left. They also have a volleyball court, football, a swimming pool and camping.

ITACURUBÍ DE LA CORDILLERA

Copaco ☎ *0518 20370/20417; municipalidad* ☎ *0518 20010*

Although Itacurubí de la Cordillera is quite a pleasant town, the principal reason for stopping here will be either to eat or to stay the night on the drive along Ruta 2 which runs from Asunción towards Coronel Oviedo and its continuation, Ruta 7, which goes on to Ciudad del Este (see *Travelling along Ruta 2*, pages 131–2). There are two plazas: one with the church, and another shady plaza adjoining Ruta 2, with swings and slides. There are a few solid colonial-style houses.

WHERE TO STAY For a modest price you can stay in the **Hotel Aguilera** (*10 rooms;* ☎ *0518 20067;* **$$**), a delightful place tucked away from the main road on the corner of the plaza that has the church. A substantial family house of character with pink colonial pillars, it has a grand sitting room and a thatched *quincho* where you can sit at tables to read or eat. To reach it turn north at the Petrobras petrol station for just one block, and you find yourself in a big grassy plaza with a football pitch and the church. Cheaper rooms have fans. There is a car park. Copaco phone *cabinas* are on the same plaza.

WHERE TO EAT AND DRINK

La Curva Ruta 2; ☎ 0518 20064; ⏱ 07.00–15.00 & 18.00, until the last customer goes. Superb restaurant right on Ruta 2, at the west end of town, good for everything from a b/fast or a light snack to a big *asado* meal. Excellent service, lots of custom, low prices. **$**

La Casona Burger bar on corner facing Hotel Aguilera. **$**

TOWNS NORTH OF RUTA 2

Although we broadly think of the Circuito de Oro as out along Ruta 2, back along Ruta 1, or vice versa, some of the very best towns to visit are not on either of those two roads. The area north of Ruta 2 is particularly interesting, with the silver of Luque, the pottery of Areguá, the beach of San Bernardino, the church of Emboscada, the leather of Atyrá and the Virgin of Tobatí. To set off on this route you can either go north from Ruta 2 at one of several places (see map on page 122), or you can get to Luque from the road that goes towards the airport (again, consult the map on page 122).

LUQUE

Copaco ☎ *021 642222; municipalidad* ☎ *021 648111*

Luque is famous for making harps and guitars, and for the silver *filigrana* (filigree) jewellery that is one of Paraguay's most beautiful traditional crafts.

GETTING THERE AND AWAY

By car If you are coming by car, take Avenida España, which turns into Avenida Aviadores del Chaco after the junction with Avenida San Martín. You will pass Shopping del Sol on your left. Keep on Aviadores del Chaco when Avenida Santa

Teresa branches off to the right. You are now on the stretch of road that goes past the harp and guitar shops of what is popularly called Luque, though it is in fact a musical barrio on the way to Luque proper, where there are more harp and guitar shops. See also *Getting out of Asunción*, pages 123–7.

At the traffic lights the road crosses Madame Lynch (the ring road), and from then on it is known as the Autopista, though it is not a real motorway. You will not stay on this road, but rather turn right. The first chance to do this is almost immediately, where there is the statue to the heroic Paraguayan woman with a child and a tattered flag ready to rebuild the country at the end of the Triple Alliance War (the Monumento a la Residenta). This road curves gently round to the left, along the edge of a green space, passing the Ñu Guazú airbase on the left and (after about five minutes) the España supermarket on the right. You pass three more harp and violin makers: Richard Sanabria, Salomon Sanabria and Dario Rojas, and then come into Luque on the Avenida General Elizardo Aquino, which goes along the side of the Plaza Elizardo Aquino and the Plaza Mariscal López, and one block later, the plaza that has the church.

It is very slightly quicker to take your right turn off the Autopista immediately after going under the road bridge, and then a quick right at the corner where the Bourbon Comebol Hotel is, and immediately left at the junction. This will take you directly into Luque. If you miss that turn by the road bridge, take the chance to turn back for the Hotel Conmebol at the next junction.

By bus If you are coming by bus, take a number 51 from Avenida Republica Argentina, just outside the Terminal, or a 30 from the centre of Asunción (but not the 30-2 with a big A in the window, that goes on to the airport rather than turning right into Luque). One block after Dario Rojas's harp shop it will turn right and shortly afterwards left, so you come into Luque slightly east of the centre. Get off at the corner where there is a taxi rank and a Sportivo Luqueño shop in the blue and yellow colours of the local football team. (They are famous, by the way, for having a pig as their mascot, which dates from the days when the fans would come into Asunción on the same train that transported pigs.) Take the road to the left, which is Dr Francia (though there is no road sign). After three blocks you will reach the plaza that has the church. You can also reach Luque by bus from Limpio and from Ypacaraí.

WHERE TO EAT AND DRINK Being so close to Asunción, you will probably not want to stay in Luque, but it does have some good places to eat.

Restaurant Real Peatonal Mariscal López 61; m 0981 515808/789242; daily except Sun eve & Mon lunch. 1st-class restaurant for both food & ambience, with a room for groups/events. Very pleasant to sit at a table outside in the pedestrian precinct amid all the old colonnades. Sophisticated menu which also has more economical pasta dishes. Takes credit cards. Live music Sat eve, especially in summer. $$$

El Español Mariscal López y Teniente Herrero Bueno; m 0981 719555; 11.00–midnight Tue–Sun. On the corner of the pedestrian street & the Plaza Mariscal López, this is a stylish bar that serves everything from a hamburger to paella, from *calamares a la romana* to an *asado*. $$

Don Vito Plaza General Aquino & also on Cerro Corá (which is the continuation of Av General Aquino). Although the photo display shows Coca-Cola & chips in every picture, Don Vito nonetheless serves good-quality *empanadas*. $

Doña Chipa Cerro Corá c/ Dr Francia; m 0983 792174. This is part of a new chain of cafés, & they serve a delicious range of *chipas*, with tantalising smells, to eat there, take away or have delivered. The *chipa a 4 quesos* (with 4 cheeses) is particularly good, but so is the rest of the range, which includes *pastel mandió* with fillings of beef or chicken, & *mbejú*. $

WHAT TO SEE AND DO Luque is centred on three plazas. One of them has the **church**, the Virgen del Rosario, which is a tall and elegant building but not particularly old. High in the apse is a painting of the Virgin giving the rosary to St Dominic, and the Virgin is also the central of three figures in the modern reredos, together with St Joseph and St Roque González. The patronal feast day is 7 October, which also falls during the time of the Expo Luque, a craft festival beginning in early September.

Facing the church on the west (on Mariscal López) is the parish centre, which has within its precincts a historic house that was the site of the **printing press** for the journal *Lambaré*, which was famous during the Triple Alliance War. Although the house has been preserved it is, unfortunately, almost completely hidden behind a high modern gate.

Two roads link this square with the other two plazas, which are adjacent to one another, separated only by a road running through the middle. One of these link roads is the **Peatonal** (that is, pedestrianised) Mariscal López, and is a most attractive street with a complete run of old colonnades along both sides. This is one of the loveliest roads in the country, and the Restaurant Real halfway along (see page 145) provides an opportunity to sit down at an outside table to savour the atmosphere.

The second road linking the church with the other plazas is the Avenida General Aquino, which is known as the **Avenida de los Joyeros** (Jewellers' Avenue) because of the number of shops selling the silver jewellery for which Luque is so

FRANCISCAN REDUCTIONS AND TOWNS WITH STRONG FRANCISCAN INFLUENCE

Name *recommended for visit	Franciscan Reduction or Franciscan Influence	Original reredos	Distance from Asunción	Departamento	Comments
Acahay	FI		103km	Paraguarí	asphalted road on way to Ybycuí
Altos*	FR	yes	66km	Cordillera	first Reduction in Río de la Plata
Atyrá**	FR	yes	66km	Cordillera	'cleanest town'
Borja	FI	yes	198km	Guairá	difficult to access
Caacupé**	FI		54km	Cordillera	principal Marian centre
Caazapá**	FR	yes (2)	228km	Caazapá	one of the finest reredos in country
Capiatá**	FI	yes	20km	Central	second most church after Yaguarón
Concepción*	FI		417km	Concepción	'Pearl of the North'
Curuguatý	FR		300km	Canindeyú	asphalted Ruta 10
Emboscada*	FI	yes	39km	Cordillera	tiny gem close to Asunción
General Artigas	FI		347km	Itapúa	asphalt road (formerly) Bobí from Coronel Bogado
Guarambaré	FR		31km	Central	early Reduction, off Acceso Sur
Itá*	FR	yes	36km	Central	very early Reduction
Itauguá*	FI		30km	Central	good museum of Franciscan art
Itapé*	FR		191km	Guairá	second Marian centre
Lima	FR		335km	San Pedro	on way to Concepción
Mbuyape´y	FI		182km	Paraguarí	difficult to access
Pirayú*	FI	yes	57km	Paraguarí	asphalt road from Ypacaraí

famous. The *filigrana* jewellery is made into earrings, brooches, cufflinks, pendants and many other forms of decoration. As you go past the two plazas and beyond it, the frequency increases until every shop is a jeweller's. One might think that there would not be enough trade to support so many shops, but in fact most of them seem to have a customer, at least on a Saturday: because Luque is so close to Asunción people can easily come here to shop. Some of the best jewellery is made in the workshop of Don Torres, between Luque and Areguá, opposite the sign to Valle Pucú. Another *filigrana* workshop between Luque and Areguá is Salvador Alvarenga's (*San Juan c/ de las Residenta;* ☎ *021 647244;* m *0971 615820*). There is also **leatherwork** in some of the shops, mostly in the form of leather-covered vacuum flasks for the iced water used in *tereré*.

The square with the church is Plaza Mariscal López, and it has a big sports area and an outside stage called Rincón Cultural (Cultural Corner). There is an old colonnade along one side (Mariscal López) and a harp and guitar shop on another side (Teniente Herrero Bueno). The adjoining square is the Plaza General Aquino, and in the middle is the **mausoleum** (🕘 *07.00–13.00 Mon–Fri, 07.00–11.00 Sat*) of General Elizardo Aquino. This round, white, tall building is more interesting than it sounds, because it is really more of a museum than a mausoleum, and has many photos of the sites associated with this famous general of the Triple Alliance War (see page 13). Born in a *compañía* (outlying hamlet) of Luque in 1825, he was responsible for building the section of railway line from Areguá to Paraguarí.

Name *recommended for visit	Franciscan Reduction or Franciscan Influence	Original reredos	Distance from Asunción	Departamento	Comments
Piribebúy**	FI	yes	91km	Cordillera	famous statue Ñandejára Guasú
Quiindý	FI		109km	Paraguarí	large town on Ruta 1
Quyquyhó	FI		163km	Paraguarí	difficult to access
San Carlos	FR		597km	Concepción	fort on far northern frontier, difficult to access
San Juan Nepomuceno	FR		249km	Caazapá	asphalted road from Villarrica
San Lázaro	FR		597km	Concepción	has caves
San Pedro de * Ycuamandyyú	FI	yes	348km	San Pedro	asphalt road from Ruta 3
Tacuatí	FR		112km	San Pedro	difficult to access
Tobatí**	FR	yes	70km	Cordillera	has twin statue to Caacupé
Valenzuela**	FI	yes	100km	Cordillera	beautiful small church
Villarrica**	FI		173km	Guairá	one of most important towns in Paraguay
Yaguarón**	FR	yes	48km	Paraguarí	finest church in Paraguay
Yataitý**	FI		161km	Guairá	capital of *ao po'í*
Ybycuí*	FI		120km	Paraguarí	famous for its park and old foundry
Ybytymí	FI		101km	Paraguarí	on the old railway line
Ypané	FR	yes	32km	Central	early reduction, off Acceso Sur
Yutý	FR	yes	313km	Caazapá	asphalt road from Coronel Bogado

Under Mariscal López, he built the trench system at Humaitá that was known as the *cuadrilátero,* and led the Paraguayan defence at the battle of El Sauce. He won the battle but was mortally wounded; Mariscal López had him decorated with a gold medal, but he died on 16 July 1866, six days after his injury.

Some of the shops selling **harps and guitars** have already been mentioned, but the best-known shops are on the road running from Asunción to the airport. Most are on the south side of the road, and the majority are run by members of the Sanabria family, all sons of a famous harp maker, and each now with his own shop. All the shops sell guitars as well, but the harp may attract more interest from visitors, being such a beautiful instrument not only in its sound but also in its appearance: most are decorated with carved details (see *Harp*, pages ix–x and *Music and folk dance*, pages 23–4). The shop owners are usually happy to talk about their work, the different qualities of harps and the different woods used.

For the **Football Museum** on the Autopista, see *Chapter 3*, page 104.

AREGUÁ

Copaco ☎ 0291 432457; municipalidad ☎ 0291 432501

Areguá must be one of the key towns to visit in a Circuito de Oro tour. It is one of three craft towns specialising in ceramics, and is the nearest to Asunción. (The others are Itá and Tobatí.) It is a lovely town, marked by an elegant church at the top of the hill and splendid colonial-type houses on the Avenida Estigarribia leading up to it. It is increasingly regarded as a prestige town, bursting with little art galleries, that merits the preservation of its architecture. A number of artists and writers have made their home here, including the distinguished novelist Gabriel Casaccia, whose striking novel *La Babosa* is set in the town.

There are streets lined with craft shops selling ceramics, with much in the way of attractive, large, unglazed flowerpots and pretty small candleholders with holes for the light to shine through. However, there is also a lot of moulded clay work that is less pleasing to European and North American taste, such as garden gnomes, along with frogs, tortoises, swans and toadstools. Another variety of mass-produced moulded clay is their typical line in crib figures, which come out in force in the pre-Christmas period, although a few artists are now beginning to make original hand-formed figures.

The chief founder of the pottery tradition was Ricardo Pérez, a late 19th-century potter who lived in the southern Chaco, and helped General Bernardino Caballero (war hero of the Triple Alliance War and founder of the Colorado party) to escape his enemies by hiding him in his big kiln and faking a fire inside. In gratitude, Caballero gave him territory in Areguá to establish a bigger pottery business.

The *fiesta patronal* (feast day of the town's patron saint) is on 2 February, the feast of Candlemas. Throughout February they have now begun to hold a fair for mangoes and food produced from mangoes. Another tourist attraction is the Expo Frutilla, or Strawberry Fair, mid August to the end of September, though strawberries are plentifully available for sale before that, from July or even the end of June. The strawberry stalls are to be found principally along the road leading to Ypacaraí, where there is a *compañía* of Areguá called Estanzuela, 2km from the town centre.

GETTING THERE AND AWAY Areguá used to be the final train station of the reactivated tourist train route (see page 119), but although that has been discontinued the station continues to be active as a craft shop. **Buses** go regularly from the Asunción Terminal, 203 (Cerro Koĩ) and 242 (La Aregueña), and you cannot miss Areguá because you will see the craft stalls lining the roads. By **car**, take the road towards the airport, but turn right just after you leave the city for

Luque. See *Getting out of Asunción*, pages 123–7. Areguá is as far beyond Luque as Luque is beyond Asunción. However, how to get through Luque and onto the Areguá road is not well signed. (You go 4 blocks past the plaza with the church until you get to the Humaitá double avenue; then you turn right for 3 blocks, then left, and carry on straight until you get to Areguá.)

Alternatively, make your way through San Lorenzo and onto Ruta 1, and after the centre of Capiata you pass the Academia Militar, where you turn left for Areguá. If you are coming from the east, you take a turn northeast for Areguá at Yparacaraí: there is no sign, but there are traffic lights at the turn. These are the three roads into the town, while on the fourth side is the Lago Yparacaraí.

TOURIST INFORMATION The Senatur tourist information centre is at La Candelaria 515 (*0291 433500*; *07.00–18.00 daily*), right in the centre of town, just a little along from the El Cántaro art gallery and on the other side of the road. On weekday mornings they can provide guides for visits within Areguá (*Gs100,000*). Their building itself, la Casona de Areguá, is of architectural interest, built in 1865 for a North American contracted by Mariscal López to make torpedoes for the Triple Alliance War.

WHERE TO STAY *Map, page 150.*

Note that you can also camp at the Club Ecológico Isla Valle (see page 152).

Hotel Restaurant Los Jardines de Areguá (12 rooms) Camino Caacupemí, Isla Valle; 021 634034; m 0984 126666; e hotel_jardines_aregua@yahoo.com; Facebook: Los Jardines de Aregua. New hotel opened 2013, run by French owners, outside town 4km along the Luque road, turn right shortly after the Copetrol service station in the direction of Isla Valle. Welcoming, peaceful, lovely gardens, big rooms & shady porticos around 3 sides of a pretty terrace. Guests have appreciated the tranquillity of not having TVs in rooms. As you might expect from the French, the restaurant is above the ordinary but not cheap. **$$$**

Hotel Aparesida Avenida del Lago 852; 0291 432421; m 0982 550221; www.laaparesida.com. 100m from lake, pool, Wi-Fi, cable TV & pool. Next door is a tiny place that sells doughnuts (*bollos*). **$$**

Hotel Restaurant Ozli (13 rooms) Av Estigarribia; 0291 432380; m 0971 325179/0982 462998. Cable TV, Wi-Fi. At the end of the Avenida del Lago, close to the station. It also has a simple café serving hamburgers & *empanadas*. Cheaper rooms with fans. **$**

Posada La Rosa de los Vientos (4 rooms) Avenida del Lago 853; m 0981 986 406. Opposite Hotel Aparesida, 2nd floor of family house. Bathroom is shared between the guests. Two rooms have AC. More expensive than most *posadas*. **$$**

Posada Sol Areguá (1 room) Domingo Martínez de Irala c/ Ricardo Pérez; m 0971 349720. One block from the church. Bathroom shared with family. **$$**

Posada Tororé (1 room) Humaitá c/ Ricardo Pérez; m 0981 801305. Five blocks behind the church in the direction of Capiatá. Unlike most *posadas*, price is per room not per person, so it is expensive for 1 person & cheap for 3. **$**

WHERE TO EAT AND DRINK *Map, page 150.*

La Cocina de Gulliver La Candelaria y Mcal Estigarribia; 0291433243; m 0971 222618; www.lacocinadegulliver.com. Attractive but unpretentious courtyard with shady trees. Spanish food – try the excellent paella. Homemade bread. Good service, recommended. There may sometimes be live music. Immediately next door is the El Cántaro art gallery (see pages 150–1). **$$**

La Vida Loca La Candelaria 807 c/ Presidente Baez; m 0982 917089; www.lavidaloca-paraguay.com; 17.30–23.00 Tue–Thu, 11.30–23.00 Fri–Sat, 10.00–21.00 Sun. Pink 2-story building, good food (especially the *milanesa* & tilapia fish) with a pleasant musical background. **$$**

Todo Casero Ricardo Pérez 807 c/ La Candelaria; 0291 432503. Just a little upmarket

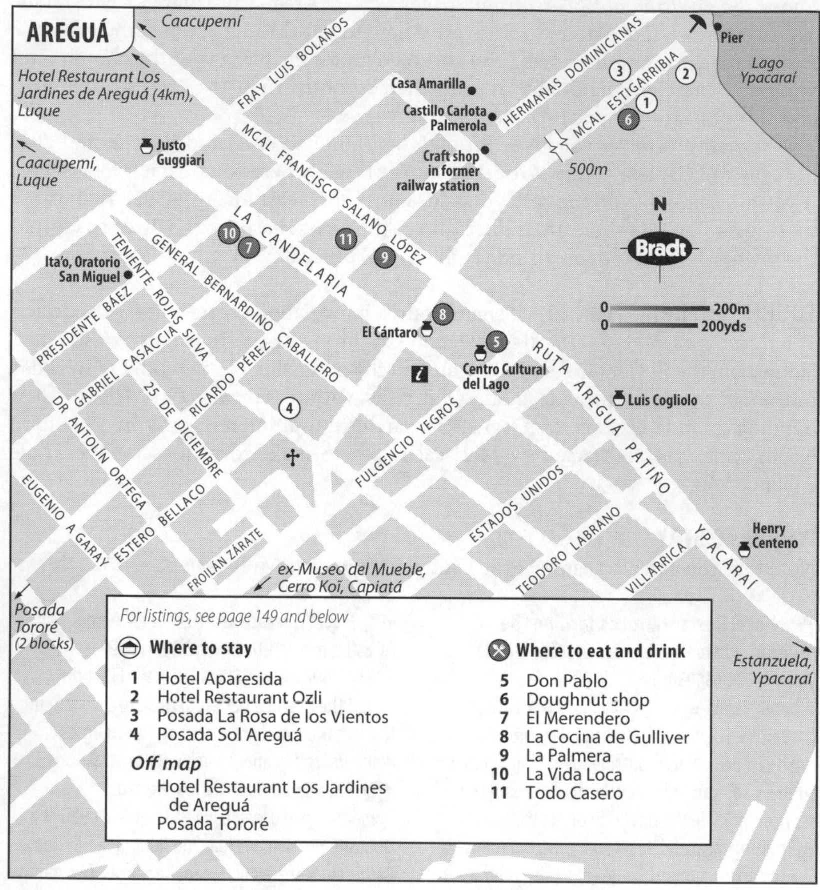

from La Palmera, which is almost opposite, this is an attractive place to eat. They serve quick snacks (pizzas, *empanadas*) & more substantial dishes. $$

✖ **La Palmera** Mcal López 555 y Ricardo Pérez; ☎ 0291 432787; m 0991 750326; lunchtime & eves Tue–Sun. Also known as the Cocina Ymá de Ña Ursula. On a corner near the station. Colonial-style balcony & a pleasant roofed eating area in the garden, delicious *asados* (Sat night & Sun lunch). Friendly people, reasonably priced food. $

✖ **Don Pablo** Yegros y Mariscal López; ☎ 0291 433137. The most popular restaurant in town, run by 3 German sisters, & decorated in quaint & rustic style with many artworks. Excellent cheap food, good Sun buffet. $

✖ **El Merendero** La Candelaria esq Gabriel Casaccia; ☎ 0291 433296; ⏲ closed lunchtime, eves after 20.00 & Mon–Tue. Nice place near craft stalls for snacks mid-morning or teatime. $

OTHER PRACTICALITIES The number for **taxis** (⏲ *24 hours*) is ☎ 0291 432301.

WHAT TO SEE AND DO There is plenty of pottery to see along the streets, both inside the shops and out in open-air markets. The main street for open air stalls of pottery is La Candelaria, but there are also 20 or 30 little pottery shops. Wandering among the shops will be the main thing you will want to do in Areguá.

El Cántaro (*La Candelaria y Mcal Estigarribia;* ☎ *0291 432954; www.el-cantaro.com*) is one of the important art galleries, with paintings, pottery, baskets and carvings in wood and stone. It is very welcoming, and has an adjoining restaurant (see page 149). It runs a Bioescuela Popular, where children have free classes in guitar, sewing, mosaic, basket-making, pottery, etc.

The **Centro Cultural del Lago** (*Yegros c/ Mariscal López; 0291 432293/432633; 10.00–17.00 Thu–Sun or later*) is next door to the Don Pablo restaurant, and is a gallery with examples from the most important potters of Areguá. There is a museum shop, a cine club upstairs and different exhibitions during the year. It is run by Ysanne Gayet (an Englishwoman) and her stepdaughter Gabriela Maldonado, with endless creativity, dynamism and good taste.

Luis Cogliolo has an art gallery just past the *policia caminera* in the direction of Ypacaraí (*Mariscal López 812 c/ Carlos Antonio López; 0291 432339; Thu–Sun*). He works in iron and wood, and makes lamps and sculptures. **Henry Centeno** is a well-known artist who has his gallery a bit further along the same road (*Mariscal López c/ Villarrica; 0291 432847; daily*). He does some landscape paintings (often with pink blossoming lapacho trees), but mostly he makes curious animals in clay, such as toucans and giraffes.

In the opposite direction, where La Candelaría ends and you turn left and then right to exit on the Luque road, is the gallery of **Justo Guggiari** (*Luis de Bolaños c/ La Candelaria; 0291 432627; Tue–Sun*), who does sculpture in metal and comes from a family of sculptors. (It was his father Hermann who did the sculpture of the soldier at Boquerón in the Chaco – see page 372 – and the metal tree trunk outside the Congreso in Asunción – see page 109.)

The **railway station** itself (down towards the lake, and to the left) has been turned into a craft shop, exhibiting and selling craft made in Areguá and other local towns.

The **Castillo Carlota Palmerola**, on Ricardo Pérez (come out of the station and turn right), is one of the most striking buildings in town, with medieval and Gothic features, including a tall round tower topped with turrets. It is now open to the public on the first Sunday of every month (*08.00–17.00; Gs10,000*), and you get a good view from the roof, especially when the lapacho trees are in flower. The castle was begun at the request of Mariscal López but not finished due to the outbreak of the Triple Alliance War, and most of it dates back to the early 20th century. It passed to the ownership of the Palmerola Ayala family, who later donated it to Dominican nuns, who still live there. Next door is the **Casa Amarilla**, a beautiful old house with elegant slim pillars, which used to operate as a sort of hotel.

The **church** of Nuestra Señora de la Candelaria was built in 1953 and is an impressive landmark, well worth walking up the hill to see, especially since the route up to it (known as the *Doble Avenida* or Double Avenue) is lined with the town's finest colonial-style architecture. At the top there is a view of Lake Ypacaraí. Houses of architectural interest are labelled with a small sign saying 'Patrimonio cultural'. Some houses are over 300 years old.

The **Ita'o** (*Presidente Báez y teniente Rojas Silva*) is a stone area where you can see the extraordinary sight of a huge ficus tree holding onto the stone by its roots, so that the grey roots and the stone almost seem to merge together. Next to it is a little round oratory of San Miguel, and on St Michael's feast day, 29 September (also the anniversary of the Battle of Boquerón), there is an important procession. To reach Ita'o from La Candelaria, turn left after passing La Vida Loca, and go uphill for two blocks.

You will also want to walk down to the lake, which has recently been improved with some benches and walkways (over the marshy ground) and a pretty pier.

There are children's swings and slides, and an environmental centre. Areguá has a **beach**, and the lake water has been very badly contaminated, but extensive work by a Korean company in early 2014 has made an improvement and it looks as though swimming may become possible again. (They have had to dredge the lake, remove vast quantities of black filth, and install a system of biodigestion to filter and clean the water, with mixed success.) The other town which has a beach on the Lago Ypacaraí is San Bernardino, with the same problems of pollution.

The **Museo del Mueble** (*Palma c/ Estación Terrena, Cocué Guazú*) was opened in 2010, but unfortunately closed again with the death of its founder, the artist Carlos Colombino, in 2013. The building itself is extraordinary and merits looking at from the outside: two huge, white, concrete slabs seem to be falling away from each other, and allowing a chink of space to open up at the top corner. 'It's a work of post-modern architecture with the idea of opening up a space of conflictive observation,' said Colombino. It is off the road to Capiatá: go past the church and follow a slight bend left and then a slight bend right to leave the principal urban area. Take the next left for nearly 2km: you leave aside the bend to the left that goes to the Estación Terrena (nothing to do with trains, but a cluster of big satellite dishes) but carry on straight for 200m, and the Colombino building is on your left.

Also just off the road to Capiatá, but on the other side of the road, is the approach to the **Monumento Natural Cerro Kõĩ**. Here is a hill with an interesting geological formation of sandstone, almost unique, but recently discovered in Egypt too. Something similar, but not quite the same, has been found in South Africa and Canada. The appearance is rather like a golden-coloured beehive, with a lot of narrow hexagonal channels, and it is believed the rock was formed 40 million years ago. There is an attendant in the car park (🕘 *08.00–16.00 daily*) to deter vandalism to cars (which used to be a problem but is no longer). From the car park there is a circuit to follow, and it is a beautiful walk, though the signposting could be improved. In 2013 over 6,000 people visited the hill, three-quarters of them in school groups. Behind Cerro Kõi is a second hill with a similar formation, Cerro Chororĩ, but it is a bit beyond the circuit and it is not recommended to go there without a guide for security reasons.

Outside town in another direction, 4km west, on the old road to Luque that runs closer to the lake than the new road, is the **Club Ecológico Isla Valle** (*Mariscal López 1844 y Vía Ferrea, Isla Valle;* ☎ *0291 432672;* **m** *0971 646285; www.islavalle.com.py;* 🕘 *entry 08.00–17.00/18.00, closes 19.00/20.00*), where they offer a service of *Pesca y Pague* ('Fish and Pay') in 20 fishponds (they lend you the fishing rod), and also have boating, horseriding, volleyball, football and a swimming pool. A great place for a day out with children. They also offer camping.

One of the companies of Areguá, Caacupemí, has a special celebration on the Feast of St Anthony of Padua, 14 June, called the **Bandera Jeré** (Flag, Spanish; All around, Guaraní). From early in the morning, groups of people take the blessing of St Anthony from house to house with the cries of '*Viva el dueño de la casa! Viva San Antonio!*' ('Long live the owner of the house! Long live St Anthony!'). They give each house a little yellow and white flag – the colours of the church – and collect from them an offering. In this way the blessing of St Anthony reaches every house, and at the end of the day everyone celebrates with dancing the polka. This celebration won third prize in the competition for the best fiesta, Pyporé Mimbí 2011. Caacupemí is 3km out of Areguá on the road to Luque.

SAN BERNARDINO

Copaco ☎ 0512 232601; municipalidad ☎ 0512 232212; www.sanber365dias.com

San Bernardino (or San Ber for short) on Lake Yapacaraí, is the number one beach resort for Paraguayans. It nudges ahead of the the river resorts such as Villa Florida, Ayolas and Cerrito, because of its proximity to Asunción, and also perhaps because of the romance of the lake that has been immortalised in the song, 'Recuerdos de Ypacaraí'. It has developed into a fashionable place among Paraguayan towns, and a good number of people from Asunción have weekend houses there. Whatever the reason for its success, it is not for the quality of the water, as the lake is polluted, and bathing is not advised.

Founded by German immigrants in 1881, the town took the name of the then president, Bernardino Caballero. Today it has some excellent hotels. There is a great difference between high season (December to February) and low season, with some establishments functioning only in the summer peak. So if you go in January you will find almost everywhere is booked up, and prices higher, but outside the summer season the hotels can be fairly empty. In late October there is a German Oktoberfest with beer and cakes and German folk dancing (shorts and braces).

GETTING THERE AND AWAY Access is from Ruta 2 after Ypacaraí (reaching that point either via San Lorenzo and Itauguá, or via Luque and Areguá). See *Getting out of Asunción*, pages 123–7 and *Travelling along Ruta 2*, pages 131–2. There is also a road that goes round the other side of the lake, but it is a dirt road, with a rickety bridge over the Río Salado, and is a very long way round. However, there is a project to asphalt the full stretch, and this work supposedly will be completed by the end of 2015.

WHERE TO STAY *Map, page 154.*

Hotel La Joya (about 6 suites) Villa Delfina c/ Ruta General Higinio Morinigo; ☎ 0512 232872; ⏲ high season only. Expensive hotel, behind the Selva Negra restaurant. It is an apartment hotel & breakfast is not served, but you can buy it in the Pueblo Hotel (see below). **$$$$**

Posada Boutique Linda India (4 rooms) Américo Vespucio y Fugger; m 0981 564424; www.posadalindaindia.com. To get to this enchanting B&B, take the 8th turn right, going northwest (away from Ruta 2) from the central crossroads where Copaco is, & it is on the second block on the left. Exquisitely decorated rooms, all with cable TV, Wi-Fi, split AC, safe. 3,000m^2 of garden with pool. Website has English version. No meals served other than ample b/fast (served until 13.00) but you can cook your own or go to one of the excellent restaurants. Late checkout 18.00. Reserve early as it gets booked out. **$$$$**

San Bernardino Pueblo Hotel (18 rooms) Paseo del Pueblo y Mbocayá; ☎ 0512 232195; e pueblohotel@gmail.com. Beautifully designed, high-quality hotel with good restaurant. Tasteful terracotta colour in rooms & solid furniture. Swimming pool, volleyball, children's playground. Wi-Fi in parts. Behind the Hotel Los Alpes, before you come to the town centre. **$$$$**

Hotel del Lago (20 rooms) Teniente Welier c/ Carlos Antonio López; ☎ 0512 232201; e gerencia@hoteldellago.org; www.hoteldellago.org. A building of character, recently renovated with style & imagination by designer Osvaldo Codas, this now counts as one of the leading hotels in the country. Situated on the plaza by the lake, it calls itself a hotel-museum & cultural centre, & has art exhibitions & a big craft shop. Round towers & Gothic windows. Chess set on table in elegant dining room. Cage with monkey & toucans on terrace. Garden has rope bridges through trees & a zip wire, provided by Aventura Xtrema. Restaurant Urutaú has excellent Sun buffet with live music, closed Sun eve & Mon. Recommended. **$$$**

Hotel Los Alpes (61 rooms) Ruta General Morinigo km46.5; ☎ 0512 232083/232399;

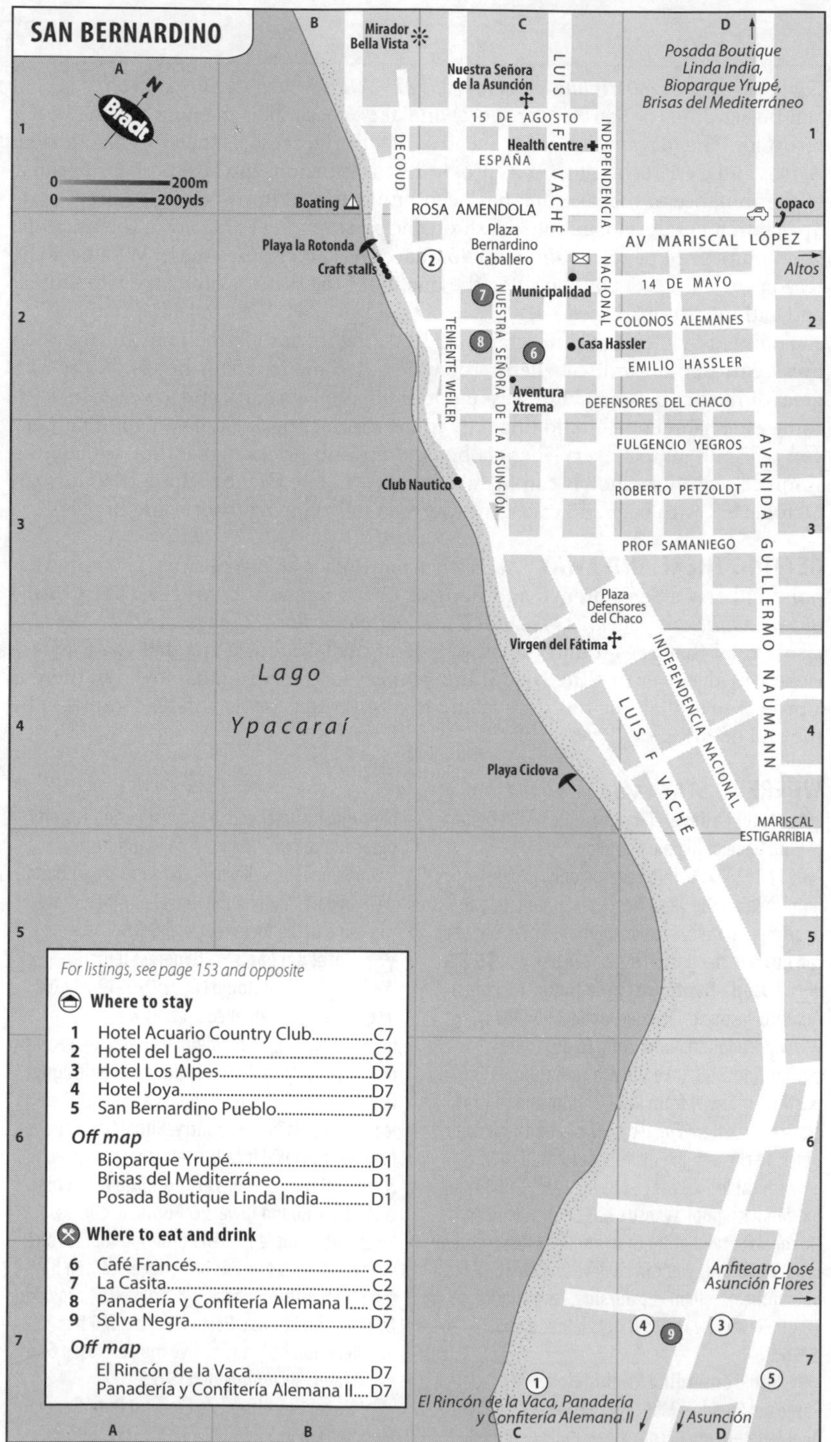

SAN BERNARDINO
Bradt
0 200m
0 200yds
Mirador Bella Vista
Nuestra Señora de la Asunción
Posada Boutique Linda India, Bioparque Yrupé, Brisas del Mediterráneo
15 DE AGOSTO
Health centre
ESPAÑA
DECOUD
LUIS F VACHÉ
INDEPENDENCIA NACIONAL
Boating
ROSA AMENDOLA
Plaza Bernardino Caballero
Copaco
AV MARISCAL LÓPEZ
Altos
Playa la Rotonda
Craft stalls
14 DE MAYO
Municipalidad
COLONOS ALEMANES
Casa Hassler
EMILIO HASSLER
TENIENTE WEILER
NUESTRA SEÑORA DE LA ASUNCIÓN
Aventura Xtrema
DEFENSORES DEL CHACO
FULGENCIO YEGROS
Club Nautico
ROBERTO PETZOLDT
PROF SAMANIEGO
AVENIDA GUILLERMO NAUMANN
Plaza Defensores del Chaco
Virgen del Fátima
Lago Ypacaraí
Playa Ciclova
MARISCAL ESTIGARRIBIA
For listings, see page 153 and opposite
Where to stay
1 Hotel Acuario Country Club C7
2 Hotel del Lago C2
3 Hotel Los Alpes D7
4 Hotel Joya D7
5 San Bernardino Pueblo D7
Off map
Bioparque Yrupé D1
Brisas del Mediterráneo D1
Posada Boutique Linda India D1
Where to eat and drink
6 Café Francés C2
7 La Casita C2
8 Panadería y Confitería Alemana I C2
9 Selva Negra D7
Off map
El Rincón de la Vaca D7
Panadería y Confitería Alemana II D7
Anfiteatro José Asunción Flores
El Rincón de la Vaca, Panadería y Confitería Alemana II
Asunción

e losalpeshotel@gmail.com; www.hotellosalpes.com.py. Very popular middle-range hotel with a good reputation. Receives a lot of groups & conventions. Pleasant garden with garden gnomes & 2 pools. Wi-Fi in part of hotel. Restaurant. At crossroads before you reach town centre. **$$$**

Hotel Acuario Country Club Ruta General Morinigo km45 y Lago Ypacaraí; 0512 232375/7; www.hotelacuario.com.py. Grandiose round building down on the beach before you reach the town, now revamped as a great & glorious sports club, with hotel accommodation too. **$$**

Bioparque Yrupé (14 rooms & 6 cabins) Avenida Guillermo Naumann; 0981 436673; Facebook: BioParque Yrupe. Ecological complex of 10ha on the edge of the lake with 75 species of native trees & 125 species of birds. Football, volleyball, 2 pools, horse carts. *Quincho*, pool, dorm for 16, *cabinas*. Good place for big groups, & they boast the biggest boat on the lake (200 passengers). **$$**

Brisas del Mediterráneo (10 rooms) Avenida Guillermo Naumann 0512 232459; www.paraguay-hostel.com. On the coast, 2km to the north of the centre, & then 200m off the road. Cabinas, pool & *parrillas*. 250m private beach. Hostel & camping. Reduced service in winter, so a prior phone call is needed in low season. **$$**

WHERE TO EAT AND DRINK *Map opposite.*

As well as the hotels above, there are the following restaurants and cafés.

Selva Negra Ruta General Higinio Morinigo km 46.5; 0512 232872; Sat, Sun out of season. Good restaurant, around corner from Hotel Joya, & part of the same group. **$$$**

Café Francés Av Luis Vaché 1005; 0512 232295; m 0981 227764; www.cafefrances.com; 10.00–22.00, closed Tue. Delightful truss-timbered restaurant that serves meals & snacks of a kind you do not usually find in Paraguay, such as foie gras, *canard à l'orange* & caviar. Low beamed ceilings & lots of atmosphere as well as the French cuisine. Run by a Frenchman with a Portuguese wife. **$$**

El Rincón de la Vaca On your right as you come into San Bernardino, before you get to Hotel Los Alpes. Restaurant at a dairy farm, so strong on homemade ice cream, yoghurt, etc. They no longer have a landline. **$$**

Panadería y Confitería Alemana I Colonos Alemanes y Nuestra Señora de la Asunción; 0512 23222; 08.00–20.00 Sat & Sun only. Meals as well as coffee shop snacks. **$$**

Panadería y Confitería Alemana II 0512 232901. Under different management. One block before Hotel Los Alpes as you come into town. **$$**

WHAT TO SEE AND DO There is a tourist office run by the Municipalidad in the town centre, in the **Casa Hassler** [154 C2] (*Luis F Vaché esq Emilio Hassler; 0512 232974;* e *sanberturismo@hotmail.com; www.sanbernardino.gov.py; 08.00–15.00 Mon–Fri, 08.00–13.00 Sat;*), which has a museum of the history of Sanber since its foundation as a German colony, and a library. It is named after a Swiss botanist who came to live in San Bernardino in 1883, and stayed more than 50 years until his death in 1937. If you would like to contract a guide to show you around, there is a group of guides coordinated by Pedro Acosta (m *0981 607829*).

Near to the Casa Hassler, on Colonos Alemanes, is an intriguing ancient tree that has been left in position as houses have been built carefully all around it. This is the neighbourhood of ice-cream parlours, mostly open only in the summer, but the main one, **La Casita** [154 C2] (m *0984 201545*), is open all year round and serves delicious homemade ices. Close to the Casa Hassler is **Aventura Xtrema** [154 C2] (*Nuestra Señora de la Asunción esq Hassler;* m *0981 682243/0961 639422;* e *info@aventuraxtrema.com.py; www.aventuraxtrema.com.py*) who offer an amazing choice of adventurous pursuits: a 4x4 drive off the roads, mountain biking, grotto walking, boat trips, cave exploration, horseriding, water skiing and diving. Perhaps the most enticing is the Hot Wheel: flying over the lake at 70mph pulled by a speedboat, which they say is for everyone – either participating or watching.

Also close to Casa Hassler, on the same street Luis F Vaché, is the **Café Francés** (see page 155). You cannot do better than eat in the Café Francés and sleep in the Hotel del Lago. The **plaza** [154 C2] where the Hotel del Lago is situated, in the town centre, has well-kept lawns and a children's playground, and a very old tree spreading its branches in the middle. If you go round the corner to the lakeside, you come to a splendid row of **craft** stalls [154 B2] selling clothes, tablecloths, *ñanduti*, *ao po'i*, pottery, and most of the usual variety of craft. **Boating** options include pedal boats, a motor launch (accompanied) or a 20-minute ride for groups in a big flat-bottom passenger boat.

If you follow Luis F Vaché down towards the fork where it branches off from the road to Ypacaraí, you come to a well-planned garden with streams, simple plank bridges, good lawns and a war memorial. Next to it is the tiny and pretty church of the **Virgen del Fátima** [154 C4]. If you continue past the fork, in the direction of Ypacaraí, you come to a **crossroads** [154 D7] which is like a secondary town centre, for you find here the famous Hotel Los Alpes, the San Bernardino Pueblo Hotel and the restaurant Selva Negra.

There are a lot of nightclubs which function only in December and January, but their names change year by year so you need to look for the information when you arrive.

The **Club Deportivo Yvytú** (*021 550154 / 661433; www.yvytu.org*) offers flights in gliders and courses of instruction. It is 800m down a dirt road, to the right of the main road that leads from Ruta 2 to San Bernardino. *Yvytú* (Guaraní) means 'wind'. You can have a 15-minute flight with a lake view in a glider or in a 1930s plane.

The ***mirador*** **Bella Vista** [154 B1] is right by the lake, and close to the town centre. On the way up, beside the steps, is an attractive church, the Virgen del Mirador, and at the top is the tall modern white statue of the Virgin, constructed in 1994 by Patricia and Roberto Ayala. You reach the top by climbing about 100 steps, or by driving up the road.

To the east of the town is a large open-air auditorium, like a Greek theatre, called the Anfiteatro José Asunción Flores, that can be used for musical or dramatic events.

ALTOS

Copaco 0512 230001/3/4; municipalidad 0512 230030/0516 262627

Altos was the very first Franciscan Reduction in the whole Río de La Plata region, and the model for later Reductions, including the Jesuit Reductions. Founded in 1580 by Luis Bolaños and Alonso de San Buenaventura, five years before the next Reduction of Itá, it was handed over to diocesan clergy in 1599.

GETTING THERE AND AWAY Altos is only 8km from San Bernardino. There are two dirt roads that lead across country from Altos to Atyrá, with picturesque views, because Altos is on higher ground than its surroundings.

WHERE TO STAY AND EAT

Finca El Gaucho (4 rooms, 2 dorms, 1 apt) 0516 252588; m 0981 976123; www.finca-el-gaucho.de Elegant, high-quality German-run guesthouse built in 2002 in 27ha, with landscaped garden & pool, reached by taking a turn left on the road between San Bernardino & Altos, & driving for 5km. Riding, fishing, hiking. **$$$**

Punta Prima (6 rooms) m 0982 170476/0982 233760; www.hotel-punta-prima.de. Great view of Lago Ypacaraí from an open terrace, on the main road between San Bernardino & Altos, 3km from San Bernardino. The restaurant has good variety & quality of pizzas, is not too expensive, & is open Fri–Sun. **$$$**

WHAT TO SEE AND DO There are two grassy plazas, almost next to each other. The first has the municipal library in the middle and the second has the church San Lorenzo de Altos: it dates from the end of the 19th century, but houses a fine original reredos. Old traditions are still strong here. On Good Friday the parish commemorates the crucifixion of Christ from midday to nightfall in an outdoor Calvary they construct beside the church, with parishioners dressed as the apostles and three carved figures on the crosses.

In a *compañía* of Altos, called Itaguazú, there is a festivity known as **Kambá Ra'angá** (black masks, Guaraní) on the feast of Sts Peter and Paul (29 June) and the adjacent days (three days in all).To reach Itaguazú turn left just as you are entering Altos, and continue along the sandy road for 3km. The event begins at 20.00. In 2013 it won the 'Pyporé Mimbi' competition for best traditional local festival in the Circuito de Oro area.

The central activity of the Kambá Ra'angá is a chasing game between young people, with costumes, masks and fire, observed by crowds around a fenced-off arena. The boys – who represent the fierce Guaicurú indigenous of the past, seeking Guaraní women – cover themselves entirely with big capes of banana leaves and wear masks: these are mostly painted stockings over their heads, although the traditional Kambá masks are finely carved in timbo wood and painted, to represent animals or ugly people. The girls have sheaves of straw which they light around a bonfire. The masked and costumed boys rush after the girls, seize them from behind, lift them up and twirl them around, while they try to defend themselves with their burning sheaves. This game is known as the 'Rúa'.

A later item in the show is when men in brown costumes like animals enter with stretchers, put 'wounded' people onto the stretchers and tip them off into the fire. After this, comically dressed dancers in masks parade in and dance in a humorous manner, falling off the stage and so on. Another act is when someone in costume (a man in a helicopter model, for example, or Spiderman) flies over the arena on a zip wire. Meanwhile, there are stalls with traditional food, and painted wooden items for sale, made locally – mostly masks, parrots and toucans. Next to the area is the little chapel which is enchantingly decked out inside: the seated statues of Sts Peter and Paul are dressed in red copes and stoles edged with yellow, and their hands are lifted in blessing. The wall behind and the ceiling above are covered with brightly coloured wooden flowers and butterflies, with a few parrots and toucans hanging from the ceiling.

EMBOSCADA

Copaco ☎ *0529 20297; municipalidad* ☎ *0529 20025*

Continuing northwards from Altos, you eventually come to Ruta 3, and the town at the junction of the two roads is called Emboscada. Here there is a little-known delight of a Franciscan-style church, dating from 1744 – tiny and precarious, with leaning door and window frames. It is complete with 70cm-thick adobe walls, wooden porticos, three reredos, a painted pulpit, carved doors and window bars and carved capitals, a couple of pews, and a hanging choir loft that you can go up to if you dare. It is only the façade of the church that is not original. The church is dedicated to St Augustine, whose statue appears at the top of the reredos, flanked by St Michael and St John the Baptist, with Sts Peter and Paul beside the Virgin on the row below. The patronal feast day is 28 August. Access to the church can be gained from the *casa parroquial* (☎ *0529 20039;* ⏱ *07.30–11.30 Mon–Sat*) and in the afternoons by ringing the sacristan Francisco Rojas (**m** *0972 897205*). If the front gate is padlocked, there is a turnstile gate at the side.

ATYRÁ

Copaco ☎ 0520 20192; municipalidad ☎ 0520 20188/05014

The 'cleanest town in Paraguay' is the tag that is customarily given to Atyrá, thanks to the efforts of a mayor in the 1990s, Feliciano Martínez, known as 'Nenecho', who promoted an ecological awareness. There are notices up in the streets such as 'The most hygienic town is not the one that gets the most cleaning but rather the one that the people dirty the least'. Its high standards have slipped a little, but it is still an attractive place to visit, especially if you can afford to stay in the Casa del Monte at the top of the hill, with its rural beauty.

As a Franciscan Reduction it was originally further north but it moved to its present site in 1672 because of attacks by both slave-traders and hostile indigenous tribes. The reredos of the church, San Francisco de Atyrá, is considered one of the finest in the country, and dates from the mid 18th century.

In late September/early October, there is an Expo Cuera (leather fair) in this street, and wood and basketware craft items are also put on sale.

GETTING THERE AND AWAY If you are driving, you want to turn north at the huge Pilgrim Cross (Kurusú Peregrino) on Ruta 2, a little to the west of Caacupé (see *Travelling along Ruta 2*, pages 131–2). As you reach the town of Atyrá, you cross the dirt road that leads westward to Altos, and eastward to join the Caacupé-Tobatí road. (If you are heading from here to Tobatí, take the fourth right from this point.) Both Altos and Tobatí are quite close to Atyrá if you go cross country on these dirt roads, and because the land is high the roads are not too muddy.

The road into Atyrá brings you up to the Paseo Indio José – a pedestrianised lane in the centre where there are stalls of leathercraft, particularly sandals. Buses from Asunción stop at this point. The bus journey takes two hours and currently costs only Gs5,000. To reach the church, go along the Paseo Indio José, turn right, and it is facing you at the top of the hill. You will pass the Municipalidad on your left, where there is a small tourist information centre.

WHERE TO STAY AND EAT

Casa del Monte (18 rooms) Monte Alto; ☎ 0520 20069/0516 250050; m 0981 570015; e hotelcasadelmonte@gmail.com; Facebook: Hotel Casa del Monte. Tourist & ecological complex, founded by a friend of Nenecho – a thoroughly Paraguayan paradise of rustic style with a little zoo. It is at the top of a hill, 2km from the town centre up a dirt road, well signed. Drive a couple of blocks past the front of the church & then turn right. If you do not have a car, they will collect you from the bus stop in the town centre for Gs25,000, or you can take a taxi. The restaurant is roofed but open at the sides, with great views. One of the bedrooms is a *choza* (round thatched hut). Little paths make fun exploration, winding around the ponds & swimming pool & among the animals, which include monkeys, macaws & peacocks, parrots & toucans, geese & grouse. Further away are pigs, sheep, goats & horses. There is sauna, massage, aromatherapy; football, volleyball, archery & ping-pong. There is a 40m² labyrinth – the only one in the country – & more than 60 species of fruit trees. They have a computer room & Wi-Fi, & they take credit cards. The hotel changed hands a few years ago & seems to have lost a little of its character. Weekdays are much cheaper than weekends. **$$**

Pytu'u Hostal (2 twin rooms) ☎ 0520 20021. Economical lodging, on a road where the buses from Asunción pass, 3 blocks south & 2 east from the front of the church. No b/fast, & no kitchen. **$**

Villa Bar Av San Antonio y 22 de setiembre; ☎ 0520 20105. Good, cheap bar serving traditional dishes. From the church, 2 blocks south & 1 east. **$**

WHAT TO SEE AND DO The old **reredos** of the church is beautifully decorated in red and gold, and has St Francis in the centre (above the Virgin), carrying a cross and a skull, and flanked to the left by St Roque. Above him is the seraph that brought him the stigmata. With more statues from the Reduction in the sacristy, the church effectively functions as a museum – the **Museo de Arte Sacro San Francisco de Asis** (*Casa parroquial:* *0520 20020;* *07.30–noon Mon–Sat & in the afternoons after about 16.00; daily mass at 18.00 winter, 19.00 summer, Mon–Sat; 08.00 & 11.00 Sun*).

The Paseo Indio José takes its name from the monument to the indigenous man who carved the Virgin of Caacupé (see box on page 142). The figure of José, complete with mallet and chisel, is actually carved out of a living tree. Although in most versions of the legend José came from Tobatí, there is also a tradition that says he came from Atyrá, specifically in the story of how he rescued the Virgin from a flood.

If you want to visit the workshop where most of the **leather goods** are made, it is called J C Artesanía en Cuero (*Av Atyrá 327;* *0520 20059;* m *0981 511031*) and is run by Julio César Maidana. It is one block west and half a block south of the southern end of the Paseo Indio José. Though they do a special line in sandals, they also produce belts, coverings for vacuum flasks and *guampas*.

The barrio **Monte Alto**, up the hill on the way to Casa del Monte, has a tall Risen Christ with outstretched arms, about 8m high, standing in a garden beside the road. Also in the same compound are other religious figures, including the pregnant woman of Revelation 12 confronted by the dragon with seven heads, and a tiny stone chapel to the Divino Niño Jesús.

Outside the town to the southeast are a couple of natural sites: a waterfall called Chorro Karumbe'ý (Guaraní 'Tortoise Water Fall'), and a hill called Cerro Kavajú (Guaraní 'Horse hill'; see under Caacupé, page 143).

The **Casa Marianela** (m *0982 101933/0972 289443;* e *marianela-atyra@gmail.com;* *07.00–noon & 13.00–17.00 daily*) is an extraordinary retreat and conference centre run by the Redemptorists with capacity for 160 people; during the above visiting hours you can ask to see the house and the murals without a problem. It is located at the northeast corner of the town, five blocks from the centre. On the gate is written 'CSSR Marianela', and a long drive leads to a stunning brick building – newly built (inaugurated in 2008) but with much ornamental detail of a medieval or moorish flavour. It has 15 or more massive murals by the artist Nino Sotelo (who also did the murals on the tower of the Caacupé Basilica, see page 143). Particularly original is the chapel, raked like a lecture theatre and with huge paintings of the Last Supper and Crucifixion by Sotelo.

TOBATÍ

Copaco *0516 262699; municipalidad* *0516 262206*

Tobatí is the furthest northeast of the little clutch of craft towns in the Circuito de Oro and is famous chiefly for wood carving and pottery. The name Tobatí in Guaraní means 'white clay', and the town also has a brick and tile industry. It is a pleasant small town with some attractive colonnades, an interesting church with some original statues from the Reductions, and a large warehouse in the Villa Artesanal which is well stocked with craft of all sorts – nearly all from Tobatí itself, showing that the town has a much broader range of craft skills than those for which it is most famous.

Tobatí is one of the oldest towns in the country, founded as a *táva* (a village for indigenous) by Domingo Martínez de Irala, in 1539 or thereabouts, some 25km to the northwest of its current position. Irala was a tough (but not ruthless) politician who consolidated the Spanish conquest throughout the Southern Cone, and is sometimes considered the founder of Paraguay. A little later, in 1583, the Franciscan Fray Luis Bolaños (see box on page 326) turned it into one of the first Christian missions, when Hernandarias entrusted all the indigenous villages around Asunción to the Franciscans for evangelisation. In the early years, Tobatí suffered many attacks from the Mbayá indigenous and in 1699 it moved to its present site. Tobatí figures importantly in the religious history of Paraguay because the Indian who carved the Virgin of Caacupé came from here, and the twin statue he made is still kept in the Tobatí church (see box on page 142).

GETTING THERE AND AROUND Public **buses** leave the Asunción Terminal every half an hour or so, from the lower platforms, reached by the subway. The bus is called La Serrana, and is slow, bumpy and tiring, taking two hours or more, because it has a lot of stops and the traffic in San Lorenzo is quite dense. It passes through Caacupé on the way to Tobatí.

If you are fortunate enough to be able to go by **car**, it will take less than half the time and is a lot more comfortable. See also *Getting out of Asunción*, pages 123–7 and *Travelling along Ruta 2*, page 131–2.

Some 8km before Tobatí you pass two ***balnearios*** (bathing places) called Ruta 63 and Ybotý 64 (m *0981 849546)*. Both have streams as well as swimming pools. Ruta 63 has better infrastructure and the focus is more on the pool, while Ybotý has a better stream and more natural beauty.

As you approach Tobatí you pass through a band of low hills with distinctive rock formations on their cliff faces: the stone has weathered to form intriguing shapes in which (with a bit of imagination) animals can be discerned: a sleeping lion, the head of a bear, and so on. There is a little chapel to the Virgen del Camino or the Virgen del Paso (the Virgin of the Way) at the foot of one of the cliffs. At the last cliff on the right-hand side, immediately before entering the town, is the prominent landmark of the Tres Caras de Indios (three heads of Indians) monument, adorned with a bunch of typical Tobatí pots. Some steps wind up the side to a *mirador* on top, from where there is an extensive view to far wooded hills in all directions.

The best place to get off the **bus** is probably at the church. This is a small town and most places can be easily reached on foot, except for the Villa Artesanal, which is a slightly longer walk.

Tobatí has an excellent service of **motor-taxis**, which are motorbikes drawing carts with a little canopy against the sun, which take two or three people. This is a more pleasant way of getting around town than by car, and very economical. There is a stop for these motor taxis where you get off the bus, and also outside the Villa Artesanal, or you can ring for one (m *0971 879604*).

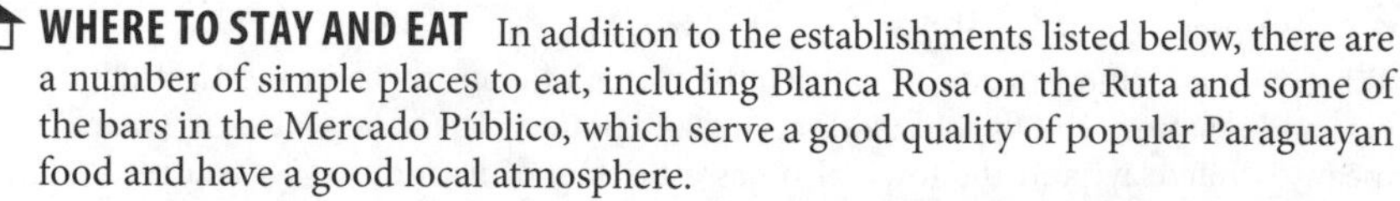

WHERE TO STAY AND EAT In addition to the establishments listed below, there are a number of simple places to eat, including Blanca Rosa on the Ruta and some of the bars in the Mercado Público, which serve a good quality of popular Paraguayan food and have a good local atmosphere.

Hotel Vista Serrana (28 rooms) 0516 262879; www.vistaserrana.com.py. New hotel on outskirts of Tobatí, big round arches, fountains, views amid hills, restaurant, swimming pool, jacuzzi, sports centre, gym. Situated 200m beyond the Villa Artesanal & 1200m from the main road into town. **$$$**

Los Manantiales (6 rooms) Puesto Pino; 021 205053 / 207039; m 0981 425498. 4km north from Ruta 2 on the road to Tobatí you pass this *estancia* which has a fine old house built of stone with antique furniture. Activities on offer include riding, trips in horse carts & walking in the woods. With neither email nor a web page, phoning is the only way of getting in touch, but it is worth it for something distinctive, beautiful & old. **$$$**

Bar Kiki (5 rooms) Estrella; 0516 262296. Rooms with private bathrooms & fans, b/fast not included in the price. Also recommended by the local people as a place to eat. **$**

FIESTAS Tobatí shares the same feast day as Caacupé, 8 December, the birthday of the Virgin. As in Itaguazú (see page 157), there is a tradition of masked figures called *kambá ra'angá* that take part in processions.

On Easter Sunday at dawn, the mass of Tupãsý Ñuvaitĩ is celebrated, with a replica of the statue of the Immaculate Conception.

For a couple of weeks at the end of October and beginning of November, there is a craft fair, which means that the exhibition at the Villa Artesanal is greatly expanded, with stalls in the forecourt.

OTHER PRACTICALITIES There is a **cash machine** at the Banco Visión.

WHAT TO SEE AND DO Tobatí is the home of **Zenón Páez** (*www.zenonpaez.com*), the most famous sculptor of wooden saints alive in Paraguay today, though he is now very old and no longer working. He was born in 1927 to a family of *santeros* (carvers of saints/saint-makers) and his children carry on the family tradition. He took very seriously the religious nature of his work, and was responsible for the statue of Cristo Rey (Christ the King) in the church of that name in Asunción. His gallery has now moved from his house to the nearby house of his daughter Sonia Páez (*Avenida Pedro Juan Caballero 1033; 0561 262763; daily until 19.00*) which is one block before the former gallery, on the same side of the main road coming into town. They still have examples of all his typical work for sale: figures of saints, painted and plain, ranging from 10cm high to 50cm or more; models of carts drawn by four or six oxen; and intricate chess sets such as examples portraying the two sides in the Triple Alliance War. Each set took him a month to carve and sells for a price that reflects that.

A block or two past the Páez house, away from the centre, is the house and shop of the Orego family (*0516 262745; daily*), who are also *santeros*. It is marked 'Santería Compostura y Pinturas' and Andrés Orego's wife, Nilda Páez, is Zenón's niece. All the traditional designs are continued, including the Holy Trinity cross (see pages 101 and 255) and the crucified woman Santa Librada. Wooden heads of Indians line the walls – another Tobatí traditional theme.

The **pottery of Tobatí** has a very distinctive style, with unglazed faces of women moulded on the rounded side of a vase, or twigs winding across the surface in a darker brown glaze. Another variant of their work is black pots (the colouring comes from mango leaves). They are more for decoration than for use, and are all made by poor women in their own homes, so there is not any obvious place where you can go to see the potters at work.

The **Villa Artesanal Ramón Ayala** (*0516 262162; 08.00–17.00 daily*) is named after another notable sculptor of Toabatí who died in 2011, and used to carve wooden pictures of house façades. The Villa Artesanal is a walk of a kilometre towards the west (towards Atyrá), or you can take a motor-taxi from the bus terminal. The turn is four blocks before the plaza that has the church in the middle, where there is a shop of domestic electrical goods and motorbikes. If you are approaching from the Asunción side, the sign on the main road is on the left-hand corner after you pass the service station on the right, and says 'Fundación Tobatí, artesanos, expo'. The Villa Artesanal is very much worth getting to because of the extensive range of high-quality craft for sale in the large warehouse. It includes work by the 400 people affiliated to the local association of artisans, many of them from the *compañías*. The works of Zenón Páez are not exhibited here, but among the better wood sculptors of Tobatí today are Hugo Esquivel, Benicio Villalba and Angel Martínez. The range of goods includes carved chairs and tables, paintings and hammocks, *ao po'i* shirts and clothing, wooden parrots in hoops and *encaje ju* tablecloths, *filigrana* silver jewellery and leather goods, as well as pottery and wood carvings.

The **church**, set in the midst of the green, was opened in 1946 (replacing an earlier Baroque church), and has twin white towers and broad side colonnades. In theory, it is open until midday, but if closed you can call at the *casa parroquial* or parish house (*0516 262300; 07.00–11.00 Mon–Sat*) directly behind the church, with grey railings, to get access. The church is normally open on Saturday mornings for cleaning, as well as for Mass (*18.00 Thu in summer, 19.00 in winter; 08.00 & 18.00 Sun in summer, 19.00 in winter*) In centre position on the reredos is the famous **statue of the Immaculate Conception** of Tobatí, which at about 1.5m high is a lot more visible than Caacupé's *Virgen de los Milagros*: the two are copies of each other, carved by the same indigenous hand, though it is the smaller Caacupé statue that gets all the visitors and all the attention. Above it is a Christ Child Saviour of the World, on the left a Virgin of Sorrows, and on the right a fine Christ of Patience, that is, Jesus sitting to rest after his scourging. These pieces are usually described as Jesuitical in style, although Tobatí was a Franciscan town (but see box, pages 174–5). The church has a full set of holy week statues used for processions.

The former parish priest, Teófilo Cáceres, has written a useful book on Tobatí, *Tobatí: Tava - Pueblo - Ciudad* (Asunción, 1995), which includes information about the statues. The book can be read in the public library (*07.00–12.30 & 13.00–17.00*) behind the Municipalidad, on a corner adjoining the plaza.

In the neighbourhood of Tobatí groups can do a **day of adventure tourism** with the company Aventura Xtrema (see page 155): you walk over the hills, explore a deep cave with head-torches, refresh yourself where there are three waterfalls of clear water, and end up abseiling down a 40m rock face (all with safety equipment). For details see www.aventuraxtrema.com.py/tobati.

VAPOR CUÉ

There is an open-air museum at Vapor Cué, 4km after the town of Caraguataý, which you reach by taking a road going northeast from Eusebio Ayala for 22km. This is a site where seven Paraguayan gunboats from the War of the Triple Alliance are kept on display, together with a monument. The boats came upriver when it was a river, but today it is nothing more than a stream. Vapor Cué is unlikely to be a particular attraction for foreign visitors, though it is of interest to Paraguayans, for whom the war still weighs heavy in the mind, and Mariscal López is seen as the great hero of tenacity in the midst of disaster. There is a government-run hotel and restaurant there, **Hotel Nacional de Turismo Vapor Cué** (*20 rooms; 0517 222395;* **m** *0976 762269;* **e** *hotelnacionaldevaporcue@gmail.com;* **$$**).

TOWNS SOUTH OF RUTA 2

The town that forms the classic route for the crossover between Ruta 2 and Ruta 1 is Piribebúy, and it is well worth a stop for its museum and church. But you can also go from Ypacaraí to Pirayú, which has an interesting church, and from there continue (on a stretch of dirt road) to Ruta 1 and the magnificent church of Yaguarón. Valenzuela is normally reached from Ruta 1, and Sapucai is normally reached from Ruta 1, but it is possible to go on a bit of rough road that unites these two towns, thus forming a longer circuit between the two principal rutas (see map on page 122).

PIRAYÚ

Copaco ☎ *0519 20302; municipalidad* ☎ *0519 20011)* Pirayú grew up under Franciscan influence from Yaguarón. The church here dates from as early as 1561 (or possibly 1567), according to a date in the choir loft. It has no fewer than five original reredos, as well as a font, confessional box, a good pulpit and a fresco of the Trinity. Ask for access at the *Casa de las Hermanas* (the Sisters' house) on the right-hand side of the church, behind the newly restored house of the first bishop of Paraguay, Basilio López (brother of President Carlos Antonio López), which has been recently turned into a cultural centre.

According to a carved date on a beam by the choir loft, the church was completed in 1661 (or possibly 1667). The steps to the choir loft are steep and very dirty, but are safe to climb. This is the only church from the period of the Reductions to have been built with a theatre (an extra room behind the high altar), and a painted backcloth was sent to the Escuela de Bellas Artes to be restored. The principal reredos is very pretty, with its grey-blue and gold colouring and seven saints, of which Sts Peter and Paul, to either side of the Virgin, are the best. Three coats of paint were removed from the reredos in an 11-year work of restoration. Profesora Gregoria Delgadillo (☎ *0519 20185/20153/20011;* **m** *0983 200486;* **e** *gregoriadelgadillo@hotmail.com*) knows a lot about the town and is willing to act as a local guide.

There is also an old railway station – the only one in the country to have two towers – and a *casa artesanal* that sells *ñanduti* and hammocks.

GETTING THERE AND AWAY It is reachable not only from Ypacaraí (see pages 140 –1) on asphalt (12km) but also from the other direction, from Yaguarón (see pages 172–6), on a good-quality *empedrado* (10km). (A dirt road of poorer quality goes from Yaguarón to Paraguarí.)

PIRIBEBÚY

Copaco ☎ *0515 212085; municipalidad* ☎ *0515 212202*

Piribebúy is the town on the link road between Ruta 1 and Ruta 2, so it is strategically placed to form part of the Circuito de Oro. Although it was not founded as a Reduction, it has a lovely church dating from that period and a reredos inside that has as its centrepiece a wonderful crucifix known as Ñandejára Guasú (Guaraní 'Our great Lord'). On 21 January they celebrate their patronal feast day.

But Piribebúy is better known for having been for a brief time the capital of Paraguay, as Mariscal López fled Asunción in the Triple Alliance War. For him and for Paraguay it was the beginning of the end that culminated with his death at Cerro Corá, in the northeast corner of the country. In Piribebúy there was a week-long battle and a massacre, and Paraguayans are proud of the heroism of the populace who fought to the death. This chapter of history is recorded in the museum.

Piribebúy is also the place where the famous *poncho de sesenta listas* is made.

GETTING THERE AND AWAY See *Travelling along Ruta 2*, pages 131–2. To reach Piribebúy from Ruta 2, take the turn south that is opposite the Chipería El

Indio – the first of many *chiperías* on Ruta 2 – and continue for 9km. When you reach the town, signed to your right, the main road comes down towards it in a southwesterly direction but at the entrance to the town it then bends a little towards the southeasterly, before straightening out and heading due south. The result of this is that when you enter the town you are heading directly south, but if you then take a left turn at the museum, you hit the main road again at a right angle, the town fitting itself into an elongated wedge shape to the west of the road.

To reach Piribebúy from Ruta 1, see *Travelling along Ruta 1*, page 169. In this case you need to turn left after crossing the stream, exactly where the main road begins to bend a little left, and this will bring you directly past the plaza with the church (on your left) to the museum (on the far corner of the next block, where you reach the main street of Piribebúy).

For both routes, see *Getting out of Asunción*, pages 123–7.

There is a **bus** (*Empresa Piribebuy;* ☎ *0515 212217*) that goes from Asuncíon to Piribebúy, passing through San Lorenzo, Capiatá, Itauguá, Ypacaraí and Caacupé on the way.

WHERE TO STAY AND EAT The best option within Piribebúy is **El Viejo Rincón** (*6 rooms; Maestro Femín López y Teniente Horacio Gíni;* ☎ *0515 212251;* **$**), an attractive, colonial-style building of character on the corner one block from the Ruta and one block from the church, with wooden columns, tables under the portico and tablecloths of typical Paraguayan lace. It has AC but no internet. There are a number of excellent places to stay and eat outside the town – see page 166.

FESTIVALS The patronal feast of Ñandejára Guasú is on the third Sunday of January, and is taken as the occasion for celebrating a festival of the *poncho de 60 listas* (see page 24) in the Club 12 de Agosto. But bigger and more popular in style is the feast of San Blas on 3 February. The little statue of San Blas, dressed in a long red cope, is in a sanctuary in the barrio San Blas, two blocks beyond the petrol station.

WHAT TO SEE AND DO When you approach from Ruta 2 you fork left to enter the town, and that road leads straight ahead to the **museum**, on the corner of Mariscal Estigarribia. Its full name is the Museo Histórico Commandante Pedro Pablo Caballero (🕘 *07.00–noon & 14.00–17.00 Tue–Fri, 07.00–11.00 Sat, 07.00–noon Sun, closed Mon; free admission*), and it is named after the Paraguayan commander in the battle of Piribebúy. The museum is in a colonial house dating from the López period. It was founded by veterans of the Chaco War and has a larger section on that war, but more interest is bound to focus on the earlier war, given the particular history of Piribebúy. Although only one room is devoted to the War of the Triple Alliance, this is not a bad place to get an overview of it, with the help of the excellent guide Miguel Ángel Romero (**m** *0971 179437*), who is also a *santero* (a carver of saints).

There are large paintings of Mariscal López and his Irish partner, Madame Lynch (known as 'Madame' because she was married to a Frenchman when the relationship with Francisco Solano López began). There is a timeline and a good map, charting the course of the war from the misconceived invasion of Mato Grosso (to the north) at the end of 1864, through the brief campaigns of Corrientes and Uruguay (to the south), to the 2½-year stand-off at Humaitá (in the southwest corner of Paraguay; see pages 232–5). In mid-1868 the Paraguayan army was pushed back to Pikysyrý (south of Asunción), but by mid-1869 all was defeat, as the sick and hungry vestiges of the army were dragged back by López, through Piribebúy and up to the extreme northeast corner of the country. Mariscal López was finally killed at Cerro Corá, on 1 March 1870, thus ending the war. See also pages 352–3.

In the battle of Piribebúy on 12 August 1869, the actual Paraguayan army was not present, but was camped out at Azcurra, near Caacupé. So the battle was fought between the 20,000-strong force of the Triple Alliance, and only 1,600 defenders. The women in particular, known as the Heroines of Piribebúy, fought with rifles, swords, bottles, bones, and anything they could lay their hands on, rather than surrender. When the cannonballs ran out, they shot with coconuts. The tenacity of the Paraguayans was astonishing, but the defeat was inevitable. It was horribly followed by the burning of the hospital of Piribebúy, with the doors locked to incinerate the 600 people inside – nurses, doctors and the wounded – in one of the most terrible atrocities of the war. Four days later, on 16 August, came the massacre of Acosta Ñu, in which an army of 3,000 children was slaughtered, who had been prepared for the battle by the schoolteacher, Maestro Fermín López, who taught them to paint the fake beards and moustaches on their faces as a way of making the enemy think they were older and stronger than they were (see in this chapter under *San Lorenzo*, page 134, and under *Villarrica*, page 318). Fermín also got the children to paint the reredos of Piribebúy yellow (see below) to preserve it from looting by the enemy.

To gain access to the **church**, ask at the museum, and the guide may take you down himself, closing the museum in the meantime. The church is one block to the east, in the middle of a green. You reach it from the back, which is the better angle from a historical point of view, because you can see the unbroken colonnade all round, supported on wooden pillars with carved capitals, and with original windows and doors. It was begun in 1733, while funds were being sought for building the larger church at Yaguarón, and when Piribebúy was finished in 1753 (according to the date on one of the roof beams) the work on the church at Yaguarón could begin. The pulpit in particular is similar to that of Yaguarón. The appearance of the Jesuit symbol IHS confirms how heavily the Franciscan churches relied on Jesuit-trained artists to build their churches. The frontage with its tower was put on later, in a different style, although the combination is quite pleasing.

There are original windows and doors, floor, pulpit, confessional boxes, niches, and a 1759 reredos. The magnificent centrepiece is the famous Ñandejára Guasú crucifix, which is articulated (it has hinged arms, so can be taken down from the cross and put in the coffin). According to some accounts, it was brought from Spain, while according to others it was brought from the Jesuit Reductions of Misiones, and it is an object of much devotion. It is flanked by the Virgin of Sorrows and the Beloved Disciple (both clothed figures), and at the top is a charming seraph – the angel that brought the stigmata to St Francis of Assisi. A modern tower over this main altar permits light to enter and show the reredos to advantage.

In 1999 there was a famous scandal when a journalist from ABC-Color, Luis Verón, denounced the restoration done to this reredos by a foreign architect, Luis Fernando Pereira Javaloyes, who in turn sued him and won the case. Despite that, the restoration proved so controversial that it was undone and the over-painting removed at enormous cost.

To get to the place where the famous *ponchos de sesenta listas* are made, you need to return to the main road and follow it south over the little stream towards the outskirts of the town. Take the second left where there is a sign saying 'Balneario Camping las Palmeras' and drive along the edge of the big sports ground. Then turn left down the grassy track at the edge of the field. Halfway down you will pass a house with a small notice saying 'Heladería San Cayetano'. It looks an unlikely place for a poncho workshop, but it is right. Rosa Segovia and her family (*Cerro León y Capitán Cristaldo;* ☎ *0515 212097;* e *poncho60lista@hotmail.com*) carry on the craft that has been handed down through generations. A *poncho de sesenta listas* is a kind of poncho made from cotton thread, so is very fine and ornamental, with a silky sheen, but is not made for warmth. It has 60 white stripes in it, and is enormously time-consuming to make, and for this reason the craft is in danger of extinction as a handmade product. It takes 22 days' work by one person to make the poncho, which will sell for less than US$200, of which more than half is the cost of so much cotton thread. It is said that Mariscal López had this kind of poncho, but that the tradition began even earlier, in the days of Dr Francia. Sometimes the poncho is made in black and white, sometimes in black, red and white, and sometimes in multicoloured stripes.

If you continue on the dirt road you took when you left the asphalt, you come to Ruta 2. This is the most direct route if you want to continue travelling east.

AROUND PIRIBEBÚY

Where to stay around Piribebúy

La Quinta (4 cabins & 8 suites) Ruta Paraguarí–Piribebúy km82.5; ☎ 021 3288484; m 0971 117444/117555; m only for GiroTigo 0982 214171; e laquinta@laquinta.com.py; www.laquinta.com.py. One of the *estancias* at the upper end of the market, a favourite of the main tour operators. Beautifully designed & the food is gourmet cuisine & in vast quantities. Lunch costs Gs92,000 currently & is a buffet, *tenedor libre*; you must reserve & pay 50% in advance, which you can do through GiroTigo to the number above. (Ask your hotel to help you do this.) All the usual activities: swimming, riding, walking, football, volleyball, ping-pong, etc. If it can be faulted, it is for being less Paraguayan in design than other places, & also for being difficult to find. There is no sign with its name on the road, & even the sign that locates it, 'Km 82.5' (ie: from Asunción), is small. It is 10km from Piribebúy & 19km from Paraguarí, on the east side of the road, & it just a little to the Piribebúy side of the Capilla de San Juan. If you do not have your own vehicle, take a bus to Piribebúy, & then one of the hourly buses towards Chololó, or a taxi from Piribebúy or Paraguarí, or more comfortably & more expensively, let La Quinta pick you up from Asunción. Charges are for 24hrs with meals & activities, or for a day, 09.00–18.00. Reservations can also be made through Apatur (see page 54). **$$$$**

Estancia La Aventura Ruta 2, km61.5; m 0981 441804; e estanciaaventura@hotmail.com; www.estancia-aventura.com. Close to the Piribebúy turn, but on the Asunción side of Ruta 2, this is a German-run *estancia* where you can ride with the gauchos, swim in the lake & play tennis. Tastefully designed with a wide colonnade to the house. Aimed principally at the German market. **$$$**

Hotel Topachi Resort (19 rooms) Avenida Nanawa y Virgen del Rosario; m 0981 322881; www.topachi.com. German-run hotel resort 7km outside Piribebúy: follow the notices from Ruta 2 after passing through Caacupé. Spa & 3 pools. Reservations only by email only. **$$$**

San Francisco Country Club Hotel Ruta Paraguari–Piribebúy km66; ☎ 0516 250301; m 0981 802253; e info@francisco-country.com; www.san-francisco-country.com. Between Piribebúy & Ruta 2, on the west side of the road. Charming round thatched huts (called bungalows), well furnished. Pool, sports areas. Cheaper bungalows have fans. **$$$**

Hotel Parador Chololó (30 rooms) Ruta Paraguarí–Piribebúy km87; ☎ 0515 212766/021 553965/551207; Facebook: Chololó Parador Turístico. Set in Chololó park (see below). Rooms & cabins, restaurant, 150m from the road. AC. No internet. **$$**

Hotel Gabriela See page 177.

What to see and do near Piribebúy

Chololó The huge Chololó park is a paradise of woods, streams and little waterfalls, but it is sometimes marred by the quantity of rubbish left lying on the ground by day trippers. The Hotel Parador Chololó (see above) is set within it, but not many people stay overnight. It is 72km from Asunción via Paraguarí and 87km via Piribebuý. It is 10km from Mbatoví.

The Eco-reserva **Mbatoví** activity centre (*Ruta Paraguarí–Piribebúy km72; ☎ 021 444844; m 0971 659820; e info@mbatovi.com.py; www.mbatovi.com.py; ⏱ closed Mon*) is a fantastic eco-adventure park among the hills between Piribebúy & Paraguarí, 10km from Ruta 1. You can reach it by getting a bus from Asunción to Paraguarí and a taxi from there. There are great views of the hills from the *mirador* Mbatoví Rovetã (Guaraní, Window of Mbatoví). The *tape saingo* (Guaraní, hanging path) takes you across four rope bridges followed by a 105m zip wire and finishing with abseiling down a 20m cliff. There is an emphasis on safety as well as excitement, and children can do the zip wire from age 6. Shoes with stout soles are best for the rope bridges. The 1,700m trail Yvaropý passes through land which according to legend was the resting place of the gods. All of the activities are good value: US$35 for foreigners and Gs100,000–Gs130,000 for Paraguayans. Payment must be made in full in advance in a bank to avoid risks of handling money on site. If you do not come in your own group you may have to wait a few days to go with another group, but at weekends and on public holidays when there is a lot of movement they can accept a booking even from just one person.

VALENZUELA

Copaco ☎ 0516 256003; municipalidad 0516 255201/3

Valenzuela is often overlooked in the Circuito de Oro, but if you are interested in reredos from the Reductions, then it is a must. But you will have difficulty getting there without instructions.

GETTING THERE AND AWAY There are a few **buses** direct from the Terminal in Asunción, at least every hour. The journey takes three hours by bus, and is very much quicker by car. If you are coming by **car** on Ruta 2 (see *Travelling along Ruta 2*, pages 131–2), then look for a turning to the south, 7km to the east of San José and 8km to the west of Itacurubí de la Cordillera. There is no road sign indicating Valenzuela, but you will know you are at the right junction when you see a café on the corner marked 'Despensa Copetín El Desvío' and a battered yellow hoarding advertising 'Cerámica Ña Virginia'. You drive for 13km on this road, which is now asphalted, and then you reach a welcome sign announcing that Valenzuela is the town of the pineapple (*piña*): there is a festival of the pineapple in January, and it is the town's principal crop.

If you are coming on the new road that runs from Paraguarí to Villarrica, then Valenzuela is reached by a dirt road going north just before Caballero.

WHERE TO STAY Just 3km beyond Valenzuela & another 1km to the right is **La Cascada** (*15 rooms; ☎ 021 552131/0516 255495; m 0981 880738/0982 215223; www.complejoturisticolacascada.com;* **$$$**), a delightful but little-known rural hideaway with a 2km ecological reserve, waterfalls, riding, football and beach volleyball. It has a sandy beach by a stream and a 4m high observation tower. There are thatched roofs over tables dotted around the grass and a painted landscape on the wall of the *quincho*. Visitors can go on a beautiful walk with a guide to two waterfalls, one with a fall of 7m and the other (more difficult to reach) 25m high. Rooms all have AC, private bathroom, sommier beds, or you can camp. Buses run to Valenzuela approximately every hour, but only two or three a day go the further 3km. The phone signal is poor, both for the landline and mobile, so you may have to try more than once.

WHAT TO SEE AND DO Valenzuela has an idyllic plaza, adorned (depending on the season) with the red blossom of the *chivato* tree. Facing the church is a monument to 'P Victor Fernández Valenzuela SJ, sublime rector de la enseñanza cristiana e insigne fundador de este pueblo' (Fr Victor Fernández Valenzuela SJ, sublime rector of Christian teaching and distinguished founder of this town).

However, according to the historian Margarita Durán, the town was founded not by a Jesuit but by a diocesan priest called Antonio Fernández de Valenzuela. On his death, the private oratory he had built turned into a parish church. What we certainly know is that the relationship between Jesuit and Franciscan art, and Jesuit and Franciscan history, is a lot more intertwined than is often supposed. The date of the foundation was 24 July 1813.

The church, though small, is a gem. The keys are in the hands of Señora Amalia, who lives a block away. Ask local people to show you her house, and do not forget to tip if she comes specially to open the church for you. The church is old but has been retouched, and the general impression has been completely altered by the addition of a modern tower at centre front, quite simple but with Gothic arches. Inside, however, you find beautiful old treasures of art, notably an original reredos – not large, but ornate, and with delightful figures and still surprisingly vivid colours. In the centre of it is an unusual tabernacle with two sliding, curved doors. On the outer sides of the tabernacle are archangels with charmingly childish proportions: St Michael trampling the demon on the right-facing side; and St Raphael with his fish on the left-facing side.

Above the tabernacle is St Joseph – to whom the church is dedicated – with a lily in his hand. Sts Peter and Paul, in papal tiara and mitre respectively, flank him on either side. The Virgin of the Assumption is at the summit of the reredos, standing as usual on a crescent moon adorned with cherubim heads. The pulpit is ancient (though the steps up to it are not) and it has a carved wooden pineapple hanging beneath it. Facing the altar is a choir gallery, which is modern, but in the original style and position. One of the notable features of this little church is the painting on the wooden bases of the pillars and the walls above them, and the arched roof above the altar, which, though simple in design, is either untouched or restored in the original style.

SAPUCAI

Copaco ☎ 0539 263200/263299; municipalidad ☎ 0539 263214

The old railway line of Paraguay – one of the first in Latin America, if not the first (the claims vary) – was built with the help of English engineers and workmen. The first stretch, from Asunción to the station Trinidad (the Botanical Gardens), was opened in 1861, and the line reached Sapucai just when the Triple Alliance War was beginning. The workshops of Sapucai were constructed in 1887, and this became the centre of the railway industry.

GETTING THERE AND AWAY See *Getting out of Asunción*, pages 123–7, and *Travelling along Ruta 1*, page 169, for getting to Paraguarí. Then take the new road that runs from Paraguarí to Villarrica (see page 315).

Posada Tapé Bolí (2 rooms) ☎ 0539 263282; m 0982 401715. Towards the north end of town. $

Posada Arroyo Porã (3 rooms) m 0981 895020/0971 242438. 3km from Sapucai & 3km from Escobar, on the north side of the road. As well as 3 bedrooms in the *posada*, there are individual cabins for 2, 3, 4 or 5 people, with AC or fans. Camping. A dammed stream forms a natural pool. Riding. **$**

WHAT TO SEE AND DO The huge shed (the width of three railway lines) where the trains used to be made is now open as a **museum** (*0539 263218; 07.00–17.00 daily; free admission*), called the Museo Nacional Ferrocarril Presidente Carlos Antonio López, after the president under whom the railway flourished, before the Triple Alliance War put an end to all development in Paraguay. It is a fascinating place of large, old fashioned rusting machinery, witness to former days of glory. There are wheels, clamps, presses, boilers, cogs, coach lights, a bronze bell, some train wagons named 'C A López' and the presidential coach with photos of famous travellers.

There is also what is known as the Villa Inglesa (English estate) which was built in 1905 for the English technicians who were working on the railway. There are about 30 of these houses, more than a century old and very solidly built. In their day they had the mod cons of the period, being the first houses in the interior to have electric light and running water. Some descendants of the English workers still live there. The English developed fruit cultivation in the country and for this reason the Guaraní word for grapefruit comes from the English: *greifu*.

As is the case with so much else associated with the railway, there is an air of time warp about the town, with its old houses and church, nestling into the side of the hills that run between Ruta 1 and Ruta 2 (the Cordillera). The *cementerio de los trenes* is the name they give to where the old dead trains lie.

Early on Saturday mornings around 07.00, some 50 women on donkeys descend from the surrounding hills on an old stone path, the Tapé Bolí, which was built by Bolivians taken prisoner during the Chaco War. They come laden with agricultural products to sell in the marketplace.

TRAVELLING ALONG RUTA 1

Ruta 1 is the highway that runs from Asunción in a southeasterly direction to the border town of Encarnación, on the Río Paraná, opposite Posadas, Argentina. This is the route to Paraguay's chief tourist attraction, the Jesuit museums of Misiones and the Ruins of Itapúa, which are described in the next two chapters. For the moment, however, we are concentrating on the places that can be visited close to Asunción, in the Circuito de Oro. All buses leaving the Asunción Terminal and heading for Encarnación go along Ruta 1, as well as those heading for Ayolas or for Pilar.

San Lorenzo is the town where the road divides into rutas 1 and 2, but it is dealt with under Ruta 2 (see pages 132–5). Remember that if you are in your own vehicle, you can take the Acceso Sur to get onto Ruta 1, as an alternative to passing through San Lorenzo (see *Getting out of Asunción*, pages 123–7).

After passing through the craft town Itá – or after the Acceso Sur joins up with Ruta 1, if you are taking that route – you go through Yaguarón, with its famous church. The one-way system does not lead you past it (except on a return journey), but if you are in your own vehicle it would be a great pity not to stop and visit it. It is the most beautiful church in Paraguay (see pages 170–1).

There is a good place to break your journey for a meal or a snack at the Frutería just before Paraguarí. All Paraguayans with cars make it a regular stopping point (see page 177).

After that, the next recommended eating place is in Quiindý not until you cross the Río Tebicuarý and reach Villa Florida, in Misiones (see pages 188–9). By then you will have left the Circuito de Oro far behind.

ITÁ

Copaco ☎ *0224 632901/632199; municipalidad* ☎ *0224 632575*

Itá was the second of the Franciscan Reductions, founded in 1585 by Luis Bolaños and Alonso de San Buenaventura, and its church is not only the earliest but has several interesting features that have been lost in other Franciscan churches. Itá is also well known as one of the pottery towns: here they claim to be the capital of pottery (though Areguá and Tobatí would rival this claim). The feast day of the patron saint, San Blas, is 3 February.

ORIENTATION The town is on Ruta 1 but spreads to the south of the highway. The main bus stop is just before the traffic lights at the junction with the road that turns off at right angles to go north to Itauguá and Ruta 2. That road is called General Caballero, and if you work westwards from there, back along Ruta 1, then the turnings are (in order) Independencia Nacional, Manuel Gamarra, Carlos Antonio López, Enrique Doldán Ibieta, Teniente Valdovinos (north side only), Curupayty, Cerro Corá, Guarambaré and San Lorenzo. This will help in locating the sites mentioned below.

There is a taxi rank on General Caballero next to the Petrobras service station by the traffic lights, and another taxi rank by a smaller Petrobras service station on Enrique D Ibieta – both on Ruta 1. The Plaza del Mercado is between Manuel Gamarra and Independencia Nacional, three blocks to the south of Ruta 1. The bus terminal is down there, next to the Municipalidad, for those buses that end their journey at Itá.

There is not much in the way of restaurants, let alone hotels, but halfway down the Plaza del Mercado, on the west side, is a *patio de comidas* on the second floor, so obscurely signed that you may not find it unless you ask.

WHERE TO STAY Not strictly speaking in Itá, but a little before it and belonging to the previous town, J Augusto Saldivar, is **Oñondivemí** (Guaraní 'Together') (*35 beds; Ruta 1 km27.5;* ☎ *0295 20344;* m *0981 441460; www.onondivemi.com.py;* **$$$**). This is one of the closest *estancias* to Asunción. Activities include football, volleyball, swimming, boating, horse carts, cycling and fishing. It has a pool, biopark and zoo with capybaras, parrots, monkeys and peacocks, plus a museum with about 200 stuffed animals native to Paraguay. There is the option of cheaper accommodation in bunk beds for groups. Book in advance, at least the day before. Reservations can also be made through Apatur (see page 54).

WHAT TO SEE AND DO The **church** is believed to have been the first Franciscan church built in Paraguay. It is dedicated to San Blas (St Blaise in English; the 4th-century bishop who healed a boy with a fishbone stuck in his throat, and is invoked by holding two crossed candles across the throat). To reach it you take Carlos Antonio López or Enrique Doldan Ibieta from Ruta 1, and the church is between the two, three blocks from the main road.

High on the tower is a charming little figure of San Blas in his mitre, with his cope and stole painted red. A plaque in the porch acknowledges the foundation of the Reduction in 1585 by the two Franciscan friars, Bolaños and de San Buenaventura. You can gain access to the church in the mornings by calling at the parish house (*Enrique Doldán Ibieta y San Blas;* ⏲ *07.00–11.30 Mon–Fri, 14.00–16.30 Sat*). It is not marked as such but is a house on a corner of the plaza, to the southwest of the church, and next door to the Escuela Juan O'Leary. There is another chance to get into the church in the evening, as it opens at 18.30 every day for Mass at 19.00, and on Sundays there is an extra Mass at 08.00.

If you are not able to gain access, at least look in through the old wooden bars of the window near the altar on the east side, which is customarily left open. Although most of the walls date from the 20th century almost everything else is original: the painted roof beams (one of which bears the words 'Ec Est Domvs Domini – Firmiter Edificata – Anno 1698'), the frescoes on the walls behind the altar, the shutters, window bars, doors, statues and reredos.

The reredos is very pleasing, not so much for the quality of the sculpture – for in this case the figures are clothed in material rather than being carved entirely out of wood – as for the harmonious composition of the whole, well lit, and with good use of the bright red that is typical of San Blas here. The liturgical red is picked up on the figure of St Peter, in a papal tiara, on the far left, and St Laurence the deacon, holding the grill on which he was roasted, on the far right. Between these figures and the central San Blas are two friar-saints in the brown Franciscan habit: St Francis of Assisi, with a skull and a book, and San Francisco Solano with a violin. The latter is particularly interesting, as it recalls the fact that this early Franciscan missionary, who worked in northern Argentina rather than Paraguay, was also a teacher of the violin, before the Jesuits arrived and developed the musical tradition of the Reductions to a much higher level. The three figures on the upper level of the reredos are (from left to right) St Anthony, the Virgin and St Joseph.

Over the arch above the chancel is a beautifully preserved Trinity fresco, and there are frescoes of angels all around the wall behind the reredos. Down the nave near the front entrance is a group around the crucifix – Mary and the Beloved Disciple. In the sacristy are more statues, and the original pulpit piled high on top of a large original chest of drawers.

The biggest selection of craft in Itá is in the long building called **CAPICI** (*Centro Artesanal de las Pequeñas Industrias de la Ciudad de Itá*; ⌚ *07.00–17.00 Mon–Fri, 07.00–noon Sat*), which is on the corner of Cerro Corá and Ruta 1. Here you can buy big garden pots, plates for hanging on the wall, cribs, banana-leaf figures, paintings, statues of San Blas, hammocks, leather bags, model dancers, crochet items, and *gallinas de suerte* ('lucky hens'). These last are a traditional Itá craft and require some explanation. The chickens have clay feathers stuck on all round them like petals, and they come in different sizes and different colours, each colour representing a wish for good fortune in one way or another: white – love; brown – friendship; grey – health; black – abundance; blue – marriage; green – hope and orange – work.

Rosa Brítez is the most famous of Itá's artisans, and is a delightful and dynamic person, quite used to being besieged by visitors. Her home and workshop is on Ruta 1 at the entrance to the town (from Asunción), on the south side, in between a bus shelter and a tiny canal and just before a petrol station. Her work is in black clay and is distinctive, typified by very round bodies. Of her 13 children, four work in pottery like her. She has her own plot of land, from which she can extract the clay, and she turns it black by baking it in the smoke of the *guayaiví* plant. Among her regular products are a series of 30 erotic poses as described in the *Kama Sutra*, shown in full graphic detail. This provoked the rage of one Catholic priest, who tried to have her workshop closed down. But her work appealed to the late pop singer Michael Jackson, from whom she received an order.

Other potters of note in Itá (and some prefer their work to that of the better-known Rosa Brítez) are Juana Marta Rodas and her daughter Julia Isidrez, whose workshop is on the road to the big national hospital of Itauguá. Look for the yellow railings and a sign with their name. There is also Gregoria Benítez and her son Celso, whose workshop is five blocks south of the CAPICI craft centre, then turn right and you will find it on the left, next to the chemist. Gregoria's brother, Marciana Rojas, invented the *gallinas de suerte* mentioned above.

The best place to pick up a bus for the onward journey is by the traffic lights at the junction of Ruta 1 and General Caballero. This is where the road to Itauguá begins, but if you continue on Ruta 1, the road will swing to the right and then leave town. Immediately south of Itá is a big roundabout where the alternative route from Asunción known as Acceso Sur joins Ruta 1 (see page 126).

The two Franciscan Reductions of **Guarambaré** and **Ypané** are reached from the Acceso Sur (see the regional map, page 122). Ypané has had its reredos returned to the church. What remains of the reredos and the old church of Guarambaré is in the Museo Bogarín in Asunción, but the modern church has an interesting statue of St Michael: call at the *casa parroquial* for access (*0293 932212*).

YAGUARÓN

Copaco 0533 232300; municipalidad 0533 232296/232368

The next town down Ruta 1 is Yaguarón, famous for being the only Reduction to have its original **church** still standing in its original form. This is a 'must-see' if you are interested in the Reductions, and although the Reduction is Franciscan, the church is on exactly the same model as in the Jesuit Reductions. If you are not in your own transport, you see it out of the window of the bus as you go through the town, travelling towards Asunción. (Travelling southwards, however, the one-way system does not lead you past it.) It is highly distinctive with its simple pitched roof, massive wooden columns and separate wooden bell tower, and is clearly visible on the north side of the Ruta, which curves around it. But if you can manage to stop and go inside, do not miss the opportunity to see this gloriously harmonious extravaganza of painted and carved wood.

Fray Luis Bolaños and Fray Alonso de San Buenaventura, his missionary companion, founded Yaguarón shortly after Itá, around 1586–87. Today, Yaguarón still has an interesting band, called Peteke Peteke, that plays traditional, indigenous music on old instruments such as the *turú* (cow's horn) and different sizes and shapes of drums. It traditionally plays on 3 February (feast of San Blas), 16 August (feast of San Roque) and the first Sunday of September.

GETTING THERE AND AWAY See *Travelling along Ruta 1*, page 169.

TOURIST INFORMATION There is a tourist information kiosk (*07.00–13.00 daily*) at the side of Ruta 1 as you approach Yaguarón.

WHERE TO STAY

Ápe Avy'áve (Guaraní, 'Here I Have More Joy') (7 rooms) 0533 232462. Small guesthouse as you leave the town, on the left-hand side of the road to Asunción. **$**

Aní Rehása Reí ('Do Not Pass By In Vain') (2 rooms) 0533 232210. Small guesthouse opposite church, with a simple, family feel. Fans, private bathrooms. The cheapest option. **$**

WHERE TO EAT AND DRINK On a corner tucked into a residential area behind the church, two blocks from the road into Yaguarón and two blocks from the road out, is **Tía Ana** (*Julia M Cueto esq Buenaventura Gamarra; 0533 232100;* **m** *0992 205308;* **$**), a friendly family restaurant.

WHAT TO SEE AND DO The **church** (☎ *0533 232229;* ⏰ *06.00–11.00 & 13.30–17.00 Tue–Sun, closed Mon; Mass times: 18.00 Sat (sometimes with choir); 08.00 Sun (sometimes with choir); 18.00 Tue & Thu winter or 19.00 summer; 06.00 Wed & Fri*) is dedicated to St Bonaventure, the Franciscan bishop-saint after whom one of the two founders was named. The sacristan, Antolín Alemán (☎ *0533 232198;* **m** *0982 995122*), attends the church all day and acts as guide. If you would like the lights put on to see the reredos better, do not forget to make a small donation for electricity costs: every Gs5,000 is a help. From time to time there is an atmospheric *son et lumière* called the *Paseo de Música y Luces*, with music from the period of the Reductions. This can be put on by day and not just at night – because the church is dark inside once the doors are shut – but it has to be organised with prior notice. Speak to Antolín Alemán or contact Osvaldo Codas, the creative spirit behind the Hotel del Lago (**e** *osvaldocodas@gmail.com*), to see what the possibilities are.

The church is large and imposing, 70m long and with 30m-wide colonnades all around it. At the date of its construction, the architecture of the Reductions was moving in favour of building stone churches such as Trinidad. The first metre of the walls in Yaguarón was in brick, but after some conflict the decision was made to continue the church in the traditional adobe and wood, rather than to experiment with the new techniques. According to the traditional methods of construction, this meant building the roof first, supported on massive tree trunks (of *urunde'ý* wood) up to 30m high, that were buried in the ground together with a good part of their root structure. The walls of adobe, up to 1.8m thick in places, were filled in later: they do not support the roof. The figure of Samson and the lion has been carved into a stone at the entrance, with the date 1755, when the church began to be built: it was finished in 1772, four years after the Jesuits were expelled from their territory further south. There is a fine choir loft over the entrance inside.

The high, painted ceiling gives us an idea of what every church in the Reductions was like originally. (That of San Ignacio Guasú, for example, had 1,600 painted ceiling panels, before it fell into disrepair and was dismantled.) Sadly, the once-painted walls were whitewashed in 1919, being considered beyond restoration.

The Franciscans called on the artistic and architectural expertise of the Jesuits in the construction of the church, and in particular for the 14m-high 6m-wide **reredos**, carved out of *peterebý* wood by a Portuguese sculptor in Buenos Aires, José de Souza Cavadas. (Later, he constructed a similar reredos for the church of Capiatá, which is still in position.) In the centre we see the Immaculate Conception, and above her the Holy Spirit. Right up at the top is God the Father, complete with orb and triangular halo to represent the Trinity. The archangel Gabriel is to his right, and the archangel Raphael to his left, carrying his usual fish. In a right-hand niche of the reredos is a third archangel, Michael, with the sword he uses to defeat the devil. The corresponding left-hand niche has St Bonaventure: he fights with the cross rather than the sword. On the door of the tabernacle is the Lamb of God.

The confessional boxes are elaborate works of art, with solomonic columns and elaborate toppings, the whole painted in meticulous detail with reds, greens and golds. The highly adorned hexagonal pulpit stands on the supportive head of a figure which could be Samson or simply an *ángel atlántico* (Atlas-like angel), and is topped with the usual dove of divine inspiration, the Holy Spirit.

In 1854 President Carlos Antonio López removed the side altar and sent 14 cartloads of precious carvings up to adorn the new church of Trinidad that he was building in Asunción: they have not yet been returned. The church of Yaguarón benefited from some restoration in 1882 and again in the 20th century.

Behind the high altar is the **sacristy**, 12m long and so elaborately decorated that it is like a whole further chapel. It has a most ornate holy cupboard, full of drawers, for keeping the vestments and sacred vessels. The roof is painted with a *trompe l'œil* dome. There is a whole series of passion statues here in the sacristy, for processions every night beginning with the Virgin of Sorrows (the Friday before Good Friday) and every night of Holy Week. There is a good articulated crucifix here. It is used on Good Friday outside the church, when there are too many people to fit inside. On

FRANCISCAN AND JESUIT REDUCTIONS COMPARED

Though the Jesuit Reductions are much more famous than the Franciscan Reductions, it is a great mistake to ignore the latter. They were the first Reductions, and the Jesuits learned from their earlier experience. The Franciscan Luis Bolaños founded a great number of Reductions, and the two Jesuits who were most energetic in founding Reductions, Roque González and Antonio Ruiz de Montoya, built on his pioneering work.

The best-known Franciscan Reductions are close to Asunción, in the area of the Circuito de Oro ('Golden Circuit'), but it is not generally realised that there were Franciscan missions over a much greater area, in nine different *departamentos* (Paraguarí, Cordillera, Guairá, Caazapá, Central, Canindeyú, Itapúa, San Pedro and Concepción) stretching from the northern frontier of the Río Apa to almost as far south as Jesús, in Itapúa. Some of the Franciscan towns were true Reductions, in the sense that they were founded by Franciscans as missions. Others were towns that grew up spontaneously where there was a need, in a region where Franciscan influence was strong, so that they used the same type of art, architecture and social organisation, but did not have a precise Franciscan founder. Both sorts are shown on the map on page 124.

One of the differences between the Franciscan and Jesuit Reductions is that the Franciscans, being friars, were prepared for continual movement rather than settlement in one place: when they moved on, or were asked to leave by the governor, the town found its way of continuing without them, for better or for worse. The Jesuits by contrast excluded other Europeans from the entire region, creating a pure Guaraní environment, where the language and culture of the indigenous could flourish, uncontaminated by the vices of drink and sexual and commercial exploitation. The Franciscans believed in working within a very dirty system to ameliorate it; the Jesuits believed in pursuing the ideal.

The Jesuits were able to avoid for their Guaraní the *encomienda* system (everywhere except in San Ignacio Guasú, which was founded on the roots of a Franciscan mission, Yaguará Camigtá). The *encomienda* meant that indigenous people were sent away for hard labour for months on end, in a kind of prisoner-of-war arrangement, because they had given armed resistance to their conquerors. It was practically slavery under another name, and the *encomienda* system was not abolished until 1803. Where the Jesuits worked with indigenous people who had gathered together of their own free will, in new territories where there had not been a European armed invasion, there was no basis for demanding the *encomienda*. But because the Franciscans worked alongside the secular Europeans, often evangelising settlements already established by the Spanish, they could not avoid it.

The Jesuit region of the Treinta Pueblos was more uncompromising and romantic, and has inflamed a huge historical nostalgia for a *Lost Paradise* (the title

Good Friday there is also a pilgrimage of young people up the hill behind the town.

The **bell tower** outside, standing to the left of the church, is a fine example of the kind that once adorned every Reduction (with the exception of those with stone churches, where it was incorporated into the church building). Though the actual pieces of wood have been renewed over the centuries, the design is original.

Josefina Plá, the Spanish scholar and artist who married a Paraguayan and made Paraguay her home, wrote of this church, and others in the Circuito de Oro:

of the book by Philip Caraman SJ, 1975, Sidgwick and Jackson). But when the Jesuits were expelled the Reductions died and were virtually abandoned within a decade or two, as churches were looted by people from Asunción who had long been envious of their riches. The Franciscan towns, however, continued growing in a more organic way with the rest of Paraguay, and escaped the destruction that befell the Treinta Pueblos.

The Jesuits brought over from Europe some of the finest composers, writers, sculptors and architects of the era, who were themselves Jesuits, and devoted the rest of their lives to the Guaraní, in circumstances of very considerable danger: 26 lost their lives as martyrs. The Franciscans were largely dependent on the Jesuits for the development of an artistic style. Although many people contrast the simpler style of what they call 'Franciscan art' with the more flowery style of 'Jesuit art', according to Darko Sustersic, probably the leading expert on the subject, the terms are a misnomer. The real contrast, he says, is to be made between art pre-Brassanelli and post-Brassanelli. Giuseppe Brassanelli (usually written in Spanish as José Brasanelli) was a Jesuit sculptor and architect who reached South America in 1691 and changed the whole dynamic of carving. The earlier style was based on the straight tree trunk, out of which a fairly static figure was carved, solidly placed on its two feet, looking straight ahead, and symmetrical in design. There are some beautiful examples of this simple design. But Brassanelli taught by example how to make the robes seem to ripple in the wind, the body to move its weight off its centre point, the head to incline and the arms to gesture. This was the arrival of Guaraní Baroque.

In terms of tourism, the Jesuit Reductions are known for their fine carved statues of saints (*imágenes*), many of which are kept in the museums of Misiones, and for their stone ruins, particularly of their great churches. But the Franciscan towns also have a beautiful artistic heritage – though a barely known one – in the form of the reredos (*retablo*), the decorative setting on the wall behind the altar, that often acts as a frame for a number of statues.

There are no extant Jesuit reredos, though there is the occasional blurry aged photograph. But if you can find someone to let you into the church of Caazapá, or Atyrá, or Piribebúy, or Tobatí, or more than half a dozen other Franciscan towns, you will see statues of saints – themselves fine works of art – set within an exquisitely carved and painted framework of harmonious colours. Yet hardly anyone knows of the existence of these reredos, and there is no tourist infrastructure yet to present them: no books, no leaflets, no postcards, no guides, no notices, no tours. It is undiscovered territory, and all the more exciting for that. The Circuito de Oro route, as offered by the tour companies, usually focuses more on craft than on reredos. Compare this lack of attention with the proliferation of over 1,500 books and academic articles on the Jesuit Reductions, albeit mostly in Spanish.

Of course, Yaguarón is not the only notable church in Paraguay: Piribebúy, though smaller and deprived of the framework of its original building, rivals it in elegance (and also in the mystery of its origin and realisation); Capiatá, a copy of Yaguarón, is very lovely, within its much reduced scale, and Atyrá, Tobatí and Valenzuela have original touches; Pirayú is very interesting. But Yaguarón has always attracted attention on a larger scale, perhaps for its proximity to the capital; and, apart from its undoubted value for its style and its fabrication, the plan and original features of the building are preserved. What is even more interesting for the scholar is to consider that it is one of the few churches remaining out of the 103 that the records tell us existed in the country at the beginning of the 1870 War.

On the feast of St Bonaventure, 15 June, the people bring beautiful small litters of saints or holy pictures, surrounded by pink flowers, to place in the colonnade of the church.

Also in Yaguarón is the **Museo José Gaspar Rodriguez de Francia** (*Calle Pirayú 325; 0533 232343; 09.00–14.00 Tue–Sun; free admission*). It is named after Paraguay's first president, because his father originally owned the house, and Dr Francia spent his early childhood there. It is a splendid house, with a colonnade on the front side, and the display is of furniture and objects of the period, with some religious art. The curator is Rosa Acevedo (*m 0981 912920*).

OUTSIDE YAGUARÓN The hill known as **Cerro Yaguarón** (tucked right up against the southwest corner of the town and not the one that is more visible from the Ruta when you have passed through the town) is traditionally the site of a big Good Friday procession of the Stations of the Cross. On the summit is an oratory and what are allegedly the footprints of St Thomas the Apostle, variously known in Guaraní as *Pa'i Zumé*, *Pa'i Tomé* and *Tumé Arandú* (Guaraní 'Thomas wise'). As you descend you pass the grotto (*gruta*) of St Thomas. Some say this was the grotto created when Pa'i Zumé destroyed seven monsters from Guaraní mythology. The neighbouring town of Paraguarí also has a hill that allegedly was connected with St Thomas (see below). According to an ancient myth, the apostle Thomas came to evangelise Paraguay many centuries before the conquest. He was left unharmed by all the wild animals and insects and revered by the people, and when he left – borne away on the crystalline river waters to evangelise other countries – he left a blessing on the *yerba* used for *mate* and *tereré*. Still today, people say the first sip from the *bombilla* belongs to San Tomás.

Agua Dulce (*Ruta 1 km56; 021 660784; m 0981 221729; e campamento@aguadulce.com.py; www.aguadulce.com.py*) is a recreation centre with outdoor activities and camping facilities, but with an emphasis on water: springs and waterfalls, swimming pool, football and volleyball. However, it is only available for hire by big groups. It is situated between Yaguarón and Paraguarí, 600m away from the main road.

PARAGUARÍ

Copaco 0531 432299; municipalidad 0531 432204

Paraguarí is one of the larger towns within the circuit, and is useful for its facilities (cash machines and food at the Frutería). It has its own ancient tradition (rather like Yaguarón) of a cave on the craggy hill, **Cerro Santo Tomás,** where allegedly the apostle Thomas lived (see above). Another craggy hill next to it is called the Cerro Hu. They are to the northeast of the town.

GETTING THERE AND AWAY See *Travelling along Ruta 1*, page 169. Paraguarí is the town from which to take the link road from Ruta 1 to Ruta 2, on the classic Circuito de Oro route. After Paraguarí it passes through some pretty hill country.

WHERE TO STAY On the road to Piribebúy, but only 4km from Paraguarí is **Hotel Gabriela** (m *0971 319219;* e *hotel_gabrielapy@hotmail.com;* **$$**). It is very quiet and lies over 50ha, surrounded by hills. It has a clean swimming pool, tennis, volleyball, basketball and crazy golf, and serves international food. There are monkeys and parrots in the grounds. Visitors can also go there for the day.

WHERE TO EAT AND DRINK Outside the town on the Asunción side, on the right if you are coming from the capital, is a the **Frutería** (*Ruta 1, km61.5;* *0531 432406;* $) where Paraguayans stop for a snack or a drink or a meal. With good-quality food, low prices, plenty of variety and decent toilets it is the nearest thing Paraguay has to a motorway café. Up the ramp is a buffet with *asado*. The fruit salad is one of the most popular options. There are also ATMs.

For **La Quinta** and **Mbatoví**, see pages 166 and 167.

WHAT TO SEE AND DO The **Museo Histórico de la Artillería** (*0531 432274;* *07.00–11.30 & 14.30–17.00 Mon–Fri*) is in a sizeable hall in the army camp, 1km from the town centre. At weekends you may be able to gain access courtesy of the military. Among the items on display is one of the cannons used to threaten the Spanish governor Velasco on the morning of 15 May 1811 when Paraguay gained its independence.

The old railway station of Paraguarí at the northeast end of town is one of the more engaging ones, in glorious isolation at the end of a long, straight road and reached up a grand flight of a dozen stone steps. It has recently been repainted.

CARAPEGUÁ

Copaco *0532 212901/21993; municipalidad* *0532 212234*

Carapeguá is the last of the craft towns on Ruta 1, until you get to San Miguel a long way south in Misiones. They make many of the same things as San Miguel: hammocks, bedcovers, ponchos and tablecloths. They specialise in a kind of cotton weave known as *ao poyví* (Guaraní 'sturdy material'), which is similar to the *ao po'í* (Guaraní 'fine material') of Yataity but with a thicker thread. They also make *encaje ju* lace, basketware and the *sombreros* with broad brims against the sun known as *sombreros pirí*. Most of the work is done in the *compañías* rather than in the town itself.

WHERE TO STAY On the left of Ruta 1 as you leave town towards the south, opposite the Corona service station, **Corona Suites** (*26 rooms; Ruta 1;* *0532 213145;* m *0976 969753/0985 328442;* **$**) offers fantastic value and modern rooms, some with minibars. It has split AC, TV (not cable) and Wi-Fi. There is no restaurant, but there is Pizzería Don Quijote next door for an evening meal (see page 178). The car park is closed at night but the night porter will open it. It is ideal for travellers driving out of Asunción in the evening and wanting to cover some miles before nightfall, and perfect if you want to do the little known boat trip to Mocito Isla (see pages 181–3), as it is close to the turn. Prices are cheaper mid-week.

WHERE TO EAT AND DRINK There are also a couple of attractive bars on the plaza.

Pizzería Don Quijote Ruta 1; m 0971 559095/484450; from 17.00 daily. Next to the Corona service station & opposite Corona Suites. Serves pizzas & other fast food. $

Maná Mariscal Estigarribia y General Caballero; 0532 212307. Excellent, popular restaurant on the plaza of Carapeguá (see below). Fills up with sports fans when there is a sporting event on TV. Does delivery. $

Ña Luz Mariscal Estigarribia y Rosa C. Cabello; 0532 212789. Stylish bar on the plaza, serves hamburgers & pizzas. $

WHAT TO SEE AND DO There are three **craft shops**. On Ruta 1 are Artesanía Susi and Artesanía Bárbara, almost opposite each other and run by sisters, near the Comedor San Carlos (another simple restaurant). For the third, turn right (west) when coming from Asunción, where a sign says '*Rastro*'. This goes past the plaza to Artesanía Mirna Mabel.

The plaza itself has a statue to General José Eduvigis Díaz, war hero of the 1866 battle of Curupayty̌. The church of Carapeguá (*normally open in the morning; Mass 19.00 Sat, 08.00 & 19.00 Sun*) has a number of carved statues of Jesuit style, including a crucifix, Christ at the column, St Joseph and the Immaculate Conception. It also has a tabernacle and pulpit from the same period.

While the Circuito de Oro is an imprecise area, Carapeguá is probably its outermost limit. But there are a few more towns on Ruta 1 before you cross the Río Tebicuarý, which fall more easily into this chapter than into the next one (Misiones).

YBYCUÍ

Copaco 0534 226500; municipalidad 0534 22396

The name Ybycuí means 'sand' in Guaraní. In modern spelling it would be written *yvycu'í*, but place names often retain an older spelling.

GETTING THERE AND AWAY If you want to visit the **Parque Nacional Ybycuí** (Gs5,000), take a turn to the left (southeast) from Carapeguá, and go through the towns of Acahay, Ybycuí and La Rosada. As you will see on the map on page 182, the town of Ybycuí is not in the park of that name, but La Rosada is – although not in the same place as the holidaymakers with their camping equipment. Acahay can also be reached from Quiindý by dirt road. The bus Salto Cristal (*021 555728*) goes there from Asunción.

WHERE TO STAY There is no accommodation in the park, but at holiday times Paraguayans turn up to camp. The little town of Ybycuí (which is not particularly attractive) has a small hotel. The **Hospedaje La Esperanza** (*0534 226320;* **$**) must be the cheapest hotel in the country, but it is successful enough to have opened a new building. All rooms have private bathrooms, TV and AC, but if you do not use the AC you pay only half the cost. Breakfast is Gs7,000 extra.

WHAT TO SEE AND DO After going through the town of Ybycuí, and before reaching the park, you pass the **house of Bernardino Caballero** (a former president and founder of the Colorado party) 10km further on. It is open in the mornings. The main road bends to the left, while the right fork divides and you go under a red, white and blue gateway to reach the pink building that was Caballero's *solariega* (summer house). There is a large statue of him on horseback and a red flag. There are two rooms, with some documents about his founding of the Colorados, and a little furniture. The grounds are well tended.

The **Parque Ybycuí** is the national park most visited by Paraguayans, for its location is within reach of Asunción. Created in 1973, it has 5,000ha with hills, woods, streams and waterfalls. There is a *zona recreativa* and a visitor centre. There is no other national park with as many waterfalls in such a small area (16). Cars are not allowed inside the park, so those who want to camp do so close to the entrance, mostly on a slope looking down towards the stream Arroyo Mina. There are washrooms for campers and a little shop. To explore the paths, you cross the stream and then it is a half-hour walk upstream to the Salto Guaraní, at 970m, or a slightly longer walk in the other direction and up a tributary to the Salto Escondido ('hidden waterfall').

A bigger waterfall, the **Salto Cristal**, with a drop of 42m, is not in the park but is in the same region: it is 15km by dirt road south of the town of La Colmena (see below).

Paraguay Safari (m *0971 545659;* e *paraguaysafari@gmail.com*) offers a two- or three-day guided tour with camping to the waterfalls, which can include the Salto Cristal.

The *zona histórica* of **La Rosada**, 3km away, is technically still in the Parque de Ybycuí. It has a well-designed museum marking the place where there was an iron foundry, reputed to be the first in South America. The foundry was destroyed in 1869 in the War of the Triple Alliance, because it was fabricating armaments, but it has been partially restored for tourists.

LA COLMENA

0537 223500; municipalidad 0537 223298

The town of La Colmena was founded by Japanese in the 1930s. It lies 25km east of Acahay (see map, page 182). Hourly buses run by Cardozo Hermanos leave the Asunción Terminal every hour until 17.00. You might want to stay a night here if you are going to the Salto Cristal in the morning, as it is a long, hard trek and you will want to start early. You can enquire at the Municipalidad for a guide, or at your hotel. For the onward journey, there are three buses a day in each direction, Carapaegua to Villarrica. The ones to Villarrica pass at 06.00, 10.00 and 13.30.

WHERE TO STAY

Hotel Fujimori 0537 223238. Has restaurant with Japanese & Paraguayan food. **$$**

Hotel Triunfo 0537 223270; m 0983 717929. Friendly woman eager to help organise guide with or without vehicle & visits to other beautiful waterfalls besides the Salto Cristal. No restaurant. Cheaper rooms have fans. **$**

SALTO CRISTAL

This famous 42m high waterfall is surely the most marvellous one in Paraguay – the Salto Monday is easier to get to, and is wider and louder, with more volume of rushing water, but with its proximity to the Iguazú Falls it can appear relatively unimpressive. The Salto Cristal, however, is distinct: elegant, secretive and stunningly high in proportion to its width. Few people reach it, because you have to be determined and adventurous to seek it out, and athletic to descend the sharp cliff that will lead you to its foot. Ocasionally people abseil down it.

It takes its name from the stream, Arroyo Cristal, which marks the frontier between the *departamentos* of Paraguarí and Guairá. The nearest town is La Colmena, and if you take the road east from there in the direction of Tebicuarymí

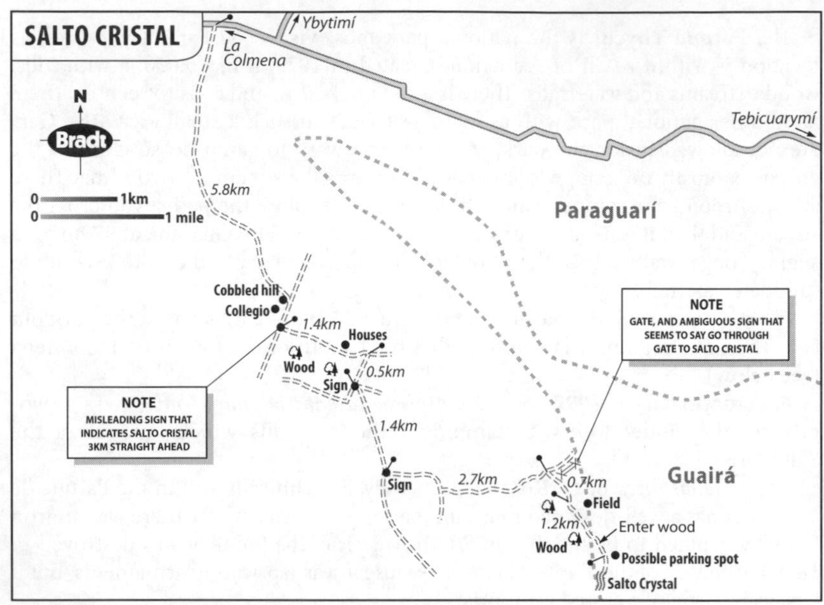

you come after 7km to a black-and-white sign reading 'Azpa – desvío a Chacra. Salto Cristal a 9km'. It is only visible if you approach from the La Colmena side. (In fact, from this point it is 14.3km to Salto Cristal.)

Follow this dirt road south, taking the turnings as indicated on the map (see above). A car can go nearly all the way, leaving you with 500m to walk through the last bit of the wood, where you will pass a house with a sign saying that Salto Cristal is on private property and you should call ☎603354. Since there is no mobile phone signal there to enable you to ring, and there is a dog guarding the house, it may be difficult to fulfil this requirement if no-one comes out to meet you, but in theory you will be asked to pay Gs10,000 entrance fee.

The path soon comes to a T-junction, and here it is best to go right first of all, as this will lead you to the top of the waterfall, where you can sit and admire the stupendous view from above, if you have enough of a head for heights. Returning to the T-junction and taking the other path, you come to a place where you can descend the cliff. There are rocks, branches and roots of trees all the way down, as well as a rope, so there is always something to hold on to, but it is quite a long way and almost vertical, so this is only for the fit and adventurous. At the bottom is the stream, but the waterfall is not yet in sight. You need to scramble from stone to stone and through shallow water for about 300m until you turn the curve and are faced with an amazing sight. There is a large pool of still water to swim in below, while thin streams of silvery water cascade vertically downwards over rocks from far above – more than 20 times the height of a man – fanning out a little as they descend. You feel you are in a very special secret place, penetrated by few adventurers before you.

SAN ROQUE GONZÁLEZ

Copaco ☎0538 20000; municipalidad ☎0538 20151

This is the next town down from Carapeguá on Ruta 1 (see *Travelling along Ruta 1*, page 169). It was founded in 1538 and until 1948 was known as Tabapý. It was the site of the battle where the Comuneros revolution was suppressed in 1735 (see page 12).

QUIINDÝ

Copaco ☎ *0536 282599; municipalidad* ☎ *0536 282553*

Quiindý (the town after San Roque González, see opposite) grew up around a chapel dedicated to the Niño Jesús (Christ Child) in 1733, built by a certain María Peralta de Figueredo in thanksgiving for having escaped in 1743 from the indigenous who had kidnapped her. The original pulpit has been taken up to the Casa de la Independencia in Asunción. Today this is a sizeable town where leather footballs are made, and you see them displayed all along the road. It has a striking church with pointed arches that you pass in the bus.

WHERE TO STAY Set back behind the petrol station on the east side of the road, on the north side of town, is **Alce's Hotel** (*18 rooms; Km108.5;* ☎ *0536 282651/282341;* **$**), which has Wi-Fi and a computer room. Like Corona Suites (see page 177), this is a good place to stay if you are looking for a hotel on your route: it is not as cheap as Corona Suites, but it is noticeably more comfortable. There is no restaurant, but you can cook your own barbecue on the *parilla* or eat at one of the places listed below.

WHERE TO EAT AND DRINK

Doña María Ruta 1, 411; m 0981 568897; ⏱ 07.00–22.30 daily. Pretty, rustic eating place by side of road, lots of cakes & pastries, also serves lunch. *Asado* for Sun lunch. Karaoke on Sat eve once a month. Good place to stop for a meal or for a coffee but you need to tell them in advance if you want it without sugar. **$$**

Copetín Don Juan Simple restaurant in the centre of Quiindý. **$**

PARQUE NACIONAL LAGO YPOÁ

The Parque Nacional Lago Ypoá is a huge area of wetlands or *humedales* (100,000ha) to the west of Quiindý, little known and barely even marked on maps, yet one of the places richest in flora and fauna in eastern Paraguay.

GETTING THERE AND AWAY A map of the area can be studied by the roadside, opposite the Frutería of Paraguarí (see page 177). A project is underway to build a passable road so people can visit this region rich in natural beauty and fauna; the secretary for tourism of the *gobernación* of Paraguarí, Alba de Bogado (☎ *0531 432979/432211;* m *0981 688080*), can give up-to-date information. Within the swamps are many islands of firm ground, or *islas*, of which Caapucú-mí is the largest. At Ykuá Ñaró Point it is said that you hear noises and see lights coming from the ghosts of the cavalry in the Triple Alliance War. You can travel through the marshes by boat, but there is nowhere to stay at present, other than a campsite.

You can get to **Mocito Isla**, set among the reeds at the north end of Lago Ypoá, if you take a turn 3.5km after Carapeguá, marked to 'Humedales de Ypoá'. Continue following signs to the *humedales* (wetlands) or to 'Mocito Isla' on 25km of dirt road. It is mostly well signed, but where a sign is missing you should turn right rather than left. You will see plenty of birds of prey and egrets and eventually pass a visitor centre (now sadly defunct), after which you come to the shore of the lake. Then you ring the family on the island. Vicente Ruiz Díaz, his wife Feliciana (m *0971 150847*)

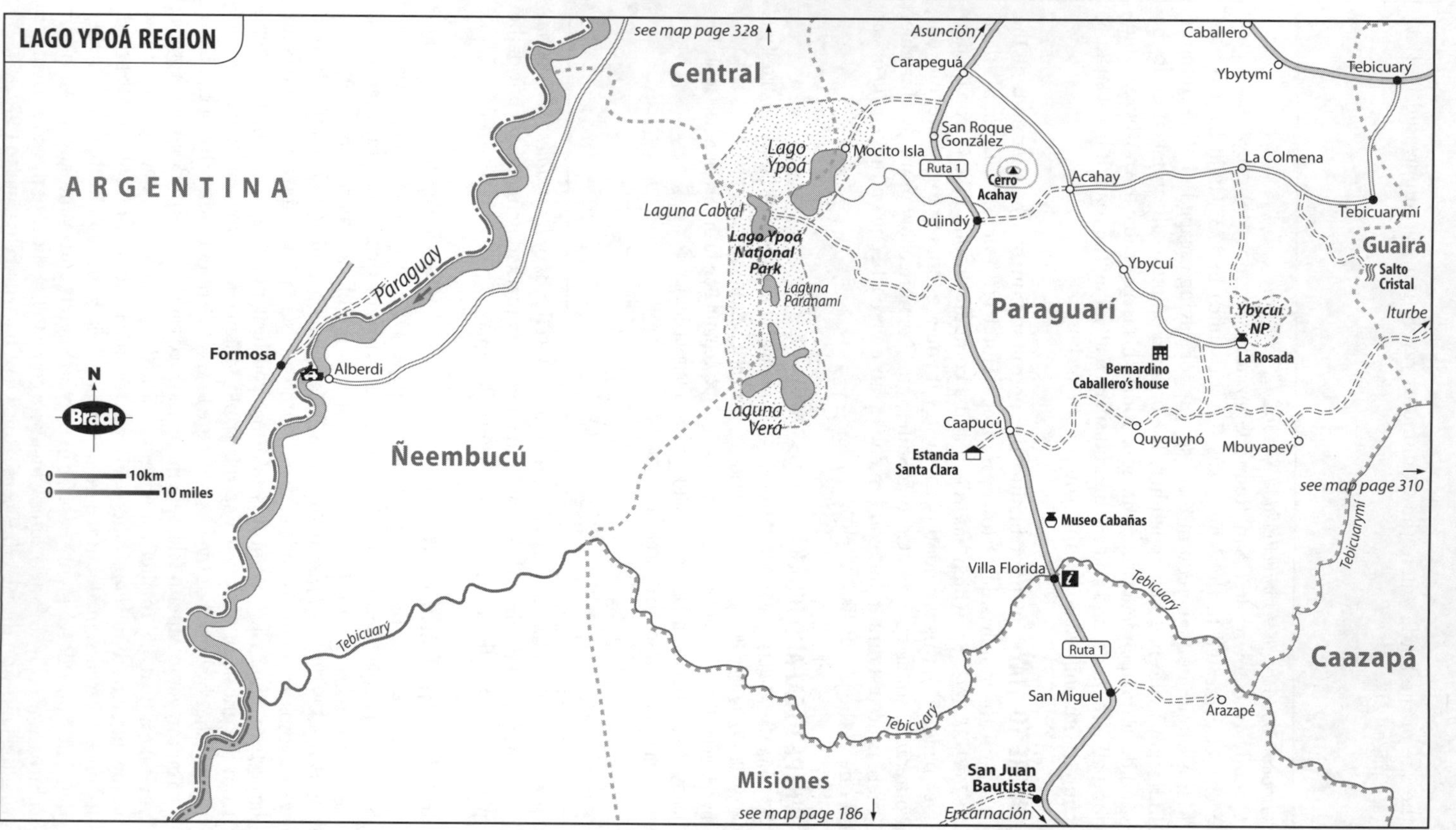
LAGO YPOÁ REGION
see map page 328
Asunción
Caballero
Ybytymí
Tebicuarý
Central
Carapeguá
San Roque González
Lago Ypoá
Mocito Isla
Ruta 1
Cerro Acahay
Acahay
La Colmena
Tebicuarymí
Guairá
Salto Cristal
ARGENTINA
Laguna Cabral
Quiindý
Lago Ypoá National Park
Laguna Paranamí
Ybycuí
Paraguarí
Ybycuí NP
Iturbe
La Rosada
Paraguay
Formosa
Alberdi
Bernardino Caballero's house
N
Bradt
Laguna Verá
Caapucú
Quyquyhó
Mbuyapeý
Ñeembucú
Estancia Santa Clara
0 10km
0 10 miles
see map page 310
Museo Cabañas
Tebicuarymí
Villa Florida
Tebicuarý
Tebicuarý
Ruta 1
Caazapá
San Miguel
Arazapé
Tebicuarý
Misiones
San Juan Bautista
see map page 186
Encarnación

and his son Silvino (**m** *0971 563297*), and they will come and collect you in their boat. You must have a Guaraní speaker with you as they do not speak Spanish, and even their Guaraní is fairly dense. They may give you a fixed price or may ask for a tip at your discretion (recommended minimum Gs50,000).

This is a tricky visit to fix up, and it is not recommended unless you have arranged with the family first, as you might be making the journey in vain: they ask for three days' notice if possible. But if you can make it, the trip is a total delight, as you waft smoothly and silently through reedy waters full of birds. The boat can take seven or eight passengers. You can take a picnic to eat on the island, or sometimes arrange a cooked meal with the family in advance. They will take you to a *mirador* (viewpoint) and are friendly and helpful, within the language limitations.

To reach Lago Ypoá (the largest lake of the area) you would have to take a track for about 20km from Ruta 1 km132, after Quiindý, and you complete the journey on a private road. But the access road is difficult and you can only do it with a 4x4, and maybe not even then. However, this area will undoubtedly be opened up in the future and will be well worth a visit.

CAAPUCÚ

Copaco ☎ *0531 280301/2; municipalidad* ☎ *0531 280279*

The last town on Ruta 1 before the River Tebicuarý is heralded with a striking monument of a *campesino* and a bull, on the right-hand side of Ruta 1, coming from Asunción. The town has a good-quality *estancia* and an interesting old house called the Museo Cabañas, practically on the main road.

WHERE TO STAY Only 6km to the west of Caapucú is **Estancia Santa Clara** (*8 rooms; Ruta 1 km141;* **m** *0981 405020;* **e** *reservas@estanciasantaclara.com.py; www.estanciasantaclara.com.py;* **$$**), with all the usual comforts and delights of an *estancia*, including riding, sulky horse carts, a mini zoo with jaguar, mountain lion and monkeys, walks, volleyball, hammocks and a pool, and there is lots of homegrown produce. Reservations can also be made through Apatur (see page 54).

WHAT TO SEE AND DO Little known but not to be missed is the delightful **Museo Cabañas** (*Ruta 1 km154;* **m** *0971 359295;* ⌚ *09.00–16.00 Tue–Sat; free admission*) or to give it its full name, Museo Oratorio Prócer Manuel Anastasio Cabañas. It is 11km south of Caapucú and about 8km before the river, but the rather battered sign gives no clue of the quality of what is to be found there, barely 1km to the east of Ruta 1. The house is also known as la Alquería de Yaguarý, but the locals call it the Cabañas Guasú (the big [house] of the Cabañas). It is not actually a big house, although the original mansion of the Cabañas family had been, which was burnt down in the Triple Alliance War. What remains is a simple 17th-century outhouse of stone and adobe, and an oratory, standing separately and of similar size.

An 1886 map inside the house helps to explain the history. Before the construction of Ruta 1 and the bridge over the Río Tebicuarý, travellers would cross the river by ferry at the Paso Santa María, and the road, such as it was, passed right by the Cabañas house. On the other side of the river, the road went past Santa María de Fe, instead of going past San Ignacio as it does today.

'Cavañas', as it is marked on the map, was therefore a key place through which everyone passed. In the time of the Jesuit Reductions it was a place to spend the night; the Comuneros revolutionaries led by José de Antequera, on their way from

Misiones to Asunción, stopped there in 1724 and fought a battle nearby; General Belgrano stopped there with his Argentinian troops in 1810, on the way to and from his defeat in the battles of Paraguarí y Tacuarý; in the time of Dr Francia there was a covert suggestion that the dictator should be deposed and replaced with the head of the Cabañas family at that date.

Today the house has been beautifully furnished with period furniture, clothing and leather-thonged bed frames. There are wooden attachments in the walls for hanging hammocks, and an old hand mill for maize or *coco*. The oratory has a beautiful Cristo de la Paciencia from the Jesuit period, which is set in an original, painted niche. The well-kept garden is charming, with a well, a cooking pot over logs, tight rows of cactus plants acting as fencing, and an ancient and unusual thorn tree. The renovation was the work of the late Carlos Colombino Lailla working with the foundation that bears his name, and the house was opened as a museum in 2002. The guide is usually Alcides González Cabañas (**m** *0971 359295*), a descendant of the original owners.

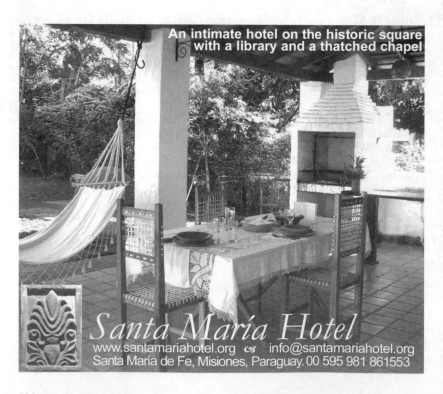

5

Misiones and the Jesuit Reductions

Departamento: Misiones; gobernación
021 7212536 / 7213034

If you have dozed off on the bus you may wake up as you cross the bridge over the Río Tebicuarý into Misiones, because of the gentle brrm-brrm of the low speed-bumps. Stretches of cream sand extend before your eyes, depending on the river level. You are now in the famous Misiones *departamento*, or the mission territory of the Jesuit Reductions – which also continue into the next *departamento* of Itapúa. (For an explanation of the term 'Reduction' see page ix.) The basic rule is: museums in Misiones, ruins in Itapúa. These two *departamentos* are Paraguay's top tourist attractions – the land of what is often called 'The Lost Paradise' or 'The Forgotten Arcadia'. Given their distance from Asunción, you need a minimum of two or three days to visit them, and five or six days to do them justice.There are four Jesuit Reductions in this *departamento*: San Ignacio, Santa María de Fe, Santa Rosa and Santiago. Passing through Misiones to the next *departamento* of Itapúa (covered in *Chapter 7*) you will find three more Reductions: San Cosme y Damián, Trinidad and Jesús. All seven are well worth visiting, and are being promoted through the government tourist office as the Ruta Jesuítica. There were once 30 such towns in the most developed, settled period of the Reducations, and they were known as the Treinta Pueblos (Thirty Towns). Founded on both banks of the Río Paraná and both banks of the Río Uruguay, today they stretch from Paraguay through Argentina and into Brazil.

HOUSES IN THE *CAMPO*

Everything in the Paraguayan countryside is strongly framed by tradition. A typical house in the *campo* will be built of brick or wood, roofed with tiles or straw, and will have two separate rooms with a roofed area between them, to give shade from the hot sun. The kitchen will be at the back – probably just a wooden hut heavily coated with smoke, with hooks to hang things from and an open log fire. There will also – always – be an outside oven called a *tatakuá*, which is like a small brick igloo sitting on the ground, with an opening at the front for access and a smaller one at the back for ventilation: a wood fire makes the bricks very hot indeed, and then the fire is taken out and the meat or *sopa paraguaya* is cooked in the residual heat of the bricks. It is much hotter than a modern oven and cooks faster. The toilet will be a latrine – called a *baño común* (common bathroom) – which will be a hole in the ground with a seat over it, within a small wooden hut with sloping corrugated iron roof, at a distance from the main building. Finally, there will typically be a well.

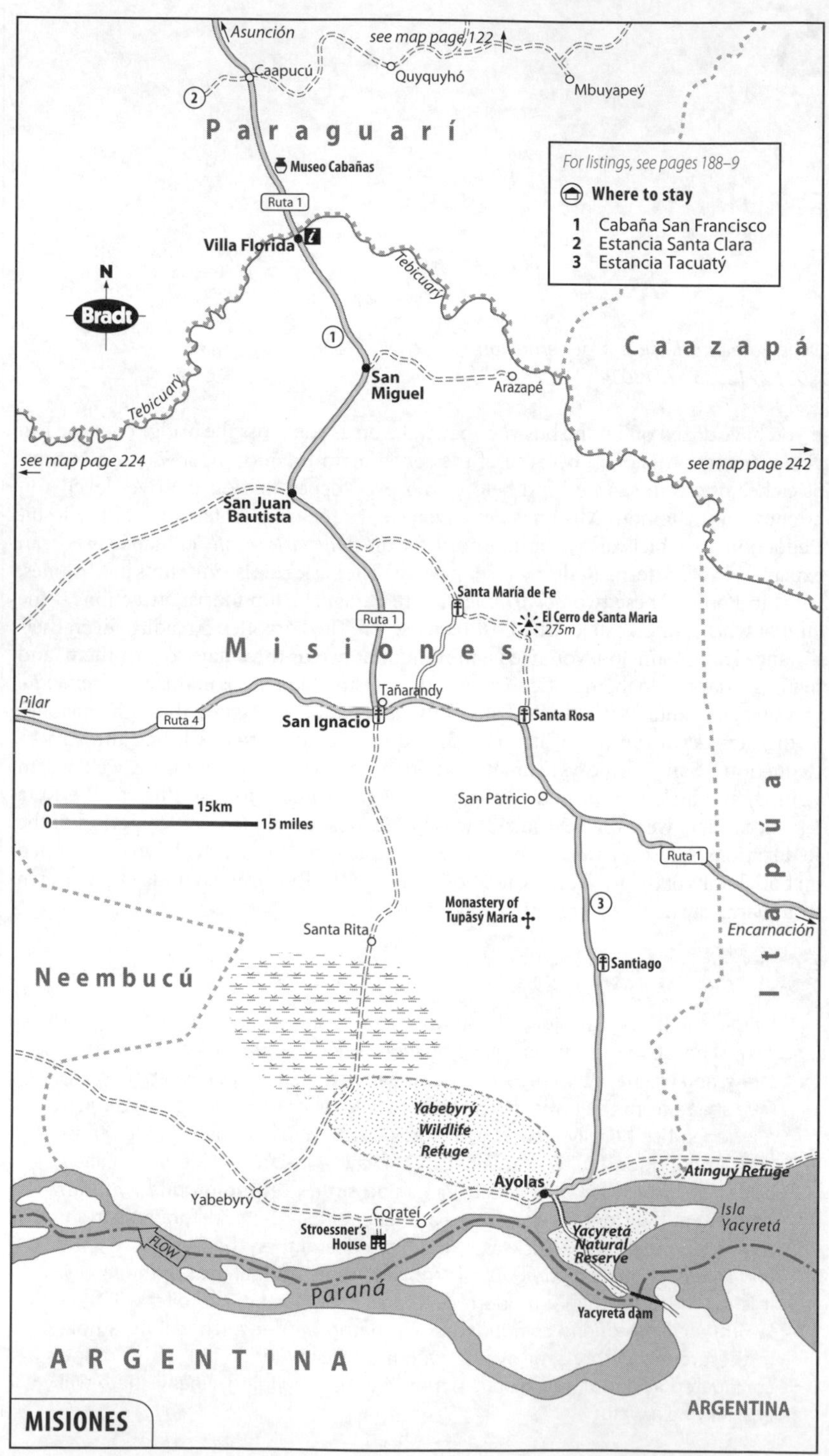
Asunción
see map page 122
Caapucú
Quyquyhó
Mbuyapeý
Paraguarí
Museo Cabañas
For listings, see pages 188–9
Where to stay
1 Cabaña San Francisco
2 Estancia Santa Clara
3 Estancia Tacuatý
Ruta 1
Villa Florida
Tebicuarý
Caazapá
San Miguel
Arazapé
Tebicuarý
see map page 224
see map page 242
San Juan Bautista
Santa María de Fe
El Cerro de Santa Maria
275m
Ruta 1
Misiones
Tañarandy
Pilar
Ruta 4
San Ignacio
Santa Rosa
San Patricio
0 15km
0 15 miles
Ruta 1
Itapúa
Monastery of Tupãsý María
Santa Rita
Encarnación
Santiago
Neembucú
Yabebyrý Wildlife Refuge
Atinguý Refuge
Ayolas
Yabebyrý
Corateí
Isla Yacyretá
Stroessner's House
FLOW
Yacyretá Natural Reserve
Paraná
Yacyretá dam
ARGENTINA
MISIONES
ARGENTINA

On the way to them you pass through some other attractive towns that were not Reductions, though they fell within the lands of the old Reductions and began as outposts or chapels on the *estancias*. Later they developed into urban centres in their own right. Of these, Villa Florida, with its beaches on the river, is a Paraguayan holiday town; San Miguel, with its woollen craft, is a popular tourist stop; and San Juan is the capital of the *departamento*.

From Villa Florida onwards, it is approximately ten minutes from town to town through Misiones.

VILLA FLORIDA

Copaco ☎ *083 240460; municipalidad* ☎ *083 240216/240404*

Before the bridge was built, you had to cross the Río Tebicuarý by raft. Until 1880 the place was known as Puerto Santa María or Paso Santa María, because it was the access to Santa María de Fe, which was once the largest of the Reductions (although now it is only a small town).

In this country, 'Florida' is pronounced with the stress on the second, not the first syllable. Because of its extensive sandy beaches – 10km of them, weather permitting – Villa Florida is a holiday resort for Paraguayans, much in the way that San Bernardino is, but with not quite the popularity because of being that bit further from Asunción. There are a number of well-off families who have houses in Asunción, farms in the country and holiday homes in Villa Florida, a stone's throw from the beach. And the hotels are chock-a-block in the summer season, which runs from December to Semana Santa (Holy Week).

The famous *dorado* fish (the 'river tiger') swims in the river and is considered the most delicious of the fishes, though since 2009 there has been a prohibition on fishing it for commercial purposes. The law is not always observed, though it may affect its availability in restaurants. But you should have no difficulty in ordering other fish dishes such as *chupín de surubí*, *milanesa de surubí*, *pirá caldo* and *caldo de mandi'í* (see box on page 217).

If you penetrate beyond the main road, you will find an attractive small town that appears to be built on grass, with just a few narrow strips of asphalt where necessary for the passage of cars. Some of the houses around the plaza are well-restored old buildings – one, called Ñande Ypý Kuéra (Guaraní 'Our Ancestors'), dates back to 1872.

ORIENTATION When you cross the bridge you will pass immediately on your left a **tourist information centre** (🕘 *only in the summer season, Dec–Mar*) and a craft shop, next to the Hotel Touring Club (see page 188). Then you pass through a toll (*Gs10,000 for cars*). Most of the town's facilities are on Ruta 1, including all three hotels, most of the shops, Copaco with its telephone *cabinas* (*on the corner of Boquerón or Agustín Pio Barrios, 4 blocks from the bridge*), and a couple of tyre repair workshops. If you need to buy swimsuits or towels, try Bodega Florida. Other services are on the **Avenida Tebicuarý**, which is a very broad grassy space, with a row of trees down the middle, a thin asphalt strip on one side, and a volleyball pitch on the other, located one block to the northeast of Ruta 1. The post office is here (*c/ Boquerón*) and a second internet service in the Panda shop (*c/ Feliciano Orue*).

Around the **Plaza Bernardino Caballero** (which is three blocks to the south of the bridge and then two blocks to the northeast, along the asphalted Jóvenes Mártires por la Democracia) you will find the Municipalidad, hospital, Casa de la Cultura and police station, and on its far corner a small supermarket and a good café.

BUS TIMETABLE: ASUNCIÓN – MISIONES

00.00	Nuestra Señora de la Asunción*	10.15	Beato Roque González (to Bella Vista on Ruta 6)	13.45	Alborada
00.30	Flecha de Oro	11.00	Yacyreta	14.00	Rysa
00.30	Encarnacena*	11.15	Ñeembucú* (to Pilar)	14.00	Ciudad de Pilar°*
01.00	Rysa*	11.30	Rysa	14.30	Pilarense (slow, to Ayolas)
03.00	Flecha de Oro	11.45	Flecha de Oro	15.00	Flecha de Oro
04.15	Alborada	11.45	Mariscal López	15.30	Pilarense (slow, to Ayolas)
05.30	Flecha de Oro	12.00	Encarnacena*	15.50	Misionera
06.30	Pilarense (slow, to Ayolas)	12.00	Encarnacena*°	16.00	Alborada* (Fri, Sat, Sun)
07.00	Alborada	12.15	Misionera	16.30	Misionera (not Sun)
07.15	Ñeembucu* (to Pilar)	12.20	Pycasú*	17.00	San Juan
07.30	Pycasú	12.30	Misionera (not Sun)	17.00	Encarnacena*
07.30	Misionera	12.50	Yacyreta	17.30	Yacyreta
08.00	Misionera (not Sun)	13.00	Alborada*	17.30	Ortega
08.30	Encarnacena*	13.05	Alborada (to María Auxiliadora on Ruta 6)	17.30	Rysa
08.45	Flecha de Oro	13.30	Nuestra Señora de la Asunción*	17.30	Encarnacena°*
09.00	Pycasú*			18.00	Ciudad de Pilar°* (not Sun)
09.30	Alborada*			18.45	San Juan

From the plaza you have a good view of the river down a couple of paths. The more westerly of these goes past the charming **church** of the Immaculate Conception, on the site of the old Jesuit chapel, but rebuilt in 1975 with help from Switzerland. In the porch is a handsome crucifix dating from the time of the Reductions.

WHERE TO STAY

Hotel Touring Club (7 rooms) 083 240205. Immediately on left as you cross the bridge, this hotel opened Dec 2009. **$$$$**

Hotel Nacional de Turismo Villa Florida (20 rooms) Ruta 1 esq Barreiro; 083 240207; m 0976 762273; e hotelnacionaldevillaflorida@gmail.com. Count 5 blocks from the bridge to find this hotel on the northeast side, set back down a driveway. One of the hotels originally owned by the government tourist office Senatur. With 11 huge palm trees growing in the inside patio, a swimming pool & substantial dark wood furniture, this is a beautifully designed hotel. However, it has struggled to keep standards up: its success in the summer does not compensate financially for its emptiness the rest of the year. It is now under new management. Wi-Fi, but it does not reach all rooms. The restaurant offers a very limited but inexpensive menu (**$$**). **$$**

Hotel La Misionera (10 rooms) Ruta 1 esq 8 de diciembre; 083 240215. Just after the Parador Touring Club, on your left as you cross the bridge into Misiones. Wi-Fi in reception. **$$**

Hotel Playa (8 rooms) Ruta 1; 083 240214. Pleasant but simple hotel next to the 'Expreso Río Paraná' sign. Traditional style around an inner courtyard. AC. Meals served according to the dish of the day. **$$**

WHERE TO EAT AND DRINK

Hotel Touring Club See above; 083 240205. A useful stop if you are driving down from Asunción, & indeed it is used as a stop by the long-distance buses Encarnacena & Crucero del Norte. Good infrastructure; service & food could improve. The garden goes down to the river, & in the summer it may be filled with animals: sheep, goats, ostriches, capybaras & many kinds of birds. **$$**

19.00	El Tigre*	22.00	Pilarense (slow)	22.50	Beato Roque González (to Bella Vista on Ruta 6)
19.30	San Juan	22.30	Alborada* (to María Auxiliadora on Ruta 6)	23.30	Ñeembucu°*
20.00	Ñeembucu°	22.30	Beato Roque González	23.30	Alborada
20.30	Yacyreta	22.30	Encarnacena°*	23.45	Pycasú*
21.00	Flecha de Oro				

* Good bus but you may have to pay a higher fare; however, fares are very low anyway.

° From San Ignacio these buses go to Pilar, not to Encarnación, and in San Ignacio you must get on or off at the Hotel Arapysandú and not at the Plaza. Most of the other buses go on to Encarnación, and a few go further, past the ruins of Trinidad to María Auxiliadora. Some go to Ayolas, which means they turn off before Encarnación.

No general timetable of this form is available from the Terminal in Asunción, except by going round every bus company and asking, or from the website www.mca.gov.py/webtermi.html by clicking on the name of every bus company, but that timetable has not been kept up to date. However, if you go to the Information window at the terminal they should be able to tell you which bus is the next to leave for your destination.

La Reja Av Tebicuarý, entre Bareiro y Agustín Pío Barrios; 083 240325; m 0981 515475; every day for lunch & supper. 5 blocks along Ruta 1 from the bridge, & then a couple of blocks to your left. There is a sign on Ruta 1. Delightful, small restaurant, full of character, lots of plants. Family atmosphere. $

Comedor Ñande Róga 083 240582. On your right after you have left town going south. Fish soups & *milanesas*, all dishes can be served up quickly. $

San Cayetano 083 240319. A clean & modern café on the corner of the plaza, serving everything from sandwiches to the substantial pot roast *asado a la olla*. $

BEACHES All of the beach facilities tend to be seasonal, from December until Semana Santa. During this period you can expect to find fishing facilities, bars, toilets, beach volleyball, campsites, sometimes horses to ride, and from some of the beaches you can hire a boatman very cheaply to take you across the river in a rowing boat. During Semana Santa there is volleyball and football on the beach, along with other activities such as athletics and searching for Easter eggs in the plaza, all forming part of 'Villa Florida en Familia'.

Caracol 5km to the east of the town. Take the 2nd turning left if coming from Asunción.

Punta Arena Caapucú A beach on the other side of the river, belonging to the Caapucú municipality.

Paraíso (Paradise) 1.5km to the west of the town. Coming from Asunción, you will see the notice pointing down a dirt road to the right – the 1st turning after the bridge. Then turn right again at the first crossroads, & left when you reach the river. This is one of the best beaches, & the closest, with the only drawback that it gets rather full. On the 1st w/end of Feb the beach is the site of a Latin American parachuting festival. For more information contact Roland Peyrat (e *contacto@republicaflyer.com*).

Yvága (Guaraní 'Heaven') Excellent beach, beyond Paraíso to the west of Villa Florida. Take the 2nd turning on the right after you cross the bridge (Feliciano Orué). The only disadvantage is the distance (5km).

Centú Cué As you leave town going south, there is a turning on the left (Narciso Corrales) which leads eventually to this attractive beach resort, 7km east of Villa Florida. This is the best place to fish for *dorado* (which is legal as long as it is not for commercial ends, & is within the fishing season).

SAN MIGUEL

Copaco ☎ *0783 248350; municipalidad* ☎ *0783 248205*
San Miguel is an important place to make a brief stop for its picturesque woollen and woven crafts. This is a wonderful place to buy hammocks, blankets, rugs, bedcovers, tablecloths, jerseys, ponchos, hats and woollen socks and gloves.

The pueblo was founded in 1725 by the Jesuits, not as a Reduction but as a house for watching over cattle in the *estancia* belonging to Santa María. There is a statue of St Michael in the church that dates from this period.

Just before you enter the town you pass a monument proclaiming the town as the 'Capital de la Lana' (Capital of Wool) with a painted statue of St Michael, but it is up the bank to the right and may be above your eye level in a bus. Next to come is a roadside stall on the left, selling painted wooden toucans and parrots, made out of the natural formation of branches and twigs. This is a speciality of San Miguel, but much better known is the display of hammocks, ponchos and blankets that people hang up for sale in front of their houses, and that you pass as you go out on the southern stretch of road. This craft in wool and cotton is picturesque if you are whizzing past in a bus, but if you are in your own vehicle it will be worth your while to stop and buy something.

As you reach San Miguel, you see the turn to Arazapé 14km to the east. This small *compañia* specialises in knitted sweaters and other woollen clothes.

WHERE TO STAY AND EAT The **Cabaña San Francisco** (*12 rooms; Ruta 1 km173;* ☎ *083 240328;* **m** *0971 216171/0985 732434;* **e** *info@francisco-country.com;* www.csanfrancisco.com.py; **$$**) is an *estancia* 5km north of the town on Ruta 1, with sports facilities, horseriding, sulky, fishing, pool and *quincho*. You must book in advance. You get off at their entrance on the main road, and they will collect you from there if you have a mobile phone to ring them, or tell them the exact time of arrival.

The **Parador San Fernando** (*Ruta 1;* ☎ *0788 248292;* **m** *0982 578784;* **$**) serves hot and cold dishes and fast food, and is within the town.

OTHER PRACTICALITIES Services in San Miguel have improved a lot in recent years. There is now a cash machine next to the Municipalidad, which is important for those who have come with insufficient cash for the craft they want to buy. The signal for Tigo and Claro mobile phones are now fine, but Personal still has a poor signal. But there is still no taxi service.

WHAT TO SEE In June (usually the second or third Thursday–Sunday; check with the Municipalidad or Copaco for the programme of events) there is a most appealing craft festival called Ovecha Ragué, which in Guaraní means sheep's hair – in other words, wool. The grassy plaza is filled with stalls selling quality craft products, but there is also a singing festival, folk dance display, cycling tournament, procession of floats and antique cars, and traditional cooked dishes on sale. Of these, batiburillo is a particular treat, and is a dish specific to Misiones: it is made of beef offal, and you eat it hot in a little dish accompanied by a stick of mandioc.

In the middle of the plaza is the little **church** of San Miguel, with a traditional bell tower beside it: in Jesuit times, this was a chapel belonging to the Santa María de Fe *estancia*, but today little is left from the Jesuit period. If you climb the tower you find two ancient bells at the top, of which the cracked one bears the words

'Santa Maria Ora Por Novis [*sic*] and 'A Nos L 12 4' (or possibly 1724). Inside the church, at the centre of the reredos is a statue of San Miguel dating back to Jesuit times, which unfortunately has been repainted in bright colours. It is an almost exact, smaller version of one of the San Miguels (probably by Brassanelli) in the Santa María Museum (see pages 206–7), with outstretched wings, angled sword and squirming serpent. To the right of the reredos is a larger San Miguel – rather a fine piece, though not from the Reduction.

The first **craft shop** you come to on the road from Asunción is devoted to the craft of Arazapé. When you reach the plaza there are two good shops: Mainumby (*0783 248288*), which has lots of things suitable as souvenirs, like tablecloths, clothes and little lace mats (both *encaje ju* and *ñanduti*, see page 24), and next to it Delmia (*0783 248232*), which has sheepskins hanging outside and specialises in the heavier items like bedcovers, mats and hammocks. Next to that is the Municipalidad.

A little further along the same road you come to a host of family-run craft shops, all with hammocks strung outside and sometimes wool hung out to dry as well. A couple of them near the end of the row – Zully (*0783 248322*) and Artesanía Muñeca (*0783 248214*) – have workshops behind, where you can ask to go in to see the clanking hand looms in action. Casa Irene (*last but one on the northeast side; 0783 248225*) has a good line in blankets. El Trionfo (*0783 248249*) has a lot of items hung up around a thatched workshop.

SAN JUAN BAUTISTA

Copaco 021 7212399; municipalidad 021 7212235; NB: all numbers in San Juan have recently changed to begin 021 7, instead of 081.

San Juan Bautista is the capital of the *departamento,* though not the principal town; San Ignacio is bigger and has more facilities. The town is famous as the birthplace of the guitarist and composer Agustín Pío Barrios, known as Mangoré (1885–1944; see box on page 196). (This claim has recently been challenged, however, by the inhabitants of Villa Florida, who maintain that he was born there.)

San Juan is the See of the diocese of San Juan Bautista de las Misiones, which has historically been instrumental in resisting the corruption and human rights abuses of successive Colorado governments. Its first bishop, Monseñor Ramón Pastor Bogarín Argaña, is the town's second most famous figure after Mangoré: his tomb and portrait have a place of special honour in the cathedral. He was courageous in opposing the Stroessner dictatorship – which wiped out the Christian Agrarian Leagues that began in this diocese – and is regarded as a quasi-martyr because he died of an untimely heart attack under the stress of the persecution, on 3 September 1976, in the year of the worst repression. It is said that from his residence he could hear the screams of those being tortured in the police cells. The most recent bishop, Monseñor Mario Melanio Medina, also had a reputation for outspoken criticism, and was the only Paraguayan bishop to support Fernando Lugo openly in his run for the presidency. San Juan was not one of the Reductions, but it began as a chapel on the *estancia* of the Reduction of San Ignacio, and was known first as Posta San Juan and then as San Juan Capillita. It has been suggested that the first chapel may have been constructed in 1697 by the Jesuit Anton Sepp – the 'father of the Paraguayan harp' and a prolific writer about life in the Reductions. In 1893 San Juan became a *municipio* independent of San Ignacio.

It is a pretty town with two attractive plazas and cobbled streets, and Ruta 1 skims along the edge rather than cutting through the middle as it does in San Ignacio. As you reach San Juan, coming from San Miguel, you will see on the right-hand side a sign welcoming you to the 'Cuna de Mangoré' (the cradle of Mangoré), the imposing Palacio de Justicia set back from the road, and opposite the law faculty of the Universidad Nacional, with a little plaza in front of it called the Paseo de los Ilustres, with plaques to Mangoré, Monseñor Bogarín and other distinguished people from the town's past. When you reach a pronounced curve to the left (*la curva*) with a triangle of grass and the big hoarding for Kurupí *yerba*, you are at Plaza Ermita, and this is where you must turn sharp right if you want to enter the town.

WHERE TO STAY *Map opposite.*

Hotel Boutique La Catedral (4 rooms) Coronel Alfredo Ramos e/ Mariscal López y Victor Z. Romero; 021 7212227; m 0971 925011; e lacatedralhotelboutique@hotmail.com; Facebook: La Catedral Hotel Boutique. Small hotel opened in 2012 near the cathedral, with sober styling. Two more rooms will be ready very soon. **$$$**

Hotel Tajý Potý Ruta 1 km195; 021 7212533; Facebook: Tajy Poty. On the left as you come into the town from Asunción, before you reach the Palacio de Justicia & on the other side of the road from it. A comfortable hotel, which despite its distance from the centre is usually full. Wi-Fi, cheaper dormitory for groups. The name is pronounced approximately 'Ta-Jew po-too' & means 'flower of the lapacho tree' – the famous pink blossom seen all over the country in spring. **$$$**

Alfa Hotel (7 rooms) Monseñor Bogarín c/ Raúl Villalba; 021 7212878; Facebook: Alfa Hotel. Small new hotel in a central location. Wi-Fi. Comfortable but without the style of La Catedral. **$$**

Hotel El Portal (6 rooms) Gumercindo Corvalán c/ Augusto Roa Bastos; 021 7213440; m 0981 246806/0985 419540; e hotelelportal@hotmail.com; Facebook: Hotel El Portal. Tucked away 100m from Ruta 1, just before the Universidad Nacional (coming from Asunción) & nearly opposite the Palacio de Justicia, this basic but modern new hotel has enclosed parking, Wi-Fi & cable TV. Charges per person, so more economical for a single. **$$**

Hotel San Juan (9 rooms) Monseñor Bogarín c/ Waldino Lovera; 021 7213331; m 0975 196230/0981 595964; hotelsjuan@hotmail.com. Budget hotel between *la curva* & the first plaza, old building, formerly called Ña Nenena. **$**

WHERE TO EAT AND DRINK *Map opposite.*

Waldorf Dr Victor Z Romero y Monseñor Rojas; 081 212209; noon–14.30 & from 20.00 daily. A former hotel now functioning only as a restaurant, conveniently situated between the 2 plazas. **$$**

Ña Tere Monseñor Rojas 499; 021 7212512. Well-established local place with good economical food. **$**

Crisol Monseñor Bogarín y Capitán Martínez; 021 7212703. Recommended by local people, on Plaza Boquerón. **$**

Pasal Monseñor Bogarín 290; 021 7212026. Next door to Crisol on the Plaza Boquerón is this *confitería* & *panadería*, which serves coffee & variety of croissants with friendly service. Good for b/fast. **$**

La Tranquera Monseñor Bogarín c/ Rosalia Candia; 021 7212711. Just before Hotel San Juan, coming from the Ruta. Meaty grills. **$**

Petrobras service station Opposite Hotel Tajý Potý; restaurant until 22.30 daily. Reliable food & a small coffee machine. **$**

OTHER PRACTICALITIES There is a **cash machine** outside the Palacio de Justicia [193 E1], and another at the Cooperativa San Juan Bautista [193 D2] (or Coopersanjuba for short). **Telephone *cabinas*** can be found at Copaco [193 D2] (*Monseñor Bogarín y Raúl Villalba).*

FESTIVALS The famous **midwinter fiesta of San Juan** falls on 24 June (see box on page 194). This is dramatically celebrated all over the country with fire and dangerous

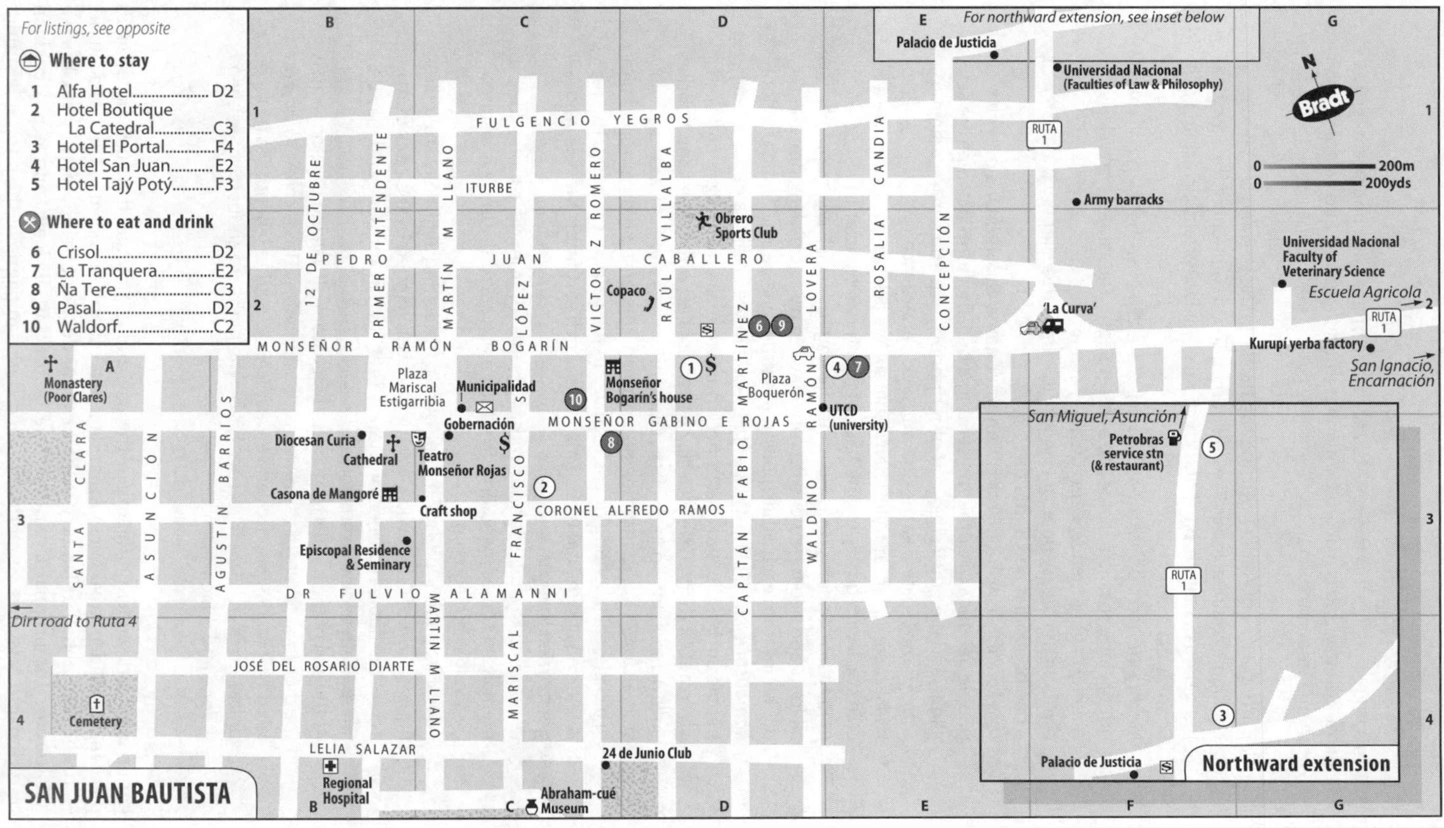
SAN JUAN BAUTISTA
For listings, see opposite
Where to stay
1 Alfa Hotel........D2
2 Hotel Boutique La Catedral........C3
3 Hotel El Portal........F4
4 Hotel San Juan........E2
5 Hotel Tajý Potý........F3
Where to eat and drink
6 Crisol........D2
7 La Tranquera........E2
8 Ña Tere........C3
9 Pasal........D2
10 Waldorf........C2
For northward extension, see inset below
Palacio de Justicia
Universidad Nacional (Faculties of Law & Philosophy)
Army barracks
Universidad Nacional Faculty of Veterinary Science
Escuela Agricola
Kurupí yerba factory
San Ignacio, Encarnación
'La Curva'
RUTA 1
0 200m
0 200yds
FULGENCIO YEGROS
ITURBE
PEDRO JUAN CABALLERO
MONSEÑOR RAMÓN BOGARÍN
MONSEÑOR GABINO E ROJAS
CORONEL ALFREDO RAMOS
DR FULVIO ALAMANNI
JOSÉ DEL ROSARIO DIARTE
LELIA SALAZAR
12 DE OCTUBRE
PRIMER INTENDENTE
MARTÍN M LLANO
VICTOR Z ROMERO
LÓPEZ
RAÚL VILLALBA
MARTÍNEZ
FABIO
CAPITÁN
RAMÓN LOVERA
WALDINO
ROSALIA
CANDIA
CONCEPCIÓN
SANTA CLARA
ASUNCIÓN
AGUSTÍN BARRIOS
FRANCISCO S
MARISCAL
Obrero Sports Club
Copaco
Monseñor Bogarín's house
Plaza Boquerón
UTCD (university)
Plaza Mariscal Estigarribia
Municipalidad
Gobernación
Diocesan Curia
Cathedral
Teatro Monseñor Rojas
Casona de Mangoré
Craft shop
Episcopal Residence & Seminary
Monastery (Poor Clares)
Dirt road to Ruta 4
Cemetery
Regional Hospital
Abraham-cué Museum
24 de Junio Club
Northward extension
San Miguel, Asunción
Petrobras service stn (& restaurant)
Palacio de Justicia

SAN JUAN FIESTA

This midwinter feast of fire, on 24 June, is one of the most important festivals in the country, and is marked by many traditional games and customs, some of them rather dangerous:

- putting a row of candles outside the house in the evening
- cooking traditional foods like *pajaguá mascada* (Guaraní 'of the Payagua indigenous'; Spanish 'bite') and *chicharõ trenzado* (Guaraní 'crackling'; Spanish 'plaited')
- kicking around a *pelota tatá* (Guaraní 'of fire'; Spanish 'ball') – a ball made out of cloth, soaked in kerosene and set alight. The game is to kick it directly at your friends, who run away screaming.
- climbing the greasy pole, or *yvyrá sỹi* (Guaraní 'tree slippery'), in search of a bag of goodies tied at the top
- *toro kandil* (Spanish 'bull torch'), another game with fire. One or two people get under a cloth representing a bull, the horns of which are set alight, and then they charge at other people, who run away screaming.
- *carrera vosá* (Spanish 'race'; Guaraní 'sack'), a sack race
- *paila jeheréi* (Spanish 'frying pan'; Guaraní 'we lick'), trying to remove a coin stuck with grease on the back of frying pan by licking it
- *jaguá jetu'u* (Spanish 'dog'; Guaraní 'refusing to move'), two people on all fours and tied together with rope have to try to crawl in opposite directions from each other, pulling the other one behind along the floor
- *kambuchí jejoká* (Spanish 'water jar'; Guaraní 'we break'), a game where people are blindfolded and turned round to make them dizzy, and then given a stick to try to break a clay water jar filled with sweets and goodies
- *gallo ñemongaru* (Spanish 'cock'; Guaraní 'we make to eat'), a cock is starved for 24 hours and then put in a bag. Unmarried girls surround him in a circle, each holding grains of maize in the palm of the hand. The cock is released and the girl whose maize the cock eats first is the one who will get married that year.
- *Casamiento koyguá* (Spanish 'wedding'; Guaraní 'from the countryside'), a dramatised comedy wedding, in which a naive and shy bride is insulted by a vulgar bridegroom
- *udas kái* (Spanish 'Judas'; Guaraní 'burn'), the setting alight of a stuffed figure (a sort of Guy Fawkes) which has been hanged by the neck from a tree. The figure has been previously drenched in kerosene and may be stuffed with explosive fireworks.
- At the end of the night's festivities, the custom of walking barefoot across the glowing embers of the remains of the bonfire. This is called *tatapỹi ári jehasá* (Guaraní 'embers over we walk'). According to legend, the feet are protected from burns if you do this on the night of San Juan. I have seen it done and there were no burns.

games after dark, either on the eve or the day, and in San Juan this customarily takes place in the polideportivo Lucio Amarilla Leiva, otherwise known as Club 24 de junio.

In the second half of January is the **Festival del Batiburillo, Siriki y el Chorizo Misionero**. The original Guaraní name of *siriki* is *chiringuí*, and it is a cocktail traditional to Misiones. Sometimes called the champagne of the poor, it is similar to the Brazilian *caipirinha*, made with white rum (*caña blanca*), a delicate kind of lemon (*limón sutil*) and soda water, and sometimes with grapefruit juice added. *Chorizo misionero* or *sanjuanino* is a sausage of chopped pork, and *batiburillo* is the speciality of Misiones (see page 395).

WHAT TO SEE AND DO The first square (the first one you reach if you come from *la curva*) is called the **Plaza Boquerón** [193 D2] and has a monument in the form of four pyramids in memory of the Chaco War, and a mural commemorating the fiesta of San Juan. Five blocks on from this square is the **Plaza Mariscal Estigarribia** [193 B2–C2], which has the cathedral on the south side, and a painted statue of the Mariscal in the centre. Another mural, commemorating Mangoré, is on the corner of Monseñor Gabino Rojas and Dr Martín Llano. On the other street that joins the two plazas is the former house of Monseñor Bogarín himself, with seven columns supporting a balustraded balcony (on the southeast corner of Monseñor Bogarín y Victor Romero).

The **cathedral** [193 B3] (*021 7212868*) is a splendid though unelaborate building in cream and beige, with a slightly Moorish aspect to the top of the octagonal tower. On the left as you enter is a carved wooden niche from the time of the Reductions, with a vine motif up its spiralling columns. It has been carefully repainted, and looks new. The main doors to the cathedral were carved by a local carpenter on the theme of the Lamb of God. Behind the altar to one side is a striking stained-glass window of the baptism of Christ, running from floor to ceiling. The statue of St John the Baptist, which is carried in procession through the streets on the night of 24 June, is a charming old piece, with the Lamb of God at the feet of the saint.

To the right of the altar is the **tomb of Monseñor Bogarín**, with an enormous painting behind it, portraying the history of this diocese, founded in 1957. Monseñor Ramón Bogarín (with the glasses) is talking to his uncle, Juan Sinforiano Bogarín, the Archbishop of Asunción, who holds the bridle of a horse. Next to him is St Luigi Orione, the Italian founder of the Sons of Divine Providence order, who prophesied to Ramón Bogarín that he would die a martyr. In the foreground, holding the hand of a child and smiling, is the bespectacled figure of P Carlos Villalba, who was to become the second bishop of the diocese. (Monseñor Medina was the third bishop.) On the left is a group of barefoot children, with a parrot, puppy, football, statue of the Virgin of Caacupé, folk-dance costume, and first communion dress.

Next to the cathedral is a large auditorium, due to be finished in 2015, that will be a concert hall and conference centre. On the next corner from that is the Municipalidad. Opposite the Municipalidad is the *gobernación* and next to it is the post office. Behind the theatre is a craft shop, and next to it, on the corner directly behind the cathedral, is the **Centro Cultural Casona de Mangoré** [193 B3] (*Coronel Alfredo Ramos y Primer Intendente;* *021 7212400;* **m** *0975 671273;* **e** *ogamangore@yahoo.es;* *08.00–20.00 daily; free admission, donations welcome*). This former home of Mangoré, where he lived with his parents for 14 years, has been converted into a little museum and cultural centre by the artist Gil Alegre and his wife Sebastiana Galeano, who live in part of the house and run painting workshops. Knock on the door to visit if it is not already open. As well as mementoes of Mangoré's life and work, there is the soutane once worn by Monseñor Bogarín. The entire block, including this house and the cathedral, has been officially declared 'of national interest'. Four blocks to the south and two to the east is a **Museo de las Victimas de la Dictadura** (*021 7212219;* *0.700–11.30 Mon–Fri*) in the former Abraham-cué prison: ask for Alberto Morel in the Oficina de Derechos Humanos (Human Rights Office) in the police station that now occupies the site. Abraham-cué was infamous for having *campesino*

MANGORÉ

Agustín Pío Barrios, Paraguay's great and legendary guitarist and composer, known as Mangoré, was born on 5 May 1885 in San Juan (or, according to other sources, in the neighbouring town of Villa Florida). He studied and travelled extensively with his music, visiting Belgium and Germany as well as almost every country in Latin America. He died of a heart attack in 1944 in San Salvador, where he had been directing a guitar school for the last five years of his life.

He was enormously esteemed by his pupils and disciples, and the English-Australian classical guitarist John Williams said that 'as a guitarist/composer, Barrios is the best of the lot, regardless of ear. His music is better formed, it's more poetic, it's more everything! And it's more of all those things in a timeless way.' In his work can be detected Baroque influence (especially from Bach), Romantic influence (especially from Chopin) and influence from Hispanic-American music (particularly Paraguayan folksong and indigenous music).

He took the professional name Nitsuga Mangoré, which is a combination of his first name spelt backwards with the name of a *cacique* of colonial times. Sometimes he wore indigenous dress to play in concerts. The photos of him, taken in many countries of the world, show a long face with thick lips and a solemn expression. He sported a moustache until the 1930s. He was a manic depressive, alternating depressed moments when he could not work with periods of hyper-intensive creativity. In 1925 he wrote a sonnet, *Bohemia*, in which he said of himself:

Yo soy hermano en glorias y dolores
De aquellos medievales trovadores
Que sufrieron romántica locura!

'I am the brother in glories and sorrows
Of those medieval troubadours
Who suffered romantic madness!'

His house in San Juan, the Casona Mangoré, has been turned into a museum (see page 195). One of the rooms in the Cabildo of Asunción is also dedicated to Mangoré, and his face appears on the Gs50,000 note.

members of the Christian Agrarian Leagues locked up and tortured during the Stroessner dictatorship, particularly in 1976, when the leagues were wiped out by the oppression. It held prisoners until recently, but a new prison has now been built outside town.

Continuing on Ruta 1 beyond the town of San Juan, you pass the **Kurupí Yerba factory** [193 G2] (*km197;* ☎ *021 7212418*) on the right, and about 10km out of San Juan, by a bus shelter, there is a turn to the left down a dirt road which is not signed but eventually comes out at Santa María de Fe.

SAN IGNACIO GUASÚ

Copaco ☎ *0782 232299; municipalidad* ☎ *0782 232218/232581*

San Ignacio Guasú (Guaraní 'big'; Spanish 'Saint Ignatius') tends to be the focus of any visit to the Reductions, being the largest urban centre and located right on Ruta 1. It is not only of great historical importance for being the first of the Jesuit-Guaraní Reductions, founded in 1609, but it is also an important town to visit, both for its museum and for its general cultural level. (There are different spellings in use: Guasu is the correct Guaraní spelling; Guazú is the hispanicised form; but the practice of this book – see box on page 279 – is to use the form Guasú, though in *Chapter 8* the Argentinian practice is followed in the spelling 'Puerto Iguazú'.)

San Ignacio has some charm as a town, though it is marred by being directly on the main road, Ruta 1, which runs right through the middle. Attempts have been made to reduce the traffic by making it one-way, but the side-effect of this is to make the traffic go faster. However, there is not much traffic yet in Paraguay as yet, not even on an international highway like Ruta 1.

In 2009 San Ignacio celebrated the 400th anniversary of its foundation with a rich programme of events and lectures; the annual anniversary of the foundation of all the Reductions is now commemorated with a week at the end of December, to mark the date of the first Mass in the first Jesuit mission. Right at the end of 1609, its two Jesuit founders, Marcial de Lorenzana and Francisco de San Martín, celebrated their first mass in the presence of the *cacique* Arapysandú, who had invited them to evangelise the area. But the Reduction was principally identified with San Roque González de Santa Cruz (see box on pages 114–15), who arrived the following year and forged its identity. He set a model for all subsequent Reductions through his town planning and immense energy and organisation. Like most Reductions, San Ignacio moved from its original site, but in this case the move was within the same region, and it had settled in its final location by 1667 (when, we are told, the original church was consecrated).

After the Expulsion of 1768 the Jesuits returned to Paraguay in 1927, and to San Ignacio in 1933, so once again San Ignacio (like Santa María de Fe, and up until a few years ago Santa Rosa) is in Jesuit hands. The Jesuit residence is on the original site of the *colegio*, and so is the museum, which must be the most magnificent standing 17th-century building in Paraguay. It now houses a collection of Jesuit-Guaraní art second only to that in Santa María de Fe. There are also a number of other interesting museums and murals in the town (mostly around the old plaza), a couple of good craft shops and monuments on the outskirts of town.

WHERE TO STAY *Map, page 198.*

Hotel Rural (8 rooms, including 1 dormitory) Ruta 1 km 230; 0782 232895; m 0975 606631/0981 809105; e gusjhave@hotmail.com. Previously known as San Ignacio Country Club, this hotel is 4km out of town on the road towards Encarnación, exactly opposite the turn to Santa María de Fe. The warm & genial host, Peruvian Gustavo Jhave, provides plenty of entertainment, with horses, swimming pool, sauna, jacuzzi, parillas, sports fields, etc. All activities included in the overnight price. You can also bring your own food & drink & spend the day there, as well as staying the night. Wi-Fi. **$$$**

Hotel 1609 (20 rooms) General Díaz esq. Cerro Corá; 0782 232603; m 0975 655444; www.hotel1609.com. Currently the top hotel in town, with carved red stone ítems in reception reminiscent of the Reductions. The slightly cumbersome name (pronounced *mil seiscientos nueve*) is the date of San Ignacio's foundation, & even the rooms have dates for their numbers (1610, 1611, etc). Frigobars, cable TV, enclosed parking. Pool under construction. No restaurant. **$$**

Hotel Piringo (10 rooms) Ruta 1 c/ Alider Vera Guillen; 0782 232913. On the approach road from Asunción, this has a good atmosphere & is a hub of activity, because the major bus lines stop here (Rysa, Nuestra Señora de la Asunción, Yacyretá & Río Paraná), & because there is a 24-hour restaurant with Wi-Fi. Apart from that, it is worth visiting to see the high-quality artworks on sale by local sculptors. Rooms are more basic than 1609 in town, although they are almost the same price. **$$**

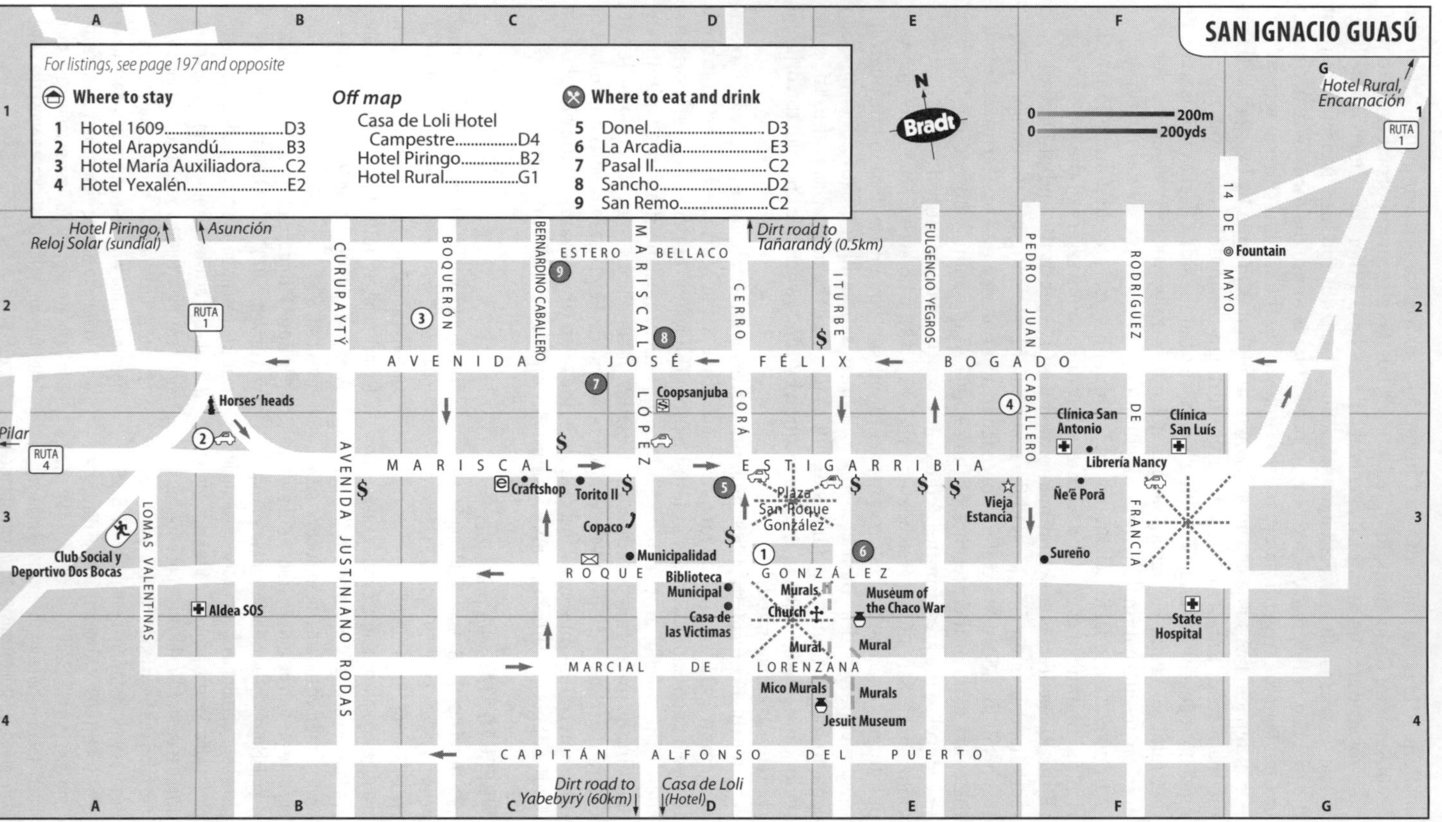
SAN IGNACIO GUASÚ
For listings, see page 197 and opposite
Where to stay
1 Hotel 1609 D3
2 Hotel Arapysandú B3
3 Hotel María Auxiliadora C2
4 Hotel Yexalén E2
Off map
Casa de Loli Hotel Campestre D4
Hotel Piringo B2
Hotel Rural G1
Where to eat and drink
5 Donel D3
6 La Arcadia E3
7 Pasal II C2
8 Sancho D2
9 San Remo C2
N
Bradt
0 200m
0 200yds
Hotel Rural, Encarnación
RUTA 1
Hotel Piringo, Reloj Solar (sundial)
Asunción
Dirt road to Tañarandý (0.5km)
14 DE MAYO
Fountain
CURUPAYTÝ
BOQUERÓN
BERNARDINO CABALLERO
ESTERO BELLACO
MARISCAL LÓPEZ
CERRO CORÁ
ITURBE
FULGENCIO YEGROS
PEDRO JUAN CABALLERO
RODRÍGUEZ DE FRANCIA
AVENIDA JOSÉ FÉLIX BOGADO
Horses' heads
Pilar
RUTA 4
Coopsanjuba
Clínica San Antonio
Librería Nancy
Clínica San Luís
MARISCAL ESTIGARRIBIA
Craftshop
Torito II
Plaza San Roque González
Vieja Estancia
Ñe'ẽ Porã
Copaco
Sureño
Municipalidad
ROQUE GONZÁLEZ
Club Social y Deportivo Dos Bocas
LOMAS VALENTINAS
AVENIDA JUSTINIANO RODAS
Biblioteca Municipal
Murals
Museum of the Chaco War
Church
Casa de las Victimas
Aldea SOS
State Hospital
Mural
Mural
MARCIAL DE LORENZANA
Mico Murals
Murals
Jesuit Museum
CAPITÁN ALFONSO DEL PUERTO
Dirt road to Yabebyrý (60km)
Casa de Loli (Hotel)

Casa de Loli Hotel Campestre (8 rooms) Marsical López 1595 c/ Coronel Rafael Franco; 0782 232362; m 0985 113640/0975 654758; e lacasadeloli@yahoo.com; www.lacasadeloli.com.py. An excellent hotel, but inconveniently placed on the furthest edge of town, 1km from the centre on the road to Yabebyrý. If you have a car it is worth it. Discreetly hidden behind a wall. Big garden, pool, *quincho*. Meals to order. **$**

Hotel Arapysandú (10 rooms) Ruta 1 y Ruta 4; 0782 232213. Strategically placed in the triangular island at the junction of the road to Encarnación & the road to Pilar, & behind a service station. Taxi rank behind it, & in front is the 'horses' heads' monument (see page 203). Restaurant all hours. Ciudad de Pilar bus-stop outside. **$**

Hotel Yexalén (16 rooms) Av Pedro Juan Caballero c/ José Félix Bogado; 0782 232600. Opened on this site in 2007, b/fast room but no restaurant, friendly people, all rooms AC, some with sommier beds. **$**

Hotel María Auxiliadora (22 rooms) Boquerón c/ José Félix Bogado; 0782 232152. Cheaper rooms have fans. No b/fast. **$**

WHERE TO EAT AND DRINK *Map, page 198.*

La Arcadia Iturbe c/ Roque González; m 0975 619171. Far & away the best restaurant in town, very reasonably priced & underused simply because it looks as though it is more expensive than it is. For this reason the opening hours are limited to lunch Tue–Sun & dinner Fri & Sat. Will open on other evenings for a group on request. Imaginative dishes, many dating back from the time of the Reductions. Brilliant hand-painted décor, since the restaurant is owned by the family of the artist Koki Ruiz. **$$**

San Remo Estero Bellaco esq Bernardino Caballero; m 0971 973583. Good pizzería with great atmosphere & service, but it's not cheap. **$$**

Pasall II José Félix Bogado e/ Mariscal López y Bernardino Caballero; 0782 233212. Coffee shop with good cakes, also open at night for beers & snacks. **$**

Donel Mariscal Estigarribia esq Cerro Corá; m 0985 245207. Good location on the corner of the main square, with tables outside. **$**

Sancho José Félix Bogado y Mariscal López; 0782 232638; all day. Always abuzz with locals grabbing lunch. Good value. Recently moved to larger premises. Wi-Fi. **$**

NIGHTLIFE The main nightlife spot is **La Vieja Estancia** [198 E3] (*Mariscal Estigarribia y Pedro Juan Caballero; 0782 232297/0782 232366; from 19.00 Thu–Sat nightclub from 23.00 or midnight onwards on Fri (karaoke) & Sat (dancing)*) Huge tree trunk outside carved into a bull's head.

SHOPPING The Liberería Nancy [198 F3] is the nearest thing to a department store. Opposite is a good shop for computer accessories and electrical goods, Ñee̋ Porã. For supermarket shopping, try Torito II [198 C3] and Sureño [198 F3].

OTHER PRACTICALITIES San Ignacio is now well supplied with banks and cash machines. There are many **taxi** ranks but at night it can be difficult to find a taxi. The most reliable places to look are on both sides of the Plaza San Roque González [198 D3 & E3] and behind the Hotel Arapysandú [198 B3] (where you can wait if need be inside in the bar-restaurant, which is open all hours). Phone numbers of taxi ranks are: 0782 232771/232715/232320/232812/232953.

WHAT TO SEE AND DO The square on Ruta 1 is the **Plaza San Roque González de Santa Cruz** [198 D3]. In the centre is a stage, where a free open-air concert of dance and folk music – Serenata Folclórica – is held every Sunday evening (excluding January, and mid-June to mid-August). Next to it is a large, if undistinguished, statue of San Roque González, portrayed as is customary with an arrow through his heart (see box on pages 114–15).

REDUCTION: A TYPICAL TOWN LAYOUT

The Jesuit-Guaraní Reductions (and to a lesser extent the Franciscan Reductions) were centred around a square – the plaza – which at times was very large indeed (such as in Trinidad). On three sides of the plaza were *casas de indios*, which were rows of single-storey buildings with a colonnade all around or at least on the two long sides. Each building would comprise eight or ten square rooms, with doors opening to front and back, and each room would be the home for a family. The houses consequently had more doors than windows: in some places there were windows as well as doors, and in other places not. In the old Guaraní huts, the buildings would also be long like this, but with the difference that all the families would live together; the Jesuits separated the families, in order to protect fidelity in marriage. Another difference was that the houses in the Reductions used improved building skills, passing from wood and straw, to adobe and tile, to brick, and eventually in some places to stone.

On one side of the plaza was the church, which was the most prominent building in the *pueblo* (town), and at times quite magnificently adorned. The bell tower was a separate wooden construction to one side or the other of the church (right up until the last Reductions, when it became an integrated part of a stone church as in Europe). On one side of the church there was customarily the cemetery, and behind that was the orchard, while on the other side was a group of buildings sometimes collectively referred to as the *colegio*, although they would include not only the school but also the priests' residence, rooms for guests, offices and a range of workshops. This *colegio* would be arranged around a couple of patios, with the Jesuits' house adjoining the church.

The most able boys studied in the school. Mostly, but not exclusively, they were the sons of the *caciques*, and, inevitably for the era, boys only. They were taught to read and write in Latin, Guaraní and possibly Spanish: Spanish was not used within the Reductions, but Latin was, in church. They also studied mathematics and music. The workshops of a Reduction could cover a wide variety of crafts: stone work and carpentry; carving – especially statues of saints – in stone and wood; painting – to decorate the church and colour the statues; weaving and making clothes; pottery, silverwork and goldwork, and ironwork – both for forging wrought-iron railings and gates, and for making firearms. The Guaraní needed guns to use in self-defence against the *bandeirantes* who from the beginning attacked and burned down the Reductions, capturing or killing the indigenous population. Out of more than 70 Reductions that were founded for the Guaraní, more than 40 were destroyed by these slave-traders coming from São Paulo in present-day Brazil.

Close to the two patios of the college, but without a fixed, regular spot for every Reduction, was the *kotý guasú* (Guaraní 'room big') for orphans, widows and other women who needed extra help and protection. There was often a small Loreto chapel somewhere in the Reduction, and a Calvary hill, but these did not have set locations.

One block behind this square is the original plaza of the Reduction, with the **church** [198 D4] in the middle of the green. This plaza does not have a name but can be referred to as the old plaza. Built in 1935, within a few years of the Jesuits' return to San Ignacio, the church is neither original nor in the original position (which in a Reduction was always on one side of the plaza and not in the middle of it), but is nonetheless a splendid building with both charm and dignity. Painted white, it has a high bell tower and balustrades, and two big palm trees flanking the doorway. Inside, the reredos has St Ignatius, St Francis Xavier and St Luis Gonzaga. There are three representations of San Roque González: there is a statue of him (holding his painting of the Virgin) in a side chapel, a painting by Nino Sotelo of the saint walking with the *cacique* Arapysandú, and another painting of the martyrdom.

Six bas-relief **murals** [198 E4] in painted cement are found beside the church and at the corner, created during the Third Meeting of Muralismo Latinoamericano in August 1999, using Guaraní traditional mythology to portray Christian-related themes. While the murals are the work of different artists from different countries, they have adopted a uniform style and technique and the same muted red, yellow and grey colour scheme. They are interesting pieces, but need some interpretation. Going from north to south, the first is called *Porã ypý rekávo* (Guaraní 'In search of the primeval beauty') and shows the hummingbird – which existed before the creation of the world – hovering Holy Spirit-like over a mother and child, in front of a row of palm trees and next to a half-made rush basket, which evokes the feather headdress out of which the woman was created in Guaraní mythology. The second is called *Sãsó* (Guaraní 'Emancipation') and shows a naked man breaking free of the ropes that bound him to a cross, while the menacing jaguar passes by. The third shows a Christ-figure stretching out his arms to distribute maize and the pipe of peace, with an indigenous decorated dish in front of him, and in his other hand an armadillo, the traditional carer of the earth. This mural does not bear a name, but it is known locally as *La Comunión* and is the work of three local artists: Koki Ruiz, Cecilio Thompson and Teodoro Meza. The fourth mural is called *Itatýpe ojehái Kurusú rapykueré* (Guaraní 'Among the stones he left the track of the cross') and shows the Good Friday procession of Tañarandý (see page 204) with its crucified figure, the crowd with lanterns, and a carpet of *apepú candiles* (candles of animal fat in bitter orange skins). The fifth is called *Yvý marane'ỹ* (Guaraní 'The land without stain') and is a strong portrayal of an indigenous man attacking a conquistador, while a fierce bat – the guardian of the sacred precincts – joins in driving the evil from the land. The last, slightly smaller mural is called *Yvytú pepó ári* (Guaraní 'On the wings of the wind') and portrays the theme of protection through three symbols: the watchful hummingbird, a large hand, and a caring mother.

Two painted murals by the Chilean artist Luis Marcos Enrique, known as Mico, are found on the walls of the Jesuit residence. They show the arrival of the conquistadors and the work of Roque González and the early Jesuits in protecting the Guaraní people. These very colourful works of a popular, almost comic-book style, were painted in early 2009, during a week's youth mission, but are now unfortunately seriously deteriorated. A considerable section of ***casas de indios*** remain around the old plaza, on both the east and west side, with their traditional long colonnades. On the east side is the Casa de Cultura and the Museo de Semblanza de los Héroes (**m** 0975 606635; ⌚ *07.00–noon & 13.00–176.00 Mon–Fri, 07.30–11.30 Sat; free admission*). This is the **Museum of the Chaco War** [198 E3], with a few items from the earlier War of the Triple Alliance. The Chaco War took place between 1932–35 (see pages 13–15), and the museum is based on a collection donated by the local pilot Ramón Martino, who was the first aviator in South America to carry out a bombardment by night (on 22 December 1934). The names of the soldiers from San Ignacio who fought in the war and survived fill six columns on a memorial board, while the names of those who died in this tragic war fill more than three columns (ie: more than a third died). In front of the museum is a monument erected in 2009 to the local soldiers who fought in the war, carved in red stone by the local artist Gerardo Farias and colleagues.

Directly facing the church is an original *casa de indios* used as a private house, which, like the Casa de Cultura (see page 201), retains its wooden pillars. (In most original houses, when the wood has rotted it has been replaced with masonry pillars.) Next to it is the parish office, the San Luis parish centre, the Municipal tourist information centre (*☎ 0782 233458, no fixed opening hours*), and then the **Casa de las Victimas** [198 D3] (*☎ 0782 233000; m 0972 185986 Bonifacio Flores; ⏲ 07.00–11.00 & 13.00–16.00 Mon–Fri; free admission*), which is an archive and documentation centre on the victims of Stroessner's repression: many of these were from San Ignacio, Santa Rosa and Santa María, where the Ligas Agrarias Cristianas (Christian Agrarian Leagues) had begun. The centre is generally attended by victims, who are most hospitable to guests, and some of them formed part of the Truth and Justice Commission that worked in the years 2004–08 to document the human rights' abuses of the 1954–89 dictatorship. After that in the row of houses comes the **Biblioteca Municipal** [000 D3] (*⏲ 07.00–noon Mon–Sat; 13.00–17.00 Mon–Fri*) which has a permanent exhibition of photos of the Jesuit Reductions taken by P José María Blanch SJ.

The **Museo Diocesano del Arte Jesuítico Guaraní** [198 E4] (*Iturbe 870, c/ Alfonso del Puerto; ☎ 0782 232223; m 0985 187824 (Estela) / 0975 685072 (Clemente); ⏲ 08.00–11.30 & 14.00–17.30 daily; Gs10,000*) is open only in the afternoons (at present), but access during the morning can often be obtained by applying to the parish office opposite the church or by telephoning in advance. From the street you can read the names of 26 Jesuit martyrs of the period of the Reductions, on a stone set high in the wall, and beginning with Roque González de Santa Cruz, followed by his two companions who were canonised along with him by Pope John Paul II on his visit to Paraguay in 1988. Alonso Rodríguez was killed as he rushed out to see what was going on as Roque González was felled with a stone axe; Juan del Castillo was killed two days later in a nearby locality as part of the same attack masterminded by Ñesú.

The museum is housed in a beautifully proportioned long building that was originally the residence of the Jesuits in the Reduction. If you go to the end of the colonnade, you can find some exposed adobe blocks which show the internal construction of the walls, almost 1m thick. There is a column from the *urunde'ý* tree, showing how some of the root structure was left intact to give the columns greater stability. On one side of the museum is the current Jesuit residence, while around the other side is an original sundial of the period, still only 20 minutes out of true, and beyond that the Jesuit retreat house, arranged around a couple of patios. Within the garden is a small area of the original floor of the church, 32m x 80m, which used to stretch down from that point to the plaza, but which was regrettably demolished in the 1920s because it was in poor repair. Destruction was cheaper than restoration. Photographs in the museum record how the church looked, inside and out, immediately before it was knocked down.

The carved wooden sculptures from the Reduction underwent restoration at the time the museum was opened, in the 1970s, under the Chilean Tito González. A second restoration a few years ago, under the direction of the Italian Donatella Salono Lippens, proved controversial. The statues in San Ignacio consequently have (for good or ill) a lucidity of colour that contrasts with the muddier tones of the old paint in a museum like that of Santa María. In 2013 all the Jesuit museums of Misiones – San Ignacio, Santa María de Fe, Santa Rosa and Santiago – were given a slight redesign by Luis Lataza, with more informative notices, although he respected the fundamental layout of their various rooms.

Among the notable works in the first room – called the Room of the Creation – is a huge and striking composition of Tobias and the Angel: the Angel is huge, and towers over Tobias, who is portrayed as a little boy grasping the hand of his angelic guardian. Another famous piece is a very feminine-looking St Michael conquering the devil. You can observe a rectangle cut out of the back of the statues: all large Jesuit statues were made this way, so that the inside could be hollowed out and the weight reduced. Some also say that it removed the sappy interior that was liable to rot. A number of angel heads are set on the wall, some with and some without the two wings that are so characteristic of angel heads in the Reductions; they were originally part of the reredos, which was an impressive work with 22 statues in niches.The next room – the Room of the Paschal Mystery – has statues of the passion and resurrection, including a pair of statues portraying the Risen Christ meeting his mother, who greets him with arms outstretched. These two statues were originally carried in procession on Easter Sunday morning, in the ceremony known as Tupãsý Ñuvaitĩ (Guaraní 'the Encounter of the Mother of God'). (There is another statue of the Risen Christ in the church of Santa María de Fe, but the best is in the museum of Santiago. The Santa María museum also has two or three Virgins which were probably Tupãsý Ñuvaitĩ statues.) The third room is devoted to the Church, and has a variety of saints, among them St Anna, and St Rose of Lima, and two pairs of saints from the reredos – Peter with his keys and Paul with his sword – and also the two founders of orders of friars: St Dominic holding a church, and St Francis holding a book. The last three of these are attributed to Brassanelli (see box on pages 174–5), as also is a statue of St Anthony of Padua. Other pieces of note are two Immaculate Conceptions (with Mary standing on the moon), one of which formed the centrepiece of the original reredos of the church, as can be seen in an old photograph on the wall of the museum.

Another saint from that reredos is the patron of the Reduction, St Ignatius. This statue is the triumphant central piece of the last room – devoted to the Society of Jesus – with three other Jesuit saints, also from the reredos – St Francis Borja with his monstrance, St Francis Xavier with his crucifix and St Stanislaus Kostka with the infant Jesus. The missing piece from the reredos is San Luis (or Aloysius) Gonzaga, which went on loan to the little chapel in the *compañía* of San Luis, and has never returned.

Do not miss the little chapel, which you must enter from the side walkway. Its reredos originally belonged to one of the side altars in the old church, with St Lucy at the top, and the central figure of the young Jesus known as the *niño alcalde* (boy mayor), representing Christ simultaneously as divine judge and incarnate child. It appears to be the work of the same sculptor who carved St Paul in the museum. This room is still in use as a chapel, and the pew is from the original church. On special occasions, a dramatisation of the original reredos of the church is put on by the Grupo La Barraca de Tañarandý (☎ *0782 22775;* **m** *0975 619171*). Called the *Museo Viviente*, the performance uses living actors dressed up as Jesuit statues. Brief though it is, it is a beautiful show. The feast day of St Ignatius (31 July) is also always celebrated in style.

Monuments at the west end of town If you leave the town centre behind and go to the west end of town, you can visit two modern stone monuments, both based on ideas conceived by Koki Ruiz (see page 204). The six **horses' heads** [198 B2] (and two horses' flanks) set on pillars outside the Hotel Arapysandú were carved by Mario Mereles, and commemorate the departure of cavalry from San Ignacio on 31 July 1932 (the feast of St Ignatius) to fight in the Chaco War.

Further out of town you come to a small hill on the south side of Ruta 1, where some stone sculptures have been set into the grass, including two tall stone slabs forming a sort of gateway. This is the **Reloj Solar** (sundial), and the idea of the piece is to compare and contrast the life of the Guaraní outside and inside the Jesuit Reductions. The sculpture is now in poor condition and some parts of it have been lost, but on one side the sundial represents the ordered daily programme that the Jesuits introduced, and on the other the leaves of *yerba mate* symbolise the unstructured life of the Guaraní in the forest.

Tañarandý Tañarandý is a *compañía* immediately to the north of San Ignacio which has gained a reputation for artistic works. The *compañía* is a charming place and should be visited if you can possibly spare the time. You can get a taxi from San Ignacio, or walk: the furthest point of Tañarandý, the chapel, is only 3km from San Ignacio. You will want to see the painted house names along the road, the craft shop Kandiré, and to go inside the chapel.

Each house along the principal dirt road **Yvaga Rápe** (Guaraní, Heaven's Road) has a colourfully painted sign outside with a picture showing the work of the owner. Most of the occupations are rural – keeping poultry, hoeing the ground and driving an ox plough – but there is also a builder, a grocer and a lorry driver. They were painted in primitive style around 2005 by a local artist Cecilio Thompson, who was tragically killed shortly afterwards when he was knocked off his bicycle. There are also carved stone owls along the road, the work of an artist called Patricio Rotela.

A couple of blocks along the road, on the left, opposite the *colegio*, is a **craft shop** called Artesanía Tacuarera (m *0985 181356*), with attractive gifts and furniture, all made out of bamboo and very professionally designed. To get to the **chapel** of Tañarandý keep straight on along the main access road until you reach it on the right, on the right-hand corner at the end of the third block. You pass three stone owls on pillars before you get there. Inside and out, it has been converted from a basically simple building into a flight of art and imagination, with painted pillars, mouldings, panels and angels, covering every inch of the walls and ceiling. The paintings were done by Teodoro Meza, Macarena Ruiz and Koki Ruiz. Particularly good is a *trompe l'œil* door that makes the church seem bigger than it is, and a striking deposition from the cross, painted by Koki Ruiz behind the altar. The keyholder, Seferino Corvalán, lives exactly opposite the church and will show you round if you clap your hands outside his door (the usual way of attracting attention when there is not a bell, though you can knock on the door if you prefer). Do not forget a small tip.

At dusk every Good Friday evening there is a torchlit **procession** of a statue of the Virgen Dolorosa (Sorrowful Virgin) accompanied by Guaraní chant. The event is free, and attracts tens of thousands of visitors from all over the country – so many people that it is now difficult to see or to hear anything. At the end there is customarily the deposition from the cross of a bust of Christ crucified, followed by the illumination of 'living pictures' (*cuadros vivientes*), in which people dress up and pose in the position of famous works of classical religious art, each group delineated within a frame. It is an extraordinarily beautiful and touching event, the initiative of Koki Ruiz, who lives in La Barraca, on the edge of Tañarandý, but with massive collaboration from the local people, who place on the dirt road more than ten thousand lit *candiles* in the skins of bitter oranges. If you go on Holy Thursday evening, to avoid the Friday crowds, you can witness the practice of the living pictures, but not the procession with *candiles*.

SANTA MARÍA DE FE

Copaco ☎ *0781 283298; municipalidad* ☎ *0781 283214*

Santa María de Fe, the most northerly of the Treinta Pueblos, is a jewel. It has the best museum of any of the Reductions, including those in Argentina and Brazil, and it still operates as a living town around its historic plaza. If you only have time for one museum and one ruin from the Reductions, try to make it Santa María de Fe for the museum, and Trinidad for the ruins. Santa María is a good place to break the journey on the way to Trinidad from Asunción, and because it is so close to San Ignacio and to Santa Rosa there is a good chance that you may be able to see at least two if not all three of these museums, without too much expenditure of time.

Santa María was once one of the biggest of the Reductions, and the main road through Misiones used to run from Villa Florida to Santa María. But it has been saved as a tranquil, unspoilt town, little more than a village, by the fact that Ruta 1 bypasses it, and goes through San Ignacio instead. In the publicity of the Ruta Jesuítica, Santa María features as the Reduction marked by 'spirituality and calm', and visitors often speak of its special atmosphere.

Santa María de Fe was one of two Reductions (with Santiago) founded in the 1630s by the French Jesuit Jacques Ransonnier in the Itatines region to the north (in present-day Brazil). In 1647 Fr Noel Berthot consolidated the settlement after it

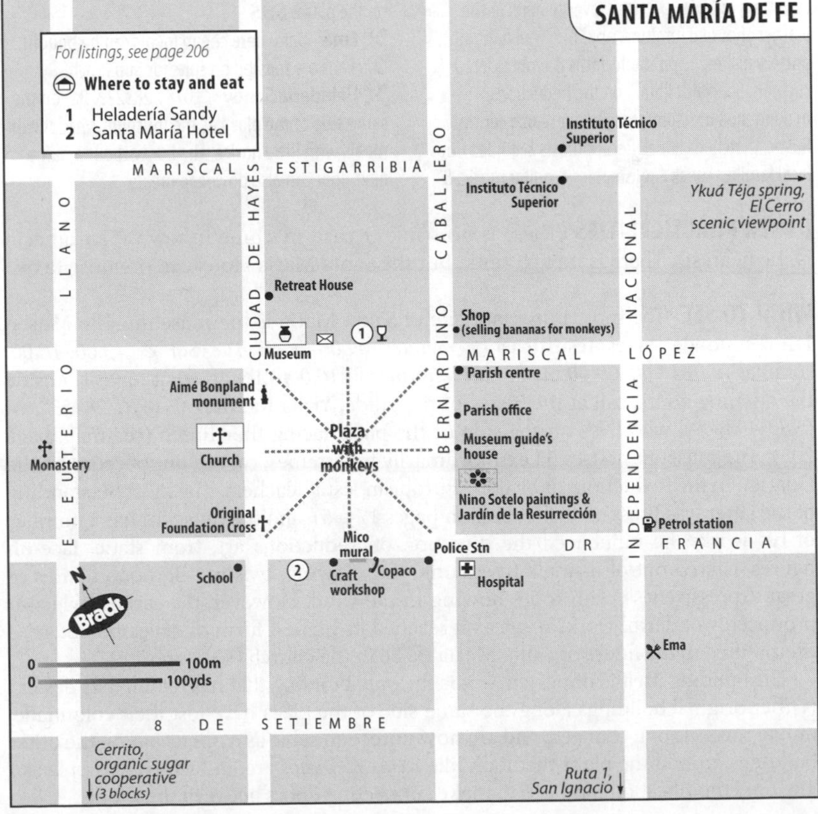

had been dispersed by attacks from Portuguese *bandeirantes*, and in 1669 it moved again, south to its present position among the Treinta Pueblos.

GETTING THERE By **car**, the journey from Asunción takes 3½ hours, and you take the signed turning to the left, 4km after San Ignacio. After 11km you arrive in the town. By **bus**, there is one direct bus each day, the Mariscal López, which leaves the terminal in Asunción at 11.45 and arrives in Santa María about 16.30; it will drop you right at the door of the hotel or wherever else you want to go to. Or you can take one of the many buses (about two an hour) that go to San Ignacio on their way to Encarnación or to Pilar (see bus timetable, pages 188–9), and then take a taxi, either from the Hotel Arapysandú or from the plaza: it will cost Gs30,000 and take 15 minutes.

WHERE TO STAY AND EAT *Map, page 205.*

Santa María Hotel (See ad, page 184) (5 rooms) 0781 283311; m 0981 861553; e info@santamariahotel.org; www.santamariahotel.org; Facebook: Santa Maria Hotel. This hotel is on the historic plaza, in a couple of buildings facing the museum. Each room is adorned with a carved stone in the wall, copies from original stones in the Jesuit Ruins. Large dining room for events & huge mango tree in garden provides a focus for sitting outside. Craftwork everywhere: in the leather-thonged furniture, appliqué wall hangings, pottery dishes, *ao po'í* tablecloths & embroidered curtains. Specialist library on the Reductions, making the hotel something of a research centre. Rustic, thatched chapel. Receptionists & guides from local families speak English. Harp & guitar music, & folk dance displays can be organised. Tours can be arranged, even to the Reductions in Argentina & Iguazú Falls; guided service in English from airport to airport. Begun in 2006 to bring work to a town with massive unemployment, the hotel specialises in introducing guests to the local people & projects. Wi-Fi, split AC, sommier beds. Meals to order. Use mobile number for 24-hour service if hotel is closed when there are no guests: you can ring from Copaco on the plaza. **$$$**

Ema Bar where cheap meals can be bought. Chickens are roasted on spits for Sun lunch. **$**

Heladería Sandy 0781 283222. Bar on the same side of the plaza as the museum. Very cheap meals with little notice. The bar without a name next door can also do cheap meals. **$**

OTHER PRACTICALITIES There is no bank or cash machine in town (San Ignacio is the nearest). There is no taxi rank, but the Santa María Hotel can organise taxis.

WHAT TO SEE The most important site of Santa María is the museum. The **Museo Diocesano de Artes Jesuíticas** (*winter 09.00–noon Tue–Sat & 13.00–16.00, summer until 17.00, 09.00–noon Sun; entrance Gs10,000*) If you want to visit outside the opening hours, call at the house of the guide, Yrma Ramírez (*0781 283332;* m *0983 458689*), who lives on the side of the plaza facing the church (see map, page 205). The museum houses 54 extraordinarily fine statues, carved out of cedar by the Guaraní in the Reduction, or by their European Jesuit teachers. The most outstanding of the latter was Brassanelli (see box on pages 174–5), and the museum has a number of his works: he influenced the direction of Reductions art, from static, face-on figures, carved out of a single tree trunk, into flowing, twisting Baroque figures of great expressiveness, with robes flowing in the wind. However, the earlier style also produced wonderful works of art as it reached its highest form of development, as is exemplified in the figure of Santa María de Fe in the church (see opposite).

The building itself is important – it is the only building that has retained its design. (Other original buildings along the same side of the plaza have lost their colonnade, or had the style of it changed, and are now unrecognisable as *casas de indios*; the other buildings around the plaza that look like *casas de indios* are, in fact, recent replicas.) The only modification has been to make connecting doors between the rooms.

The first room of the museum has some vestiges of the old church, including the wrought iron crosses that were originally on top of the church and on top of the old wooden bell tower. The second room is devoted to Jesuit saints. The three large statues of St Ignatius, St Francis Xavier and St Francis Borgia were in the original reredos of the church, above the figure of Santa María de Fe that is still behind the altar in the church (see below), and that was flanked by the figures of Anna and Joachim (or according to another theory, Elizabeth and Zacharias), now in room 5. Also in room 2 are a pair of statues of St Luis Gonzaga, and another pair of St Stanislaus Kostka, in which the smaller figure is evidently the work of a European, and the larger figure is a Guaraní copy. The Guaraní were great copyists, but each piece comes out with a distinctly Guaraní style, particularly in the face.

In the third room of the museum are statues of early martyrs: Barbara with her tower, Cecilia with a cup of martyrdom and Sebastian holding some arrows. There are a couple of Virgins here, of which at least the one in the corner – with Guaraní features – is a Tupãsý Ñuvaitĩ (see page 203): if you compare it with the Brassanelli Tupãsý Ñuvaitĩ in the preceding room, the difference of style is quite marked, although which is better is a matter of personal preference.The fourth room has two St Michaels, and facing them, in one of the original niches that would once have housed each one of the saints, is St Joseph. The fifth room has the famous crib of Santa María, which, although not quite life-size, is still very large. As well as the usual figures there is the elegant bird with a head crest known as the *perdiz* (crested tinamou in English – it is also carved on the ruined altar of Trinidad). The Christ Child was stolen from the museum in 1983, but a substitute figure has been found that fits the role quite nicely, although it was not originally carved to be a Jesus. The figure of the seated Mary clutching a book was almost certainly part of an Annunciation scene, but again fits well into this grouping, as her downcast eyes seem to be contemplating the baby on a cushion at her feet.

To reach the sixth and last room (really two rooms knocked into one) you must exit and re-enter again from the colonnade. This is the Room of the Passion, and the figures in it are powerful and poignant so that entering this room is something of a mystical experience. The Christ-on-a-donkey figure is still used liturgically on Palm Sunday (see page 210 on the Cerrito). The towering figure of Christ in the Garden of Gethsemane is said by some to have been carved by Anton Sepp, a Jesuit from the Tirol who lived in Santa María in the 1690s, during the plague that killed off 20 or 30 indigenous each day. Sepp was a prolific writer and a brilliant musician – he is known as the 'Father of the Paraguayan harp' – and was probably the best-known Jesuit of the generation following Montoya and Roque González: there is no evidence that he was also a sculptor, but it is a nice idea as the figure certainly expresses anguished petition. There is a figure of St Peter weeping as he hears the cock crow, an unusual and moving subject, and three figures of Christ at the pillar. The middle, slightly smaller piece is an extraordinarily moving and very Guaraní portrayal of Christ, with silent hurt eyes and a triangular scar on his cheek. Before the cross is one of the most expressive figures in the museum – a Virgin of Sorrows, looking upwards, utterly absorbed in the painful sight before her eyes. The next figure is the articulated Christ, whose hinged arms can be raised when he is on the cross and folded down when he is removed from it. This figure exactly fits the holes on the cross on the little Calvary hill known as the Cerrito (see page 210).

Apart from the museum itself, there are many points of interest around the plaza. The great **statue of Santa María de Fe**, which gives its name to the town, is behind the altar in the **church**, flanked by two angels, a life-size crucifix, and a Risen Christ (see page 203), all from the Reduction. This large and striking statue of Mary shows the Virgin as she is spoken of in Revelation 12, clothed in the sun, standing on the moon, and with a crown of 12 stars around her head. It is a thoroughly Guaraní portrayal of an olive-skinned woman with long black hair snaking down her back, contrasting with the fair skin, blue eyes and light-brown hair of the much more famous Caacupé Madonna (even though that too was carved by an Indian – see box on page 142). The patronal feast day of Santa María de Fe is 8 September, the Birth of the Virgin (whereas that of Caacupé is 8 December, the Immaculate Conception).

The church itself was built in 1954 and though smaller than the original church (which fell down in 1910) is in the original spot and is traditional in style, with a pitched roof supported on tree-trunk pillars. For access to the church (*Mass: Sun 18.00 winter, 19.00 summer*) ask at the parish office, in the colonnade on the opposite side of the plaza (*0781 283360; 08.00–11.00 Mon–Fri*). There is a small community of monks, the **Comunidad San José** (*0781 283359*), who sing lauds and vespers in their monastery chapel daily and are happy to receive visitors to these liturgies (*06.00 & 18.00, but times are liable to vary; ring to check*). Outside the church is a small **monument to Aimé Bonpland** (see box below), a world-famous 19th-century French botanist who lived for ten years in Santa María de Fe.

On the next corner from the Bonpland monument, just outside the Santa María Hotel, is an original **cross** – one of four that used to stand in the four corners of the plaza. The other three corners of the square now have replica crosses, planted during youth events in 2009. On a wall next to the Copaco public telephones is a brightly coloured **mural by Mico** of Fr Noel Berthot and a group of Guaraní gathered around their statue of the Virgin. The mural was painted during a youth mission, and the

AIMÉ BONPLAND

Aimé (in Spanish, Amado) Bonpland (1773–1858) qualified first as a medical doctor, but his passion was botany, and he travelled all over South America with his German friend, Alexander von Humboldt, producing drawings of plants and insects. He created a herbarium representing some 6,000 species, half of which he was classifying for the first time. There is a Museo de Ciencias Naturales Dr Amado Bonpland in Corrientes, Argentina.

After his initial long travels with von Humboldt (1799–1804) he became superintendent of the gardens of La Malmaison, home of Napoleon's wife, the Empress Josephine, but he returned in 1816 to Argentina and cultivated a *yerba mate* plantation. At a time when there were border disputes over what is now Misiones Argentina, Bonpland's alliance with Buenos Aires was seen as a threat by the then dictator of Paraguay, Dr Francia. He sent troops over the border to arrest Bonpland, and had him confined to Santa María de Fe for ten years (1821–31), where he married the daughter of the *cacique*, María Chirivé, and had two children (also called Amado and María). They lived at a place called the Cerrito (little hill) in the Taperã area on the edge of the village, where he opened a hospital and dedicated his time to healing the sick with natural medicines; he was seen by the local people as a *karaí arandú* (Guaraní 'man wise').

Eventually international pressure for his release resulted in him being thrown out of the country without his family. Instead of returning to Europe, he settled once more in the border area of Argentina, and continued cultivating *yerba mate*, until his death in 1857 in Santa Ana, Corrientes. He has descendants who still live in Santa María.

LIBERATION THEOLOGY AND THE CHRISTIAN AGRARIAN LEAGUES

Liberation theology has been mentioned, and Paraguay has made a distinguished contribution to that pivotal shift in religious thinking that burgeoned out of Latin America from the 1960s and has continued until the present day – except that, as with everything else, Paraguay's contribution has been almost forgotten. Nonetheless, what is arguably the simplest, clearest, primer in liberation theology thinking was published in Spain in 1971: *Vivir como Hermanos* (Living as brothers and sisters) by José Luis Caravias (a Spanish Jesuit who has lived in Paraguay since the 1960s, with the exception of a period of forced exile when Stroessner's police threw him out, literally, onto the streets of Argentina without documents, money or spare clothing). The book was republished in Paraguay by CEPAG in 2003.

In the early 1960s, at the same time as Brazil was developing its Christian base communities – the crucible of liberation thinking among the poor – Paraguay was making a parallel development, known as the Christian Agrarian Leagues (Ligas Agrarias Cristianas, LACs), beginning in Santa Rosa in 1960. But whereas Brazil's communities survived political persecution to become world famous, the Paraguayan LACs were totally wiped out by the bloody repression unleashed by Stroessner in 1976, in what is known as the Pascua Dolorosa (Sorrowful Easter).

Today the history of the LACs is being recovered through appliqué wall hangings embroidered in Santa María de Fe, designed by the wife of one of the torture survivors. They record key moments in the life of the leagues: *mínga* (Guaraní 'working together'), *jopói* (Guaraní 'sharing'), *escuelitas campesinas* (Spanish 'little campesino schools'), biblical reflection, the repression and torture. The sewing co-operative has a website where orders can be made (*www.santamariadefe.com*). The history of the leagues is told in a chapter of *Unfinished Journey: The Church 40 Years after Vatican II* by Margaret Hebblethwaite, the author of this book – see *Other books*, page 402, for details. See also *Museo de las Memorias*, pages 105–6.

artist Mico is a Chilean whose full name is Luis Marcos Enrique (the same who did the murals in San Ignacio – see page 201). All that side of the plaza had adobe *casas de indios* still standing until 1943, when a cyclone knocked them down.

Among the trees of the plaza lives a family of **howler monkeys**, who provide a popular tourist attraction; you can buy bananas to feed them from a greengrocer at the corner of the plaza, next to the Librería Judith. They stay in a group so once you have found one you should be able to locate another six or eight in the next tree or two – brown mothers and babies, and big black males.

Santa María has its own particular craft in the form of embroidered appliqué. The **craft workshop**, Taller de Hermandad (*see ad, page 222;* e *info@santamariadefe.com; www.santamariadefe.com;* ⌚ *07.00–11.00 & 13.00–16.00 Mon–Fri*) is located on the plaza between the Santa María Hotel and Copaco, in a reproduction *casa de indios*. The workshop is run as a co-operative of around 30 women who work in two shifts, but the afternoon group is bigger. They always welcome visits and have a selection of craft to sell: keyrings, purses, shopping bags, T-shirts and wall hangings. This is the only place in Paraguay where this colourful and intricate craftwork is done, though similar work is found in a number of other Latin American countries. Orders can be made from abroad through their website.

Another reproduction *casa de indios*, built in 2007 with substantial wooden pillars supporting a colonnade, is on the next side of the plaza (opposite the church). Though this is a private dwelling (the house of the author of this book), access can usually be arranged to see the large paintings inside by Nino Sotelo of the Jesuit history of Santa María de Fe: consult the Santa María Hotel or the museum guide about access. The same artist painted the history of the Virgin of Caacupé (see box on page 142). Behind the house is the Jardín de la Resurrección (Garden of the Resurrection), where a life-size empty tomb of Christ forms the backdrop for a five-minute display at 07.30 of Agua y Música, with little irrigation fountains playing in the rays of the sun: this is made available on a regular basis to guests of the Santa María Hotel if they wish. The town has a number of community projects. The Instituto Técnico Superior, supported by the UK charity the Santa Maria Education Fund offers free tertiary-level education and English courses to a high level: the hotel receptionists have trained there. On Sunday mornings you can witness harp classes in the Instituto and violin classes in the parish centre, where the Baroque music of the Reductions is learned alongside Paraguayan folk music.

At the east end of town is a small hill – the **Cerrito** – which was used as a Calvary in Jesuit times. The Cerrito is still today the site for the beginning of the Palm Sunday procession, with the figure of Christ-on-a-donkey, from the museum. On the opposite side of town, another old Jesuit site is **Ykuá Téja**, a spring of water that you pass on the cross-country way to Santa Rosa. It was once the source of water for the Reduction, and with a series of roofed pools it is still a place where the poor go to do their washing.

A long way further down the same road, you come to the turning for the **Cerro** (or Hill), a good hour and a half's walk away. This is a traditional place of pilgrimage for hundreds of local people on Good Friday. It has an oratory at the top and a view.

SANTA ROSA

Copaco ☎ 0858 285700; municipalidad ☎ 0858 285379

Today this town is smaller than San Ignacio, but bigger than Santa María de Fe, although historically it was founded in 1698 as an overflow Reduction from the then over-large Santa María. Its plaza has more original buildings than either of these two close neighbours, and although it has fewer statues, those it does include a few remarkable pieces. It is also the only Jesuit-Guaraní Reduction in any country to have a surviving Loreto chapel – a feature of many of the Reductions, apart from the main church – and the only one to have surviving frescoes. It has an original bell tower, not of the customary wooden construction, but of stone, which accounts for it being still standing. And it has a couple of matching stone panels on the outside of its church.

In short, Santa Rosa is a jewel that should be visited if at all possible. It is easy to take in on the way to Santiago or San Cosme y Damián, or Encarnación, as it is almost on the main road: many buses enter the town before continuing down Ruta 1. There is also a dirt road that leads there from Santa María, which is in good condition, and makes a delightful country drive.

The town is named after the Peruvian St Rosa of Lima and the patronal feast day is 30 August.

WHERE TO STAY AND EAT Within the town there are bars but no obvious restaurants. If you have a car the best place to eat is the Hotel Parador Santa Rosa just outside the town on Ruta 1 (see opposite).

Dolly Palace Hotel (8 rooms) Presidente Franco 649 e/ Av Florida y 14 de mayo; 0858 285224; e dollyhotel@hotmail.com. Half a block from the Plaza. Wi-Fi, split AC, sommier beds, internal parking. **$$**

Hotel Parador Santa Rosa (10 rooms) Ruta 1 km256; 0858 285249; m 0985 882248/0985 182190. On the north side of Ruta 1 about 1km after Santa Rosa in the direction of San Patricio. There are a variety of rural activities on offer & a massive pool. Large restaurant, good for special events. **$$**

Hotel Avenida (10 rooms) Av Florida, esq Edda B de Ayala; 0858 285358. 3 blocks from Ruta 1. **$**

WHAT TO SEE AND DO One side of the plaza has a complete row of ***casas de indios***, of which one in the middle (that of the hairdresser Don Benítez) has its original floor and wooden external door. All are actively used: most are shops, the end one is a police station, and next to that is a small **Museo de las Ligas Agrarias Cristianas** (*07.00–noon Mon–Sat*), which was a Christian community movement violently suppressed during the Stroessner dictatorship. In the plaza itself are a couple of modern **stone fountains**, both of them the work of Máximo Rotela, an artist from San Gerónimo, which is a *compañía* of Santa María. One shows some stone toads and the other portrays a figure from Guaraní mythology, Kurupí (see page 136).

The **bell tower** stands to the right of the church, and is 8m high, built out of red stone blocks. Four columns of stone have been preserved and set into the front exterior wall of the church, carved with a strong plant-based design. To gain access to the church, you pass through the parish secretary's office, which also sells the tickets to view the Loreto chapel. The original church was destroyed by fire in 1883, but the **reredos** to one of the side altars was saved and this now forms the centrepiece of the church. Delightfully, one of the cherubs perched on the top of the reredos is black, which must be one of the earliest instances of racial justice awareness expressed through art. There are a number of **saints** carved in the Jesuit period, although during the extension work on the church they have been moved for safekeeping: they include St John the Baptist with his lamb, San Isidro with his hoe, and a figure believed to be Isidro's wife.

The little **Loreto chapel** can be visited in the mornings (*0858 285221; 07.30–11.30 Mon–Sat, at other times by arrangement with Padre Joaquín,* m *0981 605423; voluntary donation, suggested minimum Gs5,000*), or sometimes at other times by arrangement. Before going inside, it is worth taking time to study this small and beautifully proportioned building, with its exquisitely carved door and window. Once inside you will see the **frescoes**, still perfectly discernible: to your left, the Last Judgement, and under it the Annunciation; to the right, Joseph's carpentry workshop; and in front of you, the legendary transport of Mary's house from Nazareth to Loreto, borne by angels through the skies. The letters QSD on the Last Judgement mural, next to St Michael, stand for the Latin words *Quis Sicut Deus?* ('Who is like God?' , the meaning of his name in Hebrew). Next to the mural of the Annunciation are the letters VCF, standing for the Latin *Verbum Caro Factum est* ('The Word was made flesh').

The most famous sculptures are the Gabriel and Mary at the Annunciation, by Brassanelli, currently displayed in front of the mural of the Annunciation. One of the most wonderful pieces in this little room is the Pietà (or *Piedad* as they say in Spanish), also probably by Brassanelli. This Mary is crazed with grief as she raises her head to howl to the heavens, her dead son in her arms notably smaller than her. It is interesting to compare this piece with the very different interpretation found in the museum in Santiago, where the *Piedad* is a classic of contemplative acceptance and breathes a spirit of enclosed tranquillity (see page 214). To either side of the door are two life-size crucifixes – not Jesus this time, but the two thieves: the good thief and the bad thief. They may have been used in an outdoor Calvary. In small painted panels facing the door are symbols of the Passion and the two figures who accompanied Jesus to the cross: his mother and the Beloved Disciple. There is also St Peter (with the keys of heaven, entrusted to him by Jesus) and St Paul (with the sword that effected his martyrdom).

SANTIAGO

Copaco ☎ *0782 20200/20393; municipalidad* ☎ *0782 20244*

Originally sited in Itatín, to the north, and called San Ignacio de Caaguazú, this Reduction changed its name to Santiago (St James) when it had to move south, because there were already two San Ignacios in the Treinta Pueblos, and one a near neighbour. It is the twin town to Santa María de Fe, and was also founded in the early 1630s and moved at the same time, finally reaching its present site in 1669. One snatch from the historical records tells us that Santiago had hundreds of costumes for the opera, which was performed on the *fiesta patronal*.

Today Santiago is notable for three things: its museum and Jesuit remains, including a lot of *casas de indios* around the plaza; its two grand *fiestas* of riding skills and dance in January; and its Benedictine monastery.

To reach Santiago you take a turn right after San Patricio, which is the road going to Ayolas. After 16km you turn left to enter the town, where there is a notice proclaiming that you are arriving in 'Santiago, capital de la tradición Misionera', and a white statue of a man in a sombrero on a horse.

 **WHERE TO STAY AND EAT** Some of the *estancias* near Santiago are linked to the Misiones-based Emitur network (*Emprendimiento Misionero de Turismo;* ☎ *0782 20286;* m *0975 626780/0983 131128*) rather than to Apatur (see page 54).

Estancia Tacuatý (18 rooms) Desvio Ayolas km10; ☎ 0782 20286; m 0975 626780/0983 131128; www.tacuaty.com.py. Now with attractive new buildings for guests, this rural hotel 5 mins before you reach the town provides excellent facilities for staying the night. Football & volleyball pitches. **$$$**

Hotel Restaurant El Tauro Plaza; m 0995 356960. A simple hotel but right on the plaza, on the far side from the church. Can take 25 people. Rooms have private bathrooms & fans (rather than AC). **$**

Hospedaje Mercado Plaza; ☎ 0782 20211. Super-simple though this little hotel is – with no private bathrooms & fans (rather than AC) – it is an original house from the Reduction, in a row of *casas de indios,* right on the plaza, so the historic sense compensates for any lack of comfort. 5 rooms, 2 bathrooms, & facilities for cooking your own *asado* in the garden, where there is a big, grassy lawn. The rate for tourists is cheap, but they take known regulars for even less, so this is definitely shoestring accommodation. **$**

Bar La Casona Plaza; ☎ 0782 20076. Hamburgers & *milanesas*, the most basic food. Occasionally they have rooms too. **$**

FIESTAS The Festival Latinoamericano de la Doma y el Folklore (doma refers to mastery over cattle) is usually held on the first weekend in January, though the date can vary. You can check with the Estancia Tacuatý that hosts it (☎ *0782 20286; see above*), Copaco, the Municipalidad or Emitur (see numbers above). The festival goes from 09.00 until sundown, and is held amidst the shady trees of the estancia 7km south of Ruta 1, and 9km to the north of Santiago, on the east side of the main road. There are bucking broncos, cattle branding and a fine display of dancing, with many troupes from neighbouring countries, as well as those performing traditional

above This train on display at the Estación de Ferrocarril in Asunción was the first to run when Paraguay opened its railway in 1861 (MM) pages 104–5

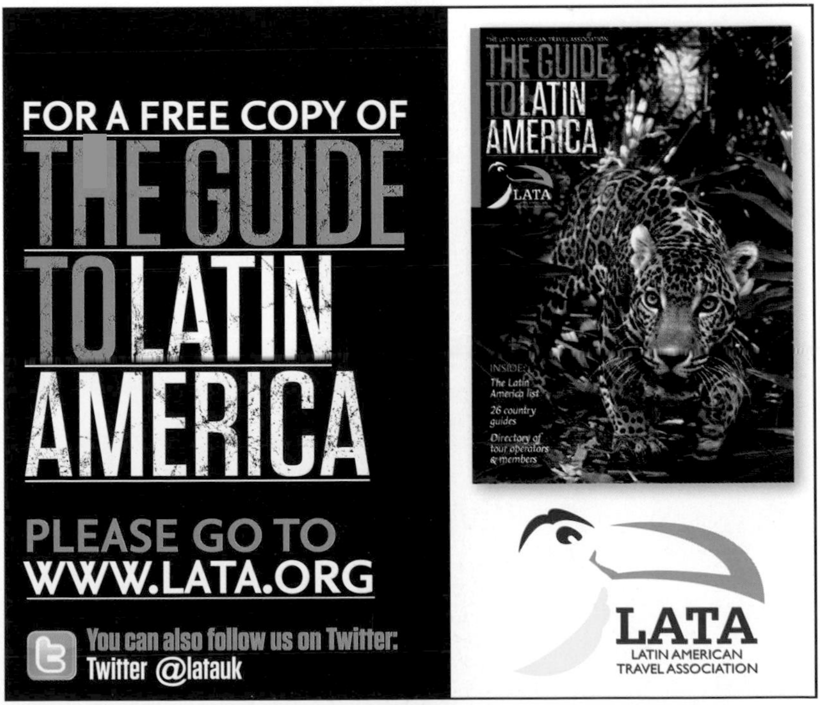

right Villarrica's cathedral was built in 1877, but one of its three bells dates from 1781 (MM) page 318

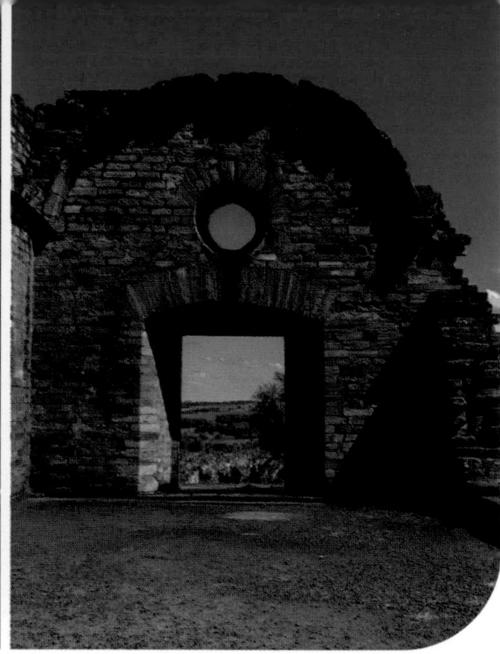

above left **Trinidad is the most evocative of the ruined Jesuit-Guaraní sites due to its surviving stone carvings** (DS) pages 247–56

above right **The Ruins of Jesús appear almost Cistercian in their austere beauty** (MM) pages 256–9

below **Franciscan *casa de índios*, Caazapá – the houses for the indigenous, like the churches, had porticos running the length of the building** (MH) page 325

above Yaguarón is the only original church from the Reductions to survive in its complete form, including the façade and the wooden bell tower (MM) pages 173–6

below left The church of San Carlos Borromeo was once one of the largest in South America, but it was the victim of cannonball fire during the Paraguayan War (MM) page 234

below right St Michael stepping on the devil, Santa Maria de Fe museum (MM) pages 206–7

above left Paraguayan hammocks are made of finely woven cotton and are widely used and sold (MM) page 190

above right A gaucho counts his cattle in the *campo* (MM) page 185

left Maká chief: a visit to the Maká village outside Asunción is easy to arrange (CM) page 120

below *Ñandutí* lacework, which is sometimes fashioned into long, elaborate dresses (DS) page x

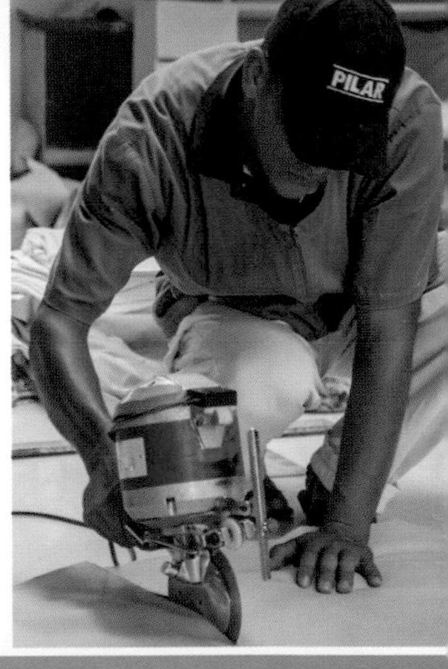

above A typical house in the *campo*, with wooden walls and a thatched roof (MM) page 185

right Visitors can gain an insight into the spinning, weaving, dyeing and printing of cotton at the Pilar factory in Asunción (MM) page 230

below Fishermen setting out on the Río Tebicuarý in Misiones (MM) page 185

above left Black howler monkey (*Alouatta caraya*) – when they howl, they make a loud repeated noise somewhere between a croak and a snore (JL) page 5

above right The jaguar is the biggest feline in the Americas (JL) page 5

below The South American coati (*Nasua nasua*) lives in low thorn and humid forests (JL) page 5

bottom The caiman (*Caiman yacare*) is a protected species found on both sides of the country (JL) page 6

above left Glittering-bellied emerald hummingbird: these birds are often seen sucking nectar from flowers (JL) page 7

above right The toco toucan (*Ramphastos toco*) is one of the most famous and most colourful birds in Paraguay (JL) page 6

right Greater rheas (*Rhea americana*) are large, flightless, silent birds (JL) page 6

below The Chilean flamingo (*Phoenicopterus chilensis*) is a common sight in the Chaco (MM) page 7

above left The *palo borracho* tree stores water in its heavily swollen trunk, and can be seen all over the Chaco (MM) page 361

above right The unusual sandstone formations of the Koĩ and Chororĩ hills near Areguá can only be found in one other place in the world (MM) page 152

left The elegant Salto Cristal is one of Paraguay's highest waterfalls at 42m (MM) pages 179–80

below Laguna Capitán is one of the salt lakes scattered to the southeast of Loma Plata (MM) page 374

Paraguayan dances. There are musical groups, and a display of caballerías (horse teams) in their colourful uniforms, including groups from Argentina, Brazil and Uruguay. Craft is on sale from all over Paraguay, and there are traditional foods to buy, such as asado a la estaca (beef barbecued on near-vertical sticks, in front of an open fire) and the speciality of Misiones, batiburillo. If you want to eat the asado, you need to take your own sharp knife, plates and cutlery. There is sometimes another mini-festival along the same lines on Saturday of Holy Week.

A very similar event, the **Fiesta de la Tradición Misionera**, takes place shortly afterwards, on a Friday, Saturday and Sunday in mid January. It takes place much closer to the town, in a big open-air stadium, which does not have the shade of the Estancia Tacuatý. It is longer established (more than 25 years old) and always very successful. Not much happens on the Friday, and on the Saturday the programme customarily begins in the evening with a procession of horse teams. The folk dance – one of the biggest attractions – takes place very late on Saturday night, which – added to the shortage of good hotel accommodation in the town – makes it difficult for visitors without cars to attend. Sunday is a full day, with branding of calves, castration of animals, bucking broncos, displays of riding skills and a bullfight. (They do not kill the bull in Paraguay, or even wound it, but simply throw it to the ground.) For information, ring the Municipalidad (see number opposite).

WHAT TO SEE Santiago has a good number of original ***casas de indios*** with colonnades around the huge, historic plaza. A statue of the Jesuit founder, Noel Berthod, was set up in 2010 on the side of the square near to the museum. Near to the church, but further along that side of the square, is a new Centro de Interpretación in the Secretaría de Cultura of the Municipalidad, where display boards recount the history of the *pueblo*.

On the other side of the church is the **museum** (🕘 *08.00–11.00 & 14.00–17.00 Mon–Sat, 09.00–11.00 Sun; Gs5,000*), in a purpose-built house constructed in reference to (but not in imitation of) the old *casas de indios*. It has toilets. At the time of writing, the guide is Karina Medina (**m** *0975 649122*). To the side of the museum is a grass-covered slope with a few remnants of the adobe walls of the old church: the slope itself is no doubt the result of the earth of the adobe collapsing. Beyond it is an excavated ground plan of what would have been the patio next to the church, with a series of rooms used as workshops, classrooms and the rooms of the Jesuits.

The museum is unique in having some brilliantly painted wooden panels, which are displayed near the entrance. There is a charming portrayal of baby Jesus and baby John hugging a lamb together, while attendant angels offer them bunches of flowers. Sheep also figure in a painting of Jesus entrusting the keys to Peter, delightfully drawn without any sense of perspective. There is a Holy Family, a Virgin and Child, and plenty of angel heads with wings.The museum is divided into three rooms, dedicated to the Incarnation (with an Annunciation and a crib), the Redemption (with figures of the Passion and Resurrection, mostly from the reredos of the original church) and Jesuit saints. The 50 or so statues are of mixed size and quality, unlike Santiago's sister town, Santa María, where all the works are large masterpieces. Some of the figures, including the crib (smaller and less complete than Santa María's) seem to show traces of Flemish influence, which is not surprising when you consider that these two Reductions were founded by Jesuits from the Belgian province. The Annunciation, too, and St Isidore and his wife, María de la Cabeza, also share in this slightly Flemish style: the 11th-century Spanish farmer saint was popular among the Jesuits as he had been canonised at the same time as St Ignatius and St Francis Xavier, in 1622. It is interesting, also, to see in the last room the first known statue of Roque González, not yet portrayed with his exposed heart, but barefoot and with one hand outstretched.

Among the statues are some works of quite outstanding quality, principally in the middle room. There are a couple of poignant portrayals of the carrying of the cross, where the face of Christ merits careful attention. The pietà (*piedad* in Spanish)is marvellous: this Mary encloses with her cloak the flopped body draped across her knees, in a spirit of absorbed contemplation that contrasts with the anguished scream of Brassinelli's pietà in the oratory of Santa Rosa. This Mary is supremely tragic, but peaceful at the same time. The best figure of the Risen Christ of any of the museums – for the Tupãsý Ñuvaitĩ procession (see page 203) – is found here, and seems to be light as thistledown as the golden robe flies up in the wind, practically lifting Jesus into the air.

Ask the guide for access to the church, where there is a large statue of Santiago el Matamoro (St James the Moor-killer) riding on his horse over the dead bodies of Muslims he has slain with his sword. Odious as this conception is to a modern-day consciousness, it has to be seen in historical context: for the Guaraní, any saint victorious in battle represented for them their victory against the slave-traders – a struggle which in fact they won by force of arms in the 1641 Battle of Mbororé: from then on they were virtually safe from *bandeirantes* and an era of peace and prosperity came to the Reductions. For this reason we find portrayals of St Michael (who defeated the devil), St Sebastian (who was a Roman centurion), St Barbara (the patron saint of explosives, because a bolt of lightning killed her would-be executioner), and now Santiago el Matamoro.

The reredos of the church has a theme of baptism, with John baptising Jesus, Peter baptising the Ethiopian eunuch, and Francis Xavier baptising the eastern Christians. This would have been a reredos in the baptistry of the original church (which was probably built in 1725 – according to the date on a bell – and fell down in 1907), but now it is behind the high altar. There is also a statue which appears to show a man praying before the Virgin, but study of the photograph of the original reredos reveals it to be Jesus praying in Gethsemane – part of a Passion sequence.

Monastery Though buried deep in the countryside, far from anywhere, the Benedictine monastery of Tupãsý María (Guaraní 'Mary the Mother of God') (☎ *0782 20034;* **e** *tupasy@itacom.com.py; www.monasterio.org.ar;* ⏱ *08.00–noon & 15.00–18.00 Mon–Sat, 10.30–11.30 & 15.30–18.00 Sun*) belongs to the municipality of Santiago. To reach it, take the 12km dirt road that goes west from the Ayolas road, 14km south of the junction with Ruta 1; it is well marked. There is another route via San Patricio, but it is not signed. The monastery was founded from Argentina in 1984, and is the only Benedictine monastery in the country. The church has been built with the basic shape of the ancient Franciscan church of Yaguarón but in a much simpler style. There is a shop that sells the produce of the monks, beautifully packaged: candles, jams, yoghurts and delicious liqueurs. The public can attend the monastic hours: 07.00 lauds followed by mass (09.30 mass on Sunday); 12.15 sext; 18.15 vespers and 20.45 compline. They can also stay in a guesthouse to make retreats.

AYOLAS

Copaco ☎ 072 222799; municipalidad ☎ 072 222384

Ayolas, on the Río Paraná, is associated with two things: fishing; and the Yacyretá dam, shared with Argentina (Paraguay's other huge hydro-electric money-earner, after the Itaipú dam, which is shared with Brazil). Huge numbers of Brazilians go to Ayolas to fish, filling the hotels in the high fishing season, which is September and October. Curiously, Ayolas has not yet developed as a general beach resort, though it could well do so. If you want a nice sandy beach, at the side of a river enormous enough to be a lake, and with a good variety of freshly caught fish for dinner, then you cannot do better than Ayolas. And you may even have the beach to yourself.

If you are a fishing devotee, Ayolas is perfect. For the day a *lancha* (motor boat) might cost Gs250,000 (for up to three people) plus fuel, which could be up to 50 litres on a long trip (currently around Gs8,000 per litre).

HISTORY The oldest part of Ayolas is the barrio San José-mí, where the present-day Hotel Ayolas is situated. It still has the best beach. The barrio San Antonio – which has nearly all the hotels – also preceded the arrival of the Entidad Binacional Yacyretá (EBY) – often known simply as '*la Entidad*', 'the Entity'.

Construction work on the project for the joint Paraguayan–Argentinian hydro-electric dam began in 1983, and at first involved building a colony for the workers: the Mil Viviendas (One Thousand Homes). In 1994 the first part of the dam was opened, and in 1998 it was completed. The former construction workers have either changed to other jobs, or moved – selling the keys to their houses to incomers. The houses themselves remain the property of EBY and form a very pleasant suburb of bungalows. The staff now at Yacyretá live in another estate built by the EBY, called the Villa Permanente, which is closer to the administrative offices, but adjoins the Mil Viviendas.

As a producer of energy, Yacyretá is associated in every Paraguayan mind with money, and there is fierce competition for the jobs there, which are extremely well paid and are generally distributed among Colorado party members as political favours. Many of those on the staff over the years have been *planilleros*, which meant that they were paid a monthly salary but did not actually have to turn up to do any work.

GETTING THERE AND AWAY To reach Ayolas take Ruta 1 from Asunción and turn right after San Patricio. There are two bus companies that go to Ayolas from the bus terminal in Asunción: Yacyretá and Pilarense. The journey takes five hours. Both companies enter Santiago half an hour before reaching Ayolas.

Pilarense leaves Asunción at 03.30, 06.30, 14.15 and 15.30. For the return journey it leaves Ayolas at 04.45, 10.30, 14.10 and 22.30.

Yacyretá leaves Asunción at 04.45, 09.00, 11.00, 12.50, 17.45 and 20.30. For the return journey it leaves Ayolas at 04.15, 08.30, 12.00, 16.00, 17.00 and 23.15.

GETTING AROUND When you reach Ayolas you go under a '*Bienvenidos a Ayolas*' gateway and a little after that is a turning to the left, which goes to the dam, but if you carry on straight there is a second turning to the left that goes to the town. You need to take this second turning, because the main road that plunges straight ahead will suddenly stop in the middle of nowhere.

When you take the turn to the town, you pass a cash machine and speed bumps, and then a turn to the right marked '*EBY Relaciones Públicas*', which is where you go if you want to visit the dam.

If you do not turn right for *Relaciones Públicas,* but continue straight on, the main road will swing right and take you round the southern perimeter of the **Villa Permanente**, and then past the left turn to the Hotel de Turismo, which marks the beginning of the **Mil Viviendas** – to the right (north) – while a turn to the left takes you into the barrio San Antonio. The Villa Permanente and Mil Viviendas are purpose-built garden cities with broad avenues, green grass and trees. The bus will pass the modern church and theatre and multi-use hall of Mil Viviendas, and will stop in due course at the terminal – a surprisingly small building, on the northern edge of Mil Viviendas. There is a shopping centre opposite.

The terminal has the only taxi rank in town, and places are quite spread out in Ayolas so it is not easy to walk everywhere. If a taxi does not show up, you could ring for one: Cristian Gómez (*072 222805;* **m** *09751 950329*); Vicente Gómez (*072 222817;* **m** *0975 649358*) or Indio (*072 222569*). He and his father are both taxi drivers, and also have an eight-seater minibus. A taxi from the Terminal to your hotel may cost no more than Gs15,000 at current prices. There is also a service of *mototaxis*, which have a little roofed trailer behind a motorbike, so they are quite adequate for journeys within the town. They charge less than half the cost of an ordinary taxi, but do not have a regular mototaxi rank, so you will need to order them through your hotel or ring for one. Try Pablo Lofuente (**m** *0984 266377*).

From the terminal, the bus will continue on to its workshop, where it waits until its next journey to Asunción, passing down **barrio San Antonio** on the way, which is (by contrast with the garden cities) a long straggly road with shops on both sides. The cheap hotels are along this road.

At the end of barrio San Antonio, you have the choice of bearing left for the barrio **San José-mí** – the oldest barrio, and closest to the best beach – or bearing right, which is the road to Corateí and eventually Yabebyrý.

WHERE TO STAY The hotels with good riverside locations are the Hotel Nacional de Turismo (the first you come to), the Hotel Ayolas (the last you come to) and the much more modest Hotel Leka (down a side road from barrio San Antonio). Most hotels in Ayolas do not include breakfast in the price.

Hotel Nacional de Turismo (20 rooms) 072 222273; **m** 0976 762277; **e** hotelnacionaldeayolas@gmail.com. One of Senatur's hotels but since 2012 under private management (along with Senatur's other two hotels, in Villa Florida & Vapor Cué, see pages 188 & 162). A driveway leads to a spacious complex, with rooms arranged along 3 colonnades facing onto a pleasant garden with palm trees. Not directly overlooking the river but has steps & a path leading through a field to the bank, making a pleasant walk – all land belonging to the Hotel. The whole hotel has been well designed & rooms have solid wood furniture. Pool & children's playground. Restaurant. Takes credit cards. **$$**

Hotel & Restaurant Ayolas (25 rooms) Plaza Juan de Ayolas; 072 222844; **m** 0983 456801; **e** hotelayolas@outlook.com; www.hotelayolas.com. Formerly known as Hotel El Dorado, this hotel is right on the river, with a very pleasant courtyard & spectacular view. It is down a cobbled road & located in the oldest barrio of the town, San José-mí. If you come in on the Yacyretá bus, & carry on beyond the terminal to the Yacyretá *taller* (workshop) where the bus is stationed until its next journey, then you will be only 200m away & can walk. If you come in on the Pilarense bus, then you may need a taxi, & you can usually pick one up at the terminal. After some years of progressive deterioration, this superbly located hotel was taken over in 2013 & the rooms have now been renovated. The restaurant opens onto a riverside terrace. Karaoke, billiards. Also has dorms. **$$**

Hotel Kadel (about 12 rooms) Barrio San Antonio; 072 222153; **m** 0971 137270. A large fish sign marks this hotel, on the north side of the road. B/fast room, thatched *quincho* at back. AC, cable TV, sommier beds, minibars, but also has budget rooms at less than half the price with just fans & shared bathroom. Wi-Fi. Some colour schemes rather jarring. **$**

Hotel Leka (14 rooms) Barrio San Antonio; 072 222270; **m** 0961 541084/0975 628138. Some 500m down a dirt track & with a small sign that can be easily missed. It is opposite 'Barcos y Rodados'

& shortly after Hotel Kadel. Right on the riverbank, this modest little place is full of character & has a stunning location, perched on the cliff above a small beach. There is a big, open b/fast room, & you can sit & eat in the shade of trees by the riverside. Has 6 dorms, rooms with fans, & a block of 8 new rooms with AC. You can order the fish meal of your choice. Has a parrot that sings as well as talks. **$**

Hotel San Antonio (12 rooms) Barrio San Antonio; m 0985 756855. Barrio San Antonio, on the south side of the road. Unbelievably cheap for an attractive, traditional-style row of rooms along a colonnade. Price does not include breakfast but is an extra at only Gs3,000. Family-style hotel with shared TV. **$**

WHERE TO EAT AND DRINK Most hotels, even the small ones, can serve good fish dishes if asked, even if they do not offer much else. Standard drinks on offer are limited in most places to beer (*cerveza*) and fizzy drinks (*gaseosa*) though in a few places you may be able to buy wine too, or order a fresh fruit juice (*jugo*).

Marimex lunch & eve from 20.00 Tue–Sun, closed Mon. Dancing sometimes at weekends, *asado* Sunday lunch. **$$**

Restaurant Lizza Set back from the road on the east side as you approach Ayolas, after the turn to Atinguý (see page 220) & after you have gone under the 'Bienvenidos a Ayolas' gateway; 072 2222756; all day every day. Definitely the place to eat, packed with character. Offers a good variety of food & drink at very low prices. Long tables covered in white tablecloths & fascinating decorations: more to see here than in most small-town museums. Hanging from the ceiling & walls are hammocks, sombreros, bird nests, ostrich eggs, baskets, gourds, armadillos, guitars & snake skins. Also on show are two types of maize mill, an ancient chair made without nails but tied together with leather thongs, & an old iron with a cavity for putting cotton & alcohol, an air pump for fanning the flames & a dial to extinguish them. A framed certificate gives a Mención de Honor to the best restaurant in Ayolas. The food is good too – with huge portions, & the service excellent: they have even been known to get out a lounger for you if you need a kip. Unbelievable value. **$**

OTHER PRACTICALITIES There is only one bank, the Banco Nacional de Fomento, in the Villa Permanente, but there are a couple of cash machines that accept all cards on the way into town in a little glass cabin right on the road after the turn,

FISH DISHES

Fish is the recommended food in Ayolas, and there are many varieties which you will not find elsewhere in the country. It can be served grilled on the *parilla* (barbecue: this is also known as an *asado,* like barbecued meat); *a la plancha* (grilled); fried (*frito*); as a *chupín* (covered with a sauce); as a *milanesa* (coated in batter); or in a *caldo* (soup).

Dorado Considered the best, and to appreciate its quality it should be cooked as an *asado*. One fish usually serves more than two people.
Surubí The only fish you will commonly find elsewhere, eg: in restaurants in Asunción. It provides good steaks of boneless white flesh, suitable for *milanesa* or *chupín*.
Pacú Suitable for *asado* or *chupín*.
Boga Suitable for *asado* or for frying. Some consider this has the best flavour of any fish for *asado*.
Bagre Small fish, suitable for frying or *caldo*.
Mandi'í Small fish, suitable for frying or *caldo*.

next to the police control and before you come to *Relaciones Públicas*. A taxi driver can take you there quickly on the excellent roads.

Fishing is prohibited from early November to late December; this period is known as the *veda*. The exact dates vary a little from year to year, and also vary between waters shared with Brazil and with Argentina. The high season for fishing is before this, in September and October.

WHAT TO SEE AND DO The main attraction in Ayolas itself is the dam, but outside of the town an excursion to the nearby Refugio Atinguý is highly recommended.

There are some attractive **churches** in Ayolas. The church in the old barrio of San José-mí is a good example of the traditional design. The church in Mil Viviendas is modern and is kept open. Triangular in shape, it is filled with light through its two walls of modern stained glass, with simple circular designs of pink, blue, green and yellow. There is a statue of St Francis Xavier (after whom the church is named). The church in the Villa Permanente is also modern and although this is the more expensive barrio, it is a less interesting church than that of Mil Viviendas.

Going to the beach is a must. One of the best **beaches** is the Playa Milenio, which you reach by taking the track round the side of the Restaurant Lizza. It has a good amount of sand and a small amount of shade (but probably enough, as you may find yourselves the only people there). The other good beach is in barrio José-mí, after Hotel Ayolas and the port. Further away is the beach of Corateí (see page 221). Swimming should be limited to close to the bank: the current in the Río Paraná is strong and dangerous.

The Yacyretá dam (*072 222276; e rrpp_ayolas@hotmail.com or milce.duarte@eby.gov.py; www.eby.gov.py; visits at 08.30, 10.00, 14.00 daily; free admission)* To visit the Yacyretá dam you must present an application with the name, nationality and passport number of each visitor. This is a simple operation that can be done in person at least half an hour before each guided visit (so do not come without your passport) or by phone or email. In high season it may be necessary to book in advance, as there are only 18 places in the minibus. The guides are knowledgeable and occasionally an English-speaking guide can be arranged with prior notice. The same visit of the dam can also be done from the Argentinian side. Over 18,000 people visit Yacyretá each year.

Head for the circular hall known as *Relaciones Públicas*: it is a short distance to the right of the main road as you arrive in Ayolas, and there are signs. There is a model of the whole area in the reception hall, and ice creams, drink and T-shirts for sale.

While you are waiting for your tour you can visit the museum next door, the **Museo Histórico Ambiental de la Entidad Binacional Yacyretá** (*072 222141; 07.00–15.30; free admission*). It can be reached through the same building, or from a separate entrance towards the main road. This is an interesting museum, so do not leave it until after the 14.00 visit, when it will be closed. In one section are old household items from the locality; in another, examples of fish floating in preservative in jars (rather stomach-churning); in another, some *japepó* funeral pots used by the Guaraní; but the most interesting part is the section of taxidermy, where you can study closely the animals, reptiles and birds you keep hearing about in Paraguay. To see the huge southern screamer (see page 9) at full size with its wings outstretched makes more impression than just to read that it has a span of 170cm – and it also makes it much easier to recognise in the wild. You can observe the difference between the marsh deer (which has antlers) and the grey brocket deer (which does not). There is a nutria, Azara's agouti, maned wolf and crab-eating fox, among others.

The visit to the dam begins with a five-minute film (usually in Spanish, although an English version also exists) which explains that Paraguay is the biggest producer of energy per capita in the world. This is partly because the population is only seven million. Paraguay uses only 10% of the energy it produces at Yacyretá, and the rest can be sold. The next stage is the bus journey over the bridge to the Isla Yacyretá and to the huge hall, nearly 1km long – so big that the staff travel around it on bicycles. Here 20 turbines work away under the floor, each one marked by a huge red circular area. At any one time, 19 turbines are functioning, permitting ongoing maintenance of all the machinery.

One interesting detail is the lift that has been constructed for the fish, particularly the *dorado*, because they go upstream to reproduce. The lift transports them to the river above the dam. It appears, however, that the arrangements are not completely successful, as there has been a marked reduction in the numbers of *dorado,* and legal measures have been taken to restrict commercial fishing of *dorado* and give the fish population time to recover.

You then cross the long dam itself, which spans the strait from Paraguay's Isla Yacyretá to the Argentinian mainland. The dam is more recent than Itaipú (see pages 293–4) and not quite so enormous. Itaipú depends on the vast power of a huge 120m drop of water (and anyone who has visited the Garganta del Diablo at the Iguazú Falls, see page 283, will know how dramatic that plunge is), whereas Yacyretá has a drop of 21.3m. For reasons of the difference in water flow, the turbines at Yacyretá turn around a vertical axis, whereas those of Itaipú have a horizontal axis.

Despite its smaller size, Yacyretá represents a major hydroelectric project, generating huge amounts of electricity, and therefore of money. The generating capacity is 20 thousand million kilowatt-hours (20,000GWh) per year. This is a lot less than Itaipú (98,630GWh) and less also than the Guri Dam in Venezuela, but more than the Aswan Dam in Egypt.There have been environmental problems associated with locating the reservoir in the upper part of the river: the flooding involved relocation of populations and loss of habitat for animals. There have also been complications such as reduced oxygen levels in the water (due to rotting vegetation) with an effect on fish population. It is estimated that 2,000 Paraguayan families live off fishing in this region, so the situation is of some concern.

On the other hand, the source of energy, being water, is perpetually renewable and is free, and the production process does not leave polluting residues. The EBY supports environmental conservation programmes such as the Refugio Atinguý (see page 220), hoping in this way to offset the negative environmental impact of the reservoir above the dam. They also use a good part of the income for socially beneficial enterprises: health and education projects, and scholarships to university for the most able pupils from poor homes.

The name Yacyretá is Guaraní and means 'land of the moon' (*jasy* 'moon', *reta* 'land'). An alternative explanation of the name is that it means 'land of the turbulent water' (*y* 'water', *asy* 'difficult', *reta* 'land'). There may be something of both meanings. As will be pointed out in *Appendix 1 – Guaraní* (see page 389), there is variety in Guaraní spelling and most place names follow the old spelling.

Reserva Natural Yacyretá On the Isla Yacyretá there is a nature reserve, and by prior arrangement with Relaciones Públicas (☎ *072 222276*) you can book a guided visit. There are three visits currently on offer: to the *lagunas*, to the sand dunes, and the path known as *Sendero Akutí Po'í* to the *mirador* (viewpoint). The booking process is the same as for the dam (see opposite).

When the dam was built, 90,000ha of land had to be flooded, with environmental as well as social damage, and in partial compensation for this, Yacyretá has committed to maintain the same number of hectares as protected areas, free from hunting, deforestation and forest fires. The visit to the dunes is great fun, with long stretches of sand to explore, up and down hills dotted with dwarf palms and the very tall (25m) arary tree (*calophyllum brasiliense*), which provides sought-after wood for furniture and flooring and is in danger of extinction. Some dunes are fixed with vegetation while others are in constant movement, blown by the wind. Hawks and vultures are common here because of the fish.

Refugio Atinguý This is a centre for conserving and breeding animals, particularly endangered species native to the area, and is effectively a well-maintained little zoo. Although past experience has indicated that you can visit simply by turning up, to be on the safe side it is advisable to follow the instructions on the Yacyretá website, which are to apply for permission in advance with the names and passport numbers of the visitors, to Relaciones Públicas (see page 215), or by phone (*0786 20050/0080 int. 1332-1444*). The website also announces official times of visits (*08.30, 11.30, 13.30, 16.30 Mon–Sat; 08.30, 11.30 Sun and holidays*).

Allow half an hour to get there and an hour for the visit. The 10km road, though broad and flat, is *enripiado,* not asphalted. After Atinguý the road carries on to San Cosme y Damián, a Jesuit Reduction just into the next *departamento* of Itapúa (reached more easily taking the turn from Ruta 1 that branches off after General Delgado).

Entrance is free, and after opening (and closing!) the gate and driving in, you find yourself in a broad grassy area with a plentiful supply of wandering greater rheas (see page 6). There are also some southern lapwings striding masterfully around the green. There is a building to your left, and beside it you enter an attractive wooded walk, where the caged animals are to be found. Nearly all are native to the area, and many are threatened species. Atinguý has a breeding area for these species, and most are set free, with only a few examples retained in 18 large cages for the public. In all there are 84 species of mammals, 144 of birds and 15 of reptiles.

Among the mammals there are capuchin monkeys, mountain lions, jaguars (which fetch US$5,000 on the black market if smuggled out of the country), anteaters with their hugely long tongues, and maned wolves (it is difficult to breed these in captivity, but Atinguý has succeeded). In a larger enclosure there are grey brocket deer. Among the birds there are examples of the mountain peacock (with black and white stripes, native to the zone, but rare), a variety of ducks and owls – all with striking colouring – and Paraguay's colourful blue-and-yellow and red-and-green macaws, which come from the Chaco.

The breeding zone is a larger fenced-off area with a small lake inside and offers protection to marsh deer, capybaras and caimans. Deer, capybaras and caimans are all considered delicacies. Although hunting them is illegal, in usual Paraguayan fashion this has no effect in discouraging the practice, apart from the fact that you are unlikely to be offered them in a restaurant in Asunción. Rheas are also in this breeding enclosure. The male does all the nurturing of the young, including sitting on the eggs for 42 days; the only thing the female rhea does is lay the eggs, and then abandon them.

Yabebyrý Wildlife Refuge To the north of Ayolas, deep in the *campo*, is the Yabebyrý Wildlife Refuge, devoted to preserving species such as the broad-nosed caiman and marsh deer. To enquire, contact the *guardaparque* Nelson Montiel (**m** *0985 763840*). A new hotel is currently being built near the entrance to the reserve.

Corateí This tiny village half an hour's journey downriver by cobbled dirt road is a pleasant place for an excursion. It has a good beach, and a number of hotels and guesthouses to cater for people who come for the fishing, many of them from Brazil. The roads in Corateí are broad and grassy and lead down to the river. A little wooden house by the beach marked as *copetín* (bar) oozes character, and does simple snacks, but only to order. Be careful about swimming: on the curvy part of the beach it is forbidden because of the strength of the current further out in the river.

Getting there and away You can reach Corateí by bus from Ayolas leaving the terminal at 06.30 or 11.00. Return buses leave Corateí at 07.00 and 15.30. If you go by taxi it will cost you over Gs100,000 each way. If you are in your own vehicle, continue straight on after the barrio San Antonio instead of turning left towards the Hotel Ayolas.

Where to stay

Quinta Corateí 021 332927; m 0983 335000; e quintacoratei@grupo3c.com.py. Very well regarded, despite the sparse info available online. Beautiful building with a striking view & unusual-shaped pool. 100m from the beach. It generally deals with groups of 8 or more, who can share the same *quincho*/sitting room. Weekends get booked out months in advance. **$$$**

Posada Vale da Lua m 0975 649009; e valedaluapy@gmail.com; http://valedaluapy.wix.com/posada. The clientele is almost entirely Brazilian – hence the Brazilian name. Recently moved, now with striking modern design evocative of tents, Wi-Fi, split AC & satellite TV. **$$**

Stroessner's house An unmarked turning to the left 5km beyond Corateí leads after a couple of kilometres to a large house on the waterfront that once belonged to President Stroessner. It is virtually abandoned, apart from a solitary policeman who is posted to keep watch day and night. Once a week they change the guard, as it is a lonely job with nothing to do except greet the very occasional visitors who come to gawp at the curiosity. The bottom floor is a covered car park, and upstairs are bedrooms in a very run-down condition, but you cannot look around inside the house. Between the house and the river is a grassy area where a helicopter could land.

If you continue west along the same road (which becomes progressively sandy) you will reach Yabebyrý after another 17km.

Yabebyrý This is a pretty village set around a grassy plaza, distinguished by having two churches next to each other. There is an old abandoned adobe church, Franciscan but of the same era as the Jesuits, with a tower that has collapsed down one side, and a more recent church (about 30 years old) beyond it. The thunderous sound of the tower's collapse could be heard all over the village on 17 May 2013, and the sight of the lopsided structure now is quite dramatic. If you approach to look inside the old church, there will be a flurry of wings and a sudden exodus of the birds that nest inside, which include swallows, doves, cardinals, woodpeckers, wood-rails and hummingbirds.

Yabebyrý was the home of Juanita Pesoa, the girlfriend of Francisco Solano López before he met Madame Lynch. He met her in a nearby *compañía* called Guardia, where he was visiting his troops. He gave her a statue of his patron saint, Francis Solano, which she later gave to the church, which then changed its dedication accordingly: before then it had been the church of the Immaculate Concepción. This fine statue, which was restored a few years ago, is still the central figure in the reredos of the new church. The Franciscan saint has a small Indian kneeling at his feet. There is also a beautiful crucifix from a similar period, with articulated arms, very long wavy black hair, wounds running blood, and an exquisitely tranquil face.

Juanita Pesoa is better known as an inhabitant of Pilar, where her house can be seen (see page 230), but she only moved there after the hurt of being replaced in the affections of Mariscal López. After the end of the Triple Alliance War she lived in Isla Umbú (see page 231–2), but her body is buried in the churchyard at Yabebyrý. There is no longer a stone to mark the spot, but the locals know where it is.

Yabebyrý was also the refuge for a year (1909–10) of the political philosopher and essayist Rafael Barrett, who was the first to write about the cruel exploitation of the *mensú* workers in the *yerba* plantations.

Getting there and away If you are not coming from Ayolas, you can reach Yabebyrý by taking the road due south from San Ignacio. It is a bad dirt road, but is now being prepared for cobbles. A driver who used to operate the Cerritano bus service for years reported that over the years he had been stranded on this road with his passengers for Christmas, New Year and Holy Week, due to rain making the road impassible. But it goes through lovely countryside, as you pass through the 40km wetlands to the south of Santa Rita, where there are wetlands on both sides of the road and birdlife is plentiful. There are many egrets and limpkins. A Yacyretá bus leaves the Plaza in San Ignacio (see page 199) at 09.30 and at 14.00 every day except Sunday. It takes two hours to travel the 62km to Yabebyrý and then goes on to Laureles and Cerrito (see pages 238–40). For the return journey the bus leaves Cerrito at 02.00 and at 14.00, so reaching Yabebyrý about 04.00 and 16.00. If it rains the bus cannot travel: you can check with the Yacyretá representative in San Ignacio (**m** *0985 330076*).

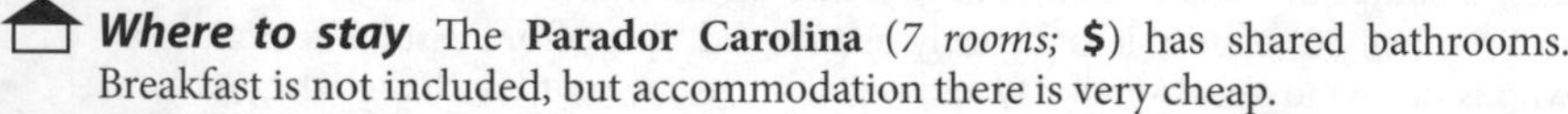

Where to stay The **Parador Carolina** (*7 rooms;* **$**) has shared bathrooms. Breakfast is not included, but accommodation there is very cheap.

Where to eat and drink Right on the square, José Allende Servín, a teacher, runs **El Buen Comer** (**m** *0981 106795;* **$**), a most hospitable and economic service for the few visitors to the village. He is also a fount of local knowledge.

6

Southwest to Ñeembucú and the Old Battlegrounds

Departamento: Ñeembucú; gobernación ☎ *0786 232334/233587*

Tucked away in the southwestern tip of eastern Paraguay, Ñeembucú is one of the wildest and most beautiful areas of Paraguay, and one of the least visited. The access point is San Ignacio. It also has the advantage of comfortable fast buses running from Asunción to Pilar, and a number of new *posadas turísticas* recognised by Senatur (see page 73). There are now *posadas* in Humaitá, Paso de Patria and Cerrito.

Pilar, the capital of the *departamento* and the gateway to the other places of interest, is a good hour and a half from the international highway Ruta 1, and is reached by Ruta 4, which is asphalted. At Pilar, the asphalt runs out. There is an *empedrado* (cobbled road) on to Isla Umbú. It continues to General Díaz, and from there to Paso de Patria the road is partly *adoquinado* (paved with concrete blocks). If you want to get away from people and into nature, Ñeembucú is a great place to go. Only in the remote northern Chaco will you find a *departamento* more sparsely populated.

In its low-lying savannahs and wetlands, bordered on two sides of a triangle by the rivers Paraguay and Paraná, the marshes of Ñeembucú are as important as they are unknown. The **birdlife** is stunning, and even the least bird-aware of visitors will be enchanted by the sight of egrets (white herons) winging above them. There are plenty of roadside hawks, southern crested caracaras, black vultures, southern lapwings, spotted nothuras, neotropic cormorants, and picazuro pigeons. Birdwatchers will want to stop and get out their binoculars where the wetlands start, as close as 20km from San Ignacio. Unfortunately, it is difficult to do this unless you are travelling by car, as the buses do not generally stop on the 1½ hour drive through empty countryside between San Ignacio and Pilar. As evening draws in, the birdsong most heard is from the giant wood-rail, the limpkin and the famous southern screamer, which is found only in South American swamps. It is a huge, heavy, distinctive bird, and its wingspan of 170cm makes it a noisy bird in flight. It has a red surround to the eye, a crest of feathers at the back of the head, black and white rings around its neck, red legs and partially webbed feet. It is usually found in pairs, and the couples, which share the incubation of eggs, are so faithful that when one of the pair dies the other often dies too. Its cries of *chahã* can be heard up to 3km away, earning it its Guaraní name.

The **wetlands** are also an attractive area for fishing, and Paraguayans can sometimes be seen fishing in the water-filled ditches right by the side of Ruta 4. Caimans are frequently hunted (illegally), and there are river otters. Most people who go down to the banks of the Paraná go for a fishing trip, but remember that the *veda* (prohibited period) runs from early November to late December. This

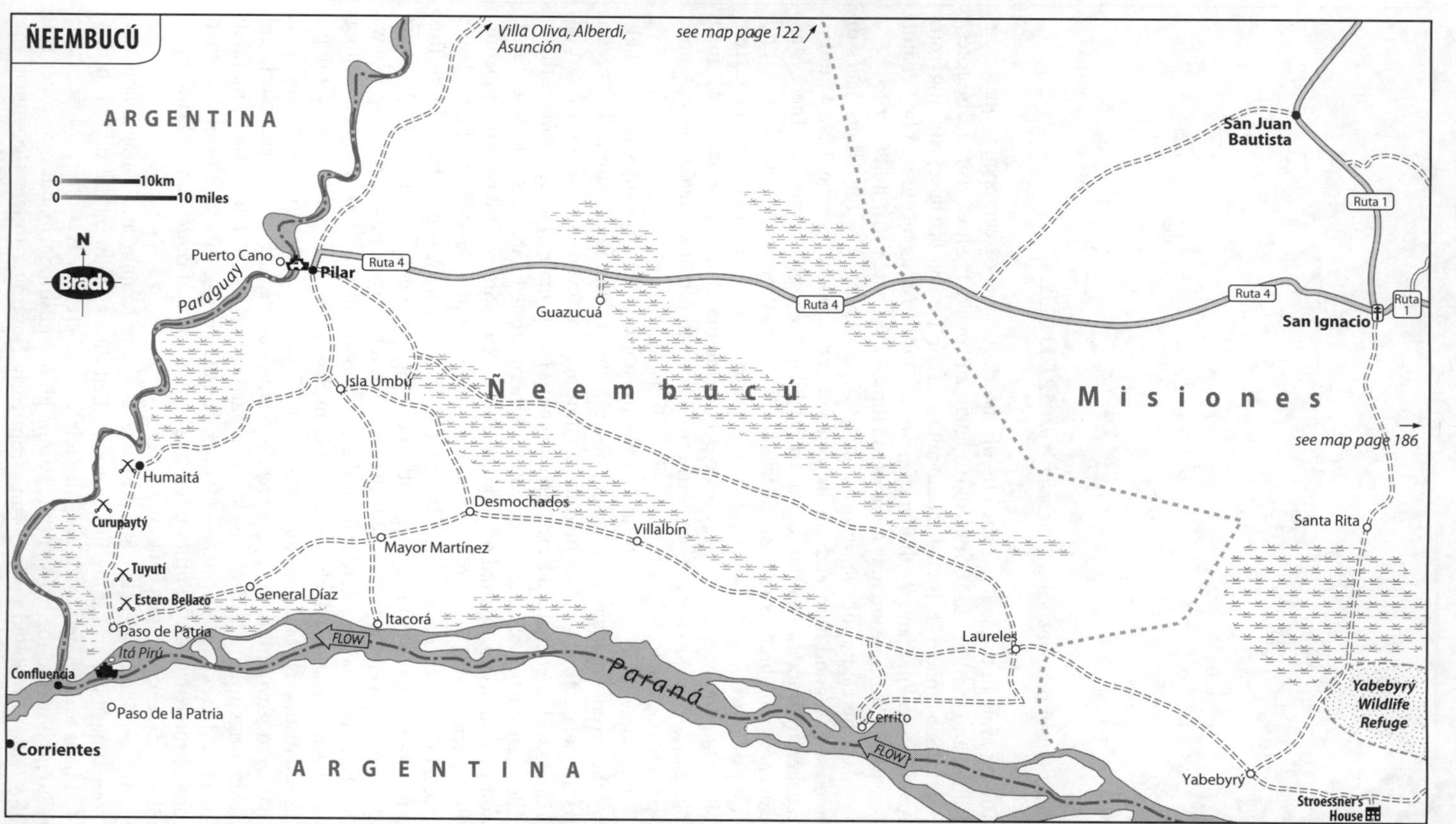
ÑEEMBUCÚ
ARGENTINA
0 10km
0 10 miles
N
Bradt
Villa Oliva, Alberdi, Asunción
see map page 122
San Juan Bautista
Ruta 1
Puerto Cano
Pilar
Ruta 4
Paraguay
Guazucuá
Ruta 4
Ruta 4
San Ignacio
Ruta 1
Isla Umbú
Ñ e e m b u c ú
M i s i o n e s
see map page 186
Humaitá
Curupaytý
Desmochados
Villalbín
Mayor Martínez
Santa Rita
Tuyutí
Estero Bellaco
General Díaz
Itacorá
Paso de Patria
FLOW
Laureles
Itá Pirú
Paraná
Confluencia
Paso de la Patria
Cerrito
Yabebyrý Wildlife Refuge
Corrientes
FLOW
ARGENTINA
Yabebyrý
Stroessner's House

period is to allow breeding to take place undisturbed and so preserve the native fish species. For waters shared with Brazil and rivers internal to Paraguay the dates of the *veda* begin about a week earlier and end about a week later. For the wetlands of Lago Ypoá, which is on the borders of the three *departamentos* of Ñeembucú, Paraguarí and Central, see pages 181–2.

Meanwhile, the **wooded areas** are still home to some threatened species such as the marsh deer, pampas deer and maned wolf. Deer are often hunted, though this is illegal. But the police, who check cars going in and out of Ñeembucú, will often allow through illegally caught game if the Paraguayan hunter politely offers a share of the goodies.

The road that runs parallel to the Río Paraná on the southern coast links up a series of fishing havens, which have excellent sandy beaches. The far southwest is also a region of great historical importance to Paraguayans, because it was where the fatal **War of the Triple Alliance** began, which figures so large in the national consciousness. This is where the Paraguayan victory of Curupaytý took place, and the defeat at Humaitá that marked the turning point of the war. The ruin of Humaitá is a familiar site to Paraguayans in the form of photographs, though few people have penetrated far enough to visit the actual sites.

Since Ñeembucú is a *departamento* rather isolated from the rest of the country, it is as well to be prepared for certain local characteristics of the hotels: they customarily price their accommodation per person and not per room; they usually do not provide breakfast, or if they do they do not include it in the price (except in Pilar, which being a bigger town has more outside influence); and they sometimes do not provide towels or top sheets unless you ask for them (*toalla* and *sábana para tapar* respectively).

PILAR *Copaco ☎ 0786 232300; municipalidad ☎ 0786 231130*

Pilar was founded by Pedro Melo de Portugal y Villena on 12 October 1779, and that date is still celebrated as the *fiesta patronal*. Although the town is out on a limb, geographically speaking, it breathes a spirit of education that is surprising for somewhere so remote. With painted wall murals adorning street after street, it is one of Paraguay's most attractive towns. It is also the gateway to visiting the main sites from the Triple Alliance War, especially Humaitá.

Pilar is known throughout the country for its cotton company, which also bears the name Pilar, and was founded by an Italian, Paolo Federico Alberzoni, who began to work there in 1929. The best sheets, towels and cotton fabrics come from the firm, which has major stores in Asunción as well as here in its town of origin, although the great bulk of its production goes for export. It is good to see the difference that a successful industry can make to a town in Paraguay: there are many attractive houses, both colonial and modern, several pleasant avenues and a lovely tree-filled plaza.

GETTING THERE AND AWAY There used to be a small domestic airport to the southwest of Pilar, and you will still see the signs to it, but there is no longer any air service.

By bus Buses run regularly from Asunción to the bus terminal in Pilar, and the journey takes about 5½ hours. San Ignacio is where you change from Ruta 1 to Ruta 4, and you reach there after about 4 hours. The best bus companies are Ciudad de Pilar (☎ *021 558393 / 0786 232980*), Ñeembucú (☎ *021 551680; 0786 230916*) and la Encarnacena (☎ *021 551745 / 0786 232468; www.laencarnacena.com.py*), which

BUS TIMETABLE: ASUNCIÓN – PILAR

ASUNCIÓN TO PILAR		PILAR TO ASUNCIÓN	
07.15	Ñeembucú	00.30	Encarnacena
10.15	Pilarense (slow)	01.00	Ciudad de Pilar (not on Sundays)
11.15	Ñeembucú	08.00	Ciudad de Pilar
12.00	Encarnacena	12.00	Encarnacena
14.00	Ciudad de Pilar	13.30	Pilarense
18.00	Ciudad de Pilar (not on Sundays)	14.30	Ñeembucú
22.30	Encarnacena	18.30	Ñeembucú
23.20	Ñeembucú	24.00	Ñeembucú

are *semi cama*, which means they have Wi-Fi and comfortably reclining seats. La Pilarense is the worst, but is no cheaper. The other company you will see, Del Sur, operates services from Pilar to the villages towards the south of Ñeembucú (see under the different villages in this chapter). Note that the bus terminal moved recently to a smart modern bus building (*Azzarini esq. 1º de marzo*), three blocks east and one block south from where it used to be on Irala c/ Tacuary. There is a big wall map of the town inside and a taxi rank outside. The old bus terminal has meanwhile been turned into a smart shopping centre, the Shopping Municipal – a dramatic change from the little stalls that used to border the buses, and one that reflects the rapid economic rise of the town over the last five years.

Coming from the other direction, there is a Ñeembucú bus (*semi cama*; Wi-Fi) that leaves Encarnación at around 08.30 and San Ignacio at around 11.00, having set off from Ciudad del Este at 04.00 (except Sun). It leaves Pilar on the return journey at 06.30 (except Sat), reaching Ciudad del Este at 17.00. If you do not catch this bus and want to reach Pilar from Encarnación, you should change buses in San Ignacio. Get off at the traffic lights (*semáforo*) as you are about to leave San Ignacio, and walk a little way left to the Hotel Arapysandú behind the stone horses' heads and the service station, on the curve of the road. Ruta 4 for Pilar begins here and you board your bus at this point, outside the hotel. If you are catching the Ciudad de Pilar, look for a man selling tickets: he generally turns up about half an hour before the bus is due. On other buses you usually pay when you board.

By car For those travelling in their own cars, the horses' heads in San Ignacio will also be the key landmark for turning onto Ruta 4. From there it is straight all the way.

By boat You can also reach Pilar by boat from Argentina or, conversely, leave Paraguay by the same route. Ferries leave Pilar every day for Puerto Cano at 07.00 (motorboat) and 08.00 (*balsa*, literally 'raft', which takes cars). From Puerto Cano you can get a bus to Mansilla (about 40km), and from there pick up another bus to Corrientes, Resistencia or Formosa, none of which are very close. The return ferries leave Puerto Cano at 13.00 (*balsa*) and 14.00 (motorboat).

GETTING AROUND Ruta 4 runs north–south but is called Irala within the town. There are traffic lights at the junction with Tacuarý and again at the junction with Colón. The bus terminal is three blocks to the east of Irala, and the centre (with the plazas and the Cabildo) six blocks to the west. There are a number of one-way streets.

LOCAL TOUR AGENCY Marecos Turismo [227 E1] (*Padre Federico Schiavoni c/ Ruta 4; 0786 232172;* **m** *0982 375125/0973 881634*) North of the bridge and west of Ruta 4, this agency organises bus trips within Neembucú, especially to Cerrito (see pages

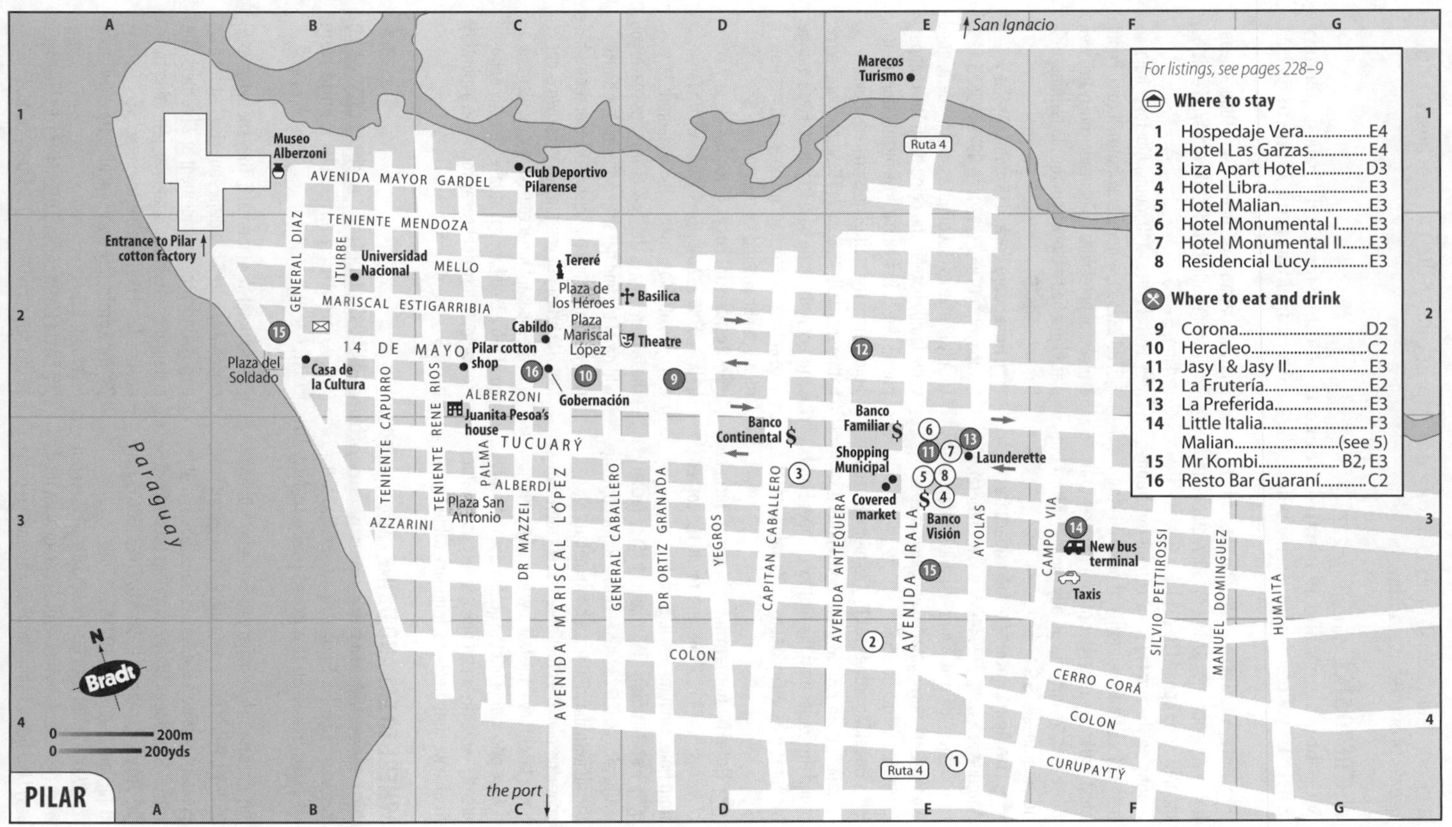

PILAR
For listings, see pages 228–9
Where to stay
1 Hospedaje Vera.....E4
2 Hotel Las Garzas.....E4
3 Liza Apart Hotel.....D3
4 Hotel Libra.....E3
5 Hotel Malian.....E3
6 Hotel Monumental I.....E3
7 Hotel Monumental II.....E3
8 Residencial Lucy.....E3
Where to eat and drink
9 Corona.....D2
10 Heracleo.....C2
11 Jasy I & Jasy II.....E3
12 La Frutería.....E2
13 La Preferida.....E3
14 Little Italia.....F3
Malian.....(see 5)
15 Mr Kombi.....B2, E3
16 Resto Bar Guaraní.....C2
San Ignacio
Marecos Turismo
Ruta 4
Museo Alberzoni
Club Deportivo Pilarense
Entrance to Pilar cotton factory
AVENIDA MAYOR GARDEL
TENIENTE MENDOZA
GENERAL DIAZ
ITURBE
Universidad Nacional
MELLO
MARISCAL ESTIGARRIBIA
Tereré
Plaza de los Héroes
Basilica
Plaza Mariscal López
Theatre
Cabildo
14 DE MAYO
Pilar cotton shop
Plaza del Soldado
Casa de la Cultura
Gobernación
ALBERZONI
Juanita Pesoa's house
TUCUARÝ
Banco Continental
Banco Familiar
Shopping Municipal
Covered market
Banco Visión
Launderette
Paraguay
TENIENTE CAPURRO
TENIENTE RENE RIOS
PALMA
ALBERDI
Plaza San Antonio
AZZARINI
DR MAZZEI
AVENIDA MARISCAL LÓPEZ
GENERAL CABALLERO
DR ORTIZ GRANADA
YEGROS
CAPITAN CABALLERO
AVENIDA ANTEQUERA
AVENIDA IRALA
AYOLAS
CAMPO VIA
New bus terminal
Taxis
SILVIO PETTIROSSI
MANUEL DOMINGUEZ
HUMAITA
COLON
CERRO CORÁ
CURUPAYTÝ
Bradt
0 200m
0 200yds
the port

238–9). Their usual form is a long day trip in one of the Del Sur buses, with an *asado* provided at midday.

WHERE TO STAY *Map, page 227.*

Most hotels are still concentrated around the old bus terminal (Irala c/ Tacuary), where travellers used to arrive before the new terminal was built a little to its east.

Hotel Las Garzas (20 rooms) Colón e/ Irala y Antequera; 0786 233130. A gleaming modern hotel opened in 2013, Las Garzas ('The Herons' or 'The Egrets') is the current frontrunner, half a block from Copetrol. Although it is the most expensive hotel it is quite a lot nicer than those that are only marginally cheaper. B/fast but no other meals. **$$**

Liza Apart Hotel (24 rooms) Tacuary c/ Antequera; 0786 232944/55; www.lizahotel.com/bienvenida.php. A long-established favourite with visitors, now upgraded with apartments. Cable TV, AC, frigobar. **$$**

Hotel Monumental II (23 rooms) Tacuary c/ Irala; 0786 230638. Well known hotel just round the corner from the slightly cheaper Hotel Monumental I. All mod cons – TVs, minibars, AC. **$$**

Hotel Monumental I (24 rooms) Tacuary c/ Ayolas; 0786 230638. Just round the corner from Hotel Monumental II. **$**

Hotel Malian (52 rooms) Irala e/ Tacuary y Alberdi; 0786 232405/232464. Right opposite the old terminal, this has a bit more buzz & character than the other hotels. Every room has had a facelift over the last few years. There is now a wide price range but the quality does not vary greatly – the cheaper rooms are very good value, as all have sommier beds, frigobars, cable TV, AC & private bathrooms. There is also a super-cheap single room with shared bathroom. Wi Fi a bit slow. Parking. **$–$$**

Hotel Libra (10 rooms) Alberdi c/ Irala; 0786 232531; e hotelibra@hotmail.com. Popular & pleasant hotel with quiet inside courtyard, well placed just half a block from the old terminal. AC but not splits. **$**

Hosepdaje Vera (18 rooms) Ayolas y Curupaytý; 0786 232130; m 0975 775825. Locally known as Ña Chiquita's, this modern, good-value family hotel is still being built. The cheaper price is due to its being a little further from centre, 1 block from the traffic lights on Irala. Private bathrooms, split AC & cable TV. Some rooms have sommier beds, some have frigobars. Fresh orange juice at breakfast, restaurant open at lunchtime, & meals can be ordered for the evening. **$**

Residencial Lucy (9 rooms) Tacuary c/ Irala; 0786 232249. Guesthouse with a family feel opposite Monumental II & restaurant Jasy. The owner, Lucy, is chatty & always has space: you will probably find her sitting outside her house ready to talk to any passer-by. Cheaper rooms have fans. No b/fast but you can buy your own & eat it in the pleasant inner courtyard with plants & a good table & sink, or eat at Jasy I directly opposite (see below). Also does cheap rooms on a monthly basis. **$**

WHERE TO EAT AND DRINK *Map, page 227.*

Not all restaurants are open at lunchtime. Fish is, of course, a speciality of the region. The La Frutería supermarket (*14 de mayo esq Antequera*) sells a wide range of fruit, making it a good place to buy breakfast.

Corona 14 de mayo y Dr Granada; 0786 232629. Pilar's top restaurant, with excellent food, pleasant outside patio, good service & reasonable prices. Now open midday as well as evenings. **$$**

Jasy I Tacuary c/ Irala; 0786 231586 & **Jasy II** Tacuary c/ Alberdi; 0786 231738; 07.00–15.00 & 19.00–23.00 daily. Modest but busy restaurants serving typical Paraguayan food. Jasy I is 3 houses along from Jasy II, which is next door to Hotel Monumental II. They specialise in reasonably priced fish dishes but also fast food & pastas. Under the management of 2 brothers, the restaurants are similar & popular, reflecting their quality. Jasy I perhaps has the edge. **$$**

Mr Kombi closed midday. Has Wi-Fi zone. Fast food. **$$**

Little Italia Alberdi e/ Chóferes del Chaco y 1o de marzo; m 0971 872073/0982 534825;

evenings Fri–Wed, closed Thu. Backing onto the new bus terminal, this new restaurant serves pizzas, pastas, *lomitos* & ice creams. Also has rooms. $$

Resto Bar Guaraní 14 de mayo y Dr Mazzeí. Pizzeria with karaoke. $$

Heracleo 14 de mayo c/ Av Mariscal Lopez; m 0975 104686; daily from early morning to late night. On the Plaza Mariscal Lopez, this restaurant has changed hands & names various times, & now concentrates on fast food & fruit juices. $$

Malian Hotel Malian (see opposite); 0786 232405. The restaurant of the Hotel Malian recently had a face lift, complementing its good Paraguayan food with attractive décor. The *caldo de pescado* (fish soup) is excellent. The Lomitería Malian (m *0975 675263*), which is the more popular, open-to-the-street part of the restaurant, wins top marks for professionalism for being the only restaurant in town to continue functioning with emergency lighting during the frequent power cuts. It also has a good *lomito arabe* & excellent service, & does deliveries. $

La Preferida Ayolas e/ Tacuarý y Alberzoni; closed evenings. Simple café with only two dishes on the menu but good homemade pasta & quick service. $

OTHER PRACTICALITIES There is a **Wi-Fi zone** in the Plaza Mariscal López [227 C2]. Among the **banks** are the Banco Continental (*Tacuary esq. Capitan Caballero*), Banco Visión (*Irala esq. Alberdi*), Banco Familiar (*Irala esq. Alberzoni).* There is a **launderette** (*lavandería*) [227 E3] next to the Hotel Monumental II. Bearing in mind that some places to stay do not include breakfast, **La Frutería** [227 E2] (*14 de mayo esq. Antequera*) is a good place to buy breakfast, because they have a good fruit selection. **Directory enquiries** for numbers in Pilar is 0786 232300.

WHAT TO SEE AND DO The adjoining plazas of Mariscal López and Los Héroes are reached by turning west off Avenida Irala (the road you come in on, with palm trees down its middle). You can take 14 de mayo, for example, and along this street, as on many others, including the plazas themselves, you will find colourful painted **murals**, generally proclaiming environmental themes. The two adjoining **plazas** are a delight – filled with trees and benches and big models of local birds and animals, such as the turtle, parrot, heron and hummingbird. Keep fit classes sometimes take place in the Plaza de los Heroés, which also has some permanent equipment for adult exercising.

The **Cabildo** [227 C2] (*Mariscal López c/ 14 de mayo; 0786 232078; 09.00–11.30 & 13.30–17.00 Tue–Fri, 09.00–noon Sat, Sun; closed Mon; free admission*) is an attractive colonial building with a first-floor balcony, and is in fact the only *cabildo* from colonial times that is still standing. It was rebuilt in 1817, during Dr Francia's presidency, but in 1824 he suppressed the *cabildo* system nationwide. It was restored in 1969. The current Director is Teresita Salcerdo.

The downstairs room is packed with items including statues from the original church of Pilar, which was knocked down during the Triple Alliance War. There is a fine St Michael, a large St Francis holding a skull, and a Christ taken down from the cross (*Cristo Yacente*). There are also a couple of columns from the original church, decorated with grapes and vine leaves, and the original tabernacle. From the Triple Alliance War there are cannonballs, and paintings of Mariscal López and of battles. The upstairs room is currently out of bounds pending the strengthening of the staircase.

At the corner of the plaza is the **Gobernación** building of regional government [227 C2] (*14 de mayo y Av Mariscal López; 0786 232210 int. 110; 07.00–13.00*), where the current secretary for promoting tourism is Gilberto Martínez (m *0981 479070;* e *turismo@neembucu.gov.py*). He can not only provide all the information you want, but – with about four days' notice – can arrange a tours of the town, a fishing trip, a visit to Isla Umbú or a tour to Humaitá or to more war sites further south.

This last is particularly valuable as bus access is extremely limited, the roads are still dirt tracks and most taxis will not go there.

At the far end of the adjoining Plaza de los Héroes, at the corner of Avenida Mariscal López y Mello, is a **monument to *tereré*** [227 C2] – the ubiquitous drink of the country – and behind is one of many picturesque old houses with a front portico. There are public toilets near this corner of the plaza. All around the plaza are educational establishments, and there is a branch of the Universidad Nacional nearer the river (*Iturbe c/ Mello*).

The largest building on the Plaza de los Héroes is the **Basilica de Nuestra Señora del Pilar** [227 D2], which has a little pointed bell tower standing apart from the main building. The carved wooden doors of the church show the Virgin of Guadalupe (Mexico) filling San Juan Diego's cloak with roses, and to the right of the main altar is a stained glass of San Roque González and his companions. Immediately inside the door of the church, to the left, is a striking crucifix that looks like bark peeling off a tree, and at its foot a glass coffin containing a remarkable and very bloodied Christ, articulated at the neck, shoulders and knees. To the left of the high altar is a series of photographs showing the five stages of the basilica, beginning with an original adobe church with a pitched roof and separate wooden bell tower, exactly like the Jesuit churches in style. Sunday masses are at 07.00 and (with rich musical accompaniment) at 19.30.

The **Avenida Mariscal López** is one of the most pleasant streets to walk down, with its central strip adorned with models of wildlife and colourful moulded pictures of the Triple Alliance War, or of the Pilar cotton factory, which has brought economic survival to the town. You also pass a large statue to the founder of Pilar, Pedro Melo de Portugal y Villena.

Not far away is the **house of Juanita Pesoa** [227 C2] (*Alberzoni c/ Tte René Rios*), who was Mariscal López's first mistress and mother of three of his children. Although she remained a rival to Madame Lynch throughout her life, she moved here from her birthplace of Yabebyrý (see pages 221–2) after the rival appeared on the scene. You can only look at the house from the outside, but there renovation is underway and it is not yet known if it will be open for visits in the future. It is a beautiful period house in colonial style, with rounded tops to the doors and windows and plaster details, so the outside is worth seeing.

A block north from there is the shop of the famous **Pilar cotton trade** [227 C2] (*14 de mayo y Palma; ☎ 0786 232386; www.pilar.com.py*), which has a big selection of rolls of fabric (all 100% cotton), sheets, towels, tablecloths, aprons and spongebags – a good place for a browse, especially if you have done the tour first of the Pilar factory itself (see below), where they give you a discount voucher.

The **Pilar factory** [227 A1] is four blocks further towards the river and two to the right. Since 2012 the guide Renee Amarilla has been offering a fabulous tour of the factory, in which you are led through huge halls buzzing with machines pumping out soft white cotton threads, as you follow through the spinning, weaving, dyeing, printing and making up of household items. There is meticulous hand quality control, and the soft, pure white, fluffy cotton is a joy to see as it dances off the machines. Book in advance to be sure of getting on a tour (*☎ 0786 232181;* **m** *0975 761853*), but you can also just turn up. Cotton used to be the principal crop of Ñeembucú, but now the company buys their raw material from Brazil.

With a separate entrance further around the walls of the factory compound is the **Museo Alberzoni** [227 B1] (*☎ 0786 234150; ⌚ 07.00–18.00 Tue–Fri, 07.00–13.00 Sat; free admission*), which tells the story of the firm, set in the house of the company's founder. If you ring beforehand they are happy to arrange a free talk with Profesor Carlos Alberto Mazo, an elderly gentleman with an extensive knowledge of the history of the town. A couple of blocks in the opposite direction down the riverside is the **Casa de la Cultura** [227 B2] (*14 de mayo y General Díaz; ⏲ 07.00–noon Mon–Fri; 07.00–11.00 Sat*), which has a permanent exhibition of old photographs of the town. This building, which faces onto the Plaza del Soldado, dates back to 1913, when it was built as the Hotel Florencia, and received many eminent guests, including ambassadors, government ministers and the composer Agustín Pio Barrios (see page 196). It is now used for harp classes and has a dance studio where many kinds of dance are taught three times a week.

The biggest annual event in Pilar is the **Fiesta Hawaiana**, which is celebrated through the night of 2 January down on the beach by the Club Deportivo Pilarense. Thousands of young people come to this event, filling the hotels, and there are flower garlands and lights in the river.

There is plenty of **fishing**: ask at your hotel, or Gilberto Martínez from the *gobernación* (see number on page 223) will gladly arrange a trip with a local fisherman.

At a short distance from Pilar are two pretty villages with notable old churches, Guazucuá and Isla Umbú.

AROUND PILAR

Guazucuá

Municipalidad ☎ *0786 231795* Just 3km off Ruta 4 from San Ignacio, and 33km before you reach Pilar, is the village of Guazucuá, which has an attractive old church, La Pura y Limpia Concepción, very similar to that of Isla Umbú (see below), although the reredos is later in style and the bell tower is now brick-built. There is an appealing Jesus on the donkey, and also a fine Christ in the coffin. The key holder is Profesora Sofía Céspedes (**m** *0985 278348*) who lives on the right-hand corner before the plaza. The church has statues of saints, carved wooden reredos, thick adobe walls and a ceiling made in the old traditional style of bamboo and mud. The name Guazucuá (Guaraní 'Deer hole') comes from the time when the people returned after the Triple Alliance War to find their village overrun with deer.

Getting there and away A bus leaves Pilar at 11.00 for Guazucuá and takes an hour (Gs10,000), but to return you would need to find your way back to the main road, because the return bus from Guazucuá does not leave until 05.00. All the buses except Encarnacena will stop for someone waiting by the side of Ruta 4. The owner of the bus, Fidel Garay (**m** *0981 107532*), who lives in Guazucuá, also has a smaller vehicle so can take someone the 3km to Ruta 4 for Gs15,000. A taxi ride from Pilar to Guazucuá or vice versa would cost at least Gs150,000 and would take half an hour.

Isla Umbú

Copaco ☎ *0786 231119; municipalidad* ☎ *0786 231000* This is a delightful little place, 12km south of Pilar, and only a couple of kilometres off the road to Humaitá. The earth down here (and in all southern Ñeembucú) is greyish yellow, unlike the red earth of most of eastern Paraguay. Like Guazucuá, the village is set in the wetlands and there are lakes on both sides of the village (*esteros*).

Isla Umbú has a gem of a **church** built in 1862 in the time of Carlos Antonio López, in the traditional style of pitched roof and colonnade, and a separate wooden bell tower which you can climb up, like a miniature Yaguarón. Palm trees line the path to the door, there are pine trees to the sides, and white flowers are dotted over the grass (depending on season). If you arrive in the morning you can gain access to the church from the parish office, on a corner of the plaza near Copaco (⏲ *08.00–11.00 Mon–Sat*). If you arrive after 11.00, ask Copaco to ring the parish secretary, who is keyholder. If that fails, a second keyholder, Ignacia Ojeda, lives on the street one block before the plaza, on the right-hand corner behind the *colegio*. Do not forget to tip if someone comes out specially. There is a painted reredos, a brick floor, carved wooden holy water stoups, carved wooden pillars, a bamboo-lined ceiling and a pretty choir loft. The patron saint in the centre of the reredos is St Athanasius. The pulpit and confessional box have been removed to the museum. Mass is once a fortnight at 08.00, with lay celebrations on the intervening Sundays, and the *fiesta patronal* is on 2 May, the feast of St Athanasius. If you have to choose between visiting Guazucuá and Isla Umbú, you will probably do better to give priority to Isla Umbú.

Everything is around this plaza – the community centre, bar, police station, Municipalidad, primary school, public library, Copaco, parish office and the museum. There is even a 'Home Stay El Portrillo' to the left of the church, where you can get a room for the night in a family house.

Named after a soldier, the **Museo Coronel Pedro Hermosa** (⌚ *08.00–13.00 Mon–Fri, 08.00–11.00 Sat; free admission*) is in the former military quarters of Mariscal López, and is well worth visiting. If you find it closed. contact the Municipalidad (☎ *0786 231119;* ⌚ *08.00–noon Mon–Sat*) and they will be delighted to open it, or ring the guide Leticia Veloso (m *0975 725840*). It has some interesting drawings showing the construction of the church at Humaitá (see page 234), a lot of rather good oil paintings of the Triple Alliance War by Bartolomé Martínez of Encarnación, and various items from the time of Juanita Pesoa, including agricultural implements, looms, trunks and a leather hammock. Juanita Pesoa – Mariscal López' mistress before Madame Lynch – married one of the few survivors of the Triple Alliance War, Coronel Pedro Hermosa of Isla Umbú, and spent her last years in the village. She also lived in Yababyrý (see pages 221–2) and Pilar (see page 230).

Isla Umbú benefitted from some support to its tourist facilities from the Universidad Americana a few years ago, with guides trained, brochures printed and an information centre opened. This has had its effect, although the local guides no longer live in Isla Umbú and the information centre is not kept open.

Getting there and away Coming from Pilar, the roundabout with the turn to Isla Umbú is unmissable. But if you are coming from Humaitá, you may be misled, first by a school marked Isla Umbú some distance before the town, and then by a turn east towards General Díaz, which comes shortly before the turn to Isla Umbú itself. There is a Del Sur **bus** (☎ *0786 233083*) that leaves Pilar for Isla Umbú at 11.30 and another at 17.00; from Isla Umbú they go on to Mayor Martínez and Itacorá. For the return journey, these buses leave Itacorá at 05.00 and at 13.00, reaching Isla Umbú at 06.00 and 14.00 respectively. So you can visit Isla Umbú comfortably in the same day by public transport, leaving Pilar at 11.30 and returning from Isla Umbú at 14.00,

HUMAITÁ

Copaco ☎ 0786 232780; municipalidad ☎ 0786 231559

Further down towards the southwest tip, where the rivers Paraguay and Paraná join, are the chief battle sites of the Triple Alliance War in its early long campaign, and the towns to visit here, with museums, are Humaitá and Paso de Patria (at the tip). Humaitá means 'ancient stone' in Guaraní, which turned out to be an appropriate name for a remote town that came to be known chiefly – or only – for its ruin of a church, destroyed by enemy bombardment. The town was originally founded by Pedro Melo de Portugal y Villena in 1778, one year before he founded Pilar.

BUS TIMETABLE: PILAR – HUMAITÁ – PASO DE PATRIA

Pilar	Humaitá	Paso de Patria	
05.00	06.30	07.15	(Ñeembucú)
10.00	11.30	12.15	(Del Sur)
10.30		12.00	(Gabriel Candia, alternate days)
17.00	18.30	19.30	(Del Sur)

Paso de Patria	Humaitá	Pilar	
04.00	05.00	06.30	(Del Sur)
11.15	12.15	13.45	(Ñeembucú)
14.00	15.00	16.30	(Del Sur)
	16.50	18.20	(Gabriel Candia, alternate days)

The journey is worth making not only for the ruin, but for the beautiful natural scenery, with egrets flying, horses and cattle grazing, and white flowers blooming everywhere.

GETTING THERE AND AWAY The journey from Pilar is 38km and you should allow 1½ hours. The only access is by **dirt road**, and when it rains these roads are impassible, although the route through General Díaz (just past the tip along the banks of the Paraná) to Isla Umbú is slightly less slippery than the coast road.

Local **buses** go from the companies Del Sur (☎ *0786 233083*) and Ñeembucú (☎ *0786 230916*), but there are only a few a day in each direction. There is also a **private minibus** that leaves the terminal in Pilar for Humaitá every other day, returning the following day (*Gabriel Candia;* m *0985 278749*). The journey all the way to Paso de Patria takes 2¼ hours.

If you go by **taxi** you can expect to pay at least Gs350,000 to go as far as Humaitá, including the wait. Arrange it in advance with the *Gobernación* (see number on page 223), or ask around among the taxi drivers near the Pilar bus terminal, but do not be surprised if they show no enthusiasm for taking you so far on such bad roads: it really needs a 4x4.

WHERE TO STAY AND EAT

Hotel Municipal (4 rooms) m 0985 283609. This elegant old house built in 1898 with big rooms & decorative tiled floors has a spectacular view from its courtyard directly onto the ruin (illuminated at night). To the front is a view of the river. This has the potential to be a fantastic hotel, but unfortunately it is run-down, often unattended & not very clean. If you can cope with these disadvantages you will find your stay memorable & at a bargain price (Gs30,000 per person). AC. No restaurant but you can eat at the restaurant opposite, La Terraza. **$**

Posada and Bar La Terraza (4 rooms) ☎ 0786 231557, 0985 279312; restaurant ⌚ 07.00–22.00. Boring modern building but well located with terrace overlooking river. The fresh orange juice is excellent & the service is friendly. Rooms above bar are very pleasant & modern, sleep 3 or 4 each, & have AC, private bathroom & TV. **$**

Posada y Bar Las Gorditas (2 rooms; sleeps 8) Heróica Resistencia; ☎ 0786 231530, 0985 735735. New restaurant, basic but well thought of, on the road into town from Pilar, just 5mins' walk from the ruin, ie: 3 blocks from the river. The Posada is not on the same site but is 2 blocks away under the same management; ask at the Bar. Shared bathroom, AC. **$**

El Bosque (3 huts, sleeps 12) Heróica Resistencia esq. Paso de Patria; ☎ 0786 231532. Economical rustic accommodation in 3 thatched huts, one with AC. B/fast not included. On a corner facing a wood with howler monkeys on one side & the owner's house on the other. Roof needed repairing on 2 of the 3 huts at the time of writing. The owner, Yolanda Verga de Candia (widow of José María Candia, who did a lot of research on the Triple Alliance War), lives next door, & she also has a private museum that anyone can visit at no cost. Look for the pink house next to Las Gorditas. **$**

OTHER PRACTICALITIES There is no Personal signal in Humaitá, although there is Tigo. There is no reliable signal for internet use anywhere south of Pilar.

WHAT TO SEE AND DO The **church of San Carlos Borromeo** was one of the biggest churches in South America in its day, accommodating a congregation of up to 5,000. President Carlos Antonio López had it built, and dedicated it to his patron saint. It was inaugurated on 1 January 1861 and only five years later was bombarded continuously by the Triple Alliance, who believed it was being used as a military base. After six months of constant cannonball fire it was left as we have it today, with fragmentary ruins of less than half the frontage. Its dramatic silhouette is one of the iconic views of Paraguay. Night floodlighting of the ruin and of the Museo Histórico (see below) was installed in 2011, and is turned on every night.

The **new church of Humaitá** (🕘 *07.00–noon & 14.00–17.00*), which backs onto the ruin, was built with bricks from the old church. It has a number of Jesuit-Guaraní statues, which Carlos Antonio López ordered to be brought to adorn his building. The repainting they have suffered has not enhanced their artistic quality, and the nine statues are clumsily placed in an overcrowded row. However, there is a delightful Gabriel, with wings and arms outstretched.

It may be surprising to find how much attention Paraguayans pay to the sites of their defeats, rather than their victories. But for them Humaitá is the 'symbol of resistance and Paraguayan heroism' (their slogan to tourists), and the sad ruins on the riverbank represent both defiance and dignity. You find the same approach in Vapor Cué, Piribebúy and Cerro Corá (see pages 162, 164–5 and 351–3). The more crushing the defeat, the more is heroism seen there. What they are most proud of is that 'a Paraguayan does not surrender'.

The **Museo Histórico** (🕘 *07.30–noon & 13.30–19.00 Tue–Sat, 08.00–11.00 & 14.00–17.00 Sun & Mon; US$2 foreigners, Gs5,000 Paraguayans. They prefer you to pay in guaraníes, but to the current value of the dollar*) is a recently designed museum in an attractive old building with a colonnade, which was originally the barracks of Mariscal López, on the old Plaza de Armas, near the ruins. The guide Juana Mendoza (**m** *0985 217404/0975 627741*) is quite knowledgeable. A wall map shows the different battlegrounds of the Triple Alliance War, which was essentially won by the Allies in this region in 1866, although Paraguay did not finally capitulate until four years later in the extreme northeast of the country. Shortly after the Allies crossed the river, the Paraguayans attacked them at the marsh Estero Bellaco, on 2 May 1866. The attack failed, but Paraguay regrouped, greatly strengthened their army to 24,000, and attacked the allies again in the First Battle of Tuyutí on 24 May 1866. Despite their increased size, the Paraguayan army suffered a devastating defeat and over half their force was killed or wounded. On 12 September 1866 Mariscal López met the Argentinian President, Bartolomé Mitre, for a conference at Yataitý Corá, but the Allies' condition for ending their offensive was the removal from power of López himself, and he refused to agree to go. Ten days later, the Alliance attacked again at the Battle of Curupaytý, but this time the Paraguayan army won an important victory. With only 5,000 soldiers against 20,000 Brazilian and Argentinian troops, Paraguay maintained its trench line. The Allies had 10,000 casualties, and the Paraguayans only 96. The museum has an interesting model of this battle, and also a reproduction of a famous painting (from the Museo de Bellas Artes in Buenos Aires) by the Argentinian artist Cándido López, who fought at Curupaytý and lost his right arm there, but subsequently taught himself to paint with his left hand, and painted the battle in 1893, 27 years after the event.

The **site of the Battle of Curupaytý** is a little to the south of Humaitá, in the *compañía* Paso Pucú, on private land belonging to the *diputado* (member of Parliament) Antonio Attis. The fortifications were designed by the English colonel George Thompson. Some trenches are still visible, and there is a simple monument with a bust of General José Eduvigis Díaz, who led the Paraguayan army. Plans are being made to improve the access road, and if you want to make the visit you should contract a local guide, perhaps by speaking to the *Gobernación* or to Professor Vicenta Miranda: the battlefield is 12km from Humaitá and a gate into an *estancia* needs to be unlocked to get there. But there is no tourist infrastructure and the place is likely to be more of interest to Paraguayans than to visitors. The same applies to other battlefields of the Triple Alliance War, such as Tuyutí and Estero Bellaco. A long wooden pier stretches from the museum down into the river. Slightly downriver, Mariscal López had a barrier built across the water, at Itá Punto, with chains and dynamite, to prevent the Triple Alliance forces from sailing north.

Another private *museo histórico* is known locally as **Casa Pilo**, and is in the house of the Candia family (*0786 231532*). It has silver plates, coins, sables, swords and cannonballs, and also some paintings and sacred images. This is the family who run the Hospedaje El Bosque (see page 233).

A teacher, Vicenta Miranda (m *0985 270690*), is a fund of knowledge on the history. Her house is on the corner behind the *colegio*, with a lot of flowers in the front patio as well as so many war remains that her house is really a museum in itself.

FISHING PUEBLOS ALONG THE RÍO PARANÁ

The great Río Paraná is 3km wide for much of its course along Ñeembucú, where it is not broken up by islands. It provides great fishing and beaches. NB: Ayolas in Misiones (see pages 214–22) and Encarnación in Itapúa (see pages 268–76) also benefit from beaches onto the Paraná.

PASO DE PATRIA *Copaco 0785 202300; municipalidad 0785 202251.* Further south, 20km from Humaitá (and 62km from Pilar), Paso de Patria is another quiet and even more remote war town. This southernmost point of Ñeembucú, where the Río Paraguay and the Río Paraná join forces, is excellent for fishing, and there are herons and water birds to be seen, some of which are endangered species.

Getting there and away Paso de Patria reachable only by **bus** on the dirt road from Pilar via Humaitá (see box on page 233) or a better road (that is in the process of being made an *adoquinado* – see page 392) from General Díaz, unless you take a **motorboat across the river** from Paso de la Patria, Argentina, which is only half an hour from Corrientes. Note that the town on the Argentinian side is called Paso de *la* Patria. The ferries all leave Paraguay at 06.00 and return from the Argentinian side at noon and 14.00 from Mondays to Fridays (Gs20,000 per person). The Argentinian immigration post is not staffed at weekends. For public transport, see page 233 on the buses that come from Pilar via Humaitá.

Where to stay and eat This is a good place to stay, because there are a couple of excellent *posadas* run by friendly and helpful people (they are relatives), where you can enjoy a good level of independence and do your own cooking but still enjoy generous help by your hosts in fixing up boat trips, etc. Typically, a big fishing group will come at a weekend, bringing their food with them to complement the fish they catch. Midweek you will probably find the *posadas* empty. There are a couple of nearby stores where you can buy basic food supplies, and if you do not want to cook you can eat perfectly well at the nearby Comedor Lilian (**$**). There are also a couple of hotels, Hotel Dorado and Hotel Paso de Patria (**m** *0985 285158*), but the personalised care and quality of the *posadas* make a hotel unnecessary.

Posada Almiper (1 room) 1½ blocks south from the southwest corner of the plaza; 0785 202257; **m** 0985 793598. Separate little house in the garden of the family home sleeps 6 in a large room. Private bathroom & basic cooking facilities in portico. Price may be negotiable, split AC, *parilla*. **$**

Posada Thaiz (3 rooms) **m** 0982 328382; **e** hilaferq@gmail.com; Facebook: Posada THAIZ. On the northeast corner of the plaza, independent house with its own kitchen, bathroom, 3 bedrooms sleeping 7–10 people, 2 patios, tables & hammock. You have to call at the next house to be attended to, not at the Posada itself, which will probably be unoccupied. **$**

Practical information In terms of **mobile phone networks**, and therefore internet access, only Tigo reaches this far south, and even that is slow. There is a new **tourist information centre** next to the museum.

What to see and do The **museum** (*14 de mayo y Paso de Patria; 0785 202254/202243;* **m** *0982 518915; 08.00–11.30 or on request*) is housed in the former barracks of Mariscal López's army, a pretty building with a colonnade and well-kept garden, although it is not quite as original as the adobe building collapsed after a flood in 1983 and had to be rebuilt. The guide, Vicente García (**m** *0985 518915*), often goes into the countryside on excavations of war remains in the afternoons, so try to let him know in advance that you would like to visit. It has the usual array of war relics: soldiers' plates and cutlery, cannonballs and coins, spades and spanners, spurs and swords, buckles and bottles, bullets and bayonets. They have been well arranged, in decorative displays. You can also see films in the museum, including a general film about Ñeembucú that lasts 15 minutes.

There is also a small private museum called the **Museo San Francisco Solano** (*one block east from the main museum,* **m** *0785 202201*) with objects from the Triple Alliance War.

An enjoyable excursion is to take a speed boat (*deslizador*) out to the point where the Río Paraná and the Río Paraguay join, called the *confluencia*. It will cost you at least Gs250,000–Gs350,000, but is worth doing, and the host of your *posada* can help make the booking, or contact Miguel Gamarra (**m** *0981 541963*). You see the extraordinary phenomenon of different coloured waters meeting but not mixing; the waters of the Paraguay at that point are orangeish, while those of the Paraná are slate blue, and an almost straight line divides the colours as the waters of the two rivers join and then make their slow way down towards the sea. The tip of the tip of Paraguay is marked at this point by a tree that juts out over the waters from the final promontory.

ITÁ PIRÚ Close to the point where the waters of the two rivers meet is the little island of Itá Pirú on the Río Paraná, which has a naval base, a *posada* and nothing else. The name in Guaraní means 'thin stone'. This is a great place to hang out among the birds and the fish, away from the world, although you need a boat to get there.

Most visitors come to fish and bring their own boat on a trailer. You could pay a boatman from the port of Paso de Patria, or once there the posada (see page 236) can hire you a boat, although this is only economical for groups.

Immediately opposite the Posada across a narrow channel is a good beach, and between the island and Paso de Patria is another good sandy beach, reachable only by water and occupied only by flocks of black cormorants (*mbiguá*). Make sure that you have long enough on your boat trip to enjoy the beach as well as to see the *confluencia*. At Paso de Patria itself the water is too deep for a beach, though there is a popular, touristy beach on the Argentinian side (although you cannot go at weekends – see page 235).

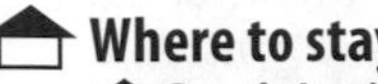

Where to stay

Posada Itapirú (5 rooms) m 0982 822596; e evayudith@hotmail.com; Facebook: Posada Itapirú. Pleasant atmosphere in this *posada* abuzz with Paraguayans engaged in fishing, so they are booked out in Jan, Feb, weekends & during Semana Santa. There is also a complete separate house for hire. AC. The *posada* includes a shop. They also offer camping. Boat hire m 0982 576084. **$**

ITACORÁ Another place frequented by the fishing community, particularly busloads from Brazil, is 50km from Pilar, at Itacorá, on the Río Paraná rather than Río Paraguay. If you are coming from Paso de Patria, take the partially *adoquinado* road east to General Díaz, which is named after the victorious general of Curupaytý and has a good beach, after which the road deteriorates. At Mayor Martínez take a little track south to Itacorá (Guaraní 'stone'; Spanish 'circle') on the coast. If you are coming from Pilar, take the road for Mayor Martínez when you get to Isla Umbú.

Getting there and away To get to Itacorá by public transport, Del Sur (*0786 233083*) runs a bus that leaves Pilar at 11.30 and 17.00, and returns from Itacorá at 13.00 and 04.00 every day.

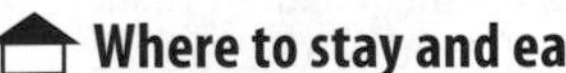

Where to stay and eat

Hotel Paranamí (12 rooms) m 0971 810650; e hotelparanami_itacora@hotmail.com. Exists exclusively for fishing trips, & for an additional fixed daily rate of Gs600,000 will include everything needed for a day's fishing (dinner, boat, fuel, guide, etc) apart from the tackle itself. No restaurant, not even for b/fast. **$$**

Hotel Itacorá (14 rooms) m 0972 479864/0985 112395. Recently expanded building with the addition of a 2nd floor. Smart & modern. No restaurant or b/fast but equipped kitchen at the disposal of guests. Can provide a boat & guide, but it is not cheap. **$$**

Comedor Ña Viki 0786 231417. Simple restaurant on the right as you enter the village. Surprisingly, it does not serve fish. **$**

Other practicalities There is another naval base here. There is no Wi-Fi to be found, and portable modems (dongles) may not work either, though you can try, as both Tigo and Personal have a signal.

Travelling onwards to Cerrito Continuing along the road that runs parallel to the coast you come to the junction with the considerably better road that runs from Isla Umbú to Desmochados. After Desmochados the next village is **Villalbín**, with its delightful monument showing a trio of a calf, a footballer and a *campesino* raising his sombrero (which you see if you approach from the east side, from Laureles). Another 33km east of Villalbín is a turn down to Cerrito on the coast.

East of Villalbín the roads are pure sand, flanked by grassy meadows and copses and sometimes marshlands, right up to Ayolas in the next *departamento* of Misiones. The birdlife is very interesting, and many birds – particularly birds of prey and owls – perch on the fence posts at the side of the road, where they can be studied at quite close hand. If there has been rain you will need a 4x4.

CERRITO This undiscovered paradise for fishing and bathing is set right on the water's edge, reached by a 15km turning off the same road running from Paso de Patria to Laureles. It has a long sandy beach and several little guesthouses. At weekends it fills up with holidaymakers on coaches from Pilar, but outside of Ñeembucú it is quite unknown. Paraguayans seeking beaches go to one of the new *costaneras* (where the sand has recently been laid) or to San Bernardino (where the water is polluted) but are unfamiliar with Cerrito. True, it is awkward to get to: the drive from Pilar takes about 3 hours, and from San Ignacio via Yabebyrý around 4 hours – and that is if the weather is good. But if people from Pilar can make it to Cerrito, then people from outside of Pilar should be able to do so too, for Pilar is now easily reached from Asunción, with some of the best buses in the country. However, you may need to be part of a group hiring a bus in Pilar in order to make a trip feasible. If you have a group, you can do this through Marecos Turismo (see page 226), but there is no reason why you should not cut out the middleman, hire the bus direct from Del Sur, and order your meals direct from the *posada* in Cerrito.

Getting there and away Del Sur (*0786 233083*) run a **bus** that leaves Pilar at noon on Mondays, Wednesdays and Fridays and returns from Cerrito at 03.00. Alternatively, you can reach Cerrito on the Yacyretá bus that passes through Laureles (see opposite).

If you are driving you take the road that goes south from the Villalbin–Laureles route. If you are approaching from the Laureles side, local people recommend the alternative route south when you are just leaving Laureles on the Villalbin road. After 8km south you reach a gate: go through it and turn right at this junction for 20km to reach Cerrito.

Where to stay In Cerrito, as in most of Ñeembucú, prices are given per person, not per room, and breakfast is not included in the price, but can generally be bought as an extra. There are not really any restaurants – just a few bars that serve snacks – but most guesthouses will cook for you, and cook well. Of course, fish is the order of every day. Most will help organise a boat for fishing with a guide (boat for day Gs300,000; guide Gs150,000; petrol around Gs200,000). When there are a lot of people there are four or five boats in the lagoon that will do trips on the lagoon or to islands, and collect you later in the day.

Posada y Bar El Pescador (9 rooms) 0788 200052; m 0983 568326. Behind the naval base, only a few houses from the shoreline, with another house 100m away adding another 7 rooms. Does the best b/fast of the guesthouses. **$$**

Posada El Puerto (7 rooms) m 0984 111818. Wonderful welcome from Abel & his wife at this house right on the shoreline. 1 room has a view over the lagoon. Some with AC & private bathrooms, others with fans & shared bathrooms, priced accordingly. Does excellent *asado de boga*. **$**

Hospedaje Chinita (6 rooms) 0788 200032; m 0985 135035. Next door to Abel lives his mother Chinita, now a little elderly but full of warmth & welcome. This guesthouse has good tables in a sitting room & in a quincho facing a well (still in operation) if you want to sit & use a computer. **$**

Posada y Bar Leti (3 rooms) 0788 200020; m 0985 294761. Four blocks from the beach, this posada has big rooms with 4 beds. 1 has a TV, & 2 have split AC. Cheap b/fast. **$**

Other practicalities Priscilano Viveros in the Municipalidad (*0788 200040;* m *0983 644456*) is happy to help with **tourist information**. In terms of **mobile phone networks**, there is a good Tigo signal, but no Personal signal.

What to see and do Cerrito has broad tree-clad avenues, a pretty little white church and, most importantly, a 2km sandy beach onto the Lago Sirena – really a river lagoon, just tucked in off the river behind a narrow headland. The sunrises over the lagoon are spectacular, and there is a good view from the little hill (*cerrito*) at the end of the village, on the riverside. A statue of President Stroessner on the hill was destroyed shortly before his overthrow from power – some locals insist it was a lightning strike, though some like to say it was a bomb.

There are three beaches: that of the Lago Sirena, right in front; on the far side of the lagoon, a beach on the Isla Martín García (lots of cormorants and gulls); and Isla Pombero, on the river (a large circle of inviting yellow sand next to an overgrown island). The latter two require a boat trip, and this is well worth doing. If there are a lot of holidaymakers, there will be a big public boat that can ferry you at low cost. If not, it is worth asking your *posada* to help arrange a private boat trip (*try Enzo Bogado,* m *0981 838233; about Gs250,000–300,000 including fuel*).

LAURELES *Copaco 0788 221000* Not far to the east from Cerrito is the town of Laureles, which has a very large picturesque square, surrounded on all four sides by traditional old houses with colonnades. The church is set in the midst of this square, and is of Jesuit style, built in 1791 and rebuilt in 1830, with a separate bell tower accessible by a wooden ladder. Also within the square, next to the church, is a large open-air amphitheatre, which is used for the annual **Fiesta de la Tradición y el Folklore**, which begins on the third Friday of January and carries on over the weekend. Thousands of people go to listen to the musical groups playing late at night in the amphitheatre. By day there are the usual stalls, horse events and *asado a la estaca* that typically enliven Paraguayan fiestas.

Getting there and away If you are coming **from Cerrito to Laureles**, there are two possible routes: one is to go north to the junction with the Villalbín–Laureles road, and then east; the other (which is considered by locals to be more reliable, although it is not usually marked on maps) is to go east along the top of the lagoon and beyond for 20km, and then take a turn north where there is a gate, which you can open (and shut, of course). After some 8km, this brings you to a point a couple of kilometres west of Laureles.

You can reach Laureles by **bus** from Pilar with Del Sur (*0786 233083*), departing Pilar at 11.00 every day, and at 17.00 on Thursdays and Sundays; the buses leave Laureles at 09.00 every day, and at 02.30 on Fridays and Mondays. If you are not exploring the rest of Ñeembucú first, it is considerably more direct to come on the Yacyretá bus that leaves the Plaza in San Ignacio Guasú at 09.30 and at 14.00, and that goes on to Cerrito after Laureles. It runs every day except Sundays, and takes you through some countryside excellent for birdwatching, with wetlands and wildlife. For the return journey the bus leaves Cerrito at 02.00 and 14.00, passing through Laureles again on the way back to San Ignacio. The journey from San Ignacio to Laureles takes 3 hours, and from Laureles to Cerrito takes a further hour. Because the bus is travelling on dirt roads, it may not always leave after heavy rains, so you should check by ringing the representative in San Ignacio (m *0985 330076*).

Where to stay There are a few very simple *hospedajes*, of which one is **Hospedaje Isabelita** (*5 rooms; San José Obrero c/ Virgen María;* ☎ *0788 221031;* **$**), a simple, economical but friendly place with a shared bathroom and fans.

TRAVELLING EAST OF LAURELES To the east is Yabebyrý (see pages 221–2), which is in the *departamento* of Misiones, and is where you turn north for San Ignacio or continue parallel to the river to reach Corateí (see page 221), Ayolas (see pages 214–15), and eventually San Cosme y Damián (see pages 241–7).

NORTHERN ÑEEMBUCÚ

We have been exploring the southern part of Ñeembucú, but there is also a vast stretch of the *departamento* north of Pilar, as you can see if you look at the coloured country map at the beginning of the book. Up in that north end of the department, the small town of Villa Oliva is also renowned for its fishing. It lies on the shores of the Río Paraguay, rather than the Río Paraná like Itacorá and Cerrito. A lot of people head to Villa Oliva to fish, especially during Holy Week (*Semana Santa*) and summer.

WHERE TO STAY

Posada y Bar El Pescador (10 rooms) ☎ 0788 200052; m 0983 568326. Behind the naval base, with 2 other houses 50m & 100m away adding another 10 rooms. Can organise boat for fishing with guide: boat for day Gs300,000, guide Gs150,000, petrol around Gs200,000. **$**

Posada Nora (2 rooms) m 0995 686151. On the river, with 7 beds, private bathroom. **$**

Posada El Triángulo (2 rooms) m 0981 858253. Double & single room, kitchen, sitting room & recreation area. **$**

UPDATES WEBSITE

You can post your comments and recommendations, and read the latest feedback and updates from other readers, online at www.bradtupdates.com/paraguay.

7

Southeast to Itapúa and the Ruins

Departamento: Itapúa; gobernación *071 202054/203252/205995*

Though Itapúa is a different *departamento* from Misiones, it includes three old Jesuit missions: San Cosme y Damián, Trinidad and Jesús. The last two of these, and especially Trinidad, have the famous, evocative Ruins that are the icon of tourism in Paraguay. There is magic in the arches of Trinidad, stepping out along the sides of the huge plaza, once athrong with activity and now inhabited only by southern lapwings with their noisy chant, and in the stone frieze of angel musicians high in the ruined church, recalling the orchestras of Guaraní musicians that once filled the building with their Baroque music. When you add to this the quality of the carved statues now kept in the modern church, Trinidad has to be credited with being the most wonderful of all the Reductions – surpassing both San Ignacio Miní in Argentina and São Miguel in Brazil, both of which, however, are far better known and receive something like 20 times as many tourists.

Jesús, only 10km away from Trinidad, is also a romantic place, and for some people it is the favourite, with its views of palm trees framed by the windows of the abandoned church. San Cosme y Damián is also captivating – the only Reduction to have original buildings standing and in use around the best part of the plaza, including the church with original statues inside. A fourth Reduction, Itapúa, was sited at Encarnación, but nothing at all remains of it, though the city has a Jesuit museum where artwork from that period is preserved.

No-one should visit Paraguay without going to the Ruins of Trinidad and Jesús, if their time in the country permits it. Both have been declared World Heritage Sites by UNESCO, and all the former Reductions have now been linked in a tourist development project called the Ruta Jesuítica, which will increasingly boost the facilities offered. But travelling from Asunción to Trinidad takes about eight hours on public transport, six hours in a private vehicle, so it is not comfortable to go there and back in a day. The best way to visit is to make Misiones the first stop, visiting at least some of the museums of Jesuit-Guaraní art on the way (San Ignacio, Santa María de Fe, Santa Rosa and Santiago). From there, Trinidad is a much easier journey. And from Trinidad, you can go on to reach the Iguazú Falls within a day (see *Chapter 8*, pages 277–94), for a triumphal conclusion to a Paraguayan holiday.

Once you leave Misiones behind, you will go through two towns with rhyming names: General Delgado and Coronel Bogado. Between the two towns is the turn for San Cosme y Damián, which stands 23km south of Ruta 1 and is a historic jewel that is well worth the excursion.

SAN COSME Y DAMIÁN *Copaco 073 275200; municipalidad 073 275253*

San Cosme y Damián has a wonderfully peaceful atmosphere, and is unique among the Guaraní Reductions because it is more than a ruin: it has been partly restored

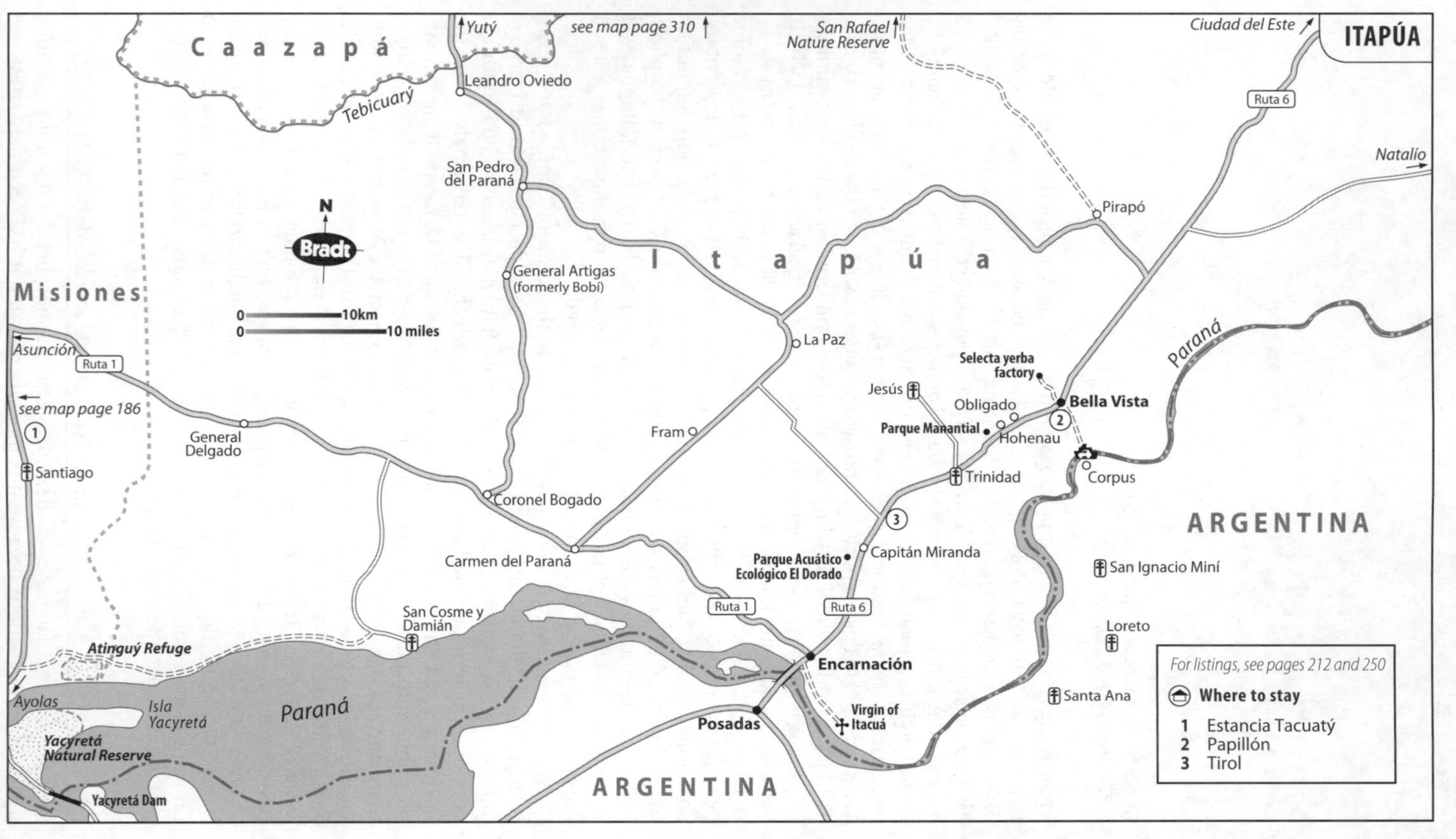

ITAPÚA
Caazapá
Itapúa
Misiones
ARGENTINA
ARGENTINA
Yutý
see map page 310
San Rafael Nature Reserve
Ciudad del Este
Natalío
Asunción
see map page 186
Ruta 1
Ruta 1
Ruta 6
Ruta 6
Tebicuarý
Paraná
Paraná
Leandro Oviedo
San Pedro del Paraná
General Artigas (formerly Bobí)
General Delgado
Santiago
Coronel Bogado
Carmen del Paraná
Fram
La Paz
Pirapó
Jesús
Selecta yerba factory
Bella Vista
Obligado
Parque Manantial
Hohenau
Trinidad
Corpus
Capitán Miranda
Parque Acuático Ecológico El Dorado
San Cosme y Damián
Atinguý Refuge
Encarnación
Virgin of Itacuá
Posadas
Ayolas
Isla Yacyretá
Yacyretá Natural Reserve
Yacyretá Dam
San Ignacio Miní
Loreto
Santa Ana
N
Bradt
0 10km
0 10 miles
For listings, see pages 212 and 250
Where to stay
1 Estancia Tacuatý
2 Papillón
3 Tirol

and has the roof on the buildings that remain, which include the still functioning parish church. It is named after two early Church twin brothers who were doctors in 4th-century Sicily, and they were chosen as patrons for two reasons: the foundation of the Reduction by an Italian Jesuit, P Adriano Formoso, in the same year that a church to saints Cosmos and Damian was restored in Italy; and the danger of plagues from European illnesses made the intercession of medical saints very appropriate.

The first settlement was near Formosa in Brazil, in 1632, in the region known as Tapé, but the area was attacked by *bandeirantes* in three successive years, and like most other Reductions it had to move. It went first to what is now Argentina, in 1638, where it joined up with Candelaria – the capital of the Treinta Pueblos – and then separated again before moving to its site in present-day Paraguay. Before the 1768 Expulsion it had over 3,000 inhabitants; 16 years after the Expulsion it had sunk to less than a third of that number.

San Cosme was famous for being an astronomical centre, under the astronomer-priest P Buenaventura Suárez, who studied Jupiter, wrote a book predicting solar eclipses and constructed a very accurate sundial that is still to be seen in position. It was Suárez who led the Reduction to this final site, and he installed in San Cosme what was only the second observatory in the continent, using local materials such as quartz crystals found on the shores of the Río Paraná, which he used as lenses. The date usually given now for the move to the present site is 1718, on the grounds that one of Suárez's books, printed in 1718, says he was already working here, but the sources are inconsistent on the dating.

The patronal feast day is 26 September.

GETTING THERE AND AWAY Though well worth seeing, San Cosme y Damián is a little tricky to get to. It is an awkward distance from both the museums in Misiones and the Ruins on the other side of Encarnación (over an hour's drive in both directions). If you are coming from Asunción on Ruta 1, then you reach the turn to San Cosme y Damián nearly an hour (60km) before you get to Encarnación. If you are in your own vehicle, then you only need to make a detour of 28km south to reach the remains. If you are on **public transport**, then the axis for reaching San Cosme is Coronel Bogado, 12km to the east of the turn.

Coronel Bogado is named after José Félix Bogado, who fought for independence in the continent under General San Martín. The town is famed for its *chipas* (maize rolls), and sellers may get on the bus to ply their wares from the Don Pipo Chipería (on Ruta 1 opposite the bus terminal). Paraguayans often stop for a snack or a meal at the Chipería Tatiana, on the outskirts, beyond the grassy triangular plaza to the east. Also recommended are the Chipería Tati and the Chipería Tía, both close to the Tatiana but on the other side of the road. Try the *chipas* that are filled with cheese and ham, or with chicken: they are delicious. You should also order the Paraguayan tea *cocido* to wash it down (with or without milk), rather than asking for conventional tea or coffee.

There is a Banco Regional with a cash machine at the west end of Coronel Bogado, as you arrive from the Asunción direction. Shortly afterwards you come to traffic lights and a modern, clean bus station (☎ *0741 252589*). There is a bus service from here to San Cosme throughout the day with two different companies, Perla del Sur and San Cosmeña, that run on alternate days but follow the same timetable. They go right down to the Reduction, which is the last stop, and the journey takes an hour. Some of the buses continue after Coronel Bogado to Encarnación. The fare at the time of going to press was Gs10,000. You can also pick up these buses further along the Ruta, by the turn to San Cosme, and save ten minutes on the journey.

Here are the quoted departure times, although they may vary when the bus has to come from Encarnación: from Coronel Bogado 09.00, 10.30, 12.00, 15.00, 16.00, 17.30; and from San Cosme y Damián 06.30, 07.30, 10.00, 11.30, 13.30, 16.00. There is also a Tigre bus which leaves Coronel Bogado at 19.00 (coming from Ciudad del Este) and goes to San Cosme to spend the night, leaving early in the morning at 04.30.

For greater comfort and speed, you can take a **taxi** and do the journey in only half an hour. There are always taxis at the terminal. A taxi driver called Anibal Bogado (m *0985 754292*), is recommended: he has a car with insurance, but he is not one of the drivers who wait at the terminal: he currently charges Gs100,000 for the round trip, or Gs120,000 to include a 2-hour wait. There is also a taxi driver in San Cosme called Carlos (*073 275294;* m *0985 797378*); this is a good service to use if you only need a lift one way, which is a good idea as it leaves you free to spend as long as you want – and there is a great deal to see and do.

WHERE TO STAY AND EAT There are now a lot of good and inexpensive posadas in San Cosme. They all include breakfast except Leoncito. Note that Stella Mary and B y G have proper restaurants as well. If you ring the Reduction in advance (*073 275315*), or even ask on the day, the guides there will help you find the best facilities for your overnight stay (but you will need to speak to them in Spanish). With the opening of the Observatory as a night-time attraction, they are doing this more and more.

Posada Aguapey (12 rooms) 073 275293; m 0981 981729. The nearest thing to a proper hotel, but being right at the beginning of the town (where there is a roundabout, opposite the police station) it is a long way from the Reduction. If you have a car this does not matter, & the Posada has a minibus (Gs15,000 per person to the Reduction). Pool. **$$**

Posada Doña Lelia (4 rooms) 073 275368. Only half a block from the Reduction, 2 rooms have private bathrooms, can cook lunch or dinner if you wish. **$$**

Posada Cielo (6 rooms) 073 275309; m 0985 210393. Refurbished rooms, comfortable beds, 2 bathrooms shared between guests, 2 blocks behind Reduction. Some rooms in separate house, others up spiral staircase. TV, hammocks. B/fast with freshly cooked *chipa* & cake. A cheaper option is to stay in a ready equipped tent with bedding, for 2 people. **$$**

Posada Aguilera (5 rooms, sleeps 20) 073 275263. Half a block from the Reduction, opposite the school. Split AC. **$**

Posada 6 Hermanos 073 275211. Traditional house, belonging to mother of a guide at the Reduction, same price as most of the other *posadas* but includes evening meal as well as breakfast. About 5 blocks from Reduction, private bathrooms, nice garden. **$**

Posada Ale (3 rooms) m 0985 811198. Can sleep 10 people, 4 blocks from the Reduction. **$**

Posada Doña Chinita (7 rooms) 073 275263. Half a block from the Reduction. **$**

Posada Leoncito (3 rooms) 073 275227. Half the price of the other posadas, & opposite the Reduction, but no b/fast. You can use the kitchen or get b/fast elsewhere. **$**

Posada Stella Mary y Rafael Mariscal Estigarribia y San Cosme; 073 275207; m 0981 474480. Usually just called Stella Mary. Very agreeable, economical local restaurant, which has now become a posada as well. Half a block behind the Reduction. Can do b/fast if your posada does not offer it. In the evening can be empty, but can get packed out at lunchtime with people from Yacyretá, so you might want to book in advance. As with all small places, you can expect good service if you give a little notice, preferably the day before. **$$**

Posada y Restaurante B y G 073 275 272; m 0985 295280. As a restaurant this is a bit bigger than Stella Mary, & still very economical. There are 4 beds in 1 room – a bit of a squash. It is just past Aguapey, on the other side of the road. **$$**

FIESTA NACIONAL DEL INMIGRANTE On the first weekend of June there is a Fiesta Nacional del Inmigrante in Coronel Bogado, with the participation of Poles,

Germans, Arabs, Ukrainians and Czechs, among others, whose families moved to the region mostly in the first half of the 20th century. The Fiesta began in 2007 and there are displays of folk dance, traditional costume and national dishes. Other towns in Itapuá that received a large immigrant population are Carmen del Paraná, Hohenau, Bella Vista, Obligado, Natalio and Piripó – not to mention Encarnación, where the Plaza de Armas celebrates the different nationalities in different sections of the Plaza de Armas.

WHAT TO SEE The **Reduction** (*073 275315;* m *0985 732956 Rolando; winter 07.00–20.00, summer 07.00-21.00 daily; foreigners Gs25,000, Paraguayans Gs15,000, local people Gs5,000; ticket is valid for Trinidad & Jesús too at no extra charge if used withn 3 days; debit and credit cards accepted; mass on Sunday at 08.00*) is the great, and indeed the only, attraction. There is no English-speaking guide and no written materials to buy, but the Spanish-speaking guides are good and helpful. Rolando Barboza does mornings (*073 275286;* m *0985 732956*) as does Mariela Cantero (m *0985 933532*), and Perla Machuca does afternoons (m *0985 732956*).

The splendid gateway which features the famous bat (*murcielago* in Spanish) at its peak has been restored in two-coloured stone. (The bat was the guardian of sacred places.) The red stones are the original pieces and the white stones complete it.

The church is an original building but was not constructed to be a church: the foundations of the projected church, never built, can be seen on the opposite side of the patio, while the present church is a long thin building, 65m x 12m, that would have been used as part of the *colegio* complex if the church had ever been completed. It now has a new roof, faithful to the original design, but the original walls are intact. The staircase up to the choir gallery just inside the entrance has now been replaced. The back section of the church was badly damaged by fire in 1899, and is partitioned off, leaving the church with more workable proportions. The ancient leather chair, with carved, gilded arms and legs and the national *mburcuyá* flower painted on its back, was sat in by Pope John Paul II when he went to Encarnación on 18 May 1988. There are 22 carved statues down both sides of the church, and though not of the quality of those in Santa María or Trinidad, there are a number of interesting pieces. Among those worthy of note are Cosmas and Damian (two big figures displayed together to the right of the altar), St Michael (a very feminine archangel, with a clearly hermaphrodite devil), the risen Christ (displayed as the central piece behind the altar), and St Isidore (with a short, flared tunic and a hoe). The figures of St Joseph and St Barbara were stolen in 2003, when the church was broken into at night, but fortunately recovered in 2007.

The building set at right angles to the church is the complex known as the *colegio*, though it also comprises a dining room, cellar and kitchen (in the corner), workshops, grain store (on the upper storey) and 18th-century latrines (outside and at the very end, out of sight). There are original painted ceilings, one original door (and the rest restored to match), some original wrought-iron window bars, some remains of original shutters, a painted cupboard, and a stone bearing the date 1764 (four years before the Jesuits were expelled). There is access up an ancient steep staircase to the high upper storey – this is the only building left from the Guaraní missions that has a second floor – where the huge *lapacho* floorboards, 12cm thick, are impressive. You can look out from the little windows towards the River Paraná, but this is not an ascent for those with no head for heights, as part of the floor is missing. There is a back entrance to the building, with stone steps, for people arriving from the river some 1,800m away.

The famous sundial is marked in 15-minute sections, and does not know summer time. The slight inaccuracies that have crept in over the years are due to visitors exerting pressure on the apparatus and the metal bar distorting.

Extensive restoration work was carried out in 1989–91, carefully following the original design. As recently as 2008, 15 painted ceiling panels were cleaned and returned to their original position. The church is still used as the local parish church, and the weekly mass is on Sunday morning at 08.00.

In keeping with the Reduction's history as an **astronomical centre**, the visit to the Reduction was complemented in March 2010 with a small planetarium, and a high-quality professional telescope for star-watching. There is also a multimedia centre, the Centro de Interpretación Astronómica Buenaventura Suárez (in honour of the Jesuit astronomer), where films are shown on astronomical themes. With these three new attractions – the multimedia centre, planetarium and observatory – San Cosme y Damián has received some ten times the number of visitors that it had before, and the visit has at least doubled in length, deserving a full afternoon and evening, or, alternatively, evening and the following morning. In either case you will need to spend the night, so as to see the stars by night, though it is disappointing if it turns out to be a cloudy night when nothing can be seen.

In the multimedia centre you will handle a heavy black meteorite and learn about Suárez's book *Lunario de un Siglo*, published in 1748 and recently republished in a facsimile edition. Among the films are ones that show the traditional mythology of the Guaraní in relation to the stars. For example, the Milky Way was the path of the tapir (*mboreví rapé*) treading every night the same path of dry leaves that shine as stars; eclipses were seen as blue jaguar (*jaguar jhový*) taking the sun or the moon in its mouth; Orion's belt was seen as three widows of war, a mother and her two daughters, later with Christian influence interpreted as the 3 Marys who stood at the foot of the cross; and the famous Southern Cross (symbol of Mercosur) is the footprint of the rhea (*ñandú pysá*), with its three toes and its heel (the African ostrich has two toes). A number of these films are available in English but due to the number of visitors to the centre it would be necessary to book a time in advance for showing an English version of a film.

The planetarium can accommodate 30–40 people, sitting in a circle, and the movement of the stars in different seasons is demonstrated on the domed screen. A group of young people from the locality were trained by astronomer Blas Servín during an 11-month course, at the end of which the best five were selected to be guides, and their knowledge is impressive as they identify constellations with a special torch, in what to the visitor appears just a formless mass of stars.

The telescope magnifies 3,000 times what can be seen by the naked eye. Only one person can look through the telescope at a time, but it is worth waiting for as this is a rare opportunity that you may find nowhere else. Among other features, the guide may show you the stars Sirius and Canopus – the brightest stars that can be seen from the earth – and planets such as Mars, Jupiter, Venus, depending on the month of the year: you can see the rings around Saturn. For detailed information about astronomy and the centre in San Cosme y Damián, see www.astropar.org.

Another small attraction in this visitor centre is a kind of astrolabe called an armillary sphere (*esfera armilar*) which shows the movement of the circles of the heavens around the earth. There are only a few of this kind of astrolabe in the world.

Another attraction of San Cosme, and one that needs even more time, is a river excursion by motorboat to the **sand dunes** of Isla Ybycuí. The Río Paraná in this area swells out to an immense width of over 30km, and the island represents the remains of a sandy hill way out in the middle, which is being slowly worn down by wind, rain and waves. It used to be an impressive 30m high, tailing off into a series of little islets of sand surrounded by water, but it is constantly shrinking, because the sand is very fine. There are various boats, some taking ten people (Gs600,000) and some taking five (Gs500,000), but only on very busy days can you join a boat that is already travelling – usually you have to form your group beforehand. Because of the distance it takes 45 minutes to an hour to reach the island: allow four hours for the round trip, and take any food, chairs, umbrellas, etc that you wish to use. Departures are usually at 08.00 and 13.00, or at other times by arrangement. It is recommended that you leave very early in the morning, but rough water can delay departure. Contact Carolina Ibarra (m *0985 110047*) for details.

Another visit of interest is to a **Guaraní indigenous community** of today, the Pindó village, which you drive through on the road to San Cosme. It is situated 7.5km from Ruta 1. Profesor Brigido Bogado (m *0984 222780;* e *pindocentrocultural@gmail.com; Gs10,000 per person*) is the teacher in their primary school, an author and a poet, and speaks excellent Spanish. Let him know a few days in advance and he can arrange a display of dance and of craft, as well as giving a historical introduction, including the deprivations that the community suffered when they were relocated as a result of the Yacyretá dam, and perhaps a talk about natural medicine too. The craft is in wood and beads, and the most typical products are small wooden animals and birds: jaguars, armadillos, caimans, toucans, owls and parrots, which are delightful and inexpensive souvenirs.

CARMEN DEL PARANÁ

Just 12km from General Bogado is the town of Carmen de Paraná, variously known as the rice capital, the cradle of independence (because the battle of Tacuarí was fought here, see page 12), and as the crucible of the races (because of immigration from Germany, Poland, Japan, Korea and elsewhere). If you are approaching from Asunción, you turn right at the junction where there is a turn left for Fram. Carmen sticks out like a shoe into the river, and has a coast road and a beach. There is a museum in the old railway station (*0762 260300;* m *0985 251037;* *08.00–noon & 13.00–17.00 Tue–Fri, 14.00–17.00 Sat & Sun*), with rooms devoted to the history of the town and the railway, and a tourist office. It also has three beaches and three *posadas*: Pytu'u (m *0984 929528*), Bon Descanso (m *0985 702930*) and LUAMS (m *0985 835672*).

TRINIDAD

Municipalidad 071 270165; www.turismojesusytrinidad.com.py

The importance of the Ruins of Trinidad and Jesús has already been stressed. This is where the 'Lost Paradise' of the Jesuit-Guaraní Reductions (1609–1768) can be dreamed about, with the inspiration of so many angels carved in stone. This is the land which has inspired so many hundreds of writers all over the world to produce books and articles, plays and films. The bibliography on the Reductions runs into thousands of items, and the conference known as Jornadas Internacionales sobre las Misiones Jesuíticas attracts hundreds of scholars every time it meets.

HISTORY La Santísima Trinidad del Paraná – 'the most holy Trinity of the (River) Paraná', to give it its full title – was one of the last of the Treinta Pueblos to be founded (in 1706, by P Juan de Anaya). It was a daughter-foundation of San Carlos, in what is now Misiones, Argentina. (San Carlos was also the name of Fr Gabriel's Reduction in the film *The Mission*.) Trinidad was first located near the

River Uruguay, but moved to its present position in 1712, just six years after its foundation. The only Jesuit-Guaraní Reduction founded subsequently was Santo Ângelo in 1707, in present-day Brazil.

The most distinctive feature of Trinidad is its use of stone for building, which has left us with beautiful ruins, while the earlier Reductions built in adobe and wood perished. There are two churches, and the bigger one – the *iglesia mayor* – is the triumphant work of the Milanese Jesuit architect Giovanni Battista Primoli (1643–1747), known as Juan Bautista Primoli in Paraguay. He arrived in the Río de la Plata region in 1717 and began his work by overseeing the completion of the cathedral in Córdoba, Argentina. He died at Candelaria (the capital of the Reductions, in what is now Misiones, Argentina) in 1747, and it is likely that the work on the Trinidad church was then carried on by the Jesuit architects who were working in the nearby Jesús (see pages 256–9), Antonio Forcada and Juan Antonio de Ribera.

The population of Trinidad reached 5,000 in its prime, and there were 30 *caciques* and herds of 25,000 cattle. (To give meat to 5,000 people at a time they needed to slaughter 30 cattle.) The first philharmonic choir of the Río de la Plata region came from Trinidad, and was functioning in the early 1730s, a few years after the great Jesuit composer Domenico Zipoli arrived in South America (1726) and began writing masses and antiphons. There was a huge choir of 200 children.

There were only a dozen Jesuit priests in total who lived in Trinidad (four of them died there), and there were never more than two or at the most three at a time in any Reduction. The parish priest shortly before the 1768 Expulsion was Fr Pierpaolo Danesi (another Italian, like Primoli from Milan, in Trinidad 1759–63), who had an interest in clock making, sculpture and the use of precious stones: it was Danesi who completed the reconstructed dome, the frieze of angels, the bell tower of the church, and other internal decorations. He died on the journey of the expelled Jesuits back to Europe. When Trinidad was taken over by Asunción, its spiritual life was placed in the hands of the Franciscans, but the decline was immediate and rapid, and 35 years after the Expulsion the Guaraní had abandoned the place.

There was some excavation of the church and the *colegio* as early as 1973 under the Italian-Venezuelan Graciano Gasparini, but the principal work was carried out in 1981–90 under the Italian Roberto di Stefano, when the discovery of the Ruins hit the national press. Some work was done on the friezes in 1985 by Juan Benavides.

GETTING THERE AND AWAY If you continue on Ruta 1 from Coronel Bogado you will arrive in Encarnación (see pages 268–76) within an hour, and from the bus terminal there you can catch another **bus** to Trinidad, which is only 30km away on Ruta 6 – the road that ends up eventually at Ciudad del Este. Some buses are very slow and take over an hour, so ask which is the best one to take for Trinidad, and you should be there in 30 minutes. A few buses continue on from Ruta 1 to Ruta 6, passing through the terminal of Encarnación on the way. Approximate times from San Ignacio are: Ortega 07.00; Ñeembucú 09.00; Beato Roque Gonzalez 13.45; Alborada 16.35.

Buses leave the terminal in Encarnación at least every hour, and if you ask to be dropped at the ruins (*las ruinas*) you will have only a ten-minute walk up the road on the right-hand side to reach them. You cannot miss them. There is a huge sign on the main road, on the far side of the town, next to a big electricity plant with lots of pylons.

But if you are in your own **car**, there is another route to the Ruins that is slightly quicker, because it bypasses the city completely. At Carmen del Paraná (see page 247), 12km beyond Coronel Bogado, you turn left, and drive for 28km as straight as a die through agricultural land, passing the Norwegian town of Fram (the wheat capital),

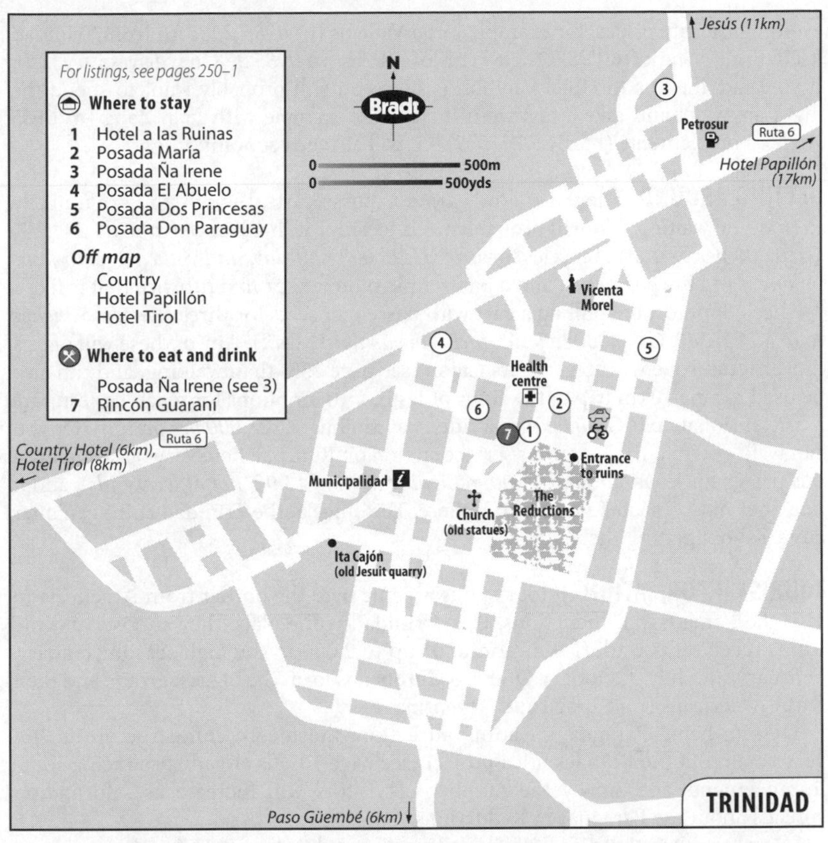

and then turn right towards Ruta 6. Do not take the first turn marked to Ruta 6, which is cobbled for over 20km, because there is a better one afterwards, which is asphalted – 'Calle M', on the right after the Upisa factory. It comes out between Capitán Miranda and Trinidad, at the Texaco service station and just before the Hotel Tirol (see pages 250–1), which is a good place to have lunch or stop for the night.

After you have gone through Fram, if you carry straight on instead of turning right for Ruta 6, you pass through the Japanese colonies of La Paz and Pirapó. Eventually you join up with Ruta 6 on the far side of Bella Vista. This route is sometimes called the Graneros del Sur (the Granaries of the South).

If you want to withdraw money on the way to the Ruins, then you may want to pass through Encarnación, for its banking facilities, rather than take the alternative route through Fram. But there are also **cash machines** 9km to the north of Trinidad, in the Colonias Unidas (see pages 259–60). There are no facilities yet for exchange or cash withdrawal in either Trinidad or Jesús.

Another way of doing the journey is to take a **taxi** for the day. This has the advantage that it takes you effortlessly to both Trinidad and Jesús, saves your energy for walking around the ruins (which on a hot day is quite exhausting), and between the two sites whisks you away for a nice lunch at either Hotel Tirol or Hotel Papillón. The disadvantage is that from Encarnación it is a bit expensive – for example, around US$100 or Gs500,000 with the taxi driver from Encarnación Miguel Benitez (**m** *0985 784634*). You can cut the cost by using a taxi from closer to the ruins and avoiding the city prices, for example Jorge Vallejos (m *0985 208446*) from Trinidad itself, Emilio Stark (m *0982 223984*) or José Rojas (m *0985 278765; drives very fast*). If you take the bus to Hotel Papillón (where you will probably want to spend the night anyway), and take a taxi from there – for example with Juan Zang (m *0985 707667*) or Clemente (m *0985 741039*) – it will also be economical.

GETTING AROUND There are now *karumbé* horse carts, though you are unlikely to find one waiting and will probably need to order it in advance (m *0985 143657; Gs10,000 per person*) , bicycles for hire (*Gs25,000 half-day, and you can get to Jesús on one if you are energetic*), and a panoramic mototaxi or *taxi turístico* that is like a 3-wheeled motorbike pulling a cart with passenger seats for three (*Andrés Sánchez* m *0985 922342; Gs70,000 to Jesús, including an hour's wait*). Any of these will offer a more picturesque way to get to Itá Cajón (see page 255) than walking, and can also be used for the 10km trip to the ruins of Jesús. Other options for reaching Jesús are a conventional taxi (*Gs80,000*) or a ride in a minibus (*Gs25,000 per person*). Or you can walk down to the Petrobras service station on Ruta 6, where very occasionally a bus passes for Jesús (*around 11.00, returning around 13.00, not at weekends*), and if one does not come, take a taxi from there. The office at the Trinidad ruins can offer advice about getting there.

TOURIST INFORMATION If tourist buses come over the border from Argentina to visit the Paraguayan Reductions, then Trinidad is the place they choose, and the Ruins receive 1,000 tourists a month, or up to 2,000 in the high season (January, February, and July–October). Of these, Europeans form the biggest group, and then Latin Americans from Brazil and Argentina.

Despite being Paraguay's leading attraction, the tourist infrastructure is still very small. But the Ruta Jesuítica project (see page 185) is already producing some improvements and slowly the number of visitors will increase as information spreads about the Paraguayan Reductions.

In early January there is a fiesta in a village 6km behind the Ruins, to the southeast, called **Paso Güembé**, where a prize is given for the largest watermelon grown. They usually reach the 20–21kg mark, and the largest ever exhibited weighed 27kg.

WHERE TO STAY AND EAT *Map, page 249.*

Hotel Papillón (40 rooms) Ruta 6 km45, Bella Vista, Itapúa; 0767 240235/240280; m 0985 784846; www.papillon.com.py. About 15km from Trinidad & despite the distance is most people's top choice for a hotel near the ruins. It is certainly a lot busier than either Hotel Tirol or Hotel a las Ruinas. Large bedrooms. As well as volleyball, basketball, tennis, ping-pong & a pool, the garden has a giant chess set where you can walk around the board as you play. Excellent buffet for only Gs55,000 (Sun Gs65,000) & even better à la carte menu. Awarded prize as successful small business by ADEC (Association of Christians in Business). **$$$**

Country Hotel (8 rooms) Ruta 6 km23,5 de Encarnación; m 0981 239468; e 0981874337@tigo.com.py; www.country-hotel.blogspot.com. A German-run family hotel, too far from Trinidad to walk to the ruins, but handily close if you have a vehicle. Set on a slope by the main road where you cannot miss it, to the south of Trinidad shortly before the *peaje* (toll point). You have to pass the *peaje* on the way & pay the toll, but it is only Gs10,000. It also advertises itself as a hostel, so check if you need to share rooms or bathrooms. Kitchen facilities, volleyball, squash, pool, camping. You can lunch here better & possibly more economically than at nearby Hotel Tirol, sitting at a table by a fountain under the pine trees, although their prices for rooms have now overtaken Tirol's. **$$$**

Hotel Tirol (60 rooms) Ruta 6 km20, Capitán Miranda, Itapúa; 071 202388/211053; e reservas@hoteltirol.com.py; www.hoteltirol.com.

py. About 10km (& 10mins) before Trinidad, this older hotel is an enjoyable place to stay, opened in 1958 & expanded in 1970. Set in wooded park behind the brick archway that comes up on the right after you leave Encarnación, well signed & beautifully designed, though dated now in its décor. There are 4 swimming pools laid out on a hillside with the rooms opening onto the pool area. It is quiet, with a spectacular view & big palm trees. The main disadvantage – for the less able – is the large number of steps between the dining area & the bedroom area, though the variety of levels is fun for the young. The restaurant food is a bit dull. Slightly cheaper than Papillón, but not much. **$$**

Hotel a las Ruinas (5 rooms) **m** 0985 828563. Located right outside the ruins of Trinidad, but has a 1-star rating on TripAdvisor, so the *posadas* are to be preferred at present. However, it is not a bad place to sit & have a drink & look at the Ruins. **$$**

Posada María (2 rooms) **m** 0985 769 812; **e** mohr.mariaester@yahoo.com.ar. Just a couple of blocks from the entrance to the Ruins, this attractive *posada* is recommended for those who do not have their own transport & want to stay overnight in Trinidad. One double room & 1 with 2 beds, both with private bathroom, Wi-Fi. Lunch or dinner can be served for Gs30,000. **$$**

Posada Ña Irene (4 rooms) **m** 0985 748308. Restaurant which also has rooms, on other side of Ruta 6, 3 blocks along the road that leads to Jesús. Shared bathroom, AC, TV. Has restaurant. **$$**

Posada El Abuelo (2 rooms) **m** 0985 749187. The rooms for guests are in a separate, pretty wooden house, with bathroom just for them. AC, 4 blocks from the road leading to the Ruins on Ruta 6. **$$**

Posada Dos Princesas (2 rooms) **m** 0985 731423. Just off the road that leads from Ruta 6 to the Ruins. Cheese, ham, cake & orange juice for b/fast. **$$**

Posada Don Paraguay (2 rooms) **m** 0985 173 598. 80m from the Ruins, with pool, bathroom used only by the guests but shared between the 2 rooms. **$**

WHERE TO EAT AND DRINK *Map, page 249.*

In addition to Ña Irene (see above), **Rincón Guaraní** (**m** *0983 657598;* **$$**) is a new restaurant just along from the Hotel a las Ruinas. It has a lively feel to it and offers anything from *empanadas* and hamburgers to bœuf stroganoff and grilled chicken. You can also go in just for a drink.

WHAT TO SEE AND DO

The Ruins of Trinidad

(*summer 07.00–19.00 or until it is dark; Paseo Nocturno Thu–Sun , winter 19.30, summer 20.30; foreigners Gs25,000, Paraguayans Gs15,000, local people Gs5,000; same ticket can be used for day visit and paseo nocturne; ticket is valid for Jesús & San Cosme y Damián too at no extra charge and lasts for 3 days; debit and credit cards accepted*) The Ruins are on the northern edge of the town. There is no landline on site currently functioning, but there are good guides with mobile phones who you can ring for information. One of the best guides, Crystian Arevalos (**m** *0982 603819;* **e** *crystiancna@hotmail.com*), speaks English. He works 13.00–22.00 except Wednesdays, but can sometimes be booked for other times on request. Other guides are Edgar Paredes (**m** *0985 772803*), Kristian Zarza (**m** *0985 712979*), Ramón Olazar (**m** *0985 722033*) and Carlos Sotelo (**m** *0985 729862*).

Trinidad is the most evocative of the ruined Jesuit-Guaraní sites due to its wonderful surviving stone carvings, and the magical isolation of the site. One of the advantages of the Paraguayan Mission route being less frequented than the Argentinian and Brazilian Reductions is that it leaves more room to dream and less room for tourist tat. Brazil's tourist infrastructure in Missões is very tasteful, and Argentina's is quite pleasant, but there is nothing quite like the experience of standing alone on the brink of Trinidad's vast plaza, and then setting off to explore. You begin by walking through the arched colonnades of the *casas de indios* and crossing the huge expanse of grass towards the big church on the far side; then make your way up the nave, past the souls in the flames of purgatory on your right where the Guaraní kept night watch over their dead, past the great pulpit of the four evangelists on the left where sermons were preached in the native tongue, and into the sanctuary. There, high above your head, but clearly discernible, 46 angels play the music of heaven, just as the Guaraní had played the same instruments in the church below.

The map near the entrance shows the **typical layout** of a Reduction, with a central plaza; *casas de indios* in parallel rows on three sides of the plaza; the church opening onto the fourth side of the plaza, with a cloister on one side, including the priests' house, college and workshops; the orchard behind it; the cemetery on the other side of the church; the bell tower next to the church; and the *kotý guasú* (house for widows and orphans) close to the cloister. What is different about Trinidad is that it had two churches: the earlier church was still pretty large, though not as big as the later triumphant work. The bell tower that you see (and that appeared on the cover of the first edition of this book) is not the one that stood at the corner of the *iglesia mayor* but the one that was close to the *iglesia primitiva*. It is sometimes called the Torre de Atalaya, or the **watchtower**, to distinguish it from the Primoli-Danesi bell tower in the corner of the *iglesia mayor*, of which there is now only a stump. (Both were of stone, unlike the wooden constructions standing that were typical of the earlier period.)

All the Reductions were built around a large **plaza**, but the plaza of Trinidad is particularly vast, measuring 200m from east to west, and 130m from north to south. This space was used for religious processions, sporting and theatrical events, as well as for the whipping of criminals. A colonnade ran all around this long building, and in the case of Trinidad it had stone Roman (ie: round-topped) arches, with a *mburucuyá* flower carved above every junction of the arches.

The ***casas de indios*** are a feature of Trinidad, as they are relatively well preserved (compared with other Reductions). Originally there were 21 blocks around the Plaza Mayor, and eight still remain as ruins: the Roman arches of their colonnades are intact on a number of these. Each block comprises between six and eight square rooms, each one for a family, with a front and back door. The rooms measured 5m x 5.7m and the walls are 80cm thick. You can still see the carved stone rosette between the arches, and pick out the form, with nine separate rooms in each block – each room the home for a different family. They were originally roofed with large tiles known as *tejas coloniales* or *tejas musleras*, because they were moulded on a man's thigh, but later on the tiles were moulded on the trunk of the *cocotero* tree, to get a more uniform size. (The downside of installing the lights for the Luz y Sonido in 2009 – see below – is that these houses are now cluttered up with cables and reflectors, which reduces the magic by day, although it adds to the magic by night: there are 16,000m of electrical, sound and video cables now strewn around the site.)

The great **church** (*iglesia mayor*) – Primoli's church – is on the south side, and is 85m long, 43m wide (including the colonnades) and 14m high (though originally the roof would have risen another 8m or so above this level). The discovery in 1759 of lime in a quarry 2km away enabled more ambitious architecture than had been possible earlier. This church in Trinidad was described by P Jaime Oliver (parish priest of Santa María de Fe at the time of the Expulsion) as 'the biggest and best of all the Missions; built entirely in stone, with a very beautiful dome, cupola and lantern of the dome; all done with great clarity, proportion and decoration. The façade and tower are superb. In short the whole work has turned out without equal in all that part of America and is even much to be envied in the principal cities of Europe.'

The church **bell tower** to the right of the façade – not to be confused with the watchtower that was a distance away – had a clock, according to the inventory at the time of the Expulsion, which was the work of P Danesi, in 1763. Trinidad was famous for bells, and had a foundry, which made bells from both iron and bronze. The bell tower of this main church had 12 bells of different sizes – some made here and others in San Juan Bautista (now known by its Portuguese name São João, being in Brazil).

The church originally had a barrel vault roof, 14m high, which was made of stone and brick, and on the exterior was covered with colonial tiles. The 1768 inventory records many side altars and reredos of gilded wood, which have been lost with time – either sacked, or destroyed by the elements.

The huge **dome** of this ambitious church, which was 24m high, collapsed twice. The first time was before the Expulsion, probably sometime between 1750 and 1756, when it fell down one night. We know the problem was the soft, porous sandstone, and the most likely theory is that the stones fell because they filled up with rainwater and doubled their weight. In the rebuild, bricks were used instead of stone, and the newly discovered lime facilitated a stronger construction. Despite this, the rebuilt dome did not last as it should have done, because after the Expulsion stones were looted from the colonnades and flying buttresses, and without this counter-tension, the dome collapsed for a second time in 1775. With the lime reinforcement it now dragged down part of the walls with it. It was never rebuilt.

The **floor** we see today is original, and beneath the centre nave were found human remains: it seems the priests were buried in the crypt – at least until their bodies could be shipped back to their home country – while the *caciques* of the *cabildo* were buried under the floor of the church, but in a foetal position in huge pots. A design of scales carved into a stone on the floor above such a grave refers to the judgement expected from God. The ordinary indigenous were buried in the cemetery to the left of the church. In a niche on the exterior is an intact stone statue of **St Paul**, with his sword, but the 12 apostles who were set in niches along the nave have been decapitated by looters who mistakenly believed that the Jesuits had hidden gold inside the soft sandstone statues.

To the right as you enter is an altar with a stone evocation of **purgatory** set above it, showing souls in flames. (In traditional Guaraní religion there was a belief in hell, which was known as *añereta*.) Dead bodies were laid out on the floor in front of this purgatory on the day before they were buried. To the left you come to the baptistery, which has a fine stone **font**, carved with the Latin baptismal formula *In nomine Patris et Filii et Spiritus Sancti* and the date 1720 (before Primoli arrived). This font was discovered buried and it is virtually intact.

As you pass up the nave you come to a beautiful, red-stone **pulpit** – all the more remarkable when you learn that this has been reconstructed out of 600 shattered fragments, though originally it had been carved out of a single stone block. It bears the symbols of the four evangelists: the angel for St Matthew, the lion for St Mark, the ox for St Luke and the eagle for St John.

At the top of the church is a large stone, carved with leaves, the *mburucuyá* flower, and large *perdiz* birds (usually translated 'partridge' but more accurately, the tinamou), which serves as the main altar: other sections of this altar, with the same design, are preserved in the cloister outside. Mass is still celebrated here on special occasions, and musicians from the Orquesta Filomúsica, together with the **Zipoli Octet**, will sometimes come from Asunción to play and sing some of the music written for the Reductions, in the context of a mass. There is no better way of experiencing the mystery of these sacred ruins.

The church originally had three internal balconies: one over the entrance, and two at the sides where children played musical instruments. High on the wall of the transepts, above the level of the frieze, are ornate windows with flying angels carved in stone. But the most remarkable and lovely feature of this church is the

frieze of angels playing musical instruments, high up around all the area of the altar and the transepts, silently and permanently echoing the music of the church. A line of angels symmetrically flanks the Virgin on each wall – shown either at the crib, or standing on the moon. Some angels are swinging incense, others playing violins and harps, trumpets and organs, bassoons and clavichords, and the *maraca*, which was a Guaraní rattle – a gourd filled with seeds. Both frieze and pulpit can be attributed to Danesi's direction.

The interior of the church was filled with **paintings** by the Catalan Jesuit Brother José Grimau, who also worked on the church of Jesús (see pages 257–8). There were originally four side altars on each side of the church, and 24 niches with statues. While the basic construction of the church was completed in six years, with 500 workers, it continued to be worked on throughout the life of the mission, with final details being added to the interior, until the 1768 Expulsion put an end to the work, leaving some side altars still to be completed.

There are two sacristies – the one on the left for the children's choir, and the one on the right for the priests – and their doorways are also surrounded by grand carved designs of pillars and pedestals, of leaves and flying angel heads. When you enter the right-hand sacristy today you find a one-room **museum** packed full of carved stones and fragments of lettering. There is a wealth of *mburucuyá* flowers and angel heads, and a fine carved stone niche, rather like the one in the 'secondary chapel' at Jesús (see page 258). There is also a modern-day model of the Reduction.

Exiting the church through the sacristy you come to the **cloister** with the *colegio*, which would have had the usual cluster of priests' rooms, school and workshop buildings set out around the patio. Some of these workshop rooms had adobe walls – now reduced to just heaps of earth – but there are some good floors intact with octagonal tiles. In the central space of the cloister, some underground and overground drainage channels have been cut: the Jesuits were expert at channelling water systems.

There is a striking stone statue of a **woman with a fan** on the pavement to the right of the church – one facet of a column, with a different figure on each side, but this side is the most easily discernible. It is not known who she represents, but she is likely to be a saint. In the shadow of the colonnade here you find another fine collection of carved remains, including a gargoyle, more fragments of the high altar, and a couple of fine angel supports.

The second church in Trinidad is also of a good size though much simpler in design and unadorned. It was built earlier and is known as the ***iglesia primitiva***. It was used while the big church was under construction, and again when the Primoli dome collapsed. The Franciscans used this church after the Expulsion.

It may be difficult to pick out the other features of this Reduction: the *kotý guasú* (next to the cloister), a reservoir for storing rainwater (in the middle of the *huerta* or orchard), a quarry (*cantera*) and a *barbacuá* (oven for drying *yerba mate*, now on private land).

A long-awaited **Paseo Nocturno** (Night Walk) was inaugurated in 2009 and operates immediately after nightfall from Thursday to Sunday. It is not really a Son et Lumiére type of light show, but a nocturnal, illuminated walk, and provides an experience of the Ruins quite different from that of daytime. The two churches, watchtower and *casas de indios* are floodlit, and 185 small lights sunk into the ground provide just enough light to find your way around, while sounds emit from 100 loudspeakers in different areas of the site – mostly music, but also birdsong and household activities – to give the effect of life going on in the Reduction, and atmospheric photographs are projected onto the walls of the *iglesia mayor*. If you are there on the right days, do not miss this beautiful experience.

The statues of Trinidad Marvellous as Trinidad is, it is still better when you discover that there are some 17 carved wooden statues of outstanding quality kept in the modern parish church, a five-minute walk away around the perimeter fence. The guides do not customarily mention these treasures, because it can be awkward to arrange access, so if you can, arrange it advance (*try* **m** *0985 810053*), but if you cannot, do not be deterred from asking on the day. As always, do not omit to tip if someone comes out specially. But you may be lucky and find the church open anyway. Sunday mass is at 08.00 and the church stays open all morning.

The only well-known carving here is a **painted wooden Trinity**, about 1m high, displayed in a painted niche. This piece is of considerable interest not only because it is the icon of this place named Trinity but also because it is the finest example of a distinctive style of portraying the three divine persons that is typically Paraguayan and at the same time deeply theological. (There are other examples in the Museo del Barro in Asunción.) The Son stretches out his arms on the cross in total self-giving, and the Father above him stretches out his arms in a complementary and parallel movement. Between the two – fruit of the cross and at the same time springing from the Father's heart – the dove extends its wings in parallel motion. And so the persons of the Blessed Trinity are shown in perfect balance. The expressions on the faces, the painted details of wounds, and the co-ordinated colour scheme of yellow, red and brown, make this a mystical and poignant piece, despite some damage to noses, hands and feet.

In early 2006 this figure was stolen, but fortunately it was recovered a few months later, in extraordinary circumstances. The story is that there was a gang of three: after the robbery, one thief died in an accident, and then the second died too, and the third thief became so fearful of divine vengeance for the crime, that he confessed. The image was recovered from the banks of the Río Paraná, where it had been buried underground, waiting to be smuggled over the river.

All the statues in the church are of high artistic quality, similar to, and as good as some of the statues in Santa María de Fe and San Ignacio. For example, a Virgin standing on the moon with the child Jesus at her feet (rather than in her arms); another more static Virgin whose child emerges out of the triangular shape of her robe (a more sophisticated version of the figure in the little chapel of San Ignacio); the crucifix (with a golden dove launching into flight from the top of the cross); and a Christ in the coffin with his sensitive face streaked with blood. Finally, there is another work quite distinctive to Trinidad showing two very large figures from another Trinity (though this time the Spirit is missing from the group). This is the Father, with the Son seated on his right hand in heaven.

Itá Cajón The former stone quarry of the Jesuits has now been opened for visits (**m** *0985 726971/0985 301098; foreigners Gs20,000; Paraguayans Gs10,000;* ⌚ *07.00–17.00 daily*), and is 700m away from the Ruins, passing through the village of Trinidad, and 500m from Ruta 6. The staff may be willing to stay open longer if you contact them in advance. A guide shows you the cliff from where the stone was cut out in step-like blocks, and you can see the long, exposed roots of an extraordinary tree called the *guapo'y*, running from the top of the cliff wall to the bottom – some 6m or more in height. There is an extensive area of 6ha where you can walk. The site has been attractively presented with native plants and is worth visiting if time does not press after visiting the Ruins.

Craft It is well worth visiting the workshop of the sculptor Vicenta Morel (**m** *0985 726971*), who does high quality work in wood and stone – especially large stone pieces made up of several panels, and copies of the angel musicians from the frieze in the church. To reach her workshop turn sharp right immediately after you have turned off Ruta 6 by the big sign to the Ruins, and it is about the fifth house along the track that runs parallel to, and very close to, the main road.

Capilla San Antonio Fanatics of the Reductions may be interested in this Jesuit-Guaraní ruined chapel, in an isolated, overgrown site 3.1km from Ruta 6, on the Encarnación side of the *peaje* (toll point), which is 5km before you reach Trinidad. Take the little road that bears west just to the south side of the *peaje* – that is, on the other side of the toll point from the two motels El Bosque and Tiger's, and on the other side of the road. When you get to the crest of the hill, there will be a notice on your right reading 'Agrogandera YSAKA…' and the tiny chapel is close to the road on the left-hand side. A temporary roof has been added to make the chapel usable, and inside there is a little altar lavishly decked with artificial flowers and a picture of St Anthony. The dry stone walling is almost all intact – though gone a bit wavy and gappy – and you can observe simple capitals at the top of columns and walls inside.

JESÚS

Copaco ☎ 071 270200; municipalidad ☎ 071 270150 www.turismojesusytrinidad.com.py

The first Jesús was founded in 1685 some 200km to the east, on the banks of the River Monday. The founders were two Spanish Jesuits: P Francisco García and P Gerónimo Delfín. Its first move was in 1691 to the area of the Río Ibaretý; then it moved again to the Río Mandisoví and Capybarý. By 1731 the population had reached 2,400. But Jesús did not settle on the present site until 1758 or 1759, only ten years before the Expulsion.

The result is that Jesús was never completed – though 3,000 indigenous are said to have worked on the construction. According to another theory, 3,000 was the population of the town at its present site. In fact, its full name is Jesús Tavarangué, which means 'what was going to be the town of Jesús'. (In Guaraní, *táva* means 'village', *-rã* means 'going to be', and *–ngue* means 'in the past'.) It has been called (by the Jesuit historian P Bartomeu Meliá) 'the pilgrim *pueblo*'. Most of the Reductions moved once or twice, but Jesús was just beginning to settle down when the end came.

The inventory at the time of the 1768 Expulsion records fields of sugar cane, two plantations of the *yerba mate* tree and seven cotton fields.

GETTING THERE AND AWAY Jesús is reached from Trinidad, and the ruins are 11.6km from Ruta 6, along a road that is now asphalted. Unless you are pressed for time, it would be a pity not to see both as they are so close, and although Jesús has less to explore, some people prefer it to Trinidad. If you are seeing both in the same day, you may prefer to go to Trinidad first, before you get too hot and tired, because it is generally considered the finer of the two. Or you may want to keep Trinidad for the cooler temperature of early evening, when it will be more comfortable to walk around.

For taking a **taxi** from Encarnación, see under Trinidad, pages 249–50. If you yourself are driving, you will see the sign to the Antigua Misión de Jesús de Tavarangué on Ruta 6, just 100m to the north of the entrance to the Trinidad ruins, but on the opposite side of the road, right by the Petrosur service station. If you are coming from the ruins of Trinidad, see page 250.

When you reach Jesús, drive straight through the village until you reach the Ruins, and then turn right to get to the entrance.

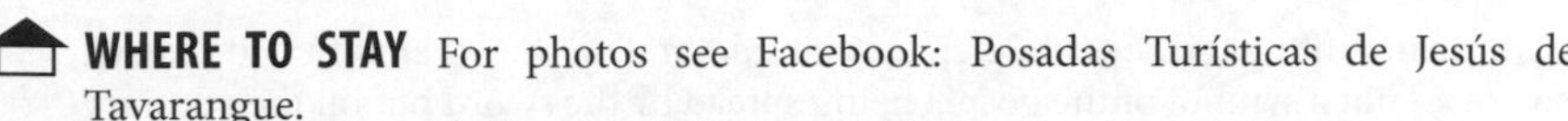

WHERE TO STAY For photos see Facebook: Posadas Turísticas de Jesús de Tavarangue.

Posada el Profe (1 room with 2 beds) m 0985 704862. About 6 blocks from the ruins. Split AC, Wi-Fi. **$$**

Posada Fabiana (1 room) m 0985 714034. Two can sleep here. There is a shared bathroom. Look for the little wooden green house about 9 blocks from the ruins. **$$**

WHERE TO EAT AND DRINK Meals can be ordered for delivery from m 0985 256220, or you can go to the **Bar La Estrella**, 2 blocks from the ruins, or the **Hamburguesería Carol**, which also does delivery, one block from the plaza where the present parish church is.

WHAT TO SEE AND DO Although Jesús is still an active town, people only go to see one thing: the **Ruins of Jesús** (*021 3281752; summer 07.00–19.00, winter 07.00–18.00, daily; foreigners Gs25,000, Paraguayans Gs15,000, local people Gs5,000; ticket is valid for Trinidad & San Cosme y Damián too at no extra charge and lasts 3 days; debit and credit cards accepted*).

The ruins have a lovely setting, being on higher ground, with vistas of palm trees framed through the windows, and there is something almost Cistercian about their isolation and austerity. Guides come and go at Jesús, but one of the best informed is Lira Hein (m *0985 734340*). There are about 100 visitors a week to the Ruins at Jesús – around a quarter of the number that visit Trinidad.

The church and the college are the principal remains in this peaceful spot with its dramatic columns and vistas, though you can also pick out something of the whole layout of the town, according to the typical design of a Reduction. There is a plan on your left as you enter, mapping out the cemetery (to the left of the church), the orchard (behind it), and priests' house, college and workshops (to the right). The *casas de indios* were arranged in rows around the plaza, which no longer exists as a plaza, but is the long grassy space you cross before reaching the church, where you can rest halfway in the shade of some trees.

The architects were Brother José Grimau (who was also a painter), Brother Antonio Forcada (who died in 1767, the year before the Expulsion) and Brother Juan Antonio de Ribera (who was the son of a famous Spanish architect, Pedro de Ribera). The 59m x 24m **church** is not so much a ruin as never completed. The 11m walls are intact, but it never had more than a provisional roof, as there was not enough time before the Expulsion to complete the work with the three vaulted roofs that had been planned. Coming from the last period of architecture in the Reductions, the church is built in stone and consequently survived, while other churches built in adobe have long since collapsed. What helped even more was the discovery of the lime quarry: the use of lime in the construction has given us walls that have remarkably withstood the battering of the elements over the centuries.

The three **doorways** into the church have a touch of Moorish influence due to the fact that the three architects who worked on the building were all Spanish: they have a three-leaved form, similar to the mosque-cathedral in Córdoba, Spain. Two **niches** on the façade between them are beautifully adorned with plant motifs down the sides: the typical Paraguayan *mburucuyá* (passion flower, representing the Passion), the *fleur de lys* (representing purity) and the leaves of the *cocotero* palm (representing the Entry into Jerusalem). The domed top of the niche is carved to represent a shell (representing baptism). Above the niches you can see the papal tiara surmounting the keys of Peter, on one side, and on the other with two crossed swords – not a symbol of the gospel being spread by the sword but on the contrary of the right of this Catholic town, under the guardianship of the Pope, to carry arms in its own self-defence. In short, Church protection lent the Reduction both spiritual protection (the keys to the Kingdom of Heaven) and temporal protection. It is assumed that originally the one niche held a statue of St Peter, and the other a statue of St Paul (whose symbol is the sword – the implement of his martyrdom).

Entering the church, the baptistry opens off to the right, and has a hole in its domed roof, for a rope to pass through to ring the bell.

There are two rows of six **columns** down the nave, with a pulpit on both sides, placed on the fourth column. Flat against the wall are further rows of tapering columns, with capitals adorned with a palm-leaf design. The plaster on these flat columns is original, made of a mixture which included animal bones, eggshells and yellow clay. Looking out from the nave through the windows and doorways you see vistas of palm trees.

Set in the corner walls above the altar are heads of angels with wings – the very typical design of the Reductions – and below them stones with **date carvings**, one reading 'S. Fra.co de Asis 1776' – a reminder that the Reduction was put in Franciscan hands after the 1768 Expulsion of the Jesuits – and on the other side 'S.to Domingo de Gúzman 13 Febrero' – suggesting that Dominicans too may have had a spell in Jesús. The new regime was not successful, and within 70 years the population of the town had sunk to just 300. The church was never finished.

There are sacristies to the right and left of the main altar, where the holes for the beams can be seen, as these two rooms had their roofs in place before being abandoned. Behind the main altar is a room usually known as the **secondary chapel**. It has an attractively carved niche, topped with flying angels and with fleur de lys designs down the sides; originally this had a little sink in it for washing the sacred vessels used in the mass.

On the ground floor of the 15m **tower** that forms the right-hand front corner of the church was a baptistery with a little domed roof. An outside staircase leads up to the higher floors. You can climb to the top of the tower and there is a splendid view: on a clear day you can see as far as Trinidad. The ground floor of the tower (that the staircase bypasses) was said to be used as a storeroom or, according to another theory, as a cell for offenders: drunkenness and polygamy were some of the offences meriting punishment.

The priests' rooms, school and workshops were substantial rooms with a very wide colonnade, around what is labelled as the ***plaza privada***, the patio to the side of the church, in the standard form of a Reduction.

Two rows of ***casas de indios*** have been excavated. The colonnade goes round all four sides, and the end rooms were larger than the others, possibly designed for the *caciques* and their families. The original floors were 50cm below the current ground level.

The work of **restoration** of Jesús began in the 1960s and continued with increasing professionalism through the rest of the century. The walls were meticulously cleaned, and fungi, lichen and micro-organisms removed. A number of walls which were leaning or falling had to be resettled in their original positions. The tower was made safe for people to climb up and see the view. The whole site was fenced off and trees were planted around the perimeter. The gateway to the site was built in a style that echoed the doors into the church. In 1993 Jesús (along with Trinidad) was declared by UNESCO a World Heritage Site.

There are now *karumbé* rides on offer at Jesús, though you are unlikely to find one waiting and probably need to order it in advance (**m** *0985 774159; Gs10,000 per* *person*). The horse carts leave from the entrance to the ruins and cost Gs10,000 per person, and at least seven people can fit in.

There is a craft shop, **Artesanía Fide** (m *0992 410236*), in the block next to the Municipalidad, two blocks on from the Bar la Estrella. It sells a wide variety of items including *ñanduti, ao po'i*, leatherwork, woodcarvings, pottery and postcards.

If you have time and sufficient interest to persist, you may be able to gain access to the current **parish church**, (several minutes' walk away), which houses original statues from the Reduction, although they are not of the quality found in Trinidad or in the museums in Misiones. To do this you should ring to arrange it beforehand if possible (m *0985 948777*), and you will need to return to the plaza in the village centre, where the church is located. If you have not rung beforehand, call at the *casa parroquial* (to the left of the modern church), or out of hours call at the house of the key holder Daniela Ayala (on the corner, to the left of the school). As always, if you have the Spanish, do not hesitate to ask – people want to help – but also do not omit to tip if someone comes out specially.

COLONIAS UNIDAS

The Colonias Unidas is the name given to three towns with a high immigrant population: Hohenau, Obligado and Bella Vista. They were all founded by Germans or by Paraguayans of German descent. Unlike European countries, where immigrants are usually poorer and struggling to establish themselves, Paraguay depends heavily on better-educated and better-off immigrants for the development of its economy. The Germans and Ukrainians, and later the Japanese, who settled in this part of the country have helped stimulate successful cultivation of rice, soya, wheat and cotton through more efficient agricultural techniques and organisation, and there are a large number of food factories in this region.

HOHENAU *Copaco* ↘ *0775 232889; municipalidad* ↘ *0775 232206* Hohenau ('high meadow' in German) is called the Mother of the Colonies, as it was the first of the three towns, and is now the one with most facilities, including branches of the Universidad Nacional and the Universidad Católica, and a Children's Villages hospital (Aldea SOS). It has a statue of a settler with an axe, called the monument to the Hachero de Oro (Golden axeman) on the Avenida de los Fundadores, close to the Centro Cultural Edwin Krug (🕘 *07.00–11.00 Mon–Sat, 13.30–17.30 Mon–Fri; free admission*), where there is a small museum of things belonging to the first immigrants. These arrived in 1900 and were children of German parents, born in Mato Grosso Brazil; but after World War I there was a much greater migration from Germany.

 **Where to stay** There are a couple of little hotels here on Avenida de los Fundadores that are less than half the price of Hotel Papillón but still have air conditioning and televisions: Hotel Kuschel (*10 rooms; exactly opposite Casa de Cultura* ↘ *0775 232364;* **$$**) and Hotel Pillat (m *0975 603548;* **$$**) .

What to see and do

Parque Manantial (*Ruta 6 km35, Hohenau;* ↘ *0775 232250/232732:* m *0985 703500;* e *manantial@tigo.com.py; www.manantial.itapua.net; Gs10,000*) The Parque Manantial is a huge nature playground, clearly signed, only just off Ruta 6 on the Trinidad side of Hohenau, and reachable by public bus. Here you can play volleyball, ping-pong and billiards, swim and trampoline, go boating or cross the stream on a hanging bicycle, take a ride in a horse cart, tractor or lorry, visit a farm, a spring or a quarry, and if you get bored with all that then there is a Wi-Fi zone as well. You can camp in the park, or stay at the nearby Hotel Papillón (see page 250).

OBLIGADO *Copaco* ☎ *0717 20028; municipalidad* ☎ *0717 20026* Obligado is just to the west of Ruta 6, and runs on from Hohenau without any clear division. It is a German-run industrial town, founded in 1912, and now dominated by the enormous Colonias Unidas food factory. See *Other practicalities* below for information on cash machines. A good **restaurant** is Los Hermanos (*Ruta 6 km39;* ☎ *07752 32497;* **$**).

BELLA VISTA *Copaco* ☎ *0767 240400; municipalidad* ☎ *0767 240219* Bella Vista is the '*yerba mate* capital', and at the crossroads of Ruta 6 with Avenida General Marcial Samaniego there is a tall monument to *yerba mate* in the form of an enormous *guampa* and *bombilla* on a white concrete support. Because the town was founded by Germans coming from the Mato Grosso region of Brazil, the *guampa* has a Brazilian shape, with a pointed bottom.

If you go left (northwest) from here for 5km, you come to the **Selecta** factory of *yerba mate* (☎ *0767 240339;* **e** *comercial@selecta.com.py; www.selecta.com.py*), which welcomes visits and has guides. The visit lasts about an hour, and you can follow the progress of the leaf right from the *yerba* tree (*Ilex paraguariensis*) through its drying and toasting and milling and years of maturing, to its final packeting for the market in Paraguay, Uruguay, the USA and – surprisingly – Japan. Let Selecta know of your visit beforehand if possible, so they can prepare a little pack of freebies and pass the names to the guard on the gate. Another *yerba* factory is Pajarito, to the southeast of the crossroads (*Av M Samaniego c/ Corpus;* ☎ *0767 240240;* **e** *info@pajarito.com.py; www.pajarito.com.py*). They too offer visits, though in practice they do not respond as readily as Selecta to such a request.

Tourist information There is a tourist information office at the crossroads called Mate Róga (Guaraní 'Mate House'), and the town's most knowledgeable person on tourism, Carlos Mallo of Koati Turismo (**m** *0985 725530;* **e** *koatiturismo@gmail.com*) can often be found there, or else at his pizzeria, Patio Mix, one block before the Casa de Cultura (*Av Marcial Samaniego y 12 de octubre;* ☎ *0767 240696;* **$**).

Other practicalities Bella Vista is perhaps best known for its Hotel Papillón (see page 250), which has an excellent restaurant.

To find a **cash machine**, if you are coming from Trinidad, turn left at the Banco Itapúa in Hohenau (which does not yet have a cash machine) and right at the Avenida Osvaldo Tischler. When this reaches Obligado (there is no division between the two towns) it is called the Avenida Dr Francia, and on the left you will pass the Banco Regional cash machine, which takes debit as well as credit cards, and a little later on the same side the BBVA, which takes Visa. There is another Banco Regional cash machine at the crossroads in Bella Vista (five blocks beyond the Hotel Papillón).

A small local industry is that of **macadamia nuts** – the round light nut often found inside a chocolate coating, which is rich in Omega 3 fatty acids and reduces cholesterol. Jars under the brandname Macbella can be bought from Mate Róga (see above).

EXCURSION TO SAN IGNACIO MINÍ

www.misionesturismo.com.ar; www.misiones-jesuiticas.com.ar; www.elbastion.com/ruinas

Note: This section contains prices in Argentinian pesos. These were accurate at the time of writing, but are highly subject to change due to monetary instability and inflation.

For many people, the reason for their trip to Paraguay is to visit the famous Paraguayan Reductions – the Jesuit missions for the indigenous that flourished between 1610 and 1768, when the Jesuits were expelled. But the old area of the Treinta Pueblos now spreads outside Paraguay, into Misiones Argentina and Missões Brazil. In Misiones Argentina the much-visited Reduction of San Ignacio Miní has extensive ruins and is a UNESCO World Heritage Site. It attracts some 300,000 visitors a year, and is easily reached as an excursion from Paraguay. Its low season is December, from the end of term up until Christmas, before the crowds begin again in January.

Also to be taken into account is that everyone who comes to Paraguay wants to visit the Iguazú Falls just outside the border, and these can be taken in as part of the same excursion. They can also be done separately by taking a bus from Asunción to Ciudad del Este and crossing into Foz (see page 279), but there are advantages in taking the route to the waterfalls that goes through Misiones Argentina and past San Ignacio Miní. The buses in Argentina are notably better; you arrive directly on the Argentinian side of the falls, which has more to explore than the Brazilian side; and you avoid Ciudad del Este, which would add a different kind of tone to your holiday. Misiones Argentina is the strip of land between the River Paraná (border with Paraguay) and the River Uruguay (border with Brazil at this point, and, to the south, with Uruguay) that you travel through from Posadas to Iguazú.

GETTING THERE AND AWAY There are various ways in which a visit to Paraguay can be conveniently combined with a trip to both the Iguazú Falls and San Ignacio Miní. You can fly into and out of Asunción, but you can also fly into and out of Foz, Brazil. You can also do an 'open-jaws' trip, flying into one airport and out of the other.

The obvious way of getting from Misiones Paraguay to San Ignacio Miní is to cross from Encarnación to Posadas. From the bus terminal in Encarnación you can cross to the bus terminal in Posadas (☎ *+54 376 4456106*) in three ways: a long-distance bus; the little shuttle bus that goes to and fro; or by taxi. The terminal is on the southern edge of Posadas, right on Ruta 12 which leads to San Ignacio Miní. Do not forget that there is sometimes (not always) an hour's time difference between Paraguay and Argentina (see page 37).

The slowest way of crossing the border is in a **long-distance bus** (which continues on to Buenos Aires) as it can be delayed for anything from one hour to five hours (in high season) while Argentinian immigration and customs do their checks. There are often Paraguayans on the bus with irregularities in their papers (such as for having overstayed their permitted time on a previous visit) and that can hold everyone up as fines are charged or bribes offered.

The **shuttle bus** goes regularly and is cheap (Gs10,000 or A$10 at the time of going to press), but, by contrast to the long-distance buses, is so fast that you may get left behind. The drivers have no patience in waiting for passports to be stamped: all the Paraguayans and Argentinians have to do is flash their identity card, and while the foreigners are waiting to have their passports vetted the bus drives off without them and they have to wait up to half an hour for the next one.

A **taxi** is easiest and quickest, but may cost about ten times as much as the shuttle bus. At the taxi rank at the Encarnación bus terminal you should specify that you want to cross into Argentina, as only some of the taxis carry the necessary paperwork. This also has the advantage that the taxi will wait while you change your money at the *cambio* office some 100m after customs. It is a good idea to get your **money-changing** done here as there are no exchange facilities in the bus terminal of Posadas.

If you are not arriving from Paraguay but **from the Iguazú Falls**, then you take a bus from the terminal in Puerto Iguazú. There is a bus about once an hour, and the journey takes five hours. The quality of the buses varies: good companies with a frequent service are Horianski (*+54 376 4455913*) and A del Valle.

If you are doing a more comprehensive tour of the Reductions and want to go to San Ignacio Miní after visiting the ruins at São Miguel in Brazil, or vice versa, then what looks a difficult journey on the map is actually quite easy. There is one bus a day run by Reunidas (*in Brazil +55 3312 1910/1495; in Argentina +54 3752 454795; e turismo@reunidas.com.br; www.reunidas.com.br*), that leaves Posadas at 11.00 every day, and reaches the Santo Ângelo terminal at 17.05 (heading for the destination Florianopolis in Brazil, via Cruz Alta). (Santo Ângelo is the nearest big town to São Miguel and was itself a Reduction.) The fare at the time of going to press was A$160 or R$40. In the other direction it leaves Santo Ângelo at 09.30 and arrives in Posadas at 15.30 to 16.00.

If you are **flying** to the airport at Posadas (*+254 376 457413/4*), then you will be arriving on an Aerolineas Argentinas flight from Buenos Aires. The Posadas Airport (airport code PSS) is 13km to the west of the city centre.

Once you are in Posadas, the journey of 60km to San Ignacio Miní is easy. Buses leave from the bus terminal for Puerto Iguazú at least once an hour, and most stop at San Ignacio Miní (but it may be at the terminal on the Ruta, just 200m past the principal entrance, rather than entering the town and turning around, as some buses do). The journey can be done in just over an hour, and it is worth getting a return ticket as the savings is considerable. It currently costs A$30 single, A$40 return. Note that in Argentina they drop the Miní and speak just of San Ignacio, just as in Paraguay thcy talk just of San Ignacio rather than San Ignacio Guasú.

Some buses will turn off the road under an arch to announce the beginning of San Ignacio, and you get off where the bus turns around to return to the main road. The ruins are now a five-minute walk away to your right (northeast). Other buses drop you at the terminal on the Ruta, which is only 200m past the entrance arch.

But there is also another, little known route from the Ruins of Misiones Paraguay to the Ruins of Misiones Argentina. You can take a **ferry** from the port (*puerto*) of Bella Vista over the river to Argentina, landing at Puerto Maní, near to Corpus, which was one of the original Reductions. Virtually nothing is left of that Reduction, and the site has not been developed for tourism, but only 15 minutes from the port of Corpus are the famous ruins of San Ignacio Miní. If you are staying at the Hotel Papillón in Bella Vista, for example, then returning to Encarnación to cross the border is something of a detour and probably unnecessary.

The ferry is called the *Balsa Mirlo*, run by the Argentinian company Vargas. It takes up to four small cars (first come, first served) and is not expensive, and then there is a small tax to pay on arrival at Argentinian customs. The ferry starts and ends its day on the Argentinian side, and it operates from 07.00 to 11.30 and then from 14.30 to 16.30. (That is the Paraguayan timetable: Argentinian time is one hour ahead, except in the Paraguayan summertime.) Unfortunately the ferry does not run on Saturdays or Sundays, although there are hopes that this will change. You need to check the ferry is running before finalising any plans – you can do so with Carlos Mallo of Koati Turismo, see page 260 for contacts, or with the ferryman Mario (*+54 9 3764 702088*) – as it sometimes breaks down and needs to be repaired.

You can also cross the river in a small and rather battered **motorboat**, which takes about 30 passengers and charges only Gs10,000 (*Señor Morel*). Dirt roads lead down to the ports on both sides, which are passable but difficult in rain. If you are a foot passenger, you may have to ring for a taxi on the Argentinian side: you cannot rely on there being a boat waiting. Carlos Mallo is happy to ring and ensure that there will be a taxi or remise to meet you on the other side. San Ignacio Miní is under 30km away, so the taxi ride is not expensive.

A third hydro-electric dam, between the dams of Itaipú and Yacyretá, has been planned for this strip of the river, near Bella Vista and Trinidad, to be called the Corpus dam, though nothing has been heard of this project for a long time now. If that is built the ferry would disappear, and there might (or might not) be facilities to cross over the dam by road instead.

GETTING AROUND Taxis are to be found outside the Hotel San Ignacio, but they look like ordinary cars. This may put off the wary, used to the rule that you never go in a car that is not an official taxi, least of all in Argentina, for fear of being assaulted and robbed; but in fact this problem is not found in a small town like San Ignacio, and it is perfectly safe.

HISTORY San Ignacio Miní is one of the oldest Reductions despite the fact that its name Miní means 'small', that is, 'younger', in contrast to the Paraguayan San Ignacio Guasú – the 'bigger', the 'older'. San Ignacio Guasú was founded at the end of 1609 while San Ignacio Miní was founded in 1610–11, in Guairá, the region to the northeast of the falls, in present-day Brazil. The founders were José Cataldino and Simón Masseta, and Antonio Ruiz de Montoya went to join them shortly afterwards. After persistent sackings by Portuguese slave-traders, who destroyed all the Reductions of Guairá apart from Loreto and San Ignacio Miní and carried off hundreds of thousands of Guaraní to sell in the slave markets of São Paulo, Montoya decided to move to safer territory below the waterfalls, in the region to the south of the River Paraná. Twelve thousand people set off in 1632, but only 4,000 arrived. The rest died from hunger or disease, or fled into the jungle.

The new San Ignacio Miní moved again, to settle on its present site in 1696, and over the next few decades the style of architecture began to change from adobe to stone. Thanks to the greater durability of stone, we have ruins today. Of the 15 former Reductions in Argentina, most have disappeared and only San Ignacio Miní has a lot to see.

The town thrived until the time of the expulsion of the Jesuits in 1768, which led to the disintegration of the Reductions. By 1810 there was no population left in San Ignacio Miní, and what had not already been stolen or fallen into disrepair was burnt down by the first Paraguayan president and dictator, Dr Francia, in 1817, in a war of border disputes between Paraguay and Argentina, and again by Paraguayan troops in 1821. Today the town is dominated by tourism.

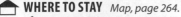

WHERE TO STAY *Map, page 264.*

Portal del Sol (10 rooms) Rivadavia 1105; +54 376 4470005/4470096; e hotelportaldelsol@gmail.com or hotelportaldelsol@hotmail.com; www.portaldelsolhotel.com. Recently built hotel close to the ruins, minor faults in design of rooms. **$$**

La Toscana (10 rooms) Hipólito Irigoyen y Uruguay; +54 376 4470777; e hotellatoscana@live.com.ar; www.argentinaturismo.com.ar/hotellatoscana. A favourite with many despite being further from the ruins & down a dirt road. Friendly service, pool, Wi-Fi, terrace with *parrilla*. **$$**

Hotel San Ignacio (9 rooms & several bungalows) San Martín 823 y Sarmiento; +54 376 4470047; e hotelsanignacio@arnet.com.ar; www.hotelsanignacio.com.ar. Right on the corner where you get off the bus, & also close to the ruins. Rooms are pleasantly updated with TVs & big en-suite bathrooms. Helpful manager. Restaurant, internet, paddle boats, parking. The bungalows are for 4 or 5. Price does not inc b/fast, but the b/fast

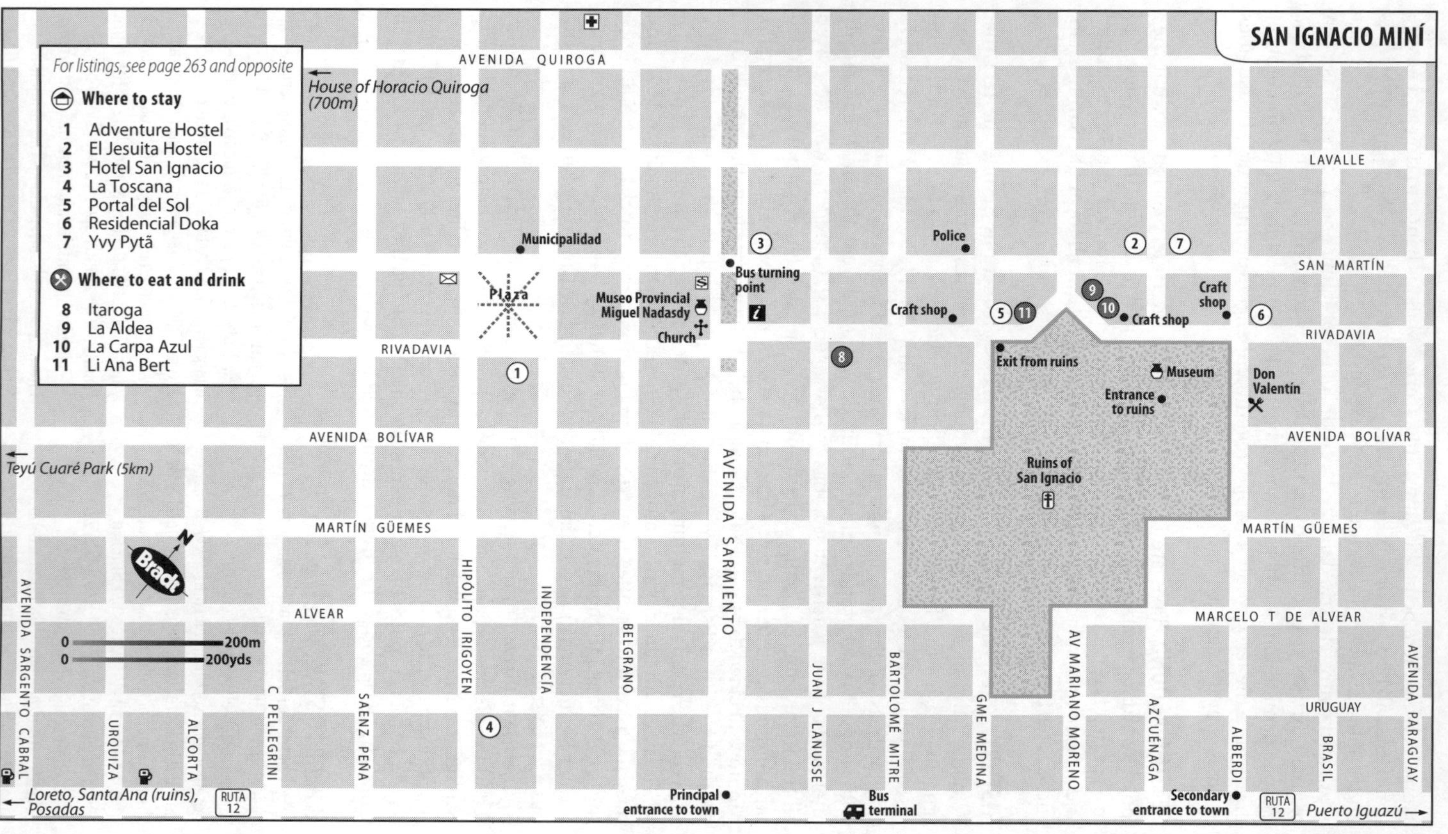
SAN IGNACIO MINÍ
For listings, see page 263 and opposite
Where to stay
1 Adventure Hostel
2 El Jesuita Hostel
3 Hotel San Ignacio
4 La Toscana
5 Portal del Sol
6 Residencial Doka
7 Yvy Pytã
Where to eat and drink
8 Itaroga
9 La Aldea
10 La Carpa Azul
11 Li Ana Bert
House of Horacio Quiroga (700m)
Teyú Cuaré Park (5km)
Loreto, Santa Ana (ruins), Posadas
RUTA 12
Puerto Iguazú
AVENIDA QUIROGA
LAVALLE
SAN MARTÍN
RIVADAVIA
AVENIDA BOLÍVAR
MARTÍN GÜEMES
MARCELO T DE ALVEAR
ALVEAR
URUGUAY
AVENIDA PARAGUAY
BRASIL
ALBERDI
AZCUÉNAGA
AV MARIANO MORENO
GME MEDINA
BARTOLOMÉ MITRE
JUAN J LANUSSE
AVENIDA SARMIENTO
BELGRANO
INDEPENDENCÍA
HIPÓLITO IRIGOYEN
SAENZ PEÑA
C PELLEGRINI
ALCORTA
URQUIZA
AVENIDA SARGENTO CABRAL
Municipalidad
Plaza
Museo Provincial Miguel Nadasdy
Church
Bus turning point
Police
Craft shop
Exit from ruins
Entrance to ruins
Museum
Ruins of San Ignacio
Don Valentín
Secondary entrance to town
Principal entrance to town
Bus terminal
200m
200yds
Bradt

served at the bar is not expensive, & is better than you get when you pay an all-inc price for B&B in a cheap hotel: you can have croissants, rolls of ham & cheese, & a fried egg. **$$**

Yvy Pytã (8 rooms) San Martín 1363; m from abroad +54 9 376 4666876, from Argentina 0376 15 4666876; e yvypyta@hotmail.com.ar. Close to the ruins, modern rooms for 2, 3 or 4, kitchen basic but with essentials. *Parrilla, quincho,* cable TV, parking. **$$**

Residencial Doka (10 rooms) Alberdi 518; +54 376 4470131. Sited just half a block from the entrance to the ruins. Clean prefab chalets. **$$**

Adventure Hostel (21 beds in dorms & 9 private rooms) Independencia 469; +54 376 4470955; e sihostel@hotmail.com; www.sihostel.com.ar. Slightly further from the ruins; from the road on which you come in, go a couple of blocks in the opposite direction from the ruins, & you will find it on the plaza, on the opposite side from the Municipalidad. Well designed & beautiful, big garden. Very international feel. Games room & they hire out kayaks & bicycles. Cicero restaurant, eat inside or out. **$**

El Jesuita Hostel (1 dorm for 6) San Martín 1291; +54 376 4470542/+54 376 462 1222; e hosteleljesuita@gmail.com; Facebook: Hostel El Jesuita. Small hostel in old house near ruins, helpful owners. Has bicycles for going to Teyú Cuaré (see pages 266–7). **$**

WHERE TO EAT AND DRINK *Map opposite.*

La Carpa Azul Rivadavia 1295; +54 376 4470096; e lacarpaazul@hotmail.com; 06.00–16.00 Mon–Sat, 07.30–16.00 Sun. Facing the wall of the ruins. Named after the capacious blue tent that houses it, with room for 350 people, behind a souvenir shop under the same management. Extensive menu. *Asado* is brought to your table on the hot grill it has been cooked on, & they also serve grilled fish. The delicious *empanadas* make an inexpensive starter. The complex has an adjoining swimming pool, volleyball & paddle boats. **$$**

Liana Bert Rivadavia 1133; +54 376 4470151. Opposite the exit from the ruins. Sells craft on the same site under the name La Negrita. They serve steaks, grilled chicken & pasta dishes, as well as good quality sandwiches, *milanesas* & *empanadas*. The food is good as well as economical, & the location is convenient. The name comes from the 3 sisters who run the establishment: Lidia, Ana & Berta. There is a phone & internet shop next door. **$$**

Itaroga Rivadavia 240 y Juan Lanusse. Nice small place with terrace, good food. **$$**

Don Valentín Alberdi 444; +54 376 4470284; 07.00–19.00. *Milanesas*, steaks, fast food. Not open late. **$$**

La Aldea Rivadavi c/ Moreno; +54 376 4470567. Pizzeria with character. Serves 2-course *menú turístico*. Open late. **$**

WHAT TO SEE

Ruins of San Ignacio Miní

(*+54 376 4470186; summer 07.00–20.00, winter 07.00–18.00 daily followed by Imagen y Sonido (image and sound show) at 20.00 in spring & summer, 19.00 in autumn & winter; foreigners A$70, Latin Americans A$60, Argentinians A$50, residents of Misiones Argentina A$20, children free under 5. The Imagen y Sonido requires a separate ticket, which is the same price as the day entrance)* The ruins are outstanding not only for their extent and their beauty, but also for their presentation. The ticket is also valid for the other Reductions of Loreto, Santa Ana and Santa María La Mayor and lasts for two weeks. The tour begins with a Centro de Interpretación, which is a series of rooms that serve as an introduction and capture the spirit of the Guaraní. You walk through a reconstructed Guaraní house, of the kind that was used when they were still in their semi-nomadic state, through a mock-up of the jungle, and into a dark room filled with phrases from Guaraní mythology, uncannily reminiscent of biblical creation stories. Passing out into a courtyard, you are on the quay where a ship of the conquistadors has arrived.

Everyone passing out into the open air is given a guided tour, which begins every 20 minutes at busy times. There are now a few guides with enough basic English to explain the essential points, though you cannot rely on there always being one available.

On the way to the church (designed by the Italian Jesuit architect, Brassanelli), you pass through rows of indigenous houses. They may lack their roofs, but the doorways, windows and columns of the galleries are all clear to see, and you get the feel of the huge plaza, with the 74m-long church over on the other side. The two biggest and most photographed remains are the columns on either side of the church's entrance, rising gloriously upwards and terminating in angels with flowing robes. The stonework that once united them in an arch has long since vanished.

From inside the church you can pass to the college, arranged around a courtyard and with all the basic structure still clear, as well as a couple of doorways with fine sculpted details. The Jesuits' residence and the workshops were on this side, while on the other side of the church were the cemetery, the orchard and the house for widows and orphans (*kotý guasú*).

The guide will also point out trees used for different functions: *timbó* for making canoes, *hakarandá* for making bark infusions, *lapacho* for making strong columns, *cedro misionero* for making harps, and creepers for making hammocks. The visit ends with a small museum containing a few archaeological remnants but it has none of the fine art statues that make the museums of the Reductions in Paraguay so remarkable.

One of the delights of San Ignacio Miní is the line of wooden street stalls that run round the outside fence of the ruins. Here you will find wind chimes and dreamcatchers, semi-precious jewellery, hand-painted T-shirts and rough-hewn wooden buttons, hats woven from maize leaves, little animals carved by present-day Guaraní out of balsa wood and hand-rolled cigars.

After dark there is a spectacular show in the ruins lasting 45 minutes, called ***Imagen y Sonido***. It happens every night, with a maximum number of 70 at a time, and if they are to put on a second showing they require a minimum number of 10. This new attraction, inaugurated in July 2009, evokes the story and the life of the Reduction through projecting virtual actors onto the walls of the ruins and onto mists of water that surge up from below ground: it begins with a projection thrown onto a tree, the *timbó,* and then the virtual characters of Guaraní, priests, conquistadors and *bandeirantes* appear at eight different stations, telling the history and presenting the daily life of agriculture, schooling, music, etc. This highly imaginative and dramatic production is in Spanish, but you can ask for an English version on headphones.

Museo Provincial Miguel Nadasdy *(Sarmiento 557; ⌚ 07.00–18.00 Mon–Sat; free admission)* Near where the bus arrives is this museum containing the collection of a Hungarian, with Stone Age remains and small statues from the Jesuit period, and a documentation centre about the Jesuit period.

House of Horacio Quiroga (*⌚ 08.00–18.00 daily; admission about A$15*) While the ruins are clearly the outstanding feature of San Ignacio Miní, it is also well worth visiting this house. Quiroga (1878–1937) was a Uruguayan writer who is attributed with having developed the short story as a Latin American literary form, and the story of his immensely tragic life is movingly told as you walk through the bamboo woods around his house, so that by the time you reach the simple building you are fascinated to see where this extraordinary writer lived. To walk there, go west, and where the map on page 264 ends and walk along the dirt road for 400m, taking the left fork where the road divides.

Teyú Cuaré The Teyú Cuaré (Guaraní 'Lizards' cave') park southwest of San Ignacio is so called because a huge lizard was reputed to live there. It is now a 170ha ecotourism reserve near the river, with seven paths and seven viewing points, looking across the Río Paraná towards Paraguay. One of the peaks in the area with a spectacular view is called **Osununú** (Guaraní 'place of thunder')

Loreto and Santa Ana (⌚ *07.00–19.00 daily*) These two Reductions are also easy to reach from San Ignacio Miní, and you will not be much delayed if you take them in on your journey. Both are a short taxi ride away (11km and 16km respectively) along the main road to Posadas. The same ticket gets you into all three Reductions. Loreto was one of the oldest Reductions, along with San Ignacio Miní, as both moved from north of the Iguazú Falls in the famous exodus led by Antonio Ruiz de Montoya (see pages 263 and 359). His body is believed to have been brought back from Perú by the Guaraní, and buried in Loreto. Santa Ana has attractive ruins, and its church was designed by the great Italian Jesuit artist Giuseppe Brassanelli (see box on pages 174–5), who is buried under the high altar.

EXCURSION TO SAN RAFAEL NATURE RESERVE

San Rafael is a Resource Management Reserve of Atlantic Forest, straddling the boundary of the *departamentos* Itapúa and Caazapá. It is one of the last sites in eastern Paraguay where you can still find large tracts of native forest. There are streams, waterfalls and dense forest. A number of NGOs in Paraguay have joined together to form the San Rafael Conservation Alliance, to protect this remaining fraction of the Atlantic Forest; they include Pro Cosara (*www.procosara.org*), which does not have a tourist arm, and Guyrá (*www.guyra.org.py*), which does. It was the first IBA (Important Bird Area) to be recognised in Paraguay, and it has more species of birds than anywhere else in the country. There are now 429 identified species – more than half the species in the whole of the country – and possibly more species not yet recognised by science. It is the only Paraguayan site to have recorded the impressive crested eagle, as well as having the harpy eagle, parrots and the famous Paraguayan bellbird, which has been immortalised in the harp piece of that name. There are tawny yellow pumas, tapirs and monkeys. The Mbyá Guaraní still lead a traditional life in this forest.

The Cerro San Rafael, just to the south of the reserve, used to figure erroneously in school textbooks as the highest hill in Paraguay. The Servicio Geográfico Militar clarified in 1988 that Tres Kandú is the highest (see pages 321–2).

WHERE TO STAY Those who wish to visit the San Rafael reserve should contact SEAM (Secretaria del Ambiente) (*021 615806; www.seam.gov.py*), but better still visit with the conservation organisation Guyrá (*Gaetano Martino, formerly José Berges, 215 esq Tte Ross;* *021 229097/223567;* **m** *0981 866383;* **e** *guyra.paraguay@guyra.paraguay.org.py; www.guyra.org.py*). On top of a hill with a view of the pastures, is the Kanguerý biological station (pronounced very approximately 'kangaroo'). It is a very special place to stay, despite the setback that their visitor's hostel was burnt down in November 2012 in an arson attack, presumably by illegal loggers who regarded the reserve as threatening their interests. However, it has been rebuilt completely, with two dormitories (six people in each), and hot water generated by solar panels. They have friendly, knowledgeable staff, including the brilliant guide Daniel Espinola (**m** *0986 649634*). Visitors should bring their own food and drink. This stay sounds expensive but when you take into account that the price includes a long and possibly difficult journey (if it rains), guides, binoculars and all activities are included, the price is reasonable. They can send an English-speaking guide from Asunción, at an extra cost.

Excursions offered include a guided walk through the forest, horseriding, a night ride to see foxes, owls, hares and other nocturnal animals, and a ride to see birds of prey. There is a constant stream of interesting birds to the station, which is a beautiful spot for relaxing in hammocks and reading books. The staff can provide binoculars and books to recognise birds. Be prepared for a lot of mosquitoes and other flying or creeping insects in this humid, almost tropical environment. Bring long trousers, a long-sleeved shirt, stout walking shoes, insect repellent and insecticide.

The Guyrá staff will collect you, possibly from the Hotel Papillón in Bella Vista, from where the journey takes two and a half hours. After 10km on Ruta 6 in the direction of Ciudad del Este, you take a small dirt road left where there is a sign to Acá. You will be driving on a dirt road for much of the way, and from November to January it usually rains for a couple of hours in the afternoon, so you should not attempt the journey without a 4x4, and even then you are likely to get lost if you have not done the route before. An alternative route is along the Graneros del Sur road that goes through Fram (see pages 248–9); before reaching Piripó you take a road north, where Alto Verá is signed.

To stay in such a beautiful and remote nature reserve, with everything made easy for you, is a special and rare kind of experience. Simon Barnes wrote (*The Times*, 14 June 2008) of his stay in the San Rafael rainforest with Guyrá: 'The place is both inhospitable and enchanting. It sucks you in, it involves you. You raise your eyes and see plants on plants on plants. Everything is soft, damp growth. If you are still enough, you can hear the trees growing.'

ENCARNACIÓN

Copaco ☎ *071 208999; municipalidad* ☎ *071 203982/204800 www.encarnacion.com.py*

Encarnación is sometimes called the Pearl of the South, just as Concepción is known as the Pearl of the North. Both have religious names: the Incarnation and the (Immaculate) Conception. But while Concepción is a quiet, pretty town, unspoilt in its isolation, Encarnación – on the border with Argentina – is a big international thoroughfare, and one of the most important cities in Paraguay, after Asunción, Ciudad del Este and Pedro Juan Caballero.

Encarnación was the site of one of the earliest Reductions founded by Roque González in 1615, bearing the full name Nuestra Señora de la Encarnación de Itapúa, or Itapúa for short. Just three years later, it moved from the left bank (where Posadas is) to the right bank (where Encarnación is), and developed a good school of painting under the French Jesuit Louis Berger. But the once-magnificent church – the work of Giuseppe Brassanelli, with three naves and a painted wooden dome – was demolished in 1848 because it had become dangerous. Today there are no remains at all. The name Itapúa has passed to the *departamento* of which Concepción is the capital. The modern bridge, nearly 3,000m long, that spans the Río Paraná to Posadas is called the **Puente San Roque González de Santa Cruz**, commemorating the fact that Roque González's foundation of Itapúa began on the Argentinian side before establishing itself on the Paraguayan bank.

Encarnación is principally of interest to visitors for two things: the carnival and the coast road. The **carnival** (*www.carnavalencarnaceno.com*), which is celebrated in February and/or March, on the four weekends prior to Lent, is the biggest and best in the country, and until a few years ago was the only one. There is a new Sambódromo for the parade, which is claimed to be the best in the region, with the exception only of Rio de Janeiro and São Paulo. It is 440m long and has capacity for 10,500 people, plus facilities for parking, toilets and sale of food. Tickets range from Gs20,000 to Gs150,000 and are sold at the Carnival office on the San José beach, in the new Sambódromo itself, at the Asunción office of the mobile phone company Tigo, and by ticket touts on the day. There is also a Carnival office in town (*Artigas 760 c/ General Cabañas;* ☎ *071 206917/8*). There are different prices for different boxes and terraces, some with seats and some without. You will probably need to buy some goggles while there, to protect your eyes from the white squirty foam that is sprayed out in great excitement by the crowd, as they watch the spectacular parades of scantily dressed dancers in enormous coloured feather costumes. It begins at 21.00 and ends about 03.00.

Hotels get booked out way in advance, so you need to book early; you will probably find it difficult to book a hotel for less than two nights, and you will also be paying a much higher price in carnival season.

The 27km coast road, or **Costanera**, has recently been built around the city centre, and especially to the west. This is part of the massive reconstruction work to compensate for the higher river level as a result of raising the walls of the Yacyretá dam. It has three principal sandy beaches – San José, Mbói Kaẽ (Guaraní, thin snake), which is just north of the bridge into the city, and Pacu-Cuá (Guaraní, home of the pacu fish), which borders the barrio San Isidro, south of the bridge to Argentina. The San José beach is now regarded as one of the most fashionable places for Paraguayans to go to relax, spawning a lot of new hotels, bars and shops. Unlike the Costanera of Asunción, the water is clean enough for bathing. Security guards patrol the area, which is well lit, and there are plans for a pier and a floating quay for motorboats.Encarnación is now a key destination for Paraguayans in the December to February summer holiday – almost half a million people went to its Costanera in summer 2012–13 – and some hotels raise their prices for this high season as well as for the Carnival.

For Paraguayans, there is another attraction in Encarnación: shopping. The Feria Municipal has some of the lowest prices in the country, and behind it is a whole new commercial centre, sometimes referred to as the Nueva Circuito Comercial. Encarnación is also important as a university city, with respected faculties of both the Universidad Nacional and the Universidad Católica, as well as the more minor universities. But it is not especially endowed in cultural life or in museums, though it has a few. It also has a sanctuary of the Virgin Mary at Itacuá, on the Río Paraná, that is attracting considerable crowds, like a mini-version of the country's main Marian site, Caacupé.

Encarnación is known for being the home city of President Fernando Lugo, but it is not only home to Paraguayans: there are also many descendants of immigrants from Ukraine, Russia, Germany, Poland, China, Japan, Korea and Arab nations, as well as a large Muslim population.

GETTING THERE AND AWAY If you are **driving** from Asunción, you will cover the 370km to Encarnación in five or six hours – six to eight by **bus**. It is straight down Ruta 1, right to the end. If you are coming from the Reductions in Misiones, allow two hours from San Ignacio by car or express bus, three by ordinary bus. If you are coming from Ciudad del Este, the journey is almost as long as coming from Asunción.

When Ruta 1 reaches the city, instead of continuing straight ahead down Avenida Dr Francia, you follow most of the traffic in turning left. After nine blocks you come to a roundabout, where there is a shop called Luminotecnia. If you are bypassing the city to go towards the ruins, you bear to the left here, and you will be on Ruta 6. But to enter the city you turn right, and the centre will now be on your right again. After ten blocks there are some traffic lights, on the corner of General Cabañas, which more or less marks the southern limit of the city centre. To your left you will now pass a large supermarket, Superseis, and then the Arthur Hotel, which is one of the best. If you continue on, you will eventually reach the bridge into Argentina.

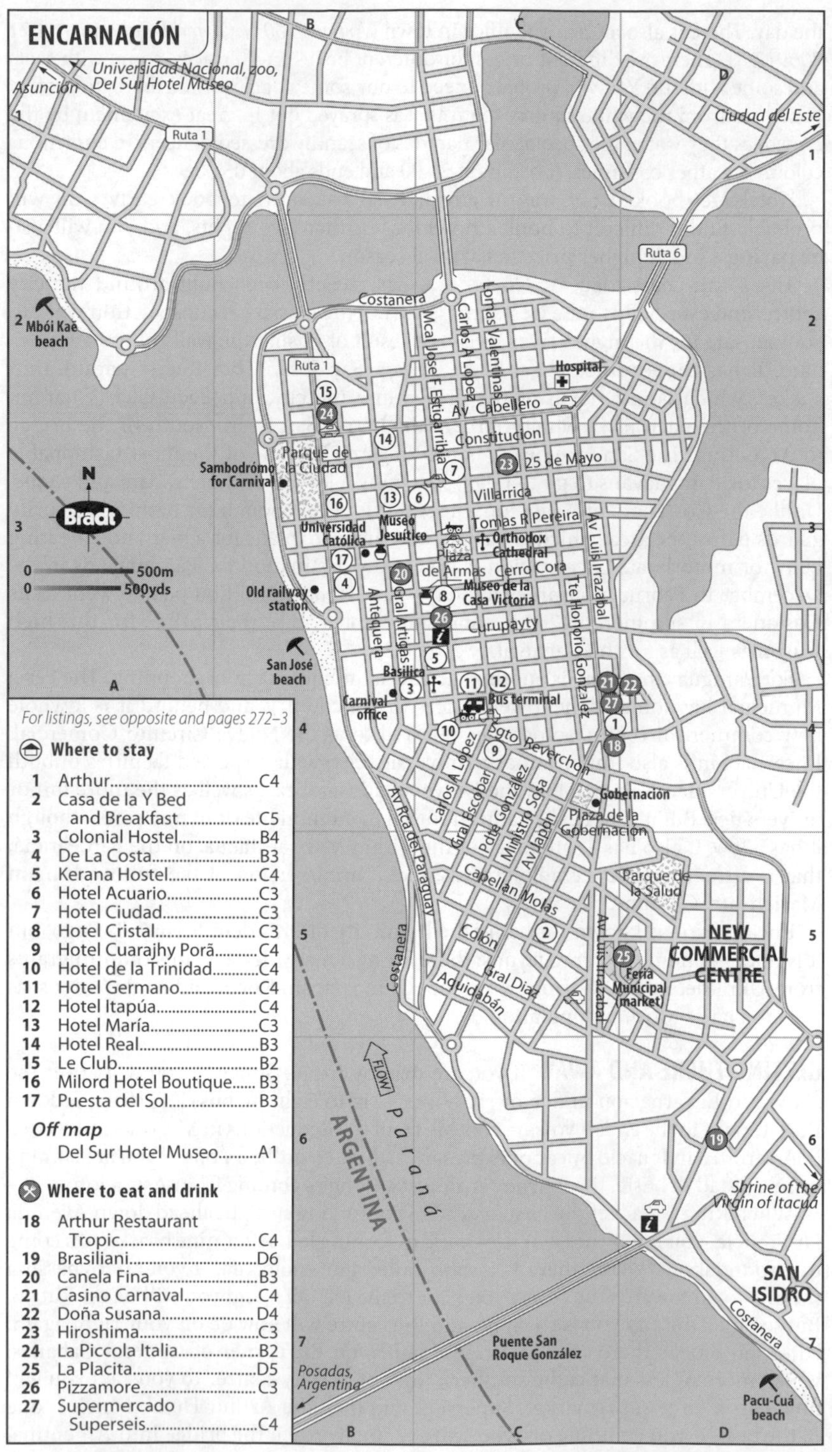
ENCARNACIÓN
Universidad Nacional, zoo, Del Sur Hotel Museo
Asunción
Ciudad del Este
Ruta 1
Ruta 6
Costanera
Mbói Kaẽ beach
Hospital
Av Cabellero
Constitución
25 de Mayo
Villarrica
Tomas R Pereira
Mcal José F Estigarribia
Carlos A Lopez
Lomas Valentinas
Parque de la Ciudad
Sambodrómo for Carnival
Universidad Católica
Museo Jesuítico
Orthodox Cathedral
Plaza de Armas
Cerro Cora
Museo de la Casa Victoria
Old railway station
Curupayty
Antequera
Gral Artigas
San José beach
Basilica
Carnival office
Bus terminal
Av Luis Irrazabal
Tte Honorio Gonzalez
Sgto Reverchon
Gobernación
Plaza de la Gobernación
Av Rca del Paraguay
Gral Escobar
Pdte González
Ministro Sosa
Av Japón
Capellán Molas
Parque de la Salud
Colón
Gral Diaz
Aquidabán
Av Luis Irrazabal
Feria Municipal (market)
NEW COMMERCIAL CENTRE
FLOW
Paraná
ARGENTINA
Shrine of the Virgin of Itacuá
SAN ISIDRO
Costanera
Puente San Roque González
Posadas, Argentina
Pacu-Cuá beach
N
Bradt
0 500m
0 500yds
For listings, see opposite and pages 272–3
Where to stay
1 Arthur C4
2 Casa de la Y Bed and Breakfast C5
3 Colonial Hostel B4
4 De La Costa B3
5 Kerana Hostel C4
6 Hotel Acuario C3
7 Hotel Ciudad C3
8 Hotel Cristal C3
9 Hotel Cuarajhy Porã C4
10 Hotel de la Trinidad C4
11 Hotel Germano C4
12 Hotel Itapúa C4
13 Hotel María C3
14 Hotel Real B3
15 Le Club B2
16 Milord Hotel Boutique B3
17 Puesta del Sol B3
Off map
Del Sur Hotel Museo A1
Where to eat and drink
18 Arthur Restaurant Tropic C4
19 Brasiliani D6
20 Canela Fina B3
21 Casino Carnaval C4
22 Doña Susana D4
23 Hiroshima C3
24 La Piccola Italia B2
25 La Placita D5
26 Pizzamore C3
27 Supermercado Superseis C4

The **bus terminal** [270 C4] (*071 202412*) is the kind of run-down place awash with people trying to sell you things, where you feel you need to watch your wallet carefully. The toilets are cramped, and the facilities for changing money minimal. If you arrive early in the morning you will find it almost impossible to get a cup of coffee, though getting a drink of *mate* is easy. All the big bus companies go from here, and there are plenty of people around to direct you to the next bus for Asunción or for Ciudad del Este, as the case may be. There are basically only two roads out of Encarnación: Ruta 1 going northwest, and Ruta 6 going northeast – as well, of course, as the road going south over the river to Argentina. Encarnación to Asunción currently costs around Gs60,000, and Encarnación to Ciudad del Este Gs50,000.

If you want to **cross the border** into Argentina, specify this before you get in a **taxi**, as not all of them carry the necessary paperwork. You can also get a **bus** to the terminal of Posadas for only Gs5,000 (see *San Ignacio Miní*, pages 260–7). There are motor launches to Argentina which leave from a port tucked away just to the north of the Roque González bridge.

TOURIST INFORMATION There is a tourist information office in the town centre [270 C4] (*Mariscal Estigarribia 1015 c/ Curupaytý; 071 205021;* e rutajesuiticapy@hotmail.com; *07.00–22.00 daily*) which can help with leaflets, maps and information, including the latest edition of *Encarnación Quick Guide*. There is also a Senatur **tourist information office** in the building with passport control, by the bridge (m *0985 794595*).

WHERE TO STAY *Map opposite.*

Just before you enter the city, there is a fabulous new hotel opened in 2014, which is also a museum, very reasonably priced. Just before you cross the first of the two consecutive bridges into Encarnación you come to the **Del Sur Hotel Museo** (*62 rooms; Ruta 1, Barrio Ita Paso; 071 207816/207846;* m *0985 146495;* e *delsurhotel-museo@hotmail.com; Facebook: Del Sur Hotel Museo;* **$$**). It is on the left if you are approaching from the Asunción side, after the compañía Juan del Paraná (on the right) and opposite the entrance to the Encarnación port (also on the right) – both of them north of the city. One room of this stunning new glass-fronted, three-storey building is a museum housing the Sacred Art collection of the late Alberto Delvalle – saints & their niches. At night the place is dramatically lit and there are tables for dinner outside. The rooms are comfortable with pastel colours, and the whole building breathes elegance. It also has a pool. Set in a wood, it must be one of the top recommendations if you do not need to be within walking distance of Encarnación.

Within the city itself, hotels have been sprouting up like mushrooms since the Costanera was built. It is no longer possible to include more than a small selection of the total, though that in itself is a sizeable list.

Hotel de la Trinidad (73 rooms) Mariscal Estigarribia esq. Jorge Memmel; 071 208099; www.hoteldelatrinidad.com.py. New hotel at the top end of the market with a touch of the Reductions, hence the name. It is closer to the bus station than to the Costanera, but as it is a 13-floor tower, with windows designed to maximise views, it has good views of San José beach. Gym, spa, pool. Restaurant Primoli. Tea room (Confitería Arasá). **$$$$**

Le Club Hotel Angel Ramón Samudio y Ruta 1; 071 208045; www.leclub.com.py. New, expensive hotel near the top end of the Costanera (just before you turn left onto Caballero, when arriving on Ruta 1). Restaurant is disappointing. **$$$$**

Milord Hotel Boutique (15 rooms) Avenida Gaspar R de Francia y 25 de mayo; 071 205839/206235; m 0985 814008;

www.milord.com.py. This small, new, luxury hotel is well located between the Plaza de Armas & the Costanera. If you think the name is a touch silly, do not be put off, as this is now considered to be the best hotel in town, & also to have the best restaurant. It was started by a couple who went to live in Paris for 4 years & learned to cook there. **$$$$**

Hotel Acuario (15 rooms) Juan L Mallorquín 1550 c/ Villarrica; 071 202676; www.acuario.com.py. Heated indoor swimming pool (16m x 8m). A couple of blocks from the plaza. Car park, Wi-Fi, minibars, cable TV. Blue-&-yellow colour scheme may not appeal to everyone. **$$$**

Hotel Cristal (85 rooms) Mariscal Estigarribia 1157 c/ Cerro Corá; 071 202371/2; www.hotelcristal.com.py. One of the old favourites, now extensively renovated. High-rise, large pool, Wi-Fi, parking, Restaurant Esmeralda. **$$$**

De La Costa Hotel (100 rooms) Av Rodríguez de Francia 1240 c/ Cerro Corá; 071 205694/200590; m 0985 142363; www.delacostahotel.com.py. One of the better hotels, though rooms are not big & it can be noisy. Swimming pool, minibars, Wi-Fi, restaurant, gym, facing San José beach & with view over river towards Posadas. 200m from the Sambodromo. **$$$**

Hotel María (20 rooms) General Artigas y 25 de mayo; 071 203282/204711; Facebook: Hotel Maria Encarnacion. Solid, reliable hotel with Wi-Fi. **$$$**

Puesta del Sol (16 rooms) 14 de mayo 44 c/ Av Rodríguez de Francia; 071 202376; www.hotelpuestadelsol.com.py. Minibar & sommier beds, 1 block from San José beach. **$$$**

Arthur Hotel (60 rooms) Av Irrazábal c/ Av Japón; 071 205246/7; e arthur_hotel@hotmail.com; www.arthurhotel.com.py. Not so long ago this was considered to be the best hotel in town, but it has now been overtaken by the new luxury hotels. It is excellent value for money compared with other hotels in the same class. Secure parking, Wi-Fi, cable TV, minibar, garden with fountain, games room, ping pong, gym, sauna, pool, computer room. **$$**

Hotel Ciudad (25 rooms) Mariscal Estigarribia y 25 de mayo; 071 202155; e cadenacuarajhy@itacom.com.py; www.hotelciudad.com.py.pizzería. The former Cuarajhy I under new management. Restaurant, Wi-Fi, car park. **$$**

Hotel Cuarajhy Porã (23 rooms) Sgto Reverchón e/ Escobar & Carlos Antonio López; 071 204922/ 206409; m 0995 366302; www.hotelcuarajhypora.com.py. Just 2 ½ blocks from the terminal. Family business dating back to 1980s. Wi-Fi, gym, sauna, car park with guard. Has cheaper rooms on the ground floor. **$$**

Hotel Real (25 rooms) Av Bernardino Caballero 170 c/ Artigas; 071 202020; e hotel_real_encar@hotmail.com. Economic hotel with simple décor, but has Wi-Fi & *quincho*. You pass it on the main road into town. Cheaper rooms have fans. **$**

Hotel Germano (9 rooms) General Cabañas c/ Carlos Antonio López; 071 203346; e gerstapf@hotmail.com. Clean & friendly family hotel, located behind the rank of white taxis. Cheaper rooms have fans & shared bathrooms. Staffed 06.00–22.00 & sometimes closed on Sun. The disadvantage – which is also an advantage for those who make last-minute plans – is that during the Carnival they do not take reservations in advance, but only offer rooms when they are vacated. Recommended. **$**

Hotel Itapúa (120 rooms) Carlos A López y General Cabañas; 071 205045; m 0985 619618; www.hotelitapua.com.py. Close to the terminal, with restaurant, minibars, cable TV, Wi-Fi & parking. Big & basic with white melamine furniture. Lower-priced rooms have fans & do not inc b/fast. Restaurant. **$**

Colonial Hostel (6 rooms; sleeps 26) General Artigas 762 c/ General Cabañas; 071 201500; m 0995 607652; e colonialhostelencarnacion@gmail.com. Shared kitchen. 300m from San José beach. **$$**

Casa de la Y Bed and Breakfast (2 rooms, sleeps 10) Carmen Castro 422 e/ Yegros y Molas; m 0985 778198; http://casadelay.wix.com/casa-de-la-y. Family-run, homemade breakfast, *quincho*, lovely garden with hammocks, personal attention. 'Y' (pronounced 'E') is Yolanda, who runs the hostel with the help of her daughter, who is an English teacher. Dorm with bunks, or double room with 2 single beds. Not quite so central, but they can collect you from the border or the bus terminal for Gs20,000. Recommended. **$**

Kerana Hostel (4 rooms) Mallorquin 950 e/ Curupayty y Kreuser; m 0986 355243/0975 139593; www.keranahostel.com. Neat, modern, well equipped. 300m from San José beach. Recommended. **$**

WHERE TO EAT AND DRINK *Map, page 270.*

he bars along the Costanera are good for a drink but do not serve good food. If you are travelling on a shoestring budget, around the **terminal** are lots of cheap *kioskos* ($) where you can grab a bite of a typical dish with the locals. Probably best is the complex directly south, with a sign 'Bar Parrillada Comedor Valle San Pedro', next to where the *karumbé* are parked.

Arthur Restaurant Tropic Av Irrazábal c/ General Brúguez; 071 205245; 11.00–14.30 & 19.00–23.00. Next door to Arthur Hotel. Good buffet. *Tenedor libre* or by weight. **$$$**

Brasiliani Ruta Internacional, c/ aduana; 071 202181; closed Mon. One of the best of the fixed price, pile-it-on restaurants (*tenedor libre*), 50m from the Puente Roque González. **$$**

Canela Fina 14 de mayo e/ Mallorquín y Artigas; 071 205080. Pizzas & other dishes in a romantic atmosphere. Same owner as Brasiliani. **$$**

Casino Carnaval Av Irrazábal y General Cabañas; 071 203836. Far more than a casino, with a snack bar, pub & restaurant, & live music every day. **$$**

Doña Susana General Cabañas c/ Av Irrazábal, behind the casino; 071 204915; www.restaurantdonasusana.com.py; Wed–Mon. Excellent Chinese restaurant with Paraguayan dishes too. Behind the Casino, rather tucked away. Also does home delivery, so you can read its menu on the website. **$$**

Hiroshima 25 de mayo y Lomas Valentinas; 071 206288; 11.30–14.00 & 19.00–23.00 Mon–Fri, 19.00–midnight Sat. Highly recommended Japanese restaurant, a great favourite of all who go there. Can be hard to get a table. **$$**

La Piccola Italia Ruta 1, 1894, c/ Avenida Caballero; 071 202344. Inexpensive Italian restaurant, serves big portions. **$$**

Pizzamore Mariscal Estigarribia/ Curupayty; 071 200452. Big pizzeria with coffee bar. Good pizzas ('artisan pizzas made with love' is their motto) but little atmosphere. **$$**

Supermercado Superseis Irrazábal y Bruguez. Next to Arthur Hotel, has *patio de comidas*. **$**

La Placita (market) Has a lot of cheap eating places (*casillas* or *kioskos*) – see above. **$**

OTHER PRACTICALITIES You can get a **shower** at the 'baño público con ducha' on the south side of the bus terminal [270 C4]. **Banks** are mostly clustered around the Plaza de Armas [270 C3]. There are three branches of **Cambios Chaco** where foreign currency can be exchanged: the most central is at Mariscal Estigarribia 1406, e/ Tomas Pereira y Villarrica (*071 209760; 07.45–17.45 Mon–Fri, 08.00–14.00 Sat*). **Taxis** can be found on the corner of Plaza de Armas (*071 204302*); radio taxis (*071 200604; m 0985 700100*). There is **car-hire** with Localiza, (*Avenida Irrazábal 1100 esq. Oscar Giménez; 071 204097; www.localiza.com.py; 07.00–noon & 13.30–18.00 Mon–Fri, 07.00–12.00 Sat*).

FESTIVALS Apart from the carnival (see below), the other main festival is on 25 March, the feast of the Annunciation, which is the patronal feast day. There is an international dance festival in July, attracting visiting groups from Argentina, Brazil and Uruguay. In September there is another dance event, the Festival Nacional del Paraná, where dance teachers explain their techniques to the public.

Encarnación Carnival The carnival (*071 200928; www.carnavalencarnaceno.com; range of prices for standing room up to good seats*) has been going since 1916, when the railway reached Encarnación, which marked a watershed in the history of the city. The Encarnación Carnival is far and away the largest in Paraguay, and is held in the Sambódromo next to the Costanera, just a touch to the east from its old site on Avenida Dr Francia. Between the new Sambódromo and the old Sambódromo is the **Parque de la Ciudad**. The Carnival takes place over three or four weekends before Lent begins, ie: in February and maybe a bit of January or March. Tickets are sold in the carnival office on the Costanera (☎ 071 200928), in Tigo offices, in the Hotel Piringo of San Ignacio, and other places; they can also be bought (for a negotiable mark-up) from private sellers outside the entrance immediately beforehand. You buy a ticket for a particular block, so it is important to choose well before paying: you should take into account not only the position in relation to the parade but also the seating arrangements, bearing in mind that you are going to be there for many hours of the night. The starting time is officially 21.00, but in practice it may be a bit later, and it goes on until 03.00 or later. There are about a dozen teams, and it takes at least half an hour for each to pass, with its succession of floats and radiant, energetic dancing girls, scantily dressed but harnessed into huge frameworks of brightly coloured feathers. The exuberant crowd, meanwhile, sprays white foam out of canisters: it is a good idea to buy the protective goggles on sale, to keep it out of your eyes, as it has bleach in it. If you are not a night bird you may not last until the end, but no matter – the whole event is hugely exhilarating and worth the hiked-up hotel prices.

WHAT TO SEE AND DO

The Costanera Encarnación today is practically synonymous with the beach – principally San José beach – and with the Costanera, that is, the new, long coast road that wraps around the city. In fact, Encarnación is almost on an island, reached by three bridges across the strait to the north. The new San José river beach, 800m long, is broad and has yellow sand, dotted with blue and green parasols, and fronted by smart bars. The water is warm and is not deep. You can hire all your beach equipment on the spot: chairs, tables, big umbrellas, loungers, floats for going in the water, and bicycles for exploring the length of the Costanera. There is free, supervised parking and clean toilets. A tourist information office is being built, and there are notices proclaiming a Wi-Fi zone.

You can take boat trips or go for long walks along the Costanera, yet find a bench to sit on every few metres. There is a lack of trees for shade, but they cannot be conjured up overnight (the Costanera has only been open since 2012). Many parks and playgrounds are being created alongside the road.

The sunsets are beautiful and majestic. At night the riverfront gleams with lights, and the lights of the Costanera over in Posadas, Argentina, are well visible and cast long reflections in the river. Best of all, it is very well patrolled so that you know that you are safe, whether by day or by night.

Having said that, in some ways it is surprising that one of the principal attractions for Paraguayan holidaymakers and weekenders is Encarnación beach, as there are better beaches elsewhere that are empty. Along the river bank of Ñeembucú there are many, and although most are difficult to get to, those in Ayolas are easy to access, and are closer to Asunción than Encarnación. Then, leaving aside the many and ample sandy beaches of the Rio Paraná, there are beaches on the Río Tebicuarý at Villa Florida (see page pages 189–90), while in the north there are lovely beaches on the Río Aquidabán (see page 342). But there are people who like the romance of deserted beaches and other people who like the buzz and the facilities of crowded beaches, and fortunately for the former, there are far more of the latter.

OTHER SITES IN ENCARNACIÓN If you come in by bus, you will arrive close to the **Basilica** [270 C4] – in other words, the cathedral – on the block that is northeast of the terminal. There are three statues from the Reductions inside the entrance to this church. Then another five blocks north of the terminal you come to the historic grassy square of the **Plaza de Armas** [270 C3]. This is an ancient square, nicely set out for walking and sitting, with a variety of trees and a little lake. It has a white monument in the middle like a mini Cerro Corá (see pages 352–3) and is divided into different squares within a square, with sections devoted to children, mothers, Ukrainians, Japanese and Germans. The last section has a plaque thanking Paraguay 'for having generously accepted' their immigrants – perhaps a veiled reference to the number of Nazis who found refuge here. There is often folk dance on Saturday nights. The Ukrainian **Orthodox Cathedral** of San Jorge [270 C3] is a handsome pale green and gold building with an onion tower on the corner of Carlos Antonio López and Tomas Romero Pereira. At weekends you can hire a ***karumbé*** (horse cart for passengers) from the corner of the Plaza de Armas (*14 de mayo y Carlos Antonio López*) and do a tour of the city. These yellow, roofed vehicles, first introduced from Brazil in 1939, now have a subsidy from the Municipalidad to continue their work, as they are regarded as something of an icon of the city. They are also found at the terminal, in the side road to the south [270 C4] (🕘 *Mon–Fri until 11.00*), next to the Hotel Río which operates as a *motel* (see *Appendix 2*, page 394) and so is not included in *Where to Stay* on pages 271–3.

From there it is three blocks west to reach the **Museo Jesuítico** at the Universidad Católica [270 B3] (*Artigas c/ Tomas Romero Pereira; ☎ 071 201485 int 250; ☎ 07.00–11.30 Mon–Fri; free admission*). This has a collection of small carved wooden statues of saints, and some construction materials. The museum was founded by historian Professor Alberto Delvalle with items from his own collection.

In the next block south, the **Museo de la Casa Victoria** [270 C3] (*Cerro Corá c/ Artigas; ☎ 071 203691; 🕘 08.00–11.00 & 14.00–17.00 Mon–Fri; free admission*) is a small museum with items from the Chaco War.

If you go along the road Cerro Corá towards the beach you will come to the **old railway station** [270 B3], which is currently completing a meticulous restoration, with as many as possible of the original bricks and doors. It will house a museum and a bar. Encarnación was the end of the line, within Paraguay, before the railway crossed into Argentina, so this was an important station.

Further south is a triangle of park called the **Parque de la Salud**, which has been recently inaugurated, similar to the park of the same name in Asunción (see pages 117–18). It has 1km of well-surfaced paths for walking or cycling illuminated by 32 lights, and there are gymnastic and games areas, as well as drinking water, toilets and showers. The idea is to promote exercise and a healthy lifestyle in a pleasant surrounding of trees and plants.

The **Feria Municipal** [270 D5] (also known as La Placita or El Mercado Municipal, or even the Zona Baja in memory of the old days, see below) is a marketplace of cheap goods. For many Paraguayans, their chief interest in arriving in Encarnación is to do some shopping at low prices in the Feria. Originally it was located in the *zona baja* – the low-lying barrio in southwest Encarnación – but when the Yacyretá dam was raised, that area was partly flooded. Since about 2006 the Feria has been housed in a new precinct on the Avenida San Roque González, on the way to the bridge, just south of the Parque de la Salud. Though some traders initially resisted the move to the new purpose-made building further from their homes, it now provides plenty of atmosphere as well as convenience for buying clothes, electrics, craft, Paraguayan cheese, chickens and vegetables. And the barrio to the east of the Feria building is now a whole new commercial zone.

Some 6km to the north of the city is a small zoo called Zoológico Juan XXIII (*entrance Gs2,000*) which has jaguars, mountain lions, anteaters, monkeys, snakes, toucans, parrots and peacocks, among other animals. From the city, after crossing the bridge towards Asunción, and before crossing the next big bridge, it is on the last road to the right: you pass the entrance to the Universidad Nacional, then there is a small roundabout for turning, and at this point take a right, left and right again.

EXCURSIONS FROM ENCARNACIÓN A new **Parque Acuático Ecológico** (aquatic park) called **El Dorado** (*🕘 10.00–19.00, Gs30,000 Tue & Wed, Gs40,000 Thu & Fri, Gs50,000 Sat & Sun; closed Mon*) opened in early 2014, 11km outside Encarnación on Ruta 6 (that is, towards Trinidad, just before Capitan Miranda). With high bouncing slides plunging into a pool, a second pool for children, and a lake for boating and fishing, it promises to offer great family fun. There is a snack bar and camping facilities. Further slides that are higher or that spiral are planned as a further investment in the future.

The sanctuary of the **Virgin of Itacuá**, 12km south of Encarnación, is rapidly establishing itself as a new Caacupé, attracting around 10,000 pilgrims each year. Near the bridge, you take a turning to the left (east) at the roundabout where there is a yellow spiral around a white pole. Then you come to a white statue of a woman carrying a fish in her hand and a basket on her head. This road, called Tupãsyrapé (Guaraní 'God's mother's road'), runs for about 9km parallel to the river, taking you through the countryside. If you do not have your own vehicle, you can reach the shrine of Itacuá by bus, taking the *linea 4*. There are also some boats that go from Encarnación to the sanctuary of Itacuá, but that is more of a leisure trip.

According to the story, in 1906 a group of fishermen in a boat noticed a woman dressed in white standing among the rocks. They identified her with the Virgin Mary. A spring of water appeared, a shrine was built, and in due course miracles were noted. Today there is a large modern basilica, shaped like a ship, with a prow sticking out towards the river, and a deep-blue shell-like niche in front of the windows. If you go around the edge of the basilica you come to the little statue set in a rocky grotto. As at Caacupé, the principal feast day is 8 December, the Immaculate Conception, and this is preceded by masses for the nine preceding days (the novena). On Sundays there are religious celebrations at 10.00 and 17.00.

A motor boat called ***Carlos Mateo*** (*Martin Eisenkolbl;* **m** *0985 762443;* **e** *yatecarlosmateo@gmail.com*) does a number of excursions from Encarnación, leaving from the beach Mbói Kaẽ (Guaraní 'thin snake'), which is not on the Costanera but just north of the bridge that brings Ruta 1 into Encarnación. The boat has 5 air-conditioned cabins and a bar, lounge and open terrace. The journey to the sand dunes of San Cosme y Damián lasts 40 minutes but the round trip lasts three hours with time spent on the beach. A trip to the Virgin of Itacuá lasts two and a half hours; and a trip around the three principal beaches of the Costanera (the third is San Isidro, to the south of San José, but before the international bridge) lasts an hour.

8

Excursion to the Iguazú Falls

The Iguazú Falls are one of the wonders of the world. Going to see a waterfall might not sound like a full day's occupation, but that is the very minimum that you need for Iguazú, and two days is still not enough for an exhaustive visit. The size, power and variety of these falls is breathtaking. They are in the region known as the Three Frontiers, where Paraguay, Argentina and Brazil meet, but the falls today are just outside Paraguayan territory, forming the border between Brazil and Argentina. Few visitors to Paraguay want to go home without seeing them.

In the time of the President Dr Francia, there were border disputes over Misiones Argentina, but Paraguayan claims were ended by the disaster of the Triple Alliance War. Paraguayans still, however, feel a certain affinity with this territory, especially since the falls have a Guaraní name. Guaraní is still spoken as the mother tongue in Paraguay while it has been virtually lost in Argentina and Brazil as a living language, with only place names surviving.

Most people who go from Paraguay to the Iguazú Falls (or *las Cataratas* as everyone calls them) travel to the Paraguayan border city of Ciudad del Este and then cross over to Foz do Iguaçu in Brazil. This is the most direct route.

However, there are many reasons for preferring the alternative route through Encarnación in the south of Paraguay, to Posadas, Argentina, and then up to Puerto Iguazú, which is the town on the Argentinian side of the falls. Encarnación is a smaller and safer place than Ciudad del Este, and travelling to Encarnación gives you the chance to visit the museums of Misiones Paraguay and the Ruins of Itapúa on the way. The journey on Argentinian buses up to the falls is more comfortable than the parallel journey on Paraguayan buses, and as you travel up through Misiones Argentina you have the opportunity to visit San Ignacio Miní (see pages 260–7). Other interesting places en route (which unfortunately fall outside the scope of this book) are the Solar del Che, where Che Guevara spent his infancy, and the Minas de Wanda. When you reach the falls, there is more to do and explore on the Argentinian side than on the Brazilian side; most people prefer the Argentinian side, although the Brazilian side has different strong points. In addition, Puerto Iguazú is a smaller and safer place than Foz, and now has some really lovely places to stay, for all budgets. Lastly, Spanish speakers may prefer to visit the falls in another Spanish-speaking country (Argentina) rather than a Portuguese-speaking country (Brazil).

If you have time, it is worth visiting both sides of the falls, although it is not possible to do both on the same day. If you try to come to the Argentinian side from Foz, the journey each way will take about 1½ hours. For this reason, this chapter covers the Argentinian town of Puerto Iguazú, before moving on to the Brazilian side and Foz do Iguaçu. The next chapter then covers Ciudad del Este, which you may need to pass through if you are going from the waterfalls to Asunción.

IGUAZÚ FALLS
see map page 296
For listings, see pages 282–3
Where to stay
1 Casa Blanca
2 Hostel Natura
3 Hostel Paudimar Campestre
4 Hotel Cataratas (Argentina)
5 Hotel das Cataratas
6 Hotel San Martín
7 Mabu Thermas & Resort
8 Posada 21 Oranges
9 Sheraton
10 Viale
PARAGUAY
(Alto Paraná)
Tatí Yupí Biological Reserve
Reserve entrance
Lago Itaipú
Paraná
Itaipú Dam
Viewpoint for Itaipú Dam
Modelo Reducio
Itaipú Dam Visitors' Centre
Museo de la Tierra Guaraní & Zoo
Polo Astronômico
Canal da Piracema
Itaipú Dam Visitors' Centre
HERNANDARIAS
Refugio Biológico Bela Vista
Acaray
Ecomuseu
AVENIDA TANCREDO NEVES
BR 277
Paraná Country Club
Airport Guaraní
Madame Chateau
Plaza Foz (dance show)
Puente de la Amistad
Lago de la República
CIUDAD DEL ESTE
FOZ DO IGUAÇU
BRAZIL
(Paraná)
PRESIDENTE FRANCO
Salto Monday
Monday
Marco das Três Fronteiras
Brazilian Airport das Cataratas (IGU)
Pto Meiro
Puente Tancredo Neves
Hito de las Tres Fronteras
Duty Free Shop
Hito de las Tres Fronteras
PUERTO IGUAZÚ
Park entrance (Brazil)
RN 12
La Aldea de la Selva
Parque das Aves
Iguaçu National Park
Aripuca
Iguazú
Productores Mineros
see map page 296
Santuario Ecológico de Santa María del Yguazú & Museo Imágenes de la Selva
Moisés Bertoni House
Aldea Fortín Mbororé
Parque Nacional Iguazú
Entrance to Iguaçu Falls (Brazil)
Entrance to Iguazú Falls (Argentina)
Estación Cataratas
ARGENTINA
(Misiones)
Estación Central
Iguazú Falls
N
Bradt
RN 12
Estación Garganta
0 5km
0 5 miles
Argentinian Airport de Cataratas (IGR)

PUERTO IGUAZÚ

www.experienciamisiones.com; www.welcomeargentina.com; www.iguazuturismo.gov.ar

Puerto Iguazú has a population of 50,000, while Foz do Iguaçu, on the Brazilian side of the frontier, has more than 300,000. Not surprisingly, then, Puerto Iguazú is a more pleasant and manageable place, where you can walk back from a restaurant at night without feeling nervous.

GETTING THERE AND AWAY

By bus If you follow the suggestion to travel to the falls through Misiones Argentina, you will take a bus **from Posadas** up Argentina's Ruta RN12 – or from San Ignacio Miní, which is *en route*. They leave approximately hourly. The quality of the buses varies: good companies with a frequent service are Horianski (comfortable, free drinks, terrible movies) and A del Valle. The journey from Posadas to Puerto Iguazú takes five or six hours, and the cost with Horianski is currently A$165 single, A$232 return (unless you stop off at San Ignacio Miní on the way, see pages 260–7). If you are arriving by bus **from Buenos Aires**, the journey takes some 17 hours and you will probably come on one of the following buses, stopping at Posadas on the way: Crucero del Norte, Expreso Singer, Tigre Iguazú, Via Bariloche or Río Uruguay.

If you are travelling by bus **from Ciudad del Este**, the journey is not difficult, as Rio Paraguay run a bus that takes you directly from the bus terminal in Ciudad del Este, through Foz, to Puerto Iguazú without stopping. Buses leave about every half hour and are very inexpensive. At Argentinian border control the bus may not wait for you to have your passport stamped, in which case you will have to wait for the next bus; but you may not want to have your passport stamped anyway if you are only going to the waterfalls, as an Argentinian stamp without the corresponding exit and entry stamps for Paraguay can leave you liable for a fine when you next want to leave the country. Take care not to miss the last bus back from Puerto Iguazú to Ciudad del Este, which leaves at about 18.00.

If you are doing this route it is advisable to get pesos while you are still in Ciudad del Este, where there are many exchange houses offering a quick service; if you wait until you are in Puerto Iguazú you may have to walk some seven blocks from the bus terminal to find somewhere to change guaraníes into pesos, with a lot more fuss and with more restricted opening hours.

Do not forget that there is an hour's time difference between Paraguay and Argentina in winter (but not in summer), and an hour's difference between Brazil and Argentina in summer (but not in winter). There is always an hour's difference between Paraguay and Brazil.

IGUAZÚ: THE NAME

There are at least five different ways of spelling Iguazú. This guide uses the Argentinian form, but in Paraguay they sometimes spell it Iguasu. In English it is usually spelt Iguassu, and in Brazil they spell it Iguaçu. It is a Guaraní name, but even that does not settle the matter as there are different ways of spelling words in Guaraní. However, according to current correct practice in writing Guaraní, it would be spelt *y guasu*. *Y* means water, and *guasu* means big. So the name means 'big water' and you could spell it Yguasú. To all intents and purposes, despite the distinct pronunciation of the *y* vowel in Guaraní, the normal pronunciation of the word is 'ig – wa – sue'.

There are also buses that go from Asunción through to Foz, but this is not necessarily a help, as they arrive at the international bus station (Rodovia) and you need to go to the local bus station (TTU) to continue your journey to Puerto Iguazú. Note that the planned bridge from Presidente Franco to Foz (see page 287) will also make travel easier from Ciudad del Este to Puerto Iguazú, although it will still be necessary to cross the Brazilian frontier.

By ferry Another way of arriving is on the little-known ferry **crossing from Paraguay** on a *balsa* (literally, 'raft', in effect a car ferry), which leaves from the port in Presidente Franco (immediately south of Ciudad del Este, and only 8km from Puente de la Amistad). The ferry takes up to 28 cars, and begins and ends its day in Puerto Iguazú, where the port is close to the Hito de las Tres Fronteras. The first crossing is at 08.30 and the last crossing from Paraguay is at 17.15; the ferry now runs seven days a week (and not just Monday to Friday as it did before 2012). It can take up to 30 cars and 90 passengers, and is very inexpensive. It principally serves local people going to do their shopping in the other country, but is a great idea for tourists too, as you cross from Paraguay to Argentina in 12 minutes, with none of the delays that can hit you on the Puente de la Amistad, and none of the nuisance, expense and delay of negotiating Foz. There is customs and passport control on both sides of the river. This route is particularly helpful for those who would need a visa to pass through Brazil, such as US citizens and Australians.

By air Puerto Iguazú has its own **airport**, the Aeropuerto Internacional Cataratas de Iguazú, 17km from the town and 12km from the waterfalls, which has flights from Buenos Aires. But though it is called International it has few if any international flights, and if you are arriving from another continent you will arrive in Foz. Both airports are called Cataratas, so the airport code is helpful to differentiate them: IGU for Foz, Brazil, and IGR for Puerto Iguazú, Argentina. For details of arriving at Foz Airport, see page 287.

Visas Holders of EU or US passports do not require visas to enter Argentina. Citizens of the USA, Canada and Australia can enter without a visa if they have paid a 'reciprocity fee' online (*www.provinciapagos.com.ar* and *www.migraciones.gov.ar*).

TOUR OPERATORS AND GUIDES The website of the local secretariat of tourism is www.iguazuturismo.gov.ar. The number of the local **Secretaría de Turismo** is ☎ +54 3757 420800. There is a tourist information office on Ruta 12 just before the junction with the road that goes to the waterfalls. Here are some tour operators:

Venteveo Turismo Av Córdoba y Misiones; ☎ +54 3757 423992; e info@venteveoturismo.tur.ar; ⊕ 09.00–19.00 Mon–Sat. Has an office in the terminal, Local 25. Helpful & efficient. Recommended.

Cuenca del Plata Tareferos 111/ Sucursal Paulino Amarante 76; ☎ +54 3757 423300; www.cuencadelplata.com. This company offers (among other attractions) a trip to a Guaraní indigenous village; see page 286.

Cataratas Turismo Av Tres Fronteras 301; ☎ +54 3757 420970; e cataratasturismo@cataratasturismoevt.com.ar. Another local tour operator, with cars & buses of varying sizes.

Caracol Avenida Victoria Aguirre 563; ☎ +54 3757 424242; www.caracolturismo.com.ar; ⊕ 07.00–21.30 daily. Big company, offering the usual tours of the National Park with a slight slant towards ecotourism & adventure tourism.

Emturi Avenida Victoria Aguirre y Balbino Brañas; ☎ +54 3757 422763. As well as the usual tours of the waterfalls they offer a visit to the Solar del Che Guevara, just over an hour away on the road to San Ignacio Miní.

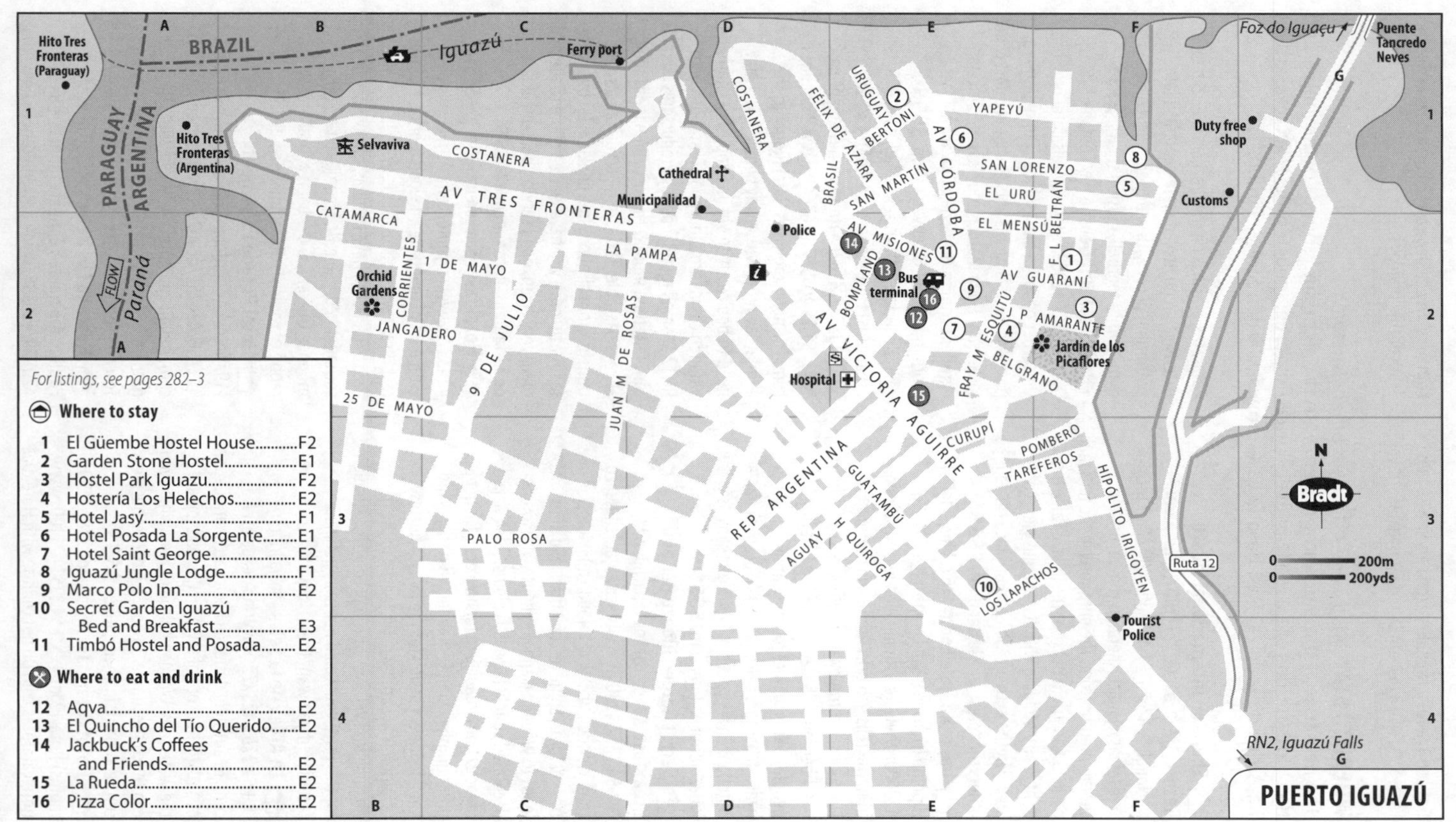
PUERTO IGUAZÚ
For listings, see pages 282–3
Where to stay
1 El Güembe Hostel House.........F2
2 Garden Stone Hostel.........E1
3 Hostel Park Iguazu.........F2
4 Hostería Los Helechos.........E2
5 Hotel Jasý.........F1
6 Hotel Posada La Sorgente.........E1
7 Hotel Saint George.........E2
8 Iguazú Jungle Lodge.........F1
9 Marco Polo Inn.........E2
10 Secret Garden Iguazú Bed and Breakfast.........E3
11 Timbó Hostel and Posada.........E2
Where to eat and drink
12 Aqva.........E2
13 El Quincho del Tío Querido.........E2
14 Jackbuck's Coffees and Friends.........E2
15 La Rueda.........E2
16 Pizza Color.........E2
Hito Tres Fronteras (Paraguay)
BRAZIL
Iguazú
Ferry port
Foz do Iguaçu
Puente Tancredo Neves
PARAGUAY
ARGENTINA
Paraná
FLOW
Hito Tres Fronteras (Argentina)
Selvaviva
COSTANERA
Cathedral
Municipalidad
Police
AV TRES FRONTERAS
CATAMARCA
CORRIENTES
1 DE MAYO
LA PAMPA
Orchid Gardens
JANGADERO
9 DE JULIO
JUAN M DE ROSAS
25 DE MAYO
PALO ROSA
URUGUAY
FÉLIX DE AZARA
BERTONI
BRASIL
SAN MARTÍN
AV CÓRDOBA
YAPEYÚ
SAN LORENZO
EL URÚ
EL MENSÚ
F L BELTRAN
AV MISIONES
BOMPLAND
Bus terminal
AV GUARANÍ
J P AMARANTE
FRAY M ESQUITÚ
BELGRANO
Jardín de los Picaflores
Hospital
AV VICTORIA AGUIRRE
CURUPÍ
POMBERO
TAREFEROS
REP ARGENTINA
GUATAMBÚ
AGUAY
H QUIROGA
LOS LAPACHOS
HIPÓLITO IRIGOYEN
Tourist Police
Duty free shop
Customs
Ruta 12
RN2, Iguazú Falls
N
Bradt
0 200m
0 200yds

Galileo Travel Avenida Victoria Aguirre 391 PB Local 5; +54 3757 424362; e info@galileotravel.com.ar; www.galileotravel.com.ar. Does excursions & adventure holidays.

WHERE TO STAY *Map, page 281, unless otherwise stated.*

The new style is all rustic and wooden, with the sights and sounds of the jungle, and there are options of this style in every price range, eg: Iguazú Jungle, Secret Garden, La Aldea de la Selva, Jasy, Posada 21 Oranges, Garden Stone, Timbo.

Sheraton Internacional Iguazú Resort [Map, page 278] (180 rooms) Parque Nacional; +54 3757 491800/0800 888 9180; e reservas@iguazu.sheraton.com.ar; www.sheratoniguazu.com. The only hotel in the national park, looking right out over the Iguazú Falls, this light & airy building with its fabulous views offers luxury in the extreme. Some rooms face the falls & others the forest, at a lesser price. **$$$$$**

Iguazú Jungle Lodge (6 cabins, 3 lofts) Hipólito Irigoyen y San Lorenzo; +54 3757 420600; www.iguazujunglelodge.com. 15mins from the falls, 7 blocks from town centre. Luxurious accommodation either in a cabin (each has 3 bedrooms & sleeps 7) or in a Loft (for 2 people). Wi-Fi, games room, swimming pool, hydro-massage, balconies, 24-hour snack bar, a notebook in every cabin. Same company as www.iguazujunglexplorer.com. **$$$$**

Secret Garden Iguazu Bed and Breakfast (3 rooms) Los Lapachos 623; +54 3757 423099; www.secretgardeniguazu.com. Wooden walkway through mini forest of trees & ferns, some rescued from land burn-offs, leads to wooden clapboard house with rooms decorated simply in pastel colours. Fresh baked bread & homemade jam for breakfast. Owner is photographer John Fernandes, who shares his knowledge & passion for the forest. Courtesy caipirinhas at sundown, Wi-Fi even in the garden, no pool, no TV. Those who stay adore it, although for this price you would normally get more facilities (if you want them). **$$$$**

La Aldea de la Selva Selva Iriapú; +54 3757 425777; www.laaldeadelaselva.com. Beautifully designed luxury accommodation of a rustic hue, out of town on the road towards the waterfalls. Wooden balconies from which you can touch the jungle. 3 pools, 2 jacuzzis, business centre, organic kitchen garden. **$$$$**

Hotel Cataratas [Map, page 278] (130 rooms) Ruta 12 km4; +54 3757 421100; www.hotelcataratas.com Do not confuse with Hotel Das Cataratas, which is on the Brazilian side. Big rooms, extensive menu in elegant restaurant, 2 large swimming pools with waterfalls; jacuzzi, sauna, gym, tennis, football, musical shows. **$$$$**

Hotel Saint George Av Córdoba 148; +54 3757 420633; www.hotelsaintgeorge.com. On corner opposite bus terminal. Big swimming pool & attractive rooms; lots of fruit at b/fast & the restaurant Doña María is top class. Helpful staff, excellent English. Jacuzzi, sauna, gym, massage room, good craft & souvenir shop. **$$$$**

Posada 21 Oranges [Map, page 278] (10 rooms) Calle Montecarlo km5; +54 9 3757 405577/416764 (from within Argentina 03757 15 405577/416764); www.21oranges.com. Formerly known as Hotel Riotropic, this is a great favourite with many people & you may need to book early to get in. Simple but charming wooden cabins around a pool. Turn south from RN12 at small roundabout by Productores Mineros, turn left, then right, & the last 700m is dirt road, always passable. Taxi service, & you can arrange transfer from airport when booking. On bus route to Iguazu, once you have walked 600m to the main road. Very clean, good service, good breakfast, but no restaurant. Recommended. **$$$**

Hotel Jasy San Lorenzo 154; +54 3757 424337; www.jasyhotel.com. Attractively designed with a lot of rough-hewn wood & brick. Library, restaurant with lots of salads, Wi-Fi in common areas. Rooms all have minibar, microwave, heating, sommier bed, cable TV. Moonlit terrace (*jasy* is moon in Guaraní) & the bar is a focal spot with a range of cocktails. Recommended. **$$$**

Hotel Posada La Sorgente (19 rooms) Av Córdoba 454; +54 3757 422756/424252/424072; www.lasorgentehotel.com. Italian-run hotel opened in 2005. Nice garden, 2 blocks from bus terminal. Restaurant La Toscana specialises in pasta & is rated highly. **$$$**

Hostería Los Helechos (60 rooms) Paulino Amarante 76; reservations +54 3757 420829/420338; www.hosterialoshelechos.com.ar.

Inexpensive restaurant open for dinner until 22.30 (no lunches). Swimming pool. Avoid rooms 31–45, which have no external windows. **$$**

Garden Stone Hostel Avenida Córdoba 441; +54 3757 420425; www.gardenstonehostel.com. Big garden (1500m^2). Every bedroom differently decorated so no institutional feel. **$$**

Marco Polo Inn Av Córdoba 158; +54 3757 425559; www.marcopoloinniguazu.com. Great advantage of this hostel is that it is right opposite the bus terminal. Dorms & private rooms, kitchen, tourist info, big lounge bar. **$$**

Timbo Hostel and Posada (7 rooms inc dorm for 14) Avenida Misiones 147; +54 3757 422698; www.timboiguazu.com.ar. B/fast in rustic *quincho*, lots of greenery, 'a little bit of the wild immersed in the centre of Iguazú', only 100m from bus terminal. Lovely design to rooms with bamboo blinds & ethnic woollen picture hangings. Meat or vegetarian *asados*. Probably the top choice in hostels. **$**

El Güembe Hostel House (sleeps 35) Avenida Gobernador Lanusse y Guaraní; +54 3757 424189; www.elguembehostelhouse.com.ar. Located 2 blocks from the bus terminal, kitchen & pool. **$**

Hostel Park Iguazu Paulino Amarante 111; +55 45 3757 424342; www.hostelparkiguazu.com.ar. Dorms & rooms, basic but clean & modern, 2mins from the terminal, pool, ping pong, book exchange. **$**

WHERE TO EAT AND DRINK *Map, page 281.*

Aqva Av Córdoba y Carlos Thays; + 54 3757 422064; reservas@aqvarestaurant.com; noon–midnight daily. Stylish restaurant, strong on meat & fish. **$$$$$**

La Rueda Av Córdoba 28; +54 3757 422531; larueda1975@iguazunet.com; lunch & eve Wed–Sun. Excellent restaurant centrally placed, about 3 blocks from the terminal. Atmosphere, imaginative menu, well-presented food, cellar (bodega) where guests can choose their wine out of 350 Argentinian varieties. **$$$$**

El Quincho del Tio Querido Bonpland 110; +54 3757 420151. Spacious restaurant & a good place for whiling away a long evening, as it has live musicians. **$$$$**

Pizza Color Av Córdoba 135; +54 3757 420206. Right next door to the bus terminal, has decent food, at reasonable prices. **$$$**

Jackbuck's Coffees and Friends Av Misiones 235; +54 3757 439985. Excellent food, coffee, service & Wi-Fi. Run by friendly Brazilians. **$$**

IGUAZÚ FALLS *(www.iguazuargentina.com; www.iguazujungle.com)* For the visit to the Brazilian side of these waterfalls, see pages 291–3.

The Iguazú Falls are a natural rock formation estimated as being 150 million years old. They were first discovered by the Spanish governor of Asunción, Alvar Núñez Cabeza de Vaca, in 1542. They are so stunning that when Eleanor Roosevelt saw them she exclaimed, 'Poor Niagara!' The reason for their drama is the large lake that is formed above – swirling round to one side so that it becomes 1,200m wide – with the result that the falls run diagonally across the river, ending in a horseshoe shape. The falls have a total length of 2,700m, and the water plunges down some 70–80m to quite a narrow channel at the bottom. There are as many as 275 separate narrow waterfalls cascading over the rocks at the rate of 1,500m^3 per second, with rainbows playing in the sun and a cauldron of spray that blurs visibility.

On the Argentinian side there are a lot of walkways which take you over parts of the river, giving you an ever-changing series of views. There are cliffs to climb up, and down with steps, and boat trips that take you over to San Martín island, and up as close as you can dare to the falling water, where everyone laughs and screams and gets soaked. Most dramatic of all is the **Garganta del Diablo (Devil's throat)** where a walkway takes you over the lake at the top until you are looking right down the 84m pit of the most thunderous fall with the spray hiding the full fearsomeness of it – a great place for photos, if you stand back. From there you can take a quiet boat ride called the *paseo ecológico*, through waters where butterflies and caimans can be seen.

There are half-hourly **buses** from the Puerto Iguazú bus terminal (though they start their journey at the Hito Tres Fronteras) to the Parque Nacional Iguazú (currently A$60 return). The journey takes 20 mins: the bus company is Rio Uruguay and the notice says 'CATARATAS/WATERFALLS'. You pay to get into the park when you arrive (*+54 3757 491469;* **e** *info@iguazuargentina.com;* *Oct–Mar 08.00–19.00, Apr–Sep 08.00–18.00; currently A$170 foreigners, A$115 under-12s and residents of Mercosur, A$65 Argentinians;* *08.00–18.00 365 days of the year*). Only Argentinian pesos are accepted, but you can get these at a cash machine by the entrance gate; there is another one inside, at the central station of the Narrow Gauge Railway. If you have opted to hire a car from the airport to give you more flexibility, you will need to pay parking (currently A$60). You must let the hire company know if you are going to take a car from Foz into Argentina, and pay an extra insurance premium, but this is usually worth doing by comparison with taxi prices to cross the border).

The entrance fee enables you to do the walks, take the trains and visit the museum – the sometimes overlooked Centro de Interpretación de la Naturaleza Yvyrá Retã (Guaraní, 'Land of Trees'), near the entrance. But if you want the boat rides, or jeep rides through the forest, then there is a choice of packages with **Iguazú Jungle Explorer** that you can buy at the terminal before you set off. There are three different packages of rides, but a green passport enables you to do them all, and although the price seems to go up steeply every year it is very much worth it. The staff wear yellow shirts and many of them speak excellent English.

The park covers 67,000ha and is the home to 2,000 species of animals and plants, including 80 species of mammals, and five kinds of cats (jaguars and mountain lions among them).

Favourites among the 450 species of birds are the toucans, hummingbirds and green parrots. The park is also incredibly rich in butterflies.

The **peak times** are January, Semana Santa and July (actually the coldest month, but when the South American *vacación de quince* – fortnight's holiday – coincides with the European holiday period). Every year more than one million people visit Argentina's side of the falls. Argentina's national park was recognised by UNESCO as a World Heritage Site in 1984, and in 2012 the falls were formally recognised as one of the 'New Seven Wonders of Nature'.

The new installations in the park have taken into account the needs of people with disabilities, and there are 6% ramps and special places for wheelchairs on the train. (The boat rides on the lower river, however, require you to climb 150m of steps.) There are also electric cars for helping anyone who is slow in moving to get around the park. There are large toilets, and braille in the Centre of Interpretation and on the menus of La Selva.

Some people recommend taking dry clothes in a rucksack, as you will get soaked in the boat tour and may end up buying them, and certainly plastic bags are advisable. Others advise doing the boat trip where you get wet early in the day to give you time to dry off, and going to the popular Devil's Throat after that, when the first wave of keen tourists has already been and gone. A hat, water and insect repellent are recommended for those doing the 3.6km Macuco Nature Trail.

There are various places to have **lunch.** The Restaurant La Selva near the entrance is the most expensive and the best, but there are cheaper places next to it and in three other locations that serve fast food. There are plenty of souvenir shops, and there are always Guaraní indigenous with their attractive gifts of feather headdresses, colourful bags and wooden animals. You are asked not to feed the coati (from the raccoon family) because it alters their natural behaviour and makes them aggressive.

THE LEGEND OF IGUAZÚ

According to Guaraní myth, the land was ruled by Mbói, a mighty snake who was one of the sons of the great god Tupã. The local *cacique* Igobí had a daughter called Naipí who was so beautiful that when she stopped to look at her reflection in the river, the waters would stop in their tracks in admiration of her. This girl was promised to Mbói, but she fell in love with a young man called Tarobá, and when the day of her consecration to the God came round, while the festivities were going on, the couple escaped downriver on a canoe. When Mbói realised what had happened he was so angry that he slashed at the earth with his snake-body and caused a terrifying earthquake, so that the waterfalls of Iguazú were created as the river rushed from one level to another, and the canoe and its occupants were swallowed up. Mbói turned Tarobá into a palm tree on the upper level of the falls, while Naipí was turned into a rock at the bottom, against which the terrifying waters of the falls would pound for perpetuity, while her lover leans helplessly towards her from an unbridgeable distance above. Mbói meanwhile lives in a cave beneath the tree and watches the torment continue through endless ages. No wonder the most fearsome drop in the falls is called the Devil's Throat (Garganta del Diablo).

There is so much to see and do that you can consider coming back the next day to complete the visit – and you get a 50% discount if you do. A special excursion is offered on the night of the full moon every month, entering the park at 19.45, 20.30 or 21.15, but places are limited so you must book. (It is currently A$550 for an adult with dinner in the La Selva restaurant). When the moon reaches its fullness it changes colour, and this is a magical and romantic excursion. For details, consult www.iguazuargentina.com.

An eco-adventure programme is offered with **Iguazú Forest** (*www.iguazuforest.com*). Activities include wet-abseiling, jungle biking, trekking, climbing rope ladders, butterfly- and birdwatching and rock climbing. An information leaflet tells you what to do if you meet a jaguar: do not run away, but face the animal and make a lot of noise, clapping your hands and talking loudly. Try to appear bigger than you are by waving your arms with any bag or item of clothing you have to hand. Do not go any closer, but withdraw slowly, without turning your back on the animal. It is very unlikely you would meet one of these large felines, but knowing what you would do if you did adds to the fun of the expedition.

WHAT ELSE TO SEE AND DO

Duty-free shop [281 G1] (*Ruta 12;* ☎ *+54 3757 421050;* www.dutyfreeshoppuertoiguazu.com; ⌚ *10.00–21.00 daily*) This massive modern shop is in between the Tancredo Neves bridge and the Argentinian customs, with fountains playing outside. It has won awards for being 'the best duty-free shop in the world'.

Hito Tres Fronteras [281 A1] (*Av de las 3 Fronteras*) This pyramidical obelisk looks out towards similar markers on the coasts of Brazil and Paraguay. Argentina has the best view of the three, because it has a bit of height, and also has a large craft store beside it, the Corredor Artesanal. Also at its side is a sort of theme park about the jungle, called Selvaviva (www.selvaviva.com; ⌚ *09.00–noon & 16.00–18.00 Tue–Sun; A$90 adults, A$50 children*), with a fish tank, bird observation point, butterfly world, spider house and ant land. See the map on page 281.

Orquidiarios [281 B2] These orchid gardens (☎ *+54 3757 423394;* 🕘 *08.00–noon & 16.00–20.00 daily*) house 20,000 natural varieties of orchids. You will find them a few blocks south of the Hito Tres Fronteras.

Jardín de los Picaflores [281 F2] (*Fray Luis Beltrán 150;* ☎ *+54 3757 424081;* 🕘 *08.30–17.00 daily*) Three blocks from the bus terminal, almost opposite the Hotel Lilian, this is a garden of hummingbirds. In Guaraní mythology, this bird, the *mainumbý* (Guaraní; Spanish *picaflor*), was the only one to have direct communication with God.

Aripuca (*www.aripuca.com.ar;* 🕘 *09.00–18.00 daily; entrance fee, first part of visit guided*) This unusual construction of massive logs (some from trees 300 years old) with a roof on top is situated 300m from the west side of the main road that runs into Puerto Iguazú. It takes the form of a trap used by the Guaraní to catch animals alive, and in and around it are exhibitions, shops and snack bars. It is designed to raise ecological awareness, as a protest against the logging that has cut these trees down. Allow an hour for the visit.

Productores Mineros (*Ruta 12, km3.5;* ☎ *+54 3757 424193; www.productoresmineros.com.ar;* 🕘 *08.00–21.00 daily*) An interesting store of semi-precious jewellery where you can watch people work, with attentive multilingual staff.

La Aldea Fortín Mbororé This is a Guaraní village which you can visit with indigenous guides, 1.5km south of RN12 (900m beyond the Posada 21 Oranges. There is no direct telephone line, but you can ask to arrange a tour at the bilingual Guaraní/Spanish school at the start of the village, and negotiate the price (they usually charge per person). You can also arrange a tour in advance through the agency Cuenca del Plata (see page 280).

Santuario Ecológico de Santa María del Yguazú & Museo Imágenes de la Selva (Museum of Statues of the Forest) (🕘 *08.00–18.00 daily*) This little chapel and museum with wooden sculptures by Rodolfo T Allou is in the midst of the forest on the banks of the river. You can reach it by walking through the National Park, and you will come to it before you reach the waterfalls. It has now become the meeting point for activities organised by Yguazú Extreme (☎ *+54 3757 423660; www.yguazuextreme.com*). They offer abseiling, rock climbing, zipline, walking in the forest and travelling in a motorboat on the river to the Hito Tres Fronteras.

FOZ DO IGUAÇU *www.pmfi.pr.gov.br*

Foz do Iguaçu is 1,065km from São Paulo, at the extreme west of the state of Paraná. It has an incredible 26,000 beds for tourists, in 161 hotels and guest houses, and more than 150 restaurants. Its principal attraction is the waterfall of Iguazú, which here is spelt Iguaçu – the second most visited place in Brazil for pleasure tourism after Rio. The number of visitors rose from a million in 2009 to 1.5 million in 2012, with the highest numbers coming from Germany, the USA and England, in addition to visitors from neighbouring Argentina and Uruguay, with Paraguay a little behind due to the lower income of most Paraguayans. The city has a growing number of smart hotels, many of them out along the Avenida das Cataratas that goes first to the airport and then to the falls.

GETTING THERE AND AROUND Travellers going to Foz may be crossing the border from Paraguay or from Argentina as part of a visit to the waterfalls, but it is also a sensible port of arrival or departure for a visit to Paraguay.

By air Flying into Foz in order to visit Paraguay is a good idea, because it is the international airport closest to the falls, where you will undoubtedly want to go at some point in your trip. You can fly in and out of Foz instead of Asunción, or you can do an 'open-jaws' journey, into one and out of the other. You can even cut out Asunción altogether, and visit the interior of Paraguay – particularly the Jesuit-Guaraní missions – without ever going to the capital city. In fact, for travellers who know they want to go to Iguazú, and are looking for other places to visit in the region to build a holiday, a trip to Paraguay is a perfect solution.

The airport (*+55 45 3521 4200/4276*) is between the town and the waterfalls, and its airport code is IGU. There are connecting flights from São Paulo, Rio de Janeiro, Brasília and Porto Alegre, with the companies TAM (*www.tam.com.br*), Gol (*www.voegol.com.br*) and Azul (*www.voeazul.com.br*); and from Lima, Peru, with LAN (*www.lan.com*). Intercontinental airlines can arrange the connection as part of their ticket. A bus from the airport to Foz will take about 45 minutes and it stops at many of the major hotels; the service is frequent and inexpensive. (R$4). If you prefer to take a taxi you can pay for it by credit card at the desk in the airport. Note that the airport is halfway between the town and the waterfalls, so you can get a bus in either direction. If you are coming from Puerto Iguazú for a flight from Foz Airport, allow at least an hour for the journey to be on the safe side.

By road To come by bus **from São Paulo** (see pages 35–6) Pluma (*www.pluma.com.br*) is one of the best companies. You can also bus in from Porto Alegre.

A bus over the river **from Puerto Iguazú**, Argentina, is quite inexpensive and leaves from the terminal. The bridge is called the Ponte Tancredo Neves (in Spanish, Puente Tancredo Neves). If you get left behind by the bus while you are having your passport stamped, you have to wait for the next bus, and you can lose a lot of time because different companies run the route and they do not accept each other's tickets. It is worth knowing that the border control into Brazil is only 800m from the Avenida das Cataratas, along which public buses go frequently, so if your bus goes off leaving you at Brazilian passport control, you have the option of walking this distance to the Avenida and catching a bus from there, whether to the waterfalls or the airport or into Foz.

You can get a bus **from Ciudad del Este**, and even a taxi is quite a reasonable price. The bridge is called the Ponte da Amizade (Puente de la Amistad in Spanish). Do not forget that there is an hour's time difference between Brazil and Paraguay. Foz is quite a cut up from Paraguay. You notice the difference the moment you have crossed the border: streets are properly asphalted, without pits and holes; there is less rubbish; there are well-ordered street signs; and in the city there are proper pavements. There can occasionally be a delay of a couple of hours in crossing the bridge from Paraguay if the customs officials are having a drive on cutting down smuggling. To ease delays, a new bridge is to be built to Foz from Presidente Franco (immediately south of Ciudad del Este), though work had not yet begun on it when we went to press.

Car hire At the airport you might just consider **renting** a car for one day to get quickly around on the Brazilian side between the waterfalls, the bird park, the Itaipú dam, the Bela Vista refuge, etc. It may work out cheaper than an all-day **taxi**, although the latter has the considerable advantage of a driver who knows where he is going. You would have to pay an extra insurance premium to take a rented car over the Argentinian border, and you will not be allowed to take it into Paraguay at all. There are a lot of car hire firms in Foz, including Avis, Hertz, Localiza and Unidas which are at the airport, and Yes – Rent a Car, which is in the centre (*Av Paraná 1132; +55 45 3025 4300; www.yesrentacar.com.br*).

TOURIST INFORMATION You may have some difficulty in insisting on getting your **passport** stamped. Travellers who are just going to the waterfalls and returning do not need a stamp in their passport, and passport control will wave you through, while taxi drivers may be reluctant to wait while you queue. But if you are not returning by the same route after seeing the falls, you can be in trouble the next time you go through passport control – if an entry or exit stamp is missing you will be fined.

At the Rodoviária (international bus terminal) [289 C2] there is a helpful **tourist information** office where English is spoken. There are also tourist information offices at the airport, at the local bus station or Terminal Urbana [289 A3] (*Av J K y Av Republica Argentina*), and in the city centre (*Centro Municipal de Turismo, Avenida das Cataratas 2,330, Vila Yolanda; +55 45 3521 8128; teletur@pmfi.pr.gov.br; 07.00–23.00 daily*). The buses to the waterfalls are cheap (R$3.50) and start from the local bus station or Terminal Urbana. They pass a number of hotels in Foz before going down the Avenida das Cataratas.

Visas are required from holders of US, Canadian and Australian passports but not from holders of EU passports. There are a large number of **tour operators and agencies**. A list can be found at www.pmfi.pr.gov.br.

WHERE TO STAY *Map opposite, unless otherwise indicated.*

Mabu Thermas & Resort [Map, page 278] (362 rooms) Avenida das Cataratas 3175; +55 45 3521 2000/0800 41 7040; www.hoteismabu.com.br. After the hotel in the national park itself, the Mabu, with under-lit fountain outside & its own heliport, must top the bill for expense, but it is an 'all-inclusive system' with no extra charges. Water from the Mabu spring flows fresh to the pools of the hotel & is renewed every 4hrs, maintaining a constant 36°C (body temperature) all day long & year round. **$$$$$**

Hotel das Cataratas [Map, page 278] (195 rooms) BR 469 km32, Parque Nacional do Iguaçu; +55 45 2102 7000; www.hoteldascataratas.com. The only hotel within the national park, 25km from Foz, 15km from airport. Refreshingly, this is not a modern building, but a pale pink, elegant Portuguese colonial-style house, set back with a green between it & the beginning of the cliff walk which has all the views. **$$$$$**

Viale Hotel [Map, page 278] (151 rooms) Rodovia das Cataratas km2.5, Vila Yolanda; +54 45 2105 7200; www.vialecataratas.com.br. 10km from the falls. Modern minimalist design with an extraordinary aluminium chute thing shaped like an elbow outside. **$$$$**

Turrance Green Hotel (96 rooms) Rua Manêncio Martins 108; +55 45 3026 4200/0800 645 2124; turrance@turrancehotel.com.br; www.turrancehotel.com.br. On the corner of the Rodovia das Cataratas. Fitness centre, home theatre, 2 swimming pools with waterfalls. **$$$**

Hotel San Martín [Map, page 278] (135 rooms) Rodovia das Cataratas km21; +55 45 3521 8088; www.hotelsanmartin.com.br. Super hotel with dark soothing wood halls, extremely close to the falls & airport. More than 2km of ecological trail in a garden of natural forest. **$$$$**

Hotel Rafain Centro (119 rooms) Av Marechal Deodoro 984; +55 45 3521 3500; reservas@rafaincentro.com.br; www.rafaincentro.com.br. Very good, very central. Do not confuse with Rafaín Palace or Rafaín Churrasquería. **$$$$**

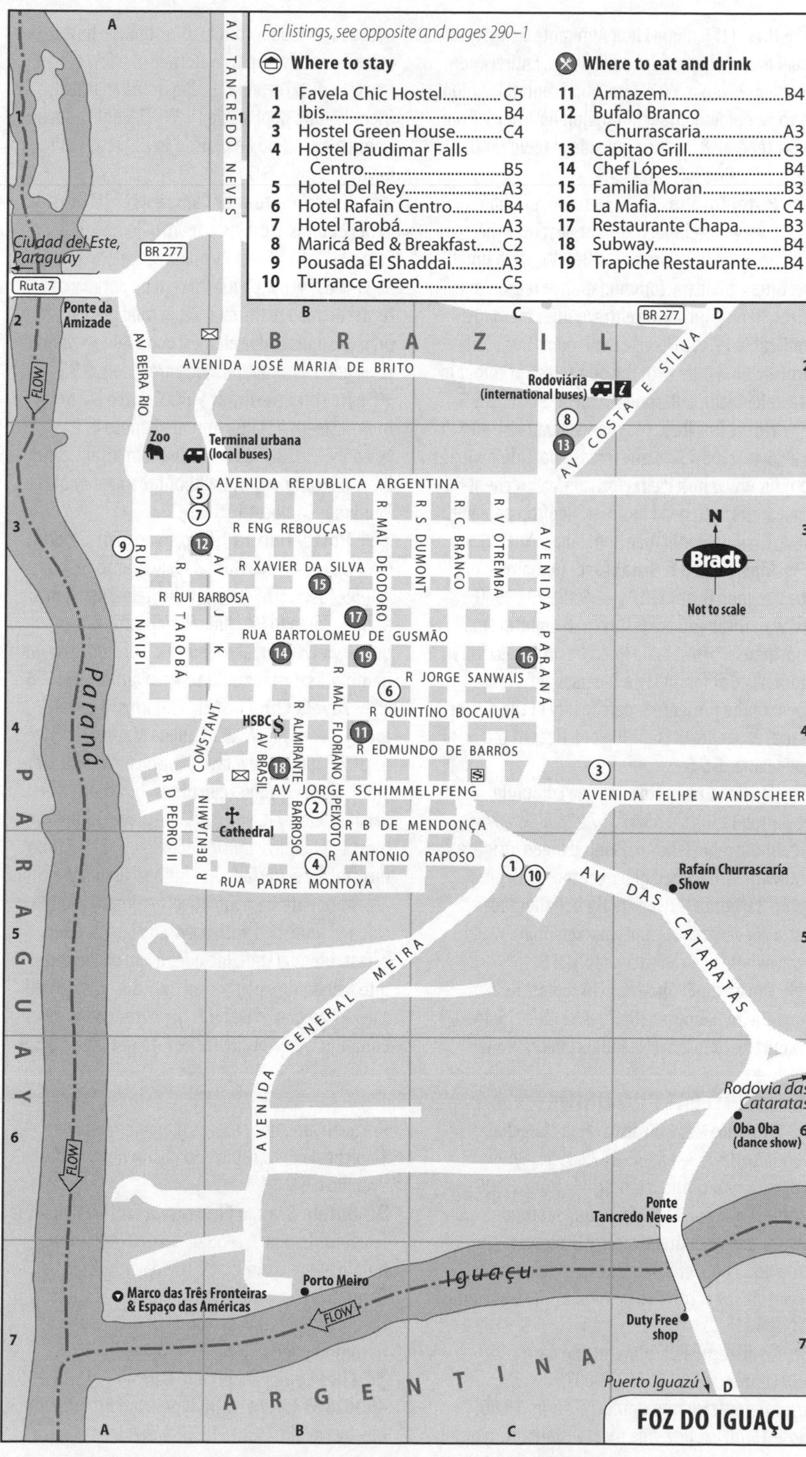
For listings, see opposite and pages 290–1
Where to stay
1 Favela Chic Hostel C5
2 Ibis B4
3 Hostel Green House C4
4 Hostel Paudimar Falls Centro B5
5 Hotel Del Rey A3
6 Hotel Rafain Centro B4
7 Hotel Tarobá A3
8 Maricá Bed & Breakfast C2
9 Pousada El Shaddai A3
10 Turrance Green C5
Where to eat and drink
11 Armazem B4
12 Bufalo Branco Churrascaria A3
13 Capitao Grill C3
14 Chef Lópes B4
15 Familia Moran B3
16 La Mafia C4
17 Restaurante Chapa B3
18 Subway B4
19 Trapiche Restaurante B4
BRAZIL
PARAGUAY
ARGENTINA
Ciudad del Este, Paraguay
BR 277
Ruta 7
Ponte da Amizade
AV TANCREDO NEVES
AVENIDA JOSÉ MARIA DE BRITO
AV BEIRA RIO
Rodoviária (international buses)
AV COSTA E SILVA
Zoo
Terminal urbana (local buses)
AVENIDA REPUBLICA ARGENTINA
R ENG REBOUÇAS
R XAVIER DA SILVA
R RUI BARBOSA
RUA BARTOLOMEU DE GUSMÃO
R JORGE SANWAIS
R QUINTÍNO BOCAIUVA
R EDMUNDO DE BARROS
AV JORGE SCHIMMELPFENG
R B DE MENDONÇA
R ANTONIO RAPOSO
RUA PADRE MONTOYA
R MAL DEODORO
R S DUMONT
R C BRANCO
R V OTREMBA
AVENIDA PARANÁ
RUA NAIPI
R TAROBÁ
AV J K
R MAL FLORIANO PEIXOTO
R ALMIRANTE BARROSO
AV BRASIL
R BENJAMIN CONSTANT
R D PEDRO II
HSBC
Cathedral
AVENIDA FELIPE WANDSCHEER
AV DAS CATARATAS
Rafaín Churrascaría Show
AVENIDA GENERAL MEIRA
Paraná
FLOW
N
Bradt
Not to scale
Rodovia das Cataratas
Oba Oba (dance show)
Ponte Tancredo Neves
Iguaçu
Porto Meiro
Marco das Três Fronteiras & Espaço das Américas
Duty Free shop
Puerto Iguazú
FOZ DO IGUAÇU

Ibis (176 rooms) Rua Almirante Barroso 866. Usual Ibis quality at economic prices. Entirely non-smoking. Minibar, Wi-Fi, etc. Good central location on corner of Av Jorge Schimmelpfeng 1 block from the cathedral, & on the right side of town for the waterfalls. B/fast is extra. **$$**

Hotel Tarobá (178 rooms) Rua Tarobá 1048; www.hoteltaroba.com.br. Just over the road from the bus terminal. A Best Western hotel, this offers quality accommodation at reasonable prices. Sauna, business centre, games room, gym, pool, cable TV, Wi-Fi, etc. Small rooms but nicely furnished in white with the odd splash of colour in a tasteful picture. Restaurant Menu Brasil. **$$$**

Hotel Del Rey (45 rooms) Rua Tarobá 1020; +55 45 2105 7500; e reservas@hoteldelreyfoz.com.br; www.hoteldelreyfoz.com.br. Excellent-value hotel with good facilities. Rooftop pool with view, small tables in rooms, minibar, Wi-Fi. **$$$**

Maricá Bed & Breakfast (4 rooms) Rua Gregorio Dotto 118; +55 45 9102 8900; www.maricabedbreakfast.com. Delightful small guesthouse, b/fast table looks beautiful, & every room has a different style & personality. It is all down to the presence & personality of the owner Maria, who speaks English. Pool. Near to the Rodoviária. **$$$**

Hostel Green House Rua Edmundo de Barros 1130; +55 45 3572 8668; www.greenhouse-hostel.com. Painted green inside & out, with lush garden greenery too. Pool, ping pong. Barbecue serving steaks or handmade burgers every night. Supermarket 5mins' walk away where you can eat cheaply. **$$**

Pousada El Shaddai (4 rooms) Rua Engenheiro Rebouças 306; +55 45 3025 4490/3; e contato@pousadaelshaddai.com.br; www.pousadaelshaddai.com.br. Guesthouse/hostel. One block from bus stop to waterfalls & a few blocks from shops & restaurants. Big Brazilian b/fast, friendly staff, pool, cable TV, Wi-Fi, English spoken. Name means 'God be praised' in Hebrew. Cash payments only. **$$**

Hostel Paudimar Campestre [Map, page 278] (2 dorms, 2 cabins, 6 rooms) Rodovia das Cataratas km12.5, cnr Av Maria Bubiak; +55 45 3529 6061; www.paudimar.com.br. Backpackers hostel on road to the falls, set in rural grounds, from private cabins to dormitories; good value, swimming pool, good information. Recommended. **$$$**

Hostel Paudimar Falls Centro (2 dorms, 3 rooms, sleeps 23) Rua Antonio Raposo 820; +55 45 3028 5503; www.paudimarfalls.com.br. Same company but without the beauty of the Paudimar Campestre. **$$**

Hostel Natura [Map, page 278] (2 dorms, 6 rooms) Alameida Burri 333, Remanso Grande; +55 45 3529 6949; www.hostelnatura.com. In a similar area to Paudimar Campestre, but even better views over lake & sunset. Pool, *quincho* with hammocks, restaurant. Taxi from airport R$35. **$**

Favela Chic Hostel (3 dorms, 2 private rooms 1 van) Rua Major Raul de Mattos 78; +55 45 3027 5060; www.favelachichosteliguassu.com. This is not everyone's cup of tea, but those who like it swear by it. Fun, sociable place, 150m from most popular live music bar in town, 125m from bus stop to waterfalls/Argentina/Paraguay. Simple accommodation imaginatively painted in favela colours, furnished with recycled objects. Good b/fast, friendly staff. Includes a van converted into a bedroom, painted all over the outside with the Mayan god of water & the Aztec god of love. Camping. See website for how to get there. **$$$**

WHERE TO EAT AND DRINK *Map, page 289.*

Trapiche Restaurante Rua Marechal Deodoro 1087; +55 45 3572 3951; www.trapicherestaurante.com.br; from 17.00 Mon–Thu, from 11.00 Fri–Sun. Seafood restaurant with great variety & pictures to help you choose. Sometimes has live music. Free transport from your hotel in the evenings. **$$$$**

Armazem Rua Edmundo de Barros 458 Centro; +55 45 3572 0007; www.armazemrestaurante.com.br; from 18.00, closed Sun. Exotic & fine meat restaurant, typically Brazilian fare, under same management as Trapiche. Free transport from your hotel in the evenings. **$$$$**

Bufalo Branco Churrascaria Rua Rebouças 530, esq. Tarobá; +55 45 3523 9744; www.bufalo.branco.com.br; midday to 23.00. Churrasquería with extensive buffet. Close to the Hotel Del Rey & on corner of Rua Tarobá. Recommended. **$$$**

Chef Lópes Almirante Barroso 1713; +55 45 3028 3334; www.cheflopes.com.br; buffet pay by weight 11.30–15.30 & menu de chef

18.00–23.00 Mon–Sat. Huge restaurant, suitable for big conventions, quality food. $$$

Capitão Grill Avenida Costa E Silva 185 Loja 312; +55 45 3027 4943. Good food, nice outside area although this busy restaurant is located on major road. Live music sometimes. $$

La Mafia Rua Watslaf Nieradka 195; 45 3026 6210. Close to the Avenida Paraná, 1 block south of Bartolomeu de Gusmão, this Italian restaurant is frequented by students & others who appreciate good pasta at accessible prices. Charming old-world Italian décor. Free transport from your hotel in the evenings. Recommended. $$

Familia Moran Rua Almirante Barroso 1968; +55 45 3025 2863. 24-hour restaurant, good variety of buffet, sandwiches, cakes, etc. $$

Restaurante Chapa Rua Bartolomeu de Gusmão 1014; +55 45 3572 8881; closed Sun. Accessible prices, good variety & service. $$

Subway Jorge Schimmelpfeng 230; +55 45 3027 7717; www.subway.com.br. Popular chain of cafés where you can choose your salad or the content of your sandwich. $$

ENTERTAINMENT Dance shows are offered by the following:

Rafaín Churrascaría Show [289 D5] Av das Cataratas 1749, km6.5; +55 45 3523 1177; from 20.45 Mon–Sat. This is the best known dance show, spanning the dance &/or music of 8 Latin American countries with more than 45 artistes. It takes place in a restaurant with capacity for 1,200 people & prices are reasonable. Obviously very much for tourists.

Iporã Lenda Show Avenida das Cataratas 1759; +55 45 3523 1177; www.iporashow.com.br; 22.00–23.30 Sat. Next door to the Rafaín Churrasquería, this show is preferred by many. The 2 shows are very similar, but this one begins with a musical presentation of the legend of Tarobá & Naipí (see page 285). There follows a glittering display ranging from salsa to the Caribbean malambo pampas.

Oba Oba [289 D6] Ponte Tancredo Neves, next to customs; +55 45 3529 9070; www.churrascariabottega.com.br; from 22.00 Mon–Sat. This show concentrates on authentic Brazilian samba & mulatas, & takes place in the *churrascaria* Bottega.

OTHER PRACTICALITIES The **banks** in Foz include HSBC, Itau and Banco do Brasil. HSBC cash machines can be found at Uniamérica, Hotel das Cataratas, Vila 'A', Hipermercado Big, Bourbon Cataratas and Cataratas J L Shopping. Other 24-hour cash machines are located in the service station at the east end of Avenida Schimmelpfeng, and on the corner of Avenida José Marin Toriot and Avenida Paraná.

Brasil is a major shopping street with wide pavements and an HSBC bank with a cash machine, at Avenida Brasil 1151, between Bocaiúva and E de Barros. It has at least three **internet** places: Posto Telefônico, opposite the department store Kamalito, between Rua Barbosa and Bartolomeu de Gusmão (*09.00–22.00 Mon–Sat, 09.00–13.00 & 18.00–22.00 Sun*); Galeria Brasil, between Sanwais and Gusmão; and the Cybercafé between Sanwais and Bocaiuva.

Voltage is different in Brazil, 110 volts (like the USA), unlike the 220 volts of Paraguay, Argentina and Europe. Most portable electronic devices these days are self-switching.

IGUAÇU FALLS (*www.cataratasdoiguacu.com.br*) For the visit to the Argentinian side of these waterfalls, see pages 283–5.

Buses to the Iguaçu Falls go from the local bus station or Terminal Urbana on Avenida J K and Avenida República Argentina. The buses are number 120, marked 'Cataratas' or 'Parque Nacional' (R$3.50) and run every 20 minutes; the journey takes about 45 minutes. They go through town, past a lot of hotels, and then along the Avenida das Cataratas: you can get on them at any point. Then you pay to get into the national park (🕘 *summer 09.00–18.00; winter 09.00–17.00, last entry 1hr before closing; R$49.20, reduction for residents of Mercosur, children 2–11 R$7.90, credit cards accepted*). If you come by car, the parking fee is R$17, and there is room for nearly 700 cars as well as 170 buses. From the entrance to the park – which is also the visitor centre – you take a shuttle bus (attractively painted with animals and birds): the first one leaves the visitor centre at 09.00 and the last shuttle leaves the Porto Canoas square by the waterfalls at 18.30. You should be warned that prices for entry and activities tend to go up steeply every year. Prices given here are for 2014.

Brazil has a much larger national park than Argentina around the falls: 185,000ha, as against 67,000ha in Argentina. But of the waterfalls themselves, Brazil owns less than Argentina: 800m, as against the 1,900m on Argentinian territory. In 1986 the Brazilian national park was recognised by UNESCO as a World Heritage Site. It protects the largest remnant of Atlantic Forest in Brazil, with a rich biodiversity that includes a number of endangered species: jaguar, mountain lion, broad-snouted caiman, vinaceous-breasted amazon, harpy eagle, peroba-rosa, ariticum and araucaria. An option in the national park apart from the waterfalls is to do the track known as the Pozo Negro – a 9km route that can be done on foot or on bicycle, leading to a 10m high observation tower with a panoramic view of both forest and lake.

A visit to the Brazilian side of the Iguaçu Falls is centred on a spectacular walk along the cliffs, the Trilha das Cataratas, with amazing views of the waterfalls opening out in front of you and changing as you go along. The best views of the falls are probably had from this side of the river, because they are facing you (rather than under your feet, as they are on the Argentinian side). The visit need not be as long as the one on the Argentinian side, but you should still allow at least three hours. You may see flocks of the water-loving swifts who build their nests just behind the falls.

The cliff walk begins outside the elegant Hotel das Cataratas, discreetly set back from the cliff edge. (It is a far cry from the prominent modern Hotel Sheraton (see page 282) in the Argentinian national park, which is marvellous when you are on the inside looking out, but rather an eyesore for those on the Brazilian bank looking across at the view of nature.) But before you arrive, there is the option of getting off the bus for the Macuco Safari Solo Selva tour (*www.macucosafari.com.br; R$85, children and over-60s half price*). This involves a 3km drive in a jeep, with a guide pointing out features of the trees and plants you pass. Then you continue on foot for 600m, before getting in a rubber dinghy to approach the waterfalls by river.

As in Argentina, there is a boat trip that runs you up close to the foot of a waterfall, where you get thoroughly wet (*www.macucosafari.com.br; R$170, children and over-60s half price*). But something you do not get on the Argentinian side is the platform beneath the falls that you walk out to, mid-stream, and from where you get a stunning view of the Garganta del Diablo above and ahead of you. There is a lift up the cliff face, and when you have gone past the last waterfalls you reach a **restaurant** called Porto Canoas (☎ *+55 45 3521 4400;* 🕘 *11.30–16.00 Tue–Sun*), which has a fantastic location right by the riverside. It is a self-service buffet – not cheap, but considering the location not unreasonable either. They have a big display of beautifully presented salads and you can sit on the terrace beside the lake, which here gives little indication that it is about to plunge over the edge in such a dramatic fashion.

You catch an introduction to the subtropical rainforest that comprises Brazil's national park in the first stretch of the Macuco Safari. It is a semi-deciduous seasonal forest with a great green canopy formed by big trees like fig, cinnamon and palm, and other species that can reach a height of 30m including laurel and cedar. Smaller trees include the rubber tree and varieties of palm. The ground is covered with ferns and grasses, while orchids and creepers adorn the trees. In the floodplain areas there are bamboos, palms and grasses. In the eastern area there survives the great Paraná pine, *Araucaria angustifolia*, symbol of Paraná state.

Endangered species of animals and birds live in the forest, protected by the big trees like the *yerba mate* tree. There are 257 species of butterflies, 18 species of fish, 12 of amphibians, 41 of snakes, 8 of lizards, 45 of mammals and 248 of birds. Among these birds you find parrots, parakeets, toucans, hawks, hummingbirds and goldfinches. Among the mammals are the jaguar and smaller wild cats, as well as the tapir, brocket deer and capybara.

A number of longer trails are offered in the national park, by foot, bicycle or electric car, under the heading of Poço Preto or **Macuco Ecoaventura** (www.macucoecoaventura.com.br; *R$135, children and over-60s half price*). The company Macuco Safari offers rafting over the rapids – a 30-minute trip (*www.macucosafari.com.br*). Yet another activity is the Campo de Desafios, or Field of Challenges, which includes abseiling, rafting and tree climbing in differing degrees of difficulty, and is situated at the beginning of the Trilha das Cataratas (*www.campodedesafios.com.br*).

Helicopter trips over the falls and up to Itaipú and the Marco das 3 Fronteiras are offered by Helisul (*Rodovia das Cataratas, km16.5; ☎ +55 45 3529 7474; www.helisul.com*). Some people say the trips disturb the bird life at the falls.

WHAT ELSE TO SEE AND DO

Parque das Aves (*Av das Cataratas, km17.1, next to zoo; ☎ +55 45 3529 8282; www.parquedasaves.com.br; ⏲ 08.30–17.00 daily; R$28*) Difficult as it is to tear yourself away from the waterfalls, this bird park is well worth a visit, and is considered the best in Latin America. It receives half a million visitors a year. Over 1020 birds from 150 different species are beautifully presented, along 1,000m of paths. Half the birds have been rescued from maltreatment or from trafficking, and most of the rest have been born in the park. Forest aviaries 8m high give scope for the birds to enjoy a habitat among trees. You can have direct contact with toucans, parrots and parakeets, and the park is also home to alligators, snakes and butterflies. There is a restaurant and a gift shop.

Getting there and away Bus 401 goes there from the Terminal Urbana, passing along Avenida J K and Avenida Jorge Schimmelpfeng and the airport on the way (R$3.60), but it is, in fact, just to the right of the Avenida Das Cataratas at the point where it turns left into the car park by the entrance to the National Park.

Marco das Três Fronteiras [289 A7](Spanish 'Hito de las Tres Fronteras') Down Rua General Meira you come to the point where the Río Iguaçu joins the Río Paraná, and three obelisks mark the meeting points of Brazil, Argentina and Paraguay. The big round building is the Espaço das Américas, a concert hall.

Itaipú Dam (*Av Tancredo Neves; ☎ 0800 645 4645/+55 45 3529 2892; www.turismoitaipu.com.br*) Itaipú Dam is fully covered in *Chapter 9*, pages 304–5. Brazil and Paraguay share the same film, the same *mirador*, and the same design and infrastructure for the basic visit (what the Brazilians call the Visita Panorâmica; *lasts 1½hrs: visits every hour on the hour from 08.00 to 16.00; R$26*). The differences are that the Brazilian side gets more visitors, because Brazil in general gets more visitors, and that you pay on the Brazilian side, while the Paraguayan side is free. Brazil also offers the option of a longer visit, the Circuito Especial (*Circuito Especial, lasts 2½hrs; R$64*), where you get into the 1km gallery, and down a staircase to the level closer to the turbines: there are certain rules on clothing for this longer circuit, and the minimum age is 14.

The Visitors' Centre is the starting point, as it is situated 12km north of the centre of Foz. To get there, take a bus going to 'Itaipu Dam' or 'Conjunto C Norte' or 'Conjunto C Sul' from the urban bus terminal. The journey takes half an hour (*R$2.85*). Within the same complex are some further attractions.

Ecomuseum (*www.turismoitaipu.com.br;* ⌚ *08.00–16.30 Tue–Sun; R$10*) You pass this museum on your left on the way to the Itaipú dam, after passing the Buddhist temple. The history of the environmental projects of Itaipú is imaginatively presented, with information about the fauna and flora of the region, ethnography, and details of how energy is generated by the dam.

Refugio Biológico Bela Vista (*www.turismoitaipu.com.br;* ⌚ *Tue–Sun; R$20*) After the Ecomuseum, you reach this down a turn to the right, before the visitor centre of the dam. The visit begins with a ride in an electric wagon along the Canal da Piracema (constructed to enable fish to bypass the dam and so go upstream to breed). Then it continues with a 2km walk in a reserve created to house the thousands of plants and animals displaced by the dam. All the buildings were built to function on alternative energy sources. The visit lasts 2½ hours and begins at 08.30, 10.00, 14.30 and 15.30.

Polo Astronômico (*www.turismoitaipu.com.br;* ⌚ *10.00 &16.00 Tue–Sun, also 19.00 Fri & Sat winter or 19.30 summer; R$19*). Opposite the visitor centre, this is a planetarium with a museum of the skies attached and an observatory for looking at the stars by night. Allow 2 hours for the visit.

UPDATES WEBSITE

You can post your comments and recommendations, and read the latest feedback and updates from other readers, online at www.bradtupdates.com/paraguay.

9

Ciudad del Este and the East

Departamento: Alto Paraná; gobernación ☎ 061 508688/518105/518109

Although Ciudad del Este has a reputation for crime and smuggling and is not somewhere you would normally choose to go for a holiday, you may well find yourself going there on the way to the Iguazú Falls (or the Iguaçu Falls – on the Brazilian side). If you take as much care as you normally would in a big city, there is no need to avoid it or to feel uncomfortable there: you may even find yourself enjoying the buzz of the place. It also has more green space than most towns: it was built to be a garden city.

What is more, immediately north of Ciudad del Este are some very interesting and attractive places that really do merit a visit: the famous Itaipú dam, the Museo de la Tierra Guaraní and the Tatí Yupí. Immediately south of the city is the Moisés Bertoni house, the home of the esteemed Swiss naturalist, hidden in some beautiful woods. Both of these are reached via what is called the Supercarretera (or Avenida Mariscal López), which is the road that runs as straight as a die from north to south, or to be more exact, from north-northeast to south-southwest. The Supercarretera is off to the left of the map on page 298, 4km from the Puente de la Amistad, and is unmissable because there is a flyover over it.

CIUDAD DEL ESTE

Copaco ☎ 061 500000; municipalidad ☎ 061 500222

Ciudad del Este was founded in 1957, in Stroessner's time, and was soon named after him – Ciudad Presidente Stroessner. The name mercifully did not survive the end of the dictatorship. It began with an airstrip, two avenues and the foundation stone of the cathedral, and subsequently grew to the point where *Forbes* magazine declared it the third-biggest commercial city in the world after Miami and Hong Kong. For Paraguayans, it is the place you go to buy a computer, if you know where to look and what you are looking for. The commercial centre, with its endless outlets selling electrical goods grouped into big shopping centres where everything is shiny and modern, is a phenomenon that nothing in Asunción can touch. But just a stone's throw away is the sordid, broken, dirty face of the third-world marketplace, which is what you first see when you enter Paraguay from Brazil.

As you walk down a shopping street like Adrián Jara, you find a unique blend of elegance and squalor, with a man with a rifle at every corner. There is litter in the streets, and lads lugging piles of flattened cardboard boxes on their heads, or tugging trolleys of heavy electronics uphill. And coming at you from all sides is the *shlik* sound of packaging tape being stretched around boxes of purchases.

As a city, Ciudad del Este has severe social problems. Children as young as seven may ask you for money, and then try to steal your mobile phone; they are known

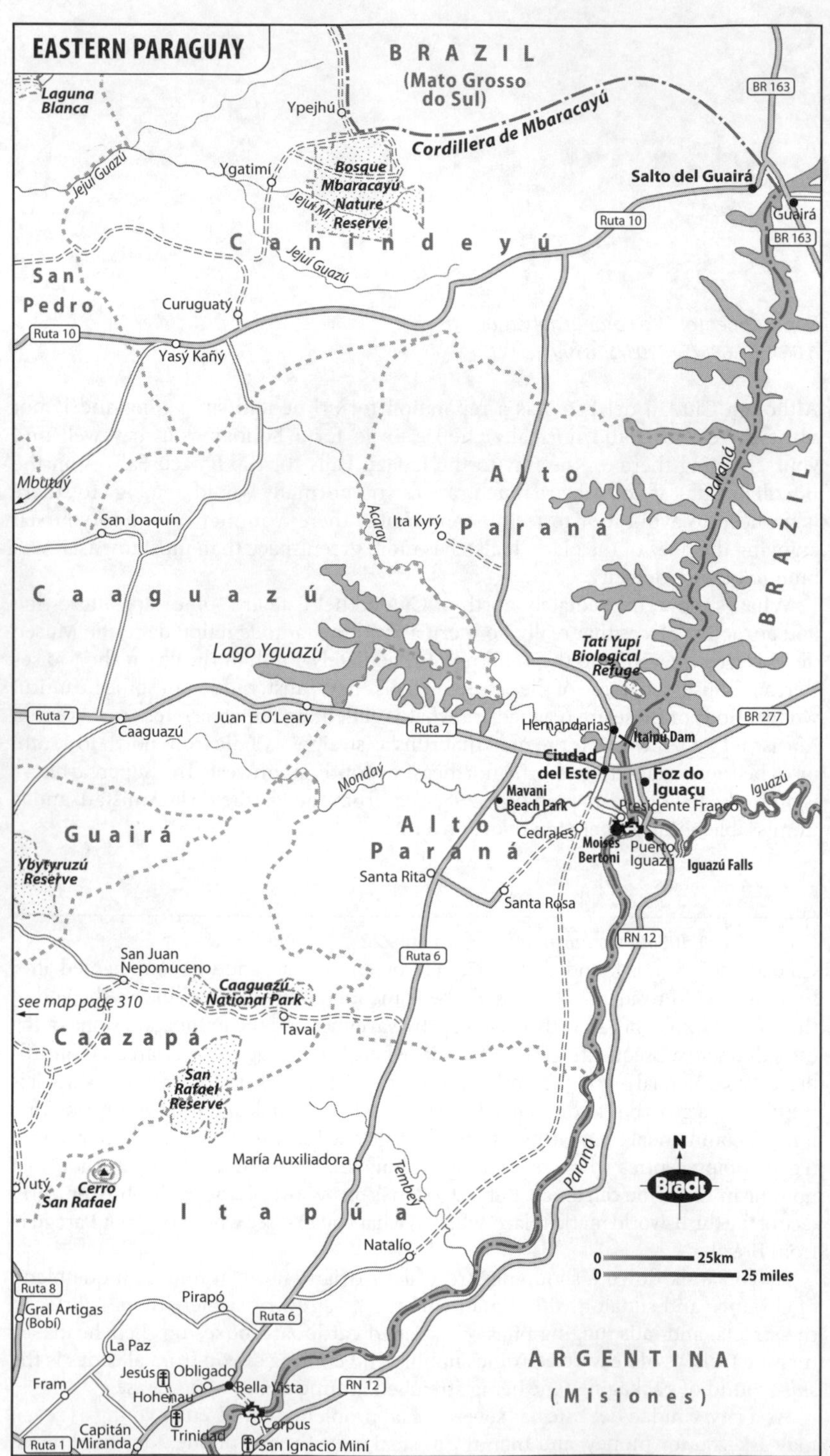
EASTERN PARAGUAY
BRAZIL
(Mato Grosso do Sul)
Cordillera de Mbaracayú
BR 163
Laguna Blanca
Ypejhú
Ygatimí
Bosque Mbaracayú Nature Reserve
Jejuí Guazú
Jejuí Mi
Salto del Guairá
Guairá
Ruta 10
BR 163
Canindeyú
San Pedro
Curuguatý
Ruta 10
Yasý Kañý
Mbutuý
San Joaquín
Alto Paraná
Acaray
Ita Kyrý
Paraná
BRAZIL
Caaguazú
Lago Yguazú
Tatí Yupí Biological Refuge
Ruta 7
Caaguazú
Juan E O'Leary
Ruta 7
Hernandarias
Itaipú Dam
BR 277
Ciudad del Este
Foz do Iguaçu
Monday
Mavani Beach Park
Presidente Franco
Iguazú
Guairá
Alto Paraná
Cedrales
Moisés Bertoni
Puerto Iguazú
Iguazú Falls
Ybytyruzú Reserve
Santa Rita
Santa Rosa
RN 12
Ruta 6
San Juan Nepomuceno
Caaguazú National Park
see map page 310
Tavaí
Caazapá
San Rafael Reserve
María Auxiliadora
Tembey
Paraná
N
Bradt
Yuty
Cerro San Rafael
Itapúa
Natalío
0 25km
0 25 miles
Ruta 8
Gral Artigas (Bobí)
Pirapó
Ruta 6
La Paz
ARGENTINA
(Misiones)
Jesús
Obligado
Fram
Hohenau
Bella Vista
RN 12
Corpus
Capitán Miranda
Trinidad
Ruta 1
San Ignacio Miní

as *pirañitas*, little sharks. There are encampments of Mbyá Guaraní – one beside the bus terminal and another beside the Centro Regional de Educación – who have come in from their ancestral grounds and resist attempts to return them there. They scrape a living in the city by begging and collecting bottles and tins from the rubbish and selling them by the kilo, and from prostitution, organised through the taxi drivers. Watch your wallet or handbag, and be prudent: at night even the Itaipú Dam suffers theft of its light bulbs.

The economy of the city depends largely on cross-border smuggling. One phenomenon is the activity of the *sacoleiros*, the word for Brazilians who cross the bridge each day to fill their bags with cheap goods from Paraguay, and return home to sell them in Foz: goods 'for personal use' are import-free, and if they do it every day they have quite a business. From time to time the Brazilians have a drive to cut down on customs-dodging at the border, and there can be long delays in getting across the bridge, optimistically named Puente de la Amistad (Ponte da Amizade in Portuguese), the Bridge of Friendship. Taxi drivers from the terminal fortunately charge a flat rate to take you to Foz, so there are no extras if you have to wait in a queue for a couple of hours to get across the bridge.

It is not recommended to accept a supposedly cut-price offer of a taxi from someone who does not do the journey regularly. The taxi drivers from the terminal know Foz (at least to some extent) and speak Portuguese to ask for directions: without this you may find yourself having to pay for a second, Brazilian taxi, which will more than wipe out any saving you thought you were making. See also pages 287–8 on crossing the border.

GETTING THERE AND AWAY

By bus If you arrive in Paraguay **from Brazil**, you may be coming in a bus from São Paulo, which is a long but comfortable journey away (see *Chapter 2*, pages 35–6). (You may find that you have to change buses on the Brazilian side of the border, because the bus companies do not want their best buses to travel on Paraguayan roads.) Or you may be coming from Foz – either from the airport (which is a good way of flying to Paraguay) or from a visit to the Iguazú Falls, which may have begun on the Argentinian side.

If Ciudad del Este is your first view of Paraguay, the contrast with Brazil will be a shock, particularly on this access road from the bridge. But bear in mind that this squalor is a far cry from the dignity, freshness and tradition of the Paraguayan *campo* that you will find when you leave Ciudad del Este behind.

A number of companies make the bus journey **from Asunción** to the terminal in Ciudad del Este (☎ *061 510421*), which is 1,500m south of Avenida Monseñor Rodríguez (the southern carriageway of Ruta 7), and not far from the river. Go down General Bernardino Caballero, past Rogelio Benítez, past San Martín, and you will come to the Estadio 3 de febrero at the corner of the next road, Eugenio A Gray. The terminal is on the far side of the Estadio. There are frequent departures all day long, and the cost is Gs60,000–65,000. The companies that go from Asunción to Ciudad del Este are Rysa, Nuestra Señora de Asunción, Crucero del Este, Pycasú, Santaniana and San Luis (generally regarded the least comfortable). Rysa costs Gs5,000 more but has more buses. The journey takes five hours, and do not be misled by Crucero del Este telling you that they do it in 4½ hours. To avoid the rather exposed and sometimes dirty toilets in the terminal, go to the 'Sala VIP' where they are much better: these facilities are for travellers on international and long-distance journeys, and your journey will count as long distance.

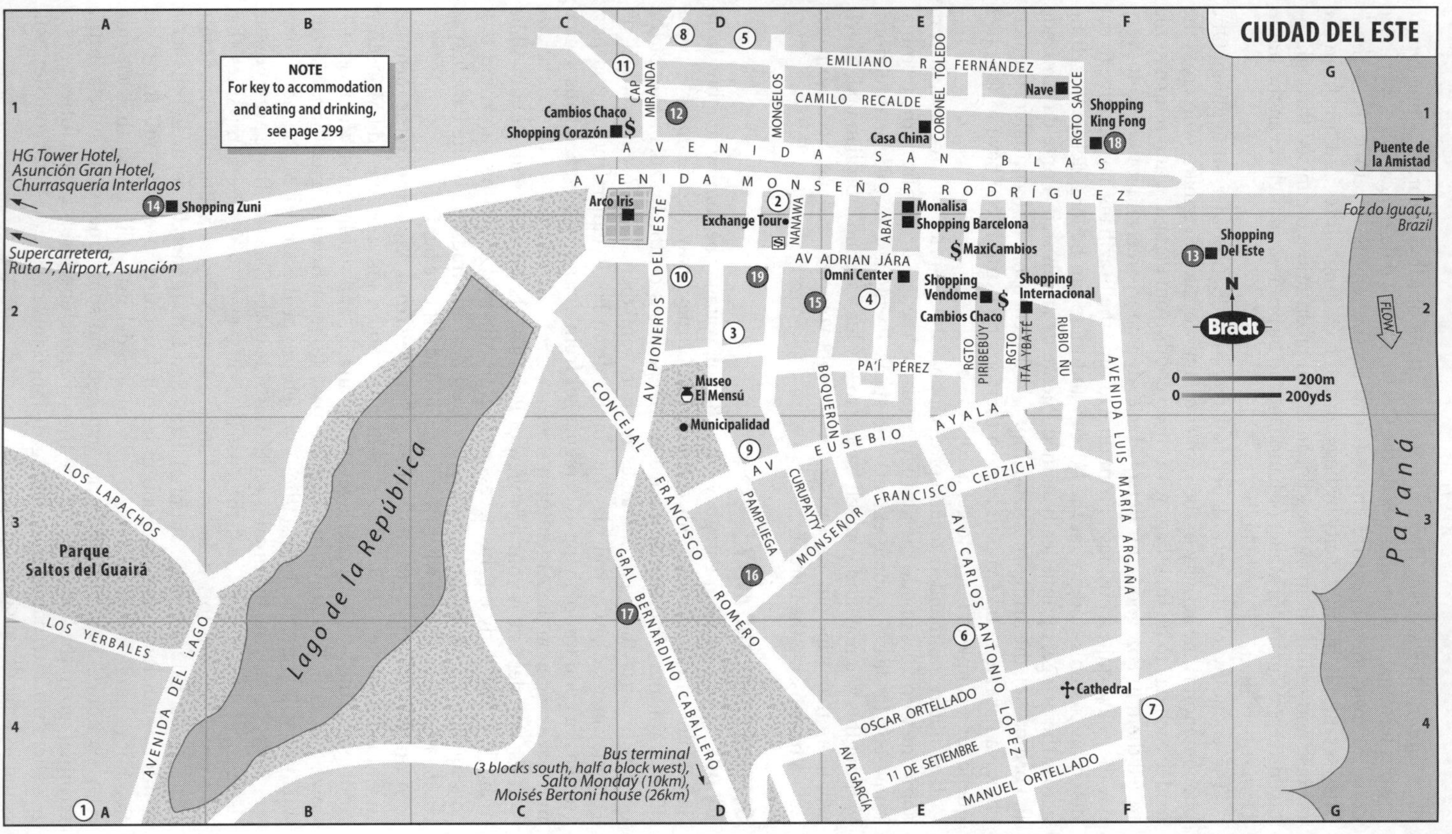
CIUDAD DEL ESTE
NOTE
For key to accommodation and eating and drinking, see page 299
Puente de la Amistad
Foz do Iguaçu, Brazil
FLOW
Paraná
Shopping Del Este
Bradt
N
200m
200yds
Shopping King Fong
Nave
RGTO SAUCE
EMILIANO R FERNÁNDEZ
CORONEL TOLEDO
CAMILO RECALDE
Casa China
MONGELOS
CAP MIRANDA
Cambios Chaco
Shopping Corazón
AVENIDA SAN BLAS
AVENIDA MONSEÑOR RODRÍGUEZ
Arco Iris
Exchange Tour
NANAWA
Monalisa
Shopping Barcelona
MaxiCambios
ABAY
AV ADRIAN JÁRA
Omni Center
Shopping Vendome
Cambios Chaco
Shopping Internacional
RGTO PIRIBEBÚY
RGTO ITÁ YBATÉ
RUBIO ÑU
AV PIONEROS DEL ESTE
PA'Í PÉREZ
BOQUERÓN
Museo El Mensú
Municipalidad
AV EUSEBIO AYALA
CURUPAYTÝ
PAMPLIEGA
MONSEÑOR FRANCISCO CEDZICH
AVENIDA LUIS MARÍA ARGAÑA
AV CARLOS ANTONIO LÓPEZ
Cathedral
OSCAR ORTELLADO
11 DE SETIEMBRE
MANUEL ORTELLADO
AV A GARCÍA
CONCEJAL FRANCISCO ROMERO
GRAL BERNARDINO CABALLERO
Bus terminal (3 blocks south, half a block west), Salto Mondaý (10km), Moisés Bertoni house (26km)
Lago de la República
AVENIDA DEL LAGO
LOS LAPACHOS
LOS YERBALES
Parque Saltos del Guairá
Shopping Zuni
HG Tower Hotel, Asunción Gran Hotel, Churrasquería Interlagos
Supercarretera, Ruta 7, Airport, Asunción

If you are coming **from southern Paraguay** – from Encarnación – there are plenty of services, and the journey takes between four and seven hours (faster at night). The bus companies include Nuestra Señora de la Encarnación, Rysa, Itapúa Poty, San Juan and Ñeembucú. The latter two go further than Encarnación, to San Ignacio and beyond. So also does Ortega but it is a bit slow. But if your only reason for the journey is to go to the Iguazú Falls then you might consider crossing over to Posadas and coming up to the falls through Misiones Argentina (see page 279).

By car If you are driving, study the instructions on pages 123–7 for getting out of Asunción. If you get onto Ruta 2 successfully in San Lorenzo then it is straight ahead all the way, with the road changing its number to Ruta 7 at Coronel Oviedo. To cover the 327km allow five hours, plus whatever stops you make.

A suitable place to stop for **a meal** would be La Nona, next to the Hotel Bertea, just before the roundabout in Coronel Oviedo (see page 311). If you want to do something more organised and imaginative to break your journey, and if you have that little bit of extra time, you could try ringing or emailing in advance to the *estancia* **Don Emilio** (*021 660791/021 603994;* m *0981 507105;* e *donemilio24@gmail.com; see page 312*), 6km to the south of Ruta 2 on the road to Villarrica, or the *estancia* **Los Manantiales** (*021;* m *0981 425498; see page 160*) just 4km north of Caacupé, and see if they can do you a lunch, or put you up overnight. An alternative way of making a reservation is through the Central de Reservas of Apatur in Asunción (*Brasil c/ 25 de mayo, 8th Floor; 021 210550 int 126;* e *turismo@tacpy.com.py; www.turismorural.org.py*). *Estancias* always require advance notice of at least a day.

By air You can fly to Ciudad del Este's Aeropuerto Guaraní (airport code AGT, from its official name of Alejo García) from Asunción and from São Paulo, but this does not allow much flexibility, as there is only one flight a day, with TAM Airlines (*021 645500; www.tamairlines.com*). The PZ706 departs from Asunción at 17.20 and arrives in Ciudad del Este at 18.05; then at 11.50 it continues to São Paulo, arriving at 14.30. In the other direction, the PZ707 departs from São Paulo at 15.30, arriving at Ciudad del Este at 16.10; it then leaves Ciudad del Este at 09.40 to arrive in Asunción at 10.25. The cost of the fare from Asunción to Ciudad del Este is currently around US$60 one way. The airport is just north of Ruta 7, some 25km west of the bridge and shortly before the junction with Ruta 6.

The office of the **airline** TAM is on the corner of Curupayty and Avenida Dr Eusebio Ayala (two blocks south of Exchange Tours).

CIUDAD DEL ESTE

For listings, see pages 301–2

Where to stay

1	Casa Alta Hostel	A4
2	Centro	D1
3	Cosmopolitan	D2
4	Guarania Hotel y Restaurante	E2
5	Hotel Austria	D1
6	Hotel California	E4
7	Hotel Casino Acaray	F4
8	Hotel Munich	D1
9	Hotel Panorama Inn	D3
10	Mi Abuela	D2
11	Santo Domingo	D1
Off map		
	Asunción Gran	A1
	HG Tower	A1

Where to eat and drink

12	Ambrosia	D1
13	Del Fuego	F2
14	Gauchiño Grill	A1
15	Gugu's	D2
16	Patussi Grill	D3
17	Patu's Bar	D3
18	SAX Bistro	E1
19	Yrupé	D2
Off map		
	Churrasquería Interlagos	A1

GETTING AROUND When in Ciudad del Este, try to leave your car in a guarded car park. If you cannot do that, a trick to avoid break-ins is to offer a local street kid a tip for keeping an eye on your car until you return.

Car hire Ciudad del Este has two car hire companies. Localiza offers car hire from the airport, or from the office on Ruta 7, the northern carriageway of which is called Avenida San Blas when it is inside the city. Alternatively, you can hire from Pycom, who have a branch in the Hotel Casino Acaray and another near the cathedral.

Localiza Av San Blas km4.5; 061 572456; 07.00–18.00 Mon–Fri; 08.00–noon Sat. Also at airport: about 7 blocks to the west of the Supercarretera; 061 683895; 09.00–13.00, 14.00–18.00 Mon–Sat; www.localiza.com.py.

Pycom 11 de setiembre 428 c/ Carlos Antonio López; 061 509485/6. Also at Hotel Casino Acaray [298 F4]; 061 504250 int. 176; m 0993 281115. e reservas@pyrent.com.py; www.pyrent.com.py.

LOCAL TOUR OPERATORS

Cosmo's Tours Curupaytý c/ Pa'i Pérez; 061 510068; e incoming@cosmos.com.py. Offers a 2-day packet from Asunción to the Iguazú Falls, staying at a hotel in Foz.

Exchange Tours/Mavani [298 D2] Av Nanawa 90 edificio Saba PB local 1; 061 500766/7/513313; e mavani@mavani.com.py; www.mavani.com.py. Exchange Tour is the travel agent & Mavani the tour operator. They offer a city-tour of Ciudad del Este.

Los Delfines Los Lapachos y los Guayabos; 061 514083; e cdedelfines2@tigo.com.py. Can take you to the different sites of the Itaipú Tourist Complex.

WHERE TO STAY *Map, page 298.*

The nicest hotels are in an exclusive estate called the **Paraná Country Club**, which strictly speaking is not part of Ciudad del Este but Hernandarias. However, it is so close and easy to reach by taxi that its hotels are included here among those of Ciudad del Este. The Paraná Country Club is fiercely protected by armed guards, and you have to tell them exactly where you are going before they will let you in. You are filmed as you enter, and you are prohibited from taking photos once you are inside the compound. You pass a row of expensive luxury-goods shops, and then come the luxury mansions, each one a mini-castle, and the golf club. Entering such a protected area, so close to such serious social problems and penury in the adjoining city, will aggravate the conscience of all but the most hardened. But once you get to somewhere like the Casa Blanca, it is such a lovely place – not so much for its luxury as for its design – that you almost forget your scruples. It is not the only hotel in the Paraná Country Club, but it is the most beautiful.

A new estate like the Paraná Country Club is being prepared now, called the Santa Elena Country y Marina Club, 28km north of Ciudad del Este, which will also have hotels. And there is shortly to open a new 4-star hotel called Megal Suites, with 70 rooms, gym, sauna, business centre, conference rooms, etc, at km3.5 (*061 502383*).

TOURIST INFORMATION

There is a new tourist office run by Senatur in the centre (*Mariscal Estigarribia y Adrián Jara; 061 511626/508810; e senaturcde@senatur.gov.py; 07.00–19.00 daily*) as well as one at the beginning of the bridge, which is manned 24/7.

Hotel Casino Acaray (50 rooms) 11 de septiembre c/ Av Luis María Argaña; ☎ 061 504250; www.hotelcasinoacaray.com.py. A well-known top-of-the-range hotel, right on the riverfront. Live shows, karaoke, casino. **$$$$**

HG Tower Hotel (260 rooms) Avenida Quito km7 Acaray; ☎ 061 578578; m 0986 102812; www.hgtowerhotel.com.py. New 11-storey hotel on edge of city centre. Heading away from the bridge, after the Supercarretera the 2nd major road on the right is Peru, & the hotel is on the next minor road right. Imaginative ideas, like a babymoon (luxury weekend for couple before their baby is born) & pay 2 nights get 3. Great playground for children. Gym, business centre, conference facilities, car rental, restaurant. **$$$$**

Casa Blanca (25 rooms) Paraná Country Club; ☎ 061 572121; www.casablancahotel.net. One of the most beautiful hotels in Paraguay. Fountain in the stairwell surrounded by plants, elegant drawing rooms, big stone fireplaces, view over the slow-moving green river. Pool, gym & sauna. Rooms are named after trees or precious stones, luxury suites very ample. It is not quite in Ciudad del Este, but rather Hernandarias, just across the Río Acaray. **$$$$**

Centro Hotel Nanawa c/ Monseñor Rodríguez; ☎ 061 514949; www.centrohotel.com.py. Smart hotel for business clientele with zany modern design. Rooms with access for those with disabilities. Conference centre. Closed circuit TV. **$$$**

Asunción Gran Hotel (103 rooms) Av Monseñor Rodríguez c/ Robert L Petit, km5; ☎ 061 573439/571853; www.asunciongranhotel.com. Business centre, sauna, hydromassage. Restaurant Los Lapachos. Access for people with disabilities. **$$$**

Cosmopolitan Hotel (10 rooms) Edificio Cosmopolitan 1, Pa'i Pérez y Pampliega; ☎ 061 501232/511030. Reception on 2nd floor, every room a suite with balcony, sitting room, dining table, fridge, plates, original numbered prints on walls. Parking. **$$$**

Hotel Panorama Inn Pampliega y Eusebio Ayala; ☎ 061 500110. On a quieter street but close to micro-centre. Spacious suites with huge mirrors, the sort of place to stay when you want to be there for a while. Lots of marble. Takes credit cards. Good restaurant. **$$$**

Hotel California (60 rooms) Av Carlos Antonio López 180; ☎ 061 500350/500378; www.hotelcalifornia.com.py. Almost opposite the cathedral. Minibars, TV, swimming pool, American b/fast, restaurant. **$$$**

Hotel Austria (48 rooms) Emiliano R Fernández 165; ☎ 061 504213/4; www.hotelaustriarestaurante.com. Business centre, parking, garden. Airy b/fast room, American b/fast, quiet neighbourhood, restaurant. **$$**

Hotel Munich (14 rooms) Emiliano R Fernández 71 y Capitán Miranda; ☎ 061 500347. Grand entrance, big rooms, good furniture, helpful manager, minibars, American b/fast with homemade bread. Quiet neighbourhood. **$$**

Guarania Hotel y Restaurante (130 rooms) Abay 146 c/ Adrián Jara; ☎ 061 500352/510385; e hrguarania@hotmail.com. AC, cable TV, parking, American b/fast. Restaurant closes 19.00. Internet open to public 07.00–20.00. Popular hotel that fills up quickly. **$$**

Mi Abuela Hotel (24 rooms) Av Adrián Jara c/ Pioneros del Este; ☎ 061 500333; www.miabuelahotel.com. Central. Lovely atmosphere to this hotel, which is almost as old as the city, & recognised as *patrimonio histórico* by the municipalidad. Nice patio, colourful, modern feel & lots of customers. Rooms have balconies, cable TV, Wi-Fi. B/fast room is full of historic photos, & the grandfather of the owner was Adrián Jara, one of the founders of Ciudad del Este. B/fast room also is a café, open to the street. Restaurant DiTrento. Loud pop music in reception will not suit all. **$$**

Santo Domingo Hotel (30 rooms) Emiliano Fernández y Emeterio Miranda; ☎ 061 500375. Plants & fountain in reception. Quiet neighbourhood. Recommended as an economical choice. **$$**

Casa Alta Hostel (4 rooms) Tacurú Pucú 20, barrio Boquerón; m 0973 508022/0983 100349; facebook.com/casaaltahostelcde. One block to the southwest of the lake, so nowhere central, but may be worth taking a taxi every time to enjoy the spacious hostel with pool, rooftop terrace & friendly people. AC, Wi-Fi, terrace, bar, lockers, kitchen for guests, cable TV. Transport for 7 guests. **$$**

WHERE TO EAT AND DRINK *Map, page 298.*

In addition to the places below, there are excellent eating places in the shopping centres; for example, in the Monalisa, the Shopping Barcelona and the Shopping Vendome.

Restaurant Madame Chateau Las Ventanas Suites Hotel, Av María de los Angeles esq Luis Bordon, Paraná Country Club; 061 574500. Smart gourmet cuisine in a very expensive hotel. Does a lot of business lunches. In the Paraná Country Club, near the Casa Blanca Hotel. $$$$

SAX Bistro Avenida San Blas, Shopping King Fong; 061 500621; www.sax.com.py; 09.00–15.30 Mon–Sat. Gourmet restaurant on top of SAX department store, particularly strong on seafood. Short but tempting menu. $$$

Patussi Grill Alejo García y Monseñor Cedzich; 061 502293/570621. One of the best restaurants, a *churrasquería*, with branches opposite the airport, in the Paraná Country Club & on Ruta 7 at km5. Pizza Hut is next door. $$

Churrasquería Interlagos Ruta 7 km5; 061 570621. This restaurant is 1km past the interchange with the Supercarretera. The crude colourful sign next door to Localiza car hire does not give a hint that this is 1 of the best restaurants in the city, with its endless offers of juicy meats, big variety of salads & vast number of waiters. The *mousse de mburucuyá* is very good. Live harp & guitar music from 20.00 on Sat, packed out as the evening wears onwards. Another branch of the restaurant is 1km east & around the corner, towards Hernandarias, on Supercarretera km26 (*0631 22464*). $$

Gauchiño Grill Shopping Zuni, 3 piso, Avenida San Blas c/ Patricio Colman; 061 505264; Facebook: Gauchiño Grill – Churrasquería; daily until midnight. Live Latin music Sat night from 21.00, live Paraguayan music Sun lunch. Inexpensive buffet or *churrasquería*. Good value. $$

Del Fuego Shopping del Este; m 0993 291142; www.bardelfuego. Smart bar & restaurant that also specialises in selling Habana cigars. Internet for customers. The Shopping del Este is very close to the customs (*aduana*) & the bridge. $$

Patu's Bar Bernardino Caballero 480; 061 506508; daily. Lively, imaginative restaurant under same management as Patussi Grill, specialising in pizzas. Across the green from the Patussi, & down a little turning off Bernardino Caballero, called 12 de junio. View over lake. $$

Yrupé Curupaytý c/ Adrián Jára; 061 509946; Facebook: Yrupe; b/fast–23.30 daily. Café/restaurant, particularly strong on birthday cakes. $$

Gugu's Boquerón y Adrián Jára; 061 512494; 10.30–21.00 Mon–Sat. Highly recommended & inexpensive Chinese restaurant bursting with Chinese customers. Good décor, lovely bathroom. One of 3 adjacent Chinese restaurants; Restaurant Garden & Mil Mil are the others, but Gugu's is the most inviting. $$

Ambrosia Restaurant Edificio Santa Catalina, Salón 1 y 2, Camilo Recalde c/ Capitán Miranda (behind Oasis); 061 501667. Large, clean café with AC. $

SHOPPING The principal sites in Ciudad del Este are the shops, especially the big shopping centres.

The **Monalisa** [298 E1] (*Carlos Antonio López e/ Av Rodríguez & Adrián Jára*) is a very smart department store. It seems to have a perfume section on every floor, and on the fourth floor is a *museo de perfumes* (just a display case with nine giant bottles). Their produce could have come straight out of a top store in Europe: L'Oréal face creams, Le Creuset saucepans, Lacoste sporting tops, Bulgari watches, and the biggest Toblerone you have ever seen in your life. They expect you to pay in dollars, not in guaraníes. Can this be Paraguay?

The **Casa China** [298 E1] is a smart department store, with nothing noticeably Chinese about it. But there is a big Chinese community in the city, as you become aware when you stumble across Gugu's Chinese restaurant.

Down the Avenida Rodríguez from Boquerón towards the bridge you will find it is all electronics shops, with stalls on the pavements too. The other side of Ruta 7 is Avenida San Blas, which is all clothes shops. At the bridge end of San Blas is the **Shopping King Fong** [298 F1] in an enormous building began in the 1990s and then abandoned until SAX took it over: when they have completed the 7 levels it will be the most luxurious department store in South America.

Parallel to Rodríguez but one block south is Avenida Adrián Jara: this is a key street for computers and electronics. You pass in turn the **Omni Center**, **Shopping Vendôme** (with its armed guards at every corner) and **Shopping Internacional** [298 E2].

Be cautious about buying cheap computer equipment in Ciudad del Este. The price will probably not be lower than you would pay with a cheap, large company in your own country; and you occasionally hear horror stories of various tricks that a traveller may be vulnerable to: boxed products may have had internal parts changed for others of lesser quality, or may even come with only paper inside instead of the equipment.

Nave [298 F1] (*Rua Regimiento Sauce esq Emiliano Fernández; ☎ 061 513397/513551; e callcenter@naveshop.com; ⏲ daily inc Sun; takes credit cards*) is one of the biggest and most reputable stores for computers, digital cameras, DVD players, etc. A significant indicator of its market is that its glossy leaflet is printed in Portuguese, and it is only just past the customs into Paraguay. 'Travel with peace of mind: declare your luggage,' it advises.

OTHER PRACTICALITIES There are no fewer than ten branches of Cambios Chaco (*www.cambioschaco.com.py*) where you can **exchange foreign currency**. One in the centre that opens early is the Itá Ybaté branch (*Adrián Jára esq Itá Ybaté; ☎ 061 511911; ⏲ 06.00–15.45 Mon–Sat*) and another that stays open late is the Shopping Corazón branch (*Avenida San Blas km1 Shopping Corazón; ☎ 061 510500; ⏲ 10.00–20.00 Mon–Sat*). MaxiCambios (*www.maxicambios.com.py*) also has three branches (*eg: Adrián Jára esq Piribebuý; ☎ 061 500122; ⏲ 06.30–16.00 Mon–Sat*). It is not difficult to find **cash machines** in Ciudad del Este.

The central area of town is spookily empty by 19.00, even in summer when it is still light, and you would not feel comfortable taking an evening walk in the deserted streets, which are watched over by armed guards by day.

There is a **map** produced by J B Producciones, but the best town plan, if you can get it, is by Ictus. You can get some maps of the city from Exchange Tours, upstairs (see page 300).

WHAT TO SEE AND DO The Lago de la República is a pleasant lake, formed by damming the Amambay stream, in parkland a little to the south of the centre. In the middle of the green is the **Municipalidad** [298 D3], an attractive single-storey building with a modern colonnade swarming with people paying their taxes and seeking to register their cars. To its left is the small house used as the **Museo El Mensú** [298 D2] (*⏲ 07.00–13.00 Mon–Fri; free admission*), which, as well as the typical museum contents of old typewriters and rusty rifles, tells the history of the city and houses the handwritten Acta de Fundación, dated 3 February 1957. It also has photos of Moisés Bertoni, displays of bows and arrows, and skins of caimans hanging up (like the ones Fr Gabriel comes across in the jungle in the film *The Mission*). To the other side of the Municipalidad is a Chinese garden.

The **cathedral** [298 F4] (*Carlos Antonio López e/ Oscar Ortellado y 11 de setiembre*) is dedicated to San Blas, designed by a Bolivian architect, Javier Querejazu. It was inaugurated in 1970 and extended in 1989. This interesting and dramatic building is built to resemble a ship and is best seen from the inside: it has a broad frontage with two side towers, and the nave then narrows to the sanctuary, where round windows like portholes lead up to a tall, thin, vertical panel of brilliant red, white and blue stained glass, portraying San Blas. The late Carlos Colombino was responsible for the San Blas window, and also for the main door, the pews and the confessionals. Most striking of all is the constant birdsong inside, from birds that live inside the building: it is said that you cannot hear the daily mass for the volume of the birdsong. To gain access, ask at the diocesan office behind the cathedral. Pope John Paul II, in his 1988 visit, gave the building a cross identical to that planted in the Dominican Republic to commemorate the fifth centenary of the evangelisation of America.

ITAIPÚ

ITAIPÚ DAM Itaipú (Guaraní) means 'the singing stone'. Visits to the Itaipú Dam (*061 599 8040; e arevalos@itaipu.gov.py; www.itaipu.gov.py; visits daily every hour on the hour from 08.00 to 17.00; free admission*) last 1½ hours. You must come with your passport and fill in a form requesting a visit. There is a good craft shop to browse in. The visit begins with a film (in English or Spanish) recounting the history of the construction. Then everyone gets in a bus, which takes them over the top of the dam to the Brazilian side, where the view is better.

The photos of Itaipú usually show it with the water thundering down the three spillways. In fact, you never see this: the spillways only operate occasionally, after there has been extremely heavy rain, and even then it is unusual for more than one to be used. The water that generates the power passes over the turbines far down beneath the surface.

To see the ***iluminación monumental*** (*19.30 Fri & Sat; free admission*) you must apply beforehand, by Thursday of the week in question, filling in a form with your full name, passport number and nationality, or sending those details by email to the address above or by phone (*061 599 8040*). The illumination in itself lasts only for five minutes, but the first two hours of the evening are devoted to a musical show they put on in the auditorium. Then you are bussed over to the *mirador* on the Brazilian side. Before the illumination begins, there is a short film about the dam, then dramatic music, and then slowly, bit by bit, the dam lights up, with gathering intensity, in subtle shades of green, orange and yellow. The alcoves in the concrete, when lit up, look like a row of stone lance heads, and all in all the dam is far more lovely than it is by day.

The Itaipú project was begun with the signing of a memorandum between Paraguay and Brazil in 1966. The formal treaty followed in 1973, but in 2009 President Fernando Lugo succeeded in renegotiating the treaty with President Lula of Brazil, to enable Paraguay to get three times as much money for the excess energy that it sells to Brazil. The problem with the treaty had been that whereas Brazil uses more energy than it produces from the dam, Paraguay, as a small country with a low population, uses much less – only 5% of its production.

For a long time Itaipú, with its 18 turbines (later increased to 20) was the largest hydro-electric dam in the world. The Three Gorges Dam in China has now overtaken it, with 26 turbines, soon to increase to 32. Itaipú was also the most expensive dam ever built – largely due to the corrupt practice of *sobrefacturación*, the normal form of which is to make out a bill for an excessive amount, and to share the surplus between the two parties to the fraud. The estimate for its construction was US$3.4 billion, but in the end it cost US$20 billion.

The dam began producing energy in 1984, and the last of the 20 generators began functioning in 2007. It now has a capacity to generate 14,000 megawatts, and each of the generators produces enough energy for a city of 2.5 million people. In 2008

Itaipú generated more than 94 million megawatt-hours. The royalties distributed to date are over US$6.6 billion – half to each country.

A 10km bypass (on the Brazilian side) called the Canal de Piracema has been created to enable fish to pass without going through the dam: they need this facility to reach their breeding areas. Today the lake of Itaipú is 200km long and holds 29 million cubic metres of water. It takes the place of the long sequence of waterfalls that formed the famous Saltos del Guairá, where the Guaraní led by Montoya lost all their statues, musical instruments and other possessions, in the great and terrible exodus from Guairá to where San Ignacio Miní is situated today (see pages 260–7).

The construction of the dam caused considerable ecological complications and required the forcible removal of 534 indigenous families, who moved to more urban conditions, with resulting damage to their socio-cultural lifestyle. The organisation Yvy Paraná Rembe'ype is still negotiating for a better settlement to compensate them for what they have lost.

ITAIPÚ'S TOURIST COMPLEX Itaipú supports (and has initiated) three tourist sites to the north of Ciudad del Este: the Museo de la Tierra Guaraní, the zoo and the Tatí Yupí Biological Refuge. Then to the south of the city are the Moisés Bertoni house (currently closed) and the Saltos de Mondaý.

The Museo de la Tierra Guaraní and the zoo are together in a complex 2km before Itaipú, while Tatí Yupí is a little further north, as it is on the lake above the dam. The Itaipú Tourist Complex (*061 599 8040; e arevalos@itaipu.gov.py*) is part of the Itaipú's programme of Integration, and Social and Environmental Responsibility.

To the north of Ciudad del Este

Museo de la Tierra Guaraní (*On the Supercarretera, 2km before you reach the Itaipú dam; 061 599 8782/8626; 08.00–16.00 Tue–Sun; free admission*) Do not miss the chance to visit this lovely museum. It opened in 1975, but still has a fresh feel to it, making use of multimedia displays, with touch-screen access to extensive information and interviews. It is divided into two exhibition halls. The first concentrates on the Guaraní world and explores what we can learn from the original inhabitants, whose descendants, the Ava Guaraní of Acaray-mí and Itanara-mí, still preserve their culture. There are baskets, feather ornaments, stone tools and earthenware pots, and interesting details about the social and religious system of the Guaraní: for example, they were traditionally buried in pots, in a foetal position, and the hummingbird (*mainumby*) was considered the only bird who could communicate directly with God (Ñandejára).

The second hall is devoted to the world of science, and has a lot of taxidermy. It has sections on the colonial gold hunters; the classification of species; the 18th-century naturalist Félix de Azara – who lived 20 years in Paraguay, when he was sent to delimit the boundary between Spanish and Portuguese territory; and the 19th-century naturalist Moisés Bertoni, one of whose achievements was to register the sweet herb *ka'a he'e* (*Stevia rebaudiana bertonii*), which is 300 times sweeter than sugar and has no calories. Finally, the displays reach the present-day achievement of the Itaipú dam.

Zoológico The zoo is situated next to the Museo de la Tierra Guaraní. The visit is with a guide (*08.00–11.00 & 14.00–16.00 Tue–Sun; free admission*). It has 12ha of ground, to permit the reproduction of rare species. In 2009 two baby pumas were born, which was considered a rare success. Pumas are an endangered species, as is the Chacoan peccary (Spanish *cerdo del monte*; Guaraní *taguá*), of which there are also examples in the zoo.

Some may prefer Yacyretá's Refugio Atinguý, but here you can see deer, rodents, snakes, otters, beavers, turtles, anteaters and howler monkeys. There is a red-billed currassow bird, a yellow anaconda snake and a broad-snouted caiman. There is a huge shiny black panther, baring his teeth and flicking the end of his tail, and three jaguars, kept in separate cages, with stiff, bristly whiskers, huge yellow teeth and big tongues, growling angrily.

The two principal kinds of Paraguayan parrot can be studied here: the blue-and-yellow macaw and the red-and-green macaw.

Tatí Yupí (*⌚ 08.30–16.30 Tue–Sun; free admission*) The Biological Refuge of Tatí Yupí opened in 2005. To visit it, you must get authorisation from the reception desk in Itaipú, but this is easily obtained. It is 3km north of Hernandarias and you cannot reach it without a car (or taxi). The refuge covers more than 2,000ha of natural wood with streams and springs, and the area is rich in animals and birds.

The activities include rides through the woods in a sulky (horse cart), on a bicycle, on horseback or on foot. In the lunch period you can stay in the refuge and walk in the central area and on the beach, but the activities begin again at 14.00. There is a good view over the lake, where dead tree stumps stick up out of the water, stripped and whitened by sun and rain, as a reminder that this lake has been artificially created by flooding. Brazil is a long way away across the lake: you can only pick out the bigger trees. The beach is of red sand, littered with tiny shells.

There are two **dormitories** with 30 beds each, where groups (often from schools, but any group is eligible) can stay for just one night, if they bring their bedding and towels. There is a kitchen, but you must bring your plates and cutlery. Reservations need to be made at least a month beforehand (*☎ 061 599 86666*), and no charge is made. There are also **camping** facilities.

Modelo Reducido (*1km before you reach the visitor centre, but go to the visitor centre first to obtain authorisation, presenting passports and documentation for any vehicle; ⌚ 08.30–15.30 winter, 08.30–16.30 summer*) Opened in 2013, the Modelo Reducido is a small-scale model of the Itaipú Dam, although it is said to be the largest to-scale model of any kind in South America. It was constructed many years ago as part of the development project of the dam, but has only recently been brought out and opened to the public, with functioning water. It is in the open air, so visits are not possible when it is raining.

To the south of Ciudad del Este The **Hito de las 3 Fronteras** is the point where the three countries of Paraguay, Brazil and Argentina abut, separated only by the Río Paraná and the Río Iguazú. Each country has placed a marker with the colours of its flag. To see this from the Paraguayan side, take the Avenida Bernardino Caballero which goes past the terminal, and then changes name to Mariscal Estigarribia. It is about 10km away. However, the best view of the Hito is from Argentina (see page 285).

The urban sprawl to the south of Ciudad del Este is really a separate town called Presidente Franco. A new bridge is planned to cross from here to Puerto Meira, though it has not yet got beyond the stage of inviting quotes for the work. Just beyond Presidente Franco, the Salto Mondaý and, a little further south, the house of Moisés Bertoni (currently closed), are both now technically taken into sites promoted as the Complejo Turístico Itaipú, and information can be obtained from the usual number (☎ *061 599 8040*), although they are not associated with the work of the dam. Some 60km further south from Ciudad del Este as the crow flies is the site of a further planned bridge to Brazil, at Ñacunday.

Salto Mondaý (🕒 *07.30–18.00 daily; Paraguayans Gs12,000*) The Salto Mondaý (pronounced in three syllables as Mon-da-ugh) cannot begin to be compared to the Iguazú Falls, pleasant though it is. It is approached through a well-kept garden, and the whole reserve covers 9ha. The waterfall has a 40m drop and there is an observation platform. There are new facilities for climbing through the trees on rope bridges (Gs30,000), abseiling and zip wire (Gs20,000). It is 10km from Ciudad del Este, and well signed, down Pioneros del Este, which turns into Bernardino Caballero. Mondaý is the name of the river on the Paraguayan side that is almost opposite (but a little bit south) of the juncture of the Río Iguazú and the Río Paraná. There are plans to open a Maharishi Reserva Natural on the other side of the waterfall from its current access point, and to install a lift up and down from the observation platform.

Monumento Científico Moisés Bertoni Dr Moisés Bertoni was an emblematic figure in the natural sciences who did research in meteorology, agronomy, biology and cartography. His little house was turned into a museum, with his manuscripts, letters and part of his library, his Minerva printing press with pedal and guillotine, skulls of animals and a reconstruction of his laboratory. This simple two-storey wooden house with a balcony, though for many years badly maintained and insufficiently attended to, nonetheless had a lovely feel to it, and the Guaraní indigenous who came to sell their goods seemed to feel at home.

Unfortunately, the long, heralded restoration, which was completed in early 2011, mysteriously led to the closing of the house to the public. All of the renovation done by museologist Luis Lataza – with ten museum rooms, the lower floor devoted to Bertoni's scientific legacy, and the upper floor devoted to the story of his life – has been sitting there ever since, gathering three years' worth of dust. The word now is that they are working on the place to provide a restaurant prior to re-opening. It is to be hoped that by the time this book is published the problem may be solved and the house opened again. To find out whether the house is open, contact the Senatur office in Ciudad del Este (☎ *061 511626*).

Getting there and away To reach the house by car from Ciudad del Este, take the Supercarretera going south, keep going straight until you reach the Avenida Mondaý junction, where you turn right, heading for Los Cedrales. You will cross the Río Mondaý quite bit upstream from the Mondaý Falls, and then you come to a wooden notice on the left indicating where you must start taking tracks across the fields to reach Moisés Bertoni. There are16km of this dirt road through soya fields. From the car park there is a magical walk through the beautiful subtropical forest that Bertoni enhanced and cherished around his house: the total extent of the land is 199ha. There are paths in the woods to explore – to the stream, a little waterfall, a little bridge and an ample sandy beach. Bertoni's grave is 200m from the house, where his remains lie, at his explicit request, 'resting in majestic plenitude beneath this majestic cypress tree'.

Since road access is not easy – allow an hour to travel the 26km from Ciudad del Este – some of the visitors to the house in the past came by boat, from Porto Meiro, Brazil, with the Macuco Safari tour operators. They still offered the trip at the time of writing, even though no-one was allowed inside the house.

MOISÉS BERTONI

Born in Switzerland in 1857, Moisés Santiago Bertoni was influenced by socialist ideas and studied law and botany. He set off for South America in 1884 with his family and a group of Swiss farmers to found a socialist colony. A few years later, drought impelled the colony to move from Argentina to Paraguay, where they lived in great poverty and hunger. Bertoni published works on Paraguayan geology, the eucalyptus, cotton-growing and oranges, and had his own printing press under the imprint Ex Silvis. He studied the Guaraní people and their language, and his calendar of rainfall has only recently been outdated by global warming climate changes. For a while he directed the Escuela Nacional de Agricultura, and was contracted by the Department of Health to collect poisonous snakes for the preparation of antidotes. In 1910 he received many awards at an international exhibition in Buenos Aires for his aromatic plants, tobacco, bark, maize, coffee, vegetable dyes, bananas and other fruits, and *yerba mate*. He discovered the properties of the plant ka'á he'e (*Stevia rebaudiana bertonii*), now gaining popularity as a natural sweetener. He supported his family of 13 children by selling bananas, coffee and firewood. He died of malaria in 1929.

Leisure facilities The **Mavani Beach Park** (*Ruta 6 km15 from Ruta 7, left bank of Río Mondaý;* e *info@mavanibeachpark.com.py; www.mavanibeachpark.com.py*) is a soon-to-open aquatic theme park with water chutes and slides, a lake with an artificial beach and a swimming pool with waves in a 260,000m² landscaped compound. If the Iguazú Falls have not exhausted your taste for water adventure, this promises to offer good family fun, although the opening is taking several years longer than anticipated and all that is open to date is a segment of the park called Eco Aventura, which offers rope bridges through trees and a zipwire. From Ciudad del Este drive out on Ruta 7 for 30km to its junction with Ruta 6, turn left (south) for 15km and it is on your left, just before you cross the Río Monday. Accommodation is planned. Information and tickets from the administrative office in the Shopping Zuni in Ciudad del Este (☎ *061 509586/9*). If you are driving up from the south, there is an office in Santa Rita, about 45km to the south of the Park, on Ruta 6 (*Av 14 de mayo, esq Av de los Inmigrantes;* ☎ *0673 221345;* m *0983 556434;* e *mavanibeachsantarita@gmail.com*).

Paraíso Golf Ranch Resort and Spa (*Km24 Monday;* ☎ *061 514548;* e *info@paraisogolf.com; www.paraisogolf.com*) This is located along a turning to your left before the toll station and airport as you drive out of Ciudad del Este. As well as a golf course, there are bungalows to stay in, a restaurant, swimming pool, riding and football.

10

Villarrica and Central Eastern Paraguay

Departamentos: Caaguazú; gobernación ☎ 0521 203782
Guairá; gobernación ☎ 0541 43274/41890
Caazapá; gobernación ☎ 0542 232777

Villarrica is hidden in the very heart of Paraguay, just as Paraguay is hidden in the very heart of South America. Contrasting with the flatness of most of the country, its *departamento* of Guairá is a region of green hills, streams and waterfalls, caves and archaeological remains. Part of the region is in the Resource Management Reserve of Ybytyruzú, which covers 24,000ha and is in the area encircled by Independencia, Mbocayatý, Villarrica, Ñumí and Garay.

Like Cordillera, Guairá is an important area for Franciscan towns (see box on page 146): it has Yataitý, Itapé, Borja, Yutý, Villarrica itself, and most important of all, Caazapá. Bobí (now known as General Artigas) is just over the border into the *departamento* of Itapúa, but is included at the end of this chapter.

When you cross west–east on Ruta 2, from Asunción towards Ciudad del Este, the mid-point stop is Coronel Oviedo, in the *departamento* of Caaguazú. Coronel Oviedo is primarily associated in most people's minds with being a road hub, with Ruta 3 leading directly north and Ruta 8 leading south to Villarrica. But if it is Villarrica you are heading for, it is better now to take the new road which runs more directly from Paraguarí to Villarrica, alongside the old railway line, cutting about an hour off the journey. At the time of going to press the final kilometre of asphalt was being completed.

The people of Villarrica have traditionally considered themselves a historic community, culturally a cut above the people of Asunción. They fought a publicity battle to try to have their *departamento* of Guairá, rather than Asunción, declared the Capital of the Harp. They sometimes even talk of Villarrica as the capital of the Republic of Guairá.

Going south from Villarrica you enter Caazapá, a *departamento* in the depths of the interior, and beyond it are miles of dirt roads, tracing their slow way until they join up with the asphalt that leads down to the main highways of Ruta 1 and Ruta 6. The asphalt is creeping upwards, but was still a long way from Caazapá when we went to press.

Caazapá is one of the least visited *departamentos* in Paraguay, because it is so difficult to access. But the town of Caazapá itself is a jewel that well repays a visit, and it has good hotels. Its dignified avenue of palm trees leads to a church that is kept open and has what may be the most beautiful reredos in Paraguay. The town was the heart of the Franciscan missionary effort, founded by the great Friar Luis Bolaños, who laid crucially important foundations for the better-known work of the Jesuits.

The three *departamentos* of Caaguazú, Guairá and Caazapá form a block right in the centre of Eastern Paraguay – that is to say, the half of Paraguay that is east of the Río Paraguay.

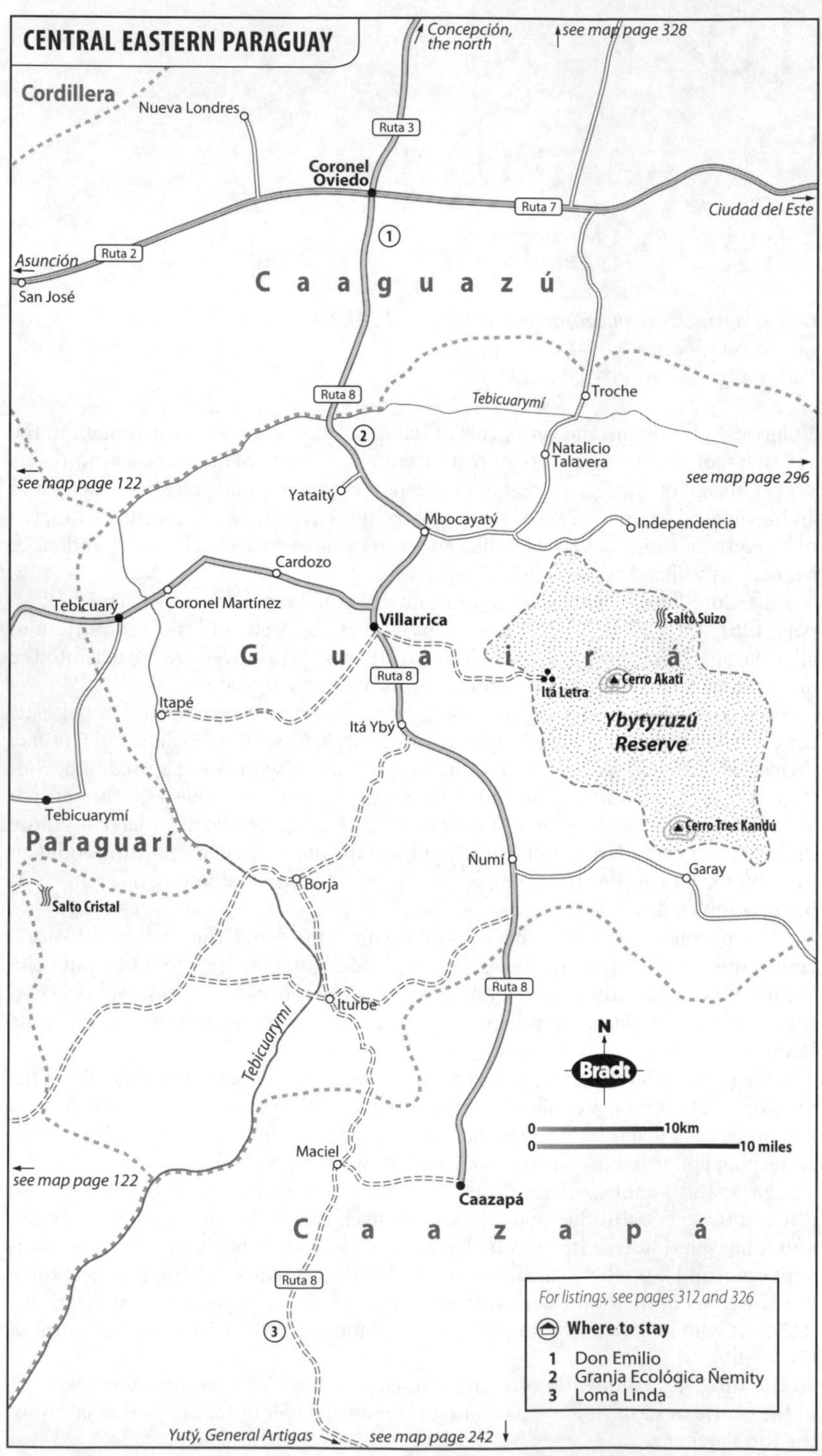
CENTRAL EASTERN PARAGUAY
Concepción, the north
see map page 328
Cordillera
Nueva Londres
Ruta 3
Coronel Oviedo
Ruta 7
Ciudad del Este
Asunción
Ruta 2
San José
Caaguazú
Ruta 8
Tebicuarymí
Troche
Natalicio Talavera
see map page 122
see map page 296
Yataitý
Mbocayatý
Independencia
Cardozo
Tebicuarý
Coronel Martínez
Villarrica
Saltó Suizo
Guairá
Itá Letra
Cerro Akati
Itapé
Itá Ybý
Ybytyruzú Reserve
Tebicuarymí
Paraguarí
Cerro Tres Kandú
Ñumí
Garay
Borja
Salto Cristal
Iturbe
Tebicuarymí
N
Bradt
0 10km
0 10 miles
Maciel
see map page 122
Caazapá
Caazapá
Ruta 8
For listings, see pages 312 and 326
Where to stay
1 Don Emilio
2 Granja Ecológica Ñemity
3 Loma Linda
Yutý, General Artigas
see map page 242

CORONEL OVIEDO

Copaco ☎ *0521 203099; municipalidad* ☎ *0521 203468*

There is little to be said of Coronel Oviedo from the tourist point of view, apart from it being the great crossroads at the very centre of the country. From the big roundabout, you go west to Asunción along Ruta 2; east to Ciudad del Este along Ruta 7; north to Pedro Juan Caballero on the road that is called Ruta 3 further along the route; and south to Villarrica on Ruta 8.

The traffic through Coronel Oviedo has been reduced a little by the new road from Paraguarí to Villarrica, and by the new stretch of Ruta 3 through Arroyos y Esteros and San Estanislao. But nothing will alter the importance of Coronel Oviedo as the mid-point on the five- or six-hour journey between Asunción and Ciudad del Este.

The **bus** station in Coronel Oviedo is set right on the big grassy roundabout, and is a busy place of hustle and bustle, with a row of orange Coca-Cola booths and as many as 13 platforms. Staff from the restaurant will rush out to hover at the windows of buses with baskets of *gaseosas* and *milanesa* rolls.

WHERE TO STAY This is a small selection from the large number of economical hotels in Coronel Oviedo.

Centro Hotel (28 rooms) Defensores del Chaco y Vicepresidente Sanchez (by the side of the Plaza de los Héroes); ☎ 0521 204610; m 0972 534766; www.centrohotel-py.com. Enclosed parking, cable TV. Rooms have wooden bedsteads & muted colours. No restaurant but guests can use the kitchen, or order food by delivery. **$$**

Hotel Bertea (52 rooms) Ruta 2 km130; ☎ 0521 202019. Range of room categories, from very cheap up to 3 times that price for better quality. **$–$$**

Hotel San Martín (28 rooms) Mariscal Estigarriba c/ Tajy; ☎ 0521 203208/202972. Another inexpensive option that you pass on the main road from Asunción. **$**

WHERE TO EAT AND DRINK The unpretentious **La Nona** (*next door to Hotel Bertea, Ruta 2 km130;* ☎ *0521 202845;* ⌚ *24/7;* **$**) is worth looking for though is not well signed. You will find it next to the much more visible Hotel Bertea, and it is under the same management. It is the regular stop for the big bus companies, which is a recommendation in itself. It has a homely charm, as the building has been haphazardly added to. It is self-service, with a choice of *asado* or hot meals, and salads.

EAST OF CORONEL OVIEDO Heading east from Coronel Oviedo, after 46km you come to the town of **Caaguazú**, which gives its name to the *departamento*. It is a timber-producing town, and is noted for the large number of motorbikes ridden there. There are a couple of large international hotels, both belonging to the Sosa network (*www.sosahoteles.com*) and aimed more at businesspeople than tourists. **César Palace Hotel** (*22 rooms; Av Coronel Manuel A Godoy y Roberto L Petit;* ☎ *0522 43096;* **$**) has pleasant rooms with subtle colours and lighting, conference rooms and a good laundry service. **Hotel Tajy** (*about 30 rooms; Ruta 7 km177;* ☎ *0522 40118;* **$**) is so similar to the César Palace that the same photos of rooms are used on both websites, but in reality the hotels are different buildings. The Tajy is slightly bigger and on the Ruta, whereas the César Palace is in the centre of town.

About 25km beyond that, at Torín, before you reach the town of Juan E O'Leary (which is just into the *departamento* of Alto Paraná), you come to the turning south for one of the more expensive *estancias* in the Apatur network, **Golondrina** (*Ruta*

7 235km from Asunción; ☎ *026 2893/4/2238;* e *centralsag@gesgolondrina.com.py;* **$$$**). If you do not mind driving 17km on a dirt road to get here, it is a beautiful place to stay, run by a Portuguese company. They have big, round bungalows, boats and fishing on the Río Mondaý, guided walks and riding.

The largest part of the *departamento* of Caaguazú stretches to the north of Ruta 7, but is remote territory and difficult to access. Here it was that a huge underground bunker was found in February 2009, which is believed to have been built by a gang of kidnappers. (Kidnapping is a scourge in Paraguay.

North of Caaguazú is the former Jesuit town of **San Joaquín,** founded in 1746, (though it was never part of the Treinta Pueblos, and is a considerable distance away from them). You can reach it from Caaguazú (67km) passing through Yhú; or you can take the asphalted road that goes north from Coronel Oviedo, and turn east after 50km, along the road that passes through Cecilio Báez (32km). Both roads are now asphalted. It has some original Jesuit statues in the church, which date back to the 18th-century foundation.

SOUTH OF CORONEL OVIEDO If instead of going east from Coronel Oviedo, you turn south towards Villarrica, then you soon pass a couple more *estancias*. Reservations at all these *estancias* can also be made through Apatur (see page 54).

Where to stay

Don Emilio (9 rooms) ☎ 021 660791/603994; m 0981 507105; www.donemilioestancia.com. Large, colonial-style house with thick walls & brick floors. Pool, & 20mins from sandy beaches of Río Tebicuary-mí. Just 6km to the south of Coronel Oviedo, at halfway point for those travelling from Asunción to Foz, 2 hours in each direction. Over 1,000ha of native woodland with deer & monkeys. Riding, trips in horse cart, walking. English spoken. **$$$**

Granja Ecológica Ñemitý ☎ 021 512028/0549 20095; m 0981 303516; e granjanemity@cu.com.py. This is 26km south of Coronel Oviedo on Ruta 8, & offers riding, horse carts & a swimming pool. Opposite this *estancia* is the short road that leads into the village of Yataitý, just 1km to the west. **$$**

YATAITÝ

Copaco ☎ *0546 20000; municipalidad* ☎ *0549 20003*

The *cuna* (cradle) of Paraguay's traditional *ao po'i* embroidery, Yataitý is an enchanting little village, with simple houses, many of which have adobe walls and thatched roofs. To reach the church and its pretty grounds, turn left off the main street.

Ao po'i (Guaraní 'fine cloth') began in the presidency of Dr Francia, when his block on imports forced Paraguayans to develop their own craft. The craft is made in many places, but nowhere is it done so intensively or with such skill and dedication as in Yataitý. Typical items are beautiful natural-coloured tablecloths of all sizes with lacy panels and lines of embroidery, and clothes, especially the brightly embroidered shirts worn by Paraguayan musicians.

The real, authentic *ao po'i* is entirely handmade from start to finish, including the spinning and weaving, but for practical reasons manufactured cloth is often used as the base. This, however, will be bought from Paraguay's high-quality cotton company, Pilar, in the town of the same name (see page 230).

All the local populace devote themselves to *ao po'i*, even the children, and it is estimated that over 2,000 in Yataitý are working at this craft. One person in the family will spin the thread, another will weave it, another will embroider and another do the lace work known as *encaje ju*. Grandmothers with failing eyesight who can no longer embroider will take part in another stage of the production process. Even the men are involved, chiefly in the ironing, which needs a strong hand after some good starching. It is all enormously delicate and time-consuming work: if one person were single-handedly to make a large tablecloth (for example), it would take her a year and a half.

Little craft shops are all along the streets, in people's houses. Digna López, known as '*la viuda de Narvajo*' (the widow of Narvajo), is one of the most highly respected craftswomen (m *0982 787572*).

For ten days in November or December there is an Expoferia, when all the local producers have stalls in the grassy Plaza General Francisco Roa in front of the church, and the full range of products is available in one place, at amazingly reasonable prices. The local *cooperativa* decides on the dates each year, and to find out when it will be held you need to ring the Municipalidad.

Yataitý is a place to visit, not to stay. When you leave, the southbound Ruta 8 reaches Mbocayatý after 7km. Here you have the choice of turning right for Villarrica, or left for Independencia.

INDEPENDENCIA

Copaco *0548 265299; municipalidad* *0548 265477*

Colonia Independencia is a German foundation, begun by emigrants in 1919 after the end of World War I. Recently, there has been another influx of people from German-speaking countries, and the town is so German that you can find a road called Berliner Strasse. If you have a European complexion you may well be addressed in German, by residents who speak faltering or heavily accented Spanish. The hotels typically have German websites ending in '.de', and sometimes even written in German.

There is a prettiness and order about the town, which has specialised in being a holiday place, full of hotels and not much else, on the edge of the Ybytyruzú nature reserve. It is a green and leafy place to stay, and has a municipal park of 3ha with a stream and a bathing place. Its slogan is 'the land of wine and sun', and it is indeed the only place in Paraguay with extensive vineyards and any beginnings of a serious wine culture.

You can reach Independencia from Ruta 8, turning east at Mbocaytý (a turn right if you are coming from Asunción on the new road from Paraguarí to Villarrica, but a turn left if you have come from Coronel Oviedo on Ruta 2). Or you can reach it from Ruta 7, turning south 18km after Coronel Oviedo: this takes you over a wooden bridge at Troche. The bus from Asunción is Ybytyruzú.

The town begins in a spread-out way along the entrance road, and many of the hotels are here. Then you turn right towards the town centre, heading towards the wooded hills of the Ybytyruzú park. At a mini-roundabout at the end of this road, you turn left for the Plaza Municipal, the stone church and the Centro Cultural. When you reach a petrol station the asphalt changes to *empedrado*. The next turn right is marked 'Salto Suizo' (see page 314), but if you carry straight on you will find your way back to the asphalt road.

Curiously, there are very few landline phones in the town: most hotels operate on mobile numbers. For internet, the signal of the Tigo or Claro modems is the best.

WHERE TO STAY

Hotels

Hotel Independencia (16 rooms) Km180; 0548 265290; m 0981 302931; e hotel-independencia@web.de; www.hotel-independencia.de. The 4th hotel you reach as you drive into Independencia. Grand entrance with a beautiful fig tree in the middle of the courtyard. Outside terrace, swimming pools, stuffed animals, internet & restaurant. **$$$**

Hotel Tilinski (20 rooms) 0548 265240. Down a gravel side road, clearly marked from the main road. Big terrace for meals. Swimming pool. Offers lunch & swimming pool for day guests. Volleyball & football pitches, stream. Restaurant offers lunch with use of swimming pool. Offers full board as well as a B&B price. **$$$**

Hotel Sport Camping (c10 rooms) m 0981 885198; e michellerickel@hotmail.com; www.hotel-sportcamping.de. The 2nd hotel you reach, on a corner opposite the (unmarked) track to Salto la Cantera. Nice big rooms in newly built thatched round bungalows. Good bathrooms. 2 swimming pools, very clean. Restaurant by pool serves simple food. Camping. **$$$**

Hotel Rowil 3 (6 rooms) m 0984 294090. Another branch of the excellent, economic Hotel Rowil group (see page 316). Cheaper rooms have fans. **$**

Posadas Turísticas

In addition to the hotels, there are now a number of Posadas Turísticas recognised by Senatur (see page 52):

Posada Ña Coti 0548 265 281; **$**
Posada Las Mercedes m 0984 612 287; **$$**
Posada George m 0981 590 243; **$**
Posada Bella Vista m **0981 323 083; $**
Posada Loli m 0983 909 080; **$**

WHERE TO EAT AND DRINK

Restaurant Austria On the left after Hotel Independencia. Cosy German restaurant with an international menu at very reasonable prices, & a swimming pool. **$$**

Restaurant Freiburg On the left after you turn south towards the Ybytyruzú park, into the town centre, where you have a view of a dramatic wooded hill ahead of you; closed Thu. Sweet little restaurant with 2 tables, 6 chairs & good food. **$$**

El Mangal Restaurant 0548 265449; m 0981 302108. In a turning left, just before the mini-roundabout (see page 313). Most dishes have German names. Outside terrace. **$$**

Restaurant Punto de Encuentro m 0981 281404/886711; lunch & eve every day. Simple, typical Paraquayan fare, *milanesa*, *lomito*, hamburger, etc. **$**

WHAT TO SEE AND DO When you rejoin the main road, after going through the town, you come to a big map before a petrol station, which marks the 'Bodega Gerhard Bühler', just past the cemetery. This is the **Vista Alegre Winery.** It does not normally offer visits for tourists. Gerhard Bühler is bringing German expertise to help Paraguay begin a wine trade, and he says Paraguay has the perfect climate for wine production. In a number of houses in Independencia you can buy grapes, but as yet there are few vineyards elsewhere in Paraguay.

If you take the turn for **Salto Suizo** (Swiss Waterfall), you will pass the Reiterhof equestrian centre (m *0981 711874*), which offers riding lessons, hacking and trips in a horse cart. To reach the **waterfall**, carry on for 8km down this dirt road, which gets progressively worse. Eventually, you can take your car no further and must walk the last stretch through the woods. When you reach the waterfall, you may be disappointed to find there is only a tiny trickle of water falling into the pool, though the drop is indeed impressive and there is a good echo. At times of heavy rainfall this would be dramatic, but then at times of heavy rainfall the road to reach it would be impassible.

Another waterfall that is more modest but closer to the main road (only 2km on foot) is the Salto la Cantera. To get there, you take a track opposite the Hotel Sport Camping. To be sure of finding it, ask for a local guide and pay a small tip (from about Gs10,000).

The hill at this end of the Ybytyruzú reserve is called Cerro Akatĩ and has an excellent view (see page 321). There is also the Cerrito, which is a conical 'little hill' on private property, and has a quarry with natural columns of sandstone, and the Cerro de la Cruz (Hill of the Cross), which is closer to the Salto Suizo.

EXCURSIONS FROM INDEPENDENCIA Victor Franco of **Aventura Sin Limites** (*Avenida Vice Presidente Luis M. Argaña,camino al hospital de Independencia;* **m** *0981 281998;* **e** *arnol_0@hotmail.com*) can organise visits to Itá Letra (see page 321) and to other places in the reserve of Ybytyruzú. He can also organise abseiling in the region, but this is only feasible for bigger groups because of the cost of the equipment and a minimum of four trained instructors. Other activities that are easier for fewer people are horse riding or going in a carro polaco (which is like a *sulky* – that is, a horse cart).

VILLARRICA

Copaco 0541 42250; municipalidad 0541 42255; www.villarrik.com

Villarrica – literally the 'rich town' – is a university city and has quite a buzz to it. Pavements are adorned with colourful produce spilling out from the shops, and there is every sign of a functioning economy: there are plenty of shops of electrical equipment and mobile phones, and prices are higher here. Many shops advertise that they change dollars and pesos – evidence of international trade – and when you go to the bus station, you seem to find more buses going to foreign destinations (São Paulo, Buenos Aires) than are going to Asunción. Villarrica has a reputation for feeling itself a rival to Asunción, and for wanting to do everything differently.

But this is to give a modern interpretation to an ancient name. The town was founded by Captain Ruy Díaz de Melgarejo on 14 May 1570, and he chose the name in the belief that there were gold and silver mines in the vicinity. The original Villarrica was in the old Guairá province to the northeast, now in Brazil, before the city suffered a series of relocations to escape the Portuguese *mamelucos* or slave-traders. Its correct, full name is Villarrica del Espíritu Santo, because it was founded on the feast of the Holy Spirit (Pentecost) (see pages 263 and 359 on the Jesuit-Guaraní exodus from Guairá).

Villarrica is known as the *ciudad andariega*, which means the city that gets up and moves. After the first two settlements in the original Guairá province to the northeast, it moved in 1634 to the source of the River Jejuí (more directly north, within present-day Paraguay), and then to the present area of central eastern Paraguay (which is now named Guairá, so the regional name moved as well as the town's name). In 1675 it was sited in Itapé (now a nearby Marian centre), moving almost at once to what is now Coronel Oviedo and in 1682 finding its final resting place on its current site, which was secured by royal permission of the King of Spain in 1701. It has had a total of seven locations.

GETTING THERE AND AROUND The principal **bus** company that runs a service from the Terminal in Asunción is Guaireña, which goes hourly (*021 551727 in Asunción; 0541 42678 in Villarrica*). It follows Ruta 2 (the east–west highway) as far as Coronel Oviedo, and then plunges directly south for another half-hour. The total journey to Villarrica takes 3½–4 hours because it is a slow bus that stops (*removido*). You could also catch Yuteña, which goes on beyond Villarrica (see page 322). There is another bus, Ybytyruzú, which leaves Asunción twice a day (*021 551727; 05.30 & 13.10*) and goes via Paraguarí and the new road, but still takes 3½ hours.

The new road through Paraguarí (see page 309 and maps on pages 122 and 310) is more direct and quicker if you are **driving**.

When you arrive you have the choice of a **taxi** – in uncharacteristically good condition for Paraguay – or a **horse cart** – which costs less than a motor taxi and is a lot more fun. The streets are full of these horse-drawn vehicles, which give considerable charm to the place. They are known as *karumbés*, which in Guaraní means 'tortoise', and they cost Gs15,000 an hour. (Encarnación is the other city famous for its *karumbés*; see page 275.)

TOURIST INFORMATION There is now a Senatur tourist information office at the north end of town [317 D1] (*Ruta 8 km165;* m *0981 747936/347425;* e *turismoguaira@gmail.com; Facebook: Turista Roga Villarrica Guaira*). Look out for blue notices saying '*Turista Róga*' (Guaraní: tourist house) before you reach town. It is in a park called Parque del Guairá, opposite the Second Infantry Division.

WHERE TO STAY *Maps opposite and on page 319.*

Hotel Musa (41 rooms) General Díaz y Curupaytý; 0541 44007; e hotelmusavillarrica@gmail.com. Stylish new hotel in the centre. Parking, split AC, cable TV, Wi-Fi. The restaurant, which is a *churrasquería*, is quite well known. **$$**

Villarrica Palace Hotel (68 rooms) Ruta 8 Blas Garay y Río Apa; 0541 43048/42832; e vph@gointernet.com.py; www.sosahoteles.com. Supposedly Villarrica's top hotel, though some visitors have been disappointed. Right at the northern edge of the town, so only suitable for those travelling by car. Large complex with grand & spacious appearance, swimming pool, sauna, gym, conference hall seating 200, enclosed parking with guard. Price rises Jan–Mar. The Restaurant Adela of the Villarrica Palace Hotel has surprisingly economical prices if you choose the set menus. Service slow. One option is to eat in the restaurant & sleep in nearby Rowil 1 or 2, which are much cheaper than Palace. **$$**

Hotel Ybytyruzú (40 rooms) Carlos A López esq Dr Bottrell; 0541 42390/40844/41507/41598; www.hotelybytyruzu.com. Also a smart, modern, large hotel, & more conveniently located than Palace. Has a lot of visiting conferences & is sometimes booked out. Wi-Fi, cable TV, pool, restaurant. **$$**

Hotel Real (10 rooms) Ruta 8 y Constitucion; 0541 44090. Cable TV. Comfortable modern hotel on the highway just south of town, behind the Barcos y Rodados service station, perfectly situated for people travelling rather than stopping, what would be called in another country a motel (but not in Paraguay!). Cable TV, Wi-Fi. **$$**

Hotel Paraíso (3 rooms) Ruta 8 km168, Mbokayaty y 2a División; 0541 40262; m 0982 797158; e info@hotel-paraiso.de; www.hotel-paraiso.de. Out of town to the north, on the west side of the road, next to an army post. German establishment (& website only in German). Models including a Nazi warship complete with swastika & bomber planes, complete Nazi air force uniform, newspaper cuttings from 1944 onwards all over wall. Also has cuttings about the *Titanic*. New pool. Well presented, family feel. German-run restaurant, good cooking, very extensive international menu, outside terrace, closed on Thu except to hotel guests. **$$**

Hotel La Familia (10 rooms) Río Apa y Mayor Bullo; 0541 40647. Small hotel tucked away near entrance to town, b/fast not included. Budget rooms with fans or AC available. **$**

Hotel Rowil 1 (c20 rooms) Pa'i Anasagasti c/ Olimpo; 0541 42852; m 0983 360066. Rooms are basic but bright & cheery & scrupulously clean. Cable TV. AC (both kinds), Wi-Fi in reception only. Restaurant. Recommended, but you need transport into the centre. **$**

Hotel Rowil 2 (8 rooms) Ruta 8 y Augusto Roa Bastos 0541 43989. Nice feel to this sister hotel to Rowil 1. A little way from the centre, but no further than the Palace, which is first choice for many. No b/fast. Cheaper rooms have fans. No internet. **$**

Hotel Guairá (12 rooms) Mcal Estigarribia y Natalicio Talavera; 0541 42369. Just a block & a half from the bus terminal. Rather old-fashioned with a certain traditional charm, though standards have slipped. Cheaper rooms have fans. **$**

WHERE TO EAT AND DRINK *Maps opposite and on page 319.*

La Tranquera Barrio Estación; 0541 42185; eves only, plus Sun lunch, closed Mon. Opposite the old railway station in the south of city, to the south of the railway line, this is a high-quality restaurant both for food & ambience, located in a position that may come up in the world when the

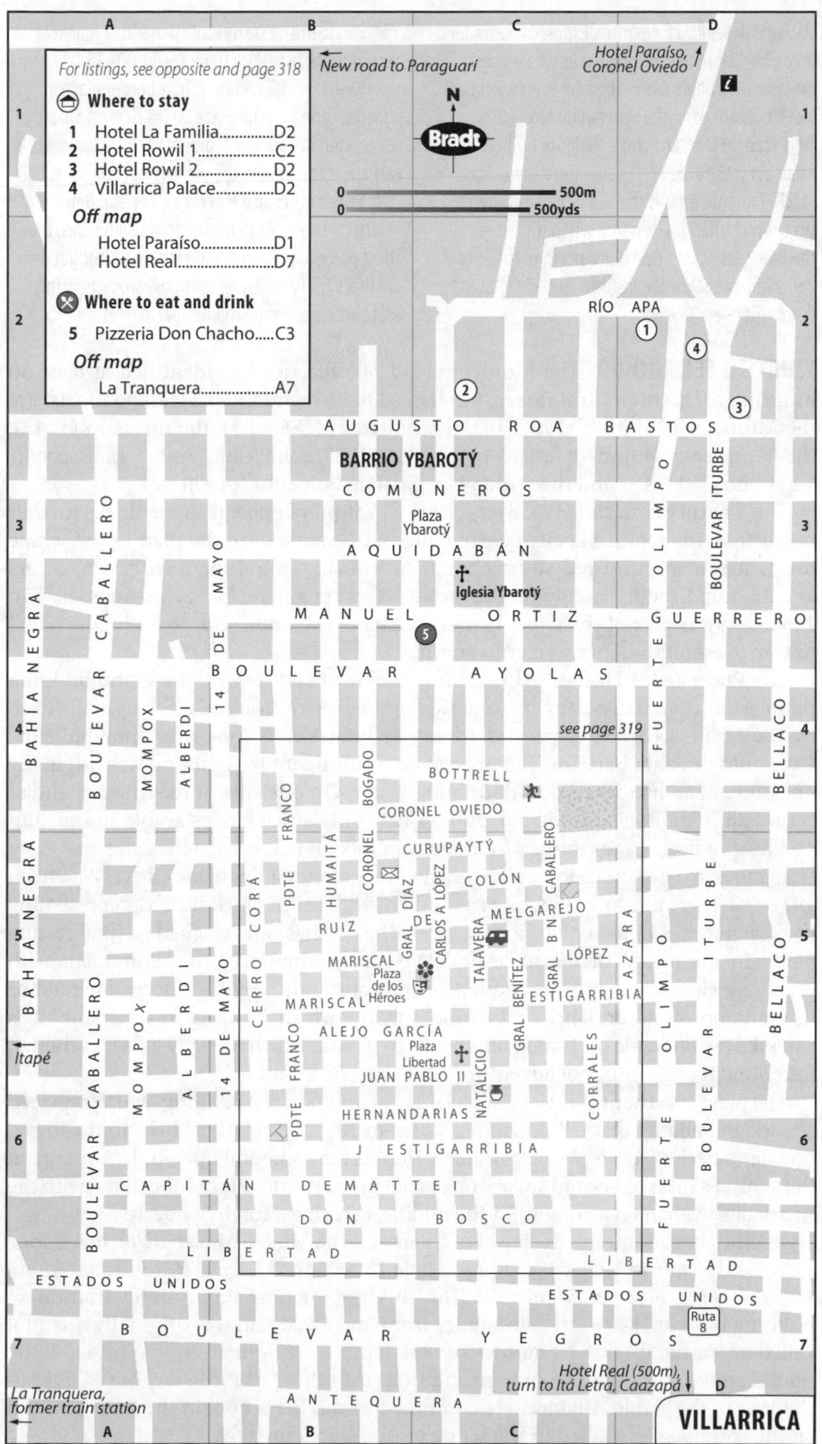

VILLARRICA
For listings, see opposite and page 318
Where to stay
1 Hotel La Familia.............D2
2 Hotel Rowil 1...................C2
3 Hotel Rowil 2...................D2
4 Villarrica Palace..............D2
Off map
Hotel Paraíso...................D1
Hotel Real........................D7
Where to eat and drink
5 Pizzeria Don Chacho.....C3
Off map
La Tranquera...................A7
New road to Paraguarí
Hotel Paraíso, Coronel Oviedo
N
Bradt
0 500m
0 500yds
RÍO APA
AUGUSTO ROA BASTOS
BARRIO YBAROTÝ
COMUNEROS
Plaza Ybarotý
AQUIDABÁN
Iglesia Ybarotý
MANUEL ORTIZ
GUERRERO
BOULEVAR AYOLAS
BOULEVAR ITURBE
OLIMPO
FUERTE OLIMPO
BELLACO
BAHÍA NEGRA
BOULEVAR CABALLERO
MOMPOX
ALBERDI
14 DE MAYO
see page 319
BOTTRELL
CORONEL OVIEDO
CURUPAYTÝ
COLÓN
MELGAREJO
LÓPEZ
ESTIGARRIBIA
FRANCO
BOGADO
CORONEL
HUMAITÁ
PDTE
DÍAZ
GRAL
DE
CARLOS A LÓPEZ
CABALLERO
BN
GRAL
AZARA
RUIZ
MARISCAL
Plaza de los Héroes
TALAVERA
BENÍTEZ
CERRO CORÁ
ALEJO GARCÍA
Plaza Libertad
JUAN PABLO II
NATALICIO
HERNANDARIAS
J ESTIGARRIBIA
CORRALES
CAPITÁN DEMATTEI
DON BOSCO
LIBERTAD
ESTADOS UNIDOS
Ruta 8
BOULEVAR YEGROS
ANTEQUERA
Itapé
La Tranquera, former train station
Hotel Real (500m), turn to Itá Letra, Caazapá
A B C D
1 2 3 4 5 6 7

station is developed for tourism. Exposed beams, tiled floors, life-size models of indigenous where guests can have their photo taken. Stage for events. *Parilla* & salad, but can provide for vegetarians too. $$

Pizzería Don Chacho Teniente Guillermo Arias; m 0982 818978; ⌚ evening daily & Sun lunch. Teniente Arias is the same road as General Díaz, which changes its name when it crosses the Boulevar Ayolas. One block north of the Boulevar, on the corner. Inside & outside space. Recommended. $$

Restaurant Danykar Bogado c/ Mariscal Estigarribia; ☎ 0541 41648; ⌚ 11.00–15.00, 18.00–01.00 daily. Pizza & hamburger place in good location on the Plaza de los Héroes. Smartly decorated in dark red & brown with tables inside & also over the road in the plaza itself. $$

Supermercado Herrero General Benítez c/ Mariscal López. As in most Paraguayan cities, the best place to pick up a good meal at a budget price, with a variety of dishes to choose from, is in the café attached to the main supermarket. $

WHAT TO SEE AND DO The Municipalidad of Villarrica has identified at least **80 buildings of architectural interest** that need to be maintained. Heading the list are the Municipalidad itself (1907–13), the cathedral (1883–91), the museum (1842), the Franciscan church Iglesia Ybarotý (1944–57), the Club Social El Porvenir Guaireño (1917–19) and the Banco Nacional de Fomento (c1900).

The **Ybarotý church** [317 C3], on Carlos Antonio López, is three blocks further north than the top of the city centre plan, but is marked on the plan of the whole town. It is a splendid red-stone church of Romanesque design, with two towers and 25 round-topped arches on the façade. It was begun by Fr Carlos Anasagasti in 1944, and this part of the street is named Anasagasti after him, changing its name to Carlos Antonio López as it goes south.

The **Plaza de los Héroes** [319 B3] is at the town centre, with the grand building of the Municipalidad occupying one side of the square. The site was originally used by the Jesuits as a cemetery, and when the Franciscans took over they built the Convento de Santa Bárbara. The present early 20th-century building was originally one-storey and had its second floor added later. On one side of the Municipalidad is the Salon Auditorio Municipal, built in 1911–14, which has a sizeable auditorium and hosts a lively programme of Paraguayan folk and classical dance classes.

Plaques in the Plaza de los Héroes tell the story of the battles of the Chaco War, from 1932–35. There is also a tall white monument with seven vertical slabs, representing the seven moves of the city (see page 315). The city has now reached its final resting place 'in the region of the majestic Ybytyruzú' (announces the monument with grandiose eloquence) and 'the coquettish and constantly moving Villarrica maintains its tradition of culture and aristocratic nobility, which has rocked its cradle. It is caressed by the gentle perfumed breeze of Ybytyruzú, which lovingly lulls it as though to remind it of a century of adventures and cruel persecution.'

The present **cathedral** [319 C3] is a large cream-coloured building, which replaced a wooden building that fell down in a storm in 1877. Of the three bells in the tower, one dates back to 1781. You are unlikely to find the cathedral open unless you go at the time of a mass. A second square opens out in front – the **Plaza Libertad** – with the figure of a woman on a column in the middle, carrying a torch of liberty.

Behind the cathedral is the jewel of Villarrica: the **Museo Maestro Fermín López** [319 C4] (*Natalicio Talavera esq Juan Pablo II;* ☎ *0541 41521;* ⌚ *07.00–18.00 Mon–Fri, 8.00–11.00 Sat; free admission*). The museum is a long single-storey traditional building built in 1842 with colonnades front and back, and was originally a school called La Patria. It takes its name from the famous schoolmaster who initiated the school and led his pupils from here and from the school of Piribebúy out to fight in the War of the Triple Alliance. He continued to run his school in the trenches, and all the children were killed in the battle of Acosta Ñu in 1869.

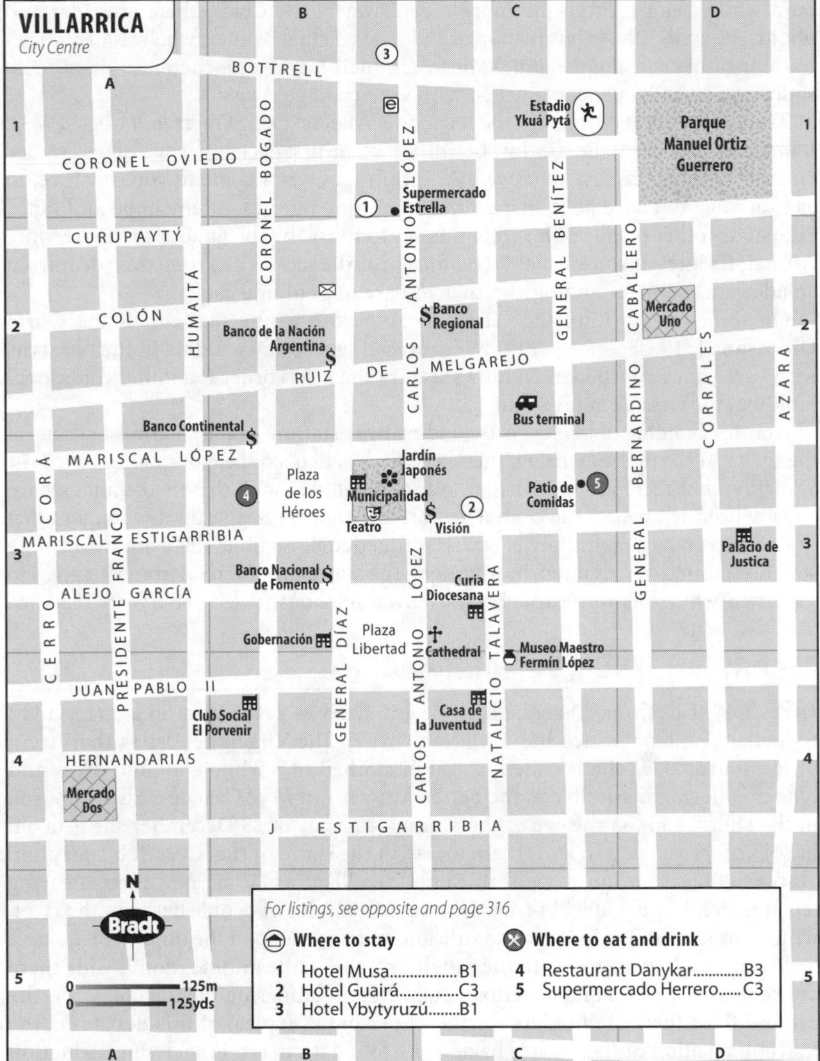

In 1972 the decision was made to turn it into a museum and today it houses a charming collection of historical items. There is a useful display board about the Itá Letra carvings (see page 321) and the different theories about their origin. The first room to the left of the reception is devoted to the indigenous and houses a huge wooden canoe, 6m long, hollowed out of a single tree trunk; there are bows and arrows, woven fibre bags, a pestle and mortar, wooden sandals and a feather headdress. A couple of historical rooms follow, with old postcards and dance trophies, old printing blocks and vinyl records, old musical instruments and kerosene lamps, old coins and notes from all over the world.

Going back further to the time of President Carlos Antonio López (1844–62) there are padlocks, candlesticks and rosaries. From the Triple Alliance War (1864–70) there are rusty sabres and spurs and bayonets, and a portrait of Mariscal López on a white charger. From the more recent war of the Chaco there are rifles and photos. From the illustrious Bishop of Villarrica, Felipe Benítez, who was Paraguay's leading thinker in the Second Vatican Council (1962–65), there are dainty silk shoes and an episcopal hat adorned with green and gold tassles.

The final room is devoted to the local poet Manuel Ortiz Guerrero (1894–1933). It includes the bars of the window beside which he first declaimed one of his famous Guaraní love poems, '*Ne rendápe ajú*': 'From far away I come to you, my love, to gaze at you. You have been living for a long time in my soul, my hope and faith.' Like many other poems of his, this was set to music by the famous composer José Asunción Flores. If you are lucky, you may hear the sounds of a harp class drift from an adjacent room, reminding you that you are in a cultural capital.

On the corner behind the cathedral and close to the museum is the **Curia Diocesana** [319 C3] – a beautifully restored single-storey building in the old style, with some unusual wooden windowsills. On the next corner is another traditional building, the Casa de la Juventud.

Another building of interest is the old **railway station**, in the southwest corner of the town. At the time of writing, there were hopes to open the old station as a tourist attraction, but there are no concrete plans as yet. A few of these old stations have already been re-opened: the central station in Asunción is now a museum, and that of Areguá is now a craft shop as well as a functioning station. There are many more stations waiting to be restored, mostly along the line of the new road from Paraguarí to Villarrica, which follows the route of the railway line constructed in the years 1884–89.

EXCURSIONS FROM VILLARRICA

TAPÉ Day trips from Villarrica include a journey of 21km west on a dirt road to the village of Itapé, which has a Marian shrine. The Virgen del Paso (The Virgin of the Journey), as she is called, is a doll clothed in a white and gold dress and blue mantle, not dissimilar to the better-known Virgin of Caacupé. She is housed in the church, but on the eve of the annual feast day of 18 December she is taken in solemn procession to a tiny sanctuary on the shore of the River Tebicuary-mí. To reach the shrine, go straight through the village as far as you can go, bearing left at the end, and you will reach the riverbank. A lot of people bathe in the river, which has steps down to it on one side and a sandy bank on the other. You go up a little staircase to gain access to the sanctuary, and in the minute room inside there are sellers of rosaries and crucifixes squashed in alongside the devotees. On the ground floor there are holders for the blue candles typical of this devotion. The Marian devotion of Itapé dates back to its foundation as a Franciscan Reduction in 1678. Today Itapé competes with Itacuá, Encarnación, for being the second Marian site of the country after Caacupé.

Buses go to Itapé from the Villarrica terminal, or you can take a taxi. On 18 December there are a lot of buses, and huge crowds go for the day. After the morning mass, people stay to bathe in the river, and there is a party atmosphere. To stay the night in Itapé, try the **Hospedaje Juanita** (*4 rooms;* ☎ *0554 250218;* **$**).

A little museum has recently been formed on an upper floor of the church, the **Museo Fray Buenaventura de Villasboa** (☎ *0554 250207;* 🕘 *08.00–16.00 Sat*), which has some sculptures of Franciscan saints from the time of the Reductions. If you find it closed, ask one of the neighbours of the church to help you find the keyholder: the principal person in charge of the museum is Franciscan Fr Nelson Vega, who lives in Itapé, but there is also a local teacher who may be able to help. The story of Itapé is in a little booklet that can be bought from Fr Vega (Gs10,000).

ITÁ LETRA Heading east from Villarrica, into the Ybytyruzú nature reserve, you can explore some ancient, enigmatic writing in the rock, the meaning of which is not known. They are not dissimilar from the rock carvings at Gasorý near Pedro Juan Caballero (see pages 353–4), and it is believed that the two sites are related. A date of 2000–4000BC has been suggested. Incredible as it sounds, a number of people believe them to have been carved by Vikings.

Itá Letra (Guaraní 'stone; Spanish 'letter') is at Tororõ, about 18km from Villarrica. A taxi from Villarrica will cost a minimum of Gs220,000 for the 24km of difficult dirt roads. The better of the two roads branches eastwards off Ruta 8 on the southern outskirts of Villarrica immediately past the Barcos y Rodados service station and Hotel Real. You will know you are getting close to Itá Letra when you pass a notice saying '*Tororõ, Reserva de Recursos Manejados, Yvyturuzú*'. This is a region of wooden houses and donkeys. After about 20km you reach Itá Letra site, on the right-hand side of the road. The rock face is quite close to the road in the garden of a family house, and has more than 50 inscriptions, some with parallel lines, like railway lines or like rakes, others with circles, curves and irregular shapes, all seeming to have some definite significance that has been long lost in time.

From Itá Letra you can in theory continue through the Ybytyruzú reserve to visit the hill **Cerro Akatĩ**, which has an excellent view down to Independencia, some 25km on from Itá Letra, before returning by road to Villarrica. But in practice the road is barely transitable, so only do it if you have a 4x4, the weather is good and you enjoy exploring.

A good alternative to finding your own way in your own vehicle is to go with a guide from Independencia, from **Aventura Sin Limites** (m *0981 281998; see page 315*). They can take you in a vehicle to the top of the hill Cerro Akatĩ, with its lovely view, and accompany you on a 2km walk downhill to Itá Letra. At the time of writing, for two people this would cost a minimum of Gs150,000 for the vehicle and Gs75,000 for the guide.

CERRO TRES KANDÚ An excursion to the top of Paraguay's highest hill, Cerro Tres Kandú (Spanish 'hill of three'; Guaraní 'bumps'), is worthwhile, but needs a little organisation. Tres Kandú is 842m high, while Cerro Akatĩ – on the other side of the Ybytyruzú reserve – is 697m high. There are two routes up Tres Kandú, corresponding to which side of the hill you climb and who is the owner of the territory: one is done through a company called Naturaleza Pura (see page 322); the other is known as the *Campamento Mariano* and is organised through the Franciscans of Villarrica (*P Marcelo Benítez;* ☎ *0541 42657;* m *0981 311641;* e *marbemarti3@hotmail.com*). This region is historic Franciscan territory.

The *Campamento Mariano* route to Tres Kandú has been developed by Professor Angel Aristides Troche (m *0984 113895*) who lives in nearby Garay, 20km southeast of Villarrica (see regional map, page 310). He is a former councillor and retired teacher who has dedicated himself to promoting the walk as a spiritual pilgrimage. You can take a car up a difficult dirt road from Garay to where there is a recently built chapel – a replica of the Portiuncula chapel of Assisi (where St Francis received his vocation) – and next to it a stone retreat house (*sleep up to 30; take your own food, kitchen, cooker, fridge freezer; minimum offering Gs25,000 per night*; *contact Marcelo Benítez as above*). The Franciscans interpret 'retreat' broadly, whether for a Christian retreat or for just a quiet time at peace with nature. Then at 450m, into the woods, there is a big cross and the walk up the hill begins. There is a series of the mysteries of the rosary carved in stone – the work of a Paraguayan Salesian priest-artist, Gustavo Laterza. Further up there is a Way of the Cross, where the steeper ascent begins.

If you want to climb to the summit of Tres Kandú you will need a guide (*currently Gs100,000*), without whom it will be impossible to find the way through the numerous little paths up the mountain. Professor Troche recommends setting off at 07.00, carrying with you ample water (2 litres if it is hot) and something sweet to give you energy. You should also take sun cream, insect repellent and a hat or cap. But be warned that it is a challenge, as the slope is very steep, and when you come down you may be dismayed to see the guide galloping down like a mountain deer while you slip and slither much more slowly, grabbing on to roots to stop you falling. It is all part of the experience.

The alternative way of climbing the hill is to organise it through Naturaleza Pura in Asunción (☎ *021 223128; Manuel Almada* **m** *0982 759121 or Roberto Cubas* **m** *0982 379706*). You may still need a guide – and they charge an entrance fee of Gs55,000 – but the route is well marked with signs that indicate how far you have come and how far you have to go. Allow 2½ hours for the ascent.

CAAZAPÁ

Copaco ☎ 0542 232299; municipalidad ☎ 0542 232201

Caazapá is one of the earliest and most important of the former Franciscan Reductions, and was founded by Friar Luis Bolaños himself in 1607 (two years before the Jesuits founded their first Reduction at San Ignacio Guazú). When you arrive in Caazapá, you may gasp in delight at finding such an attractive town so deeply hidden in the countryside. At the initial little roundabout you are welcomed by a statue of Luis Bolaños, simply attired in his Franciscan habit and carrying a cross and a staff. From here a splendid avenue of palm trees leads to the plaza and the church, with its stunning reredos. To the right is the cemetery where there is a smaller and older chapel, also with an original reredos. To the left the road leads on to the famous spring, Ykuá Bolaños – a name unfortunately now linked in everyone's mind with the tragic fire at the Ycuá Bolaños supermarket in Asunción in 2004, when 400 people died.

There are still very poor areas in the countryside around the town, but a number of better-off politicians, lawyers and businessmen have property in the area, with the result that Caazapá appears a surprisingly well-kept and well-off town. It was well off even as a Reduction, because of its excellent cotton and tobacco production, and the decoration of the church was as fine as those of the Jesuits, while the quantity of gold exceeded the Jesuit churches. (This is reported by Félix de Azara, the Spanish naturalist and military officer who was sent in 1781 to determine the border dispute between the Spanish and Portuguese colonies.)

GETTING THERE AND AWAY The town is 51km south of Villarrica on Ruta 8, and is asphalted all the way. For reaching Villarrica on the new road from Paraguarí, see page 309; in a private car you can now reach Caazapá in 2 hours and 40 minutes by this route, while the route through Caacupé and Coronel Oviedo is slower and longer, taking four or five hours.

The **bus** that goes to Caazapá direct from Asunción is the Yuteña (☎ *021 558774*), which leaves ten times a day and continues, via Maciel, to Yutý (see page 327). Guaireña (☎ *0541 551727*) has a service once a day, leaving Asunción at 16.45. The journey takes 4½ hours. Or you could take one of the frequent Guarieña buses to Villarrica, and make your way on from there, as it is a more comfortable service.

The road south from Caazapá to Coronel Bogado on Ruta 1 (see pages 243–4) is in the process of being asphalted, but the work has begun at the southern end and so far has reached Yutý, which is about halfway.

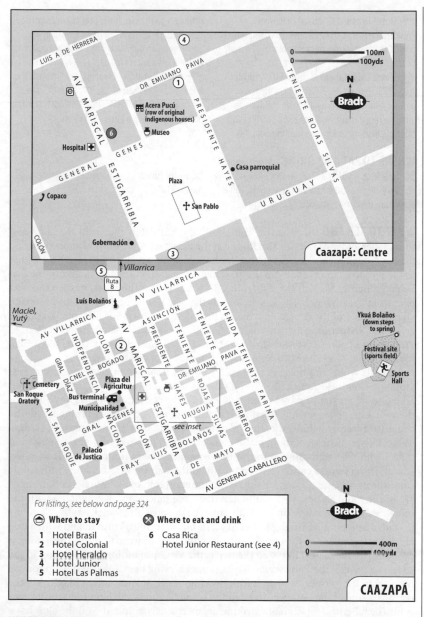

Caazapá: Centre

CAAZAPÁ

For listings, see below and page 324

Where to stay
1 Hotel Brasil
2 Hotel Colonial
3 Hotel Heraldo
4 Hotel Junior
5 Hotel Las Palmas

Where to eat and drink
6 Casa Rica
Hotel Junior Restaurant (see 4)

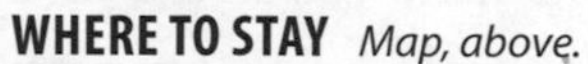

WHERE TO STAY *Map, above.*

Hotel Las Palmas (20 rooms) 0542 232264; m 0991 951339. The first hotel you reach, on Ruta 8 before the roundabout, on the right. Modern, clean & very pleasant, good facilities – just a bit far out, though the town is small so walking would not take long. Internet, swimming pool, enclosed parking. Café next door under same management is also modern & clean but sells only basic snacks. **$**

Hotel Junior (10 rooms) Presidente Hayes 437 esq Dr Paiva; 0542 232060; m 0981 309777; e hoteljunior_@hotmail.com. Tucked 1 block behind the plaza, this recently expanded hotel is smart & colourful. Wi-Fi. Restaurant. **$**

Hotel Brasil (12 rooms) Dr Paiva y Presidente Hayes; 0542 232285. Pleasant, simple hotel. Diagonally across from Hotel Junior. Friendly people. Wi-Fi. **$**

Hotel Colonial Av Mariscal Estigarribia; 0542 232290; m 0982 425850; e azujunisa@hotmail.com. A block & a half down the avenida after the roundabout. Traditional old building with colonial pillars, good location fronting onto the road with palm trees. Rooms set around a spacious hall which serves as b/fast room & restaurant. There is also an outside bar in a thatched *quincho* where *asados* are served. **$**

Hotel Heraldo (7 rooms) Sor Victorina y Ada Estigarribia; 0542 232391. On south side of plaza. Sommier beds & AC. Bottom floor is family house, upper floor is hotel. Restaurant. **$**

WHERE TO EAT AND DRINK *Map, page 323.*

Casa Rica 0542 23248; m 0981 321015; every evening. Bright bar on the avenida, half a block from the Plaza. Fast food. **$**

Hotel Junior (see page 323) Restaurant has menu del dia. **$**

WHAT TO SEE AND DO The two churches – the San Pablo church in the plaza and the smaller, older oratory of San Roque at the cemetery – are both kept open during the day, which means there is no hassle about seeking out key holders to have a look at the reredos. However, if you do find them closed, then the key holder of the San Pablo church is Ña Kali (m *0984 158228*), who lives on the plaza, next to the *casa parroquial* (see below). The key-holder to the San Roque oratory is Doña Genara, who lives behind the cemetery, which is behind the oratory. For information on the art of the Reduction, you can talk to Sonia Espinola in the Municipalidad (*0542 232201; 07.00–13.00 Mon–Fri*) or María Helena Ines Ramírez (*0542 232380;* m *0961 968871*) who is knowledgeable about the history of the town.

With its white and beige octagonal tower, **San Pablo** is an elegant church, with Gothic arches inside and a brown and yellow tiled floor. It is not old, but is rendered all the more enchanting by the birdsong inside the church and by the loveliness of the well-kept plaza outside, filled with a variety of attractive, blossoming trees. The beautiful **reredos** behind the altar is a model of the very best Franciscan design. There are six niches, set in an elaborately carved framework of plant designs, and pillars with twisted fluting on the bottom row and straight fluting in the row above. It is all in very good condition and mostly in the natural wood colour, with subtle colour features. The statues of saints (with the exception of St Francis, bottom right) are of the more static style usually described as Franciscan, as compared with the more exuberant postures and flowing robes of the post-Brassanelli style.

Balancing Francis, on the left, is St Dominic, carrying a church, and with a dog at his feet (emblem of the order because of the play of words on the Latin *domini canis*, dog of the Lord). Between the two is the Virgin, standing on the moon in the style so typical of the Paraguayan Reductions, carrying her Child. In the top row we have, from left to right, St Joseph with the child Jesus, St Paul, and St Blas. In all, the reredos is one of the best preserved in the country, and is a delight of harmony and skill. The tabernacle itself has a striking geometric design in red, and the altar has a chequered design of gilded wood.

The **sacristy** of the church contains a number of carved saints from the Franciscan period, including a Virgin and a St Joseph, which are taken out for display or procession on the corresponding saints' days. The ***casa parroquial*** or parish house (*0542 232286; 07.00–noon Mon–Fri*) faces the church. It contains silver items, including halos from saints, and an engraved ciborium with hanging silver bells, that were made in the workshops of the Reduction. The silversmiths of Caazapá were well known and used to export their work to many places.

Opposite the San Pablo church is a small **museum** (⌚ *08.00–noon & 13.00–17.00 Mon–Fri; free admission*). If you want to visit at a weekend, contact Nilda Escurra (m *0981 757645*) or the Municipalidad (☎ *0542 232201*). This is an old building, well restored, and bearing the name 'Fray Juan Bernardo' – the name of a Franciscan who worked with Luis Bolaños. It contains a selection of indigenous bows and arrows, old machines, furniture, photos and war relics. Around the back of this is a well-restored row of indigenous houses from the Reduction, labelled **Acera Pucú**: *casa de indios*. (Acera means 'pavement' in Spanish, Pucú means 'long' in Guaraní; *casa de indios* means 'indian house'.)

To reach the **oratory of San Roque**, return down the avenue with the palm trees for three blocks, and when you get to the Omar supermarket on the right, turn left down Coronel Bogado until you get to the cemetery. This little chapel is in the middle of the cemetery. It dates back (at least in its main structure) to 1779, and is a small and simple structure, built of adobe and wood. But with its huge pitched roof, making a broad surrounding portico, it appears bigger than it really is. While the Jesuit Reductions tended to have a secondary chapel called the Capilla de Loreto, the Franciscan Reductions would typically have a secondary chapel dedicated to San Roque, but this oratory of Caazapá is the only surviving example.

Inside is an exquisite carved and painted reredos, with San Roque in the centre, a crucifix above, and to either side paintings of Franciscan saints. Tragically, the original San Roque – an exquisite figure full of character, with halo, hat, staff and dog – was stolen a couple of years ago, and has been replaced by a more modern plaster San Roque. With the exception of San Roque and the crucifix, these paintings are flat, which is unusual in a Paraguayan reredos. Not to be confused with the 17th-century Paraguayan Jesuit martyr San Roque González, San Roque was a medieval French saint who devoted his life to the care of plague victims, contracted the disease himself, and lived in the wilderness with a festering wound on his leg, where a dog would bring him food and lick his sores. In art, he is portrayed with a wound on his thigh and a dog, as we see in this example: Roque points with dignity at his wound while a black dog leaps up to lick it.

Return to the plaza and continue for a couple of blocks to Luis de Bolaños, turn left (east) and go straight on until you reach the sports field (*cancha*) and sports hall (*poli deportivo*). If you cross the field, in the far corner you will come to some steps that lead down to the **Ykuá Bolaños** spring. (*Ykuá* in Guaraní means 'water hole'.) It is said to be a spring miraculously created by Luis Bolaños himself with a touch of his staff on the bare rock (or, some say, by lifting a heavy stone) in response to the challenge of a *cacique*, who complained of the thirst the group was suffering, and said they would all become Christians if Bolaños could produce water, but if he could not the Franciscan would be put to death. The spring never lacks water, even in times of drought, and according to local legend brings favours to those who are in love. The saint is carved on the back wall of the spring, with his miraculous staff and surrounded by indigenous. There are stepping stones to the source of the water on the left-hand wall.

Fiesta de Ykuá Bolaños The foundation of Caazapá on 10 January is celebrated annually in magnificent style, together with the fiesta patronal, 25 January, which is the feast of the Conversion of St Paul. Over the weekend closest to the 25th, the streets are decorated with ribbons and paintings and there are concerts every night in front of the San Pablo church. There is a *cena de gala* (grand dinner) on the Thursday night, the Festival of music on the Friday night, a horse show on the Sunday, and an exhibition of craft and local produce (Expo Feria) all week long. There are bullfights

LUIS BOLAÑOS

Luis Bolaños was the Franciscan precursor of the Jesuit-Guaraní Reductions. Born in Seville in about 1549, he was recruited for the South American missions by another Franciscan, Fray (Friar) Alonso de San Buenaventura, who was to become his companion and colleague in founding a large number of Reductions. They arrived in 1575, and Bolaños spent the next 50 years working in the Guaraní missions. As well as establishing a pattern for the Reductions, he did outstanding work on the Guaraní language, producing the first grammatical notes and vocabulary list of Guaraní. The publications of the famous grammar by Antonio Ruiz de Montoya drew on Bolaños's earlier work. He also translated the important catechism of the 1583 Third Council of Lima into Guaraní, and his version was officially endorsed by the 1603 Synod of Asunción as the teaching tool that must be used with the Guaraní people.

The Jesuit Bartomeu Meliá has written in homage of Luis Bolaños: 'With his Franciscan disposition, simple and straightforward like the indigenous, itinerant like them, a lover of nature, austere and unambitious for riches, cordial and affectionate like the Guaraní, he travelled the country, getting to know the indigenous by name. He shared their life in their own *chozas*, ate their rough food and won them over with love and with music, which attracted them irresistibly.' His remains are in an urn in the San Francisco church of Asunción (see page 113).

and rodeos from Wednesday to Friday. The Festival Ykua Bolaños of Friday night is a mega concert, attended in 2014 by 18,000 people, with the best musical groups from Paraguay and the neighbouring countries playing in the *cancha* (before the Ykuá Bolaños spring) from 21.00 to 06.00 or 09.00. For confirmation of the programme each year ring the Municipalidad or one of the hotels.

NORTH FROM CAAZAPÁ **Iturbe** is a little place 20km northwest of Caazapá reachable only by dirt roads, of interest principally for being the village where the great Paraguayan novelist Augusto Roa Bastos grew up. It lies behind his great work about life in the countryside, *Hijo de Hombre*. It is situated on the stream Tebicuarý-mí, and has a disused railway station, as do many other villages in the locality. One day perhaps these attractive historic stations will all be developed into museums or craft shops, as has been done in Asunción and Areguá.

SOUTH FROM CAAZAPÁ

Where to stay The Loma Linda estancia (*45 beds; 27km south of Caazapá, via Maciel; 021 282243;* m *0981 402713; www.estancialomalinda.com;* **$$$**) is 16.8km south of Maciel and down a little turning on the right. It offers horses, bike rides, a swimming pool, gardens, fishing and a games room. There is a pretty view of the tower of the Perpetuo Socorro church. The name means 'lovely hillside', as there is a gentle hill here in an otherwise flat plain. Reservations can also be made through Apatur (see page 54).

More Franciscan towns The road south is still called Ruta 8 even though at the time of going to press the next considerable stretch is still dirt road. However, asphalting is spreading northwards up it from Coronel Bogado and has already reached Yutý, which is one of the Franciscan towns on this road. At present, on the dirt road, allow a couple of hours to travel the 87km to Yutý from Caazapá. The other Franciscan town, a little further south, is General Artigas.

Yutý is the end of the line for the Yuteña bus. Yutý was also founded by Luis Bolaños (in 1610), but was originally was further south, where San Cosme y Damián is today. Its present site is close to a hill of magnetic rock, called Itá Karú (Guaraní 'the stone that eats'). Yutý was also a former stop on the railway line. The old church no longer exists.

General Artigas, which is actually over the departmental boundary into Itapúa, used to be called Bobí, but its once-charming old church and wooden bell tower are no longer standing. For information ring the *casa parroquial* (*0743 20098*) or the Municipalidad (*0743 20016*). From 1795 Bobí was actually a hub of communication because it was a post office stop between Asunción and Buenos Aires. But at 29km from the nearest asphalt in Coronel Bogado (see pages 243–4), it is certainly not a hub of communication today.

You can carry on driving from Yutý right down to Coronel Bogado on Ruta 1, close to the San Cosme y Damián turn, and the Tebicuarý bus (*021 558774*) covers this route.

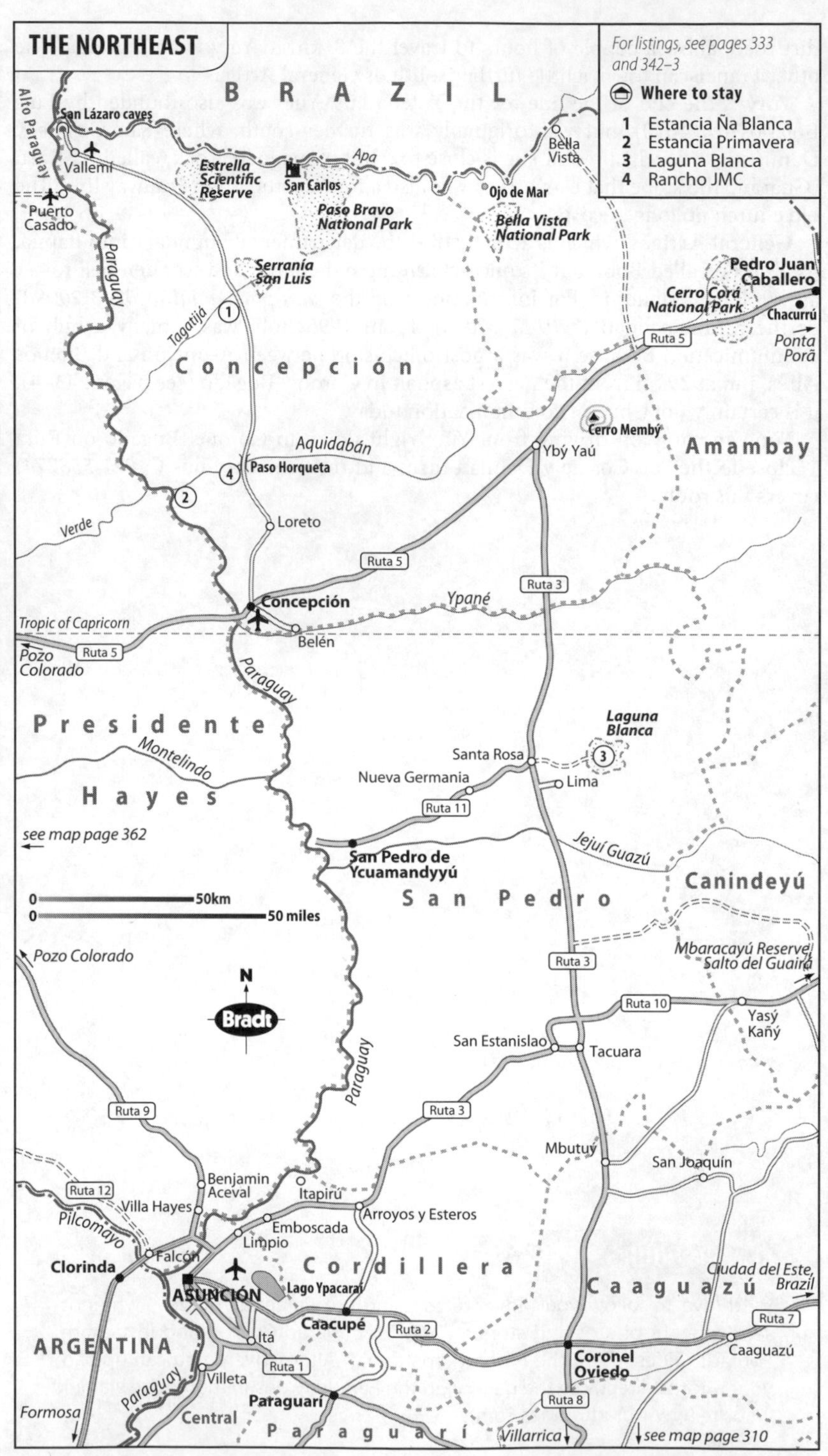
THE NORTHEAST
For listings, see pages 333 and 342–3
Where to stay
1 Estancia Ña Blanca
2 Estancia Primavera
3 Laguna Blanca
4 Rancho JMC
BRAZIL
San Lázaro caves
Alto Paraguay
Vallemí
Puerto Casado
Estrella Scientific Reserve
San Carlos
Apa
Bella Vista
Ojo de Mar
Paso Bravo National Park
Bella Vista National Park
Paraguay
Serranía San Luis
Tagatijá
Pedro Juan Caballero
Cerro Corá National Park
Chacurrú
Ruta 5
Ponta Porã
Concepción
Cerro Membý
Ybý Yaú
Amambay
Aquidabán
Paso Horqueta
Verde
Loreto
Ruta 3
Concepción
Ypané
Tropic of Capricorn
Belén
Pozo Colorado
Presidente Hayes
Montelindo
Laguna Blanca
Santa Rosa
Nueva Germania
Lima
Ruta 11
see map page 362
San Pedro de Ycuamandyyú
Jejuí Guazú
Canindeyú
0 50km
0 50 miles
San Pedro
Mbaracayú Reserve, Salto del Guairá
Pozo Colorado
N
Bradt
Ruta 10
Yasý Kañý
San Estanislao
Tacuara
Ruta 9
Mbutuý
San Joaquín
Benjamin Aceval
Ruta 12
Itapirú
Villa Hayes
Arroyos y Esteros
Emboscada
Pilcomayo
Limpio
Falcón
Clorinda
Cordillera
Ciudad del Este, Brazil
ASUNCIÓN
Lago Ypacaraí
Caaguazú
Caacupé
Ruta 2
Ruta 7
Itá
ARGENTINA
Coronel Oviedo
Caaguazú
Ruta 1
Villeta
Ruta 8
Paraguarí
Formosa
Central
Paraguarí
Villarrica
see map page 310

11

Concepción and the Northeast

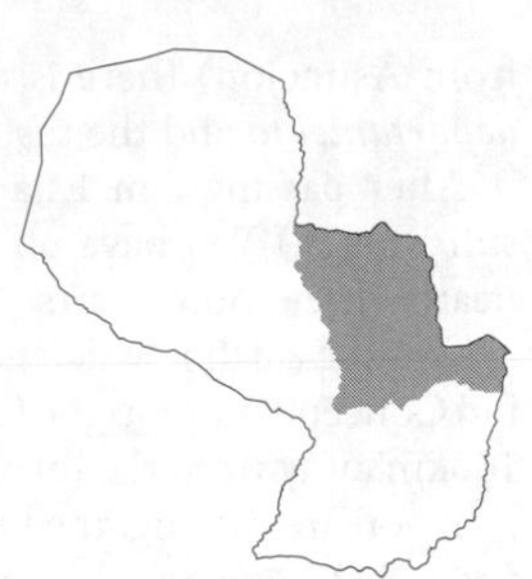

Departamentos:
San Pedro; gobernación ☎ 0342 222136/222517
Canindeyú; gobernación ☎ 046 242394/242088
Concepción; gobernación ☎ 0331 242207/242718
Amambay; gobernación ☎ 0336 272214/274610

Over 97% of Paraguay's population live to the east of the Río Paraguay, but there is less tourist activity in the large northeastern expanse of Paraguay than in the southeast with its old mission towns.

Pedro Juan Caballero, capital of the *departamento* of Amambay, on the border with Brazil, is the largest city in the northeast, but it has a reputation for crime. However, the historic park of Cerro Corá surrounded by dramatic hills is worth seeing if you can spare the time to make the long journey. There is also a new development of adventure tourism called Chacurru, which aims to bring in more visitors.

Concepción, capital of the *departamento* of the same name, is a very different kind of town: it is sleepy but charming, with prettily painted Italianate buildings. It has upgraded its hotel facilities over the last five years.

South of Concepción is the *departamento* of San Pedro, with its capital of the same name: this is deep rural territory, but rather than sleepy it is the seat of present-day *campesino* unrest, particularly relating to land reform questions.

Dead centre of this region is the beach resort and biological station of Laguna Blanca, which is both delightful and interesting for nature lovers.

In the east-northeast is the Bosque Mbaracayú nature reserve, which takes new strides every year to attract those interested in ecological tourism.

GETTING THERE AND AWAY

BY BUS See under the respective towns below.

BY CAR By private car, it used to be quicker to do the Chaco route if you are heading for Concepción, if you were confident of your vehicle, for the Chaco is a wasteland with few garages, telephones or places to eat. But at the moment the asphalt on the Chaco route is badly deteriorated, with big holes in the road that you need to negotiate carefully.

At present, therefore, it is best to drive north up Ruta 3, through eastern Paraguay. The roads are good and you have the chance to see some places on the way, and there are services along the route. Start from Asunción on the Ruta Transchaco, but instead of crossing the bridge into the Chaco carry straight on through Limpio and San Estanislao on Ruta 3 – a good, modern road (though single carriageway) that cuts off the corner of the longer route through Coronel Oviedo. It is also known as *Acceso Norte*. At 25 de diciembre (129km from Asuncion) there is a toll station that marks the entry into the San Pedro *departamento* and the rest of the north.

After passing San Estanislao you turn left for the north at Tacuara. (This is still Ruta 3.) You have now been travelling for a couple of hours or so, and after nearly three more hours you get to Ybý Yaú (which quaintly means, in Guaraní, 'we eat the earth'), which is where you reach Ruta 5 and must turn either left (west) for Concepción or right (east) for Pedro Juan Caballero. Both are approximately 100km away from the turn. The whole of this route is on decent asphalt.

If you are driving, the best places to break the journey are at San Estanislao (see pages 332–3) or Santa Rosa (see page 333).

BY AIR There is once again a service of small planes that fly to Concepción and to Vallemí, with a small company called SETAM. See boxes on SETAM flights (and for emergencies, on chartering planes) on pages 380 and 381.

TRAVELLING ALONG RUTA 3

TOWARDS ARROYOS Y ESTEROS After you have left Asunción and passed through Limpio, whether by car or bus, you take Ruta 3, heading for Emboscada, which has a jewel of a church and is included in the Circuito de Oro. You then pass through Arroyos y Esteros, on the way to San Estanislao.

Where to stay

San Guillermo 021 225285/446630; m 0981 410542; e marbains@hotmail.com. At only 35km from Asunción, before you get to Emboscada, this is one of the *estancias* closest to the capital, where the Río Piribebúy flows into the Río Paraguay. It has a jetty, chapel & pool, & is a good place for fishing or just relaxing. Reservations can also be made through Apatur; see page 54. **$$$**

Mbuni (5 dbls & 4 bungalows) Nueva Colombia, 50km northeast of Asunción; m 0981 992491; www.mbuni.de. An ostrich farm, *granja de avestruz*, which takes guests as well as rearing rheas. To get there, turn right at Emboscada, left in between Copaco & the Centro de Salud, along Profesor Méndez Mendoza, then briefly left at the end, & right along the dirt road for 250m. You will come to a bridge over the stream to your right & then Mbuni. From Emboscada it is 10km. Attractive modern rooms with African motifs (*mbuni* is an African word for 'ostrich'), pool, jacuzzi, football, volleyball & 9ha. You can eat ostrich meat & drink ostrich egg liqueur in the newly opened El Massai restaurant (*Sun lunch, or on other days by prior reservation for minimum of 4 people*). The website is in German but you can change it to Spanish. **$$$**

Hotel Olivares (4 rooms) Mariscal López 104 y 14 de mayo, Arroyos y Esteros; 0510 272070; m 0981 473082/0971 596531. Excellent, small family B&B, 56km from Asunción, handy when travelling on Ruta 3. At the Puma petrol station turn right (coming from Asunción) for 4 blocks, & you will find the hotel behind the hamburger bar. Attractive old building, modern bathrooms, split AC, garden with mango tree & well, cloth napkins at b/fast. Internet in the attractive plaza, a couple of blocks away. There are cheaper rooms with fans. **$$**

Where to eat and drink

The best place to eat is the bar next door to the Hotel Olivares, where they will cook a good, fresh *lomito* (**$**). Alternatively, there is a restaurant, Ña Selva (**$**), within walking distance on Ruta 3 where they have more dishes to choose from, buffet style.

EXCURSION TOWARDS THE RÍO PARAGUAY If you are up for some historical exploration in an area where few people go, an excursion can be made from Arroyos y Esteros to the Capilla Olivares in Itapirú, the last *compañía* of Arroyos y Esteros, on the west bank of the Río Manduvirá, close to where it joins the Río Paraguay. The chapel was built by President Carlos Antonio López and has been restored and declared a *patrimonio nacional*. There are buses that go to Itapirú, but you need to allow time for this journey.

On the way you go past an interesting old house called Puerto Bello. There is also a delightful holiday site on the Río Manduvirá, called Puerto Naranjahai. At the Farmacia La Providencia in Arroyos y Esteros, turn north off Ruta 3, on a cobbled road almost opposite Ña Selva. When it forks, go right, and travel through four *compañías*: Tacuarindy, San Antonio, De Carmen and Itá Pirú. When there is a tall chimney on the left, 17km from Arroyos y Esteros, you will come to a sign reading 'Bienvenido a Puerto José Bello'. After the Despensa Mauchi, bear right again, until you come to an elegant old house nestling all alone in the fields. This is what is left of the Puerto Bello *estancia*. The *Puerto* ('port') refers to one on the Río Manduvirá which flows past here, a tributary of the Río Paraguay.

Puerto Bello The house is also sometimes referred to as the Campos del Manduvirá. It looks bigger than it is, because it is built in elegant Italianate style and the façade has a flight of nine steps leading up to a columned portico. But if you go around the back you find that the rooms are few and small. They are, however, covered with paintings as though to show windows onto river landscapes, or birds, fish and flowers. One painting shows the ruins of Humaitá, from the War of the Triple Alliance (see pages 13 and 234–5). According to local belief, the house belonged to Madame Lynch, the consort of Mariscal López, and the details of the painting, the elegance of the architecture, the smallness of its size and its proximity to the Capilla Olivares (see below) would all seem to support that. The locals also believe that treasures and gold of Madame Lynch and Mariscal López are buried nearby, in tunnels under big stones or in boats deliberately sunk in the river. However, the date painted on the murals is 1918 – but Madame Lynch left the country in 1870, so there is something of a mystery.

Puerto Naranjahai Continuing up the cobbled road that runs parallel to the Río Manduvirá, the cobbles eventually turn to dirt, and while the road turns sharp left, you continue straight ahead on a lesser track. There is a gate to an *estancia* straight ahead and a sign that reads 'Oñondivepa', but you follow the track round to the right, and then to the left for 1km until you reach the entrance to the Puerto Naranjahai (**m** *Asunción office 0981 270242;* **m** *at the port 0984 278450;* **e** *puertonaranjahai@gmail.com; www.puertonaranjahai.com;* **$$**). This is an attractive holiday site where you can stay in a private room or a dormitory or a bungalow, or come for the day, or camp, and where the activities include motor launch trips, kayaks, fishing and horse riding. The property has been beautifully prepared, with notices indicating vegetable gardens and the names of trees. When boating on the river you may be able to see toucans and vultures. There are discounts for mid-week visitors.

Capilla Olivares To reach this chapel of President Carlos Antonio López is not cheap, as you have to approach it by hiring a boat from Puerto Naranjahai, and the fuel alone will cost at least Gs200,000. There is no access by land because you would have to cross land belonging to four different owners, and one of the gates is padlocked. However, river access is what it was originally built for.

As the Río Manduivrá flows into the Río Paraguay there is a big island called the Isla Banco'i, and where the island ends there is a sign on the left bank reading 'Rancho Tío Ile'. The chapel is only just visible from the river beyond this sign. It has a triangular pediment supported on four pillars, and there is a small bell tower with a cupola.

Built for Carlos Antonio Lopez and dedicated to his patron saint, Charles Borromeo, the chapel was, in fact, inaugurated three months after his death in 1862. There was a huge inauguration ceremony for the small chapel, with the slaughter of 42 cows and 34 sheep, enough to feed some 10,000 people. Despite this, the unpredictable Mariscal Lopez was furious when a five-column article was published praising its design, because he considered it a private chapel. As many as 84 masses were celebrated there before the outbreak of the war, less than two years later.

The chapel then fell into disrepair, until the state restored it after a fashion in 1992, but not to the standard considered fitting by the present owner. His son, Arturo Alvarado (m *0984 152934*) lives nearby and is intent on restoring it bit by bit to its original design, and enabling visitors to come, inevitably by the river route.

SAN ESTANISLAO (*Copaco 0343 20200; Municipalidad 0343 20454*) San Estanislao, commonly known as Santaní (for Taní is Stanislaus in Guaraní), is a good place to eat or sleep on the way to the northeast. It was an old Jesuit *doctrina* (something on the way to being a Reduction) but its chief claim to fame was for being a barracks for the army of Mariscal López in the War of the Triple Alliance. There are three plazas, but the most interesting is the Plaza Bernardino Caballero, with its imposing church with colonnades on both sides in traditional style. Facing the plaza is the museum, housed in the former military barracks, and it displays military remains, a few Jesuit statues (not of the best) and the 6m-long skin of the *mbói jaguá* snake (Guaraní 'snake dog', so named because of the barking noise it makes in the mating period).

According to local legend, anyone who bathes in the River Tapiracuái will be enchanted with the desire to return to Santaní.

To get to San Estanislao by car, see pages 329–30; any of the buses going to Pedro Juan Caballero will pass through here (see page 347).

The patronal feast day is 13 November.

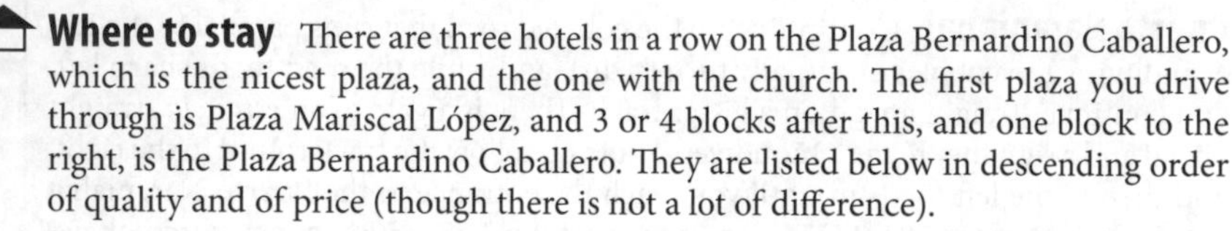

Where to stay

There are three hotels in a row on the Plaza Bernardino Caballero, which is the nicest plaza, and the one with the church. The first plaza you drive through is Plaza Mariscal López, and 3 or 4 blocks after this, and one block to the right, is the Plaza Bernardino Caballero. They are listed below in descending order of quality and of price (though there is not a lot of difference).

Hotel Safuan (12 rooms) Adolfo Mello y Defensores del Chaco; 0343 20294/20096; e hotelsafuan@hotmail.com. On the corner of the plaza. Will do meals if you order in advance. Pleasant b/fast room on 1st floor with balcony. Recommended. **$**

Hotel Neri's Defensores del Chaco c/ Adolfo Mello; 0343 420421; m 0976 827247. The middle one of 3 siimlar hotels. **$**

Hotel Maracaná (18 rooms) 0343 20282. Also overlooks plaza, a few houses down towards the museum. AC, TV. **$**

Where to eat and drink

Churrasquería Sabor Brasil 0343 21095. As you leave San Estanislao on the road towards Tacuara, next to the Esso station. On the way you pass another eating place that sells *lomito arabe* (a kind of steak). **$$**

Restaurant Colonial On the corner near the church. The sign *Molino de Maiz* is more visible, & refers to the antique maize mill in the same building. More of a bar than a restaurant, but a pretty place to eat or have a drink, with tables on the portico overlooking the plaza, surrounded by greenery, & substantial old carved wooden pillars. Menu simple but featuring typical Paraguayan fare. **$**

Travelling north or west from San Estanislao Rejoining the route, you turn left at Tacuara to go north. This is still Ruta 3, although you feel that you are joining another main road (which goes north to Concepción and south to Coronel Oviedo).

If by contrast you go west from San Estanislao, you come to Itacurubí del Rosario, after 44km, which has an annual festival towards the end of January called called Ykuá Salas, when awards are made for outstanding personalities of sport, journalism and tourism.

SANTA ROSA AND SURROUNDS Continuing north up Ruta 3, about 65km after Tacuara you come to the River Jejuí, and about 25km north is the turn to Lima, which is just 3km to the east of Ruta 3. It has a pleasant diocesan retreat house and an old adobe church. And 7km further north you come to Santa Rosa.

Santa Rosa itself is an extended sprawl of buildings along the main road, and turns out to be a good stopping place for travellers. The **Hotel Cristal** (*km325; 30 rooms;* ☎ *0451 235442;* **m** *0971 43271/0981 710489;* **$$**), halfway through Santa Rosa on the east side of the road, is new and well designed, with excellent facilities, including a pool, car park, football pitch and Wi-Fi. Its prices are a bargain, and it is doing such a roaring trade that booking in advance is recommended. It has recently opened the Churrasquería Cristal next door, with very cheap prices.

About 0.5km further on is a recommended restaurant, the **Boi de Oro** (**m** *0971 836950;* **$$**), on the west side of the road. It is run by a Brazilian and is an excellent *churrasquería*, with good, fresh salad, though it can be easily missed because of its modest exterior.

If you are going to Concepción or Pedro Juan Caballero, you continue going north from Santa Rosa for another 105km, to the end of Ruta 3 at Yby Yaú, where you make your choice of Concepción (left, see pages 337–42) or Pedro Juan Caballero (right, see pages 346–51).

LAGUNA BLANCA (☎ 021 424760/452506; **m** *0971 167600/0981 588671;* **e** *lagunablanca@tigo.com.py or consulta@lagunablanca.com.py;* www.lagunablanca.com.py; *reservations can be made directly from their website or through Apatur (see page 54;* **$$**) Close to Santa Rosa is the beach resort and nature reserve of Laguna Blanca, one of the most beautiful natural places in Paraguay. It is 270km from Asunción.

Getting there and away At the southern end of Santa Rosa is a crossroads with no signs. This is where you turn west if you want to go along Ruta 11 to San Pedro, 77km away (see pages 334–7), and also where you turn east through an enchanting country landscape to reach Laguna Blanca, some 27km away along a dirt road that has not yet been asphalted. After crossing four bridges you come to a water tank on stilts. Turn right here and cross another bridge, then left shortly afterwards, to reach the gate of Laguna Blanca. Only those with prior reservations can enter.

If you are coming by public transport, there are two buses a day from Santa Rosa: at 12.30 (Galaxia) and 14.30 (La Paraguaya). They pass by the entrance to Laguna Blanca on their way to Santa Barbara, but the final destination is Carapaí. For the return journey they pass at about 07.30 and 10.30. On a Sunday there is only one bus, La Paraguaya. It leaves Santa Rosa at 14.00 and Laguna Blanca for Santa Rosa at 11.00.

What to see and do This is a private reserve dedicated to agriculture and tourism – one of the best of its kind in South America. The beach has fine white sand, and there are little thatched roofs to give shade on the sand at the water's edge, which, with the brilliant blue of the sky, the varying greens and blues of the water, the little line of reeds and the distant margin of trees, makes it a very lovely spot. A number of activities are on offer, including beach volleyball, and you can hire almost anything you might want there: snorkel, kayak, rowing boat, horse, tent, mattress, hammock, lounger, chair, table and sunshade. At night you can gaze up at the stars in the great quietness. Prices are reasonable: Gs20,000 for a day visit; Gs20,000 for a main course; Gs30,000 per person for camping (up to 100 people); Gs100,000 per person for a bed (but that includes a free hammock, barbecue grill, loungers and beach umbrella). The rooms have either a double bed or two sets of bunks (up to 20 people), and have fans. You need to take your own towels, and 50% of the cost must be paid in advance by bank deposit.

The foundation **Para la Tierra** (m *0985 260074; www.paralatierra.org*) has opened a biological station here. You can volunteer for between one and six weeks, and you pay around US$700–900 a month. There is a small biological museum.

The reserve's uniqueness comes from its location at the point where three important and threatened ecoregions meet: the Upper Paraná Atlantic Forest to the south, the Cerrado to the north, and the Bosque Central. The natural lake, Laguna Blanca itself, is classed as an 'Important Bird Area' and is home to a number of threatened and endangered species. It has great biological diversity: since 2010 seven new species have already been discovered.

One of the endangered species is a nocturnal bird called the white-winged nightjar, which is known to breed here, and in only two other locations worldwide. It is estimated that there are 200 such birds at Laguna Blanca, and only another 300 in the world. Its habitat is under threat by the continued expansion of cattle ranching and genetically modified soya production, which is eating into the Cerrado region.

Any birdwatcher will be enthused by the great variety of birds in this region. You can rent a tent and a hammock, or you can stay in Santa Rosa and just come in for the day. Inexpensive meals are available. You can relax on the white sand beaches on the shores of the crystalline lake, and go rowing, paddleboating, kayaking or snorkelling. Or you can walk or go riding in the mix of low forest and grassland known as *cerrado*, which is a fragile ecosystem characterised by scrub or grassland growing on very sandy earth – white in colour, hence the name Laguna Blanca ('white lake'). There are sand dune hills to climb. This is the southernmost point of the cerrado, which stretches up into Brazil. One of the welcome characteristics of this very distinctive sandy terrain is that there are no mosquitoes. It is also very rich in fauna.

SAN PEDRO DE YCUAMANDYYÚ

Copaco 0342 222499; municipalidad 0342 222252; gobernación 0342 222136

San Pedro de Ycuamandyyú (variously spelt Ycuamandiyú or Yukuamandyju in Spanish, or 'Saint Peter of the Cottonfields Spring'), was founded in 1786 by the Portuguese, and still has a number of houses of a Neoclassical style from the period of the two López presidencies (see box on page 125 for the Franciscan influence in its foundation). It is sometimes said to be the poorest place in Paraguay. The access road from Santa Rosa (on Ruta 3) has been asphalted since 2008. On the way you pass through only one village, Nueva Germania. This unfortunately misguided enterprise was a 19th-century German experiment in creating a place where pure Aryan blood could flourish, founded by 1887 by Dr Bernhard Förster and his wife Elisabeth Nietzsche, sister of the philosopher. It was a ghastly failure, but there are still a few families of German extraction there who speak German.

San Pedro is identified as the approximate locality where the Portuguese explorer Alejo García was murdered by hostile indigenous in 1525: he is sometimes attributed with being the 'discoverer' of Paraguay. The town is now most famous for being the place where Fernando Lugo was bishop before becoming president of the Republic in 2008. This popular and charismatic bishop attracted to San Pedro the Latin American Congress of Basic Ecclesial Communities in 1996, which gave the town a brief moment of glory after which it sank again into its forgotten corner.

San Pedro is also known for being the seat of the most vociferous and at times violent *campesino* discontent, particularly over the issues of land reform and the purchase of land by Brazilian planters of genetically modified crops, with all the issues of health that have arisen through the use of poisons to clear the land.

Geological studies suggest that there may be oil in this *departamento*, and an exploratory perforation is planned for 2014.

GETTING THERE AND AWAY Buses from Asunción do the 320km in about six hours. Nasa (*021 551731/558451*) leaves Asunción at 21.30, and for the return journey leaves San Pedro at 22.00. Santaniana (*021 551607/551722*) leaves Asunción at 07.15 and 10.15. The fare is currently a modest Gs60,000. Buses also run directly from San Pedro to Ciudad del Este and Pedro Juan Caballero. You arrive on the Avenida Juana María de Lara and stop at the bus terminal (*0342 223017*) five blocks past the plaza.

There is a little airport on the Avenida Luis María Argaña but no regular service, and now that the road is asphalted there is no longer a need for even the rich to charter a private plane. For directions on driving, see pages 329–30.

WHERE TO STAY *Map, page 335.*

Photos of a number of other hotels can be found on Facebook: Secretaria De Turismo Gobernacion de San Pedro Paraguay.

Hotel Santa Ana (33 rooms) General Diaz c/ Independencia Nacional; 0342 222706. 4 blocks before you reach the central plaza, & 1 block to the north, near the Petropar service station. The most used & most recommended hotel. Has Wi-Fi in most rooms, AC (some split), some sommier beds. **$**

Hospedaje Santa Elena Independencia Nacional esq San Roque; 0342 222377; m 0971 812973; e everferlez@hotmail.com. AC, private bathrooms, Wi-Fi, cable TV. **$**

Hotel Giyoka (7 rooms) Av Antonio Ortigoza c/ Pancha Garmendia; 0342 222311. Ask for the house of Dr Gala in barrio Fátima. Near to la Ande (electricity office). Though it is a family house the rooms have AC, private bathrooms & TV. No b/fast. **$**

Hotel P L (25 rooms) Braulio Zelada c/ Jejuí; m 0961 813611/0971 463203. Hotel opposite terminal. AC & cable TV. Wi-Fi in reception. Good value. **$**

WHERE TO EAT AND DRINK *Map, page 335.*

Restaurant Anamar Eusebio Ayala esq Gral Caballero; 0342 222284; all day every day. Look for the low, bright red walls. The best restaurant in town. B/fast from Gs10,000. **$$**

Pachi Pachi 0342 222237. 1 block from the centre in a colonial building. The specialities are horsemeat & steak with onions. **$**

Emporio de los Alfajores Mcal Estigarribia c/ Iturbe; 0342 222282; 07.15–16.00 daily. Cheap restaurant, good service. Hot & cold midday buffet midday. **$**

OTHER PRACTICALITIES The traditional style of this town is maintained by the use of the little horse cart for passengers, known as the sulky, and by ox carts. There is a regional hospital and a private clinic. There are not many internet facilities but there is one internet place near the Hotel Victorino.

The **patronal feast day** is 29 June (feast of saints Peter and Paul) and the anniversary of the foundation is 16 March, when there are celebrations and fishing competitions.

For entertainment there is the **nightclub** Guajira Pub.

WHAT TO SEE AND DO The town centre is the **Plaza Mariscal Francisco Solano López**. Around the sides of this plaza are the cathedral, the *gobernación* (*0342 222136*), the Municipalidad and the little Museo de Antigüedades Alejo García (*for access contact the departamento de Cultura of the Municipalidad, 0342 222181*). The *polideportivo* (multi-purpose sports hall) practically fronts the plaza as well, and next to it is the Casa de Cultura, a historic old building with a portico.

San Pedro has a striking, historic **cathedral** in traditional Paraguayan style, dating from 1854 (during the presidency of Carlos Antonio López), with a double pitched roof, a portico supported on pillars, and a wooden bell tower standing apart. Inside are 18th-century wooden statues of the saints, folky in style and clothed, including St Peter. There is a fine old reredos.

On Tuesdays, Wednesdays and Saturdays there is a *feria campesina* (peasant market) on Vicente Ignacio Iturbe, immediately behind the Municipalidad, selling vegetables, meat and craft. It is flanked by an attractive mural. Craft is sometimes sold on the **Paseo de los Artistas**, a pedestrian road by the side of the *gobernación*, where there is a mural of Rigoberto Fontao Meza, a local musician who wrote songs in Guaraní in the first half of the 20th century.

A rather splendid monument in the **Plaza General Marcial Samaniego**, like a mural on a jigsaw piece with a hole in it, commemorates Alejo García, the Portuguese explorer who passed through this region in 1524 and is considered by some to be the founder of Paraguay. A nearby cross, Kurusú García, is in memory of his death at this approximate spot at the hands of the indigenous in 1525. (*Kurusú* is 'cross' in Guaraní.)

Walking around the town centre you will find a large number of attractive old buildings, particularly in the area south of the **Avenida Braulio Zelada** and Independencia Nacional. If you walk along Zelada, every block has a house of architectural interest, and these buildings fall into two types. There are the traditional houses with pitched roofs and colonnades the length of the building, of the style built in the Jesuit-Guaraní Reductions and continued long after. One of the oldest is the house of the Salomón family (Zelada y Estigarribia), dating from around 1800, and a couple of blocks west along Zelada is an attractive corner house belonging to the Campos Ross-Cassanello family, dating from about 1850. But there are also a number of grander houses with **Italianate façades**, set on corners with the door on the angle. They have tall façades, flat roofs, and many have high rounded doorways and plaster decoration above the windows. The most grandiose of these is the Seccional Colorado (Independencia y Colón), and another attractive one is the house of the Ferreira family (Yegros y Colón), built around 1900.

San Pedro is only 3km from the Río Jejuí, just before it runs into the Río Paraguay. The road from San Pedro to **Puerto'í** (the little port on the River Jejuí) leads south, while the main asphalted road to Puerto Antequera on the River Paraguay – about 24km away – branches off to the right. When you are nearly at Puerto'i you turn right for the beach, or left for the embarkation point for going to the island of Alejo García, more than 2,000m long. If you have turned right, you will come to a white-sand **beach**, and you can hire a rowing boat. At the east end of this beach is the **Restaurant Anabar** and at the west end is a Club de Caza y Pesca (hunting and fishing club). A pale pink D-shaped structure near to the river marks the spot of the *ykuá mandyjú* (cottonfields spring) which gives its name to the town.

CONCEPCIÓN

Copaco ☎ 0331 242800; municipalidad ☎ 0331 242212

One of the most attractive Paraguayan towns and sometimes known as the Pearl of the North, Concepción is quiet, picturesque and historic. (Encarnación is the Pearl of the South.) It has a number of lovely buildings constructed by Italian immigrants, typically painted yellow with white highlights, and the green cupola of the cathedral makes a welcoming sight ahead of you as you arrive.

Concepción was founded in 1773 by Agustín Fernando de Pinedo, close to the existing settlement of Belén (see pages 341–2), as a centre for growing *yerba*, for dominating the Mbaya indigenous and for defence against the Portuguese who were always trying to extend the boundaries of Brazil. A century later, in 1864, Mariscal López set off from here with 2,500 soldiers to attack the Mato Grosso of Brazil. In 1884 it became a municipality. Money was invested here in the expectation that it would be the nearest non-Chaco town when oil was found in the Chaco, but we are still awaiting that moment – hence its somewhat sleepy dignity.

GETTING THERE AND AWAY For instructions on getting to the northeast by car, see pages 329–30.

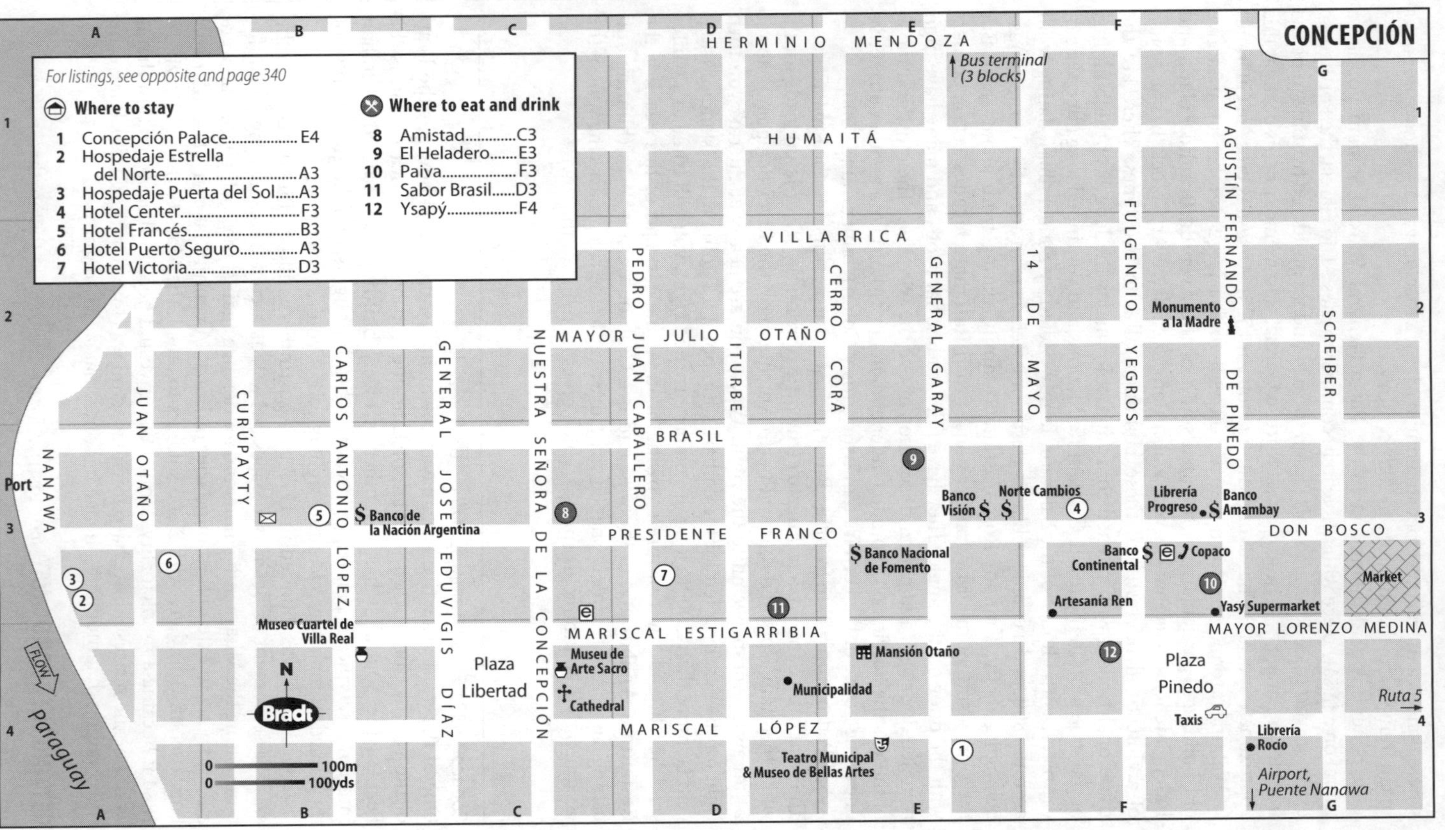

CONCEPCIÓN
For listings, see opposite and page 340
Where to stay
1 Concepción Palace.................. E4
2 Hospedaje Estrella del Norte.................................A3
3 Hospedaje Puerta del Sol......A3
4 Hotel Center..............................F3
5 Hotel Francés............................B3
6 Hotel Puerto Seguro..............A3
7 Hotel Victoria........................... D3
Where to eat and drink
8 Amistad.............C3
9 El Heladero.......E3
10 Paiva..................F3
11 Sabor Brasil......D3
12 Ysapý.................F4
HERMINIO MENDOZA
Bus terminal (3 blocks)
HUMAITÁ
VILLARRICA
MAYOR JULIO OTAÑO
BRASIL
PRESIDENTE FRANCO
MARISCAL ESTIGARRIBIA
MARISCAL LÓPEZ
NANAWA
JUAN OTAÑO
CURÚPAYTY
CARLOS ANTONIO LÓPEZ
GENERAL JOSE EDUVIGIS DÍAZ
NUESTRA SEÑORA DE LA CONCEPCIÓN
PEDRO JUAN CABALLERO
ITURBE
CERRO CORÁ
GENERAL GARAY
14 DE MAYO
FULGENCIO YEGROS
AV AGUSTÍN FERNANDO DE PINEDO
SCREIBER
DON BOSCO
MAYOR LORENZO MEDINA
Port
Paraguay
FLOW
Banco de la Nación Argentina
Museo Cuartel de Villa Real
Plaza Libertad
Museu de Arte Sacro
Cathedral
Municipalidad
Mansión Otaño
Teatro Municipal & Museo de Bellas Artes
Banco Nacional de Fomento
Banco Visión
Norte Cambios
Librería Progreso
Banco Amambay
Monumento a la Madre
Banco Continental
Copaco
Artesanía Ren
Yasý Supermarket
Market
Plaza Pinedo
Taxis
Librería Rocío
Ruta 5
Airport, Puente Nanawa
Bradt
N
0 100m
0 100yds

By bus Buses take six to eight hours to reach Concepción from Asunción, and most people prefer to travel on a night bus. Some take a route through the Chaco, via Pozo Colorado, which can be quicker, but often these are the older, less comfortable buses. The others come up Ruta 3 via Ybý Yaú, The companies travelling to Concepción are Nasa, Golondrina, Pycasú, Santaniana and Ovetense, of which the best are Nasa and Santaniana. The phone number of the Concepción bus terminal is 0331 242744.

A lot of buses travel between Concepción and Pedro Juan Caballero, including Nasa and Cometa del Amambay, and the journey may take as long as five hours; it is under three hours by car. See box, page 50, for the phone numbers of the bus companies.

To get to Vallemí (further north than Concepción on the Río Paraguay) by car is a further five hours. It is slow because you are on dirt roads for a good part of the way. By bus it is even longer. The asphalting of the road between Concepción and Vallemí was two-thirds complete at the time of going to press. You can also get to Vallemí by plane, if you manage to get a seat (see page 344).

If you need an exit stamp to leave Paraguay towards the north, you can get one in Concepción, although it is not a border town. The office is at Identificaciones (*Coronel Martínez c/ Cerro Corá; 0331 241937*). There is a border control at Carmelo Peralta on the Río Paraguay, but it is not open at night, so sometimes it is necessary to get this stamp in advance of reaching the frontier.

By air You can now travel to Concepción by plane (see boxes on pages 380 and 381). The airport is to the south of the town, but not as far south as the Puente Nanawa.

ORIENTATION Concepción spreads for about 25 blocks east to west until it reaches the River Paraguay, and then hugs its banks. You are likely to drive in on General Bernardino Caballero, which turns into Mariscal López after crossing the Avenida Agustín Fernando de Pinedo – the big avenue that cuts the town in two, running north to south. The centre, with the Municipalidad, the cathedral and the Plaza Libertad, are all on this road, but most of the hotels and shops are on Presidente Franco, two blocks to the north. If you arrive by bus you can ask to get off in the Avenida if you want to walk to your hotel, or continue to the terminal 'Yakare Valija', eight blocks north of Presidente Franco, and take a taxi. The phone number of the Concepción bus terminal is 03312 42744.

If you need a taxi while you are exploring the town, there is a taxi rank on the corner of Plaza Pinedo. Alternatively, try Señor Paniagua (m *0971 808271*) or Faustino Cabrera (m *0972 422587*).

WHERE TO STAY *Map opposite.*

Concepción Palace Hotel (58 rooms) Mariscal López 399 esq General Eugenio Garay; 0331 241858; www.concepcionpalace.com.py. The town's top hotel, opened in 2011, with business centre, pool, lounge for smokers & solar panels. Tagatiyá restaurant has a more economical menu ejecutivo at lunch on weekdays. **$$$$**

Hotel Puerto Seguro (16 rooms) Pr Franco y Juan Otaño; 0331 241895/6; www.hotelpuertoseguro.com. Good accommodation with rustic-style furniture, split AC, Wi-Fi, pool & supervised parking. **$$$**

Hotel Francés (55 rooms) Pres Franco y Carlos Antonio López; 0331 242383; www.hotelfrancesconcepcion.com. Old establishment in a building full of character on an elegant corner site. Pool & car park. This is also a recommended place to eat. **$$$**

Hotel Victoria (27 rooms) Pres Franco esq Pedro Juan Caballero; 0331 242826/242256. Old, characterful building with colonnades & balconies, & a mural in the courtyard. Owners are knowledgeable about *estancias* to the north of Concepción. Has 2 restaurants: the lunch restaurant doubles as the b/fast room, while in the evening they open a restaurant over the road, Quincho del Victoria, with an excellent *asado*, to leave the rooms quiet for guests. Sometimes has live music. **$$**

Hotel Center (54 rooms) Franco c/ Yegros; 0331 242584/242360. The cheapest hotel if you do not mind its reputation for not being a suitable place for respectable girls. Hotel Victoria costs only marginally more & has more to be said for it. Wi-Fi in reception. **$$**

Hospedaje Puerta del Sol (3 rooms) Nanawa c/ Presidente Franco; 0331 242185. Facing port, friendly, private bathrooms, cheaper rooms have fans, b/fast not included. Pay per person. Internet not far away. **$**

Hospedaje Estrella del Norte (6 rooms) Nanawa c/ Mariscal Estigarribia; 0331 242400. Next door to Puerta del Sol & similar. **$**

WHERE TO EAT AND DRINK *Map, page 338.*

Sabor Brasil Mariscal Estigarribia, e/ Iturbe y Cerro Corá; 0331 241415/243394. Facing the Municipalidad is a good Brazilian restaurant, where you can sit in a roofed, open area & enjoy not only excellent food but also the view of the elegant building opposite with its gardens & fountains. (Note that the Muncipalidad faces two directions, & this restaurant is on the road listed above & not on Mariscal López.) Formerly known as Toninho y Jardin.**$$**

Amistad Presidente Franco y Nuestra Señora de Concepción. Popular, busy restaurant & bar, full into the early hours. **$**

El Heladero Brasil y General Garay. Attractive, modern café. **$**

Paiva Avenida Pinedo e/ Presidente Franco y Mariscal Estigarribia. Good cheap restaurant where you pay by weight. **$**

Ysapý Mariscal Estigarribia y Fulgencio Yegros. Pizzeria that produces good food quickly & cheaply. **$**

Casa Puerto after 01.30 Sat nights. Popular nightclub with disco.

SHOPPING There is a corner **craft shop** called Artesanía Ren on Mariscal Estigarribia y 14 de mayo [338 F3]. It specialises in leather goods, sandals, clothes and *guampas* for *tereré*. A good **supermarket** is Yasý (*Avenida Pinedo y Mariscal Estigarribia*), where a lot of people go to buy lunch (by weight), although you cannot eat there. One block east of Avenida Pinedo, between Don Bosco and Mayor Lorenzo Medina, is a daily covered market with good fresh produce and fish. It is fun to explore.

OTHER PRACTICALITIES There is an **internet café** on Presidente Franco [338 F3] (*e/ Av Pinedo y Yegros*) and Wi-Fi in the plaza around the Municipalidad.

FESTIVALS The **feast of María Auxiliadora** (Our Lady Help of Christians) is on 24 May, and the foundation of the city is celebrated on 25 May. On 31 May there is a **procession** down the Avenida Agustín Fernando de Pinedo with floats relating to the history of the town. **Expo Norte** (*www.exponorte.org*) is a major agricultural show that comes to Concepción in the last week of August or the first week of September, and is held in the Campo de Exposiciones, 4.5km on Ruta 5. The **feast of the Immaculate Conception of Mary** is on 8 December, when there is a procession of a statue of the Virgin from the cathedral.

WHAT TO SEE AND DO Tourist enquiries can be directed to the Municipalidad (*0331 242212*). The massive white **statue of María Auxiliadora** dominates the Avenida Agustín Fernando de Pinedo. Situated outside the Salesian church of San José (also worth visiting) at the junction with Mayor Julio de Otaño, it is called the

Monumento a la Madre or Monumento a la Virgen, and was inaugurated in 2002. You can climb a few stairs to a platform at the feet of the mother to enjoy the view. At night when it is floodlit it looks even more dramatic. There is a display of old tractors, carts, vehicles and mill machinery along the Avenida Pinedo, known as the **Museo al Aire Libre**.

The **cathedral** [338 C4] on the Plaza Libertad (*Nuestra Señora de la Concepción, e/ Mariscal Estigarribia y Mariscal López,* ☎ *0331 242382;* ⌚ *every morning*) is a tall and striking building in yellow and white, not old but Classical in feel and with clean, elegant lines. The altarpiece depicting the empty tomb with angels and soldiers is the work of the famous Paraguayan artist Carlos Colombino, who specialises in wood creations. Some large and unusual birds inhabit the small garden to the front and side, and the facing plaza is very pleasant. There is a small **Museo de Arte Sacro** next door (⌚ *08.00–noon& 15.00–17.00 Mon–Fri, 08.00–noon Sat*). The **Museo Cuartel de Villa Real** [338 B4] is one block away (*Mariscal Estigarribia y Carlos Antonio López;* ⌚ *07.00–noon Mon–Sat, & at other times on request to* m *0971 803951; free admission*), in a 19th-century building that was once the barracks for Mariscal López's army, beautifully restored in 1998. It houses the wheels of the wagon that once transported Madame Lynch's piano on the great retreat to the northeast, in the War of the Triple Alliance. There are also sabres, military pictures and trumpets, indigenous feather headdresses, and bows and arrows. There is a Museo Civico Municipal in the **Teatro Municipal** [338 E4], (⌚ *07.00–noon Mon–Sat, & at other times on request to* m *0971 80395*) on Mariscal López, an elegant yellow and grey building one block to the east of the Municipalidad. In the five rooms of these museums you will find some oil paintings and miscellaneous old objects including pre-Colombian pots, a grand piano and an old printing press. Also in the same building is the Biblioteca Municipal, which has more visitors than the museum.

Inside the **Municipalidad** [338 D4] on the Mariscal Estigarribia side there are two very large and fine oil paintings: one shows the foundation of the city by Agustín Fernando de Pinedo (with the river, the soldiers, the indigenous and a Franciscan priest); the other shows the battle of Nanawa (a victory of Paraguay over Bolivia in the Chaco War).

The old building still used as a **post office** [338 B3] on Presidente Franco y Curupaytý is an elegant corner house, constructed in 1915, a couple of blocks from the port. It is marked Correos y Telegrafos, and was restored with Spanish assistance. The **Mansión Otaño** [338 E4] has been well restored and since 2008 has housed a museum of contemporary art. Other attractive **Italianate houses** are the Mansión Isnardi, Mansión Albertini and the Villa Ida.

At the port you can hire a boatman to take you to an island where there is a little church and a beach for swimming.

The imposing bridge over the Río Paraguay is called the **Puente Nanawa** [338 G4]. A little to the south of the city, it carries you into the Chaco, which feels almost like another country, so different is it in terms of soil and landscape. There is a project to build a *Costanera* (coast road) for 8km from the Nanawa bridge upwards. This would be flanked on one side by a sandy beach and on the other by fashionable shops, bars and restaurants. The old port is also being restored as a tourist attraction.

EXCURSION TO BELÉN Belén can be visited as a short excursion from Concepción, as it is only 21km to the southeast, along a dirt road. Buses run from Concepción several times a day: you can get details from the Terminal, and board the bus at the roundabout on the edge of town. It is sited exactly on the tropic of Capricorn, and is a little-known Jesuit Reduction though not one of the famous group of eight in

Misiones and Itapúa in the south of the country that formed part of the famous Treinta Pueblos. The Reduction of Belén tends to be forgotten because it was founded in 1760, only seven years before the Expulsion of the Jesuits, so had little chance to establish itself, and also because it was an experimental venture among the warlike Mbaya indigenous, with none of the success of missions to the more pacific Guaraní. Though a couple of local historians have written books about Belén recently, and this is the oldest settlement in the entire area, the truth is that there is very little to see. The present school is in an original building, but it could benefit from some restoration.

Where to stay and eat 16km from Concepción on the road to Belén is **Granja El Roble** (m *0985 898446*; e *dirk_peter_g@hotmail.com*; *www.paraguay.ch*; **$$**), run by a German who speaks English and is married to a Paraguayan. Follow the sign 2km before Belén. On weekdays you can be picked up from Concepción between 10.00 and 11.00 for free, or for Gs120,000 at other times. A taxi to El Roble costs the same. The owner explains: 'El Roble is a place of nature. Consequently there are frogs in the rooms and snakes in the bushes.' Meals are with the family, and they can cater for vegetarians.

THE FAR NORTH

If you are not under time pressure, an exploration of the vast range of land north of Concepción is an adventure. There are little-known *estancias*, extensive national parks, a remote 18th-century fort and riverside caves. Consider going one way by boat and the other way by bus, or taking a plane out. Be careful about getting a hire car stuck in the remote dirt tracks if rain comes.

There is a Nasa bus at 05.00 from Concepción that goes all the way to Vallemí, but more buses run during the day to closer places.

LORETO Driving north from Concepción for 25km you come first to Loreto, which was not a Reduction, although from its name it sounds as though it might have been. There are several buses per day, every hour or two, which you can take from the bus terminal. There is a rather attractive monument as you enter the town, like a mini-chapel in the middle of the road, blue and white with a tiny dome and cross. Take note too of the 10m bell tower at the church, modelled on the bell tower at Yaguarón (see page 175) but built in 2005.

ESTANCIAS These *estancias* are outside of the Apatur network, being remote from Asunción. Ring first to reserve and get instructions: you may be able to travel by bus and be picked up at a convenient point. The Río Aquidabán, north of Concepción, has some of the finest beaches in the country, with big stretches of proper yellow sand, but the best accommodation is by the stream Tagatijá Guazú, which is famous for its crystalline waters.

Estancia Ña Blanca 0982 917792. 94km from Concepción. Straight up the dirt road that goes to Vallemí, crossing the Rio Aquidabán & going the same distance again. When you reach the Tagatijá Guazú stream it is on your left. Small waterfalls, clear water, beautiful scenery. Snorkelling, walks, camping. Also has rooms for guests, & can take groups. Visits only by prior reservation. Named after the owner, Blanca Ferreira de González. **$$**

Rancho JMC (8 rooms) m 0983 776495. The easiest to get to, at Paso Horqueta, a little village on the Río Aquidabán, 45km from Concepción via Loreto – an hour's journey on the bus that goes to Vallemí. There is a private beach where you can camp, or you can camp at the house. No meals provided but you can use the kitchen. **$$**

Estancia Primavera 0331 242045; m 0971 247648; e nievecae@hotmail.com. 46km from Concepción, on the Río Aquidabán. Simple place offering camping & at most 2 rooms, fans rather than AC, but with lovely isolated beaches. Riding. Off the beaten track, & the road is very bad. You'll need a 4x4, but they can accompany you from Concepción. **$$**

NATIONAL PARKS There are also some national parks far to the north of Concepción – Parque Nacional Paso Bravo, Serranía San Luis and Parque Nacional Bella Vista. You are advised to first ring SEAM (Secretaria del Ambiente) (*021 615806; www.seam.gov.py*), who can help facilitate your visit. They all have a park ranger who can act as a guide.

The **Serranía San Luis** reserve is a triangle of 10,0000ha to the east of the road going north from Concepción to Vallemí. It was declared protected in 1991 and is characterised by dense forest and rugged rock formations, and protects the water basins of the streams Tagatijá Guazú, Santa Isabel and La Paz. The Tagatijá Guazú has rapids, waterfalls and clear pools, with a wide variety of fish, including *boga, piký, morenita, mandi'í* and *dorado*. Three threatened varieties of macaw (hyacinth, red-and-green and blue-and-yellow) thrive in San Luis. There are also capuchin monkeys. The park ranger lives in the southern point of the reserve and has beds for visitors.

Adjoining the fort is the extensive Parque Nacional **Paso Bravo** (93,612ha) which was formed as recently as 1998, and is named 'Wild Pass' after the stream that runs through it. It is principally savanna territory and also has caverns and hills. There is little or no visitor infrastructure.

Where to stay and eat

It might sound fun to stay in the 18th-century fort of **San Carlos**, now restored with Spanish aid and supposedly converted into a hotel, on the northern frontier with Brazil. There is a beach and rapids, and you can kayak on the River Apa. But take into account the difficulty of getting there. San Carlos is 220km from Concepción. After crossing the River Aquidabán at Paso Horqueta, drive along this dirt road for 84km in the direction of Vallemí and you will reach a cart track at Cruce Primavera which is the turning for San Carlos del Apa. If you do not get lost in the network of tracks (in no circumstances should you even attempt this without a guide), you will reach San Carlos after another 40–50km. The journey can only be made by 4x4 vehicles, and you may find it a long way to go for rather little. The tracks are better for approaching it from the east side, from Bella Vista, but this is very much longer. One visitor did make it there and enjoyed it, but he went by helicopter. There is a ferry (*balsa*) from Caracol, Brazil, and this is a better route if you are determined to get there: in mid 2014 plans were made public for the Brazilian state of Mato Grosso do Sul to finance the construction of a bridge across the river. Information about San Carlos and about the possibility of staying in the fort can be sought from the Municipalidad of San Carlos (*0351 230707*).

VALLEMÍ (*http://ciudadvallemi.tripod.com)* Vallemí is located in the top northwest corner of this northeast section of Paraguay, right on the River Paraguay and very nearly as northerly as the Río Apa, which marks the frontier with Brazil. Vallemí is a cement-producing town, and one of the striking things about it when you get off an aeroplane from the south is the totally different colour of the earth: instead of rich reddish brown it is very distinctly grey – cement-coloured, in fact. There is a quarry of *piedra caliza*, which is the raw material for making cement. The second striking feature is the simply enormous number of donkeys.

Getting there and away To get to Vallemí from Concepción by car takes about five hours. It is slow because you are on dirt roads for a good part of the way, but this should improve as the asphalting of the road between Concepción and Vallemí was two thirds complete at the time of going to press.

By bus it is a bit slower. There are only two buses a day, both leaving Concepción in the early morning and taking five or six hours. TTL (*0331 242320*) leaves Concepción at 05.00, and Nasa (*0331 232744*) leaves at 06.00.

The best way to get to Vallemí is to **fly**, and the cost is quite reasonable (see box, page 380). The main problem with flying is getting a ticket, as the thrice weekly flights are always full, and you are advised to book a long time in advance.

Where to stay and eat

Hotel La Brasilera (9 rooms) 0351 230636. This hotel run by Brazilians is fairly central. Cable TV, private bathrooms, AC, continental b/fast. Restaurant both for guests & for the public. **$$**

El Prado Hotel (8 rooms) 0351 230324/230545. Near port with river view, cable TV, AC, American b/fast, helpful owner. **$$**

What to see and do There are more than 50 **caves** in the region of Vallemí, the most notable of which are the Caves of San Lázaro just before the Río Ápa, which forms the border with Brazil. They are marked by stalactites and stalagmites, and there are guided visits to some of them, although up until now the difficulty of getting there has meant that they have had few visitors. San Lázaro is a small village only 6km from Vallemí. The (nearly finished) asphalted road from Concepción will no doubt make a difference to the number of visitors. There is also a proposal to build a bridge across the Río Ápa, to bring in visitors from Brazil.

On a level with Puerto Casado (which is on the other bank, see page 379) is the Caverna Tres Cerros (the first to be discovered), the Santa Caverna (so named because on stalactite resembles the Virgin) and the Caverna Risso (where you can do abseiling). Near Vallemí is the Caverna Camba Hopo (with little tunnels and with a striking view of the river from inside the cave). Near San Lázaro is the Caverna Santa Elena and the Caverna San Lázaro – the best known, since the caves are often generically referred to as the Cavernas de San Lázaro. The Vallemí-based guide, César González (**m** *0985 170952;* **e** *arvatur@hotmail.com*), will bring necessary equipment such as helmets, ropes, torches.

CRUISING THE RIO PARAGUAY Taking a boat up the River Paraguay is a beautiful and relaxing experience. The scenery is as wild and natural as you could possibly hope for, and the time span is in another world. Be patient with the relaxed Paraguayan approach to time: you may be told a boat has been cancelled and then find it leaves anyway, or that it is going to leave and then find it is cancelled, so be prepared to hang around. Sadly the luxury cruiser, *Crucero Paraguay*, no longer runs, but the *Aquidabán*, which takes passengers as well as cargo, is now the best option, and is full of local people and local life.

There are a couple of cargo boats that might take a passenger if they have room (the Guaraní and the *Cacique*), but they do not do so as a general rule and they do not have a fixed timetable; these two go as far south as Asunción, but the *Aquidabán* begins at Concepción and goes north, and has a regular weekly timetable. Then there is the *Ten Catén* (*0336 274200*), but it caters more for Brazilian fishing trips, as does the *Siete Cabrillas* (**m** *0971 817486/0981 361985*), which is available for contract by groups of up to 22 people, at a minimum rate of US$700 for a day trip, not including food. If you go north as far as Río Negro and Tres Gigantes in the Siete Cabrillas it will take at least 8 days and cost around US$15,000.

Travelling on the ***Aquidabán*** (*0331 242370/242435 Mondays;* m *0972 678695/551589; reservations Colho de Zouza agency* *0331 242435/242370 Mon & Wed–Fri 07.30–12.30*) by contrast, is very economical. It is a great experience, both for seeing nature and for being in a simple Paraguayan group of travellers, off the tourist trail. You need to allow time for this trip. You will have all day long doing nothing but gazing at the passing bank – which is beautiful but repetitive - so take plenty to read and plenty of insect repellent. You may witness the hunting of capybaras, and see them stretched out and gutted on the deck. The boat is something of a floating shop, and at every stop you will see people swarm on to do their shopping. This means that the boat is much fuller going upstream from Concepción than on the return journey. Some people prefer to do the downstream journey to have more space, while others prefer the upstream journey because there is more going on.

In terms of food, take with you what you can, though on board you can buy simple supplies from the cargo – beer and longlife milk and fizzy drinks but probably not water. Usually you can also pay for a portion of the hot meals the crew are preparing for themselves if they have enough (eg: breakfast Gs10,000; supper Gs20,000), but do not rely just on this.

In terms of sleeping, there are two options: a berth or a hammock. The berths (Gs30,000) are very basic, may have thin or bumpy mattresses, and will not have sheets or blankets. You can book the whole cabin of four berths (Gs100,000) for privacy, even if travelling alone. But being in a hammock on deck is a dream, both by day and by night: you are in your own private space but can also watch what everyone else is doing. You must consult the crew about using a hammock as space is limited, and they will probably put it up for you, pulling it taut, which is much more comfortable. They sometimes have hammocks to hire (Gs30,000), but if possible take your own, with a couple of ropes: you can buy hammocks in Asunción, in the Plaza de la Libertad or on the street in Palma near Turista Róga. Some disadvantages people have mentioned with hammocks are that they find it noisy on deck, that they are too tall to fit in comfortably, or that they are concerned about the security of their belongings. You should keep your valuables tucked up with you or under your pillow.

Reservations, both of the journey and of berths or cabins, should be done with the Colho de Zouza agency (see above). Note that Tuesday is sailing day, so there is no one in the office because the staff have gone down to the port. The boat leaves around 10 or 11, and you may get a reservation on the day, but again it may be full. To be sure, book a few days before, or if that is not possible, arrive early, say 8 am.

The *Aquidaban* takes three days to get to Bahía Negra, the most northerly point in Paraguay that you can reach by public boat. Puerto Casado is approximately one day's journey, and Vallemí (on the east bank) is only a short distance further. Shortly after that, eastern Paraguay comes to an end and you have Brazil to your right. Isla Margarita is a half-day journey further; from this island you can you can get a small boat (*canoa*) to Carmelo Peralta on the Paraguayan bank, if you need to. You arrive in Fuerte Olimpo two days after leaving Concepción. Bahía Negra is reached on the third day - around 8 am on Friday. Remember that travelling upriver is slower than travelling downriver: the boat goes upstream at 12km/h, and downstream at 18km/h. So the return is two days rather than three, and the boat is back in Concepción on Sunday. The fares from Concepción are currently Gs65,000 to Puerto Casado; Gs 110,000 to Fuerte Olimpo; Gs120,000 to Bahía Negra.

If you want to double check on details about boats on the river, the most reliable information can be got by ringing the Prefectura de Puertos in Concepción (☎ *0331 242560*). Since they are the navy, responsible for policing the river, they have the most accurate up-to-date knowledge, and are always willing to help.

Here is a checklist of things you might want to take. Food, drinking water, whisky (can be traded for food on the boat), all the cash you might need before returning to Concepción or further south, food in airtight containers, insect repellent, suncream, sunhat, hammock or sleeping bag or both (depending on time of year), rope, reading material or audio material or games to pass time, towel, soap, toilet paper, flip flops, binoculars, torch, lock for luggage.

PEDRO JUAN CABALLERO

Copaco ☎ 0336 272299; municipalidad ☎ 0336 272212

Pedro Juan Caballero (usually known just as Pedro Juan) is a large city and the capital of the *departamento* Amambay. The city is named after one of the *Próceres* of Independence, whose statue stands in the Plaza Panchito López. This is the furthest city away from Asunción (536km), and has a reputation for poverty and all the problems associated with poverty in big cities. There are plenty of armed guards to be seen on the streets, watching over the shops. In the first five months of 2014 the police reported 38 murders, of which 24 (more than one a week) were by paid assassins, generally shooting from motorbikes. 'There are hardly any common crimes – robberies from shops or muggings or car thefts,' said the police chief, 'but the assassins have their tentacles in drug-smuggling.'

It was founded in 1894 as a stopping point for wagons carrying *yerba* from Concepción to Brazil, and since then has profited from trade of all sorts with its larger neighbour. The **Shopping China** [348 D7] is a vast warehouse on Ruta 5 that sells everything you can think of, and serves as a prominent local landmark. It claims to be the biggest shopping centre of imported goods in the whole of Latin America. There is a Paraguayan flag outside it, and that is all there is to mark the

PEDRO JUAN CAVALLERO

The name of the city is spelt 'Pedro Juan Caballero' with a 'b', while the surname of the man is more correctly spelt with a 'v' – 'Cavallero' – insofar as you can talk of correct spellings in Paraguay, where the old tradition is that a legitimate variety of spellings can be used, so long as the name is pronounced the same. (In Spanish, 'b' and 'v' are pronounced the same.)

Cavallero was born in Tobatí in 1786 and as a soldier took part in the 1811 defence of Paraguay against the attempt to make it subject to Buenos Aires in the newly independent Argentina. But he is most famous for being one of the *Próceres* of independence on 14 and 15 May the same year (see page 12). In the meeting of the first National Congress, Cavallero was elected as one of five members of the new junta governing Paraguay. Dr José Gaspar Rodríguez de Francia eventually became the first president of the Republic, but when he turned into a dictator his former colleague Cavallero took part in a conspiracy against him. A coup was planned for Holy Week 1820, but it was anticipated by Francia, and Cavallero was imprisoned in the house which is now the Museo Bogarín, where he chose to commit suicide on 13 July 1821 rather than suffer execution (see page 103).

boundary with Brazil. It is typical of this crime-ridden city that the only comment on one internet tourist forum is from a Brazilian reporting the theft of his car from the Shopping China car park.

The Brazilian frontier actually runs right through the city, though the part on the Brazilian side is called by the Guaraní name Ponta Porã, which was once the name for Pedro Juan too. Ponta Porã is in the state of Mato Grosso do Sul.

Locals advise you not to cross into Brazil with your car, as the Brazilian police are vigilant and tough, charge large fines and may even confiscate your vehicle. However, the frontier is so invisible that it is difficult not to cross it: one side of the road you are in Paraguay and the other you are in Brazil, with nothing to show the difference other than the change of language on the shop signs. The particular street that has the frontier running down the middle of it is called Dr Franco, and the grass strip in the middle is a no-man's land where Brazilian assassins chuck bodies at night so they can be reported as found dead in Paraguay.

There is ongoing deforestation in the region, which is now principally devoted to cattle rearing. Soya, maize and manioc are the principal crops, not to mention marijuana, of which this area is said to be the capital. It has been estimated that Paraguay produces 48 million kilos of illegal marijuana each year. Smuggling abounds.

Almost 10% of the population is indigenous, mostly from a branch of the Guaraní called Paĩ Tavyterã.

GETTING THERE AND AWAY See pages 329–30 for the main part of the **car journey from Asunción**. The drive from Ybý Yaú to Pedro Juan is stunning, because of the almost vertical, round-topped, red rocky hills that shoot up out of the plain, of which the most striking of all is the double-peaked Cerro Membý (Spanish 'Hill'; Guaraní 'child of a mother') only 1km from the road. To find your way to the city centre, turn left (northwest) at the Copetrol service station on Ruta 5. You will then be on Carlos Antonio López, and 22 blocks ahead you will come to the Plaza Panchito López. Close to the plaza you come to an Esso station on the left, which has a wall map of the city.

If you are coming by **bus**, the terminal (*0336 272708*) is located on the western corner of the Laguna [348 B3]. The companies that travel here are La Santaniana, Nasa, Cometa Amambay and Ovetense. The journey goes via rutas 3 and 5 and takes eight hours. Nasa and Cometa del Amambay do the journey from Pedro Juan Caballero to Concepción. Occasionally, you hear of backpackers leaving Paraguay for Brazil by this route to Ponta Porã. The Paraguayan passport control, for your exit stamp, is at Naciones Unidas 144 (*08.00–noon & 13.30–19.00 Mon–Fri, 08.00–noon Sat*). The *aduana* (customs) is on O'Leary and Pitiantuta.

There is a little airport but no regular flights.

TOURIST INFORMATION There is a new tourist office run by Senatur (*Avenida Dr Francia c/ Curupaytý; 0336 274642/274638; m 0985 582749; e pedrojuan@senatur.gov.py; 07.00–12.30 & 13.30–17.00*), which has internet facilities and a room for showing audiovisual materials.

 **WHERE TO STAY** *Map, page 348.*

If you are coming to Pedro Juan in your own transport and just to pass the night, there is no need to enter the city, and a couple of small hotels on the outskirts could serve you well, such as the Bertea or Las Vegas in the San Blas barrio (see page 349).

Hotel Eiruzú (60 rooms) Mariscal López esq Mariscal Estigarribia; 0336 272435/273162/+55 67 431 2555; e interhoteis@uol.com.br; www.grupointerhoteis.com.br. Belongs to the Brazilian

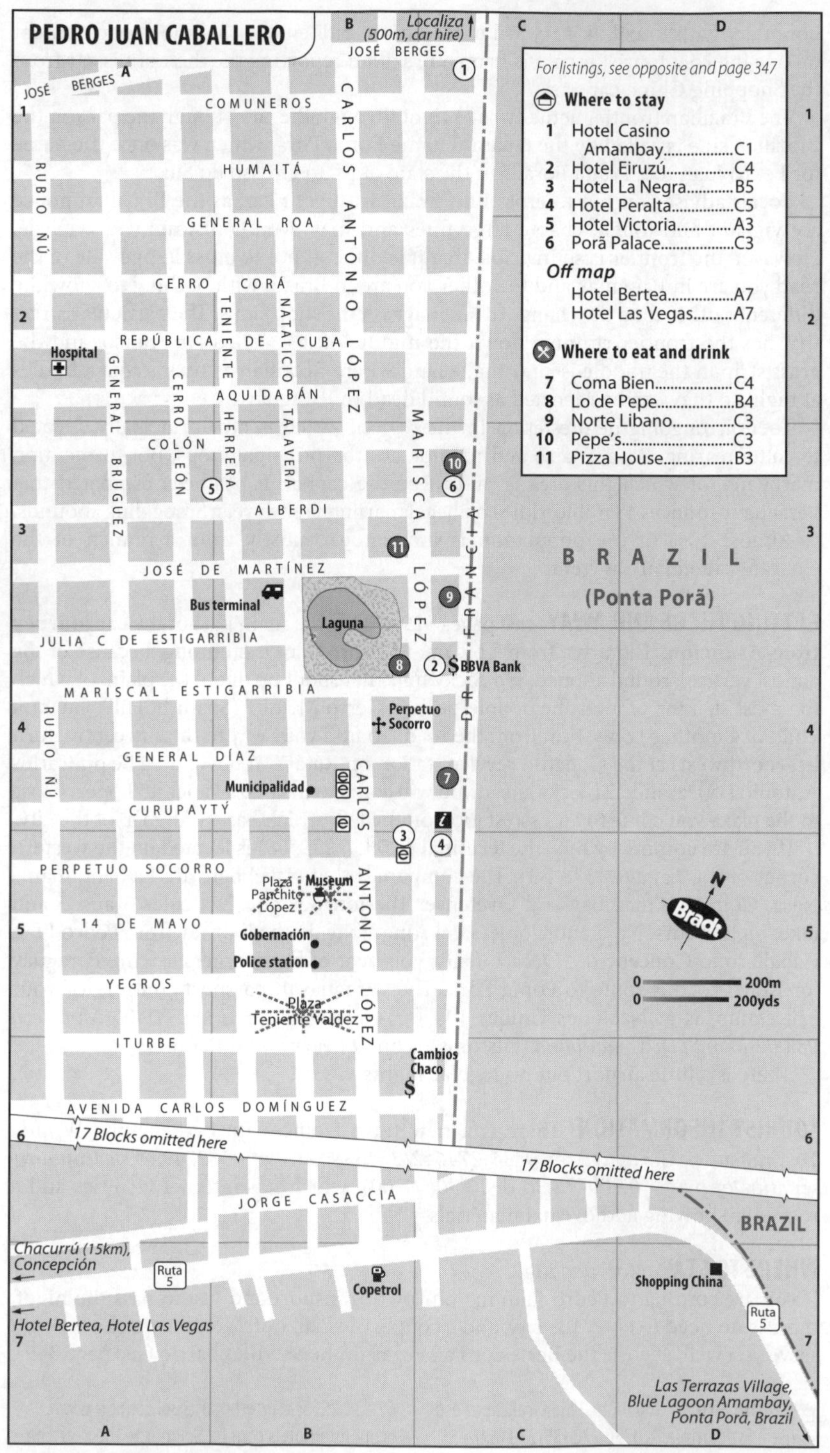
PEDRO JUAN CABALLERO
Localiza (500m, car hire)
For listings, see opposite and page 347
Where to stay
1 Hotel Casino Amambay.................C1
2 Hotel Eiruzú.................C4
3 Hotel La Negra.............B5
4 Hotel Peralta.................C5
5 Hotel Victoria..............A3
6 Porã Palace...................C3
Off map
Hotel Bertea.................A7
Hotel Las Vegas...........A7
Where to eat and drink
7 Coma Bien.....................C4
8 Lo de Pepe....................B4
9 Norte Libano.................C3
10 Pepe's............................C3
11 Pizza House..................B3
JOSÉ BERGES
COMUNEROS
HUMAITÁ
GENERAL ROA
CERRO CORÁ
REPÚBLICA DE CUBA
AQUIDABÁN
COLÓN
ALBERDI
JOSÉ DE MARTÍNEZ
JULIA C DE ESTIGARRIBIA
MARISCAL ESTIGARRIBIA
GENERAL DÍAZ
CURUPAYTÝ
PERPETUO SOCORRO
14 DE MAYO
YEGROS
ITURBE
AVENIDA CARLOS DOMÍNGUEZ
JORGE CASACCIA
RUBIO ÑÚ
GENERAL BRUGUEZ
CERRO LEÓN
TENIENTE HERRERA
NATALICIO TALAVERA
CARLOS ANTONIO LÓPEZ
MARISCAL LÓPEZ
DR FRANCIA
Hospital
Bus terminal
Laguna
BBVA Bank
Perpetuo Socorro
Municipalidad
Plaza Panchito López
Museum
Gobernación
Police station
Plaza Teniente Valdez
Cambios Chaco
BRAZIL
(Ponta Porã)
Bradt
N
0 200m
0 200yds
17 Blocks omitted here
17 Blocks omitted here
BRAZIL
Chacurrú (15km), Concepción
Ruta 5
Copetrol
Shopping China
Hotel Bertea, Hotel Las Vegas
Las Terrazas Village, Blue Lagoon Amambay, Ponta Porã, Brazil

hotel chain Inter Hoteis, though it is in Paraguay, 1 block away from Brazil. Seems pricey for Paraguay but in this rather seedy city you may feel the extra money is worth it. Internal parking with 24hr guard, internet, sauna & swimming pool. **$$$$**

Porã Palace (50 rooms) Dr Francia c/ Alberdi; 0336 273021; www.porapalacehotel.com. Big hotel catering for bank officials & commercial travellers, half from Paraguay & half from Brazil. Minibars, pool & restaurant. **$$$$**

Hotel Casino Amambay (41 rooms) Dr Francia y José Berges 01; Brazilian address for the same place is Av Internacional 3474; 0336 271140/272200/272963; www.casinoamambay.com. The casino is in a huge & elegant hall with chandeliers, sofas & gaming tables. Not everyone's cup of tea but fun for those who like that kind of thing. Parking is on the street but there is a 24hr guard. **$$$**

Hotel Las Vegas (23 rooms) Ruta 5 San Blas; 0336 271575. On Ruta 5 before you enter the city, on the north side of the road after you have gone under the big arch. Modern, with less character than the Hotel Bertea next door, but has Wi-Fi in all rooms. Minibars. **$$**

Hotel La Negra Mariscal López 1342 c/ Curupayty; 0336 274603/272262/270656. In the heart of the city. Simple, modern rooms but good value. The best rooms are on the top floor. There is a pleasant b/fast room, a car park & it is conveniently situated right next door to a bar. Cheaper rooms have fans. **$**

Hotel Bertea (30 rooms) Ruta 5 y Rubio Ñu; 0336 271958. On Ruta 5 before you enter the city, on the north side of the road after you have gone under the big arch. Striking & agreeable hotel, with friendly people. All rooms have AC, TV & private bathrooms. No internet at present. It tends to be full Mon–Fri with commercial travellers (unless you book in advance), but there is room at w/ends. **$**

Hotel Victoria (21 rooms) Tte Herrera 778 y Alberdi; 0336 272733. Basic but clean, & a couple of mins walk from the bus terminal. AC. **$**

Hotel Peralta (8 rooms) Mariscal Lopez 1257 y Curupayty; 0336 272017. Family hotel in the heart of the city. No meals, not even b/fast, but there are plenty of places to eat b/fast nearby, eg: Hotel La Negra. TV. Cheaper rooms have fans. **$**

WHERE TO EAT AND DRINK *Map opposite.*

A decent packed lunch suitable for picnicking can be bought at the **Copetrol service station** out on Ruta 5, which will serve you well if you are going to spend the day in a nature reserve (see pages 350–1).

Pepe's Dr Francia 758; 0336 272375. Recommended. Just round the corner from the Hotel Porã Palace, a little expensive but that is to be expected since there is a live group playing traditional Paraguayan folk music every night. Portions are large. **$$$**

Lo de Pepe Mariscal López c/ Mariscal Estigarribia; 0336 272796; 11.00–14.30 & 18.00–23.30 Tue–Sun. International menu, fish is the speciality. **$$**

Coma Bien Dr Francia c/ Curupayty; m 0976 834199. Brazilian restaurant, nothing elaborate. **$$**

Norte Libano Dr Francia c/ José de Martínez; 0336 270384. Middle Eastern fast-food place near the Laguna. Try the *lomite arabe*. **$$**

Pizza House Mariscal López y José D Martínez; 0336 273497. Just to the north of the Laguna. **$$**

SHOPPING A new shopping centre called Las Terrazas Village is under construction. It will not include a supermarket, but rather a grouping of 220 small shops, as well as bars and restaurants and a plaza for recreation, all enclosed in an area with security guards. The site is just 25m from the Brazilian border.

OTHER PRACTICALITIES There is **car hire** with Localiza [348 C1] (*P Juan José O'Connor; 0336 273452; 07.00–11.30, 13.00–17.00 Mon–Fri; 07.00–11.30 Sat*) Avenida Dr Francia (the last street of Paraguay) turns into Juan José O'Connor just off the map on page 348 to the north, and Localiza is within the building marked Lider Máquina, close to the hypermarket Portis, 500m north of the Hotel Casino Amambay.

There is a **Cambios Chaco** [348 B6] at Mariscal López 1797 esq Carlos Dominguez (🕘 *07.00–19.15 Mon–Sat*).

A big estate of houses and flats in a parkland of flowering trees is currently under construction 5km from Pedro Juan. It is called **Blue Lagoon Amambay** after the turquoise-coloured artificial lake of nearly 4ha that will form its heart. There will be football, basketball, volleyball and tennis, as well as a couple of theme parks.

WHAT TO SEE AND DO One of the more pleasant places within the city is the Laguna Punta Porã, generally just known as the **Laguna** [348 B3–4] – the 'lake' – which is a large plaza occupying four blocks, with a lake in the centre. In the past there was just a spring of water here, which made it a stopping place for carts transporting *yerba mate* and other products. The Laguna is now right in the heart of the city, and is taken as iconic of the city.

Another square, the Plaza Panchito López [348 B5], has the **statue of Pedro Juan Cavallero** and a small **museum** situated in the middle. The museum does not have a great deal to offer, though there are old saddles and typewriters, busts and pictures of national and local figures, and a stuffed jaguar. The **church of Nuestra Señora del Perpetuo Socorro** [348 B4] was one of the first churches in town to have been built and has an attractive triple stained-glass window portraying local people. It has sometimes been attractively floodlit at night. But Pedro Juan Caballero is not the sort of place where people go for tourism – unless it is the commercial tourism of Brazilians, going to and fro across the border for purposes of shopping or smuggling. Pedro Juan is, however, a necessary springboard for visiting the natural sites nearby.

NATURE RESERVES CLOSE TO PEDRO JUAN Though the *departamento* of Amambay needs urgent action to stop the serious deforestation, there is still a wealth of **trees**, with many areas remaining wooded. The trees here are taller than in the rest of the country, and under the canopy of their branches grow long creepers and giant ferns, which have given the name to the *departamento*: Amambay (Guaraní 'fern'). The rare *peroba* tree (*Aspidosperma polyneuron; yvyraromi* in Guaraní) grows in this region. It can grow 30m high, and its pinkish wood is excellent for flooring and furniture: most of it has been exported to Brazil, usually illegally. In terms of **fauna**, you can find the marsh deer, the jaguar, the caiman, the blue-and-yellow macaw and the bell bird. The bell bird is very strongly associated with Paraguayan culture because of the famous folk song *Pajaro campana* written by Felix Pérez Cardozo.

Because of the location of the rocky hill range (*cordillera*) down the Brazilian frontier, most of the nature reserves have cliffs that can be used for abseiling. Here are some reserves nearby, where you can picnic and go for walks, but you are unlikely to find a guide, except at Cerro Corá (see pages 351–4).

Reserva San Luis 30km from Pedro Juan, a patch of virgin forest inside an *estancia* of 12,000ha. Riding & abseiling.

Reserva Y'Ambué Explorable paths, waterfalls. Abseiling. 8km away from Pedro Juan, down a dirt road. 20ha. Camping capacity for 20 people.

Reserva Fortuna Guazú Paths, waterfalls, including 1 with drop over 38m. Abseiling. 8km away from Pedro Juan, of which only 1km is on a dirt road. Natural pools for bathing. Camping capacity for 40 people.

Parque Ecológico Sol y Luna 17km back down Ruta 5 in a place called Chirigüelo. Paths, waterfalls, pools, abseiling. Camping capacity for 60.

Granja ARA 27km from Pedro Juan, of which 7km are dirt road. The farm (*granja*) covers 100ha. Paths, waterfalls, pools, abseiling. A 50m roofed area gives protection against sun & rain. Camping capacity for 60. Holiday bungalows for 8.

CHACURRÚ ECOTURISMO (m *0983 776 069; www.chacurru.com.py)* This new adventure tourism enterprise opened recently. (It was initially advertised as Chakurrai, but the name was changed due to problems in registering the brand name it was changed to Chacurrú, which is the name of a bird that is local to the region). Chacurrú is the name of a bird that is local to the region. It is 15km from the centre of Pedro Juan Caballero, and you look out for signs when you are approaching the city on Ruta 5.

The main activity at Chacurrú is the 'Canopy Tour', an aerial walkway through the treetops, over a series of rope bridges, each slightly different in design, culminating with a 130m *tirolesa* (zip wire), and finally *rappel* (abseiling) down a drop of 28m along the side of a waterfall. It is similar to what is offered at Mbatoví (see page 167).

The Chacurrú complex is lovely to walk in, with its paths and streams, and covers 25ha, of which nearly half come into play on the Canopy Tour. There is also a viewpoint over the landscape of Amambay. Chacurrú responds to the growing interest in nature tourism, and is an attempt to stimulate the tourist industry in an area of notable natural beauty that is not much visited by foreigners except Brazilians from over the border.

PARQUE CERRO CORÁ AND THE SURROUNDING AREA

Because Cerro Corá is regularly visited, it is not necessary to follow the general rule for visiting the national parks, which is to contact SEAM (Secretaria del Ambiente) beforehand in Asunción. This famous but remote park is best known for being the site of Mariscal López's death and the country's final capitulation in the Triple Alliance War. But, in fact, it includes two other attractions: a pleasant nature walk to Cerro Muralla, and the eco-archaeological reserve of Gasorý, where there are cave writings. There is also a pleasant beach on the shores of the Río Aquidabán. The park covers more than 12,000ha and was declared a national park in 1976. It is visited by 9,000 people a year, of which 40% are foreigners.

GETTING THERE AND AWAY Although Cerro Corá is a household name in Paraguay, few Paraguayans have ever ventured that far. Tourists rarely travel as far as Pedro Juan, but if you do, then Cerro Corá is easy to reach, by taxi or your own vehicle, as it is only 30km or so to the west on the main road, Ruta 5. The entrance to the park is clearly marked, on the northern side of the road.

OTHER PRACTICALITIES At the national park of Cerro Corá there is a rota of park rangers or *guardabosques*, and the principal guide Hilario Cañete (m *0981 996496*) is ideal – a good-humoured, easy companion, with great knowledge of his subject. (He does not speak English.)

The **three tours of Cerro Corá, Cerro Muralla and Gasory** can be comfortably done in a day, but you must bring your own lunch as there is nowhere to buy food. Do not attempt to do any of these tours without a guide. High season for visits is September to November, which is when a lot of schools make trips. There is a visitor centre with a museum (🕘 *08.00–17.00 daily, all year round*). You can camp in the park for free.

CERRO CORÁ The name Cerro Corá, which means 'hill circle' in a mixture of Spanish and Guaraní, is one of the most famous names in Paraguay, being the **site of the death of Mariscal Francisco Solano López**, who is still regarded by Paraguayans as their country's greatest hero, while outsiders more often see him as one of the world's cruellest dictators (see also pages 13, 164–5, 234–5 and the box below).

The historic sites are shown by the guide in ascending order of land level, beginning with the **stream Aquidabaniguí** (which later becomes the Río Aquidabán as it approaches Concepción). This is where López died with the famous words 'I die with my country', or according to some 'I die for my country', after having been wounded by a lance in the side, a sword in the head and a bullet in the heart. Going up the slope you pass a row of 16 **busts** of soldiers and priests who were among the 450 people in this final camp: most, however, were women, children and the elderly, who were starving, to the point of eating the leather soles of their shoes.

Above this on the ascent is a huge white **monument** resembling a series of white spires on a platform: this marks the site of the encampment, and there is an airstrip for receiving government representatives for the annual memorial celebration of 1 March. The surrounding hills formed a natural screen, but deserters told the allied army where López could be found.

THE TRIPLE ALLIANCE WAR: INTERPRETATIONS

Paraguayans see the Triple Alliance War as a war of genocide, under which their compatriots showed exemplary courage in the face of certain death: this consciousness is deeply engraved in the Paraguayan sense of national identity. The perception of the Brazilians, Argentinians and Uruguyans was that they were ridding the continent of a dangerous dictator, who posed a major threat to the continent, was prepared to see his country utterly destroyed rather than give up his position, and cruelly tortured and killed huge numbers of his compatriots as suspected traitors in his desperation to hang onto power. This view tends to be shared by Europeans, whose assessment is based on the reports of British men working under him as engineers and doctors. 'No surrender' was the heart of the conflict, seen by one side as supreme courage and by the other as supreme selfishness.

Mariscal López has gone down in Paraguayan history as the country's greatest hero, with the catchphrase '*un paraguayo no se rinde*' (a Paraguayan does not surrender). In his final speech in Cerro Corá on 1 March 1870, the day he was to die, addressing the dozen or so crippled, starving and half-naked men who now constituted his army, he declared in grand fashion: 'The victor is not the one who remains alive on the battlefield, but the one who dies for a beautiful cause. We will be vilified by the generation that emerges from the disaster, that will carry the defeat in their souls, and in their blood, like a poison, the hatred of the victor. But other generations will come, and will do us justice, acclaiming the greatness of our immolation'. That rehabilitation of Mariscal López did in fact take place, in the aftermath of the Chaco War, when his remains were placed in the Panteón. Every 1 March is a national holiday, the Día de los Héroes, marking the date of his death in 1870.

Meanwhile, his Irish partner, Madame Lynch, has been presented as the darling of the poor, not because she did anything for them, but because she was disliked and rejected by the society ladies of Asunción at the time.

Higher still is an avenue leading to a huge **white cross** with a hollow centre, throughwhich the wood behind can be seen: the sensation of nature breaking through the frame of death has been movingly captured. Just beyond this is the actual site of the original grave, which Madame Lynch dug with her bare hands for her lover and one of their sons, the 16-year-old Coronel Panchito López. In 2011 a new monument was built on this spot, with a granite slab bearing the Mariscal's words '*Vencer o morir*' ('Win or die').

Panchito was shot after his father when he attacked an enemy soldier with the cry, 'A Paraguayan colonel does not surrender.' Madame Lynch is said to have wrapped herself in a Union Jack as a sign of being a non-combatant while seeking to bury the bodies, and to have paid three gold bars and some fine French cloth for the permission to do so. The rest of the army was almost naked, but she was a woman who maintained her style until the end.

A nearby **tree**, an *arbol kurañái*, has a place in the story. According to some it is where a soldier hid to watch the burial. According to others it is where Madame Lynch left a notice saying the grave was 40 paces to the east of that spot. In 1936 the grave was dug up and the remains of Mariscal López (by that time just hair and kneecaps) were transported to the Panteón in Asunción (see page 111).

CERRO MURALLA The walk to Cerro Muralla begins from a very discreet path that you would never find without a guide, a few kilometres to the east of the entrance to the park. Go to the park first, and the guide will accompany you to the path. It is a beautiful walk, through a wood, over a wooden suspension bridge, along a red earth path, turning right through white sandy terrain where there are low trunkless palm trees (*jata'í*), and cactus-like plants with thorns on the leaves (*bromelia*). Then you pass through another wood and up a short climb to a rocky peak, from where there is a magnificent view over all the surrounding countryside and especially over the dramatic humps of hill-rocks: Cerro Membý, Cerro Guyrá Kuembá and Cerro Guaiguyog. The name Cerro Corá (hill corral) comes from the way these hills form a sort of circle. Allow a couple of hours maximum.

In the cracks of the rock you can see a species of orchid with a red flower only found in this *departamento*, the *sininpia amambayensis*. There are many examples of the *ficus* (common name *matapalo*) that grows in the forks of other trees; it is not a parasite but sends down long roots to the ground and eventually the mother tree dies because the ficus draws out all the nutrients from the soil. The seeds are deposited by toucans (of which there are many here) that eat the fruit.

In the area there are mountain lions and capybaras, and other large animals that are in risk of extinction such as the marsh deer, anteater and maned wolf. Typical trees are the *palo borracho* (Guaraní *sumu'ú*) which is found more extensively in the Chaco, the cedar (Spanish *cedro*; Guaraní *ygarý*), the *jacaranda* (Guaraní *ka'í jepopeté*), the *palo de vino* capped with yellow flowers in January, and the beautiful, tall *lapacho* (Guaraní *tajý*) that bursts into pink blossoms in September and is such a distinctive feature of Paraguay.

GASORÝ The ancient cave writings of Rancho Gasorý are found a little way outside the national park, on private land, but the guide Hilario has permission to take visitors there if they are accompanied. (Sadly, unaccompanied visitors cannot be trusted not to scratch their own initials in the rock.) A short walk past an indigenous settlement leads to some cliffs that slope away inwards, and here a large number of engravings or runes can be clearly seen. They are estimated to be 4,000 to 6,000 years old. Some are like a lot of parallel lines. Others form a divided U shape that might possibly be a female sexual symbol. Nobody knows their origin, and though the most obvious explanation is that they were carved by indigenous peoples, none of today's indigenous know anything about their history. Other theories contend that the Vikings or Celts came here and left their form of writing.

There are other cave writings, but those of Gasorý are the best ones to visit. Those at **Cerro de la Serrana** (closer to the Cerro Muralla, but south of the road on the way to Lorito Picada) can only be visited very early in the day and only then with some risk: large wasps nest under the shifting cave floor and are liable to be enraged by people walking over them. The local indigenous say they have found further cave inscriptions – more extensive and much better than either of those mentioned – but it is a full day's walk to journey there and back. Anyone keen enough to go on this expedition will need to take also a Guaraní interpreter, for the indigenous speak hardly any Spanish: ask Hilario or another guide at the Parque Cerro Corá.

THE FAR NORTH OF CERRO CORÁ

A dirt road some 70km to the west of Pedro Juan Caballero on Ruta 3 leads north and eventually reaches the little town of **Bella Vista** (*Municipalidad* ☎ *038 238226*) on the Río Apa, which is simple but pretty and has nice beaches and some boating. There are a couple of very simple *hospedajes*: Gloria (☎ *038 238494*; **m** *0975 853443*) and Refugio del Teju (**m** *0973 876194*). Unfortunately, it can only be reached by driving some 75km on a dirt road, though of the superior sort known as *terraplen*. The little Río Apa forms the northern frontier of Paraguay, and there is a bridge here to the Brazilian town of Nossa Senhora de Fátima.

A little paradise called **Ojo de Mar** (Eye of the Sea) is located about 120km from Pedro Juan and 50km from Bella Vista towards the southwest, close to the Río Apa, and close to the border between the *departamentos* of Concepción and Amambay, in a place called Colonia Rinconada – a remote corner of the world if you ever want to find one. Plunging with determination through thick subtropical vegetation you reach a mysterious little round lake of clear green water which was caused by a volcanic eruption 250 million years BC and according to legend has no bottom. Locals say that people who try to cross the 100m width of the lake have found themselves swallowed up by a mysterious force from below the water. Until recently the rare white crocodile could be found here and there is still a rich variety of fish.

Travellers looking for Ojo de Mar in 2007 discovered an amazing underground aquatic cavern almost 100m deep and 300m across, with various tunnels, all practically hidden by vegetation. It was named Kururú Kuá (Nest of Toads) and is a rare geological phenomenon because it is formed of sandstone.

THE EAST-NORTHEAST

So far we have been travelling to the north-northeast of the country, up Ruta 3 and Ruta 5. If instead of going directly north up Ruta 3, you take the Ruta 10 turn 12km north of the Tacuara junction, you pass into the Canindeyú *departamento* and reach a whole different area of the country – the east-northeast. Eventually, some 250km later, you reach the capital of Canindeyú: Salto del Guairá, on the Brazilian border. This is one of the least known regions of the country, though it has some of the greatest variety of fauna.

For the 165km to the east of Curuguatý, as far as Salto del Guairá, you are in what is effectively Brazilian territory within the Paraguayan state: Portuguese is spoken and the Brazilian currency, the real, is so predominant that even the Paraguayan police charge their fines in reais, not in guaraníes. Inhabitants are known as *brasiguayos*, meaning Brazilians who have occupied Paraguay. They have done so to find more land for growing genetically modified soya, and you will see it stretching from horizon to horizon for miles on end, on both sides of Ruta 10. You will also see frequent notices announcing the presence of the pesticide Roundup.

Paradoxically, on the edge of this ecological invasion is one of the most lovely and important nature reserves in the country, the Bosque Mbaracayú, which is reached via the town of Curuguatý. It is beginning to make an important mark on tourism, and the surrounding villages are improving facilities for visitors. See also the regional map for *Chapter 9*, page 296.

CURUGUATÝ *Copaco ☎ 048 210200/210299; Municipalidad ☎ 048 210226/7.* The name 'Curuguatý' is best known for being the site of scandalous massacre of six policemen and 11 *campesinos* on 15 June 2012 – a put-up job for deterring occupations by landless peasants and for levering President Lugo out of power. Fourteen innocent *campesinos* were subsequently jailed for supposed conspiracy, in order to protect the immunity of those who were really responsible for the deaths. The phrase '*Qué pasó en Curuguatý*' ('What happened in Curugutaý?') is one that you may see in graffiti or in publications, especially in Asunción, where the battle for justice is still being fought.

If you want to visit the site of the Curuguatý massacre, you should continue past the turning to the town, for another 40km on Ruta 10 in the direction of Salto del Guairá. For several years after the massacre there was an encampment at the roadside edge where you could speak to *campesinos* in the group that were ambushed during their peaceful demonstration – and it may still be there.

The town itself is a short distance north off Ruta 10. Ironically, the entrance is heralded with a notice proclaiming '*Libertad, Entendimiento, Orden…*' ('Freedom, Understanding, Order…'). To get to the plaza, which has a Wi-Fi zone, a taxi rank and a number of bars, turn left one block after the Financiera El Comercio.

Getting there and away The principal **bus** service to Curuguatý from Asunción is with the company Canindeyú (☎ *021 555991; Gs50,000*) and they run five services a day, with a journey time of about five hours. San Jorge (☎ *021 554877*) also have two services a day, and they go on to Villa Ygatimí, which takes another hour. See below under Bosque Mbaracayú. The number of the bus terminal in Curuguatý is ☎ 048 210262.

Where to stay

Hotel El Tigre 14 de mayo c/ 3 de noviembre; ☎ 048 210706; m 0983 946295. Bedrooms set around a courtyard, where wooden slatted hammocks are strung. Tiger theme to the décor. Half the rooms have split AC. Mostly commercial travellers Mon–Fri. **$**

Hotel Bello Horizonte (31 rooms) 14 de mayo esq. Juan José Rotela; ☎ 048 210335; www.bellohorizonte.com. Opposite El Tigre & bigger & cheaper, but without its charm. **$**

Where to eat and drink

Curtisom At the north end of town, on the road parallel to the main street, between police station & Barcos y Rodalos petrol station; ⊙ from 20.00. This Brazilian restaurant has more buzz than most. It serves pizzas & hamburgers & has tables both outside & under a roof. **$$**

El Buen Gusto II A block or 2 north of Hotel Tigre, on the right. Has chickens on spits. **$**

Juan Pabla Next door to the Hotel El Tigre; ⊙ from 20.00. A decent, simple restaurant. **$**

What to see and do There is a small **city museum** (◷ *07.00–13.00 daily*) with indigenous, industrial and historical items behind the Municipalidad (☎ *048 210226/7*), but you may wish to reserve your chief attention for the very interesting **Solar de Artigas** (◷ *07.00–11.00 Mon–Fri*). As you leave town in the direction of Villa Ygatimí, you turn left exactly where the asphalt ends, and the house is 200m down the road, on the right. Do not be deterred if you find it closed: the key holder Sonia Acosta (**m** *0983 486346*) lives opposite, in a green house, and is delighted to open it up to visitors (who come rather few and far between), no matter if they arrive within the official hours or not.

José Artigas (1764–1850) was a great Uruguayan politician, of egalitarian and federalist convictions, whose vision in the context of the newly independent South American states was finally defeated. Artigas had to seek exile, which was granted by Paraguay's Dr Francia in Curuguatý, and this small house is built on the site – and in the style – of the house where he lived out the last 24 years of his life. The house has been well presented as a museum by the Uruguayan government, who opened it in 2012 and inspect it monthly to check that the quality of their work is being maintained.

BOSQUE MBARACAYÚ (*Reserve* ☎ *021 3284980; Reserve* **m** *0985 261080/0971 282850; Asunción office* ☎ *021 608740/2 & 600855;* **e** *reservasmbaracayu@gmail.com; www.mbertoni.org.py*) The extensive Bosque Mbaracayú nature reserve is tucked up by the elbow of the Brazilian border, and with its infrastructure of information and tasteful rooms for guests, this is now one of the most interesting and attractive nature reserves to visit.

The origin of the reserve was in the work of anthropologists Kim Hill and Magdalena Hurtado, from the University of Emory, Atlanta, USA, who opposed an attempt by the World Bank to sell lands of the indigenous Aché people for commercial development. The forest's future came under threat, and they also received death threats before the reserve was created. The Mbaracayú Reserve is now well supplied with 18 trained park rangers, including some from the Aché people.

Getting there and away Driving to the Bosque Mbaracayú takes six hours from Asunción (375km). After passing through San Estanislao on Ruta 3, take Ruta 10 in the direction of Salto del Guairá. After 70km you turn left for the town of Curuguatý (see pages 355–6), and from there you carry on up the same road, which is no longer asphalted, for a further 42km to reach Villa Ygatimí, crossing the River Jejuí Guazú and then the River Jejuí-mí on the way. Some 9km after Villa Ygatimí you reach the turn right to the reserve, which is located 65km from Ruta 10, The journey will take you 2½ hours on a good day, because you are on dirt roads. If it rains a 4x4 is needed to reach the reserve.

It is a good idea to spend a night in Curuguatý before beginning the last leg, but if the road is asphalted (and there are demands for that to happen) then the advice may change.

If you want to spend a night in Villa Ygatimí instead of Curuguatý, you could try **Posada Tere Kañy** (☎ *0347 20023;* **m** *0982 325256;* **$**).

The reserve cannot be reached directly by public transport, but you can take an overnight bus (*company San Jorge;* ☎ *021 554877; depart Asunción 23.30; Gs60,000*) to Villa Ygatimí, arriving around 07.30, and from there you can be picked up, if a vehicle is available, for a cost of Gs250,000 (1–4 passengers). Another bus leaves Asunción at 14.00 for Villa Ygatimí but arrives too late for a pick-up. The principal bus company for this area is Canindeyú (☎ *021 555991; see page 355*), but their buses only go as far as Curuguatý, and Villa Ygatimí is a further two hours away. However, consult the people in the reserve about your best transport options.

The tour operator DTP Tours (☎ *021 221816;* **e** *info@dtp.com.py,* www.dtptour.com.py) also arranges visits to the Mbaracayú Reserve with meals and transport included.

Where to stay and eat To stay in the Bosque Mbaracayú, contact the Fundación Moisés Bertoni who administer the reserve and have their office in Asunción (*Prócer Argüello 208 e/ Mariscal López y Boggiani;* ☎ *021 608740;* **m** *0985 261080;* **e** *mbertoni@mbertoni.org.py; www.mbertoni.org.py*). You should apply at least two weeks in advance, and complete a form by email. You should allow at least three days at the reserve to see the principal sites, and to make the long journey worthwhile. Take lots of insect repellent, and binoculars if you have them. The Mbaracayú Lodge, officially opened in 2012, has 13 beautifully designed rooms and the prices are reasonable for the quality offered (**$$$**). There is Wi-Fi. Payment is in cash or by cheque.

The website has a version in English, but the best part of it – the film – is a little tricky to find: select Mbaracayú and then Mbaracayú Lodge. Even if you don't understand the Spanish, you will get the feel of the place.

What to see and do The visit to Mbaracayú is extremely interesting in all sorts of ways. First of all, you will be introduced early on to a young guide from an agricultural school for 150 local girls (including some indigenous) on the same site. She will show you the school and take you for your first short walk through the wood, helping you recognise the song of the famous and rare bellbird or *pajaro campana*, about which a famous piece of harp music has been written, or the toucan – another iconic bird of Paraguay. You get a feel of a dynamic, living project in the presence of these young girls studying to become technicians in environmental sciences. (Another place where a hotel is linked to an agricultural school is at Benjamín Aceval – see page 364.)

Secondly, you are also given the chance of a visit (*Gs10,000*) to the local community of Aché at the Arroyo Bandera settlement, where there are 25 families. The Aché are hunters and gatherers who have only recently come into contact with the rest of civilisation, but they now have electricity, water, a health centre and a school in this community. You can ask to see them fire arrows into the air, and buy a bow and arrow for yourself, or a fan woven from the leaves of the *pindo* palm tree. It may occasionally be possible, with sufficient notice, to spend a day hunting with them (*Gs150,000*), and witness their ancestral knowledge of how to track and trap animals.

In terms of nature study, you are in the region of the Atlantic forest of Alto Paraná – of which only 7% remains after deforestation. It has 89 species of mammals, including pumas, jaguars, tapirs, capuchin monkeys and maned wolves, and 411 species of birds, including 30 endangered species. This is the only place in the country where some species of birds unique to Paraguay may be commonly seen; for example, the horned screamer, the white-wedged piculet and the buff-bellied wren. Also found in the reserve is the powerful but rare harpy eagle, with its 7cm claws.

There is an excellent guide, Jovino, and a number of activities on offer, including early-morning birdwatching and late-night star gazing. On the walks through the forest you will be shown epiphyte and liana creepers above you, and tracks of tapirs and deer at your feet. You will see leaves of the *parirí* plant that the Aché use as plates and spoons, the *yvíra* from which they extract the strong fibre to make bags, and the *anastesia ka'aguy* that they use for its natural anaesthetic properties. The guide will point out the peroba tree (*Aspidosperma polyneuron*; Guaraní *yvyraromí*), a tree much sought after for furniture making and parquet flooring, because of the hardness and the deep pink of its wood, but in danger of extinction. The *yvyra'ro* is similar but has a very distinctive bark, with deep fissures making little waves up and down the trunk. You will see the ditches where animals go to eat the natural salt deposits, and the underground dens of the *akutí*, which have seven or eight exits to fool predators. You will see quantities of blue butterflies (*panambi hový*) and possibly the distinctive red head of the woodpecker (*carpintero*).

One morning's walk will take you to Arroyo Morotĩ ('white stream' in a mixture of Spanish and Guaraní). Another longer expedition, further north, leads to the 40m Salto Karapá waterfall, where you can climb safely (and with rather an excessive amount of safety equipment) from the top to the bottom. There is canoeing on the Jejuí-mí stream.

There is a trip along the 40km track that runs east–west through the reserve to the cerrado Aguara Ñu – quite a different ecoregion with its sandy, acid soil – and you will climb a 17m observation tower to gaze as far as the eye can see. The cerrado here is 6,000ha in extent, accounting for 10% of the reserve. Dwarf palms (*yata'í* or *butia paraguayensis*) cover the terrain, with a yellow-flowering tree (*palo vino*, for the wine-red colour of its sap, or *vochysia tucanorum*), a tree with a corky bark (*kurupa'ý kurú* or *anadenanthera colubrina*), a miniature and delicious form of guava (*guavirá mí*), grass, and hardly anything else.

In the evening, as you eat your meal, it is a delight to see foxes (*aguara'i*) come close to the house to scavenge.

YPEJHÚ If you want to explore further in these remote regions, Ypejhú is not far away – 35km north from Villa Ygatimí. It is on the edge of the hill range (*cordillera)* bordering Brazil, and has 20 waterfalls, including the 100m-high Salto Itá Kambý ('milk rock', so named for the whiteness of its foam). There is abseiling at Salto Yaguareté, which is 50m. Long sleeves and boots are advisable to guard against mosquitoes. The guide Lupe Rios can be contacted directly (**m** *0982 137691*).

Where to stay and eat There are several options for staying overnight. Alternatively, you can buy a 3-day packet trip to Curuguatý, Villa Ygatimí and Ypejhú which includes transport from and to Asunción (*information from* **m** *0981 226039;* **e** *turismo@mbertoni.org.py*). But it is expensive because of the long distances travelled, and the time span of three days does not do justice to all there is to see.

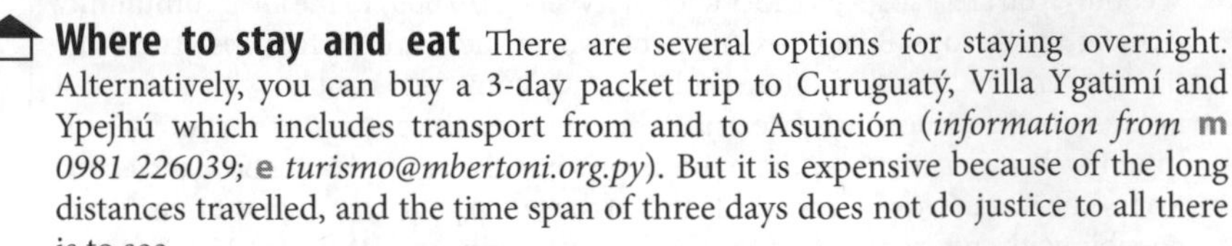

Hotel Restaurant Internacional m 0982 565 684/0973 620 724. Being on the border with Brazil, it is easy to be 'international' here. **$**

Posada La Familia m 0982 104835. Another family home that has opened up to receive guests. **$**

Posada Tajý Potý m 0981 641840. The name means 'the flower of the lapacho tree' – the beautiful pink blossom so characteristic of Paraguay. **$**

SALTO DEL GUAIRÁ (*Copaco* ☎ *046 242299; Municipalidad* ☎ *046 242206; www.guiasaltodelguaira.com*) Salto del Guairá, at the point furthest east of the Canindeyú *departamento*, 165km further east from the turn to Curuguatý, has grown into a sizeable city. It has rapidly expanded from 15,000 to 45,000 inhabitants in the last few years, from the economic stimulus of waves of Brazilians pouring over the borders to do their shopping. According to the staff in the Municipalidad, 95% of its movement is 'shopping tourism' – principally clothes, computers and electrical equipment – and it has been described as a mini Ciudad del Este.

This is a far cry from the hazardous Saltos del Guairá (the Falls of Guairá) that were famous for their role in the Jesuit-Guaraní exodus of 1631, and from which the city takes its name (albeit in the singular). There had been some seven major Falls (*Siete Caídas* or *Siete Saltos*) close to this spot, followed by many smaller ones over a long distance to the point where the Río Paraná joins the Río Iguazú, some 100km to the south, just after the latter river crashes over the famous Iguazú Falls. The Jesuit Antonio Ruiz de Montoya had to lead 12,000 Guaraní to negotiate their way past the Falls in their flight from the slave-traders. The journey was beset by hunger, disease and natural obstacles, and only 4,000 arrived safely in what is now Misiones Argentina. All their possessions, including fantastic carved statues and musical instruments, were launched over the massive Guairá waterfalls on rafts and smashed to smithereens, while the Guaraní struggled through the jungle on the bank. But since the formation of the hydro-electric project of the Itaipú dam, the dramatic Saltos del Guairá have been replaced by a tranquil feeder lake, and only the Iguazú Falls remain, on the Río Iguazú.

Getting there and away The **buses** that go to Salto del Guairá from Asunción are Ovetense (five a day), Canindeyú (four a day), Pycasú (two a day) and San Jorge (one a day); see page 50 for phone numbers. The journey takes eight hours via Ciudad del Este, or seven hours via Curuguatý.

If you are **driving**, see page 356 on getting to Mbaracayú. Then just carry on Ruta 10 until you reach Salto. If you are coming from Guairá, Brazil, the Ponte Ayrton Senna bridge (Brazilian at both ends) is a good 3km to the north as the crow flies. Some 5,000 cars cross it every working day, destined for Salto, and three times that number at weekends. After the bridge the road heads northwest, skirting a forest, and then there is a turn east into Paraguay and the road bends back on itself to descend to Salto del Guairá.

There is also a ferry or *balsa* (*08.00–17.00 Mon–Fri; Gs5,000 foot passengers; Gs15,000 cars*), which goes every hour on the hour and comes directly into Salto.

Getting around The bus terminal is on Defensa Nacional, three blocks east of the Avenida Paraguay, which is a broad road that runs south–north right through town. Two blocks down the Avenida to the left (south) you come to the *rotunda*, a big roundabout with a picture of the falls. Four blocks to the right (north) you come to a crossroads with the Avenida Bernardino Caballero, where you will see signs left to the airport (which is too small for passenger planes) and right to the *balsa* and *aduana* (customs).

If you are driving, as you reach the city on Ruta 10 there is a slight kink in the road towards the right, and shortly afterwards you turn 90 degrees left and find yourself on the Avenida, one block south of the rotunda. Then you pass the Shopping Kristal on the left, then the Municipalidad on the right, before reaching the junction with Bernardino Caballero. There is parking all down the middle of the Avenida.

If you continue straight on along the Avenida after this junction, you pass the Queen Anne Shopping on the right, then the Casino, Shopping China (on the left) and Shopping Salto (also on the left).

Where to stay

Hotel Casino 7 Saltos Resort (62 rooms) Ruta Internacional 29 de diciembre, km4,5; 046 243206; www.7saltos.com. Large new (2012) smart hotel with spa & pool, 4.5km north of town, before the turn towards the bridge. **$$$$**

Tower's Turismo Hotel (28 rooms) Carlos Méndez Gonzalves y El Maestro; 046 242096/242399; www.grupotowers.com. From the Avenida, turn right for 2 blocks at taxi *parada* 6 before Shopping China. Has a gym, pool, posh reception with comfy sofas & modern décor. **$$$$**

Hotel Lago Vista (17 rooms) Av Paraguay esq Camilo Recalde; 046 242957/242130; e lagovista-hotel@hotmail.com. One block south of where Ruta 10 joins the Avenida. Nice but busy, security guard, Wi-Fi. **$$$**

Hotel JR (24 rooms) San Miguel c/ Avenida Paraguay, 241; 046 242653; m 0984 321823. Mid-range. 3 blocks after the *rotunda* & 3 blocks before the 2nd roundabout, turn left just before Farmacia San Miguel. **$$$**

Hotel Santa Ana (26 rooms) Primera Junta Municipal c/ Bruno Otte; 046 242457; e santaana.saltos@gmail.com. Nicest looking of the modest places, but busy. Attractive garden, AC, TV, no Wi-Fi. A block in to the left as you enter town, before you turn left onto the Avenida. **$$**

Where to eat and drink

La Taberna 046 242220; 07.30–23.30 Tue–Sun. In the centre, 100m from the rotunda on the north side. Widely recommended. Self-service, hot dishes & salads. **$$$**

Dina Pizza On the top floor of Shopping Queen Anne; until 20.00. Pizzas, pastas, beer, no wine, excellent cocktails (try the Pina Colada). Good service & presentation. Menu in Portuguese but they accept guaraníes. **$$$**

La Varanda 046 243080. Brazilian restaurant on the Avenida, after the Shopping Queen Anne & the Casino. **$$$**

What to see and do There is not a lot to do apart from going shopping. A projected shopping centre, to be called Shopping Liberty (because it will have a big imitation Statue of Liberty outside) is going to have an ice rink inside – the first ice rink in Paraguay. This shopping centre will be on the Ruta Internacional, north of town, just 100m from the customs (*aduana*).

Not to be confused with the Bosque Mbaracayú Reserve run by the Moisés Mbertoni foundation (see page 357), there is a much smaller nature reserve with the same name of Mbaracayú (m *0983 675692; Asunción office* m *0973 864711*) bordering on Salto del Guairá just to the north. You reach it by turning right from Avenida Paraguay onto Yegros, and then it is 1km along on the left. It is not normally open to the public but persistent bird watchers have been known to negotiate their way inside, and researchers with appropriate authorisation and paperwork have no problem.

A fabulous Museo de las Aguas is planned on the riverside, with a block dedicated to 'Water for Life', expressing the importance of water for the future of the world, and including a library. Another block will be dedicated to 'Life in Water', an aquarium where the fish can be viewed from an underground glass tunnel. The project is the work of Italian architect Ettore Piras, who designed the night walk of Trinidad, and will include a multi-coloured illuminated fountain. But work cannot start on it until the *costanera* (coast road) is built, and they are still waiting for that.

UPDATES WEBSITE

You can post your comments and recommendations, and read the latest feedback and updates from other readers, online at www.bradtupdates.com/paraguay.

12

The Chaco

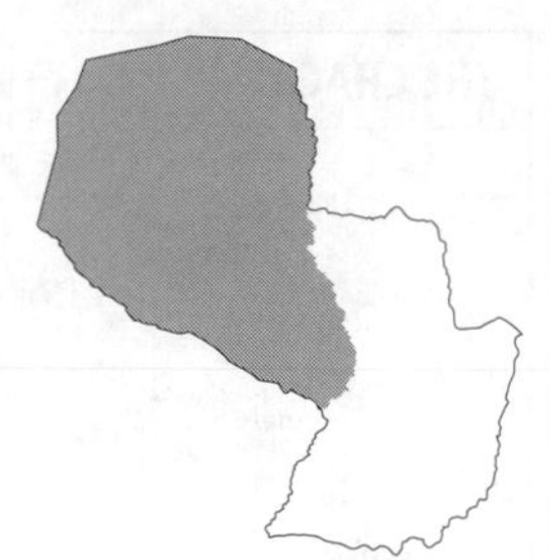

Departamentos: Presidente Hayes; gobernación *0226 262403*
Boquerón; gobernación *0491 432052/432051*
Alto Paraguay; gobernación *021 440961/0497 281005*

If you like your travel to be an adventure in remote regions, you might be interested in going to the Chaco. This is a chapter for explorers rather than regular tourists.

The Chaco has been called the Green Inferno. It is a sort of desert, though that may puzzle the visitor who begins to drive through and sees green vegetation everywhere and pools of water. In the southern Chaco, the earth is a grey, salty clay, unlike the red earth of eastern Paraguay, and few plants can tolerate it. What rainfall there is sits uselessly in ponds where the salt content makes it unfit for either drinking or promoting vegetation. This humid Chaco ecoregion goes up approximately to Pozo Colorado, traversed by tributaries from the Río Paraguay. Above that is the dry Chaco.

The tropic of Capricorn passes through the Chaco, at the level of Pozo Colorado, so most of the Chaco has a tropical climate, with greater heat than the more populated areas of eastern Paraguay, and with dry and rainy seasons. There is hardly any rainfall in the dry season (March–September).

The scenery is scrubland and totally flat (except for the Cerro León mountain in the north) and is used for cattle grazing, divided into huge *estancias*. The few houses you will see from the road – the Ruta Transchaco – are the poorest kind of wooden hovels, either thatched or with rusty corrugated iron roofs. Later on, in the affluent Mennonite settlements, you will see that even the mansions tend to have corrugated iron roofs: it is the best way of collecting rainwater.

In this arid and inhospitable land, almost every tree has thorns. The most distinctive trees are the *karanda'ý* and the *samu'ú* (*Chorisia insignis*). The former (*Copernicia alba*) is the Chaco palm tree, taller and more decorative than the *cocotero* of western Paraguay: the trunk, split in half, makes excellent walls – as can be observed in the Pa'i Pukú school (see page 366) – and the foliage forms a rounder circle at the top of the trunk, with a more intricate silhouette. It is not found all over the Chaco, but a couple of hours south of Filadelfia you can see plenty, down to Asunción. The *samu'ú*, or *palo borracho* in Spanish (drunken pole), sometimes known in English as the bottle tree, is a tree that stores water in its heavily swollen trunk. Thorns sit on this fat trunk, and further up the tree narrows before splaying out into delicate foliage. It is a very distinctive tree, much associated with Paraguay. During the Chaco War, the *samu'ú* was hollowed out to make a hiding place for an armed guard.

A beautiful, fragrant wood that only grows in the South American Chaco is *palo santo* (*Bulnesia sarmientoi*) or 'holy wood'– a protected tree with a slow growth rate of 200 years to develop fully. It produces a beautiful, hard, fragrant, olive-green wood that is much used in craftwork. It survives in this dry climate because its leaves are small and leathery. Also distinctive to the Chaco is the white *quebracho*,

popularly known in English as the break-axe tree. The indigenous eat the purple fruit of the cactus, and *poroto del monte* (wild beans). Another Chaco fruit that is good to eat is the *nistol*, which is like a small apple.

Until a few decades ago, the Chaco was inhabited only by indigenous, and it was not entirely clear whether it belonged to Paraguay or to Bolivia: both countries believe that it had always been theirs, and a variety of interpretations can be seen in maps of the time. The situation changed when the US Standard Oil company, which was working in Bolivia, announced that there was oil in the Chaco. Meanwhile Royal Dutch Shell encouraged Paraguay to hold on tightly to its territory. It suddenly became important for both countries to confirm their claim to the land, and Bolivia also had the motivation of needing access to the River Paraguay, to have a route to the sea for exporting it.

In 1925 Bolivia began to build forts in the Chaco to stake their claim, and a bitter war was fought in appalling conditions of drought – the War of the Chaco, or as Paraguay prefers to say, the War for the Defence of the Chaco, 1932–35. Paraguay basically won the war, though it was disappointed in being obliged by international pressure to cede some land back to Bolivia in the final settlement. In total, about 100,000 men had lost their lives in the war.

The oil, if it exists, has not yet materialised (although as recently as June 2014 the London-based company President Energy announced it was drilling a large area of 34,000km² in the north west Chaco, east of Neuland, with the hope of opening up 'a significant new hydrobarbon province'). But winning the war had huge symbolic importance for Paraguay, as a sign of national dignity after being so extensively destroyed in the earlier War of the Triple Alliance. But blame is also laid on Britain and the USA for encouraging a conflict to protect their respective economic interests.

The Chaco covers almost 300,000km², and accounts for 61% of Paraguay's territory, but only includes 3% of its population. It would be even more uninhabited had it not been for the arrival of the **Mennonites**, a Christian pacifist church originating in Switzerland which has been wandering the earth for 400 years seeking a land where they can live out their beliefs apart, without being absorbed into the local population. In 1927 they began to arrive in the Chaco, in a migration they describe as 'unsurpassed by anything in history since the Pilgrims sailed from Delft Haven'. Although they were arriving during the tensions immediately leading up to the Chaco War, they had no fear because their pacifism kept them safe from reprisals, and a Paraguayan government charter granted them exemption from military service. Since then they have been turning the desert into a land of fertility and plenty, so that today the Mennonite towns of Filadelfia, Loma Plata and Neuland are attracting internal immigration of Paraguayans from eastern Paraguay, looking for work.

WITHIN REACH OF ASUNCIÓN

Crossing the Puente Remanso bridge feels like going into another country because it is sizeable and has a customs post (*aduana*). Immediately after the bridge is a big junction where you choose either to go north (for the great wild) or to take the western road that runs parallel to the river and takes you to the border with Argentina, and beyond that to Clorinda. About 4km before the border is a crossroads and a café, the Copetín Al Paso. The road south goes to the village of Chaco'i, which almost faces Asunción on the northern bank of the Río Paraguay. (Chaco'i can also be reached by boat from the port of Asunción, which is more fun.) Down the same turning you can take another right (west) marked 'Barrio Monte Pila' which will take you to a footbridge to Clorinda, Argentina. But you can only cross here if you have a Mercosur identity card; there is no passport office.

If you go north at the crossroads you skirt the little town of Falcón, and continue on the very poor and pitted road that is Ruta 12, running parallel to the Río Pilcomayo. It leads to a few military outposts, but nowhere else that you are likely to want to visit. Although there is a bridge at General Bruguez, leading to General Belgrano, Argentina, it is kept locked.

But if you go north as soon as you cross into the Chaco, at the Puente Remanso, (ie: turn right rather than left), you come to a couple of towns, both in easy reach of Asunción. The first is Villa Hayes, and the second is Benjamín Aceval.

Villa Hayes is named after US President Rutherford B. Hayes, who awarded the territory to Paraguay in a boundary dispute with Argentina after the Triple Alliance War, but the large statue of a man on a horse that you drive around is not of him but of Mariscal Estigarribia, hero of the Chaco War.

The town is set mostly to the right (southeast) of the Ruta: turn right at the traffic lights between Petrobras and the Banco Visión, and follow the avenue down to the river. There is a very pleasant frontage on to the Río Paraguay, with a statue of Benjamin Aceval (the Paraguayan diplomat who took the documents to Hayes) looking out over the river. You can watch the water weeds drifting down the river and observe people fishing. If you turn right you come to a small municipal museum bearing the name Don Salvador Garozzo Simon, but you may find it closed even during its announced opening hours (*09.00–noon & 15.00–18.00 Wed–Sun*). Work is currently beginning on forming a Parque Costero (coastal park) along this very attractive riverfront, which will offer boat trips: it is anticipated the construction work will take four years to complete.

Only five minutes further along the Ruta Transchaco is **Benjamin Aceval**, with the lovely and interesting Hotel Cerrito at its further end (see below). Just south of the Hotel Cerrito, on the same west side of the road, is a **monastery** of Discalced Carmelite nuns, who are enclosed. You are welcome to go and talk to a sister through a special window that offers better protection than a grille, because you cannot even see the outline of the person you are talking to (*08.00–11.00 & 15.00–17.00 Mon–Sat, except in Lent and Advent; mass 06.45 Mon–Wed & Fri–Sat, 07.00 Sun & Thu*).

WHERE TO STAY AND EAT

Hotel Cerrito (16 double rooms, but total capacity 250 persons) Ruta 9 (Transchaco) km46.5; 0271 272799; www.hotelcerrito.com.py. Reached along a short lane (800km) on the west side of the road at the north end of town. This hotel is run by pupils at an agricultural school, the Escuela Agrícola San Francisco, which was originally run by Franciscan friars, but is now a project of the Fundación Paraguaya (*www.fundacionparaguaya.org.py*), a non-profit-making organisation. (Another such hotel-agricultural school supported by the same foundation is at Mbaracayú; see page 357.) The pupils are trained in agronomy & hotel work, with alternate weeks in the fields & in the hotel. The hotel has most impressive facilities: there is a large, attractive lounge, & the bedrooms are tastefully decorated (dorms with bunks, lockers & fans; double rooms with private bathrooms & split AC; self-contained bungalows). Organic food is grown on site. You can spend a day with the students as they go about their activities of organic cultivation, & rear pigs, chickens & rabbits. There is craft from the nearby Toba Qom (Guaicurú) indigenous community; a visit can be arranged. Wi-Fi, cable TV, cycling, billiards, ping pong, horse carts & facilities for conferences. Particularly suitable for big groups as there is a shortage of rooms with private bathrooms, but also offers an opportunity for anyone to visit the Chaco without a long journey (40mins from Asunción). Price depends on package. **$$**

La Casona Ruta 9, km44 – Carlos Antonio López c/ Humaitá; 0271 273061; m 0983 151119. Comfortable recommended restaurant with Paraguayan & international food; but they also do fast food like pizzas, *lomitos*, *chipas* & ice creams. To have more choice than the one *plato del día* it is a good idea to book in advance. **$$**

TRAVELLING ALONG THE RUTA TRANSCHACO

Most of the traffic that crosses the bridge Puente Remanso over the Río Paraguay, immediately to the north of Asunción, turns sharp left and takes a short stretch of Ruta 12 to the frontier with Argentina. On the Paraguayan side of the border there is Puerto José Falcón (close to Nanawa), and on the Argentinian side Clorinda, and then, 200km south, the more substantial town of Formosa. This is the most frequent route by which Paraguayans go to Buenos Aires – by bus. (The alternative bus route to Buenos Aires via Posadas is used by Paraguayans who live further south, in Misiones or Itapúa.) The border post is at the Río Pilcomayo, and is open 24 hours.

If you turn north just before Falcón, Ruta 12 will take you parallel to the Río Pilcomayo, as far as the Parque Nacional Tinfunque, a nature reserve on the humid Chaco ecoregion. Beware, however, that only the first stretch of this road is asphalted, and when you get to Tinfunque there are no provisions for visitors.

If, however, you want to visit the central Chaco, turn right and go up Ruta 9, known as the Ruta Transchaco.

BY BUS Once it has passed Villa Hayes (12km) and Benjamín Aceval (11km), the Ruta Transchaco continues for miles and miles with no civilisation in sight. After about an hour you will notice that it is a rarity to pass a vehicle coming in the opposite direction. The road plunges straight ahead until it narrows to a tiny gap on the horizon, in which you will occasionally see the distant dot of another vehicle coming towards you. The advantage of going by bus on this deserted road rather than by car is not only that it is cheap, but that if the vehicle breaks down it is somebody else's problem.

The bus companies that serve the towns up the Ruta Transchaco are Nasa/Golondrina (☎ *021 551731*) and Stel Turismo (☎ *021 551680*); for more details see below under the different towns, and also the section on arriving by bus from Bolivia, on pages 36–7.

BY CAR Though the drive through the Chaco is exceedingly long, there are often opportunities to see interesting fauna. In addition to having a rich bird life, the Chaco is the habitat for many mammals too, and as you drive along the Ruta Transchaco, you may see foxes, deer and armadillos.

There is a plan by Senatur (the ministry of tourism) to provide observation towers on the Ruta Transchaco, with information, both written and audio, about what you can see. If this is realised, it will be a reason for considering making the journey by car rather than by bus, which at present is the recommended option.

If you decide to drive, here is a list of where you can find food, drink and in some places a bed on the Ruta Transchaco, beyond Villa Hayes and Benjamín Aceval:

Bar-Parador Tacuara km101 **$**
Bar-Parador Río Negro km170 **$**
Bar-Parador Montelindo km210 **$**
Parador Pirahú km249; m 0972 700683/389889. Recommended. **$**
Bar-Parador Ka'i km243 **$**
Restaurant-Parador Touring Pozo Colorado, km270 (see page 366)
Hotel-Restaurant Búfalo Bill km283. m 0981 496549 Lake & mini-zoo. **$$**
Hotel-Restaurant Los Pioneros km 410 ☎ 0491 432170; m 0981 327966. **$$**
Hotel del Touring km443 (see page 369)

After that, you are on your own, and you still have another 300km or so to go to the frontier. The usual crossing point is from the military outpost of Infante Rivarola, Paraguay, which brings you to Villa Montes, Bolivia. This involves swinging west from La Patria, from where there is another road, not yet asphalted, going in a more northerly direction to cross the frontier at Hito III, after the military outpost of General G E Garay. You are strongly advised to take the asphalted road.

Until a very few years ago, the asphalt ran out somewhere in the middle of the road to Bolivia, and if you were crossing in the rainy season you were liable to be stuck in the mud for several days on end, without access to food or water. One traveller said this was the best bit of his journey, because he forged such strong friendships with the other stranded passengers. Be that as it may, the road is now asphalted all the way to Bolivia, but not the side roads – except for the one leading to Concepción. However, the asphalt has already deteriorated badly in places, so that there are pits in the road that could damage your vehicle if you drove fast through them. This is particularly so from about 50km before Filadelfia, until Mariscal Estigarribia, and also on the east–west stretch that links Pozo Colorado with Concepción, with the result that this is no longer the preferred bus route from Asunción to Concepción.

If you want to **drive** your own vehicle, and to leave the main road to go on dirt roads, then you will need to hire a 4x4 from a company such as Touring Cars (*Yegros 1045 c/ Tte Fariña;* ☎ *021 375091/447945;* e *reservas@touringcars.com.py; www.touringcars.com.py*) – but at a price: see page 70 for an idea of the cost.

The advice of the local Paraguayan guidebook, *La Magia de Nuestra Tierra*, should be taken to heart before you plunge into the terrain of interminable dirt tracks: 'Remember, before you try to have an adventure in the Chaco, that it is an inhospitable, desert territory, where many people have died of thirst. It is easy to get lost because it is flat and lacks points of reference.' For this reason no details are given here of the dirt road that takes you to the border at Hito IV, or of the bridge into Argentina at Pozo Hondo, which crosses the Río Pilcomayo near the triple frontier of Paraguay, Argentina and Bolivia.

TOURS If you want to visit the Chaco with a guide, Touring (*Touring y Automovil Club Paraguayo, Brasil c/ 25 de mayo;* ☎ *021 210550;* ⏲ *08.00–17.00 Mon–Fri, 08.00–noon Sat;* e *info@tacpy.com.py; www.tacpy.com.py*) offers a trip of up to 3 days, visiting Loma Plata, Filadelfia and Boquerón. Whereas you can visit Loma Plata and Filadelfia perfectly well by yourself, taking the bus, Boquerón is a bit more complicated – though it still might be preferable to ask the tourist office in Filadelfia (where they speak superb English) to arrange your guided tour to Boquerón, starting from Filadelfia. For more exploratory tours into the interior of the Chaco you should only go with people who really know the terrain. More details are given in the course of this chapter.

THE HUMID CHACO, UP TO POZO COLORADO

After 2½ hours of hard driving, you come to the **Escuela Pa'i Pukú** (*Ruta Transchaco km156;* ☎ *0891 8033*) immediately on the right of the highway. If you get a chance to visit this educational establishment, take it: it has been beautifully and simply constructed, with a chapel built from tree trunks and full-throated birdsong in the garden painstakingly constructed by the pupils, with fertile earth and water transported in buckets. The school is run for the children of poor families in far-flung *estancias*, and the furniture made by the pupils is highly sought after. It can be ordered through the Asunción office of the foundation (*Defensa Nacional 846;* ☎ *021 226699;* e *fundacionpaipuku@rieder.net.py*).

POZO COLORADO Another couple of hours or more of hard driving will take you to Pozo Colorado, some 250km northwest of Asunción, and about one third of the way up the Chaco. Here you can find petrol, a mechanic to mend your car and a hotel to stay the night. If you are travelling to Concepción via the Ruta Transchaco (whether by bus or car) you will turn sharp east at Pozo Colorado. Work is currently underway to improve that 138km of poor asphalt from Pozo Colorado across the Chaco to the Nanawa bridge and Concepción.

Where to stay The **Parador del Touring** (*Ruta 9 km270;* m *0971 395750;* **$$**) is run by the national motoring organisation TACPy (see *Tours*, above).

FILADELFIA

Copaco ☎ 0491 432012; municipalidad ☎ 0491 433374/6

Filadelfia (about 70km further north than Boquerón), Loma Plata and Neuland are three Mennonite towns, sited close to each other right in the middle of the Chaco, more than halfway up. Filadelfia is 13km north of the Ruta Transchaco. Loma Plata is also to the north (21km), and Neuland is 20km to the south.

In Filadelfia there are recognised groupings of other nations and races, although the Mennonites run the town through their *cooperativa* and comprise 30% of the population. There are four indigenous communities – the Nivaclé, the Guaraní, the Lengua and the Ayoreo – who account for 60% of the population. The remaining 10% are Latinos – that is, Paraguayans, Argentinians and Brazilians who are neither Mennonites nor indigenous. Each grouping lives in its own barrio, like a self-enclosed colony.

The economy of Filadelfia is based in big companies producing dairy products, and peanuts for export.

GETTING THERE AND AWAY Filadelfia is the easiest to access of the Mennonite towns and has most to see. You would be advised to use it as a base, from where you can visit the other towns if you wish. Some **buses** to Fildelfia go on to Loma Plata, and others do not. The main bus company serving the area is Nasa (*☎ 021 551731 in Asunción; ☎ 0491 432492 in Filadelfia*), which also uses the name Golondrina. Nasa buses leave the Asunción Terminal at 06.00, 14.30, 21.15, 22.00 and 23.00, and the journey takes around six hours. For the return journey, Nasa buses leave Filadelfia at 07.00, 13.00, 14.30, 21.00 and 22.00. The first two of these buses go via Loma Plata. Buses from Stel Turismo (*☎ 021 558051*) leave the Terminal in Asunción at 19.00 every day and go to Loma Plata as well as Filadelfia, but their buses, though good in quality, have more stops and arrive in Filadelfia at 02.00 (*Gs80,000*). The return journey is made from Filadelfia at 18.00.

If you are driving **your own vehicle**, you can find petrol at the service station on the corner of the turn to Filadelfia, and in Filadelfia itself there are five petrol stations. If you are stuck at night-time, it is worth knowing that there is a 24-hour service station in Neuland.

GETTING AROUND You can buy a map of Filadelfia in the post office on Avenida Hindenburg. The town is composed of wide, long avenues of grey clay, but the two principal *avenidas*, Hindenburg and Trébol, are asphalted. They cross at the Second Monument (see page 370), close to the Hotel Florida.

Here is the sequence of the streets on the usual grid system. Going south of Trébol you come to in order: Unruh, Industrial, Chaco Boreál, Boquerón, Palo Santo, Amistad and Carayá. Heading north from Trébol: Bender, Asunción, and several more streets, going into Mennonite territory. From Hindenburg, if you go east you come to: Miller, Gondra, Harbiner-Strasse, Quebracho, etc. Finally, going west from Hindenburg: Estigarribia, 25 de noviembre, Urundeý and Concordia.

If you are staying in Filadelfia's Hotel Golondrina or the Hotel Florida, the **bus** will take you to the door. Otherwise, the principal bus stop is known as the Parada de Nasa (or as Agencias), which is on Chaco Boreal, three blocks south and half a block east from the Second Monument. There is a **taxi** rank around the corner on Hindenburg.

The **bus** journey from Filadelfia to Loma Plata takes half an hour, and can be done with the company Nasa (*☎ 0491 432492*). One bus leaves Filadelfia at 07.00 and passes through Loma Plata on its way to Asunción, and another at 13.00. For

MENNONITE TOWNS

Contrary to expectations in this remote and arid land, the towns founded by the Mennonites are modern cities, where many things work as well as, or better than, they do in Asunción. It is difficult to imagine a starker cultural contrast than that of Germanic peoples and Paraguayan Latinos, and the Germanic influence here produces a different kind of culture. Phones work, electricity does not fail, window frames fit, and schools open like clockwork even in the torrential rain. Large supermarkets are better stocked than in most other parts of the country, even though it is a six-hour hard drive to their source of supply in Asunción.

The Mennonites were given the most difficult of all terrains to farm, but in the course of a few decades they have turned it around to the point where Paraguayans are flocking in, in search of work – indigenous from the rest of the Chaco, and Latinos from the east of the country. But the Mennonites keep a tight control on the positions of power: only those who can establish their Mennonite ancestry can gain a place in their barrios, which are full of mansions and fruit trees, and the financial bonuses of the *cooperativa* (the civic organisation that runs everything) are reserved for Mennonites alone. While the other races live better here than in the places they came from, they also feel they are locked forever into being second-class citizens. They receive at least the legal minimum wage, but the cost of living is double here what it is in the rest of the country.

Loma Plata was the first Mennonite town, founded in 1927 by settlers from Canada, who in turn had come from Russia (where they had gone to in 1789, after a time in Prussia, from 1535, and in Holland, from 1530). Filadelfia was founded in 1930 by Mennonites coming more directly from Russia, fleeing the Stalinist regime and the repression of peasants. Neuland was not founded until after World War II.

There are also Mennonites in eastern Paraguay, where they hold onto their group identity by conservative practices that mark them out as different: the men wear black dungarees, and the women flowery, gathered dresses and headscarves. The Chaco Mennonites, by contrast, are culturally and economically progressive, and look like an ordinary group of modern, educated Germans.

the return from Loma Plata , there is a bus (coming from Asunción) that passes through Loma Plata at about 14.00 on its way to Filadelfia.

TOURIST INFORMATION Everything in the Mennonite towns is run by the local Mennonite co-operative, which here is called the **Fernheim Cooperative** (www.fernheim.com.py; *they have a English version of their website).* The tourist information office is just one of the services run by the co-operative. It is situated next to the museum (☎ *0491 417380;* **m** *0985 820746;* **e** *turismo@fernheim.com.py;* ⏲ *07.00–11.30*), and it offers access to the museum and can arrange guided tours not only to the town but to other places in the Chaco. They speak good English, and have guides who also speak English and Spanish, as well as their native German (though they are not always available as they have to take other jobs to make a living). If you want to visit Boquerón (see pages 371–2), or anywhere else in the region, this is probably the best place to ask (but for the salt lakes see page 374). They are in the process of becoming a proper tour operator with the name Conretur.

A tour company called **Gran Chaco Turismo**, which began a few years ago, is still in business, although it no longer has an office open to the public. Norbert Epp (m *0981 223974* ; e *info@granchacoturismo.net; www.granchacoturismo.net*) who runs it, has to work as a teacher and is not always available for a tour. Guided tours can be in Spanish, German or English, and outside of Filadelfia most of the tours proposed are to one or other of the ports on the Río Paraguay, although in principal he can take you to almost anywhere in the Chaco.

WHERE TO STAY

Hotel Florida (40 rooms) Av Hindenburg e/ Unruh y Trébol; 0491 432151/5; e hotelflorida@fernheim.com.py; www.hotelfloridachaco.com. Generally agreed to be the best hotel. Opposite the museum. Excellent food, good service, pool & a pleasant inside courtyard. Rooms in old building are cheaper. **$$**

Hotel del Touring (16 rooms) Cruce Filadelfia, Ruta 9 km443; 0493 240611; m 0981 216759; [email] hoteltouringchaco@gmail.com. Not in Filadelfia itself, but on the Ruta Transchaco. Pool, restaurant. **$$**

Estancia Iparoma m 0981 940050; www.estanciaiparoma.com. A little way out of town (19km), but worth the journey. Take Hindenburg (the north-south road in Filadelfia) & continue north of town for 12km, then right & after only 140m left, so you are continuing directly north, then follow the signs. They will collect you at no cost if you stay more than 3 days. Horse carts, riding, swimming in natural mineral pools, watch cattle daily routine. Camping. Day visits. Also offers tours. **$**

Hotel Golondrina (49 rooms) Av Hindenburg 635-Sur; 0491 432643/43111; e info@hotelgolondrina.com; www.hotelgolondrina.com. The next recommendation after the Florida, 5½ blocks south of the Second Monument, & 1½ north of the Third Monument. White tiled floors, TVs, restaurant (closed Sat eve). There are cheaper rooms with fans & fewer facilities. **$**

Los Delfines Unruh esq Miller; 0491 432376. This place 1 block south & 1 block east of the Second Monument is more modest & much cheaper, with a more Latin feel. Plebeian, slightly seedy, bit of a motel in the Paraguayan sense (see page 394), but if you can cope with that it has a buzz of the kind you do not find in the German establishments. Cheaper rooms have fans & shared bathrooms. Restaurant. **$**

WHERE TO EAT AND DRINK

Hotel Florida See above. Has a good reputation for food. **$$**

Girasol Calle Unruh c/ Hindenburg 126-E; 0491 432078. Considered one of the best restaurants. **$$**

El Rincón In the shopping centre Portal del Chaco, at the entrance to the town, next to the monument where the Ruta Transchaco meets the town; 0491 432496. Extensive menu & even a simple hamburger & salad is excellent. On Sat night & Sun lunchtime they offer *asado* & a buffet. **$$**

Restaurant Boquerón Boquerón c/ Miller; 0491 433788. In the shopping centre Boquerón, 1 block to the south from the Parada de Nasa. Has a *patio de comidas* with excellent quality food at cheap prices. **$**

Spazio Restaurant Opposite Remi (see below); 0491 433626. Fast food. **$**

Restaurant Remi Calle Unruh c/ Gondra y Miller. Modest pizzeria & ice cream parlour, opposite Spazio, mostly for young people. **$**

OTHER PRACTICALITIES Next door to the Hotel Florida is El Mensajero – a **bookshop** that sells indigenous crafts as well as books and postcards. There is an Itaú bank in the Portal del Chaco shopping centre (at the entrance to town), with a cash machine. The **post office** is on the corner opposite the museum. Mennonite businesses observe strict **opening hours** (*07.00–11.30 and 14.30–18.00*), and only the supermarkets stay open an hour or two longer. By 20.00 it is a dead city, apart from inside the restaurants.

WHAT TO SEE AND DO An ambitious new *Centro de Interpretación* for the Chaco is currently being designed for Filadelfia, to open in 2015. It will include thematic circuits on fauna, flora, history and local culture, as well as observation platforms, cycle tracks and paths for walking.

The **Museum** (☎ *0491 417329;* ⏲ *07.00–11.30 Mon–Sat*) is next to the tourist office, and occupies two adjacent buildings, on Avenida Hindenburg e/ Calle Unruh y Trébol. Jakob Unger had been the first of the pioneers to propose a scientific study of the fauna of the Chaco. One of the buildings is an original house of the colony. On the ground floor it contains a collection of Mennonite bits and pieces, including a butter churn, and the printing press for the Mennonite paper *Mennoblatt*, which is still published today. Upstairs are items used by the indigenous (bows and arrows, bags, etc) and relics of the Chaco War.

In the second building (which was previously a primary school) is the natural history section, with many stuffed animals, including a jaguar, armadillo, coati, puma, anteater, wolf, tapir, tree sloth, skunk and boa constrictor. There are also 210 out of the 250 bird species in the Chaco, and a large section devoted to insects. There is a new room with a display on trees and wood of the Chaco, and there is a section on the history of the town. The museum has a pleasant garden – the Plaza de los Recuerdos – and the **First Monument** erected in town, a small obelisk, placed in 1955, on the 25th anniversary of the foundation of the town.

The **Second Monument** was put up on the 50th anniversary, and is not far away, in the centre of the junction of Avenida Hindenburg and Avenida Trébol. The **Third Monument** (erected on the 75th anniversary) is a more ambitious affair at the entrance to the town (Hindenburg y Carayá): five figures of varying heights hold up a ring with a cross in the middle. It looks its best at night when it is floodlit, and resembles a crown.

There are three principal **Mennonite churches** in town, and the one on Avenida Hindenburg (two blocks north of the Librería El Mensajero) includes an old church, now used as a dining room, as well as the modern ramped church they use today, with simultaneous translation for visitors.

The zoo in Parque Eirene was closed a few years ago, because of the costs of providing regular veterinary attention to the animals.

It is not recommended to visit the indigenous communities unless you have an introduction: the people do not like being gazed at like animals in cages. However, there is an opportunity at carnival time, when the **Guaraní** in Filadelfia issue a general invitation over the radio for anyone to join them in their annual festival.

The **Areté Guasú** ('Big Day') of the Guaraní people coincides with Carnival (that is, just before Lent, in fact the Sunday, Monday and Tuesday before Ash Wednesday). It is even referred to as their Carnival. It takes place in Filadelfia in the social club of their barrio, which is an open, roofed area. The condition of attendance is that you must join in the dancing – which can be quite energetic, and may include being rolled in mud. They wear long costumes and masks – of tigers, pigs or frightening faces of dead ancestors. There are good spirits in white that invite people to join the dance, and bad spirits in black who take people out and throw them in the mud. The music is played on their traditional instruments, such as flutes and drums. The tradition is to dance three days and nights without stopping (in teams) and to drink *chicha*, a drink of the fermented fruit of the *algarroba* – a tree that grows only in the Chaco. The third day has the most people. The Guaraní in Filadelfia now speak the same Guaraní as the rest of Paraguay, though originally the dialect was distinct.

The **Lengua**, also known as the Enxet (variously spelt Enlhet) are a little shorter and have rounder faces. They moved to Filadelfia in the early 1980s, when they came (like the other indigenous peoples) to seek work for the men in the construction industry, and for the women in domestic work. They are now losing touch with their traditional communities in the *campo*. The married Lengua women wear long skirts covering their ankles.

The **Nivaclé** are known for the beauty of their women. In the old system of leadership, the leader would be someone who had fought tigers or showed similar physical prowess, but with the move to urban life, leaders are now elected who can read and write. The Nivaclé tend to be Catholic, evangelised by the Oblates (order of priests) who came out to the Chaco in 1925, and the Sisters of St Joseph of Cluny are working with them now. (The other principal evangelisation in the Chaco was initiated by the Salesians, in the north reaches of the River Paraguay.) The Nivaclé come out in force for a monthly mass in the **church of San Eugenio de Macenod**, which has a vividly painted back wall behind the altar showing a surprisingly feminine Christ crucified and a balanced pair of male and female Christian evangelists. The Nivaclé all sit on the right of the church, while the Guaraní sit on the left with the other racial groupings that make up this lively Catholic congregation, principally Brazilians and Germans.

The **Ayoreo** are semi-nomadic and are the people who have been least changed by the process of development. Their presence in Filadelfia was a point of conflict in the past, when they were seen as a danger to their neighbours, and they were removed from Filadelfia. But a smaller group returned after a while to seek work, the women mostly in prostitution and the men in unskilled labour. The Ayoreo people are the ones who make the very attractive fibre bags, coloured in earthy browns and reds. They also sometimes sell honey that they have collected from the wilds. They do not at present have a designated barrio.

BOQUERÓN

Boquerón is a little to the south of Filadelfia, just off the Ruta Transchaco to the west, but you will probably want to go to Filadelfia first and do Boquerón as an excursion. It is the site of the most famous battle of the Chaco War, and the victory of Boquerón is a national feast day celebrated on 29 September. (The other national holiday relating to that war is the Paz del Chaco, the declaration of Peace, on 12 June.)

In 1928 the fort of Boquerón was taken by Bolivia, but then taken back by Paraguay. In July 1932 Bolivia took the fort again, and in September the same year it was retaken by Paraguay, in a costly and bloody siege that marked a decisive victory for Paraguay. The fort was considered important because it had a small lake, in this dry terrain. It still took Paraguay another three years to push the Bolivians right out of the Chaco, and the peace settlement was not signed until 1938.

GETTING THERE AND AWAY It is worth the effort to visit the site: it is respectful, informative and tragic. However, it is not easy to find as there are no road signs, and no people around to ask. The safest way to get there is to go with a guide from the tourist office (see page 368), and although it will cost half a million guaraníes, most of that is the inevitable cost of the transport. Failing that, take a **taxi** for the 70km from Filadelfia, which will probably cost more than Gs400,000, or at least to get someone from the locality who knows the roads to accompany you if you are in a hire car.

WHAT TO SEE AND DO The Boquerón site (m *Carlos Aguero 0981 242420;* 🕘 *07.00–17.00 Wed–Sun; free admission*) is officially closed on Monday and Tuesday, but it is still possible to visit if you walk in: the gate will be closed to vehicles and the museum will be closed but you can walk around. The guide Carlos Aguero lives at the site and is well informed. There are no facilities for English-speakers. The site is mostly visited by Paraguayan school parties. Sadly, it is not yet visited by Bolivian groups.

Triumphalism is kept to a minimum, perhaps because the site is owned by the pacifist Mennonites. Inside the museum of rusty battle relics there is a tribute of 'Eternal gratitude to the heroes of the Chaco!' from a Paraguayan school, but alongside it is a text that reads: 'Paraguay, America and the World should learn from their history that wars impoverish populations and sow hatred amongst people. No more war and violence between brothers!'.

On a hillside facing the museum is the memorable figure of a stainless steel soldier running, the work of artist Herman Guggiari. The soldier has a large hole in his chest where his heart should be, but the hole is the shape of the map of Paraguay: it makes a powerful point. The monument that most expresses the idea of reconciliation was placed in 2004 by the presidents of both Paraguay and Bolivia. Two huge stainless steel leaves ripple in parallel, not touching, representing the two countries at war, and a plaque renders 'homage to the fallen, who in offering their blood constructed the foundations of peace and confraternity that today unite our peoples'.

The fort was surrounded by a 4km circle of trenches, with lookout posts every 5m from where the Bolivians shot down the approaching Paraguayan troops. Some 1,200 Bolivians guarded the fort, and 8,000 Paraguayans attacked. Their only way of taking the fort was by crossing a field where there was no cover, other than by piling up in front of them the gunned-down bodies of their companions. With huge carnage over 20 days, the Paraguayans inched forward behind walls of flesh three bodies high, and took the fort on 29 September 1932.

The Paraguayan cemetery is placed in this field, where most of them died, and a mass of tightly spaced white crosses indicates where there was a huge common grave. The Bolivian cemetery is placed inside the trenches, where they died. Next to the Bolivian cemetery is a twin grave with a simple tree-trunk headstone where a Paraguayan and a Bolivian lie buried together. Captain Tomas Manchego of Bolivia and First Lieutenant Fernando Velázquez of Paraguay became friends when Manchego was a prisoner in Paraguay, prior to the formal outbreak of war, and they met again in a Bolivian hospital, when both men were wounded and dying. They left instructions that their bodies were to be buried in a joint grave.

LOMA PLATA

Copaco ☎ 0492 253240; municipalidad ☎ 0492 252254/252163

Loma Plata has less of a mixed community than Filadelfia, and there is a much more German feel to the town. The streets are all called *Strasse*. Some people do not speak any Spanish, and most speak it hesitatingly and with a strong accent. If you are not a Mennonite, you feel an outsider – except that any fair-skinned person is assumed to speak German and is liable to be addressed in that language.

The big Trébol factory in Loma Plata supplies good-quality milk products to all over the country. There is an Escuela Agricola (agricultural school) run by the *cooperativa*.

GETTING THERE AND AROUND The **bus** company Nasa (or Golondrina) (☎ *0492 252521;* ☎ *021 551731 in Asunción*) has three buses a day that go to Loma Plata, leaving the Terminal in Asunción at 06.00, 14.30 and 23.00. The journey from Filadelfia to Loma Plata takes half an hour, and can also be done also with Nasa. There is a service that leaves Filadelfia for Loma Plata at 07.00, and it leaves Loma Plata at 13.00 for the journey to Filadelfia, so you can get there and back comfortably within a day.

A detailed **city plan**, marking every building but with very small print and nothing marked on it that you might want to visit, can be bought from the *cooperativa* (upstairs from the supermarket).

Taxis can generally be found at the bus station.

TOURIST INFORMATION If you are on a day visit and arrive early, you can get off the bus at the *cooperativa* and look for the office of information and tourism (*0492 252301/52401/52501;* m *0981 200535;* e *turismo@chortitzer.com.py;* *07.00–11.30*). It is situated to the left of the Cooperative and to the right of the museum, and the name of the Cooperative here is Chortitzer (www.chortitzer.com.py). Someone from there will offer to act as a guide and driver, but you should cover the costs of the petrol, at least. A further contact for tourism is Patrick Freisen (m *0983 569922;* e *patrick@chortitzer.com.py*) – currently the chief tourism officer.

WHERE TO STAY

Loma Plata Inn (22 rooms) 0492 253235/6. Probably the best hotel, shimmering white. Spacious rooms, the closest hotel to the Nasa bus terminal, & next to a good restaurant, Chaco's Grill. **$$**

Hotel Mora (38 rooms) Calle Sandstrasse 803; 0492 252255; m 0981 213040. Pleasant front courtyard with a private, family feel. You are expected to speak German but the manager has a little Spanish. Variety of rooms at range of prices. Taxi service. **$$**

Hotel Algarrobo (23 rooms) 0492 252353. Very accessible, both for location & price. You pass it on the access road. **$$**

Pension Loma Plata 0492 452829. Clean, simple accommodation. Pool. **$**

WHERE TO EAT AND DRINK

Chaco's Grill Calle sin nombre c/ Manuel Gondra; 0492 252166. Adjoins the Loma Plata Inn. Has a Chopp Haus (German pub) as well as a restaurant section, & a good outside area for eating. Comfortable walking distance from bus terminal. **$$**

Yakare Hu m 0981 200652; lunch & dinner. On the access road to town, this new restaurant has good food & a warm atmosphere. **$$**

Restaurant Norteño Calle 3 Palmas 990; 0492 252447; m 0981 202447. A Latin place, constructed of airbricks, with relaxed atmosphere & good variety of meat dishes. Slow service, clean bathrooms. Comfortable walking distance from bus terminal. **$**

OTHER PRACTICALITIES There are several **banks** in Loma Plata, including some with cash machines.

WHAT TO SEE AND DO There is not a lot to see in Loma Plata, but there is a small **museum** (*0492 252301*) with photographs showing the tough history of the Mennonite colonisation, since their first camp in 1921 – hoes and watering cans and horse carts, and a group of the first nurses. The visitors' book shows that travellers do make it here from Japan, Canada, Australia and Europe.

You can also have a guided tour of the Trébol factory, and of a meat processing plant. The **first Mennonite church of South America** may also be of interest – the Osterwick church, inaugurated in 1932.

SALT LAKES

To the southeast of Loma Plata is an area of **salt lakes** (*lagunas saladas*), which is a paradise for flamingos, herons and coscoroba swans, and also attracts migratory birds such as plovers. It is a Ramsar site (wetland of international importance, designated under the 1971 Ramsar Convention). The origin of the salt lakes is that this part of South America used to be sea, 60 million years ago.

The biggest lake is at Campo María, 58km east-southeast of Loma Plata, with an observation tower that is great for birdwatchers. Even the shape and colour of these curvy salt lakes, with their pale beaches, is beautiful, but the view from the air is best of all. If you cannot afford to go as far as Campo María on the difficult dirt roads, there is a winding river leading up to it, known as Riacho Yacaré (Spanish and Guaraní 'Caiman Creek'), and along it a much smaller lake, Laguna Capitán, just 24km southeast of Loma Plata, which also has flamingos.

Tours can be arranged by the tourist office in either Filadelfia or Loma Plata (which is closer to the lakes), or with Estancia Iparoma (see page 369) or Gran Chaco Turismo (see page 369).

WHERE TO STAY AND EAT

Campamento Laguna Capitán m 0983 344463. This house is run by the Cooperative of Loma Plata, & they can arrange your visit. AC, Wi-Fi. **$**

Chaco Lodge Norbert Epp of Gran Chaco Turismo owns this house, which is close to Campo María, the biggest of the salt lakes. Unlike the Campamento Laguna Capitán, there is no resident manager, so visiting cannot be guaranteed. **$**

MARISCAL ESTIGARRIBIA

Copaco 0494 247298; municipalidad 0494 247201-3

Further northwest of the group of Mennonite towns on Ruta 9 you come to Mariscal Estigarribia, which is not Mennonite. This really is a remote town: coming north from Asunción you feel you have reached the furthest outpost of human existence. On the other hand, coming south from Bolivia you feel you have finally arrived at civilisation and are on the home run. It has a population of 1,000.

Named after a famous general in the Chaco War, Mariscal Estigarribia's chief claim to fame is its vast but unused jet airport, an extraordinary white elephant in the middle of nowhere (see opposite).

The visit of Pope John Paul II to Mariscal Estigarribia in 1988 drew massive crowds. He had a big rally with the indigenous in Santa Teresita, a barrio on the outskirts of the town, at km520, where there are various indigenous communities, including Guaraní and Nivaclé. Native people came from all over the Chaco to the celebration.

GETTING THERE AND AROUND You can get to Mariscal Estigarribia with the **bus** company Nasa/Golondrina (*021 551731 in Asunción; 0494 247282 in Mariscal Estigarribia*), which currently has buses leaving Asunción at 14.30 and at 22.00, passing through Filadelfia first. They leave Mariscal Estigarribia for Asunción at 12.30 and 20.00 (*Gs100,000*). If you go to Mariscal by **taxi** from Filadelfia, it will cost around Gs500,000 or more for the 80km.

There is no taxi service in Mariscal Estigarribia, but you need transport to get around the surprisingly spread-out town, so if you do not come in your own vehicle you will need to persuade someone to turn into a taxi driver for you – not usually an insurmountable difficulty in Paraguay if money is offered. To the west of the Ruta are the extensive military quarters, the old cathedral (which was built in the midst of them) and the lake. The civilian town is to the east of the Ruta, and is a long thin town with a couple of kinks along its length as it follows the line of Ruta 9. The bus terminal is near the beginning of the town. There is a roundabout at each kink, allowing access to and from the Ruta. The Municipalidad serves as a point of reference, and it is close to the roundabout at the first kink.

WHERE TO STAY The Hotel de Transito is not open to the public, but is only for official delegations to the military or to the airport.

Hotel La Estancia (15 rooms) 0494 247250; m 0975 513371Hotel behind the Municipalidad, formerly known as Hotel Laguna, now taken over by a Uruguayan & renovated. Restaurant. Cheaper rooms have fans. $

Parador Lucho m 0981 827187. At the roundabout by the military base head towards the Ruta Transchaco for 1,000m. The hotel is just 50m from the Ruta. $

WHERE TO EAT AND DRINK

Tuna Bar 0494 247390. Typical simple eatery. Close to the entrance to the town. $

Restaurant Texas 0494 2473248; m 0961 170542. Another simple restaurant. 3 blocks from Parador Lucho; m 0961 170542. $

Hamburguesería Malaika 0494 247222; every day. No street name, but it is behind the military base: it would be best to ask for directions when you are there, as it is not easy to find. Friendly people. $

WHAT TO SEE AND DO The **airport** Luis María Argaña is worth going to gaze at, as a huge, unused enigma constructed in 1988 by the USA. The local people are quite proud of it, but will tell you that they do not want the US army moving in: there was an attempt to bring in 1,000 US troops around the end of 2005 and the local people blocked the plan. The runway is 3.5km long – the longest runway in the country – but is used more for car racing (in the annual Chaco Rally, see page 376) than for actual aeroplanes. The base is capable of housing 16,000 troops, has an enormous radar system, huge hangars and an air traffic control tower. It has never been used, other than fleetingly, and (as a surprise bonus) for Pope John Paul II to meet the indigenous in 1988. You have to get out of your car and enter on foot if you want to pass the gate. The official US line is that they have no plans to open a base here, and that the airport 'was constructed at a time when the Paraguayan government envisioned developing a free-trade zone in its northern Chaco region to help develop the area'. With a population of only 1,000 and no local industry looking for air freight, something is fishy here.

Other than the airport you should visit the **cathedral and the museum** adjoining it. The cathedral is modern and was opened in 2000. Do not miss the fine, striding figure of Mary carved in wood by Miguel E Romero of Tobatí (one of the artisan towns famous for woodcraft, see pages 159–62). The museum (*ask at the Oblate house next to the cathedral for access; 0494 247217*) has a large image of the Virgin of Guadalupe as you go in. (This dark-skinned Madonna is a Mexican painting that has become the principal Marian icon for the whole of Latin America.) The museum houses a strange mixture of items considered to be of interest: craftwork by the Nivaclé, a poncho, an enormous cooking pot, old saddles, vestments and items of early technology such as a sewing machine, telephone, radio, camera and typewriter. There are also bullets from the Chaco War.

The **old cathedral** (*la antigua catedral*) is in another part of town. It is a substantial and attractive red-brick building, whose principal fault was its location: sited in the midst of the military camp, it was inaccessible for the civilian population. One of its features is the tomb of the much loved Pa'i Pukú (Guaraní 'tall priest'), Monsignor Pedro Shaw OMI. He was the Apostolic Vicar of the Pilcomayo region and died in 1984 at the age of 59. He was known for his love of the people, his travel round the

Chaco on horseback, and a number of development projects, most especially the Pa'i Pukú school (see page 366). The diocesan radio station is also named after him.

Rally Transchaco This annual motor-racing event (www.transchacorally.com.py) runs over a vast area but is centred around Mariscal Estigarribia. The exact route varies every year: in 2013 stages 1 and 2 were in the Filadelfia/Pozo Colorado area, and the third stage in a big circle stretching from Mariscal Estigarribia to the Bolivian border. The competition began in 1971, inspired by the African Safari Rally, and has happened every year since then, bar two. It takes place in mid-September, and attracts around 70,000 people – more than any other sport in Paraguay except football. It attracts huge media attention as well as crowds of followers on, who unfortunately have got a bad name for the event, leaving behind their debris of beer cans and motor oil containers, while the cars plough up the dirt roads and make them unusable for the local population. For information consult the website above or the motoring organisation **Touring y Automovil Club Paraguayo** (*25 de mayo y Brasil;* ☎ *021 210550/53; www.tacpy.com.py*).

Pigeon shooting 'Paraguay is synonymous with the world's best pigeon shooting', says the website of one US agency specialising in shooting tours (*www.staffordadventures.com*). This surprising, specialist area of tourism is centred on the central Chaco, and shooters stay either in the Picazuro Lodge near Neuland, or in the Florida Hotel of Filadelfia, or in one of the *estancias*, such as Estancia Palo Santo S A (*4 rooms & 7 bungalows;* ☎ *0493 240690;* e *denisdbertrand@gmail.com*), 80km south of Neuland, run by a Belgian, a Frenchman and a Canadian, or Estancia Faro Moro, which is run by North Americans. The pigeons descend when the Mennonite farmers harvest their sesame, sunflowers, sorghum or peanuts, and the shooting season is mid-February to May/June. The great majority of the shooters come from the USA, and this is big business. (See also page 30.)

NORTH OF MARISCAL ESTIGARRIBIA For the location of the National Parks in the northern Chaco see the map on page 8.

Adjoining the Ruta Transchaco in its most northerly stretch is the national park **Médanos del Chaco**, which covers 514,000ha. It belongs to the Dry Chaco Ecoregion – what they call the green desert. The *médanos* are sand hills, which carry a fragile covering of vegetation, consisting of dry woods and bushes. There are jaguars and mountain lions, tapirs, and a graceful, fast-moving animal called the guanaco, which is a sort of humpless camel, related to the llama.

This is a region of different kinds of wild boar or peccary. The collared peccary (*kure'í*) is not uncommon, while the white-lipped peccary (*jabalí*), which looks very similar, is dangerous and is prone to attack people. The *kure'í* has a white collar, but the *jabalí* has a white beard. There is a third kind of peccary, the *taguá*, which is so rare that it was believed for many years to be extinct until it was sighted again in the Chaco in 1975. It looks like the *kure'í* except that the hair on its shoulder sticks up almost like the spikes of a porcupine.

There are also a lot of the large lizard known as *tejú guasú*, about which there was a scandal in 2014 when the government passed a resolution to permit the hunting of 214,000 of these big lizards, for their skins. It was overturned following a mass protest on social media.

It is possible to stay in this region, in the **Campo Iris reserve** (a little southwest of the Médanos) – which has the only lagoon in the area, attracting wild animals who come to drink. The visit is organised through Guyrá Paraguay (see page 76). Like the

Médanos, Campo Iris has tapirs, and also some species found nowhere else in the world: not only the Chaco peccary, but also the Chaco guanaco and the Chaco tortoise.

Over 100 species of reptiles have been recorded in Campo Iris. There are also many rare birds including the crowned solitary eagle, greater rhea, Chaco chacalaca, Chaco blue-fronted Amazon, Guira cuckoo and brushland tinamou.

On the other side of Médanos del Chaco is another national park, the Defensores del Chaco, which is the largest conservation area in Paraguay (780,000ha). It includes the only near-mountain for hundreds of miles around, Cerro León. Strictly speaking, this is a grouping of about 46 hills over an area of just 40km, rising to a maximum height of 604m above sea level. Cerro León has tapirs, peccaries, jaguars and (true to its name) mountain lions or pumas. The jaguar, which is a threatened species, illegally hunted, needs at least 3,500ha of wild to survive in. The jaguarundi can be observed around here, throughout the year, and in winter pairs can be seen. If you want to go there, it is 263km each way, on dirt roads, and will take three days, in a 4x4 vehicle, but it is not impossible for the determined, if they can find a guide. Gran Chaco Turismo used to offer this tour (see page 369), but they may no longer have personnel free to take you. You could ask at the Filadelfia tourist office, or arrange with Guyrá (see page 76) to go to Campo Iris, which is a small reserve between Médanos del Chaco and Teniente Enciso.

The **Teniente Enciso National Park** is a smaller nature reserve, closer to the Transchaco road. It covers 40,000ha and has dense, thorny vegetation, almost impenetrable. The trees include the white *quebracho* ('break-axe' tree) and the *samu'u* (bottle tree).

THE PANTANAL

Going up the Ruta Transchaco is not the only way of exploring the Chaco, though it does take you through the centre of the region. You can also go north of Asunción up the Río Paraguay, which borders the Chaco to the east, so the places on the Río Paraguay form another area of the Chaco that can be visited. You may reach these Chaco river towns by boat, which is slow, but you are more likely to arrive by bus, overland from the Ruta Transchaco, or in some cases by plane. If you go far enough north up the Río Paraguay you reach the Pantanal – perhaps the most gloriously exciting excursion anyone can make anywhere in Paraguay.

Fuerte Olimpo is the gateway to the Paraguayan Pantanal. Getting to that point is quite feasible, though it takes a little time. Beyond Fuerte Olimpo is where you really get inside the Pantanal, and also where travel becomes difficult.

More than 60 million years ago, the centre of South America was a sea. This explains why there are still expanses of salt lakes in the Chaco (see pages 373–4). Movements of the earth's surface led to the formation of the Andes, and the north–south depression to the east of that range is the Pantanal. It is the flat land around the Río Paraguay, of which 70–80% floods in the rainy season, from December on, raising the water level by some 5m. This makes it become enormously fertile territory for flora and fauna, but very inhospitable for human beings. The average temperature is 32°C in summer and 21°C in winter. In the time of the Jesuit missions the Pantanal was called simply La Laguna. The Pantanal is principally associated with Brazil, but in fact 5% of this territory is in Paraguay.

The Pantanal is considered one of the most important and beautiful ecological sanctuaries of the planet. The tall *karanda'ý* palm with its fan-like leaves abounds, and the *karaguatá* is a low-growing bromelid with bright-red, thorned leaves and white flowers. The pink *ipés* blossoms on trees, the *aguapé* (Spanish *camalote*) fills the waters with a green carpet and keeps the waters fresh, and the huge 30cm wide flowers of the Victoria Regia open at night. There are water hyacinths, water lilies and water lettuces.

The Pantanal has the largest faunal concentration in the Americas, and has been estimated to contain 650 species of birds, 260 of fish, 160 of reptiles, 80 of mammals and 6,000 of insects, not to mention 1,800 species of plants. Emblematic of this paradise of flora and fauna is the jabiru stork, which has a black head and neck and a red collar, and a wingspan of 2m. It feeds richly on the fish, frogs and insects left behind by the floods.

The marsh deer has long, wide hooves with a membrane between its toes, so it can run on the swampy ground. There are caimans, lizards and iguanas, tapirs, wild pigs (or peccaries), coati, the paca rodent, eight species of armadillo, and all five species of Paraguayan monkey. The handsome and dangerous jaguars are the most striking of all the animals. The bird life is spectacular, with herons, ducks, cormorants, scarlet ibis, spoonbills and toucans, and there is the world's largest population of blue hyacinth macaws. The early hours of the morning and the last hours of daylight are when there is most activity from the birds.

The density of human population in the Pantanal is only 0.14 per km^2; the population includes a small number of Chamakoko indigenous (also known here as the Ishir).

GETTING THERE AND AWAY

By air After a pause of some years, there are once again planes to the northern ports of the Río Paraguay (which also go to Concepción and Vallemí on the eastern bank). The prices are quite reasonable and this is now the best way to travel to these remote places. Details of these flights with SETAM are given in the box on page 380.

You can also charter a **private plane**, but it is very expensive (see box, page 381).

By bus It is a long way to go to the upper reaches of the Río Paraguay by bus. You will be travelling over dirt roads, the buses are infrequent, and if it rains they will not go at all. However, if the day the bus travels coincides with the day you want to travel, it is faster than going by boat. **Stel Turismo** (☎ *021 558051*) goes to Puerto Casado twice a week, and before the floods of 2014 it was going three times a week to Fuerte Olimpo, which is the start of the Pantanal, and twice a week to Bahia Negra. A small company called **Turismo** goes to Bahia Negra once a week. Details of these buses are found under the respective towns, below.

By car If you really want to drive so far on such unmarked terrain without asphalted roads, you will need to hire a 4x4, for which see page 70.

By boat Halfway between Puerto Casado and Fuerte Olimpo the Paraguayan boats stop at the Brazilian port of Porto Mortinho. This is a backdoor into Paraguay and onto the Río Paraguay. But remember the difficulties that may afflict you on your way out of the country if your passport was not stamped when you entered.

Aquidabán If you do not want to pay for a flight, but want to be a pioneer in exploring the Paraguayan Pantanal beyond Fuerte Olimpo, then take your mosquito net, your hammock (you can buy one in the open-air market behind the Panteón in Asunción), a couple of good ropes, your first-aid kit, insect repellent, sun hat, camera, and a very long novel, and take the *Aquidabán*, which leaves Concepción on Tuesday at 11.00 and goes to Puerto Casado, Fuerte Olimpo, Puerto Leda and **as far as Bahía Negra**, arriving at dawn on Friday. (See pages 344–5 for full details of the *Aquidabán*'s timetable and prices, and pages 337–8 for how to get to the starting point of Concepción.)

This is a great trip for an adventurer with time to spare, because of the beauty of the scenery, the sense of freedom and release from time pressures, the personal space and comfort of your own hammock strung taut and high over the boat's cargo, the support from the tight community of the boat's crew, the novelty of seeing them hunt capybaras and gut them on the deck before chucking them whole into a massive freezer. Some basic provisions can be bought on board, but you should supplement them with your own food, and enough water for several days.

But what do you do if you want to go beyond Bahía Negra? The only way is by river, but there are no scheduled boats. You have to get private boat transport. See below on Tres Gigantes.

PUERTO CASADO (*Copaco* ☎ *0351 230693/230696; Municipalidad: ring Copaco & ask to be put through*) On some maps Puerto Casado is marked as La Victoria, and the SETAM airline refer to it as La Victoria, too. Halfway between Concepción and Fuerte Olimpo, it is not itself in the Pantanal, but it is the most southerly town of this riverside region, on the way to the Pantanal. It is a delightful but dying place on the west bank of the Río Paraguay, shortly before eastern Paraguay comes to an end, with the town of Vallemí and the caves of San Lazaro on the opposite bank (see pages 343–4).

Once economically thriving with the tannin industry of the now defunct firm Carlos Casado SA, it has something of the feel of a ghost town, with the old factory, and the unused railway station once built by the company, falling into disrepair. Mariscal José Félix Estigarribia, a hero of the Chaco War, had a house here, and an ancient carob tree (*algarrobo*) in his garden, beneath which he used to sit, is marked with a plaque. The town served as a gathering point for the troops in the Chaco War, before they were sent to the front.

In 2000 the local people were roused into panicked demonstrations when they suddenly discovered that their town had been bought up by the Moonies, as part of a 400,000ha purchase of land in the region, for purposes unknown. Years of legal and parliamentary wrangling followed to try to recover the independence of the town.

Getting there and away The best way to get to Puerto Casado is by **plane** with SETAM (see box, page 380). The local contact in Puerto Casado is **m** 0984 494775. There are two **buses** a week to Puerto Casado with the company Stel Turismo (☎ *021 558051*), which leave Asunción from the corner diagonally opposite the Terminal on República Argentina, where the company's office is, next to the big corner shop Faro. They leave at 19.00 on Tuesday and Friday, and the journey takes 12 hours. They leave Puerto Casado at 09.00 Wednesday and Saturday. The fare is currently Gs120,000.

To get there by **boat**, see above. There is a small ***hospedaje*** at the Bar Coelho (**m** *0982 327386*).

CARMELO PERALTA Halfway between Puerto Casado and Fuerte Olimpo is Carmelo Peralta, which has a passport office (🕘 *07.00–19.00 daily*) where you can get an exit stamp. It is opposite the Isla Margarita, and the town on the Brazilian side is called Porto Murtinho. There is a project to build a bridge between the two towns.

From Carmelo Peralta you can do a tour in a **barco hotel** (hotel boat), of which there are a number. Francisco Fernández, for example, charges Gs2,800,000 per person for a cruise lasting from Saturday to Thursday, with all meals included; his boat *Barco Hotel El Paraíso* has 3 bedrooms and can take 12 passengers. Most of the clients are Brazilian, which is not surprising as this place is rather hard to reach

FLIGHTS TO NORTHERN PARAGUAY

The company SETAM (*Servicio de Transporte Aereo Militar;* ☎ *021 645885;* ⊙ *07.00–11.00 & 14.30–17.00 Mon–Fri; outside these times you can ask for information and make a reservation with Capitan Giménez,* ☎ *0983 117964*) is now operating regular flights from Asunción to the north. The stops are Concepción, Puerto Casado (= La Victoria), Vallemí, Fuerte Olimpo and Bahía Negra.

The plane leaves on Monday, Wednesday and Friday, and is generally full, so it is important to reserve a place one or two weeks beforehand, which you can do by phone, and then pay on the day in cash. (When the river was flooded in 2014 and bus travel was no longer possible to some destinations, it was necessary to make a reservation a month or two months in advance.) The cost is surprisingly reasonable (currently between Gs250,000 and Gs300,000).

The plane leaves Asunción at 07.00 but you must arrive an hour beforehand, at 06.00. The flight to Concepción takes 45 minutes, and most subsequent legs of the journey take approximately 40 minutes. The plane takes off again 15 to 30 minutes after arrival on each airstrip, and it reaches **Bahía Negra** around 11.00. The return journey begins without further delay.

The planes do not go from Silvio Pettirossi (the international airport in Asunción), but from the military airbase (*aeropuerto militar*) which you pass on the *autopista* shortly before reaching the international airport, on the left. The luggage allowance is 10kg, and the plane takes 18–26 passengers.

Information on flights to the north has always been subject to frequent change, so it is important to telephone for the latest update. At the time of writing there was no information available online.

on the Paraguayan side. You can fish, or just enjoy the relaxing trip. Others who run a similar service are Francisco Salinas (**m** *0982 362410*), José Segovia (**m** *0985 238351*) and Ana Flavia Benítez (**m** *0982 332743*).

FUERTE OLIMPO (*Copaco* ☎ *0497 281000; Municipalidad* ☎ *0497 281155*) With hills rising behind it, and the attractive cathedral of Maria Auxiliadora, there is a pleasant, airy feel to this town, which is capital of the *departamento* of Alto Paraguay and known as the gateway to the Pantanal. It is 782km from Asunción by road, beginning with the Ruta Transchaco for 415km up to Cruce de Pioneros, then a dirt road for 367km.

Fuerte Olimpo is halfway between Puerto Casado and Bahía Negra. It has a number of tourist attractions, including the **Fuerte Borbón**, built in 1792; the name of the place was changed from Borbón to Olimpo by President Carlos Antonio López, who wanted to break the old colonial ties. There is a **Centro de Información Ambiental y Turística** in the town centre (☎ *0497 281117*). Young people have been trained to be guides. A good person to talk to is Profesora Cristina González de Méndez (☎ *0497 281049*).

Getting there and away Before the floods of 2014 the bus Stel Turismo was going three times a week to Fuerte Olimpo. At the time of going to press, the floods had cut this service off for many months on end, and it remained to be seen if the same service would be resumed. However, assuming that the service does return to the former pattern, the bus does the journey three times a week, leaving Asunción at 19.00 on Monday, Wednesday and Friday from outside the company's office, diagonally opposite the Terminal on República Argentina (*021 558051*) , next to the shop Faro. The journey takes 15 hours in good weather, 20 hours if it is not so good. The buses leave Fuerte Olimpo on Monday, Wednesday and Friday at 08.00, and the fare is currently Gs165,000.

Another and more pleasant way to arrive is by **boat** from Concepción: the *Aquidabán* arrives from the south at about midday on Thursday, and from the north at about 20.00 on Friday. See page 378 for details and for getting there by plane (*local contact for SETAM:* m *0982 331449*).

Where to stay and eat

Hotel AA 0497 281017. Beautiful & atmospheric with its river-facing rooms along a wooden balcony on stilts. Simple rooms, but with private bathrooms & AC. Total capacity for 42 people. Excellent home-cooked food, lots of fish. **$$**

Hotel Chaco Pantanal 0497 281021. A second choice of a more solid terrestrial variety. **$**

What to see and do The **indigenous museum** has items by the Ayoreo, Chamokoko and Maskoy. There are slings for honey pots and for babies, feather headdresses, stone tools, lances, arrows, wooden shoes, a stone pipe for smoke-making, etc. A **visit to the Chamokoko** (or **Ishir**) community of Virgen Santísima can be arranged, which may include a display of craft for sale, a welcome from the *chamán* and a trip in a boat.

The **Tres Hermanos hill** has 535 steps up, and from the summit you have a magnificent view over both Paraguay and Brazil. There are opportunities for all-day **motorboat trips** to see flora and fauna, particularly caimans, or for going in a rowing boat or a *piragua*, which is slightly broader than a *kayak*.

If you carry on north from Fuerte Olimpo, you are seriously into the Pantanal. If adventure tourism in one of the most remote spots on the planet is what you want, then this is it.

PUERTO LEDA You will probably reach Puerto Leda (halfway between Fuerte Olimpo and Bahía Negra) in the middle of the night. This is where Japanese Moonies are carving out of the wild a beautiful city for their adherents, with plantations and swimming pool, and are now planning to build a university. Before them, there was nothing except a police station, in the midst of inhospitable territory inhabited by mosquitoes, jaguars and caimans. You are now properly into the Pantanal. At some times of year you may need a special helmet to stop the mosquitoes flying into your mouth when you speak. See page 378 for how to get there.

BAHÍA NEGRA This is a small town of a thousand or so inhabitants. It only has electricity only up until midnight, which is a considerable nuisance for the

CHARTERING PLANES

Monomotor planes (which take three to five passengers) cost less than bimotor planes (which take five to nine passengers), but whichever plane you take, expect to pay over US$1,000, plus extra for the pilot's waiting time during a tour of several days. You can charter planes from **Aerotax** (*021 645523/645616/021 646523; www.aerotax.com*) or **Airmen SA** (*021 645980/021 645990; m 0981 909761/415473;* e airreservas@gmail.com).

economy, because fridges cannot be trusted, so any cattle have to be taken 700km to a slaughterhouse. There is currently a plan to bring Chilean engineers with Chinese technology to install turbines that will run off channelled and pressurised river water, and so create 24-hour electricity. This is a town where landlines were out of action for more than two years without repair because a tower fell down.

Getting there and away In Bahía Negra there is no bank or internet, and before the floods of 2014 an overland **bus** reached there only twice a week. If it returns to its former timetable, Stel Turismo (*021 558051*) will leave Asunción from the agency's headquarters, diagonally opposite the Terminal, next to the big corner shop Faro on República Argentina, at 19.00 on Tuesday and Thursday. The journey takes 18 hours if you are lucky. The bus leaves Bahia Negra at 08.00 Thursday and Saturday. The fare was Gs200,000 before the floods.

To get there by **plane**, see the box on page 380 (*local contact for SETAM:* m *0982 306234*).

To get there by **boat**, see page 378. The *Aquidabán* goes no further than Bahía Negra. If you want to carry on north into wilder and wilder country, then you need to hire a private boat, for example from Ramón García (*'Alichi';* m *0982 469942*). If you are going to Tres Gigantes, the people of Guyrá Paraguay will come and fetch you in their motorboat. There is a Paraguayan naval base here (and another further south at Isla Margarita, halfway between Fuerte Olimpo and Puerto Casado, and opposite Colonia Carmelo Peralta).

Where to stay

Ignacio Ortiz (10 rooms) m 0983 461553. Better quality hotel than the other pensiones. AC, TV, minibar, private bathrooms. Motor boat available for river trips. All meals provided to order. **$$** [100,000 per pers]

Pensión Doña Blanca (2 rooms) m 0983 667582. Family pension, very cheap, clean, friendly. Shower, latrine. Meals on request. **$**

Pensión Doña Piquita (9 rooms) m 0981 777686. Very cheap, bathroom with flushing toilet, but shared. **$**

Pensión Hombre y Naturaleza (3 rooms) m 0982 898589/862543. Enchanting small guesthouse with 10 beds in 3 rooms, created by Spanish NGO of the same name. Hotel is built of palm trees with mosquito netting filling the gaps. Very basic, but has water & flushing toilet. Often booked out because it appeals to foreigners. **$**

Where to eat and drink

Copetín Aldito m 0984 154646. Bar that can serve meals to order. The homemade bread is good. $

Don Silva m 0982 329297. By the plaza, empanadas to order. $

Hamburguesería Rosi Open-air patio, other dishes besides hamburgers on request. $

About 20km north of Bahía Negra is a junction of rivers at a point called Hito XI Tripartito, which is where the three countries of Paraguay, Brazil and Bolivia meet. If you take the Río Negro from there (the smaller river, going more directly north) you will continue along the Paraguayan border until you reach Hito X, which is a little over 40km further north, and is as far as you can go without leaving Paraguay. The west bank is Paraguay, and the east bank is a tongue of Bolivia that pokes down between Paraguay and Bolivia to Bahía Negra. (The Hitos, one to ten, are boundary markers between the Río Pilcomayo and the Río Paraguay, and straight lines drawn from one to the next mark the frontier between Paraguay and Bolivia.) The river is called Río Negro because of algae that give a black tinge to the water. If you are

TROPIC OF CAPRICORN

The Tropic of Capricorn passes through the southern Chaco, at 23.4° of latitude, and marks the most southerly point at which the sun can be seen directly overhead at noon: this occurs at the December solstice, when the southern hemisphere is tilted towards the sun to its maximum extent. The name was chosen because the constellation of Capricorn rises above it at the summer solstice. This line runs immediately south of Pozo Colorado in the Chaco, and Concepción in eastern Paraguay. When you are north of the Tropic people tend to talk of the dry season and the rainy season (December to April, approximately), rather than winter and summer.

planning to leave the country by this route, it can be done by taking a private motor boat to Puerto Busch in Bolivia. But you need to think ahead about your exit stamp. Theoretically it should be done at the customs office and passport control in Carmelo Peralta (*see page 379;* ⌚ *07.00–19.00 daily*). If you are travelling on the *Aquidaban* this is impossible to do, as you will pass there in the middle of the night, but it can sometimes be arranged at the office of Identificaciones in Concepción.

On the Paraguayan bank is the **Parque Nacional Río Negro**, covering 30,000ha, which protects the Pantanal against damage from deforestation, water contamination and uncontrolled fishing and hunting. Apart from anything else, the wetlands of the world are essential for storing over 40% of the earth's carbon monoxide, and their degradation releases a large amount of carbon dioxide.

TRES GIGANTES Just before Hito X you come to the Estación Biológica Tres Gigantes, 40km from Bahía Negra, which is the research station run by the non-profit-making organisation Guyrá Paraguay, which specialises not only in birdwatching (*guyrá* is 'bird' in Guaraní), but the preservation of the entire ecosystem. You contact them through their Asunción office (*Gaetano Martino, fomerly José Berges, 215 esq Tte Ross;* ☎ *021 229097/223567;* **e** *birding.paraguay@gmail.com; www.guyra.org.py*). To see photos of Tres Gigantes on their website, choose 'Conservation Areas'. The same organisation also offers a tour to the Parque San Rafael (see pages 267–8).

Tres Gigantes is so named because this is the only place in the world where you can see the giant armadillo, the giant anteater and the giant otter. They can be observed taking the sun on the shore or walking through the woods. The tours on offer have walks along jungle tracks, including at dawn, fishing, boat trips after nightfall with lights to see the caimans and capybaras, and navigating the streams in a rowing boat or a speedboat (*deslizador*). The iguana hangs from the trees, the caiman patrols the water, and the yellow anaconda slithers silently through this natural paradise. It takes time, money and determination to reach this remote spot, as far north as you can get on the river without leaving Paraguay, but it is highly recommended, and around 50 people are getting there each year. This must count as one of the wildest and most remote holidays in the world.

At Tres Gigantes there are three rooms, each with its own bathroom, and the house holds 12 guests. One room has a double bed and sofa, and the other two have bunk beds. Activities are walking, boating, fishing, observing the wildlife, and just relaxing in this extraordinary place. The wooden house is very attractive. It has a spacious dining room, and there are hammocks outside downstairs. Upstairs is a balcony protected by mosquito netting. Prices are Gs100,000 per person per night, plus Gs100,000 for meals, and the boat to collect you from Bahía Negra costs Gs700,000 return.

Appendix 1

LANGUAGE

SPANISH

Pronunciation

Consonants are as in English, except that *b* and *v* are pronounced the same (in Paraguay, aim more for a *v* sound). There is no *w* except for foreign words like *whisky*. The *h* is silent. The *j* is pronounced (in Paraguay) like an English *h*. The *t* and *d* are pronounced very lightly.

If *c* is followed by *i* or *e* it is pronounced like an *s* (in Paraguay); otherwise it is hard. The same with *g*: if it is followed by *i* or *e* it is pronounced like an *h*; otherwise hard. To make an English *qu* sound you use *cu* in Spanish. The Spanish *qu* is pronounced like a *k*.

The *r* is lightly rolled, and the *rr* strongly rolled. The *ll* is pronounced *l-y* but the *l* bit almost disappears. There are very few double consonants in Spanish. The *ñ* is also pronounced with a *y* sound: *n-y*.

Vowels are pronounced short and each one is separate. A *y* at the end of the word is pronounced like the vowel *i*.

Examples:

prohibido (forbidden) = pro-i-bi-do
cada (each) = ka-da
cielo (sky) = see-eh-low
aceite (oil) = a-say-ee-tay
causa (cause) = cow-za
gato (cat) = ga-to
Jorge (George) = hor-hay
cuesta (it costs) = ques-ta
que (that) = ke
caballo (horse) = ka-val-yo
niño (child) = nin-yo
ley (law) = le-ee

The **word stress** falls on the penultimate syllable unless the last syllable ends in a consonant other than *n* or *s*, in which case it falls on the last syllable. Exceptions to this have an acute accent on the stressed syllable.

Examples:

cocotero (palmtree) is said *cocotéro*
ciudad (large town) is said *ciudád*
viernes (Friday) is said *viérnes*
miércoles (Wednesday) is written with an accent

Basic grammar

Nouns have masculine and feminine forms. eg: *el sol* (the sun); *la luna* (the moon).
Adjectives agree with the nouns and are usually placed after them. There are forms for the masculine singular, feminine singular, masculine plural and feminine plural, eg: *los pueblos antiguos* (the old towns); *las casas blancas* (the white houses).
Adverbs normally have *–mente* on the end of the feminine form of the adjective.

Verbs conjugate as in most other European languages, into 1st, 2nd and 3rd person singular, and 1st, 2nd and 3rd person plural. In Paraguayan Spanish the usual 2nd person singular pronoun is *vos* rather than *tú* as in Spain, but it is quite acceptable to use *tú*. The *vosotros* form (2nd person plural) of Spain is never used, except when reading texts written in Spain: even for friends and family the word used is *ustedes*.

Vocabulary

Essentials

Good morning	*buen día/buenos días*	How are you?	*¿Cómo estás?*
Good afternoon	*buenas tardes*	Pleased to meet you	*Mucho gusto*
Good evening	*buenas noches*	thank you	*gracias*
Hello	*hola*	Don't mention it	*De nada*
Goodbye	*chau/adios*	Cheers!	*!Salud!*
My name is…	*Me llamo …*	yes	*sí*
What is your name?	*¿Cómo te llamas?* *¿Cómo se llama usted?*	no	*no*
		I don't understand	*no entiendo*
I am from England/ America/ Australia	*Soy de Inglaterra/ los Estados Unidos/ Australia*	Please would you speak more slowly	*¿Podría hablar más despacio por favor?*
		Do you understand?	*¿Entiende?*

Questions

how?	*¿cómo?*	when?	*¿cuándo?*
what?	*¿qué?*	why?	*¿por qué?*
where?	*¿dónde?*	who?	*¿quién?*
what is it?	*¿qué es?*	how much?	*¿cuánto?*
which?	*¿cuál?*		

Numbers

1	*uno*	17	*diecisiete*
2	*dos*	18	*dieciocho*
3	*tres*	19	*diecinueve*
4	*cuatro*	20	*veinte*
5	*cinco*	21	*veintiuno*
6	*seis*	30	*treinta*
7	*siete*	31	*treinta y uno*
8	*ocho*	40	*cuarenta*
9	*nueve*	50	*cincuenta*
10	*diez*	60	*sesenta*
11	*once*	70	*setenta*
12	*doce*	80	*ochenta*
13	*trece*	90	*noventa*
14	*catorce*	100	*cien*
15	*quince*	1,000	*mil*
16	*dieciseis*		

Time

What time is it?	*¿qué hora es?*	tomorrow	*mañana*
its…am/pm	*son las ….am/pm*	yesterday	*ayer*
today	*hoy*	morning	*mañana*
tonight	*esta noche*	evening	*tardecita*

Days

Monday	*lunes*
Tuesday	*martes*
Wednesday	*miércoles*
Thursday	*jueves*

Friday	*viernes*
Saturday	*sábado*
Sunday	*domingo*

Months

January	*enero*
February	*febrero*
March	*marzo*
April	*abril*
May	*mayo*
June	*junio*
July	*julio*

August	*agosto*
September	*setiembre*
October	*octubre*
November	*noviembre*
December	*diciembre*

Public transport

I'd like…	*me gustaría …*
… a one-way ticket	*pasaje de ida*
… a return ticket	*pasaje de ida y vuelta*
I want to go to…	*quiero ir a …*
How much is it?	*¿cuánto cuesta?*
What time does it leave?	*¿a qué hora sale?*
What time is it now?	*¿qué hora es ahora?*
The bus has been…	*El colectivo está …*
… delayed	*atrasado*
… cancelled	*suspendido*
economy class	*común*
with reclining seats ('half-bed')	*semi cama*
with fully reclining seats ('bed car')	*coche cama*
platform	*plataforma*
ticket window	*ventanilla*
timetable	*horario*
from	*de*
to	*a*
bus station	*terminal*

railway station	*estación de ferrocarril*
airport	*aeropuerto*
port	*puerto*
bus	*colectivo/omnibus*
local town bus	*colectivo/linea*
train	*tren*
plane	*avión*
boat	*barco*
ferry (across river)	*balsa*
motorboat	*lancha*
rowing boat	*canoa*
car	*auto*
4x4	*cuatro por cuatro*
taxi	*taxi*
minibus	*minibus*
motorbike/moped	*moto*
bicycle	*bicicleta*
arrival/departure	*llegada/salida*
here	*acá/aquí*
there	*allá/allí*
bon voyage!	*!buen viaje!*

Private transport

Is this the road to…?	*¿es éste el camino a …?*
Where is the service station?	*¿dónde queda la estación de servicios/ el surtidor?*
Please fill it up	*tanque lleno, por favor*

I'd like… litres	*quiero … litros*
diesel	*gasoil/diesel*
unleaded petrol	*nafta sin plomo*
I have broken down	*mi auto se descompuso*

Road signs

give way	*ceda el paso*	toll	*peaje*
danger	*peligro*	no entry	*prohibido el paso*
entry	*entrada*	exit	*salida*
detour	*desvío*		
oneway	*contramano*		

Directions

Where is it?	*¿dónde queda?*	east	*este*
Go straight ahead	*siga derecho/adelante*	west	*oeste*
turn left	*doble a la izquierda*	behind	*detrás de …*
turn right	*doble a la derecha*	in front of	*delante de …*
… at the traffic lights	*… al semáforo*	near	*cerca de …*
… at the roundabout	*… a la rotonda*	opposite	*en frente de …*
north	*norte*		
south	*sur*		

Street signs

entrance	*entrada*	toilets – men/women	*baños/sanitarios caballeros/damas*
exit	*salida*	information	*información*
open	*abierto*		
closed	*cerrado*		

Accommodation

Where is a cheap/ good hotel?	*¿dónde se encuentra un hotel barato/ bueno?*	… a room with a bathroom	*… una habitación con baño privado*
Could you please write the address?	*¿podría escribirme la dirección por favor?*	How much it is per night/person?	*¿cuánto cuesta por persona/por noche?*
Do you have any rooms available?	¿tiene *habitaciones disponibles?*	Where is the toilet/ bathroom?	*¿dónde está el baño?*
I'd like …	*me gustaría …*	Is there hot water?	*¿tiene agua caliente?*
… a single room	*… una habitación simple*	Is there electricity?	*¿hay luz?*
… a double room	*… una habitación doble*	Is breakfast included?	*¿está incluido el desayuno?*
… a room with two beds	*… una habitación con dos camas*	I am leaving today	*salgo hoy*

Food

Do you have a table for … people?	*¿Tiene mesa para … personas?*	Please bring me…	*Por favor, tráigame …*
… a children's menu?	*… menu de niños?*	… a fork/knife/ spoon	*… tenedor/cuchillo/ cuchara*
I am a vegetarian	*Soy vegetariano/-a*	Please may I have the bill?	*La cuenta, por favor.*
Do you have any vegetarian dishes?	*¿Tiene algún plato vegetariano?*		

Basics

bread	*pan*	cheese	*queso*
butter	*manteca*	oil	*aceite*

pepper	*pimienta*	sugar	*azúcar*
salt	*sal*		

Fruit

apples	*manzanas*	mango	*mango*
bananas	*bananas*	oranges	*naranjas*
grapes	*uvas*	pears	*peras*

Vegetables

carrot	*zanahoria*	[green/red] pepper	*locote/moron*
garlic	*ajo*	potato	*papa*
onion	*cebolla*		

Fish

tuna	*atún*	fish	*pescado*

Meat

beef	*carne (de vaca)*	pork	*chancho/cerdo*
chicken	*pollo*	sausage	*chorizo*

Drinks

beer	*cerveza*	tea	*té*
coffee	*café*	water	*agua*
fruit juice	*jugo de fruta*	wine	*vino*
milk	*leche*		

Shopping

I'd like to buy…	*me gustaría comprar …*	Do you accept…?	*¿Se acepta …?*
		credit card	*tarjeta de crédito*
How much is it?	*¿cuánto cuesta?*	travellers' cheques	*cheques viajeros*
I don't like it	*no me gusta*	more	*más*
I'm just looking	*sólo estoy mirando*	less	*menos*
It's too expensive	*es demasiado caro*	smaller	*más pequeño/chico*
I'll take it	*lo voy a llevar*	bigger	*más grande*
Please may I have…	*¿Podría darme …?*		

Communications

I am looking for…	*estoy buscando*	embassy	*embajada*
bank	*banco*	exchange office	*cambio*
post office	*correo*	telephone centre	*Copaco*
church	*iglesia*	tourist office	*oficina de turismo*

Health

diarrhoea	*diarrea*	antiseptic	*antiséptico*
nausea	*náusea*	tampons	*tampones*
doctor	*doctor*	condoms	*preservativos/condones*
prescription	*receta*	contraceptive	*anticonceptivos*
pharmacy	*farmacia*	sun block	*protector/bloqueador solar*
paracetamol	*paracetamol*		
aspirin	*aspirina*		
antibiotics	*antibióticos*		

I am …	*soy …*	I'm allergic to…	*soy alergico/-a a …*
… asthmatic	*asmático/-a*	… penicillin	*penicilina*
… epileptic	*epiléptico/-a*	… nuts	*nueces*
… diabetic	*diabético/-a*	… bees	*abejas*

Travel with children

Is there a…?	*¿Hay …?*	nappies	*pañales*
Do you have…?	*¿Tiene usted …?*	babysitter	*niñera*
… infant milk formula?	*leche en polvo para bebé?*	Are children allowed?	*¿se permiten niños?*

Miscellaneous

my/mine	*mi/mis*	that (close)	*ese/esa/eso*
your (sing)	*tu/tus*	that (far)	*aquel/aquella/aquellos/aquellas*
his/her	*su/sus*		
our	*nuestro/-a/-os/-as*	expensive/cheap	*caro/barato*
your (pl)	*su/sus*	beautiful/ugly	*lindo/feo*
their	*su/sus*	old/new	*viejo/nuevo*
and	*y*	good/bad	*malo/bueno*
but	*pero*	early/late	*temprano/tarde*
some	*algún/alguna/algunos/algunas*	hot/cold	*caliente/frío*
		difficult/easy	*dificil/facil*
this	*este/esta/esto*	boring/interesting	*aburrido/interesante*

GUARANÍ

Accents Words in Guaraní are regularly accented on the final syllable. This means that accents are marked only when the stress falls somewhere other than on the last syllable, eg: *ndaipóri* (there is not). In Spanish, however, words are regularly accented on the penultimate syllable, and accents are marked when the stress falls somewhere else, eg: *fotógrafo* (photographer). When including a Guaraní word in a Spanish text, therefore, the Spanish rule is followed, and accents are put on the final syllable of a Guaraní word, eg: *Se fueron a Caacupé* (They went to Caacupé). In this guide the same practice has been followed in order to help pronunciation: accents have been put on the final syllables of Guaraní words (even though in pure Guaraní they would not be marked), to help the reader remember how to pronounce them. This can be particularly helpful in the case of *jopará* terms (mixed language) like *sombrero pirí*. An accent on a final 'y' is often omitted, probably because of the difficulty of finding it on a Spanish keyboard.

Translation In the many instances of compound phrases using both Guaraní and Spanish words, I have given a translation that distinguishes the language of each, eg: *pelota tatá* (Spanish 'ball', Guaraní 'of fire'). Where the language of the original is not specified, it is Spanish.

Spelling Another consequence of *jopará* is that Guaraní words are sometimes spelt in the Spanish way (eg: *yacaré* for *jakaré* – caiman) and Spanish words sometimes in the Guaraní way (eg: *kandil* for *candil* – torch). This guide tries to be consistent but there are moments when consistency has to give way to general usage. It is useful, also, to be aware that you will come across a variety of spellings in Guaraní. Attempts at standardisation of Guaraní spelling have replaced the hard 'c' with a 'k', the 'z' with an 's', the 'y' with a 'j' and the 'x' with a 'ch'. Proper names have not kept up with the changes: we write Caacupé and not Ka'akupé; the Argentinians write Puerto Iguazú but the Paraguayans write San Ignacio Guasú; the usual spelling of the dam shared with Argentina is Yacyretá and not Jasyretá; but we have always written Che Guevara and not Xe Guevara. You will also find a variation between the use of the 'v' and the 'b' (which sound the same when pronounced by Spanish-speakers) and the 's' and the soft 'c'. The same street in Asunción has one street sign saying 'Tabapy' and another saying 'Tavapy'.

The sixth vowel In addition to a, e, i, o and u, Guaraní has a sixth vowel written 'y' and pronounced a bit like 'oo' and a bit like 'ugh': really, it cannot be explained without demonstration. In addition to this, all vowels have nasalised forms, and this is marked with a tilde. So there are 12 vowels in all: a, ã, e, ẽ, i, ĩ, o, õ, u, ũ, y and ỹ. A Guaraní speaker will wrinkle his or her nose when pronouncing ỹ.

Consonants A number of consonants are missing from the Guaraní language – b, c, d, f, q, w, x and z. But there are a number of extra consonants not used in the Latin alphabet, though they are written in the Latin form with two letters – mb, nd, ng, nt and rr. Finally, there is abundant use of the glottal stop, which is called the *puso* and written as an apostrophe '; it is treated as a consonant and put at the end of the alphabet. A common word with the *puso* is *mba'e* (thing).

Greetings Learning a language that has no European roots is difficult but intriguing, as so many things are completely different from the expectation. Since this is one of the delights of discovering Paraguay, a few of the most basic points of grammar are included here. It is a surprise to find that there is no word for 'hello' or 'goodbye', but the regular greeting is *mba'ẽichapa* (how are you?), and the most common dismissal is to say *jahá* (let's go), and *jajetopáta* (we'll see each other), which is in any case a *jopará* word.

Plurals You do not add 's' to form a plural, and indeed, there is no plural form, either of nouns or of verbs. Sometimes the word *kuéra* is put after a noun to indicate a plural, and *hikuái* is sometimes put after verbs. Otherwise, the context indicates a plural.

Verb 'to be' Continuing with the surprises of a non-European language, there is no verb 'to be', but this is indicated by saying 'I [am] the one', 'you [are] the one', etc: *che ha'e, nde ha'e,* etc.

Question marks There are no question marks written in Guaraní.

Numbers In strict Guaraní, numbers only go up to five: *peteĩ, mokõi, mbohapý, irundý, po,* the last being the word for 'hand'. Then there is 'many' *hetá*, and 'few' *mbový*. In practice, the number you most frequently hear is 'one', *peteĩ*, and for the rest the Spanish numbers are often

EMERGENCY

Help!	*!socorro!/!ayuda!*
Call a doctor	*llame al doctor*
There's been an accident	*ha ocurrido un accidente*
I'm lost	*estoy perdido/-a*
Go away!	*!váyase! !fuera!*
police	*policía*
fire	*incendio*
ambulance	*ambulancia*
thief	*ladrón*
hospital	*hospital*
I am ill	*estoy enfermo/-a*

used. But further numbers in Guaraní have been constructed out of combinations of the first five, and they are used by speakers trying to avoid *jopará*: eg: *poteĩ* (6), *pokõi* (7), *poapy* (8), *porundy* (9), *pa* (10), *pateĩ* (11), *mokõipa* (20), etc.

First person plural There are two words for 'we', the inclusive and the exclusive, and corresponding conjugative forms; *ñande* means 'me and you (and perhaps others)', while *ore* means 'me and others but not you'. For example, when talking about God to other people, you say Ñandejára (Our Lord) because God is the Lord of the people you are talking to, but when addressing God you say *Ore Ru* (Our Father) because God is not the Father of himself.

Conjugating Verbs are conjugated at the beginning of the word rather than at the end, eg: *apuká, repuká, opuká, japuká, ropuká, pepuká*: 'I laugh', 'you (s) laugh', 's/he laughs', 'we (incl) laugh', 'we (excl) laugh', 'you (pl) laugh'. *Japuká* corresponds to the pronoun *ñande*, and *ropuká* corresponds to the pronoun *ore*. There is no third person plural form, because the third person singular form is used.

Prepositions In Guaraní the prepositions come after the noun and so are called *pospociones*, eg: *kokuépe* (in the field), where *-pe* means 'in' or 'at'.

Prefixes and suffixes There are a host of prefixes and suffixes that subtly modify the meaning, so that a line of poetry in Guaraní may consist of two or three words, and need ten or 12 words to capture its sense in Spanish or English. The word 'hallowed' in the Lord's Prayer, *toñembojeroviákena*, has four prefixes and two suffixes added to the verb *(a)roviá* (believe). The prefixes express the sense of the optative, the reflexive, the idea of making something happen, and the first person plural. The suffixes express the sense of command and of politeness in making the command.

Appendix 2

GLOSSARY

See also box on *Craft*, page 25.

adoquinado	road paved with blocks, usually with small octagonal concrete blocks
almacen	store, corner shop
aó po'i	(Guaraní) a traditional form of embroidery
arroyo	stream
bandeirantes	lit. flag-bearers, used of Brazilians who invaded the Reductions to hunt for slaves
baño moderno/ baño común	flushing toilet/latrine
barrio	neighbourhood
bombilla	metal straw for drinking *tereré* or *mate*
bosque	wood
bungalow	not a poor dwelling but a fashionable one-room holiday house, often thatched
cabildo	(colonial) representatives who administer the town; the building they use
cabinas	telephone boxes
cacique	indigenous leader
camino de tierra	dirt road
camioneta	jeep, van
campesino	person living in the *campo*, peasant
campo	countryside
candiles	candles made from animal fat in an *apepú* (bitter orange) skin
carpincho	capybara
casa parroquial	parish house
celular	mobile phone
cerro	hill
chip	SIM card, microchip
chipa, chipa guasú, chipa so'ó	(Guaraní) see *Food glossary*, below
chipería	shop that sells *chipa*
choza	hut of indigenous
churrasquería	Brazilian-style restaurant where a lot of roast meats are served
coche cama	sleeper (on bus)
cocotero	Paraguay's most typical palm tree
colegio	secondary school
compañía	a small village in the countryside, attached to a larger town or *pueblo*
común	'common' or ordinary, eg: a third-class bus

cooperativa	1) credit union; 2) firm run by its workers, eg: of craft workers, or of Mennonites
Copaco	(Compañía Paraguaya de Comunicaciones) state telephone network, previously called Antelco
copetín	small café
correo	post, email address
criollo	born in Latin America, but of Spanish parents
cucaracha	cockroach
departamento	political division of country, like a province
deposito	left luggage, storeroom
diferencial	of buses, a superior class
Don	term of respect for a man, like *Señor*
ejecutivo	of buses, a superior class
empedrado	road covered with small stones, cobbled
empresa	company, particularly of bus company
encomienda	packet sent by bus instead of through the post; hard labour for indigenous in colonial times
enripiado	road covered with smaller stones or fine gravel
encaje ju	(Spanish, Guaraní) traditional Paraguayan lace
estancia	country estate
festival	show of music and dance
fiesta	party
fiesta patronal	feast day of a town, on the day of its patron saint
Fray	Friar (of Franciscans)
frigobar	minibar
gaseosa	fizzy drink
gobernación	regional government office, at the level of the *departamento*
guampa	cup for *tereré* or *mate* (different for each), see page 22
guarania	form of Paraguayan traditional music, in minor key
guardabosque, guardaparque	park ranger
H	*Hermano* ie: Brother (religious)
Hna	*Hermana* ie: Sister (religious)
heladería	ice-cream parlour
hospedaje	small hotel, hostel
iglesia	church
imagen	statue
intendente	mayor
interno	extension (of telephone)
IVA (impuesto de valor agregado)	Value Added Tax
jopará	(Guaraní) mixture of Guaraní and Spanish
karumbé	horse cart for tourists, within a town
kotý guasú	(Guaraní, in Reductions) house for widows and orphans
lapacho	large tree with beautiful pink (or yellow) blossom, used a lot in building
lavandería	launderette
librería	stationery shop, bookshop
linea baja	landline
lomito	thin steak in a roll of bread
maraca	instrument to shake, like a rattle
mate	hot tea-like infusion made with *yerba*

mburucuyá	national flower of Paraguay, much sculpted in the Reductions; corresponding fruit
mensú	(Guaraní) late 19th-century and early 20th-century agricultural worker, in the region around Hernandarias, whose work conditions especially on the *yerbales* made him a slave
mestizo	mixed race, with Spanish and indigenous blood
mini carga	putting some credit onto a mobile phone
mirador	viewpoint, lookout point, observation tower
monte	wild wood
motel (Cupido, del Bosque, Pasión, etc*)*	hotel for amorous liaisons, renting rooms by the hour
Municipalidad	town council, town hall, area of jurisdiction of same
Ña	(Guaraní) term of respect for a woman, like *Señora*
ñanduti	(Guaraní) traditional spiderweb lace
P or *Padre* or *Pa'i*	Father (ie: priest)
palo santo	fragrant hardwood used for small carvings
parrilla	grill, barbecue
patio de comidas	group of restaurants in one food hall
peatonal	pedestrian precinct
pesebre	crib
plaza	square
polka	form of traditional dance music, in major key
poli deportivo	or just *poli* for short; multi-use sports hall, a large roofed area with semi-open walls
Próceres	the people who effected the independence of Paraguay
propina	tip
pueblo	town or village
puente	bridge
quincho	roofed area without walls, especially with a barbecue
rancho	small country house
rappel	abseiling
reducciones	reductions (as in Jesuit-Guaraní Reductions)
remedios	herbs with medicinal qualities used in *mate* or *tereré*, or in infusions like tea
remise	taxi, especially Argentinian
retablo	reredos, the decorative setting on the wall behind the altar, that in the Reductions acted as a frame for statues
río	river
ruta	main road
selva	wild wood
semáforo	traffic lights
Semana Santa	Holy Week, especially Maundy Thursday to Easter Sunday
sombrero	broad-brimmed hat
sommier	a sommier bed indicates a deep, high-quality, sprung mattress (see pages 52–3)
split	the better kind of air conditioning (see page 53)
sulky	horse cart for tourists, in the countryside
tatakuá	(Guaraní) traditional brick oven, shaped like igloo (almost every house in the *campo* has one in the garden)
telefax	joint telephone and fax line
tenedor libre	restaurant where you can eat all you want for a fixed price

tereré	iced tea-like infusion made with *yerba*
tigre	literally tiger, but used for jaguar
tirolesa	zip wire
veda	period when fishing is prohibited, early November to late December, to allow the fish to reproduce
ventilador, aire	fan, air conditioning
yerba	plant used for *tereré* and *mate*
yerbal	plantation of *yerba* trees

FOOD GLOSSARY These are traditional foods, such as are served all over the country (but less so in the cosmopolitan restaurants of Asunción). Some of these names are in Guaraní, others in Spanish.

albóndigas	meatballs usually made with breadcrumbs
apepú	bitter oranges
arrollado	strip of meat rolled up
asado	the favourite meal of Paraguayans – a barbecue. It can include beef, chicken, pork and sausages, or any combination.
asado a la estaca	more special kind of *asado* cooked on long wooden spits stuck in the ground next to an open fire. It is generally offered at big, public events, but you need to take your own sharp knife, plates and cutlery.
asado a la olla	pot roast
batata	not potato, but sweet potato. It is eaten as much as or more than ordinary potatoes.
batiburrillo	a delicious speciality of Misiones, made by stewing together all the beef innards
bife	beef steak
butifarra	sausage made of chopped pork
caldo	soup or broth
caña	Paraguayan spirit made from sugar cane, similar or identical to rum. The cheapest *caña* is very rough but the fine Aristocrata or Tres Leones – Etiqueta Negra, at the top end of the market, still costs barely more than US$2.
carnaza	meat without bones
carne	literally 'meat', but in fact used to mean 'beef', the principal meat of Paraguay
chicharõ trenzado	traditional dish in which strips of meat are plaited together and then fried
chipa	sold as a snack on the streets and in buses, this roll is not made of bread but of maize flour and cheese
chipa guasú	a great favourite: like *sopa paraguaya* but made with fresh, tender maize instead of maize flour.
chipa so'ó	a kind of *chipa* with a meat filling
chancho	pig, and so, pork
choclo	corn on the cob, fresh and tender as opposed to dried and hard
chorizo	sausage
clérico	a cross between a dessert and a drink, made from fruit cut up and served in wine. It is served only at Christmas.
cocido	a tea-like drink made by caramelising the *yerba* leaf; Paraguay is neither a tea country or a coffee country, but *cocido* is a delicious alternative. It can be served with milk or without.

delivery	this is now the standard term for restaurants that deliver takeaway food
dorado	a large river fish, usually grilled, and considered to be the finest fish on the market
dulce de leche	a sweet spread for putting on bread
empanada	very common snack or light meal, like a Cornish pasty but filled with a beef and egg mixture, or with other fillings
guiso	meat stew usually cooked with rice
kavuré	a pastry mixture with egg and cheese, wrapped around wooden spits and cooked by an open fire, coming out in a long cylindrical shape
leche de vaca	literally 'cow's milk', the term is used to distinguish fresh milk from longlife milk bought in cartons
locro	a variety of white maize generally cooked in a meat stew
lomo	flank of beef used for steak
mandioca	white root vegetable, in English 'mandioc' or 'yucca', peeled, boiled and served with most meals like bread or potatoes, eaten with the hands
mamón	papaya, usually served as a jam, and usually heavily sweetened to appeal to the Paraguayan palate
mate	see page 393
mbejú	delicious breakfast dish or snack like a firm pancake but made from mandioc flour, maize flour, pork fat and cheese
media luna	croissant
miel de abeja	honey
miel negro	treacle, a side-product of sugar processing
milanesa	an escalope of beef or chicken coated in breadcrumbs and fried
ñoqui	what Italians call *gnocchi*
pastel mandi'ó	*empanada* made with minced mandioc
poroto	beans, kidney beans
queso paraguayo	Paraguayan cheese, excellent for cooking, but not designed to be eaten on its own
rorá	a savoury dish made of boiled maize flour, usually a breakfast or a supper dish
so'ó apuá	meatballs usually formed with maize flour
sopa paraguaya	a maize cake eaten as accompaniment to a dinner or on its own, and made from milk, maize flour, pork fat, onion, cheese and eggs. It has its origin in a soup that turned out too thick, made by the cook of President Carlos Antonio López: she put it in the oven and so created a new dish.
surubí	the most common fish, with firm white flesh and no bones
tallarín	what the Italians call *tagliatelle*, often served with a chicken sauce
tortilla	a Paraguayan *tortilla* (quite different from a Spanish *tortilla*) is a savoury pancake, sometimes fried with green vegetables inside, particularly *acelga* (chard); a common supper dish
tereré	see above
vorí vorí	a stew, often of chicken, with dumplings
yacaré	crocodile (or, strictly, speaking) caiman. Now a protected species, but Paraguayans pay no attention to the law. However, restaurants can no longer serve it.

Appendix 3

SELECTIVE LIST OF FAUNA

In most cases, the Guaraní name is the one that Paraguayans will be most familiar with.

ENGLISH	LATIN	SPANISH	GUARANÍ
BIRDS			
bellbird, bare-throated	*Procnias nudicollis*	*pájaro campana*	*guyrá campana*
cormorant, neotropical	*Phalacrocorax brasilianus*	*biguá*	*mbiguá*
duck	(various)	*pato*	*ypé*
eagle, crowned	*Harpyhaliaetus coronatus*	*águila coronada*	*taguató hový apiratí*
eagle, harpy	*Harpia harpyja*	*harpia*	*taguató ruvichá*
egret, snowy	*Egretta thula*	*garcita blanca*	*itaipyté*
flamingo, Chilean	*Phoenicopterus chilensis*	*flamenco austral*	*guarimbó pytã*
heron	(various)	*garza*	*hokó*
hummingbird	(various)	*picaflor*	*mainumbý*
kingfisher, ringed	*Ceryle torquita*	*martín pescador grande*	*javatï*
lapwing, southern	*Vanellus chilensis*	*tero tero*	*tetéu*
limpkin	*Aramus guarauna*	*carau*	*karãu*
macaw, hyacinth	*Anodorhynchus hyacinthinus*	*papagayo azul*	*guaʼá hový*
macaw, blue-and-yellow	*Ara ararauna*	*paraguayo amarillo*	*guaʼa saʼyjú*
macaw, red-and-green	*Ara chloropterus*	*guacamayo rojo*	*guaʼá pytã*
nightjar, white-winged	*Eleothreptus candicans*	*atajacaminos de alas blancas*	*yvyjaʼu morotĩ*
owl	(various)	*lechuza/buho*	*suindá*
piculet, ochre-collared	*Dryocopus galeatus*	*carpintero cara canela*	*ypek˜uũ*
potoo	*Nyctibius griseus*	*guaimingue*	*urutaú*
rhea, greater	*Rhea americana*	*avestruz*	*ñandú guasú*
screamer, southern	*Chauna torquata*	*chajá*	*chahã*
seriema, black-legged	*Chunga burmeisteri*	*saria patas negras*	*sarïa hũũ*
seriema, red-legged	*Cariama cristata*	*saria patas rojas*	*sarïa pytã*
spoonbill, roseate	*Platalea ajaja*	*espátula rosada*	*ajajai*
stork, jabiru	*Jabiru mycteria*	*tuyuyú cuartelero*	*jabirú*
stork, maguari	*Ciconia maguari*	*cigüeña*	*mbaguarí*

stork, wood	*Mycteria Americana*	*tuyuyú*	*tujujú kangý*
tinamou, brushland	*Nothoprocta cinerascens*	*perdiz de monte*	*ynambú sĩsĩ*
toucan, toco	*Ramphastos toco*	*tucán grande*	*tukã guasú*
vulture, turkey	*Cathartes aura*	*cuervo cabeza roja*	*yryvu akã virãi*
woodpecker	(various)	*carpintero*	*ypekũ*

REPTILES

anaconda, yellow	*Eunectes notaeus*	*anaconda del sur*	*kurijú*
boa constrictor	*Boa constrictor*	*boa*	*mbõi ro'ý*
caiman	(various)	*jacaré*	*jakaré*
iguana, common	*Iguana iguana*	*iguana*	*tejú*
lizard	(various)	*lagartija*	*tejú*
snake	(various)	*culebra/serpiente*	*mbõi*
tortoise/turtle	(various)	*tortuga*	*karumbé*

AMPHIBIANS

frog	(various)	*rana*	*ju'í*
toad	(various)	*sapo*	*kururú*

MAMMALS

Azara's agouti	*Dasyprocta azarae*	*aguti bayo*	*akutí sayyú*
anteater, giant	*Myrmecophaga tridactyla*	*oso hormiguero*	*jurumí*
armadillo	(various)	*armadillo*	*tatú*
armadillo, giant	*Priodontes maximus*	*armadillo gigante*	*tatú carreta*
capybara	*Hydrochaeris hydrochaeris*	*carpincho*	*capi'í yvá*
coati, South American	*Nasua nasua*	*coati*	*koatí*
deer, grey brocket	*Mazama gouazoupira*	*corzuela parda*	*guasú virá*
deer, marsh	*Blastocerus dichotomus*	*ciervo de los pantanos*	*guasú pucú*
deer, pampas	*Ozotoceros bezoarticus*	*ciervo de las pampas*	*guasutí*
fox, crab-eating	*Cerdocyon thous*	*zorro*	*aguara'i*
Geoffroy's cat	*Leopardus geoffroyi*	*gato montes*	*tiríka*
guanaco	*lama guanicoe*	*guanaco*	*guasu cacá*
jaguar	*Panthera onca*	*jaguar*	*jaguareté*
jaguarundi	*Herpailurus yaguarond*	*gato moro*	*jaguarundi*
lion, mountain/puma	*Puma concolor*	*puma*	*jaguá pytã*
monkey, brown capuchin	*Cebus paella*	*mono capuchino*	*ka'í paraguay*
monkey, howler	*Alouatta caraya*	*mono aullador*	*karajá*
nutria	*Myocastor coypus*	*nutria*	*kyjá*
otter, giant	*Pteronura brasiliensis*	*nutria gigante*	*kyjá guasú*
peccary, Chaco	*Catagonus wagneri*	*quimilero*	*taguá*
peccary, collared	*Cari tajacu*	*pecarí de collar*	*kure'i*
peccary, white-lipped	*Tayassu pecari*	*jabali*	*tañykatí*
tapir, South American	*Tapirus terrestris*	*tapir*	*mborevî*
wolf, maned	*Chrysocyon brachurus*	*lobo de crin*	*aguará guasú*

Appendix 4

FURTHER INFORMATION

LOCAL GUIDEBOOKS If you would like to supplement this guidebook with a local guidebook, there are a few (very few) that have been published within Paraguay, and that can be bought in a few (very few) places in the country. They are in Spanish, and do not have as much information as your Bradt Guide, but they have some nice pictures, and also some reference details that are not in this guide.

Jaha (Guaraní 'Let's go'), first published 2009 and regularly updated. Available as a pdf file, downloadable from the Senatur website, or in leaflet form. This guide is a fairly comprehensive list of tourist facilities all over the country, with a wealth of contact details but no other kind of text. It is in Spanish only, and in tiny print so it fits onto one large fold-out sheet making a 16-page leaflet. Excellent reference tool, but not designed to be read through. Distributed free by Senatur (*Palma 468 e/ Alberdi y 14 de mayo; ☎ 021 494110; www.senatur.gov.py; ⌚ 07.00–19.00 daily including Sun & holidays*).

La Magia de Nuestra Tierra , Fundación en Alianza, 3rd edition 2012. ISBN: 978 9 99533 797 1. This is the top choice: A4 size, 266 pages, all with colour pictures. (The first 2003 edition was just in black and white.) It manages to say something about practically every town in Paraguay. Well planned and laid out, accurate in its information. With its large number of photographs it makes an excellent souvenir even if you cannot read Spanish. The maps are much improved in the new edition. The problem, as always with books in Paraguay, is to know where to get hold of a copy – even in the capital city where it is published – but if you have failed to pick one up at the airport, it can be bought from the offices of the Fundación (*Juan de Salazar 486 e/ San José y Boquerón; ☎ 021 222215; www.enalianza.org.py; ⌚ 08.00–17.30 Mon–Fri*), or from the bookshop called Books (see page 93), or possibly from Petrobras service stations.

Paraguay: Guía Turística TACPy, Touring y Automovil Club Paraguayo, 2010. No ISBN. This is the second choice, and again is just in Spanish. Handy size (13 x 24.5cm) and extensively illustrated in colour, with every other page entirely photos. It is strong on maps, with a lot of fold-out maps at the back (though it lacks an overall map to find your way among them). Its weak point is that it has very little text on each place, and is more like an annotated catalogue of places with map references. It is a little better distributed than *La Magia*, and can be found in some service stations, as well as direct from the office of the motoring organisation Touring (*Brasil c/ 25 de mayo, up a ramp to the right of the service station;* ☎ *021 210550; ⌚ 08.00–17.00 Mon–Fri, 08.00–noon Sat*).

TAP Guia: Paraguay Westfalenhaus Verlag SA, fifth edition, no date. ISBN: 978 9 99539 250 5. The first serious attempt at a guidebook to the country, but now superseded by more recent books. The same dimensions as a Bradt Guide but much heavier, because of the glossy paper used. Because it is written in three languages – Spanish, German and English – the amount of information that fits into this heavy book is limited. Earlier editions had a useful Itinerario de Transporte Público Metropolitano (which showed the route of each bus line) but this has been omitted in the latest edition. Available from the Hotel Westfalenhaus (*Sgto 1° M Benitez 1577 c/ Santísima Trinidad;* ☎ *021 292374/292966*). US$15.

GUIDEBOOKS IN ENGLISH

Box, Ben *South American Handbook 2014* Bath, Footprint, 2013. ISBN: 978 1 90726377 4. Covering every other South American country, this guide has 41 pages on Paraguay, which is a tiny proportion of the whole.

Box, Ben *Footprint Focus: Paraguay* Bath, 2011. ISBN: 978 1 908206 27 5. Slim and small 80-page mini guide. It covers Asunción, the Iguazú Falls, and a very few other places very briefly (in 35 pages including listings), but a good size for the pocket.

Goldberg, Romy Natalia *Other Places Travel Guide: Paraguay* USA, Peace Corps Writers, 2012. ISBN: 978 1 93585 011 3. The second dedicated guide to Paraguay, with 336 pages. Written by the daughter of a Peace Corps volunteer and aimed at a young, low-budget market. Strong on the Chaco and trips up the Río Paraguay.

Rough Guide to South America on a Budget 2012. ISBN: 9781409363989. Also available for Kindle or iPhone, etc. This guide gives Paraguay only 25 pages, but it is handy for those wanting to travel far and wide with not more than one guidebook. Also available in EPUB, MOBI and PDF.

Rough Guide Snapshot to Paraguay: South America on a Budget. A short economic guide but with maps, listings and basic information. Available in EPUB format for use on mobile devices, and MOBI for Kindles.

South America on a Shoestring 12th edition, Lonely Planet, August 2013. ISBN: 978 1 74179894 4. Also available in EPUB, MOBI, PDF, and for download in separable chapters, so you could just choose the Paraguay chapter, which is 32 pages long. (Only French Guiana, Guyana and Suriname are briefer.)

GENERAL INTRODUCTIONS TO THE COUNTRY

Lambert, Peter and Nickson, Andrew *The Paraguay Reader: History, Culture, Politics* Durham and London, Duke University Press, 2013. ISBN: 978 0 82235 268 6. Fascinating collection of nearly 100 short pieces, usually no more than five pages long, covering the history of the country up to the impeachment of Lugo, and with a section on what it means to be Paraguayan, all translated into English. They also have a Facebook group you can join: The Paraguay Reader.

Morrison, Marion *Let's Visit Paraguay* London Macmillan Publishers 1987. ISBN: 0 333 44991 6. Simple 96-page introduction covering past and present, written in Stroessner's time. A historical record rather than a guide for today.

Munro, Robert ed. *Paraguay 200* England, 2011. ISBN: Collection of essays by different authors on a variety of topics touching national identity, beautifully produced, and published in time for the bicentenary of independence. Available from Robert Munro (e *robert@munro.me.uk*) £14.99 plus p&p.

NATURAL HISTORY

Attenborough, David *The Zoo Quest Expeditions: Travels in Guyana, Indonesia and Paraguay* This is an abridged edition of a book first published in 1980. Ten chapters are devoted to Paraguay and the quest for the Giant Armadillo. Available in hardback and paperback. Clark, Peter T *Guia de los Parques Nacionales y Otras Areas Silvestres Protegidas del Paraguay – Guide to Paraguay's National Parks and other Protected Wild Areas* Paraguay, Servilibro, 2004. ISBN: 99925 3 298 X. Bilingual edition, in Spanish and English.

Kohn Patiño, Celia Edith and 5 other authors *Fauna Silvestre del Paraguay – Wildlife of Paraguay* Paraguay, 2007. ISBN: 99925 913 1 5. Bilingual edition, in Spanish and English.

Lowen, James *Pantanal Wildlife: A Visitor's Guide to Brazil's Great Wetland* Bradt Travel Guides, 2010. ISBN: 978 1 84162 305 4. A comprehensive introduction to the best place to watch wildlife in South America, and beautifully illustrated throughout, this Bradt guide is the only portable book to cover all the main wildlife groups while focussing exclusively on the Pantanal. Includes both Brazil and Paraguay.

Narosky, Tito and Yzurieta, Dario *Guia para la Identificación de las Aves de Paraguay* Buenos Aires, Vazquez Mazzini, 2006. ISBN: 987 9132 13 0. In Spanish. Illustrated with clear, coloured line drawings, this is the most comprehensive printed guide available, and is easy to use because the index includes the Latin, Spanish and Guaraní name of each bird.

JESUIT–GUARANÍ REDUCTIONS

Abou, Selim *The Jesuit 'Republic' of the Guaranís (1609–1768)* New York, UNESCO/Crossroad Herder, 1997. ISBN: 0 8245 1706 7. A coffee table book with not only good pictures but excellent, reliable text.

Caraman, Philip *The Lost Paradise* London, Sidgwick and Jackson, 1975. ISBN: 0 283 98212 8. Also published by Seabury in the USA in 1976. Still regarded by many as the classic history in English of the Jesuit-Guaraní Reductions. The author was a Jesuit and drew heavily on Cunninghame Graham's book below.

Cunninghame Graham, R B *A Vanished Arcadia* London/Melbourne/Auckland/Johannesburg, Century, 1988. ISBN: 0 7126 1887 2. Republication with introduction by Philip Healy of work originally published by Century in 1901. Opened up the Jesuit-Guaraní Reductions to the English-speaking world, after Cunninghame Graham returned enthused from a trip to Paraguay in 1871.

Gott, Richard *Land without Evil: Utopian journeys across the South American Watershed* London/New York, Verso, 1993. ISBN: 0 86091 398 8. A travel book with a solid study of the old Jesuit history woven in, but more about Bolivia than Paraguay.

Jaenike, William F *Black Robes in Paraguay: the success of the Guaraní missions hastened the abolition of the Jesuits* Minneapolis, Kirk House, 2007. ISBN: 1 933794 04 6. A detailed historical study.

McNaspy, Clement J *The Lost Cities of Paraguay: art and architecture of the Jesuit Reductions* Chicago, Loyola 1982. Old book but still a staple reference by this US Jesuit who became a leading expert on the Reductions and lived in Paraguay for many years. Black-and-white photographs by José María Blanch, also available in Spanish.

McNaspy, Clement J *Una Visita a las Ruinas Jesuíticas* Paraguay, CEPAG, 1987. First edition was in 1981. Slim travel guide in Spanish to the Paraguayan Jesuit-Guaraní Reductions, plus San Ignacio Miní and São Miguel. Very dated.

Montoya, Antonio Ruiz de *The Spiritual Conquest: a personal account of the founding and early years of the Jesuit Paraguayan Reductions* St Louis, Institute of Jesuit Sources, 1993. ISBN: 1 880810 02 6. Translated by Clement J McNaspy and others. An excellent modern English translation of Montoya's great work of 1639, with useful notes. Recommended, if you can get hold of a copy.

TRIPLE ALLIANCE WAR AND MADAME LYNCH

Cawthorne, Nigel *The Empress of South America: the true story of Eliza Lynch, the Irishwoman who destroyed Latin America's wealthiest country and became its national heroine* London, Heinemann, 2003. ISBN: 0 434 00898 2. See Rees below.

Lillis, Michael and Fanning, Ronan *The Lives of Eliza Lynch: scandal and courage* Dublin, Gill & Macmillan, 2009. ISBN: 978 07171 4611 6. A new exploration of Madame Lynch and the reasons for her bad reputation. Something of a reply to the four books published only a few years earlier by Rees and Cawthorne, Enright and Tuck.

Lillis, Michael *Eliza Lynch: Queen of Paraguay* Dublin, Gill and Macmillan, 2014. A Kindle version of Michael Lillis' research for his 2009 publication. Masterman, George Frederick *Seven Eventful Years in Paraguay: a narrative of personal experience amongst the Paraguayans* USA, Kessinger. ISBN: 978 781432 699109. Facsimile edition of book published in 1870 by the once Chief Military Apothecary of Mariscal López.

Rees, Sian *The Shadows of Elisa Lynch: how a nineteenth-century courtesan became the most powerful woman in Paraguay* London, Hodder Headline, 2003. ISBN: 0 7553 11140. This and Cawthorne's book, above, are fairly similar – readable, historical studies.

Schofield Saeger, James *Francisco Solano López and the Ruination of Paraguay: Honor and Egocentrism* New York/Toronto/London, Rowman & Littlefield, 2007. ISBN: 978 0 7425 3755 2. A serious study by the Professor of History at Lehigh University.

Washburn, Charles Ames *The History of Paraguay Volume 1* USA, Elibron Classics, 2005. ISBN: 978 1402 161414 90000. Facsimile edition of 2-volume work published in 1871 by the once US Minister to Paraguay 1863–68. A Kindle edition was released in 2014.

FICTION

Bolt, Robert *The Mission* England, Penguin, 1986. ISBN: 0 14 009869 0. A novel surrounding the episodes that became the screenplay.

Enright, Anne *The Pleasure of Eliza Lynch* London, Jonathan Cape, 2002. ISBN: 0 224 06269 7. Not dissimilar to the Rees and Cawthorne histories, but this one is a novel. It is well done.

Grisham, John *The Testament* USA, Doubleday, 1999. ISBN: 0 385 49380 2. Compelling thriller set partly in the Pantanal, actually on the Brazilian side of the river, but similar to Paraguay on the other bank.

Trower, Philip *A Danger to the State: a historical novel* San Francisco, St Ignatius Press, 1998. ISBN: 0 89870 674 2. A novel of the political intrigue leading up to the Expulsion of the Jesuits.

Tuck, Lily *The News from Paraguay* USA/London, HarperCollins, 2004/2005. ISBN: 0 00 720799 9. Yet another book about Madame Lynch, which might have been omitted from this bibliography had it not won the US National Book Award.

OTHER BOOKS

Berrigan, Daniel *The Mission: a film journal* San Francisco, Harper & Row, 1986. ISBN: 0 14 009869 0. Daniel Berrigan, Jesuit and peace activist, played the part of a Jesuit in the film.

Caravias, José Luis *Vivir como Hermanos: reflexiones bíblicas sobre la hermandad* Paraguay, CEPAG, 2003. ISBN: 99925 849 6 3. Republication of a pioneering book on liberation theology first published in 1971 in Spain (because of the dictatorship of Stroessner in Paraguay). Caravias was expelled by Stroessner. Only in Spanish. Available from Librería de Ediciones Montoya/CEPAG, see page 93.

Gayet, Ysanne *The Paraguay River: a Boat Trip to the Pantanal* Paraguay, 2010. ISBN: 978 99953 926 1 1. Account of the author's boat trip, illustrated with colour photos and reproductions of paintings by Ysanne and indigenous artists. Available in Books, Asunción or from the Centro Cultural del Lago, Aregua.

Gimlette, John *At the Tomb of the Inflatable Pig: Travels through Paraguay* London, Hutchinson, 2003. ISBN: 0091794331. Riddled with little errors, but a good read. The author's friends seem to be all well-off people in Asunción, which leads to a slightly one-sided perspective.

Hanner, Eloise *Posted in Paraguay* USA, Peace Corps Writers, 2014. ISBN: 978-1935925415. The story of the author and her husband's posting to the town of General Artigas as Peace Corps volunteers in their late forties. Also available for Kindle.

Hebblethwaite, Margaret *From Santa María With Love* London, Darton, Longman and Todd, 2011. ISBN: 978 0 232 52885 5. An edited selection of this author's monthly columns in the international Catholic weekly, *The Tablet*, about living in the Paraguayan campo.

Ivereigh, Austen, ed *Unfinished Journey: The Church 40 Years after Vatican I* New York/London, Continuum, 2003. ISBN: 0 8264 7100 5. Includes chapter on Paraguay's Christian Agrarian Leagues by Margaret Hebblethwaite.

Nickson, R Andrew *Paraguay* Oxford/Santa Barbara/Denver, Clio Press, 1987. ISBN: 1 85109 028 2. A bibliography, now rather out of date. Volume 84 in the World Bibliographical Series.

Nickson, R Andrew *Historical Dictionary of Paraguay* Scarecrow Press, 1993. ISBN: 081082 643 7/978 0 81082 643 4. Major reference book, but not cheap. Revised, enlarged and updated.

O'Shaughnessy, Hugh *The Priest of Paraguay* London/New York, Zed Books, 2009. ISBN: 978 1 84813 313 6. The background to the election of President Fernando Lugo.

Stover, Richard D *Six Silver Moonbeams: the life and times of Agustín Barrios* Mangoré Querico Publications, 1992. ISBN: 978 09632 233 19.

Van Houten, Lynn *Flavors of Paraguay: 101 authentic Paraguayan recipes* Petaluma CA USA, Anteater Press, 1997. ISBN: 0 9659173 9 8. Simple spiral-bound book with the families of adopted Paraguayan children in mind.

BOOKSHOPS Books in Spanish have been kept to a minimum, but inevitably some of the titles in this bibliography are available only in Paraguay, and even then, may be out of print. For bookshops in Asunción where you may be able to pick up some new or second-hand books from this list, see pages 93–4.

DVD *The Mission*, written by Robert Bolt and directed by Roland Joffé, stars Robert de Niro and Jeremy Irons, 1986.

WEBSITES

www.oanda.com/currency/converter and **www.xe.com/ucc/full** Two websites showing the Guaraní exchange rate. In English.
www.senatur.gov.py The Paraguayan government tourist office. In Spanish.
www.paraguay.travel An alternative address for the Senatur website (above).
www.dgeec.gov.py For up-to-date statistics on Paraguay. In Spanish.
www.abc.com.py *ABC-Color* newspaper online.
www.ultimahora.com *Ultima Hora* newspaper online.
www.seam.gov.py For Paraguay's nature reserves in the National Parks. The letters stand for *Secretaria del Ambiente*. In Spanish.
www.guyra.org.py For ecotours. Click top right for the site in English.
www.birdlist.org/paraguay Checklist of birds in Paraguay. In English, Spanish and other languages.
www.faunaparaguay.com In English and Spanish. A wealth of information on wildlife, but some of the links do not work, and some of the opportunities offered are more in the aspiration than the reality. Invaluable for detailed data on wildlife (click the image gallery).
www.faunaparaguay.com/listbirds.html For birds. (This page is listed separately as it is not clear how to reach it from the home page.)
www.faunaparaguay.com/butterflies.html For butterflies. (This page is listed separately as it is not clear how to reach it from the home page.)
www.artesania.gov.py For craft. In Spanish.
www.mca.gov.py The city of Asunción website, with many links to museums, etc. In Spanish.
www.asuguia.com For activities in Asunción.
www.mca.gov.py/webtermi.html The website of the Asunción bus terminal, full of out-of-date information, but gives you something to start from. In Spanish.
www.portalguarani.com Site for Paraguayan literary texts, music, works of art, films, etc.
www.uninet.com.py Various interesting and useful links to cultural sites in Paraguay. In Spanish.
www.facebook.com/VisitParaguay.Travel For those who prefer Facebook pages to ordinary websites (and many Paraguayans do) Senatur now has a Facebook page as well as the website above.
www.worldbirds.org/v3/paraguay.php BirdLife International database.

www.yagua.com A portal much used by Paraguayans, with a lot of useful links, and always up to date. In Spanish.
www.clasipar.com.py The principal website of classified ads.

For visiting San Ignacio Miní and other Reductions in **Argentina** (all in Spanish):

www.turismo.misiones.gov.ar
www.misiones-jesuiticas.com.ar
www.elbastion.com/ruinas

Not within the scope of this book, but here are the key websites you need if you want to travel by bus from Paraguay to visit the Jesuit-Guaraní Reductions in **Brazil** (all in Portuguese):

www.reunidas.com.br for buses from Posadas to Santo Ângelo.
www.rotamissoes.com.br for the Jesuit route in Brazil.
www.saomiguel-rs.com.br for information about São Miguel.
www.missoesturismo.com.br for information on visiting the Reductions in Brazil.
www.caminhodasmissoes.com.br for pilgrimage walks from Reduction to Reduction.
Bolivian sites where you can order sheet music of what was once played in the Paraguayan Reductions, including many Zipoli pieces: Bolivian Chiquitos book order.
www.festivalesapac.com In Spanish.
www.verbodivino-bo.com In Spanish. This is the publisher of the books distributed by APAC.

APP

Ruta Jesuítica 360° New app for the Jesuit Reductions of Paraguay.

Index

Page numbers in **bold** refer to major entries; those in *italics* indicate maps.

A Todo Pulmón 10
abseiling 143, 162, 167, 179, 285, 286, 293, 307, 315, 344, 350, 351, 358
Acceso Sur (road) 68, 126, 169
Acceso Norte (road) 329
accommodation **52–4**
see also estancias; places by name
Acosta Ñú, battle of 13, 134, 165, 318
addresses xii
air conditioning 53
air travel
chartering planes 381
getting around 51
getting there and away 33–4
Northern Paraguay 380
prevention of DVT 43
airports
Asunción **68–9**, 123–4
Ciudad del Este 299
Concepción 330, 339
Foz do Iguaçu 287
Mariscal Estigarribia 374, **375**
Puerto Iguazú 280
Alberdi 37
Alberzoni, Paolo Federico 225
La Aldea Fortín Mbororé (near Puerto Iguazú) 286
algarroba (tree) 37
Aloft Asunción 77
Alto Paraguay *departamento* 361, *362*
Alto Paraná *departamento* 10, 295, *296*, 311
Altos 121, 125, **156–7**
Amambay *departamento* *328*, 329, 346, 350
anaconda 306, 383
Anaya, Juan de 247
André, Arnaldo xi
anteater, giant 6, 10, 220, 276, 306, 353, 370, 383
Antequera, José de 11–12, 183
ao po'i x, 22, 24, 25, 177, 309
ao poyví 177
Apatur 54
Aquidaban boat 344, **345**, **378–9**, 381, 382
aquifer 10
Aquino, General Elizardo 147–8
Arapysandú 197, 201
Arasunú 115
Arazapé 190, 191
Archivo Nacional (Asunción) **111**
Archivo del Terror (Asunción) 106
area 2
Areguá 25, 100, 105, 119, 121, 129, **148–52**, *150*
Arete Guasú (Filadelfia) 370
Argaña, Luis María 16, 108
Argentina
currency 47, 260–1
ferries to/from 37, 262, 280
Puerto Iguazú 279–86
San Ignacio Miní 260–7
see also Buenos Aires, Triple Alliance War
Argentinian Reductions ix
Candelaria 243, 248
Corpus 37, 262
Loreto 265, **267**
San Ignacio Miní ix, 241, **260–7**, *264*, 277
Santa Ana 265, **267**
Santa María La Mayor 265
Aripuca (Puerto Iguazú) 286
armadillo 6, 247, 365, 370, 378, 383
Arroyos y Esteros 311, **330**
Artigas (road) 67
Artigas, José 356
arts 58
Assumption (feast day) 11, 66, 111
astronomical centre (San Cosme y Damián) 246
Asunción **66–120**
access roads 67–8, 123–7, *126*
bañados 44, 66, 67, 68, 71, 100
banks 96
bookshops 93–4
bus travel 44, 69–70
Cabildo 98, **99–100**, 106, 109, 113, 196
Casa de la Independencia 12, 67, **98–9**
cathedral 98, **106–7**
Cementerio de la Recoleta 115–16
Centro Familiar de Adoración 118
cinemas 89
couriers 96–7
craft shops 91–3
Cristo Rey church **113**, 115
Cuatro Mojones 123
department stores 95
La Encarnación church 106, **112**
entertainment and nightlife 89–91
excursions 119–20
getting around 68–72
getting there and away 67
history 66–7
hospitals 95
language courses 97
Manzana de la Rivera 98, **99**, 106, 112
maps *72–3*, *74–5*, *79*
Mburuvicha Róga 68
Mercado Cuatro 26, 68, 95
Monument to the Marzo Paraguayo 98, **107–8**
municipalidad 90
museums 100–6
see also Museo
orientation 67–8
Palacio de López (Palacio de Gobierno) 67, 98, **112**
Panteón 13, 79, 97, **111**, 352, 353
Plaza de los Héroes 97, 98, **110**
Plaza Uruguaya 98, **111–12**
port 112
post offices 60, 96, 104
railway station 98, 104–5
Recova, La 92, 98, 112
Sajonia 68
Santísima Trinidad church 106, **117**, 136, 173
shopping 91–5
sports stadiums 90
Sunday in 106
swimming pools 97
Teatro Municipal 91, **110**
Terminal 50, 68, 127
theatres 90–1, 110
Universidad Católica 107
Villa Morra 68
walking tour 97–8
what to see and do 97–119
where to eat and drink 84–9
where to stay 77–83
Asunción Convention and Visitors' Bureau 76
Asunción Golf Club 118
Atinguý, Refugio **220**, 306
Atlantic Forest 4, 9, 10, 267, 292, 334
Atyrá 4, 121, 125, 136, 142, **158–9**, 175
Autopista (road) 67, 69, 100, 123
Avenida Ñ Guasú (Asunción) **70–1**, 119
Aventura, La (*estancia*) 166
Aviadores del Chaco (road) 67
Ayolas (town) 28, **214–22**
Ayolas, Juan de 11
Azara, Félix de 305, 322

Bahía Negra 345, 378, 379, 380, **381–3**
bañados 44, 66, 67, 68, 71, 100
Bandera Jeré (Areguá) 152
Barbero, Andrés 103–4
Barnes, Simon viii, 268
Barrett, Rafael 222
Barrios, Agustín Pío *see* Mangoré
Basilica (Caacupé) 143
Basilica (Encarnación) 275
Basilica Nuestra Señora del Pilar 230
Basti, Abel 14
batiburillo 190, 194, 195, 213
Bay of Asunción 9, 71
beaches
Areguá 140, 152
Ayolas 215, 216, **218**, 235, 274
Carmen del Paraná 247
Cerrito 238, 239
Corateí 221
Encarnación 235, 269, **274**
Laguna Blanca 333–4
Mavani Beach Park 308
Río Aquidaban 274, 342, 351
Río Paraná 235, 237, 238, 239, 247, 274
San Bernardino 123, 140, 152, 154, 155
Villa Florida 187, **189–90**, 274

Bela Vista (Brazil) 37
Belén 341–2
Belgrano, General Manuel de 12, 184
Bella Vista (Amambay) 37, **354**
Bella Vista (Itapúa) 27, 37, 259, **260**
Bella Vista, Parque Nacional 9, 343
bellbird 2, **7**, 267, 350, 357
Benítez, Bishop Felipe 320
Benjamín Aceval 357, 363, **364**, 365
Berger, Louis 268
Berthot, Fr Noel 205, 208
Bertoni, Moíses 295, 303, 305, 306, **307–8**
Biblioteca Nacional (Asunción) 115
birdwatching 4–5, 9, 220, 235, 239, 267, 285, 357, 383
  bellbird 2, 7, 267, 350, 357
  cormorant 9, 223, 237, 239, 378
  egret 7, 181, 223
  flamingo 7, 9
  heron 7, 9, 235, 373, 378
  hummingbird 7, 9, 221, 293
  lapwing 7, 220, 223, 241
  macaw 6, 220, 306, 343, 350, 378
  mountain peacock 220
  nightjar 9, 334
  potoo 9
  rhea 6, 220
  scarlet ibis 378
  selective list of birds 397–8
  seriema 9
  southern screamer 9, 223
  spoonbill 378
  stork 9, 378
  tern 9
  tinamou 7, 9, 377
  toucan 6, 9, 276, 293, 378
Blue Lagoon Amambay (San Pedro Caballero) 350
boat travel 37
  ferries **37**, 226, 235, 262, 280, 359
boat trips
  Asunción 106, 120
  Encarnación 276
  Iguazú/Iguaçu Falls 284, 292
  Pantanal 378–9, 381, 383
  Río Paraguay 344–6
  Río Paraná 236–7, 238, 239
Bobí 125, 309, 327
Bogado, José Félix 243
Bogarín, Francisco Xavier 12, 99
Bogarín, Monseñor Juan Sinforio 103, 195
Bogarín, Monseñor Ramón Pastor 191, 192, 195
Bolaños, Luis 21, 125, 142, 160, 174, **326**
  founded Altos 156
  founded Caazapá 309, 322
  founded Itá 170
  founded Tobati 160
  founded Yaguarón 172
  founded Yutý 327
Bolivia, bus from 36–7
  see also Boquerón; Chaco War
Bolivian Reductions 22
bombilla xi, 26, 42, 260
Bonpland, Aimé 26, **208**
bookshops 93–4
Boquerón (battle and site) 15, 366, **371–2**
Boquerón *departamento* 361, *362*
Borja 309
Bosque Mbaracayú 4, 9, 10, 329, 355, **356–8**
Brassanelli, Giuseppe 175, 191, 203, 206, 207, 211, 214, 266, 267, 278
Brazil
  bus to/from 35–6
  flights from 33
  Foz do Iguaçu 286–94
Brazilian Reductions ix
  Santo Ângelo 208, 262
  São João 253
  São Miguel 241, 262
breakfast 52
bribes 50, 62
Brítez, Rosa 171
budgeting **48–9**
Buenos Aires (Argentina) 11, 12, 67
  bus to/from 34–5, 261, 279, 315
bus travel
  in Asunción 44, 69–70
  getting around Paraguay 49
  leaving Asunción 127
  safety 44, 45–6
  telephone numbers **50**
  timetable to Humaitá 233
  timetable to Misiones 188–9
  timetable to Pilar 226
  to/from Bolivia 36–7
  to/from Buenos Aires 34–5
  to/from neighbouring countries 36
  to/from Paraguay 34–7
  to/from Sáo Paulo 35–6
  websites 36
butterflies 5, 293

Caacupé 121, 123, 125, 129, 131–2, **141–4**
Caaguazú (town) 311
Caaguazú *departamento* 10, 12, 309, *310*
Caapucú **183–4**
Ca'aro 115
Caazapá 175, **322–6**, *323*
Caazapá *departamento* 174, 267, 309, *310*
Caballero, General Bernardino 148, 154, 164, 178
Cabaña San Francisco 190
Cabañas, Salvador 27
Cabeza de Vaca, Alvar Núñez 283
cabildo 11, 229
Cabildo (Asunción) 98, **99–100**, 106, 109, 113, 196
Cabildo (Pilar) 229
cabinas 60
caiman 6, 220, 223, 247, 283, 292, 303, 306, 350, 378, 381, 383
Calle Última (road) 123
Cámara de Empresas Artesanas del Paraguay (CEAP) 25
Cámera de Diputados 18, 109
Camino Franciscano xi, 121
campesino unrest 329, 355
campo, houses in the 185
Campo Iris 376–7
Campos Cervera, Hérib 92
Candelaria (Argentina) 243, 248
Canindeyú *departamento* 174, *296*, *328*, 329, 354, 358
Capiatá 25, 121, 125, 129, **135–7**, 176
CAPICI craft centre (Itá) 171
Capilla Olivares 330, **331–2**
Capilla San Antonio (near Trinidad) 256
Capitán Miranda 249
capybara 6, 118, 170, 220, 293, 345, 353, 379, 383
car hire **50–1**
  Asunción 50, 69, **70**
  Ciudad del Este 300
  Encarnación 273
  Foz do Iguaçu 287–8
  Pedro Juan Caballero 349
Carapeguá 25, 100, 121, **177–8**
Caravias, José Luis 209
Cardozo, Félix Pérez 23, 350
Carlos III (Spanish king) 11
Carmelo Peralta 379–80
Carmen del Paraná 245, **247**
carnival (Encarnación) 268–9, **273–4**
carpincho see capybara
Casa Bicentenario de las Artes Visuales (Asunción) 113–14
Casa Bicentenario de la Literatura (Asunción) 113
Casa Cueto (Asunción) 113
Casa de la Cultura (Pilar) 231
Casa de Gásperi (Asunción) 115
Casa de la Independencia (Asunción) 12, 67, **98–9**
Casa de la Música Agustín Barrios (Asunción) 114
Casa de las Victimas (San Ignacio Guasú) 202
Casa del Monte (Atyrá) 4, 125, **158**
Casa Hassler (San Bernardino) 155Casa Josefina Pla (Asunción) 114–15
Casa Jure (Asunción) 114
Casa Marianela (Atyrá) 159
Casa Pilo (Humaitá) 235
Casa Viola (Asunción) 99
Casa Zanotti (Asunción) 115
Casaccia, Gabriel 92, 148
casas de indios 139, 200, 201, 206, 209, 210, 211, 212, 213, 251, 252, 254, 258, 325Casas del Bicentenario (Asunción) 113–15
cash machines 47
Casona de Mangoré (San Juan Bautista) **195**, 196
Castillo Carlota Palmerola (Areguá) 151Castillo, San Juan del 114, 115, 202
Cataldino, José 263
Cathedral de San Blas (Ciudad del Este) 303–4Cathedral (Villarica) 318
Cathedrals (Mariscal Estigarribia) 375–6
Catholic Church 21–2
Cavallero, Pedro Juan 12, 99, **346**, 350
Cavernas de San Lázaro **344**, 379
Cecilio Báez 312
cedar 10, 353
Cementerio de la Recoleta (Asunción) 115–16
Central *departamento* 4, 121, *122*, 174, 225
Central Eastern Paraguay **309–27**, *310*
Centro Familiar de Adoración (Asunción) 118
cerrado ecoregion 4, 9, 334, 358
Cerrito 223, 237, **238–9**
Cerro Akatí 314, **321**
Cerro Chororĩ 152
Cerro Corá (battle and site) 4, 13, 111, 163, 165, 234, 275, 329, 350, **351–4**
Cerro Corá, Parque Nacional 9, **351–3**
Cerro Cristo Rey 143
Cerro de la Cruz 314
Cerro de la Serrana 354Cerro Kavajú 143
Cerro Koĩ 152
Cerro Lambaré 37, 68
  mirador 119
Cerro Léon 3–4, 361, 377
Cerro Membý 347, 353
Cerro Muralla 351, **353**
Cerro Porteño 27
Cerro San Rafael 4, 267
Cerro Santa María 210
Cerro Santo Tomás 176
Cerro Tres Kandú 4, **321–2**
Cerro Yaguarón 176
Chaco 4, 9, 10, 37, 329, **361–83**, *362*
Chaco War 13–15, 67, 169, 201–2, 203, 352, 361, 362–3, 370, 371–2, 374, 379
Chaco'i 106, **120**, 363
Chacurru (ecoturismo) 329, **351**
Chagas disease 40–1

charities 62–3
chartering a plane 381
chemists 57, 95
chicha 370
Chilavert, José Luis 27
chiperías 132
Chololó park (near Piribebúy) 166–7
Christian Agrarian Leagues *see* Ligas Agrarias Cristianas
churches, visiting 58
cinemas 58, 89
Circuito de Oro 120, **121–84**, *122*
  Altos 121, 125, **156–7**
  Areguá 25, 100, 105, 119, **148–52**, *150*
  Atyrá 4, 121, 125, 136, 142, **158–9**, 175
  Caacupé 121, 123, 125, 129, 131–2, **141–4**
  Capiatá 25, 121, 125, 129, **135–7**, 176
  Carapeguá 25, 100, 121, **177–8**
  Emboscada 121, **157**, 330
  Itacurubí de la Cordillera 121, 132, **144**
  Itauguá x, 24, 25, 121, 125, 129, **138–40**
  Luque x, 25, 67, 120, 121, 129, **144–8**
  Paraguarí 121, **176–7**
  Pirayú 121, 125, 129, **163**, 176
  Piribebúy x, 24, 25, 121, 123, 125, 129, **163–7**, 175, 176, 234, 318
  San Bernardino 28, 121, 123, **153–6**, *154*
  San Lorenzo 67, 121, 127, 129, **132–5**, *133*
  Sapucai 105, 114, 119, 121, 129, **168–9**
  suggested routes 128–31
  Tobatí 4, 25, 121–3, 125, 142, **159–62**, 175, 176, 375
  Valenzuela 121, 125, 129, **167–8**, 176
  where to eat and drink 129
  where to stay 128–9
  Yaguarón 76, 117, 121, 123, 125, 136, 163, 165, **172–6**
  Ypacaraí 25, 121, **140–1**
Ciudad del Este 51, 226, 261, 277, 279, 287, **295–304**, *298–9*
  excursions from 304–8
  getting around 300
  getting there and away 297–9
  other practicalities 303
  shopping 295, **302–3**
  tour operators 300
  what to see and do 303–4
  where to eat and drink 302
  where to stay 300–1
climate 2, 4, 28–9
Clorinda (Argentina) 37, 363
coati 5, 378
cocotero 252, 257, 362
Colombino, Carlos 101, 102, 152, 184, 304, 341
Colonias Unidas 14, 249, **259–60**
Colorados 13, 15, 16, 18
communications **58–61**
Comuneros, Revolución de los 12, 181, 183
Concepción 25, 125, 268, 329, **337–41**, *338*, 383
  getting there and away 337–9
  what to see and do 340–1
  where to eat and drink 340
  where to stay 339–40
Concepción *departamento* 174, *328*, 329
Congreso Nacional **109–10**
conquest 10–11
conservation 8–10
consulates 32
Copa America 27
Copa Libertadores 27
Copaco 60
Corateí 221
cordillera 4, 37, 169, 350
Cordillera *departamento* 4, 121, *122*, 174, 309
Córdoba (Argentina) 248
cormorant 9, 223, 237, 239, 378
Coronel Bogado 241, **243–5**, 327
Coronel Oviedo 309, **311–12**, 315
Corpus (Argentina) 37, 262
Corpus Dam 3, **263**
Correa, Julio 92
Correo Central (Asunción) **104**
Corrientes (province, Argentina) 3, 164, 208
Corrientes (town, Argentina) 13, 36, 67, 226
Cortes, President Horacio 15, 17–18, 27
Costanera (Asunción) 106, **116**
Costanera (Concepción) 269, **274**
costume, folk dance 22
cotton 230
Cotur 76
Country Clubs 54
  Hotel Acuario 155
  Paraná 300
  San Francisco 166
  San Ignacio 197
coups 13, 15, 100, 346
couriers 96–7
craft **x**, 24–5, 121
  ao po'i x, 22, 24, 25, 177, 309
  ao poyví 177
  Areguá 148, 150–1
  Asunción craft shops 58, 91–3
  encaje ju x, 22, 24, 25, 101, 162, 177, 191, 312
  filigrana x, 24, 25, 144, 147
  Itá 170, 171–2
  ñandutí x, 22, 24, 121, 138, 139, 140
  poncho de sesenta listas x, 24, 123, 164, **165–6**
  San Miguel 190, 191
  Santa María de Fe 209
  santeros 135, 137, 161
  sombreros pirí 22, 177
  Tobatí 159, 161–2
  Trinidad 255–6
  see also Circuito de Oro
credit cards 47, 53
crime 44–6, 295–7
Cristo Rey church (Asunción) **113**, 115
Crucero Paraguay 344
cruising the Río Paraguay 344–6, 378–9
  see also Aquidabán
Cuatro Mojones 123
Cubas Grau, Raúl 16, 108
cultural etiquette 61–2
culture 23–7
Curia Diocesana (Villarica) 320
currency 2, **46–8**
Curuguatý 355–6
Curupaytý, battle of 13, 223, 225, **235**
cycling, Asunción 71

Danesi, Pierpaolo 248, 252
deer 306
  grey brocket 220
  marsh 220, 225, 350, 353, 378
  pampas 225
Defensores del Chaco (road) 123
Defensores del Chaco, Parque Nacional 377
deforestation 4, 9–10, 220, 347, 350, 357, 383
Delfín, Gerónimo 256
Delvalle, Alberto 271
dengue fever 38–9
departamentos
  Alto Paraguay 361, *362*
  Alto Paraná 10, 295, *296*, 311
  Amambay *328*, 329, 346, 350
  Boquerón 361, *362*
  Caaguazú 10, 12, 309, *310*
  Caazapá 174, 267, 309, *310*
  Canindeyú 174, *296*, *328*, 329, 354, 358
  Central 4, 121, *122*, 174, 225
  Concepción 174, *328*, 329
  Cordillera 4, 121, *122*, 174, 309
  Guairá 25, 174, 179, 309, *310*
  Itapúa 174, 185, 241, *242*, 267, 309
  Misiones 4, 185, *186*, 241
  Ñeembucú 4, 223, *224*, 225, 235, 240
  Paraguarí 4, 121, *122*, 174, 179, 225
  Presidente Hayes 361, *362*
  San Pedro 125, 174, *328*, 329
Dequení 63
Díaz de Melgarejo, Captain Ruy 315Díaz, General José Eduvigis 235
diphtheria 38
directory enquiries 60
disabled travellers **45**, 62
Don Emilio (*estancia*) 54, 299, **312**
dorado 187, 217, 219, 343
driving rules 50–1
Duarte Frutos, President Nicanor 16, 108
DVT (deep-vein thrombosis) 43

Eastern Paraguay **295–308**, *296*
  see also Central Eastern Paraguay
Ecomuseum (near Itaipú Dam) 294
economy 18
ecoregions 4
education 22
egret 7, 181, 223
El Sauce, battle of 148
electricity
  Brazil 291
  Paraguay 2
embassies 32
  Argentinian embassy 90
  US embassy 68
Emboscada 121, **157**, 330
Emitur 54, 212
encaje ju x, 22, 24, 25, 101, 162, 177, 191, 312
Encarnación 119, 226, 261, **268–76**, *270*
  excursions 276
  getting there and away 269–71
  what to see and do 273–6
  where to eat and drink 273
  where to stay 271–3
Encarnación church, La (Asunción) 106, **112**
encomienda deliveries 61
encomienda system 11, 174
entertainment 58
  see also places by name
Entidad Binacional Yacretá (EBY) 215
Escuela Pa'i Pukú 366, 375
España (road) 67
Estación de Ferrocarril (Asunción) 98, **104–5**
Estadio Defensores del Chaco (Asunción) 90
estancias (in general) 9, 187, 190, 191
estancias (to stay at) 29, **53–4**
  La Aventura 166
  Cabaña San Francisco 190
  Casa del Monte 125, **158**
  Chololó 166–7
  Don Emilio 54, 299, **312**
  Faro Moro 376
  Finca El Gaucho 156
  Golondrina 54, **311–12**

Granja Ecológica Ñemitý 312
Laguna Blanca 54, **333–4**
Loma Linda 54, **326**
Los Manantiales 54, **160–1**, 299
Mbuni 54, 330
Ña Blanca 342
Oñondivemí 54, **170**
Primavera 343
Quinta, La 54, **166**
Rancho JMC 342–3
San Guillermo 330
Santa Clara 54, **183**
Tacuatý 212
Ykuá Satí 54, **83**
Estigarribia, General José Félix 15, 363, 374, 379
etiquette 61–2
Eusebio Ayala (road) 68, 127
exchange rate 2, **46**
exchanging money 46–8, 68, 96
exodus from Guairá 263, 267, 305, 315, 359
Expo 91
exports 2, 18
Expulsion of the Jesuits 11, 109, 175, 197, 243, 248, 254, 256, 261, 263, 342

Falcón 37, 363, 364
Faro Moro (*estancia*) 376
fauna 4–7, 397–8
Fe y Alegría 63
Febreristas 15
Feria Municipal (Encarnación) 269, **275**
Fernando de la Mora (road) 68
Fernando de la Mora (town) 67, 91, **131**
Fernando VII (Spanish king) 12ferries **37**, 226, 235, 262, 280, 359
Festival del Batiburillo, Siriki y el Chroizo (San Juan) 194
Festival Latinoamericano de la Doma y el Folklore (Santiago) 212–13
Festival Mudial del Arpa (Asunción) 91
festivals and feast days **56–7**
Fiesta Hawaiana (Pilar) 231
Fiesta Nacional del Immigrante (Coronel Bogado) 244–5
Fiesta de la Tradición Misionera (Santiago) 213
Fiesta de la Tradición y el Folklore (Laureles) 239
Fiesta de Ykuá Bolaños (Caazapá) 325–6
Filadelfia 14, 363, 366, **367–71**
filigrana x, 24, 25, 121, 144, 147
Finca El Gaucho 156
first-aid kit 43–4
fish dishes 187, **217**
fishing viii, 54, 112, 152, 170, 189, 190, 214, 215, 221, 223–5, 231, 276, 312, 326, 331, 344, 383
Río Paraná 235–40
flag 2
flamingo 7, 9
flora 7–8
Flores, José Asunción 24, 111
folk dance 23–4, 58, 212–13, 273
food and drink **55–6**
fish dishes 217
food glossary 395–6
health issues 42–3
football x–xi, 27, 90
see also Museo de Fútbol Sudamericano
Forcada, Antonio 248, 257
Formosa (Argentina) 37, 226, 243, 364
Formoso, Adriano 243
Fortín Mbororé 286
Foz do Iguaçu 34, 277, 279, 280, 284, **286–94**, *289*
Fram 247, 248, 249, 268
Francia, Dr José Gaspar Rodríguez de **12**, 15, 99, 103, 111, 184, 263, 309, 346, 356
buildings of his period 138, 229
museum in Yaguarón 176
and Roa Bastos 92
town planning 67
Franciscan towns and Reductions ix, 22, 121, *124*, **125**, **146–7**, 200
Altos 121, 125, **156–7**
Atyrá 4, 121, 125, 136, 142, **158–9**, 175
Bobí 125, 309, 327
Borja 309
Caacupé 121, 123, 125, 129, 131–2, **141–4**
Caazapá 175, 309, **322–6**, *323*
Capiatá 25, 121, 125, 129, **135–7**, 176
Concepción 25, 125, 268, 329, **337–41**, *338*, 383
Curuguatý 355–6
Emboscada 121, **157**, 330
Guarambaré 103, 125, 172
Itá 25, 121, 129, **170–2**
Itapé 125, 309, 315, **320**
Itauguá x, 24, 25, 121, 125, 129, **138–40**
Lima 333
Pirayú 121, 125, 129, **163**, 176
Piribebúy x, 24, 25, 121, 123, 125, 129, **163–7**, 175, 176, 234, 318
Quiindý 121, **181**
San Carlos 125, **345**
San Lázaro 125, 344
San Pedro de Ycuamandyyú 10, 125, 329, 334–7, *335*
Tobatí 4, 25, 121–3, 125, 142, **159–62**, 175, 176, 375
typical layout 200
Valenzuela 121, 125, 129, **167–8**, 176
Villarrica 309, **315–20**, *317*, *319*
Yaguarón 76, 117, 121, 123, 125, 136, 163, 165, **172–6**
Yataitý x, 24, 25, 309, **312–13**
Ybycuí 121, **178**
Ypané 103, 125, 172
Yutý 309, 326, **327**
Franciscans 11, 19, 21, 22, 99, 321
see also Bolaños, Luis
Fuerte Borbón (Fuerte Olimpo) 380
Fuerte Olimpo 345, 377, 378, **380–1**
Fundación Moíses Bertoni 357, 360
Fundación Paraguaya 63

Galería Central 95
Garay 309
García, Alejo 10, 335, 337
García, Francisco 256
Garganta del Diablo (Iguazú Falls) 283, 292
Gasorý 321, 351, **353–4**
Gaucho, Finca El 156
General Artigas 309, **327**
General Delgado 241
General Díaz 235, 237
General G E Garay 365
geography 3–4
gobernación 18, 60
GOL airline 33
golf 118, 308
Golondrina (*estancia*) 54, **311–12**
González de Santa Cruz, San Roque 19, 109, **114–15**, 174, 201, 202, 268
statues, paintings and plaques 114, 201, 230, 325
government 18
see also Colorados; Febreristas; Liberales
Graneros del Sur 249, 268
Granja ARA 351
Granja Ecológica Ñemitý 312
Grimau, José 254, 257
Guaicurú 10, 19
Guairá (Brazil) 37, 359
Guairá *departamento* 25, 125, 174, 309, *310*
guampa xi, 26, 260
Guarambaré 103, 125, 172
Guaraní language viii–ix, 20–1, 115, 326, 389–91
guarania 23–4
guaraníes (currency) 2, **46–8**
Guasch, Antonio 21
Guazucuá 231
Guevara, Ernesto 'Che' 277
Guggiari, Herman 98, 372
guitars 24, 25, 100, 114, 141, 144, 145, 147, 148, 196
Guyrá Paraguay 9, **76**, 118, 267, 268, 376, 377, 382, 383

harp ix–x, 23, 24, 91, 100, 114, 121, 144, 148, 191, 309, 357
health **38–44**
helicopter rides 71, 293
hepatitis 38
Hermosa, Coronel Pedro 232
Hernandarias 11, 160, 300
heron 7, 9, 235, 373, 378
history of Paraguay **10–18**
Hitler, Adolf 14
Hito III 365
Hito IV 366
Hito X 382
Hito XI 382
Hito Tres Fronteras 285, 306
Hohenau 259–60
hostels 52, 77, 82–3
hotels
types of 52–3
see also places by name
House of Horacio Quiroga (San Ignacio Miní) 266
House of José Asunción Flores (Asunción) 111
houses in the campo 185
Humaitá 223, 225, **232–5**
Humaitá, battle of 13, 148, 164, 225, 232, 234
hummingbird 7, 9, 221, 293

Ictus 51
Iguaçu Falls (Brazil) 277, **291–3**
iguana 378, 383
Iguazú Falls (Argentina) 241, 261, 262, 277, *278*, **283–5**, 359
legend of 285
name 279
Iguazú Forest 285
Imagen y Sonido (San Ignacio Miní) 266
Immaculate Conception (feast day) 142
Immaculate Conception, statue of (Tobatí) 162
immigrants 2, 153, 244–5, 259, 269, 275, 337
independence 12
Independencia, Colonia 14, 309, **313–15**
indigenous ix, 19–20, 120
Aché 19, 101, 357
Áva Guaraní 305
Ayoreo 19, 101, 110, 367, 371, 381
Chamakoko 19, 101, 378, 381
Guaicurú 10, 19, 114, 157
Guaraní people today ix, 19–20, 23, 25, 101, 247, 286, 367, 370, 374
Lengua 19, 20, 101, 367, 370–1
Maká 19, 20, **120**
Maskoy 19, 20, 381

Mataco 19
Mataguayo 19
Mbayá 142, 160, 337, 342
Mbyá Guaraní 19, 25, 101, 267, 297
Nivaclé 19, 25, 367, 371, 374, 375
Paĩ Tavyterã 19, 134, 347
Zamuko 19
Indio José 125, 142, 159
Infante Rivarola 365
inoculations 38, 39, 40
insect repellent 38, 41, 42, 46
Instituto Paraguayo de Artesanía (IPA) 25
insurance, travel 38, 45
international dialling code 2, 60
internet 53, **60**
Irala, Domingo Martínez de 11, 107, 159–60
Isla Umbú 222, 223, **231–2**
Isla Yacyretá 219
Itá 25, 121, 129, **170–2**
Itá Cajón 255
Itá Enramada 37
Itá Letra 315, **321**
Itá Pirú 236–7
Itá Punto 235
Itacorá 237
Itacuá 276
Itacurubí de la Cordillera 121, 132, **144**
Itaipú Dam 3, 22, 215, 263, 293–4, **304–6**
Itapé 125, 309, 315, **320**
Itapirú 330, 331
Itapúa *departamento* 174, 185, 241, *242*, 267, 309
Itauguá x, 24, 121, 125, 129, **138–40**
itineraries, suggested 29
Iturbe 326

jaguar 5, 118, 183, 201, 220, 247, 276, 284, 285, 292, 293, 306, 350, 357, 370, 376, 377, 378, 381
Jardín Botánico y Zoológico (Asunción) 106, **118**
Jardin de los Picaflores (Puerto Iguazú) 286
JB Ediciones 51–2
Jesuit Reductions ix, 11, 174–5, 185–7
Belén 341–2
Jesús 185, 241, **256–9**
San Cosme y Damián 185, 220, **242–7**
San Ignacio Guasú 174, 185, **196–204**, *198*, 226, 262, 263
Santa María de Fe 25, 63, 142, 185, 197, 202, 203, *205*, **205–10**
Santa Rosa (Misiones) 101, 185, 197, **210–12**
Santiago 185, **212–14**
Trinidad 25, 185, 200, 205, 241, **217–56**, 249
typical town layout **200**, 252
see also Argentinian Reductions; Brazilian Reductions Jesuits
in 17th and 18th centuries ix, 11, 12, 20, 21, 22, 26, 109, 113
in 20th and 21st centuries 15, 21, 63
Expulsion 11, 109, 175, 197, 243, 248, 254, 256, 261, 263, 342
and Franciscans 125, 174–5
Jesuit art 99, 100, 103, 197, 202–3, 206–7, 213–14, 241
see also Jesuit Reductions; Ligas Agrarias Cristianas Jesús 185, 241, **256–9**
JMC, Rancho 342–3
Joffé, Roland xi
John Paul II, Pope 15, 103, 114, 143, 202, 304, 374
Juan E O'Leary 311

ka'ã he'e 308
Kambá Kua 131
kambá ra'angá 1, 131, 161
Kangueŕy biological station 267
karanda'ý 25, 361, 377
karumbé 258, 275, 316
Kurupí 117, 136, 211
Kurusú Peregrino 131, 158

La Colmena 179
La Patria 365
La Paz 249
Lago Ypacaraí 3, 71, 123, 151, 152
Lago Ypoá 3, 9, **181–3**, *182*, 223
Laguna Blanca 9, 329, **333–4**
Laguna Punta Porã (San Pedro Caballero) 350
Lambaré 11, 37, 67, 68
land without evil *see yvý marane'ý*
language 2
Guaraní viii–ix, 20–1, 115, 326, 389–91
Spanish 384–9
lapacho 2, 7, 10, 66, 151, 245, 266, 353
laptops 46
lapwing 7, 220, 223, 241
Latourrete Bo, Nicolás Darío 103
Laureles 239–40
leishmaniasis 40
Liberales 13, 15
liberation theology 209
life expectancy 2
Ligas Agrarias Cristianas 15, 191, 196, 202, 209, 211
Lima 333
Limpio 25, 69, 123, 124, 141, 145, 329, 330
literature 92
Llano, Mariano 14
Loma Campamento 91
Loma Linda 54, **326**
Loma Plata 14, 363, 366, 368, **372–3**
Loma San Jerónimo 106, **116–17**
López, Bishop Basilio 163
López, Maestro Fermín 165, 318
see also Acosta Ñu, battle of
López, Mariscal Francisco Solano López **13**, 67, 110, 111, 112, 221, 230, 331
busts, paintings, statues 98, 104, 109, 164, 319–20
in Triple Alliance War 103, 105, 134, 148, 149, 163, 164–5, 234, 235, 236, 332, 337, 341, 351–3
López, Palacio de 13, 67, 99, 100, 102, **112**
López, Panchito 111, 353
López, President Carlos Antonio **12–13**, 17, 111, 119, 125, 169
and architecture 67, 92, 99, 103, 107, 109, 118, 173, 234, 331–2Lorenzana, Marcial de 197
Loreto (Argentina) 265, **267**
Loreto (Concepción) 342–3
Loreto Chapel (Santa Rosa) 210, **211–12**
Los Manantiales 54, **160–1**, 299
luggage 46
Lugo, President Fernando x, 12, 16–17, 108, 191, 269, 304, 335, 355
Lula, President 304
Luque x, 25, 67, 120, 121, 129, **144–8**
Luz y Sonido 173, 274, 304
see also Imagen y Sonido
Lynch, Eliza 13, 110, 115, 164, 221, 230, 331, 341, 352, 353

macademia nuts 260
macaw 6, 220, 306, 343, 350, 378
Macchi, President Luis González 16, 108
Macuco Ecoaventura (Iguaçu Falls) 293
Macuco Safari (Iguaçu Falls) 292–3
Madame Lynch (road) 123
Maká 19, 20, 25, 120
malaria 39
mammals 4–5, 398
Mangoré 2, 100, 191, 195, **196**
Manzana de la Rivera 98, **99**, 106, 112
maps 51–2, 71–2
Marco das Três Fronteiras (Foz do Iguaçu) 293
Marian movement 123, 140, 141, 315, 320, 375
Mariano Roque Alonso 67, 91
marijuana 2, 347
Mariscal Estigarribia 366, **374–6**
Mariscal López (road) 68, 124
Martínez de Irala, Domingo 11
Martino, Gerardo 'Tata' 27
Marzo Paraguayo 16, 98, **107–8**
Masseta, Simón 263
Masterman, George Frederick 103
mate xi, 26–7
Mavani Beach Park 308
Mbaracayú reserve *see* Bosque Mbaracayú
Mbaracayú reserve (near Salto del Guairá) 360
Mbatoví activity centre (near Piribebúy) 167
Mbiguá 106
Mbocayatý 309, 313
Mbororé, battle of 214
Mbuni (*estancia*) 54, 330
mburucuyá 2, 7, 253, 254, 257
Mburuvicha Róga 68
Médanos del Chaco, Parque Nacional 376–7
media **61**
medical services, Asunción 95
Medina, Monseñor Mario Melanio 191, 195
Meliá, Bartomeu 256, 326
Melo de Portugal y Villena, Pedro 225, 232
Mendoza, Pedro de 11, 66
Mengele, Josef 14
Mennonite towns 368
Filadelfia 14, 363, 366, **367–71**
Loma Plata 14, 363, 368, **372–3**
Neuland 14, 334, 363, 367, 368, 376
Mennonites 361, 363, **368**
Mercado Cuatro 26, 68, 95, 106
mestizo 11, 21, 125
Metrobus 70
Mico (Luis Marcos Enrique) 201, 208–9
Migliorisi, Ricardo 101, 103
Misiones *departamento* 4, 185, *186*, 241
The Mission (film) xi, 247
missions 11
Missões (Brazil) 115, 251
mobile phones 46, 58–9
numbers in Argentina 59
Mocito Isla (Lago Ypoá) 181
Modelo Reducido (Itaipú) 306
monasteries 214, 364
money **46–8**
monkey 276, 378
capuchin 5, 220, 357
howler 5, 209, 306
Montoya, Antonio Ruiz de 11, 174, 263, 267, 305, 326, 352
Monument to the Marzo Paraguayo (Asunción) 98, **107–8**
Monumento a la Madre (Concepción) 340–1
Monumento Científico Moisés Bertoni 307Monumento Natural Cerro

Koĩ 152
Moonies 381
Morel, Vicenta 255
mosquitoes 38, 39, 41–2, 358, 378, 381, 383
motels 52
motor racing 376
mountain lion *see* puma
mountain peacock 220
municipalidad 18, 60
Museo Alberzoni (Pilar) 230–1
Museo Andrés Barbero (Asunción) 103–4
Museo Bogarín (Asunción) **103**, 107, 346
Museo Boggiani (San Lorenzo) 134
Museo Cabañas (Caapucú) 183–4Museo Coronel Pedro Hermosa (Isla Umbú) 232
Museo Cuartel de Villa Real (Concepción) 341
Museo de Arte Sacro (Asunción) 103
Museo de Arte Sacro San Francisco de Asis (Atyrá) 159
Museo de Bellas Artes (Asunción) 101–2
Museo de Fútbol Sudamericano (Asunción) **104**, 148
Museo de Historia Natural del Paraguay (San Lorenzo) 135
Museo de la Casa Victoria (Encarnación) 275
Museo de la Ligas Agrarias Cristianas (Santa Rosa) 211
Museo de la Silla de Asunción (MUSA) **102–3**
Museo de la Tierra Guaraní (Itaipú) 305
Museo de las Aguas (Salto del Guairá) 360Museo de las Memorias (Asunción) 15, **105–6**, 209
Museo de las Victimas de la Dictadura (San Juan Bautista) 195–6
Museo del Barro (Asunción) **100–1**, 255
Museo del Mueble (Areguá) 152
Museo del Barro (Asunción) **100–1**, 255Museo Diocesano del Arte Jesuítico Guaraní (San Ignacio Guasú) 202–3
Museo Diocesano de Artes Jesuíticas (Santa María de Fe) 206–7
Museo El Mensú (Ciudad del Este) 303
Museo Fray Buenaventura de Villasboa (Itapé) 320
Museo Histórico (Humaitá) 234–5
Museo Histórico Ambiental de la Entidad Binacional Yacretá (Ayolas) 218
Museo Histórico de la Artillería (Paraguarí) 177
Museo Histórico Commandante Pedro Palo Caballero (Piribebúy) 164
Museo Imágenes de la Selva (Puerto Iguazú) 286
Museo Jesuítico (Encarnación) 275
Museo José Gaspar Rodriguez de Francia (Yaguarón) 176
Museo Maestro Fermín López (Villarica) 318–20
Museo Mitológico Ramón Elías (Capiatá) 136–7
Museo Nacional Ferrocarril (Sapucai) 169
Museo Provincial Miguel Nadasdy (San Ignacio Miní) 266
Museo San Francisco Solano (Paso de Patria) 236
Museo San Rafael (Itauguá) 139–40
Museo Zoológico Francisco Schade (San Lorenzo) 135
Museum (Filadelfia) 370
Museum (Santiago) 213–14
Museum of the Chaco War (San Ignacio Guasú) 201–2
museums, visiting 58
music 23–4

Ña Blanca (*estancia*) 342
ñandutí x, 22, 24, 25, 121, 138, 139, 140
national anthem 17
national holidays 57
national parks *see* Parque Nacional
natural history **4–10**
nature reserves 8, *8*
Nazis 14, 275
Ñeembucú *departamento* 4, 223, *224*, 225, 235, 240
Ñesú 115
Neuland 14, 334, 363, 367, 368, 376
newspapers 61
Nicanor Duarte Frutos, President 16, 108
nightjar, white-winged 9, 334
nightlife, Asunción 89
Northeast Paraguay *328*, **329–60**
Nuestra Señora de la Candelaria (Capiatá) 135–6
Nueva Germania 14, 334
Ñumí 309

Oblates 371
Obligado 259, **260**
oil 335, 337, 362, 363
Ojo de Mar 354
Olimpia football club 27, 68
Oliver, Jaime 252
Oñondivemí 54, **170**
opening hours
museums and churches 58
restaurants 55
shops 57
Operation Condor 105
OPM 15
Oratorio del Santo Rey Baltasar (Capiatá) 137
Orquidiarios (Puerto Iguazú) 286
Orthodox Cathedral (Encarnación) 275
Ortiz, Diego 21
Ortiz Guerrero, Manuel 114, 320
Osununú 267
otter, giant 383
Ovecha Ragué (San Miguel) 190
overland routes 37
Oviedo, Lino 16, 108

Pablito Róga chapel (Caacupé) 141
packing 46
Páez, Zenón 161, 162
Pa'í Pukú (Pedro Shaw) 375–6
Pa'í Pukú, Escuela 366, 375
pájaro campana see bellbird
Pájaro Campana (song) 24, 350, 357
Palacio de Gobierno *see* Palacio de López
Palacio de Justicia (Asunción) 106
Palacio de López (Asunción) 13, 67, 98, **112**
palo borracho see samu'ú
palo santo x, 24
pampas 4
Pantanal 3, 4, 9, 29, 41, **377–83**
Panteón 13, 79, 97, **111**, 352, 353
Para La Tierra 62, 334
Paraguarí 121, **176–7**
Paraguarí, battle of 12, 184
Paraguarí *departamento* 4, 121, *122*, 174, 179, 181, 225
Paraíso Golf Ranch Resort and Spa (near Ciudad del Este) 308
Paraná Country Club (Hernandarias) 300
Paraquaria 11
Parque Acuático Ecológico El Dorado (near Encarnación) 276
Parque das Aves (Foz do Iguaçu) 293
Parque de la Salud (Asunción) 117–18
Parque de la Salud (Encarnación) 275
Parque de la Solidaridad (Asunción) 116Parque Ecológico Sol y Luna 350
Parque Manantial 259–60
Parque Nacional Bella Vista 9, 343
Parque Nacional Cerro Corá 351–4
Parque Nacional do Iguaçu (Brazil) 292–3
Parque Nacional Iguazú (Argentina) 284
Parque Nacional Lago Ypoá **181–3**, *182*
Parque Nacional Médanos del Chaco 376–7
Parque Nacional Paso Bravo 9, 343
Parque Nacional Río Negro 383
Parque Nacional Teniente Enciso 377
Parque Nacional Tinfunque 364–5
Parque Nacional Ybycuí 178, **179**
Parque Ñu Guazú (Asunción) 118
parrot *see* macaw
Paseo Carmelitas 87
Paseo Nocturno (Trinidad) 254
Paso Bravo, Parque Nacional 9, 343
Paso de Patria 37, 223, 232, **235–6**Paso Güembé 250
Paso Horqueta 343
Paso Santa María 183, 187
passion flower *see mburucuyá*
Paz del Chaco 371
PE (pulmonary embolism) 43
peccary 6, 118, 306, 376, 377, 378
Pedro Juan Caballero 37, 329, **346–50**, *348*
Peramás, José Manuel x
Pérez, Ricardo 148
peroba (tree) 350, 358
Perón, Juan Domingo 14
Pesoa, Juanita 221, 222, 232
house of (Pilar) 230
Pettirossi (road) 68
pigeon shooting viii, **376**
Pilar 37, 222, 223, **225–31**, *227*
Pindó village (near San Cosme y Damián) 247
Pinedo, Agustín Fernando de 337
pique 41
Pirapó 249
Pirayú 121, 125, 129, **163**, 176
Piribebúy x, 24, 25, 121, 123, 125, 129, **163–7**, 175, 176, 234, 318
Piribebúy, battle of 234
Plá, Josefina 92, 175
planes, chartering 381
planetarium 246
Plaza de la Democracia (Asunción) 110
Plaza de la Libertad (Asunción) 110Plaza de los Héroes (Asunción) 97, 98, **110**
Plaza de los Héroes (Villarica) 318
Plaza Juan E O'leary (Asunción) 110
Plaza Uruguaya (Asunción) 98, **111–12**
polio 38
politics 18
polka 23
Polo Astronômico (near Itaipú Dam) 294
poncho de sesenta listas x, 24, 123, 164, **165–6**
Ponta Porã 37, 347
population 2
Port (Asunción) 112
Porto Mortinho (Brazil) 37, 379
posadas **52**, 223

Posadas (Argentina) 34, 37, 261, 262, 279
post offices 60–1, 96
potoo 9
poverty viii, xi, 18, 20, 44
Pozo Colorado 361, **366**, 383
Pozo Hondo 366
Presidente Franco 37, 280, 306
Presidente Hayes *departamento* 361, *362*
Primavera (*estancia*) 343
Primoli, Giovanni Battista 248, 252
Próceres de la Independencia 12, 67, 99, 346
Próceres de Mayo (road) 68
Productores Mineros (Puerto Iguazú) 286
Protestant churches 22, 118
Provincia Gigante de Indias 11
Proyectadas (roads) 68
public holidays 57
Puente de la Amistad 280, 287, 295, 297
Puente Nanawa (near Concepción) 341, 366
Puente Remanso (Asunción) 120, 363, 364
Puente San Roque González de Santa Cruz 268
Puerto Antequera 337
Puerto Bello (*estancia*) 331
Puerto Busch (Bolivia) 383
Puerto Cano (Argentina) 37, 226
Puerto Casado 344, 345, 378, **379**
Puerto Iguazú (Argentina) 37, 277, **279–86**, *281*, 287
Puerto José Falcón *see* Falcón
Puerto Leda 378, **381**
Puerto Meira 306, 307
Puerto Naranjahai 331
Puerto'í 337
puma (mountain lion) 5, 220, 276, 305, 376
Pyporé 121

quebracho 361–2, 377
Quiindý 121, **181**
La Quinta (*estancia*) 54, **166**
Quiroga, Horacio 266

rabies 39–40
radio stations 61
railway 13, **119**, 148
railway stations
  Areguá 151
  Asunción central 98, **104–5**
  Encarnación 275
  Pirayú 163
  Sapucai 169
  Trinidad 118, 168
  Villarrica 320
rainfall 61
Rakiurá Resort Day 119–20
Rally Transchaco 376
Rancho JMC 342–3
Ransonnier, Jacques 205
Ravizza, Alejandro 92, 107, 111, 117
Recova, La (Asunción) 92, 98, 112
red tape 31–2
Reductions' layout **200**, 252, 257, 266
  see also Franciscan Reductions; Jesuit Reductions
reforestation 9–10
Refugio Atingúy **220**, 306
Refugio Biológico Bela Vista (near Itaipú dam) 294
religion 21–2
reptiles 6, 398
reredos 146–7, 175, 324
  see also Franciscan Reductions
Reserva Fortuna Guazú 350
Reserva Natural Yacyretá 219–20
Reserva San Luis 350
Reserva Y'Ambué 350
residence permits 31
restaurants **55–6**
  see also places by name
rhea 6, 220
Ribera, Juan Antonio de 248, 257
Río Aguaray Guazú 3
Río Apa 3, 37, 125, 174, 343, 344
Río Aquidabán 3, 342, 343, 352
Río Capybarý 256
Río Confuso 3
Río de la Plata 11, 12Río Igauzú 359
Río Jejuí Guazú 3, 315, 333, 337, 358
Río Mandisoví 256
Río Manduvirá 331
Río Mondaý 307, 312
Río Negro 3, 9, 344, 382–3
Río Negro, Parque Nacional 383
Río Paraguay 3, 4, 37, 120, 223, 235, 240, 331, 339, 341, 343, 364, 377–83
  cruising 344–6, 378–9
Río Paraná 3, 4, 37, 125, 185, 214, 223, 225, 243, 263, 268, 359
  fishing pueblos 235–40
Río Pilcomayo 3, 4, 19, 364, 366, 382
Río Salado 3
Río Tapiracuái 332
Río Tebicuarý 3, 183, 185, 274, 320
Río Uruguay 248, 261
Roa Bastos, Augusto 2, 15, **92**, 326
Rodríguez, President Andrés 15–16
Rodríguez, San Alonso 113, 114, 115, 202
Rodríguez *santeros* (Capiatá) 137
Romero, Elvio 92
Roosevelt, Eleanor 283
Roque, San 114
  see also González de Santa Cruz, San Roque
La Rosada (*zona histórica*) 179
Ruins of Jesús 257–9
Ruins of San Ignacio Miní 265–6
Ruins of Trinidad 251–5
Ruiz, Koki 201, 203, 204
Ruta Jesuítica xi, 185, 205, 241, 250
Ruta Transchaco 67, 123, 361, **364–6**, 371, 377

safety **44–6**
St Joseph of Cluny sisters 371
saints and their symbols 138
Sajonia (Asunción) 68
Salazar y Espinosa, Juan de 11, 66, 109
salt lakes 373–4, 377
Salto Cristal **179–80**, *180*
Salto del Guairá 4, 37, 305, 354, **358–60**
Salto la Cantera 314Salto Mondaý 305, 306, **307**
Salto Suizo 314
samu'ú (tree) 353, 361
San Baltasar (feastday) 91
San Bernardino 28, 121, 123, **153–6**, *154*
San Blas (Itá) 170–1
San Buenaventura, Alonso de 156, 170, 172, 326
San Buenaventura church (Yaguarón) 172, **173–6**
San Carlos (Argentina) 247
San Carlos (Concepción) 125, **343**
San Carlos, ex-Seminario de 109
San Carlos Borromeo (Humaitá) 234
San Cosme y Damián 185, 220, **241–7**
San Estanislao 311, 329, **332**
San Eugenio de Macenod (Filadelfia) 371
San Francisco, Cabaña 190
San Francisco de Atyrá 158, 159
San Francisco church (Asunción) 113
San Guillermo (*estancia*) 330
San Ignacio Guasú 114, 174, 185, 191, **196–204**, *198*, 226, 262, 263
San Ignacio Miní (Argentina) ix, 241, **260–7**, *264*, 277
San Joaquín 4, 312
San Juan Bautista **191–6**, *193*
San Juan fiesta 192, **194**
San Lázaro 125, 344
San Lorenzo 67, 121, 127, 129, **132–5**, *133*
San Lorenzo de Altos 157
San Luis, Serrania (reserve) 343
San Martín, Francisco de 197
San Martín, General José de 243
San Miguel 25, 187, **190–1**
San Pablo church (Caazapá) 324
San Pedro *departamento* 125, 174, *328*, 329
San Pedro de Ycuamandyyú 10, 125, 329, **334–7**, *335*
San Rafael Nature Reserve 9, 10, **267–8**, 383
San Roque González (town) 121, **180–1**
  see also González de Santa Cruz, San Roque
San Roque oratory (Caazapá) 324, **325**
Santa Ana (Argentina) 265, **267**
Santa Clara (*estancia*) 54, **183**
Santa Cruz, Roque xi, 27
Santa Maria Education Fund 63
Santa María de Fe 25, 63, 142, 185, 197, 202, 203, *205*, **205–10**
Santa María La Mayor (Argentina) 265
Santa Rosa (Misiones) 101, 185, 197, **210–12**
Santa Rosa (San Pedro) 333
Santa Teresa (road) 125
Santa Teresita (Boquerón) 374
santeros 135, 137, 161
Santiago **212–14**
  fiestas 24, 56, **212–13**
Santísima Trinidad church (Asunción) 106, **117**, 136, 173
Santo Ângelo (Brazil) 248, 262
Santuario Ecológico de Santa María del Yguazú (Puerto Iguazú) 286
São João (Brazil) 253
São Miguel (Brazil) 241, 262
São Paulo (Brazil) ix
  bus from 35–6, 287, 297, 315
  flights from 33
Sapucai 105, 114, 119, 121, 129, **168–9**
savanna 4, 223, 343
scarlet ibis 378
SEAM (Secretaria del Ambiente) **8**, 135, 267, 343, 351
Selecta *yerba mate* factory (Bella Vista) 27, 260
Selvaviva theme park (Puerto Iguazú) 285
Semana Santa 28, 117, 187, 189, 204, 284
Senate 109
Senatur 51, **73–5**, 91
Sepp, Anton ix, 23, 191
seriema 9
Serrania San Luis (reserve) 343
Servicio Geográfico Militar 51, 267
SETAM (airline) 51, 330, 378, 379, 380, 381, 382
sex, attitude to 62
shopping 57–8
  Asunción 91–5
  Ciudad del Este 295, **302–3**
  Encarnación 269, 275
  Iguazú Falls 285
  Pedro Juan Caballero 346, 349
  Salto de Guairá 258–9, 360

Shopping China (Pedro Juan Caballero) 346–7
Shopping Multiplaza (Asunción) 47, 94
slavery ix, 11, 12, 107, 115, 137, 158, 174, 200, 214, 263, 315, 359
smuggling 297, 346, 347, 350
snakebites 41
Solar de Artigas (Curuguatý) 356
sombreros pirí 22, 177
Son et Lumière
  Itaipú Dam 304
  Trinidad 254
  Yaguarón 173
  see also Imagen y Sonido
sopa paraguaya 55, 185
SOS Children's Villages 62
Sotelo, Nino 143, 159, 201, 210
southern screamer 9, 223
spoonbill 378
stork 9, 378
Stroessner, President Alfredo 14, 15, 92, 191, 209, 295
  Stroessner's House (near Corateí) 221
Suárez, Buenaventura 243, 246
summertime 4
sun hats 46
sun protection 46
Sustersic, Darko 175
Synod of Asunción 107, 326
Szarán, Luis 24

Tabapý, battle of 12, 181
TACPy *see* Touring and Automobile Club Paraguay
Tacuara 330, 333
Tacuarý, battle of 12, 184
Tacuatý (*estancia*) 212
Tacumbú 68
Tagatijá Guazú 9, 342, 343
tajý 2, 7, 353
Taller de Hermandad (Santa María de Fe) 209
TAM Airlines 33–4, 51, 287, 299
Tañarandý 25, **204**
Tapé 320
tapir 5, 357, 376
tatakuá 116, 185
Tatí Yupí biological refuge (Itaipú) 306
taxis 49–50
  in Asunción 69
Taylor, Alonso 105, 112
Teatro Municipal (Asunción) 91, **110**
Tebicuarý, battle of 12, 184
telephone services 58–60
television channels 61
temperatures 4, 28
Teniente Enciso, Parque Nacional 377
tereré xi, **26–7**
  monument to (Pilar) 230
Terminal (Asunción) 50, 68, 127
  tern 9
tetanus 38
Teyú Cuaré park (near San Ignacio Miní) 266–7
theatres 58, 90–1, 110
Thomas, apostle 176
Thompson, George 235
Three Frontiers 277, 285, 293, 306, 366
tierra sin mal see yvý marane'ý
timbó 10, 266
time 2
tinamou 7, 9, 377
Tinfunque, Parque Nacional 4, 364–5
tipping 48, 58
Tobatí 4, 25, 121–3, 125, 142, **159–62**, 175, 176, 375
toilet paper 61
Tordesillas, Treaty of 10
Torín 311
Tororõ 321
toucan 6, 9, 276, 293, 378
tour operators
  Argentina 30
  Asunción 76–7, 128
  Brazil 30
  Ciudad del Este 300
  Foz do Iguaçu 288
  Puerto Iguazú 280–2
  UK 29–30
  USA 30
Touring and Automobile Club Paraguay 51, 54, **75–6**
tourist information
  Asunción 73–6
  Ciudad de Este 300
  Encarnación 271
  Villarica 316
trains *see* railway
transport companies 71
Transporte Aerio Militar *see* SETAM
travel clinics 44
travellers' cheques 48
travelling positively 62–3
Treinta Pueblos ix, 11, 12, 174–5, 185, 206, 243, 247, 261, 342
Tres Gigantes 379, 382, **383**
Tres Hermanos hill (Fuerte Olimpo) 381
Tres Kandú 267
Trilha das Cataratas (Iguaçu Falls) 292
Trinidad 25, 200, 205, 241, **247–56**, *249*
Trinidad church (Asunción) 106, **117**, 136, 173
Triple Alliance War 13, 17, 67, 119, 140, 147, 149, 163, 179, 225, 232, 351–3, 363
interpretations **352**
museums 164–5, 232, 234–5, 236, 318–20, 341
Tropic of Capricorn 9, **383**
Tupã 131, 137, 285
Tupãrenda retreat house (Ypacaraí) 140
Tupãsý María monastery (Santiago) 214
Tupãsý Ñuvaitĩ 203, 207, 214
Tupãsý Ykuá (Caacupé) 143
Turista Róga 51, 73, 91, 98
typhoid 38

Universidad Católica (Asunción) 107

vaccinations *see* inoculations
Valenzuela 121, 125, 129, **167–8**, 176
Vallemí 330, 339, 342, **343–4**, 345, 379, 380
Vapor Cué 121, **162**, 234
Velsaco, Bernardo de 12
Vickery, Tim x, 66
Villa Artesanal Ramón Ayala (Tobatí) 161–2
Villa Elisa 67
Villa Florida 28, **187–90**
Villa Hayes **363–4**, 365
Villa Montes (Bolivia) 365
Villa Morra (Asunción) 68
Villa Oliva 240
Villa Ygatimí 355, 356–7
Villalbín 237
Villarrica 309, **315–20**, *317*, *319*
  excursions from 320–2
  getting there and away 315–16
  what to see and do 318–20
  where to eat and drink 316–18
  where to stay 316
Viñas Cué Ecological Park 118
Virgen del Paso (Itapé) 320
Virgin of Caacupé 141, **142**, 159, 320
  see also Indio José
Virgin of Itacuá (near Encarnación) 276
visas 31, 280, 288
Vista Alegre Winery (Independencia) 314

walking, Asunción 71
Wasmosy, President Juan Carlos 16
weights and measures 2
wetlands 4, 9, 223–5, 373–4, 377–83
white-winged nightjar 9, 334
Wi-Fi 53
wine production 314
wolf, maned 5, 220, 225, 353, 357
women travellers 46
World Cup x–xi, 27
World Heritage Site, UNESCO 241, 258, 261, 284, 292
World Wide Fund for Nature 62

Yabebyrý **221–2**, 232, 240
Yabebyrý Wildlife Refuge 9, **220**
Yacyretá Dam 3, 22, 214–15, **218–19**, 247, 263
Yacyretá Island 9, **219**
Yacyretá Reserve 219–20
Yaguarón 76, 117, 121, 123, 125, 136, 163, 165, **172–6**
yakaré see caiman
Yataitý x, 24, 25, 309, **312–13**
Ybarotý church (Villarica) 318
Ybotý 160
Ybý Yaú 330, 333, 339, 347
Ybycuí 121, **178**
Ybycuí, Parque Nacional 178, **179**
Ybyturuzú (Resource Management Reserve) 4, 309, 314, 315, 321
Ycuá Bolaños supermarket fire/shrine (Asunción) 67, **117**, 322
Yegros, Fulgencio 99, 103
yellow fever 38
yerba mate 26–7, 293
  monument to (Bella Vista) 260
  see also Selecta *yerba mate* factory
Ykuá Bolaños spring (Caazapá) 325
Ykuá Satí (*estancia*) 54, **83**
Ypacaraí 25, 121, **140–1**
see also Lago Ypacaraí
Ypané 103, 125, 172
Ypejhú 358
Ypoá *see* Lago Ypoá; Parque Nacional Lago Ypoá
Yutý 309, 326, **327**
yvý marane'ý xi, 10, 201

Zipoli, Domenico 23, 248
Zoológico (Itaipú) 305–6
Zoológico Juan XXIII (near Encarnación) 276

INDEX OF ADVERTISERS

LATA 2nd colour section
Santa María Craft 222
Santa María Hotel 184
Wanderlust 404